HISTORY OF SCOTTISH LITERATURE

Maurice Lindsay is a well-known poet, broadcaster and prolific writer on many aspects of Scottish life and literature. Among his books published by Robert Hale are: *The Burns Encyclopedia, Robert Burns: The Man, his Work, the Legend, Glasgow*, an entertaining autobiography, *Thank You For Having Me*, and three volumes of verse, *A Net to Catch the Winds, The French Mosquitoes' Woman* and *Requiem for a Sexual Athlete*. He is also the compiler of *A Book of Scottish Verse, Scottish Comic Verse, Modern Scottish Poetry, Scotland: An Anthology* and *An Illustrated Guide to Scotland 1837*.

Formerly Director of the Scottish Civic Trust, and until recently Honorary Secretary-General of Europa Nostra, he was made CBE in 1979 and had the honorary degree of Doctor of Letters conferred on him by the University of Glasgow in 1982.

HISTORY OF

ROBERT HALE · LONDON

© *Maurice Lindsay 1977 and 1992*
First edition 1977
First paperback (revised) edition 1992

ISBN 0 7090 4802 5

Robert Hale Limited
Clerkenwell House
Clerkenwell Green
London EC1R 0HT

Printed and bound in Great Britain by
Mackays of Chatham PLC, Chatham, Kent

CONTENTS

To the memory of my friend Alexander Scott,
poet and pioneer in the teaching
of our national literature

INTRODUCTION

The purpose of this book is to present to the general reader a full account of Scottish literature. It is, of course, necessary to qualify this statement, since Gaelic literature does not come within the compass of the survey except in so far as where, briefly in the latter part of the eighteenth century and rather more extensively in our own day, the traditions of the Gaelic speakers of Scotland and the literature of the non-Gaelic speakers have impinged upon each other.

Although the book is sub-divided by category—under the headings Poetry and Prose in the earlier period, Poetry, The Novel, Drama and General Prose later on—the division by centuries is interpreted with sufficient flexibility to allow for such natural dividing-points as the Union of 1707 and the outbreak of war in 1914. Clearly, the rediscovery of the Makars of the fifteenth and sixteenth centuries by the writers of the Eighteenth-century Revival, and the re-awakening of interest in Scots and Gaelic among the Scottish Renaissance writers indicates an obvious continuity. But in recent years several studies have been written the purpose of which was to establish a continuing "thread" binding more firmly together a literature in three languages over many centuries. The difficulty is that no two scholars agree as to where the "thread" runs.

At one extreme, for example, Kurt Wittig, attempted to trace a recurring Celticism in *The Scottish Tradition in Literature* (1958). He achieved his threaded necklace—the traditional Celtic snake with its tail in its mouth—only at the cost of discarding half the available beads. Equally narrowly, David Craig, in *Scottish Literature and the Scottish People, 1680–1830* (1961), attempted to establish a retrospective pattern of embryonic radicalism. Such attempts to impose a personal concept of order upon any aspect of history simply will not do.

While it is true that, for instance, the Celtic love of colour has probably influenced Scottish poetry and, more recently, Scottish painting; true also that radicalism, or an expressed awareness of the rights of the underdog is as evident in *Rauf Coilyear* in the fifteenth century as in *The Thrie Estatis* during the sixteenth, the satires of Burns in the eighteenth and the novels of Grassic Gibbon in the twentieth, these are no more than recurring facets of a complex and constantly changing interplay of racial, religious and environmental characteristics with historical circumstance. I have therefore avoided any temptation to try to establish a unifying theory and adjust the facts to suit it.

It is more than seventy years since a survey of this kind has been undertaken. Much has happened since 1903, when J. H. Millar's *A Literary History of Scotland* covered the ground with scholarly detail, launching at the same time an attack upon the sentimental Kailyard school of Barrie, Crockett and Maclaren, then still in high fashion. While it is certainly my hope that this book may be of practical use and interest to scholars, especially students of the subject in the fifth and sixth forms of schools and in Scottish Universities, its main purpose is to encourage readers to share something of the enthusiasm and delight which the literature of my own country has given me during a busy lifetime. If Scottish literature is to survive as a living force, then it is essential that it should be read, enjoyed and discussed, not just by the increasing number of academics professionally concerned with the subject, but by those who still read for pleasure.

Following the example of that most distinguished Scottish critic, David Daiches, in his excellent popular work *A Critical History of English Literature*, I have been inconsistent in the matter of texts, modernizing spelling and punctuation where not to do so might have resulted in unnecessary difficulty or even misunderstanding, in particular removing the *is* ending where clearly it was not meant to be pronounced, but otherwise altering nothing that affects sound or sense. In an age of specialization, it is inevitable that where matters of scholarly detail are concerned, some reliance must be placed on the work of others. I have tried to acknowledge such expertise wherever I have made use of it. The overall balance and the enthusiasm for its subject which I hope this volume mirrors, reflect, however, my own views and personal emphasis.

PREFACE TO SECOND EDITION

As I remarked in the Introduction to the first edition of this book, it is primarily intended for the general reader rather than the scholar – academics usually only prescribe books by fellow academics! – although, of course, I hope that it may not be without interest to professional students of Scottish literature. I have taken the opportunity of correcting a number of mistakes and misprints that occurred in the original text.

CHAPTER ONE

The Fifteenth Century and Before

When surveying the span of Scottish literature, it is necessary to establish a reasonable point in time at which it begins.

In A.D. 844, Kenneth Macalpin, King of Scots, succeeded to the Pictish crown, and so joined together the two most important Celtic states in the Northern part of these islands. Three Celtic languages, as well as Norse and Northern English, were then being spoken in different districts of what is now Scotland.

The success of Malcolm II, who drove the forces of Canute from north Northumbria in 1018, led to the formation of the provinces of Lothian and the Merse. There was further consolidation in 1034, when Duncan I inherited not only the northern and eastern parts of the realm, but also the once predominantly Welsh Kingdom of Strathclyde in the south-west. While the Norwegian grip upon their Scottish colonies in the mainland and the Western Isles was prized loose by Alexander III's victory over the storm-tossed soldiers of Hakon at Largs in 1263, Orkney and Shetland did not come into Scotland until 1490.

We know nothing of whatever literature may have been produced in those divisions of Scotland which existed during the Dark Ages. Indeed, only a handful of Gaelic manuscripts written earlier than the tenth century have survived in Scotland, although rather more have found their way to places of preservation in Europe.

The pressures against Gaelic—or Scots, as it was originally called, after the colonizers of Dalriada, who came from Ireland—must have increased after Malcolm II's annexation of northern Northumbria. They certainly grew still stronger following Malcolm III's marriage to the shipwrecked Margaret, daughter of an English prince and sister of Edgar Aetheling, the legitimate heir to the English throne then occupied by William the Conqueror. Her influence resulted in ancient practices relating to the dating of Easter and the style of tonsure peculiar to the Celtic Church, being replaced during her lifetime by the customs of Rome. Throughout the reigns of her sons Edgar, Alexander I and David I, the Scottish Court became increasingly European. Men more fitted by the breadth of their experience than the old Gaelic chiefs, came into positions of authority to match the dangers of the times. In spite of a brief and ineffectual Gaelic revolt, crushed with Norman help, after the deaths of Malcolm and Margaret within four days of each other, the long, slow retreat of the old Celtic culture into the remotenesses of the Highlands and Islands—which it is not my purpose here to follow—took on the sad momentum of inevitability.

Through the Norman marriage of one of Margaret's sons, and the strong Anglo-Norman interests of their successors, the influence of France impressed itself on early medieval Scots literature as vigorously as it did upon that of Scotland's southern neighbour England, where Anglo-Saxon alliterative tradition retreated from Court circles and gradually died out in monastic aridity. French fashions took its place: the long narrative poem known as the "romance", which satisfied the medieval passion for storytelling; the extended didactic poem, often moralistic, death being then an earlier visitant and more constant familiar; and the popular song. Couched in a kind of Northern English common to both sides of the Border, this new literature soon infiltrated Scotland.

Some of the earliest song fragments that have come down to us are unmistakably Scottish in feeling, exulting over defeats inflicted on Edward I, the "Hammer of the Scots", during the Wars of Independence, when the pillaging and counter-pillaging of marching soldiers must have resulted in the accidental destruction of works of learning and literature as fearsome as the loss deliberately created two centuries later by the Reformers bent on destroying clerical libraries. One such early "mokkyshe ryme" celebrates an English repulse during the siege of Berwick in 1296.

> What wenys King Edward with long shanks   [why imagines
> To have won Berwick all our onthankys?   [unthanks
>   Gaas pykes him,   [let us mock
> And when he hath it
>   Gaas dykes him.   [fence him round

Even more bristling with understandable hatred and scorn is this fragment, evidently sung by Scots girls after Bannockburn and, incidentally, carrying chorus-phrases which recur in later Scots and English popular songs.

> Maidens of Englonde, sore may ye mourn
> For your lemmans ye have lost at Bannockisborne!   [lovers
>   With hevaloghe.
> What wenyth the King of Englande   [why imagine
> So soon to have won Scotland?
>   With rumbyloghe.

Crude enough stuff, as political versifying usually is; yet such chance flotsam from the surface of distant days, when literature was poorly recorded, still wears something of the colour of those passions which went to the making of Scotland the nation. Although the interest it arouses is historical rather than literary, this cannot be said of the third surviving fragment, which in its original form must have been the oldest of them all. It is a Cantus, quoted in the fifteenth-century language of Andrew of Wyntoun's *Oryginale Cronykil of Scotland*.

When Alexander our King was dede
That Scotland led in love and le   [law
Away was sons of ale and brede,   [abundance
Of wine and wax, of gamyn and glee.   [game
Our gold was changit into lede,
Christ, born into virginity,
Succour Scotland and remede
That stad is in perplexity.   [beset

These eight anonymous octosyllabic lines vividly depict the loss of trade, comfort and security, which must have depressed the daily lives of ordinary people for many years after the outbreak of the Wars of Independence.

The first nameable shadow perceptibly stirring at the far end of Scottish poetry is that of the soothsayer Thomas of Erceldoune, otherwise known as Thomas the Rhymer. His prophecies are said to have included an accurate prediction of the death of Alexander III, who broke his neck when his horse fell from a cliff at Kinghorn in Fife, on a dark night in 1285. Thomas is said to have lived in the thirteenth century, and has been credited by some, including Sir Walter Scott, with the authorship of the Northern English metrical romance, *Sir Tristrem*. The "evidence" to support this attribution depends upon an ambiguous reference in the *Chronicle* of Robert Mannyng, a near contemporary of Thomas, and upon whatever may be read into the opening lines with which the only known surviving copy of *Sir Tristrem* begins.

I was at Erceldoun,
With Thomas spak y thare;
Ther herd y rede in roune
Who Tristrem got and bore.

However, there is nothing particularly Scottish about the language or treatment of this "gest" or tale, and nothing to connect it with that Thomas who, according to ballad lore, became too familiar with the Queen of the Fairies, and paid the appropriate price.

In his "Lament for the Makaris", Dunbar lists a whole gallery of poets not even a scrap of whose works have come down to us. High in priority among those whom Death had recently removed we find the "gude Sir Hew of Eglintoun". Some critics have tried to connect Dunbar's Sir Hew with one "Hucheon of the Awle Ryale" (perhaps meaning "aula regis", or king's palace), whom Andrew of Wyntoun refers to with deference, telling us that:

> . . . men of gude discretion
> Suld excuse and love Hūchoune   [should
> That cunnand was in literature.   [cunning
> He made the *Great Gest of Arthur*   [tale
> And the *Awntyre of Gawane*,   [adventure
> *The Pystil of Swete Susane*.   [epistle
> He was curious in his style,
> Fayre of facund and subtille   [eloquent
> And ay to pleasans and delyte
> Made in metre mete his dyte,   [adapted metre to his purposes
> Little or nocht, nevertheless
> Waverand fra the suthfastness.   [wavering from the truth

There undoubtedly was a real Sir Hew Eglintoun about the palace of
that High Steward of Scotland who afterwards became Robert II. This Sir
Hew, along with John Barbour and others, was on several occasions an
auditor of the Exchequer, died in 1376, and was buried in Kilwinning
Abbey. But there is nothing at all to connect him with any of the poems
attributed to him by Wyntoun—*The Pystil (Epistle) of Swete Susane*, an
alliterative rhymed re-telling of the story of Susanna and the Elders, and
the *Awntyre of Gawane*, a work which has not been definitely identified—let alone the lengthy list of Northern English pieces, including *The
Pearl* with which from time to time others have credited him.

We therefore come to the first substantial work both attributable to a
known poet and written in Scots, though this language was described by
all Scots writers prior to Gavin Douglas as "Inglis", to distinguish it from
"Ersche" or Gaelic, with which it co-existed. This poem, *The Bruce*, in
temper and feeling is unmistakably the work of a Scot. Conceived in the
French romance form of such tales as *Fierrabras* (which Bruce actually reads
to a party of his men while waiting for his followers to be ferried across
Loch Lomond), *The Bruce* is the work of Eglintoun's fellow-auditor of the
royal accounts, John Barbour (?1320–95), a scholar who in all probability
had spent some time at the Universities of both Oxford and Paris, and who,
for the thirty-eight years before his death, filled the office of Archdeacon of
Aberdeen.

Barbour seems to have been paid ten pounds for his poem by King
Robert II in 1377, and to have been granted an annual pension of twenty
shillings the following year, the amount being increased to ten pounds
annually from 1388. While it is to Andrew of Wyntoun that we owe confirmation that Barbour was actually the author of *The Bruce*, it is to Barbour himself that we are indebted for several of the facts of Bruce's life.

Not many of the things said to have happened in this poem, written only
forty-six years after the hero's death, have been found wanting when put

against the testimony of other contemporary records. Even Barbour's alleged error of confusing Bruce the Claimant with his grandson, Bruce the Patriot King, has been shown by Agnes Mure Mackenzie[1] to depend upon the interpretation of the poet's word "ar" (before). Having just finished speaking about Bruce the Claimant, Barbour then refers again to "this lord I spak of ar," i.e. to Bruce the Patriot, with whom he has previously told us, in line 25, his book will deal. That the poet should still have been accused of committing such a blunder in Dr Mackenzie's day is strange for, as T. F. Henderson pointed out as long ago as 1898,[2] Andrew of Wyntoun included lengthy quotations from *The Bruce* in his *Cronykil of Scotland*. These differ in some respects from the direct Barbour texts. But after:

> This lord the Brwss I spak of ar
> Saw all the Kynryk swa forfayre . . . [Kingdom so distressed

the Wyntoun text adds:

> When all this saw the Bruce Robert
> That bore the crown some eftirwart.

Barbour's purpose in writing was clear enough. He wanted to firm the resolve of the Scottish nation by relating the adventures of a rough-hewn larger-than-life Scottish hero-king, modelled for literary purposes on Alexander the Great, who, to medieval listeners of tales, was the hero *par excellence*. Robert the Bruce's immediate successors were cast in a less heroic mould than their great forebear, and the new generation needed a patriotic reminder. Furthermore, the taste for tales about the heroes of antiquity, which had lasted throughout the Middle Ages, was beginning to be satiated. Here was a modern national hero in whose lifetime the poet had been born.[3] Barbour was thus fulfilling a political as well as an historical purpose; and, so far as we know, doing it in a way absolutely new: as new as the way in which Sir Walter Scott was once again to reanimate medieval history four hundred years later. Not only Barbour's love of action and the human qualities which sustain it invite such a comparison. Like Scott, too, Barbour used his skills to make the telling of history yield both the satisfaction of a work of art and a strengthening of patriotic pride.

In any case, the chronicling traditions of the period allowed the casual combining of myth with fact. Chronicling narrators happily stood aside from time to time to make way for the embellishments of dubious parallels drawn from the literature of the Classical world. Thus, Barbour's "truth", as A. M. Kinghorn[4] has observed, was "truth of account of successive incidents, military tactics, details of battles and skirmishes and accuracy of chronology rather than truth of motive on the part of the hero." That the romantic approach to history, Scott's approach, was also Barbour's he tells us himself.

Stories to read are delitable,   [delectable
Suppose that they be nocht but fable;
Then suld stories that suthfast were   [truth
And they war said on gude manner,
Have double pleasance in hearing,
The first pleasance is the carpying   [discourse
And the tother the suthfastness   [telling truly
That schaws the thing richt as it wes;
And suth things that are likand
Til mans' hearing, are pleasand.   [to
Tharfor I would fain set my will,
Gif my wit micht suffice thartil,   [if, thereto
To put in writ a suthfast story,
That it last ay furth in memory,   [forth
Swa that na length of time it let,   [so
Na ger it haly be foryet.   [not allow it be wholly forgotten
For auld stories that men reads
Represents to them the deeds
Of stalwart folk that livit ar,   [before
Richt as they then in presence war.

Insofar as Barbour's poem is a narrative of heroic deeds, then it is indeed a "romance"* in the medieval sense of the term. Barbour himself saw it as such, for after his prologue he announces:

Lordings wha likis for til hear,   [to
The Romanys now begins here.

It is nevertheless ultimately as an historian that Barbour presents himself, using the octosyllabic couplet, which was already the common vehicle for this purpose in England and France. He excels in describing real events that took place only a generation removed from his own youth, and in catching the sounds and colours of action. The build-up of Bruce's character is achieved through the sustained reiteration of the soldierly qualities which

* Originally a composition in a "Romance" language stemming from the Latin tongue during the Dark Ages. By the eleventh century its main homes were in France. The *Chanson de Roland* and *Huon of Bordeaux* are twelfth-century examples of the *chansons de geste*. *Launcelot du Lac* typifies Arthurian Romance. *Aucassin et Nicolette* is a thirteenth-century example of *Romans d'Adventure*. Guillaume de Lorris's *Roman de la Rose* (completed by Jean de Meung in the latter part of the thirteenth century) had international influence. Germany possesses the *Nibelung's Ring*, while from England come *Havelok* and *King Horn*.
Romance enmeshes historical and folk material which has no correspondence in ancient literature. Romance laid the foundation of modern prose fiction, its passion for story telling never having been assuaged. It eventually gave rise to the conception of Romanticism, encouraging energy, fancy and freedom as opposed to the lucidity and order of Classicism.

carried him triumphantly through skirmishes and battles, and of his compassionate day-to-day chivalry, which made him a legend even to such ordinary folk as the old woman at whose house the fugitive king, seeking shelter, arrived in 1306.

> All that travelled ere
> For sake of ane, are welcome here.
> The King said, "Gude dame, what is he
> That gars you have sic speciality   [makes
> Til men that travels?" "Sir, perfay,"
> Quod the gude wife, "I sall yow say.
> Gude King Robert the Bruce is he
> That is richt lord of this country".

The character of Sir James Douglas, on the other hand, is described in greater detail, perhaps to provide a more human contrast and thus a foil for the hero; or perhaps merely in order to be able to liken the Douglas to the hero of Troy.

> . . . he was nocht sa fair, that we
> Suld spek greatly of his beauty:
> In visage was he somedeal gray,   [somewhat
> And had blae hair, as I hear say;
> But of limbs he was weil made,
> With banes great and schuldrys braid.   [shoulders
> His body was weil made and lean,
> As they that saw him said to me.
> When he was blyth, he was lufly,
> And meek and sweet in company:
> But wha in battle micht him see,
> All other countenance had he.
> And in spek lispit he some deal;   [speech
> But that sat him richt wonder weil;
> Til gude Ector of Troy micht he   [to
> In mony thingis likit be.

Once Barbour warms to his theme, he tells his epic story racily: from Bruce's ride north as an outlaw with all the might of Edward swung against him, to the final chivalry of that battle in the Holy Land in which the Black Douglas carries the great king's heart in a casket against the Saracens, its miraculous retrieval from the midst of the enemy, and its return to Scotland, with the Douglas's body, for burial at Melrose. In between, among the most vividly narrated incidents are Bruce's adventures in the mountains (Book 3); the siege of Kildrummy Castle (Book 4); Bruce's slaughter of the traitors (Book 5); the feats of the king's impulsive brother,

Sir Edward Bruce (Book 9); the taking of the castles of Linlithgow, Roxburgh and Edinburgh (Book 10); and the last fight of Edward Bruce (Book
18). Barbour has a sharp eye for effective detail as, for instance, in the episode of the women gathering up the spent English arrows during the
defence of Berwick (Book 17), and running with them to their menfolk
desperately defending the ramparts.

The greatest moments of the poem, however, are the famous address to
Freedom (Book 1), and the vigorous description of the Battle of Bannockburn. Writing, as he was, when an elderly king too feeble to command the
turbulent times had succeeded to the throne of Scotland, Barbour must
have felt some apprehension that the bad old days could easily return; the
days when English sherrifs hanged whom they pleased, and English soldiers left ordinary folk with no certain rights.

> Ah! Freedom is a noble thing!
> Freedom mais man to have liking;
> Freedom all solace to man gives;
> He lives at ease that freely lives!
> A noble heart may have nane ease,
> Na ellis nocht that may him please,   [nothing else but
> Gif Freedom fail; for free liking   [If
> Is yarnit owre all other thing.   [to be desired
> Na he, that ay has livit free,
> May nocht know weil the property,
> The anger, na, the wretchit doom
> That is couplit to foul thralldom.
> But gif he had assayit it,
> Then all perquer he suld it wit;   [by heart
> And suld think Freedom more to prys   [prize
> Than all the gold in world that is.

The same proud spirit rings through these lines as sounds out in the Declaration of Arbroath[5] drawn up in Latin in 1302, probably by Bernard of
Linton, and sent to the Pope by the Second and Third Estates of Scotland.

> Yet at last, by His help Who heals and sains the wounded, we are freed
> from these innumerable evils by our most valiant Sovereign, King, and
> Lord, King Robert, who to set free his heritage and his people faced, like a
> new Maccabaeus or Joshua, with joyful heart toil, weariness, hardship, and
> dangers. By the Providence of God, the right of succession, those laws and
> customs which we are resolved to defend even with our lives, and by our
> own just consent, he is our King: and to him who has brought salvation to
> his people through the safeguarding of our liberties, as much by his own de-
> serving as by his rights, we hold and choose in all things to adhere. Yet
> Robert himself, should he turn aside from the task that he has begun, and

yield Scotland or us to the English King and people, we should cast out as the enemy of us all, as subverter of our rights and of his own, and should choose another king to defend our freedom: for so long as a hundred of us are left alive, we will yield in no least way to English dominion. We fight not for glory nor for wealth nor honour: but only and alone we fight for Freedom, which no good man surrenders but with his life.

Sentiments such as these could only be supported in medieval times by skill in battle, strengthened by that courage which rises out of high national morale. At the culminating moment of the Battle of Bannockburn, it was exactly this kind of well-led courage that carried the Scots victoriously through the *mêlée*.

For when the Scots ynkirly   [especially
Saw their faes sa sturdily
Stand into battle them again,
With all thar micht and all thar main
They laid on, as men out of wit;
For whar they will full strak micht hit,
Thair micht no arming stint thar strak;
They to-fruschit them they micht owre-tak,   [dashed in pieces
And with axes sic duschis gaff   [sense blows, gave
That they helmys and heidis claff.

It is not just its determined patriotic purpose, its strong portrayal of moral and physical defiance—which, for better or for worse, played so considerable a part in forming the character of the Lowland Scot—that gives *The Bruce* its Scottish temper. The poem abounds in touches of a grim ironic humour which we would now acknowledge as being typically Scots. Thus, when Sir Richard Clare sends out spies to bring back an estimate of the size of the Scots army, the English scouts report the numbers to be so few as scarcely to make "half a dinner". When a party of English forragers return with only one cow, Earl Warren calls it the "dearest beef" he ever saw. There is also that grisly castle scene in which a cell where meal, malt, wine and the blood of beheaded prisoners has been mixed together, is described as "the Douglas's larder".

It is a pity that two other poems with which Wyntoun credits Barbour are lost. One, *The Brut*, seems to have been an account of the supposed descent of the Britons from that moment when Brutus, himself a descendant of Aeneas of Troy, is alleged to have arrived in Britain and founded the line of British kings who reigned until overthrown by the English. The other lost poem, *The Stewartis Oryginalle*, apparently traced the genealogy of the royal house of Stuart from Ninus, the builder of Nineveh, to the then reigning Scottish monarch, Robert II. Some writers have also attributed to Barbour, on quite inadequate evidence, fragments of a *Siege of Troy*, and a diffuse piece, *Legends of the Saints*.

Yet, even without these lost works, in *The Bruce*, Barbour provides Scots poetry with a firm and enduring foundation. Its obvious faults, which need not be laboured, are that its author employs a somewhat limited vocabulary, and is an accurate, rather than an adventurous or even a particularly musical, metrist. But with a little effort and a good glossary, the poem may still be read with pleasure.

The same can hardly be said of Andrew of Wyntoun's *Orygynale Chronykil of Scotland*. Wyntoun (?1355–1422) seems to have come of a good Scots family. He began his clerical career as a canon regular at St Andrews, but by 1395 had been elevated to the position of prior of St Serf's Inch, the island in Lochleven on which Mary, Queen of Scots later found herself a prisoner. There, with only his books and his fellow clerics for company, Wyntoun passed his quiet days, troubled towards the close of his life by sudden bouts of illness which, he tells us, made him hasten the completion of the final book of the poem. Wyntoun's purpose in writing, like Barbour's, was also political: the tracing of Scotland's independence from the moment of the Creation to his own day in order to sustain national morale, missing out original treatment of Bruce's life solely because of his admiration for Barbour's poem—whose octosyllabic couplets, incidentally, Wyntoun imitated, explaining:

> In Bruce his book has gert be seen   [caused to be seen
> Mair wycely treted into writ   [more cleverly
> Than I can think with all my wit.

Barbour's wit was that of a widely-read, well-travelled scholar, familiar with men and affairs; Wyntoun's, that of a dry, if conscientious recluse. There is historical value, however, in the last part of his work, which covers the ninety years that had passed since Bruce's death. But so far as literary value is concerned, the already quoted "cantus" by the other, justly admired anonymous older hand, gleams like a jewel in a vast setting of paste.

One of the interesting sidelights on Wyntoun's work is his explanation of why the Scots then disliked the English so much, the current cause being the recent capture of James I at sea by an English pirate during peacetime.

> It is of Inglis natioune
> The common kend conditioune   [known
> Of Truce the virtue to forget,
> And reckless of gude Faith to be.
> Where they can there Avantage see
> There may na Band be maid sa ferm
> Than they can mak their will their term.

Even more interesting is the earliest recorded encounter between Macbeth and the three weird sisters:

A nicht he thoucht in his dreaming
That sittand he was beside the King
At a seat in hunting, swa
Intil a leish had grewhunds twa,
He thocht while he was swa sittand
He saw three wemen by gangand,   [going
And thai wemen than thoucht he
Three weird sisters mast like to be.
The first he hard say, gangand by,   [heard
"Lo, yonder the Thane of Crwonbawchty."   [Cromarty
The tothir woman said again,   [the other
"Of Moray yonder I see the Thane."
The third then said, "I see the King."
All this he heard in his dreaming.
Soon eftir that, in his youthade,   [in his youth
Of thir thanedoms he Thane was made;   [those
Syne neist he thocht for to be King.   [then next
Fra Duncan's days had taen ending.

Thus Wyntoun plodded stolidly on, having given to Shakespeare, through Holinshed, a myth which was to prove dramatically fruitful. Its creator, or recorder—Wyntoun was a credulous believer in the superstitions and legends current in his own day—was himself quite willing to excuse Macbeth for "taking the ending" of Duncan's days on the grounds that the murderer:

All time ayssyd he to wirk   [used
Profitably for Haly Kirk.

Today, Andrew of Wyntoun may be left to the attention of historians.

This is not true, however, of the author of *The Actis and Deedis of the Ilustre and Vaillyeand Campioun Schir William Wallace, Knicht of Ellerslie*, whom tradition claims to be a minstrel known to us as Blind Harry (*c.* 1450–1491). The historian John Major (1469–1550) is our authority for this attribution. We are further told that Harry was blind from birth, and that he composed his poem during Major's infancy. From the Lord High Treasurer's accounts, we know that one "Blin Harry" received payments for reciting to James IV. Presumably the poet died soon after 1492, the year of the final entry.

Although *The Wallace* was written long after the death of its hero, it is an obvious companion piece to *The Bruce*. Blind Harry's political purpose was

similar to Barbour's. As it happens, Harry's poem also has historical significance, in that it is what Walter Scheps has called "the fullest—and virtually the only—account of the life and achievements of its hero."

Yet Harry is obviously writing for artistic effect, perhaps even for
spoken effect, since some of his lines can only be made to scan if inconsistent
variations of pronunciation are allowed. Though he is a less conscientious
historian than Barbour, the few facts of Wallace's life-story that can be
verified independently do not show Harry much at fault. It is not now possible to determine if he really did have as a source-book a Latin life of Wallace by John Blair, said to have been the knight's chaplain. Nor is it possible
to overlook the absurdity of the incidents known to be entirely the creation
of Harry's fervently patriotic imagination, which was also doubtless responsible for frequent palpable exaggerations, like his caricature description of the dimensions of Wallace's stature.

Harry's enthusiasm leads him to march Wallace southwards almost to
the gates of London, from which a terrified Edward sends out Eleanor his
Queen, to suggest a peaceful solution to the troubles between their two
nations. With dignified chivalry, Wallace repulses this purely fictitious
gesture. Only then could the supposedly frightened English king be prevailed upon to sally forth and deal with the invading Scots.

The physical exaggeration in Harry's descriptions of Wallace's many
recorded personal combats has sometimes been attributed to the poet's lack
of sight. Yet however much Blind Harry's colourful falsifications may
pain historians, late twentieth-century generations, nourished on a visual
diet of Hollywood films and television "soap-operas" based on the lives of
historic characters, would agree with the poet that in tales (or "gestis", as
they were still called in his day), fact need not necessarily determine what is
made to happen.

The eleven books of *The Wallace* are written mostly in decasyllabic couplets, the first known instance of the almost continuous use of this measure
in a major work of Scottish literature. It cannot be denied that Harry's
heroics contribute to the tedium which long stretches of his poem provoke,
the more so since he is usually content to relate embellished surface details
rather than probe motives or sketch character.

His battle scenes, though filled with descriptive detail, somehow do not
quite re-create the smell and heat and confusion of the scene as do
Barbour's descriptions of fights. This rout of a trapped English force by the
Scots is a case in point.

Atour the rock the laif ran great din.	[on top of, rest
Some hang on crags, richt dulfully to dee.	[rocks, sadly
Some lap, some fell, some floterit in the sea.	[leap
Na Southeran on lif was levit in that hauld,	[left, alive, hold
And them within they brint in powder cauld.	[burnt

There is a vivid sea-scene in connection with Wallace's crossing to France (Book 9), a journey now known actually to have taken place. For a voyage that was to lead to Wallace's encounter with, and triumph over, the Red Reiver at sea, there were bustling preparations as the ship was made ready.

Seamen he feeit, and gave them gudely wage;   [hired
They wanted nocht of wine, victual nor gear.
A fair new barge richt worthy wrocht for war.
With that they were a gudely company
Of waillet men, had wrocht full hardily.   [chosen, made
Bonalis drank richt gladly in a morrow,   [farewell cups
Syne leave they took, and with Sanct John to borrow,
Boatis were shot, and fra the rock them sent;
With glad hertis at aince in they went;   [once
Upon the sea they rowit hastily.   [rowed
The seamen then wirkand full busily   [working
Anchors wound in wisely on ather side;
Their lines cast and waitit weil the tide;
Let sailsis fall, and has their course ynom: [sails let down, course set
A gude gay wind out of the richt airt come.
Frekis in forestem rulit weil their gear,   [persons, prow
Leadis on luffboard, with a lordly feir,   [taking a sounding by throwing a
        weight overboard, companion
Lancis lead out to look their passage sound,   [sounding-leads dropped
With full sail thus fra Scotland forth they bound.

One of the most moving passages in the poem is Wallace's lament over the body of his comrade-in-arms, Sir John Graham.

When they him fand, and gude Wallace him saw.
He lichtit doun, and hint him fra them aa   [hid
In armis up. Beholdand his pale face,
He kissit him, and cryit aft, "Alas!
My best brother in world that ever I had,
My aefauld friend when I was hardest stad,   [single-hearted, beset
My hope, my heil, thou was in maist honour,
My faith, my help, my strengthist in stour,
In thee was wit, freedom and hardiness,
In thee was truth, manheid and nobleness,
In thee was rule, in thee was governance,
In thee virtue withouten variance,
In thee lawte, in thee was great largeness,
In thee gentrice, in theee was steadfastness.
Martyr thou art for Scotland's richt and me;
I sall thee venge, or ellis tharfore dee.

Although Harry is not generally regarded as a so-called "Scottish Chaucerian", the influence of Chaucer on that passage is obvious. It is even more obvious on the apostrophe before Lady Wallace's death, one of the few lyrical interludes with which Harry varies his lengthy text:

> Now leave thy mirth, now leave thy hail pleasance.
> Now leave thy bliss, now leave thy childis age,
> Now leave thy youth, now follow thy hard chance,
> Now leave thy lust, now leave thy marriage.
> Now leave thy luve, for thou shall loss a gage
> Whilk never in erd sall be redeemt again.   [earth
> Follow fortune and all her fers outrage.   [fierce
> Go leif in war, go leif in cruel pain.   [live

Similar to the French *ballat royal* form (*ababbcbc*) this stanza was used both by Chaucer and by Dunbar, with whom, indeed, it was a particular favourite.

In spite of *The Wallace's* romancing, its stretches of wordy tedium, Harry fills out many of his minor characters with skill, and carries the story forward to its tragic end in a restrained and dignified manner. Wallace's betrayal by Menteith is portrayed with vivid simplicity, the smooth nobleman uttering false assurances, Wallace standing silent with the rope round his wrists. In the same way, Harry's understatements in the execution scene are effective. Having refused to admit himself Edward's subject, Wallace is condemned to death by butchery, and denied the services of a priest before his execution. Appalled by the king's inhumanity, the Archbishop himself gives Wallace absolution. He is then persistently bothered in his last moments by an official priest, as both Mary, Queen of Scots and Montrose were similarly pestered.

Thereafter, as Harry puts it:

> . . . Lord Clifford, that knicht,
> To let him haif his Psalter buik in sicht.
> He gert a preist it open before him hauld,   [got
> While they til him had done all that they wald.
> Steadfast he read for ocht they did him there . . .
> Gude devocioun sa was his beginning
> Conteynd tharwith, and fair was his ending.

Harry wisely spares us the details of his hero's end, which included castration, half-hanging and disembowelling.

Wallace survives in a single copy dated 1488, copied by the hand of one John Ramsay, a scribe also responsible for one of the two surviving manuscripts of *The Bruce*. Harry's poem was first printed in 1508. A revised version, Protestantized to suit the Reformation temper, appeared in 1570. Subsequently it went through more editions than the work of any other Scottish poet before the arrival on the literary scene of Burns and Scott. Eight editions were brought out during the seventeenth century, and several in the eighteenth. In 1722 William Hamilton of Gilbertfield produced a "modern" English version, which thereafter outdid the original in popularity. Hamilton's heroic couplets in the Augustan manner are certainly threadbare stuff. One sample will suffice, the lines preceding those describing the sea voyage already quoted in the original:

Towards his voyage Wallace does advance,
And at Kirkcudbright shipping takes for France;
With fifty brave stout Scottish gentelmen
Above what I describe can with my pen.

The impact of the Gilbertfield version of *Wallace* on Burns, however, was immense. He told Mrs Dunlop, a descendant of the patriot, in a letter dated 15th November 1786: "The first books I met with in my early years, which I perused with pleasure, were the lives of Hannibal and Sir William Wallace."

To Dr John Moore, in the autobiographical letter of 2nd August 1787, Burns reveals the effect their life stories had on him: "Hannibal gave my young ideas such a turn that I used to strut in raptures up and down after the recruiting drum and bagpipe, and wish myself tall enough to be a soldier; while the story of Wallace poured a Scottish prejudice in my veins which will boil along there till the flood-gates of life shut in eternal rest."

James Hogg, who liked to think that the poetic mantle of Burns had fallen across his shepherd's shoulders, also reacted strongly to the Wallace story: "It was . . . in the eighteenth year of my age, that I first got a perusal of the *Life and Adventures of Sir William Wallace* and the *Gentle Shepherd**; and though immediately fond of them, yet (what you will think remarkable in one who hath since dabbled in verse) I could not help regretting deeply that they were not in prose . . ."; certainly a fair enough response to Hamilton's efforts.

More immediately, however, the impact of the original *Wallace* was considerable on the anonymous author of *Lancelot of the Laik*, an expanded paraphrase of the French prose romance *Lancelot du Lac*. He, too, uses decasyllabic couplets varied with occasional stanzas of Chaucerian pattern. As M. M. Gray has pointed out: "The descriptions of nature at the beginning of the different books . . . bear a strong resemblance to the similar descriptions at the beginning of Harry's *Wallace* from which they were probably imitated." With the anonymous translation from the French of part of the *Romaunt of the Rose*, or with such Arthurian romances as the

* By Allan Ramsay.

Northern English *Sir Gawain and the Green Knight*, or romances like *Sir Graysteil* and *Roswall and Lillian*, in octosyllabic metre and once enormously popular in Scotland though also probably of English origin, we need not here be concerned.

By the time Harry was writing, the romances and tales of the heroes of antiquity had already had their day. A people accustomed to the violent conditions of the Wars of Independence had come to learn that heroism must wear a modern face. Indeed, *Ane Ballat of the Nine Nobles*, written during the latter part of the fourteenth century, devotes a stanza each to Hector, Alexander, Caesar, Joshua, David, Maccabaeus, Arthur, Charlemagne, and Goddfrey, then includes as ninth in heroic succession:

> Robert the Brois throu hard feichting,
> With few venkust the michty King   [vanquished
> Of Ingland Edward, twice in ficht
> That occupyit his realme bot richt . . .   [without

Two other anonymous poems of the period, however, are worth our attention. The first is *The Tail of Rauf Coilyear, how he harbreit King Charlis*, which was first printed by Robert Lekprevik at St Andrews in 1572, though it was probably written about 1475. M. P. McDiarmid's curious suggestion[6] that it might well be the work of Blind Harry cannot possibly be proved. The credit therefore must go to that most prolific of all Scots authors, Anon.

The story seems to be based on an incident which befell Philip, Duke of Burgundy, one winter's night in 1458. Apparently he lost his way and became separated from his attendants in the forest of Sogne, eventually finding shelter in "La Cabane d'un Chabonnier". In the morning his attendants duly made up with him, and the reunited party rode in procession back to Brussels.

The poet, however, applies this adventure to Charlemagne, and treats the royal episode with vigorous humour. It is a story that has many parallels, ranging from King Alfred and the Shepherd through Henry VIII and the Cobbler to King James II and John Hewson. *John the Reve*, a popular ballad almost contemporary with *Rauf*, also treats of a similar instance, and Dunbar, urging the betterment of his own position at Court to James IV in *Schir, Remember*, reminds his tardy royal patron of those:

> Gentle and semple of every clan,
> Kin of Rauf Colyear and John the Reif.

Rauf is couched in a stanza formerly much used for serious romances, suggesting to some critics that it was intended as a deliberate burlesque. To us, the important point about this French tale is that it has been thoroughly Scoticized. The storm which blatters down upon the proud royal rider is a

Scottish storm:

And as that royal rode owre the rude muir
him betide ane tempest that time hard I tell.
The wind blew out of the east stiflie and sture,
the drift durandlie draif in mony deep dell.   [lastingly drove
Sa fiercely fra the firmament, sa fellounlie it fure   [fared
there micht na folk hald na fure on the heich fell.   [further
In point they war to perish, they proudest men and pure,
in thae wichit wedderis there wist nane to dwell,   [weather
Amang thae mirk mountains sa madlie they mer,   [they were bewildered
  be it was prime of the day
  sa wonder hard fure they   [proceeded
  that ilk ane tuik ane seir way   [separate
    and sperpellit full fer.   [dispersed, far

Ithand wedderis of the east draif on sa fast   [continual weathers
it all to blaisterit and blew that thairin baid.
Be they disserverit, sindrie midmorn was past.
There wist na knicht of the Court what way the King raid.
                                [no Knight knew which way

Struggling over "the wild muir in blinding storm", the king came upon a "cant carl", (a rough, gossipy fellow) whom he asked to bring him to "some harberie" or shelter. The collier took him to his home "among the fellis hie", (high fells), mistaking his king in weatherbeaten clothes for an ordinary traveller. Once the collier had attended to the horses, he indicated to the king to go through the door of the house first. The well-bred king urged the collier to lead the way; whereupon the collier, unaware of the niceties of courtly manners, took the king by the back of his collar and propelled him forward.

While the two men warmed themselves by "ane bricht brynand fire", Rauf called on his wife, Gyliane, to prepare supper. The meal ready, the collier bade the king take Gyliane's hand to the table. Once again the king politely beckoned his host to do the honours. This time the collier, under the impression that he was being mocked, grew angry at the king and "hit him under the ear with richt hand". The king staggered across the hall, whereupon the collier ordered his wife to take the guest's hand and proceed "to the buird" (table) telling the king:

Sir, thou art unskilful and that sall I warrand.
Thou byrd to have nurtour aneuch and thou hes nane,   [should, breeding
Thou has walkit, I wis, in mony wold land.
The mair virtue thou suld have to keep thee fra blame.
Thou suld be courtes of kind and ane cunnand courtier.

Thocht that I simple be,
do as I bid thee.
The hous is mine, pardie,
    And all that is here.

This sturdy collier is, in fact, an ancestor of Lyndsay's John the Common
Weill not yet fallen on evil times. The king, though never before "thus
gait-leird" (taught in such a manner), took it all in good part, and they sat
down together to a meal of rabbits, venison and game poached from the
king's own forests, and accompanied by wine, as a result of which they
found themselves "fure into fusioun" (warmed into agreement). Back
round the fire again, Rauf boasted of his prowess at hunting the king's deer
then tried to find out something about the background of his mysterious
guest. All the king would say was that he was a groom in the Queen's
Chamber, and that he was called Wymond of the Wardrobe.

Next morning, as the king was leaving, he asked Rauf to deliver him a
load of coals at the palace. Against Gyliane's advice, Rauf duly turned up at
the palace, where he quarrelled with Sir Roland, a knight instructed by the
king to watch for the collier's coming. On gaining admittance to
"Wymond", he finds him dressed "in claes of clean gold", and exclaims:

"In faith he is of mair state than ever he me told.
Allace, that I was hidder wylit,   [hither wiled
I dreid me sair I be begylit!"
The King privily smylit
    When he saw that bald.   [bold one

To the collier's dismay, the king then proceeded to regale the other
knights with an accurate account of what had happened the previous
evening, asking his followers what should be done to one who had
behaved thus towards his sovereign. The knights suggested that hanging
might be a suitable punishment. Instead, the king, appreciating Rauf's true
worth, dubbed him a knight, as one "worthy to ga to fecht Goddis faes",
(worthy to go and fight God's foes).

Clad now in armour and mounted on a horse, Sir Rauf sets out to find
and defeat Sir Roland. Instead, he encounters a huge knight riding on a
camel. Rauf charges. The combat ends with them both unhorsed and fighting on foot, until Sir Roland appears and separates Sir Rauf from his adversary, who turns out to be none other than the Saracen knight Magog, on his
way to the king with a declaration of war against France. But all ends happily. Sir Rauf becomes Marshal of France, and sets up a hostelry for stran-
gers on the moor where he first met the king.

Rauf Coilyear retains a flavour of the old-fashioned alliterative style abandoned in England for more than a century, but which reappeared in Scotland in the fifteenth century and was frequently resorted to even by

Dunbar.

The other popular poem of the time is *Cockelbie's Sow*, a semi-nationalized tale referred to by, among others, Gavin Douglas in his *Palice of Honour*:

> I saw Rauf Coilyear with his thrawin brow,   [determined
> Crabit John the Rauf and auld Cowkellpis sow.

Cockelbie's Sow is written in short irregular couplets, reminiscent of those in Skelton's later *Colin Clout*. It has been suggested by T. F. Henderson that the author of *Cockelbie's Sow* must have decided to adjust the popular regular octosyllabic couplet form usual for the telling of tales to his own rough couplets with lines of three "fyttes".

Introduced by a short "Prohemium" in irregular heroic couplets, the poem tells the tale of Cockelbie, the owner of "a simple black sow", who sold the beast for three pennies. As it is a country tale, the poet warns us not to expect too much in the way of sophistication:

> . . . I will say of my fantasy
> Some solacing to glaid this company,
> But for God's love and his apostle, Peter,
> Pardon the foolish face of this mad metre,
> Sen the sentence too feil is fantastic   [since, much
> Lat the letter and language be suchlike.
> Sen all the world changes so many faces,
> I trust I will cast cases upon cases,
> And so lat see what case you think most nice.

We are told that:

> The first penny of the three
> For a girl gaif he;
> The second fell in a furde;   [a ford through a burn
> The third he hid in a hoarde.   [hoard

We are then asked:

> Now whilk penny of the three
> Wes best bestowit, say ye?

The poet provides his own answer:

> The girl for the time plesit,
> But the penny that wes hid
> I hold least gude did.

So he begins with the tale of the second penny, which had fallen into a ford across a burn. The finder of it used it to buy a little pig. This pig, however, was stolen by a harlot who lived nearby and wanted to throw a party, to which she invited all the least reputable characters in the community. The poet has plenty of alliterative fun with her guest list, which includes:

Ane apostita frier,   [apostate friar
A pervert pardonair   [crooked pardoner
Ane practand palmair,   [experienced beggar
A witch and a wobstare,   [weaver
A milygant and a mychare . . .   [cheat, sponger
An old monk, a lecheur,
A drunken drechour,
A double-toungit counsalour . . .

The company duly assembled, they propose to kill and roast the pig. However, the "puir pig gaif a roar", which brought an alliterative company of rescuers swarming onto the scene:

Gruntillot and Gamald,
Wrotek and Writhneb,
Hogg evir in the eb,   [ever
With the halkeit hoglyn   [hacked pig
Suelly Suattis Swankyn,
Baynell bred in the bog,
Hog hoppit owre hog,
Mage of the Millhill,
Grom Gym of the Gill . . .

And so on. They made a very great noise:

With sic a din and a dirdy,   [bustle and confusion
A ganoy and a hirdy girdy,   [annoyance
The fules all afferd were,
And the harlot hurt there
With bare Tuskis tooth.
And for to say the very sooth,
In that fellon affray,   [pretty
The little pig gat clean away.

Meanwhile, the noise made by this gang of would-be rescuers aroused the neighbours who, alarmed at such an assemblage of rascals, sallied out to protect their sheep and cattle:

Stock horns blew stout,
Mony ane ischit out.   [issued
Gilby on his grey mare,
And Fergy on his sow fair,
Hoge Higin by the hand hint,   [pig, led
And Symy that was sun-brint,   [sun-burnt
With his lad Lowry
And his gossip Glowry.

At the same time, another group of neighbours was advancing from a
different direction. When the two groups identified each other, they
forgot for the moment what had brought them out, and began dancing together. Thanks to the variety of items in this impromptu programme,
which the poet dutifully lists, the names of many old tunes that are lost, as
well as of a few which have come down to us, are catalogued:

Some *Perdowy*, some *Troly Lolly*,
Some *Cock Craw thow whill day*,   ["Hey, now the day daws"
Twysbank and *Terway*,   ["Tweedisbank"
Some *Lincoln* some *Lindsay*
Some *Jolly Leman, dawes it not day?*
Some *By yon woodside sings*
Some *Late, late on evenings* . . .

At last, worn out with music and dancing, the two companies remembered their purpose, and:

Fell on the foirsaid sottis
And ourthrew all the idiots
Both of the swyne and the men.

What did it amount to?

All this grit brawling,
Babbling and other thing
Was for a pig as ye heard sayn,
Yet he escapit unslain.

In the second part, Cockelbie, without explanation, becomes a Frenchman, the girl, Adria, bought with the first penny, a beauty whom he treats
as a daughter, but gives eventually as wife to his son Flannisie. Flannisie and
his Adria so impress the king and queen that the two are given an earldom
to be called Flandria (Flanders), a bringing-together of their names.

In the third part, couched without much alliteration in heroic couplets,
Cockelbie takes the third penny out of its hiding-place and buys two eggs,
which he gives to his godson, Cockalb. Cockalb's mother thinks the gift an

insult, so Cockelbie's hen-wife uses them to found a chicken farm, Chantecler, Pertelot and Sprutok hatching further progeny till from the proceeds Cockelbie is eventually able to give his godson £1,000; an early example of the value put upon Scots thriftiness and business acumen.

We owe the survival of *Cockelbie's Sow*, like so much of the poetry of the period, to the manuscript prepared by George Bannatyne (1545–c. 1608), who was born in Newtyle, Forfarshire, but became a wealthy merchant in Edinburgh. When the plague struck the Capital in 1568, Bannatyne retreated to Newtyle, where he passed his time copying out, presumably from texts already in his possession, works by the poets he most admired.

Much of our fifteenth- and sixteenth-century heritage has undoubtedly been lost. But for Bannatyne's patient enthusiasm, even less would have come down to us.

Several other early pieces of the same period have escaped loss or destruction, among them *King Berdok*, a poem about a monarch of Babylon who lived in summer "intil ane bowkail stock" (cabbage stock) but changed his winter abode to a "cokkil shell", which no doubt provided warmer quarters. He wooed a lady who turned out to be a daughter of "the king of Fairy". The unlucky earthly monarch then found himself up against not only the outraged Fairy king, but also his somewhat surprising allies, the Kings of Pictland, Portugal, Naples and Naverne. In most unroyal fashion, this alliance of royals trained guns firing raw dough at Berdok, who had hidden in the chimney-flue of a lime-kiln. Mercury, however, took pity on him, and turned Berdok into a fern bush.

And when they saw the buss waig to and fra,   [bush
They trow'd it was ane gaist, and they to ga;
Thir fell kings thus Berdok would haif slain.
All this for lufe, luvers sufferis pain.
Boece said, of poetis that wes flour,
Thocht lufe be sweet, aft syiss it is full sour.   [often afterwards

King Berdok is an early example of the narrowness of the dividing line between the realms of fact and fancy in the Scottish poet's imagination.

One other minor alliterative piece deserves mention, that unearthly love-story about *The Gyre-Carling*, (water sprite) who lived in the Tinto Hills and ate the flesh of Christians. One, Blasor, fell in love with her, and tried to take her by force. The Carling laughed at him, and by a crude related exuberance from another part of her anatomy, produced Berwick Law. Once again, "the King of Fairy" intervened, besieging her with dogs gathered from places as widely separated as Dunbar and Dunblane. The dogs gnawed the stones around her, so she changed herself into a sow, went "gruntling owre the Greek sea" and in Asia achieved the double feat of becoming Queen of the Jews and marrying Mahoun.

The Gyre-Carling was one of the tales with which Sir David Lyndsay used to divert the child eventually to become James V. Perhaps it proved little more alarming than the later popular nursery-tales of the brothers Grimm.

In any case, long before Bannatyne's devoted quill pulled these old-fashioned fanciful diversions back from impending oblivion, a new and freshly personal note had sounded its way into Scottish poetry: a note which, as Agnes Mure Mackenzie points out, harks back ultimately "to those Provençals of the twelfth century from whom, through Italian, derives so much Northern work we are accustomed to think of as Renaissance."

King James I of Scotland was born in 1394. As Wyntoun rightly stated, during a time of truce on 22nd March 1406 while on his way to France, the young king was captured at sea by an English pirate, and handed over to Henry IV at Westminster. For the next eighteen years he was virtually a prisoner, although after Henry V succeeded to the throne, the king of the Scots was moved to Windsor and treated with great kindness. James accompanied Henry to France in 1420. When, two years later, the English king died there, James returned to England with the body. Negotiations were soon begun for James's release. For the enforced detention of their sovereign over a period of some eighteen years, the Scots were asked to pay £40,000 towards his keep, a sum reduced by £10,000 when James fulfilled another English condition in February 1424 by marrying a noble English-woman, the Lady Joan Beaufort.

In 1783, William Tytler first published the poem we know today as *The Kingis Quair* (The King's Book), which Tytler had unearthed in a manu-script collection of poems by Chaucer and other poets now in the Bodleian Library at Oxford. The poem had been copied by two different hands, the writing in each case dating from the late fifteenth century. At the beginning of the poem, but on the opposite page and in another hand, author and title are stated. At the end of the poem, in the handwriting of the second copyist, a colophon in Latin ascribes the poem to "James the First, the illus-trious King of Scots". While the evidence for royal authorship is thus per-haps slightly open to question, the poem certainly describes James's experiences during the latter part of his captivity, including his falling in love with the Lady Joan. The poem may well have been begun in 1423, and finished a year or so later, perhaps after James's return to Scotland.

Medieval scribes could hardly have forseen that their casual noting of what was then doubtless common knowledge among the learned would one day be subjected to the probing of later scholars hot for certainties.

The case against royal authorship is based on the author's claim to be a:

. . . sely youth, of nature indegest,   [immature
   Unrypit fruit with windis variable,
Like to the bird that fed is on the nest
And can nocht flee; of wit weik and unstable . . .

At the time of writing, James must have been about twenty-eight or twenty-nine, although for seventeen years or so he had lived as one dependent on the whims of others, very much in the situation of a fed bird as yet unable to fly.

Comment has also been made upon the unlikelihood of a not over-modest Stuart king deigning to compare his status unfavourably with that of the Lady Joan:

The fairest and the freschest yonge floure
That ever I saw . . .

Obviously the poet is simply using the common vocabulary of love's hyperbole.

In support of the royal authorship, there is the additional testimony of John Major. Major was born thirty years after James I's death, and stated quite clearly that the king made a poem about the queen before he married her. Perhaps the best way to leave the matter is to misquote the schoolboy's verdict on the Shakespeare–Bacon controversy, and say that if *The Kingis Quair* was not composed by James I, then it must have been written by another man of the same name.

As Walter Scheps has pointed out, *The Kingis Quair* synthesizes in masterly fashion the widely translated beliefs of Boethius, current common medieval courtly beliefs and conventions, and the literary influence of Chaucer.

Anicius Manlius Severinus Boethius (*c.* 480–524) in his *De Consolatione Philosophiae* adumbrates a situation in which his sorrows are bringing premature old age upon him, until the majestic personification of Philsophy appears, questions him about the nature of his grief, finds that his absence of self-knowledge is the cause of his trouble, and introduces him to Fortune. She ennumerates the blessings Boethius has in the past enjoyed, but laments the impermanent nature of anything she can bestow. Philosophy then propounds that true happiness is to be found only in the all-powerful God. Boethius, however, wishes to know why an all-powerful God should allow evil to exist. This raises the question of man's free-will in relation to God's foreknowledge. Philosophy's answer is that God remains a fore-knowing spectator of events, able to dispense rewards or punishments, according to whichever way our actions go, without affecting the eternal quality of His vision.

In James's poem, this Boethian situation provides a binding intellectual thread which holds the substance together. The poet, a prisoner unnaturally sorrowful for one so young, sets down accurately the variable extremes of youthful moodiness, accentuated and abnormally prolonged by the writer's enforced circumstances:

Among thir thochtis rolling to and fro,
  Fell me to mind of my fortune and ure;   [fate
In tender youth how she was first my foe,
  And eft my friend, and how I got recur   [recovery
Of my distress . . .

He then builds up with great skill the metaphor of himself as a rudderless boat, drifting with windless sails. This reflects his own "unsekerness", or aimlessness. He cries to Calliope, the chief of the muses, for help, and receives it in the form of an analysis which equates "the lack of wynd" with the absence of inspiration for his "lytell tretyse small" and the boat with "the matter whole of all".

Drifting boat and youth, united now in simile, are captured by a pirate and delivered to the enemy. After long years of captivity, the poet looks out of his prison window, sees the beautiful girl with whom he falls in love, and laments anew his inability freely to win her.

A voice tells him not to be afraid, and in a dream he finds himself "ascending upward ay fro sphere to sphere", until he arrives in the presence of Venus. There, he finds lovers of all ages and conditions who have served that goddess rather too whole-heartedly. Because she realizes that her newest suppliant requires more positive mental bracing than she can provide, she passes him on to Minerva, the goddess of wisdom. In true Boethian manner, Minerva tells him that man's will operates most freely when it is under wisdom's "governance". However, since the poet is in love with a young woman, the best that Minerva can do is to return him to earth and recommend him to the attention of Fortuna. "Governance" will at least help him to deal with her vagaries. Taken by Good Hope into Fortuna's presence, she promises the poet her assistance, but warns that the nature of her wheel on which he could ride is:

. . . evermore
After ane hicht, to vale and give a fall,
Thus, when me liketh, up or down to fall.

She takes him by the ear to help him onto the wheel; whereupon the poet wakens up.

The structural idea of the dream-sequence originated in the commentary on Cicero's *Somnium Scipionis* by Ambrosius Theodosius Macrobius, who flourished during the first two decades of the fifth century. Macrobius's moral elevation of Cicero's fragment, as one classicist tartly puts it, "gave the work a popularity in the middle ages to which its own merits have little claim."

James's other influences are less recondite. Obviously he was familair with Chaucer's "Knight's Tale", in which the imprisoned knights Palamon and Arcite first see a pretty girl, Emily, in a formal garden, and have doubts as to whether she be goddess or woman, just as had James (although his imprisonment was not, of course, fictitious). Clearly, James had also read "Troylus and Criseyde", since that poem contains a rudderless boat image; and there is a further parallel between the heart-shaped ruby given by Criseyde to Troylus and that worn by Joan Beaufort. Chaucer also made use of the Macrobian dream device. Another influence is Lydgate's *Temple of Glass*, to which *The Kingis Quair* bears a certain overall general similarity, or "family likeness".

Attitudes and conventions, such as the garden scene and the function of the birds in it, the elaborate description of Joan Beaufort's dress, her dominant position as what we would call today a love-object, and the notion of male love as an insatiable thirst, are all part of the courtly paraphernalia of medieval literature. But what is not, and what ultimately matters most, is the warmth and urgency of the poet's handling of the more personal episodes, particularly his unconventional celebration of married love.

> Blissit mot be the hëye goddis all
>   So fair that glitteren in the firmament!
> And blissit be thare might celestial,
>   That have convoyit hale, with one assent,   [conveyed whole
>   My lufe, and to so glad a consequent!
> And thankit be Fortune's axeltree—   [axle-tree
> And wheel, that thus so well has whirlit me.
>
> Thankit mot be, and fair and lufe befall
>   The nichtingale that, with so good intent,
> Sang there of lufe the notis sweet and small,
>   Where my fair hertis lady was present,
>   Hir with to glad, or that she further went!
> And thou, geraflour, not ithankit be   [gillyflower
> All other flouris for the lufe of thee!
>
> And thankit be the fair castell wall,
>   Where as I whilom lukist furth and lent.
> Thankit mot be the sanctis marciall,   [of March
>   That me first causit hath this accident.
>   Thankit mot be the green bewis bent   [boughs
> Through whom, and under, first fortunyit me
> My hertis hele and my confort to be.   [health
>
> For to the prescence sweet and deletible,
>   Richt of this flour that full is of plesance,
> By process and by menys favourable   [means

First of the blissful goddis purveyance,
   And syne throu long and true continuance
Of veray faith in lufe and true service,
I come am, and yet farther in this.   [in this wise

Unworthy, lo! bot only of her grace,
   In lufis yoke, that easy is and sure,
In guerdoun of all my lufis space   [reward
   She hath me tak, her humble creature.
   And thus befell my blissful aventure
In youth of lufe, that now, from day to day,
Flourish ay new, and yet further, I say.

That tone is new in Scottish poetry. While the *rime royal* stanza is handled with ease, the curious mixture of Scots and Chaucerian English is a variety which, we are told, was never spoken. This not only adds emphasis to the claim of royal authorship, but sets a precedence in linguistic assimilation for the purposes of literature followed five hundred years later by another and greater poet.

It seems reasonably certain that two very different but equally important germinal poems forming a natural pair must also be credited to James I: "Christis Kirk on the Green" and "Peblis to the Play". In the Bannatyne manuscript of 1568, "Christis Kirk" is directly ascribed to the king. John Major, in his Latin *History of Great Britain* of 1521, credits the same poet with "Peblis to the Play". Attempts to credit James V with the poems rely on an assertion by Thomas Dempster, an inaccurate historian, made in 1627, and completely overlook the statements of both Bannatyne and Major.

Together, these two poems founded the Scots tradition of descriptive pieces of rural merry-making in which rough humour and pace are matched; poems of colour and movement viewed by an observer of superior social standing armed with a formidable technical skill. Indeed, Allan H. Maclune thinks that "the intricacy of the metrical form alone precludes the probability of a folk origin."[7]

"Peblis to the Play" describes the journey of some country people to the town of Peebles to enjoy the annual Celtic "Beltane", or May Day, festival. Young girls get out their best clothes before setting off; groups begin to arrive, singing or proceeded by a piper; boys and girls pair away to enjoy the games and the dancing. Two men get into a fight over the bill in a Peebles tavern, the fight spilling into a brawl in the street outside. A cadger (carrier), who happens to be standing near by gets drawn into the *mêlée* and is rigorously beaten, until he is pulled out of the gutter and calmed down by his wife. The persistently belligerent are clapped into the stocks, while Will Swane seeks to restore good-humour by suggesting that all of them dance. This they do, to the skirl of the pipes. The scene ends with the young men and women kissing each other tearful and lingering farewells, until the next feast day.

The intricate stanza form, as T. F. Henderson has pointed out, combines ballad and romance patterns. Each of the two common ballad-form quatrains are held together by an interlocking rhyme scheme. The "bob" of two syllables and the returning "wheel" of the first line, common to all the stanzas, produces the effect of a refrain. The heavy alliteration—a device practised in Scotland long after it had been abandoned in England—is reminiscent of Northern romances like *Sir Tristrem*.

Here is the scene in which the cadger's wife rescues her husband from the fracas outside the pub.

His wife came out, and gaif ane shout,
And be the foot she gat him;   [by
All be-dirten drew him out;   [covered in dirt
Lord God, richt weil that sat him!   [became him
He said, "Where is your cubroun knaif?"   [low-born
Quod scho, "I reid ye, lat him   [advise
Gang hame his gaits." "Be God," quod he,   [go his own way
"I sall anis have at him
            Yit,
Of Peblis to the play."

"Ye fylit me, fy, for shame!" quod scho;   [defiled
"See as ye have drest me!   [see how
How feel ye, sir?" "As my girdin brak,   [pony-girdle
What meikle devil may lest me?   [hinder
I wait nocht weil what it wes,   [don't know
My awn gray meir that kest me,
Or gif I wes forfochtin faint
And syne lay down to rest me,
            Yonder
Of Peblis to the play."

"Peblis" survives because Sir Richard Maitland included it in his personal manuscript anthology, completed about 1587. "Christis Kirk", however, was copied both by Bannatyne and by Maitland.

"Christis Kirk" begins with a dance on the village green—there is a smack of the Scots country dance measure in the verse rhythm—together with the usual accompanying flirtations. There then follows a mock-archery contest between Robene Roy and Jock, who shoot at each other. Fortunately, both are so bad at aiming that neither is hit. Once again, a well-lubricated general brawl develops, but this time continuing over the end of the poem.

When all wes done, Dick with ane aix   [axe
    Come furth to fell one futher.

Quod he, "Where are yon hangit smaix   [mean fellows
    Richt now would slain my brother?"
His wife bade him ga hame gub-glaikes,   [idle boaster
    And sa did Meg his mother.
He turned and gaif them baith their paiks   [drubbing
For he dust ding nane other,   [strike no other
        men said
At Christis Kirk on the Green.

"Christis Kirk" trails off with a vigorous description of a wedding celebration. No doubt it was the absence of a well-defined conclusion that led Allan Ramsay to add some supplementary stanzas to the poem, achieving in the doing one of his raciest and most genuine Scots pieces.

A third poem, cast in the "Christis Kirk" stanza, and possibly by the same hand, is "Symmie and his Brudder", which tells of two St Andrews peasants who disguise themselves as begging friars, the "brudder" doing so well that he is able to marry a rich widow. "Symmie and his Brudder" also seems to lack an ending, perhaps because it has obviously suffered mutilation in Bannatyne's transcription.

Apart from what might be called a likeness of tone in such poems as Dunbar's "The Ballad of Kynd Kyttock" and his "Amends to Telyours", Sir David Lyndsay (in his "Justing of Barbour and Watson"), and Alexander Scott (in his "Justing and Debait") were directly influenced by James I's country pair. Both the Lyndsay and the Scott pieces feature mock tournaments, Scott's poem even using the "Christis Kirk" stanza. However, the family they begot produced several thriving generations that were to include Fergusson's "Leith Races" Burns's "The Jolly Beggars" and "The Holy Fair" and William Tennant's "Anster Fair", to list only some of its more distinguished members.

The first major poet of the fifteenth century is Robert Henryson (1425?–1506?). Very little that is certain is known about his life. It has been suggested that he may have belonged to the family of Henderson of Fordell. It is possible that he studied abroad and that he had legal training. His name is included among the incorporated members of the then eleven-year-old Glasgow University, dated 10th September 1462, as "the venerable master Robert Henryson, licentiate in arts, and bachelor in decrees". Presumably, therefore, he either lectured in law at Glasgow, or was already so eminent that the University decided to honour him.

However, on the title-page of his principal work *The Morall Fabillis of Esope the Phrygian*, he is said to be a "Schoolmaster in Dunfermline", and he is therefore generally assumed to have taught at the grammar-school attached to Dunfermline Abbey. A certain admonitory tone does certainly show itself in some of his poems, although more characteristic is a wry sense of humour which accords with the story of his death put out by Sir Francis Kynaston when he translated Chaucer's "Troylus and Criseyde" and

Henryson's *Testament of Cresseid* into Latin in 1635. Kynaston tells us that, "being very old", Henryson died "of a diarreha, or fluxe", and that a few hours before his demise, a wise woman came to his house and told him that if he wanted to be cured, then he must go to a certain tree at the end of his orchard, and walk round it thrice, repeating the rhyme:

> Whikey tree, whikey tree,
> Take away this fluxe from me.

The old poet protested that he was too weak to do this, and proposed instead that he should go three times round his table, chanting:

> Oaken burd, oaken burd,
> Gar me shit a hard turd.

The "wise" woman thought herself mocked, left the house in a rage, and as a result, it seems, "Mr Henderson, within half a quarter of an hour, departed this life." Probably his death occurred shortly before Dunbar wrote his "Lament for the Makaris" in 1506, where it is said of death that:

> In Dunfermline he has done roune
> With gud Maister Robert Henrison.   [just

Henryson's work is wide in range and variety, though it lacks either the spectacular verbal fireworks or the erratic passion which make Dunbar so exciting a poet. Throughout Henryson's poetry a general air of assurance and calm prevails, even when he is most troubled before the prospect of Man's instability, as in "The Abbey Walk" or humorously worldly-wise, as so often in the moral fables. As Edwin Muir puts it: "He lived near the end of a great age of settlement . . . an agreement had been reached regarding the nature and meaning of life, and the imagination could attain harmony and tranquility."[8]

This is nowhere more clearly demonstrated than in the *Fables*, where there is on the whole a welcome absence of aureate diction, a native freshness in the observation of the changing seasons, and a gently controlled use of musical rhetoric, often employed to point out contrast and similarity between the ways of mice and men. Unlike Chaucer, Henryson does not make his animals' personifications reflect too obviously the tastes and fashions of men. Henryson's creatures remain true to their kind.

Thus, in "The Taill of the Paddok and the Mous," the smallness and timidity of mice in general is delightfully characterized:

> Upon ane time (as Esope culd report)
> Ane little mous come til ane river side;   [to
> Scho micht not wade, hir shankis were sa short;
> Scho could not swim; scho had na horse to ride:
> Of very force behovit hir to bide,

And to and fra beside that river deep
Scho ran, cryand with mony piteous peep.

"Help over! Help over!" this silly mous can cry,
"For Goddis luve, somebody over the brym!"   [flood

In the "The Tail of the Uponlandis Mous and the Burgess Mous", the
plain homely speech of the two mice is much nearer that spoken in Fife
than what might have been heard at Court. Having tasted the "rude diet"
of her sister, the sophisticated town mouse asks:

. . . "Sister, is this your daily food?"
"Why not?" quod scho, "Is not this meat richt gude?"   [asked

"Na, be my saul, I think it bot ane scorn."
"Madame," quod scho, "ye be the mair to blame;
My mother said, sister, when we were born,
That I and ye lay baith within ane wame . . ."

The country mouse is induced to visit her urban sister, and they make
their way through the stubbled corn to the spence, or pantry, which is the
town mouse's home. The first mouse-meal is charmingly described:

Eftir where they disposit were to dine,
Withoutin grace they wesche and went to meat,
With all courses that cukis culd devyne,—   [cooks devise
Mutton and beef, strikin in tailyeis greit;   [tails
Ane Lordis fair thus couth they counterfeit,—
Except ane thing, they drank the watter clear,
Insteid of wine; bot yet they made gude cheer.

In the midst of their enjoyment, however, the Spenser, or steward,
arrives

. . . with keyis in his hand,
Oppinnit the dure, and thame at dinner fand.

The gentle barb of Henryson's humour is deployed on the ensuing scut-
tle for safety:

They taryit not to wesche, as I suppose,   [wash
But on to ga wha that micht formest win.
The Burgess had ane hole, and in scho goes;
Her sister had no hole to hide her in.

Fortunately, the Spenser had no leisure to seek them out. But the town mouse had no sooner calmed her country sister down and persuaded her to resume the meal, when "in come Gib hunter, our jolie cat".

Once again the town mouse bolts to her hole; but Gilbert plays with the country mouse, until she manages at last to creep between the wall and a skirting-board.

This second terrifying experience was too much for the country mouse, and gladly she leaves her sister's "mangerie . . . mingit all with care" for the safety of her country den.

> Als warm as woll, suppose it was not greit,   [as warm as wool
> Full beinly stuffit, baith but and ben,   [comfortably
> Of beans, and nuttis, peas, rye and wheat.
> Whenever scho list, scho had aneuch to eat,   [pleased
> In quiet and ease, withoutin any dreid;
> Bot to her sister's feast na more scho yeid.   [went

Other fables which show understanding of animal ways and relate the human in the animal to the animal in the human, include several in which the Fox or the Wolf, or both, are shrewdly depicted. One of the best is "The Fox's Confession to the Wolf", a masterpiece of good-humoured satire. As penance for his sins, the fox is forbidden all flesh till after Easter. He therefore goes to the seaside to catch fish. The sight of water, however, shakes his resolve, and he exclaims:

> . . . Better that I had bidden at hame
> Nor been ane fischer in the Devil's name.
>
> Now mon I scraip my meat out of the sand,
> For I have neither boats nor net, nor bait!

While absorbed in the contemplation of this difficulty, he sees a passing herd of goats, from out of which he steals "ane lytell kid".

> Syne owre the heuch unto the sea he hies,   [hillock
>   And tuke the kid be the hornis twane,   [by
> And in the watter outher twyis or thryis,   [either
> He dowkit him, and til him can he sayne: [ducked
>   "Ga doun Schir Kid, cum up Schir Salmond agane!"   [drench
>   While he was deid; syne to the land him dreuch,   [till
> And of that new made salmond eit aneuch.

Each fable ends with a *moralitas*, and it has often been observed that these *moralitates* plod somewhat heavily after the pace of the shrewd and humorous tales they follow. Yet this seems a narrow verdict in an age which reacts almost hysterically against moral judgement of any kind. Many of Henryson's *moralitates* merely point the human footnote to the animal ways. Some, like the *moralitas* in "The Taill of the Wolf and the Wedder", catch us out, so to say, by underlining for us the vulnerability of our own sympathies. In this fable, a Wedder (wether) comes to the aid of a shepherd whose dog has died. The Wedder suggests that it should be shorn and clad in a dog's skin. It could then perform the dead dog's function as guardian of the flock. At first all goes well, and the shepherd found that he "wantit not ane Hog". Our sympathies are thus attracted to this useful, ingenious and apparently well-intentioned creature.

Then one day the Wedder vows to catch the Wolf, who has made off with a lamb. Henryson introduces heavy alliteration to emphasize the mock-heroic nature of the proceedings:

> Went never Hound mair haistelie fra the hand,
> When he was rynnand maist raklie at the ra,   [recklessly, rope
> Nor went this wedder baith over mois and strand,   [moss
> And stoppit nouther at bank, bush, nor bra;   [bush
> But followit ay sa ferslie on his fa.   [fiercely

The Wolf exerted himself to the uttermost, for "weil he kennit the keenness of the doig", and even threw the Lamb away to enable him to increase his speed. But all in vain, for "ay the nearer the Wedder he couth bind him".

The chase ends suddenly and dramatically, with the Wedder closing in on the Wolf.

> The Wedder followit him baith out and in,
> Whill that ane brier-busk raif rudlie off the skin.

Things are as they are, we are reminded, not as we would have them seem; and the humiliated Wolf takes his sure revenge.

> I have been oftymis set in grit effray;
> Bot (be the Rude) sa rad yit wes I never
> As thou has made me with thy pretty play.
> I schot behind when thou overtuke me ever;
> Bot sikkerlie now sall we nocht dissever!
> Then be the crag-bane smertlie he him tuke,   [neck-bone
> Or ever he ceissit, and it in-schunder schuke.   [ceased, apart

The poet, having trapped us into sympathizing with the glory-seeking Wedder, turns his *moralitas* on those "presumpteous" enough to forget their station, the keepers-up with the Jones:

Out of their case in pride they clym sa hie
That they forbeir their better in no steid,
Whill sum man tit their heillis over their heid.   [heels

Superficially, Henryson is the most Chaucerian of all the Scots Makars
(as the poets of the fourteenth, fifteenth and early sixteenth centuries
should be called, rather than "Scottish Chaucerians", their differences, not
their similarities, being what ultimately matter) in that his favourite stanza
is either the *ballat royal*, using three rhymes, *ab, ab, bc, bc*, or the seven-line
rime royal stave.* He also sometimes uses the Chaucerian nine or ten-line
interwoven stanza. But in the *Fables*, Henryson shapes and colours his
Chaucerian heritage to his own Scottish ends in subject-matter, tone and
imagery.

To a considerable extent, he also does so in "The Testament of Cresseid"
his continuation of Chaucer's "Troylus and Criseyde". As Burns did in
"The Vision", Henryson immediately establishes the northern climatic
conditions in which he is living and writing. Outside:

The Northin wind had purifyit the air,
And shed the misty cloudis fra the sky;
The froist freisit, the blastis bitterly   [frost froze
Fra Pole Artick come whisling loud and schill.

—a scene instantly recognizable to anyone who has lived on either side of
the Forth. But the poet settles down comfortably in his room.

I mend the fire and beikit me about,   [warmed
Then took ane drink my spreitis to comfort,
And armit me weill fra the cauld thairout;
To cut the winter nicht and mak it short,
I took ane quair, and left all other sport,   [book
Written be worthy Chaucer glorious,
Of fair Cresseid, and worthie Troylus.   [lustie

Having finished with Chaucer, he then took another imaginary
"quair" in which he found "the fatal destiny/Of fair Cresseid, that endit
wretchitlie." Cast aside by her new lover, Diomeid, once he had "gotten
his desire", Cresseid goes back to her father. Although old Calchas is a
priest and keeper of Venus's temple, Cresseid is ashamed to show herself
openly in the temple.

Instead, she steals off to pray in a secret oratory, reproaching Venus and
Cupid for leading her into putting all her trust upon her physical beauty, so
that she believed: "The seed of luve was sawin in my face."

She then swooned, and in a Macrobian dream sequence—without

* So called because it was used by King James of Scotland.

which a large-scale poem of the period would have been as incomplete as a nineteenth century French opera without a ballet—the gods of the ancient world appear in the form of the seven planets. Cupid accuses Cresseid of blasphemy against Venus, his mother, and Saturn, the oldest planet, along with Cynthea, the moon, are told to pass and then deliver judgement on her. Struck by Saturn's frosty wand, she becomes a leper, awakens from her dream, and rushes to a mirror to reassure herself. She finds instead that she has indeed been smitten with the most savage and dreaded illness known to the medieval mind. The realism with which Henryson describes her appearance has led to speculation as to whether or not Henryson may have practised as a physician as well as a schoolteacher; an idle speculation, surely, since every place of any size had its leper colony, its "hospitall at the townis end". Thereafter, following a painful scene with her father, Cresseid is conducted to the "spittal" to beg with the other outcasts "efter the law of lipparleid."

One day Troylus rides by, returning from a victory against the Greeks. Cresseid's sight has gone, so she does not recognize him. Indeed, she is so physically transformed that Troylus also fails to recognize her. Yet she does remind him painfully of the Cresseid of old; so strongly, indeed, as to make him on impulse throw his purse to her. From the other lepers, astonished at her good fortune, she learns the name of her benefactor, and swoons. Before dying, she sends him back the ruby ring which was the first gift she received from him.

Troylus in turn swoons with "great sorrow" when the ring is delivered but then pronounces the only possible verdict admissable in the Court of Love, whose conventions the poem honours.

> . . . I can no more—
> Scho was untrue, and woe is me therefore.

Nevertheless, he has her buried beneath "a Tomb of Merbell gray", which in gold letters carried the simple epitaph:

> Lo, fair ladies! Cresseid of Troyis toun,
> Sometime countit the fleur of womanheid,
> Under this stone, late lipper, lyis deid.   [leper

Henryson's poems were collected for the first time in 1865[9], and in the climate of Victorian public belief, Cresseid was assumed to have exemplified Christian moral standards, her soul redeemed by repentance and love. Yet this is to read into a relentlessly honest retelling of an old tale a significance not justified by anything Henryson actually wrote. Cresseid is a tragic figure, in that she was only partly responsible for her own downfall. But she is not a Christian tragic figure, since even under her affliction her concern is not regret for her infidelity, but simply that other women should not fall victim to men's deception as she did, her "message" that to ensure male fidelity, women should themselves be faithful in love, and not be so foolish as to chide the gods. It is "frivoll Fortoun", that same lady onto whose wheel James I sought to climb in *The Kingis Quair*, whom Cresseid mainly blames for her downfall; not herself. Her sorrow is for the loss of Troylus and for her royal way of living; in other words, worldly regret for her stupidity and the loss of her pleasures, not repentance for sin. She accepts that she made a wrong decision, but is still sure that the cause of her misfortune lies not with herself—"Fortoun is fickle, when scho begins and steers", and as she now realizes, she "clam upon the fickle wheel sa hie". To a modern reader, the tragedy is the more intense just because Henryson intrudes no Christian comfort upon the resolution of this clash between human freewill and the inflexible gods whose power extended over:

> . . . all thing generabill   [created
> To rule and steir be their great influence,   [by
> Wedder and wind, and courses variable.

Over everything, in fact, except moral choice.

Besides the *Fables* and "The Testament of Cresseid", fourteen other poems by Henryson have come down to us. Of these the most considerable is "Orpheus and Eurydice". It is based on Nicholas Trivet's version of the Orpheus legend as narrated by Boethius, and makes somewhat heavy use of musical terms taken from Boethius's *De Musica*. Except for Orpheus's heart-felt cry "Where art thou gone, my lufe Euridice?", used as a chorus-line in two stanzas, much as "O false Cresseid and true knicht Troylus" is used in "The Testament of Cresseid" Henryson's version of the Orpheus legend is so far inferior to the Middle English "Sir Orfeo" that it has little to commend it. The main poem smells of the candle, and in quite the most tedious of all his *moralitates*, the poet explains that Orpheus is the union of Phebus (wisdom) and Calliope (eloquence), and so represents the intellec-tual element in man's soul. Euridyce represents temptation and desire, while Orpheus's fatal backward look is the triumph of worldly lust over reason. However, it is significantly the case that in this skilfully versified manipulation of medieval literary stock-in-trade conventions, the livelier moments evoke the poet's own Scottish scenery.

The medieval fascination for death is reflected in "The Three Deid Pollis", a poem dominated by three skulls in a row (whether real, like the heads of criminals spiked for long months in public places, or represented in effigy, as in tapestries, is not made clear). With their staring sockets of bone, the "lusty gallands gay" and the ladies with white paps enhanced with jewelry, are reminded that they, too, will one day have similar "holkit" heads. From this grim text, Henryson the preacher urges the living to eschew pride and seek heavenly mercy, especially the old for whom death must come soon. Without the fearful force of the recurring

image of the three staring deathsheads, this poem would be as conventionally unnoteworthy as is "The Reasoning betwix Death and Man", a dialogue between arrogant Man and Death, with Man assuring Death that
there is:

> . . . non sa wicht, or stark in this country   [strong, unbending
> But I sall gar him bow to me on forss.   [make, strength

—but ending with Man pleading:

> Jesus, on thee, with piteous voce, I cry,   [voice
> Mercy on me to haif on domisday.

"The Reasoning Betwix Age and Youth" is another dialogue, in which
the two ways of looking at life are pointed by the alternating refrains, that
of Youth's being:

> O Youth, be glaid in to thy flowris grene

—while that of Age is:

> O Youth, thy flowris fedis fellone soon   [fades desperately soon

"The Prais of Aige" seeks to persuade us that the wisdom of the years is
more rewarding than the hot pursuits of youth, advancing the Christian
theory that "The more of age, the nearer heaven's bliss."

"The Abbey Walk" urges us to accept our earthly lot, whatever it may
be, remembering that all is vanity. It has the resignation of a Christian
preacher certain beyond question of his understanding of the ordered balance of values between earth and heaven; the sort of assurance that the ambitious Dunbar lacked temperamentally, and which for twentieth-century
man has long since ceased to hold general validity.

"The Want of Wyse Men" and "Against Haisty Credence of Titlaris"
are satires against corruption in the administration, reflecting something of
the journalistic tone to be found in Maitland or Lyndsay. One backbiter is
vividly described:

> Within ane hood he hes ane double face,
> Ane bludy tongue, under a fair pretense.

"The Bloody Serk" would seem to prove, by its stanza form and metre,
that the ballad was well and truly established in Henryson's day. It tells the
tale of a king's beautiful daughter imprisoned by a giant and rescued by a
knight who, however, is wounded so severely that he dies, giving his
bloodstained sark or shirt to his lady so that she may look on it and remain

celibate: hardly the stuff from which timeless masterpieces are made, particularly when the *moralitas* reveals the king to be the Trinity, the lady the Soul of Man, the giant Lucifer and the knight Christ.

Of Henryson's remaining poems, only two are worthy of notice: "Sum Practysis of Medecyne" because of the surprising length to which Henryson goes, in heavily alliterative verse, to mock the admittedly useless (if not positively lethal) medieval remedies of the ancients. While Burns's "Death and Dr Hornbook" was directly inspired by the continuing use of traditional medical recipies and supposed cures, Henryson is mocking the recipes themselves.

The finest of all Henryson's minor poems is undoubtedly "Robene and Makyne" a dialogue between two rustic lovers, in the style of the French *pastourelle*. While Robene is anxious only to keep his sheep, Makyne does her unsuccessful best to lure him on, even telling him how to set about making love.

> Be heynd, courtas, and fair of feir,   [gentle
> Wise, hardy and free;
> So that no denger do thee dear,
> What dule in dern thou dree,
> Preiss thee with pain at all poweir—   [strive
> Be patient and privie.

When, later, Robene changes his mind, it is Makyne who is no longer interested, reminding him:

> The man that will nocht when he may
> Sall haif nocht when he wald.

Robene now tries his hand at sexual enticement, but fails. So Robene remains unsatisfied, while Makyne laughs at his discomfiture. It is a neatly constructed little pastoral drama, the moral being left to speak for itself.

Henryson's work needs to be read in quantity before the measure of its quality becomes fully apparent since, unlike Dunbar, he is not a supreme master of the virtuoso piece. Yet his poetry impresses by the power and manipulation of its rhetoric, by the naturalness of much of the imagery, and because despite the range of subject, in tone and style, as Isabel Hyde remarks, it is "more all of a piece".[10] The "piece" uses some of the same strands employed by both Chaucer and Dunbar: the ultimate fabric is very much Henryson's own.

By comparison, Dunbar, is not only a man of moods, of extreme exultations and dejections, but a virtuoso deploying his brilliant technique upon several styles, all of them—whether the aureate, the vernacular, the secular or the religious—shot through with contrasted lights, and characterized by energetic brush-strokes. For these reasons, the phrases which use the medieval literary man's stock-in-trade—phrases like *A per se, Fyre on flint, hair like golden wire*—stand out more sharply in his poems than they do within the gentler contours of Henryson's work.

We know a little more about William Dunbar (1460?–1520?) than about the schoolmaster of Dunfermline, but not much. Dunbar is believed to have come from East Lothian, possibly descending from a branch of the family of the Earls of Dunbar, and to have graduated Bachelor of Arts at St Andrews University in 1477, and Master in 1479. He may then have become a Franciscan novice during which period, he tells us in "How Dunbar was Desyred to be Ane Frier", he preached as far afield as Calais and Picardy. However, a vision of St Francis urging him to become a monk turned out to be, in fact, a devil in the likeness of a friar, who disappeared "with stink of fiery smowk", leaving Dunbar resolved to become instead a member of the secular clergy, and hopeful of securing a rich benefice.

For a time he seems to have been a civil servant, journeying to France in 1491 as Secretary to a Scottish embassy. He was certainly a member of the Embassy which went to England in 1500 to discuss the proposed marriage of James IV with Margaret Tudor, after a Spanish match had been declined. He welcomed the Princess's arrival in Scotland for her marriage to the King in 1503, with an aureate flourish beginning:

Now fair, fairest, of every fair,
Princess most pleasant and preclare,   [famous
The lustiest one alive that been,   [most beautiful
 Welcome of Scotland to be Queen!

He travelled north with the Queen in 1511, addressing one of his "official" poems to the city of Aberdeen, after it had mounted a pageant in the Queen's honour:

Blyth Aberdeen, thou berial of all tounis,
 The lamp of beauty, bounty, and blythness;
Unto the heaven ascendit thy renoun is
 Of virtue, widsom, and of worthiness;
 Hie nottit is thy name of nobleness.   [high
Into the coming of our lusty Queen,
 The wall of wealth, guid cheer and mirriness,
Be blyth and blissful, burgh of Aberdeen.

The monarch at whose Court Dunbar was employed was himself a cultured scholar, passionate and religious, a lover of beauty in the arts and in women, yet with a Renaissance impulsiveness which was in the end to lead to his undoing. While Dunbar seems to have been the particular favourite of the less cultured Queen (whose intellectual shortcomings are perhaps unflatteringly emphasized in Holbein's portrait), he features in the Lord High Treasurer's accounts as the recipient of a pension of £10 per annum from 1500. It was raised to £20 in 1507, and to £80 in 1510. But to one in whom high ambitions had been kindled when a very young child—as Dunbar himself tells us:

> I wes in youth, on nurice knee,   [nurse's
> Called dandillie, bishop, dandillie.

—it must indeed have been galling to be denied a benefice the least rewarding of which would have been worth about £100 per annum, which he so ardently desired, and in pursuit of which he vainly addressed numerous poetic reminders to the King. A gap in the registry of payments occurs from August 1513 to August 1515. When the records re-open Dunbar's name no longer features. Yet "When the Governor past into France" has been attributed to Dunbar by the Maitland Manuscript. If this attribution is correct, then this event, dating from 1517, would seem to extend Dunbar's life by a further two years. On the other hand, the poem of about 1520 beginning "We Lordis hes chosen a chiftane mervellous", included in some nineteenth-century editions of Dunbar's work, is so far below his general level of technical accomplishment that its attribution seems unlikely. So we cannot be sure just how long after Flodden, to which disaster he never once referred in his surviving poems, this brilliant, disappointed man disappeared from the scene.

His poems, or most of them, might easily have made an equally elusive departure from our heritage, because only a mere handful of them were printed by Chepman and Myllar in 1508. The bulk of his work survives almost by accident, through the Bannatyne, Maitland, Asloan and Reidpeth manuscripts. The first collected edition of his poems did not appear until 1834.

Dunbar's personal poems tell us quite a lot about his character, his moodiness and deep depressions contrasting with bouts of exuberant exultation. Today, he would probably be described as having a manic-depressive temperament. In "On His Heid-Ake", we learn that he suffered from migraine, and that:

> Full oft at morrow I uprise,
> When that my courage sleeping lies,
>   For mirth, for menstrallie and play,   [music
>   For din nor dancing nor deray,
> It will nocht walkin me no wise.

The Scottish medieval winter, with its poorly illuminated, lengthy darkness, its dampness and its draughtiness, must indeed have made grim enduring. Dunbar certainly seems to have found it so:

Whone that the nicht dois lengthen hours,
With wind, with hail and heavy schours,
   My dule spreit does lurk for schoir,   [sure
   My hairt for langour does forloir

For laik of simmer with his flours.
I walk, I turn, sleep may I nocht,
I vexit am with heavy thocht;
   This world all oure I cast about,
   And ay the mair I am in dout,
The mair that I remeid have socht.

Yet he was well aware of the subjective nature of many of his black moods, and sometimes made a rather forced effort to master them, as in "Ane His Awin Enemy", which concludes with the exhortation:

Now all this time lat us be mirry,
And set nocht by this warld a chirry,
Now, whill thair is gude wine to sell,
He that does on dry bread wirry,
I gif him to the Devil of hell.

The best known and most powerful of these personal poems is the "Lament for the Makaris", sub-titled "When he Was Sek". The liturgical use of the tolling refrain *"Timor mortis conturbat me"* is put to telling effect as Dunbar recounts the manner in which death has removed one by one the poets he admired or knew, leading to the inexorable conclusion:

Sen he hes all my brether tane
He will nocht lat me lif alane;
On forse I man his next prey be: [must
   Timor mortis conturbat me.

Remembering his religious vocation, Dunbar ends this tolling roll-call of the dead with what sounds a somewhat bored and perfunctory affirmation of the belief expected of a Christian:

Sen for the deid remeid is none,
Best is that we for dede dispone,
Eftir our deid that lif may we:
   Timor mortis conturbat me.

Significantly, perhaps, his fear of death is unaltered in this final refrain.

One of the dead poets listed in the Lament—most of the work of all of them has totally disappeared—deserves attention.

Dunbar says of him:

Gud Maister Walter Kennedy
In point of dede lies veraly,
Great ruth it were that so suld be . . .

Yet this same Kennedy was Dunbar's opponent in "The Flyting of Dunbar and Kennedie".

Flyting was an ancient practice, possibly of Celtic origin. The hereditary Celtic bards who earned their livelihood by singing the praises of their patron king or chief, were held in high honour, and expected suitable treatment and recompense when they appeared at the courts of other rulers. A slighted bard always had at his command a good line in invective, and his maledictions were much feared by the superstitious as supposedly bearing the power to cause physical harm.

Dunbar, though a Lowlander, must have come into contact with some aspects of Gaelic culture at the court of James IV, since the names of Gaelic readers also appear in the Treasurer's accounts. Indeed, Dunbar's incredible command of intricate rhyme schemes, metres and stanza-constructions has some affinity with the traditional "strait forms" rigid in metrical structure which Gaelic bards had to master before the proud title of *fili* was granted to them.

In this particular flyting, the scurrilous abuse the two poets hurl at each other in thickly alliterative stanzas, is so exhaustive, as George Bruce has suggested, as to be reminiscent of some Celtic sculpture in which the artist pursues this or that detour to the point where his entire working surface has been filled. The laws of libel restrain the modern journalistic heirs of the flyters: which is perhaps just as well. Though at least one other Scottish poet worthy to rank with Dunbar has indulged freely in the practice of flyting, albeit usually in over-inflated prose, it is hard to have much patience with mere name-calling, here apparently not even seriously intended to wound:

Conspiratour, cursit cocatrice, hell caa,   [crow
    Turk, trumpour, traitour, tyran intemperate;
Thou irefull attircop, Pilate apostata,   [spider
    Judas, jow, juglar, Lollard laureate;
    Sarazene, symonyte provit, Pagan pronunciate,
Machomete, mansworn, bugrist abhominable,   [sodomite
Devil, dampnit dog, sodomyte insatiable,
    With Gog and Magog grete glorificate.

In other circumstances, too, poet Dunbar's mocking spirit sometimes made his religious habit sit a little oddly; as for instance, in "The Testament of Mr Andro Kennedy", where, in Goliardic manner, the poet uses liturgical responses in direct association with secular observations to produce a mood of dark comedy:

I will na preistis for me sing
   Dies illa, Dies ire;
Na yit na bellis for me ring
   Sicut semper solet fieri;
Bot a bag pipe to play a spryng,
   Et enum ail wosp ante me . . .   [a bunch of straw, the sign of an ale house

It is surely possible that his merciless flaying of John Damien, a priest with scientific pretensions whose attempted flight on bird-wings from the walls of Stirling Castle ended in disaster, but who was nevertheless a favourite of the king's, could have had something to do with the royal failure to grant the longed-for benefice. "The Fenyeit Freir of Tungland" is attacked for his alleged pretensions as a wielder of cures:

In leechcraft he was homecide;
He would haif, for a nicht to bide,
A haiknay and the hurt man's hide,
   So meikle he was of myance.   [resources
His irons was rude as ony rauchter,   [rafter
Where he leit blude it was no lauchter,
Full mony instrument for slauchter
   Was in his gardevyance.

His attempt to fly wearing wings made from bird's feathers brought all the birds of the air to attack him. Dunbar's extravagant exhuberance is given full play:

And ever the cuschetts at him tuggit,   [doves
The rooks him rent, the ravens him druggit,
The hudit craws his hair furth ruggit,
   The hevin he micht not bruke. . . .

The golk, the gormaw, and the gled   [cuckoo, cormorant, kite
Beft him with buffets whill he bled;
The sparkalk to the spring him sped,
   As fierce as fire of flint . . .

Dunbar cannot have been a man with whom it was wise to fall out, as James Dog, Keeper of the Queen's Wardrobe, discovered when Dunbar complained to their common mistress:

When that I schaw to him your wrytin,
He girns that I am red for bytin;
I wald he had ane havye clog:
Madame, ye heff ane dangerous Dog!

When that I speak til him friendlike,
He barkis like ane midding tyke,
War chassand cattle throu a bog:
    Madame, ye heff a dangerous Dog!

The rhyme on the Wardrobe-Keeper's name is sustained through six
stanzas, a minor example of the ease with which Dunbar exercised consum-
mate artistry in whatever metre or stanza he chose.

Rhyming exuberance and verbal energy characterize "The Dance of the
Sevin Deidly Sins". There are earlier examples of the practice of repeating
the rhyme of the concluding line to link two six-line staves together, but
few with the energy and self-confidence in which Dunbar portrays each of
the sins. Like many Scots writers after him, Dunbar was on familiar poetic
terms with the Devil, through whom the poet took the strongest of all his
swipes against Highlanders and their Gaelic culture:

Than cried Mahoun for a Heleand padyane;   [pageant
Syne ran a feind to feche Makfadyane   [fetch
    Far northwart in a nuke:
Be he the correnoch had done schout,   [lament
Erschemen so gadderit him about,   [Irishmen
    In Hell grit room they tuke.
Thae tarmegants, with tag and tatter,
Full loud in Ersche begowth to clatter,
    And rowp like revin and rook: [raven
The Devil sa devit wes with their yell,
That in the deepest pot of hell
    He smorit thame with smuke.

The anti-Highland prejudice and the rhyming virtuosity tumble out in a
furious use of the bobwheel device against Donald Odhar (the Gaelic for
"brown") the grandson of the last Lord of the Isles. Between 1503 and
1507, Donald led a formidable rising against centralized Scottish authority
as represented by the king. To royalist Dunbar, whose "Epetaffe for
Donald Owre" was a trifle premature, in that after forty years' imprisonment Donald survived to lead another unsuccessful rising, there were no
two sides to the question: and, indeed, the poet was to be proved right:

Of the fals fox dissimulator,
Kynd hes every theif and traitor;
    Eftir respite
    To work dispite
    Moir appetite
        He hes of natour.

War the fox tame a thousand fawd,   [fold
And grace him gevin als oft for fraud,
  War he on plane
  All war in vane,
  From hens again
    Micht not him haud.

Unlike Henryson, Dunbar did not look with much kindliness on his fellow men. His expressed pity was usually for himself, whether complaining (understandably) to the king about a poem of his being "magellit" by one Mure—

That fool, dismemberit hes my metre,*
And poisoned it with strang salpetre,
With richt defamous speech of lords,
Whilk with my colours all discords.   [which

—or complaining that benefices are unevenly distributed at "every feast"—

Bot, Lord! how petiouslie I luke,†
Whone all the pelf they pairt amang thame. . . .   [money

—or reproving the merchants of Edinburgh, not only for the "stink of haddocks and of skates" about the entrances to the city, but because the common people are too much in evidence—

At your hie Cross, whar gold and silk
Sould be, there is bot cruds and milk;   [curds
And at your Trone bot cokill and wilk,
Pansches, puddings of Jok and Jame . . .‡   [tripe

It is doubtful if Dunbar even looked with much greater kindness on women. True, his greatest satire—the only poem of his in unrhymed alliteration to survive, and indeed the last great poem to be written in this old style—"The Treatis of The Twa Maryit Wemen and the Wedo" does not moralize or condemn. It simply shows three women in a pleasant twilit garden, having drunk their rich wines together, as later ladies might have drunk tea, talking frankly about what interests them most: their sex lives. One woman's man was old and useless. The other woman's husband, "A hur maister, the hugeast in erd" had worn himself out by his affairs with

* "Complaint to the King Against Mure."
† "To the King."
‡ "To the Merchants of Edinburgh."

other women. The widow had had two husbands: one "ane hair hogeart, that hostit out flewme", the other a rich merchant who paid dearly for her favours while "ane secret servand, richt sober of his tongue" more satisfactorily supplied her sexual needs in secret, so that she could still be:

> . . . haldin a haly wife owre all the hail shire,
> I am sa piteous to the poor, when there is persons mony.
> In passing of pilgrimage I pride me full meikle,
> Mair for the praise of people na ony perdoun winning.

Having eavesdropped on these amiable ladies, the poet ironically asks:

> Of thir three wantoun wiffis that I haif written here,
> Whilk wald ye waill to your wife, gif ye suld wed one?

Still more delightful, and rather easier to enjoy, is "The Ballad of Kynd Kyttock". Scholars like to note that although contained in the Chepman and Myllar publication of 1508 (the only surviving, though mutilated, copy of which is in the Advocates' Library, Edinburgh) following "The Twa Maryit Wemen" and "The Lament for the Makaris", both subscribed "quod Dunbar", while in the Bannatyne Manuscript it is followed by "Man, sen thy lyfe", also "quod Dunbar", its authenticity is not fully established. Indeed, W. Mackay Mackenzie finds it "remarkable . . . that if this poem had been known to be by Dunbar, neither sources should have said so." It seems to me much more unbelievable that a poem so much in Dunbar's style and demonstrating such a high degree of technical mastery should be by some other poet of equal stature, of unknown name, and without anything of similar accomplishment to his credit.

A cheerful alewife dies of drouth (thirst) and sets out on her journey to Heaven, getting a lift from a newt riding on a snail. She manages to jink (dodge) past St Peter, and so get through the gate. God is so amused at the way she has outwitted His doorkeeper that she is allowed to stay, living soberly for seven years during which she acts as Our Lady's henwife. But at last she decided that "the ale of Heaven was sour", slipped out for a drink, but this time got caught by St Peter as she tried to get back in again. Now, therefore, she keeps an alehouse between earth and Heaven; and Dunbar urges:

> Friends, I pray you hertfully,
> Gif ye be thirsty or dry,
> Drink with my guddame, as ye ga by,
> Aince, for my sake.

Dunbar's ceremonial pageant poems are, with one exception, his least successful pieces. The Latinized aureate diction he felt necessary to deploy upon such high occasions arises from the same absence of confidence in the spoken language of the day as led the Augustans to evolve their stilted poetic diction (fish becoming "the finny tribe", and so on) and led Knox and the later Reformers to have the Bible made available in English rather than in the native Scots commonly in everyday use at the time of the Reformation.

"The Thirssil and the Rose" was written to celebrate the King's wedding, and follows the same convention as Chaucer's "The Parliament of Foules" written for a similar ceremony. Dunbar's wedding piece is adroitly done, the colours resembling enamel-work, or the stained-glass windows and stained-glass work of the late English Pre-Raphaelites. As Agnes Mure Mackenzie has remarked, "the close is an enchanting chorus of bird-song, whose rhyme-royal takes on a strange chiming harmony . . . individual and beautiful, the suggestion of the choiring of many voices that is one of Dunbar's greatest gifts".[11]

The best of these pieces is his love-allegory "The Goldyn Targe", full of the colours of leaves and flowers, and birdsong newly refreshed by the sunshine following rain. A ship bearing the choice of Venus's chivalry approaches

. . . agayn the orient sky
A sail als white as blossom upon spray.

The gods and goddesses disembark, and there follows a masque as dramatic as are some of Browning's dramatic monologues where the action is contained within the poet's personal telling. Reason, armed with a golden targe, defends the poet against the assault of Beauty, but is blinded and so overcome. Like most allegories of the kind, it is all a dream. When the poet awakes, he pays generous tribute to "reverend Chaucer, rose of rethoris all", and, rather more surprisingly, to "moral Gower, and Ludgate laureate."

The kind of music for its own sake which Dunbar displays in these poems resounds with still grander tones in his two finest religious poems, although his supreme piece of rhyming virtuosity is displayed in a third, "Ane Ballat of Our Lady", where he uses an octave of alternating rhyming lines of four and three accents, enriching the four accented lines by two internal rhymes, the Latin refrain preluding a three-line bobwheel.

Hail, sterne superne! Hail in eterne,
    In Godis sicht to shine!
Lucerne in derne, for to discern   [darkness
    Be glory and grace divine!   [By
Hodiern, modern, sempitern,
    Angelical regyne!
Our terne infern for to dispern   [fierceness

Help, rialist rosyne.
Ave Maria, gratia plena!
Yearn us, gubern, virgin matern,   [govern
Of reuth baith root and ryne . . .   [pity: stem

There is something of the *toccata*, the dazzling keyboard performance for
its own sake, about this.[12] There is much more to both "Of the Nativitie of
Christ" and its companion piece, "Of the Resurrection of Christ".

In the former, the great sounds build up, the Latin refrain providing the
pedal part, until the whole organ crashes forth in a breathless paean of
praise:

Sing, heaven imperial, most of hicht,
Regions of air mak armony;   [harmony
All fish in flud and fowl of flicht
Be mirthful and mak melody:
All *Gloria in excelsis* cry,
Heaven, erd, sea, man, bird and best,   [beast
He that is crownit abone the sky
Pro nobis Puer natus est.

The same controlled build-up of sound and steady expansion of image is
similarly displayed in "Of The Resurrection of Christ", with its sonorous
opening:

Done is a battle on the dragon black,
Our campioun Christ confoundet hes his force;
The yetts of Hell are broken with a crack,   [gates
The sign triumphal rasit is of the croce,   [cross
The divillis trymmillis with hiddous voce,
The sauls are borrowit and to the bliss can go,
Christ with his blud our ransonis dois indoce: [ransoms
Surrexit Dominus de sepulchro.

One has to turn to the *Mass in B Minor* of Bach to find any parallel to
triumphal artistic religious assertion of this supremely confident sort.

Dunbar's obsession with his own problems together with his lack of tenderness and understanding of human love, may make his poetic stature
seem less than that of either Burns or MacDiarmid (neither of whom, however, are without other human weaknesses and intolerances equally
reflected in their art). Nor, any more than Henryson, was Dunbar possessed of Chaucer's compelling narrative power. But Dunbar's greatness is
his own, reflecting the recurring extremes of joy and dejection, and a general absence of that Henrysonian middle way of balanced moderation

which was, and is, a marked characteristic of Scottish literature, in spite of Gregory Smith's invention of "the Caledonian antisyzygy", or zig-zags of extreme contrary moods. Most of the world's national literatures are equipped with some kind of an "antisyzygy", without which diverse tensions could not be fully energized. But, as the work of Burns confirms, the middle of the contradiction can contain as much of genius as the tip of either zig or zag!

The last of the poets of substantial output, most of whose work belongs to the sixteenth century, at any rate in spirit, is Gavin Douglas (1475?–1522), third son of Archibald "Bell-the-Cat" Douglas, whose family more than once seemed to offer the challenge of rivalry to the royal line. Like his senior, Dunbar, Douglas studied at St Andrews, and later also at Paris. As well as Divinity, he is thought also to have studied civil law. In 1496 he was priest at Monymusk, Aberdeenshire, after which he became parson of Linton and rector of Prestonshauch—the old name for Prestonkirk—before obtaining the Provostship of the Collegiate Church of St Giles in Edinburgh.

There he remained, a prosperous and powerful churchman, for twelve years walking the same Royal Mile as the senior and greater poet, Dunbar, who remained a Court hanger-on unable even to get "ane kirk scant coverit with heather".

The death of James IV at Flodden must finally have ended Dunbar's hopes of advancement. The harassed City Fathers, however, within a fortnight of the worst and most threatening disaster ever to have befallen Scotland, found time to nominate Douglas, the lesser poet, a "free burgess of the city", without charge.

It must have seemed to them a politically prudent move, since Douglas upheld the pro-English faction. Indeed, Douglas was soon one of the Lords of Council, bent upon achieving the marriage of the widowed queen with his nephew, the sixth Earl of Angus, head of the Red Douglas family. As so often with political manoeuvrings, however, the expected rewards did not follow. Not even the queen and her brother Henry VIII could persuade the Pope to appoint Douglas Archbishop of St Andrews. The poet had in the end to be content with the bishopric of Dunkeld, given to him in 1515. Unfortunately for him, however, before he could take up the appointment, the Regent Albany, upholder of the French and nationalist factions and enemy of the Douglas house, returned to Scotland. The poet spent a year incarcerated in the castle of St Andrews on the somewhat spurious grounds that confirmation of his appointment had only been obtained because of the interference of the English king.

Thereafter Angus, for his own reasons, made peace with Albany, and the poet was released. He even became once more sufficiently trusted politically to be sent from Dunkeld to Rouen to complete negotiations for a Franco-Scottish treaty against England. But intrigue and ambition coursed in the Douglas blood. No sooner had Albany returned to France than the poet and his nephew were again hard at work to secure the return of Douglas power. Though at first successful, they failed to persuade Cardinal Wolsey and Henry VIII to stop Albany's return in 1521. Uncle and nephew had then to flee to England. Stripped of his bishopric, deserted by his nephew and befriended mainly by Lord Dacre, the poet spent his last year in exile, dying of the plague in September 1522. He was buried in the Royal Chapel of the Savoy.

Apart from some rather dull lines on "Conscience" the only known works of Gavin Douglas to survive are his long and elaborate allegory "The Palice of Honour", a short, possibly incomplete allegory, "King Hart" and *The XIII Bukes of Eneados of the Famous Poete Virgile Translated out of Latyn Verses into Scottis Meter*.

"The Palice" was written at Linton, and published in Edinburgh in 1579, by which time an edition had already appeared in London. "King Hart" survived through the Maitland Manuscript. The Virgil translation was published in London by William Copland in 1553, and reissued in Edinburgh in 1710 by Thomas Ruddiman with corrections from the Ruthven Manuscript in Edinburgh University Library. Other manuscripts are the Elphinstone, also in Edinburgh Library, one in Lambeth Library, and one for long in the possession of the Marquisses of Bath at Longleat. Although the first collected edition of Douglas's works, edited by John Small, appeared in 1874, it was not until our time that the Scottish Text Society undertook a properly collated and complete edition.

In his own day Douglas achieved a high reputation in England, as the contemporary publication of his poems in that country testifies. There are even those who have claimed that his work laid the foundations of English blank verse. Such eminent Scottish critics as T. F. Henderson, writing in the 1890s and J. H. Millar, pronouncing his judgement a few years later, were, however, unwilling to allow him much of a place in the hierarchy of the so-called "Golden Age" of Scottish poetry. More recently, it has been left to Agnes Mure Mackenzie and Kurt Wittig to restore the balance a little.

I must confess that I find it hard to derive much pleasure from "The Palice of Honour" even if it is inspired by a genuine desire to seek out how honour may be secured, and whether or not, as some have claimed, it inspired Bunyan's equally joyless allegory, the *Pilgrim's Progress*.

Douglas's "pilgrim", in approved medieval fashion, falls asleep in a "garden of pleasure" on a May morning. He dreams that he is in the middle of a forest, beside a gloomy river in flood. After the manner of the infinitely superior "Golden Targe" of Dunbar, in which nine-line stanza-form of *abaabbab*, varied by *aab aab bcc*, "The Palice" is also couched, there appears a procession of sages, led by Queen Minerva followed by a curious collection of characters out of classical antiquity, and then by Venus and her court, with Cupid in attendance. Her followers indulge in a little far from spontaneous music-making:

Proportions fine with sound celestial,
Duplat, triplat, diatesseriall,
Sesqui altera, and deculpa resortis
Diapason of mony sindrie sortis . . .

—which might have pleased Boethius in Elysium, but hardly excites the twentieth-century reader. However, these learned sounds inspired the dreaming poet to strike up a ballad of his own, a little number about inconstant love. This act can perhaps only be matched in terms of literary rashness by Tam o'Shanter's cry of approbation on viewing the witches dance in "Alloway's auld haunted kirk" some two hundred and fifty years later. Less fortunate than Tam, who escaped, Douglas's dreaming poet was promply arrested and arraigned before the court of Venus. His defence— that he is a spiritual man void of learning—fails, and he is found guilty. Before sentence can be pronounced, however, an extraordinary Court of poets appears on the scene, attending the Muses. Who should be there but:

Great Kennedie, and Dunbar yit undeid,
And Quintine with ane huttok on his heid.   [hood

—to say nothing of:

Geoffray Chaucèir as *a per se* sans peir
In his vulgare, and moral Johne Gowèir.

On Calliope's pleading, Venus frees the poet on "payment" of a poem in her praise. In the care of a nymph provided by Calliope, the poet sets out on his journey to the Palace of Honour, passing, amongst other topographical and historical features, the fountain of the Muses, where both Ovid and Virgil happen at that moment to be reciting. Near the summit of a marble rock, they come upon a brimstone pit full of the tortured, vociferous slothful. The poet is vouchsafed a view of the miserable state of the world, followed by a counterbalancing view of the State of Grace. The good Bishop of Dunkeld had scant patience with the conventions of the Court of Love , telling his readers:

Childer to engender use Venus, and nocht in vain;
Have na surphat . . .

and may well have had reformer's urgings troubling both his conscience and his muse. The Palace itself, which sounds rather like a Highland exercise in Gothic revivalism, with its

Pinacles, fyellis, turnpekkis mony one,   [round turrets
Gilt burnest touris whilk to Phoebus shone,
Skarsment, reprise, corbell and battellings . . .   [escarpment

—contains Venus on a throne, as well as a mirror that enables the poet to see at a glance every earthly deed. Having been introduced to the staff of the Palace of Honour's household—Constancy, Liberality, Discretion, Conscience, and so on—the nymph leads the poet into a garden. We are spared further tediums by his carelesness in falling into the moat, the water of which wakes him from his dreamful sleep. Douglas himself, however, does not spare us a *tour de force* in praise of Honour, the internal rhymes building up stanza by stanza, until we reach the climax of complexity, though lacking the genius that redeems the same manner of performance in the hands of Dunbar.

> Hail rois maist chois, till clois thy fois greit micht   [rose
>   Hail, stone whilk shone upon the throne of licht,
> Virtue, whais true sweet dew owrethrew all vice,
>   Was ay ilk day, gar say the way of licht;
> Amend, offend, and send our end ay richt.
> Thou stant, ordant as sanct, of grant maist wise,
> Till be supplie, and the hie gree of price   [degree
> Delite the tite me quite of site to dicht,   [soon, shame
> For I apply schortlie to thy devise.

Whatever this is, it certainly is not poetry. Its cunning craftmanship is medieval and backward-looking, its energy entirely derived from the manipulations of rather meaningless sounds.

There are some who claim higher merit for "King Hart". Certainly, this allegory of the Heart of Man as king in his castle surrounded by courtiers like Strength, Wantonness, Green Lust and Disport, who attempt to influence his judgement, is less sheerly tedious. The French *ballat royal* octaves are smoothly managed, and the opening stanzas give a vivid picture of what may well have the ambience of the Stuart court.

> King Hart, into his cumlie castle strang
>   Closit about with craft and meikill ure,   [toil
> So seemlie wes he set his folk amang,
>   That he no dout had of misaventure:
>   So proudlie wes he polist, plain and pure,
> With youthheid and his lustie levis green;
>   So fair, so fresh, so likely to endure,
>   And als so blyth as bird in symmer schene.

> For wes he never yit with schouris shot,   [showers
>   Nor yit owrerun with rouk, or ony rain;   [mist
> In all his lusty lecam nocht ane spot,   [body
>   Na never had experience into pain,

Bot always into liking, nocht to layne—   [to tell the truth
  Onlie to love and verrie gentilness
He wes inclynit cleinlie to remane,
  And wonn under the wing of Wantonness.   [live

King Hart sends Youthheid and Fresh Delight to investigate the passing of Dame Pleasaunce from her nearby castle, and they manage to get themselves captured. So King Hart himself goes out to give battle, is wounded and captured, one of his attendants being Dame Beauty. His love-sickness therefore naturally worsens, until Dame Pity sets him free. In the end Old Age, Conscience and Sadness force Dame Pleasaunce out of her own castle, and Wisdom and Reason return to King Hart's establishment in time to be around when Decrepitude arrives to deliver the final wound.

But it is really upon his translation of the *Aeneid* into heroic couplets, and his own contribution in the form of an original Prologue to each book, that Douglas's poetic reputation ultimately rests. He may simply have been galled to better Caxton's abbreviated and severely altered version of Virgil's poem published in 1490, when Douglas was still a teenager. He may have been aware of the Erse version in the manuscript *The Book of Ballymote*, compiled by the monks of Ballymote, in Sligo, sometime before 1500; or the French version, *circa* 1500, by Octovien de St Gelais. In any case, the direct stimulus to attempt himself so huge a task came from Douglas's cousin, the captain of the ship *Great Michael*, Henry, Lord Sinclair.

It is also worth noting that this is the largest-scale work of any consistent quality ever to be attempted in Scots verse.* And it is the first complete verse translation in either Scots or English, in every way superior to Caxton's severely mutilated *Aeneas*, and according to Ezra Pound,[13] superior even to Virgil's original, a view that few classicist would sustain, although others have found Douglas more vigorous and closer to the soil.

Douglas expresses a clear idea of how the style of the verse should match the social degree of the subject, when he tells us that:

The muse suld with the person agree algait.   [in every way

He distinguishes clearly between the old-fashioned, heavily alliterative style, which he reserves for country themes and subjects (including the most famous of the original Prologues) and the direct manner he feels is more appropriate for noble happenings:

The ryall style, clepit heroical   [royall, called
Full of wirship and nobleness owre all,
Suld be compilit but tenchis or void word,   [without taunts

* Its nearest rival, *The Buik of Alexander*, Sir Gilbert Hay's lengthy verse-life of Alexander the Great, written a century or so earlier, is so prosily tedious as to be virtually unreadable.

> Kepand honest wys sportis where they bourd,   [wine, jest
> All loose language and lichtness lattand be,   [letting
> Observand beauty, sentens and gravity.

Although he was the first of the Makars to call his language "Scottis"—a description hitherto applied to Gaelic or Erse—and he tells us that he has done his best to "mak it braid and plain", using "na Sudroun, but our own language", he freely admitted his inability to abide by his own purist standards.

> Nor yit so clene all Sudron I refuse   [Southern
> Bot some word I pronounce as nichtbours doys,   [does
> Like as in Latin bene Greek termis sum,   [Greek
> So me behovit whilom, or than be dum,   [behoved, rather than
> Some bastard Latyne, French or Inglis oiss   [use
> Whair scant was Scottis—I had nane uther choys.   [choice

The rough power of Douglas's rendering of Virgil can be gauged from the culminating moment of Dido's vain attempt to persuade Aeneas not to obey the injunction of the gods to sail on to Italy.

> What! will thou flee from me? Allace! Allace!
> By all thir tearis tringling oure my face,   [there
> And by that richt hand umwhile thou me gave,   [formerly
> Sen to myself nocht ellis left I have
> Now, wrechit caitiff; by our troth plychting eik,
> And by our spousage begunnin, I thee beseik,
> Gif ever ony thank I deservit towart thee,   [if
> Or aucht of mine to thee was leif, quod she,   [dear
> Have mercy of our lineage ready to spill;
> Gif time remains yet thou hear prayeris will,
> This fremmit mind, I pray you do away.   [strange
> For thee I have been hatit this mony a day,
> With all the people of Affrik, and with the king
> That rules the land of Numida and ring;   [reigns
> For thee my own Tyrianis are with me wraith,
> For thee is womanheid went and worship baith;
> And my first fame, laud and renownye,
> Whareby I was raisit to the starnis hie.
> Ready to die and myselvin to spill;
> My sweet guest, whom to thou leave me will?
> My guest, ah God! how all thing now in vain is,
> When of my spouse none other name remainis!

Effective though this is, it is through the best of his original Prologues that Douglas makes his most important contribution to Scots literature. He wrote of the countryside of Lowland Scotland as he saw and experienced it, the first of our poets to portray landscape at large for its own sake in verse. Apropos the long summer evening, painted in the Thirteenth Prologue:

Yonder doun dwines the evin sky away,   [sinks, evening
And up springis the bricht dawning of the day,
Intil ane other place nocht far in sondir,
Whilk to behold was pleasans and half wondir.

—W. P. Ker remarked: "He sees a new thing in nature . . . and in naming it he gives the interpretation, also, the spirit of poetry: 'pleasance and half wonder'."

To us, of course, it is no longer a new thing. During the eighteenth century, James Thomson, in *The Seasons*, took up where Douglas left off, and carried this Scottish absorption with nature south, where it became one of the main ingredients of the Romantic movement. But new it certainly was when Douglas first depicted the dreariness of a Scottish winter in the Seventh Prologue:

Sour bitter bubbis, and the showris snell,   [blasts, keen
Seemit on the sward ane similitude of hell,
Reducing to our mind, in every steid,
Ghostly shadows of eild and grisly deid,   [age
Thick drumly skuggis derknit so the heaven;
Dim skyis oft furth warpit fearful levin,
Flaggis of fire, and mony felloun flaw,
Sharp soppis of sleet, and of the snipand snow.
The dowie ditches were all donk and wait,   [dank, wet
The low valley flodderit all with spate,
The plain streetis and every hie way
Full of flushis, dubbis, mire and clay.   [big and little puddles
Laggerit leas wallowit fernis shew,   [muddy meadows, withered
Broun muirs kithit their wisnit mossy hue,   [made known
Bank, brae and boddum blanchit wox and bare;   [bottom
For gurll weather growit beastis hair;
The wind made wave the reid weed on the dyke;   [red, stone wall
Bedovin in donkis deep was every syk;   [immersed, ditch
Owre craggis, and the front of rockis seir,   [cliffs, varied
Hang great ice-schoklis, lang as ony spear;
The grund stude barren, widderit, dosk and grey,
Herbis, flouris, and grasses wallowit away;   [withered
Woods, forrests, with naked bewis blout,   [desolate
Stude strippit of their weid in every hout,   [wood

So busteously Boreas his bugle blew.
The deer full dern doun in the dalis drew;
Small birdis, flockand throw thick ronis thrang,   [branches
In chirming and with cheeping changit their sang,
Seekand hidlis and hirnis them to hide   [hiding-places
Fra fearful thudis of the tempestuous tide.

Douglas's ability, often exploited to blend sight and smell in a single image, should perhaps encourage us to battle with his large crop of strange words, some of them possibly archaic even in his own day. Here is how he fixes for us, in a line and a half, the gloaming: that long dying of a northern mid-summer evening, when dusk and dawn almost mingle:
   All byrnand reid gan wax the evin sky,
   The sun enfyrit hail . . .   [began to grow

And while the bat takes off on "hir peelit letheren flicht":
   Out oure the swyre swimmis the soppis of mist.   [gorge, clouds

To-day the Prologues, or parts of them, are included in every Scottish anthology; but in an age from which the influence of "the Classics" has largely receded, Douglas's "savouring" of Virgil's *Eneados* is now mainly the property of specialist students of our literature.
   His poetry apart, two of Douglas's injunctions are worth remembering—his advice to the reader:

   Consider it warely, read ofter than anis,   [once
   Weill, at an blenk, slee poetry nocht ta'en is.   [cunning

—and his injunction to his critics:

   Gif I have failit, boldly reprove my ryme,
   Bot first, I pray your, grape the matter clean,
   Reproach me nocht whill the work be ourseen   [until, overseen
   Beis nocht ourstudious to spy a mote in my ee
   That in your own a ferry-boat cannot see!
   And do to me as ye would be done to.

There speaks not so much the high-born man of action—on whose regal dignity of bearing the scholar Erasmus commented—as the perennial creative artist forever suspicious of the hacks who may half-read his work and denigrate it out of frustrated envy.
   Time, that most relentless denigrator, has all but destroyed Heriot, and Traill, and Sir John Ross, and "gude gentil" Stobo, who may or may not have been the author of that pleasant tale-telling, *The Three Priests of Peblis*,

couched in fluent narration that rarely rises above the level of skilful versifying. In calling Dunbar's flyting opponent Kennedy "greit", Douglas presumably measured the force of his judgement, a thing we cannot do, since we have only his artificial invective, a brief "Farewell to Love", and a simple, sober elegy, "In Prais of Age" to go by.

In later chapters, it will be necessary to make a division between poetry and prose. During the period covered by the present chapter—roughly up to the year 1500—poets whose latter productive years overlapped the somewhat artificial boundary of the beginning of a new century have been included. But Scots prose prior to 1500 is so sparse in quantity, and so poor in quality, that it merits little more than a footnote.

The oldest surviving examples of Scots literary prose are by Sir Gilbert Hay, who seems to have been one of the earliest graduates of St Andrews University. He went to France in the early 1420s, where he became chamberlain to Charles VII. He was with William Sinclair, Earl of Orkney and Caithness at Roslin Castle in 1456, when he translated a fourteenth century treatise by a Benedictine monk, *L'Arbre de Batailles*, or *The Buke of the Law of Armys*, and from another French treatise, *Livre de l'Ordre de Chevalerie*, *The Buke of the Order of Knychthede*. From a Latin treatise, *Secreta Secretorum*, Hay produced *The Buke of the Governance of Princes*.

Hay's views on the practical duties and responsibilities of knighthood—those also of Barbour and Wallace—balance the more widely appreciated amorous and chivalric attitudes romanticized by later writers.

> Knychthede is a grete honour, maryte [united] with a grete servitude . . .
> Knychthede was ordanyit to manetene [support] and defend haly Kirk . . .
> [and] to defend his natural lord and manetene him . . .
> Office of Knychthede is to manetene and defend wedowis, maidens, faderless and moderless barnis and poor miserable personis and piteable, and to help the wayke [weak] agayne the stark, and the pure [poor] agayn the rich; for oftymes sic folk are, be [by] mair stark na they, pelit and derobbit [pillaged and robbed] and . . . put to destruction, and poverty for fault of power and defense. And because all sic deeds is wikkitness, crueltee, and tyranny, tharfor is the ordre of Knychthede ordanyit, as in that point amang the lave [in this respect among the rest] to gainstand. And gif a knycht himself be manetenor or doare of thir thingis, he is unworthy to bear the ordre for his wikkitness.

His views on soldierly morale, from *The Buke of the Law of Armys*, could hardly be gainsaid:

> Syndrie folk there is, that hes the body rycht lytill, and yit that have the hert and curage grete, and that is a Grace of God . . . Certaynly, nocht force na strenth corporale makis a man to win the bataill. Bot force spirtuale, that is to

say, hardy curage makis victory . . . But where baith is fundyne togeder,
better wor.* [that would be better.]

Hay was probably asked or commissioned by the Earl to make these
Scots translations.

Because most scholars during this early period finished their education
abroad, and in many cases themselves remained on the Continent in a
teaching capacity, such prose as they wrote—much of it theological—was
couched in Latin. Even if there had been any other incentive to write in the
vernacular, there would have been no possibility of them having had any
general readers. The work of historians like John Fordun (d. *circa* 1385),
the author of *Scotichronicon*—later continued by the Abbot of Incholm,
Walter Bower (d. 1449)—and that of the Principal of King's College,
Aberdeen, Hector Boece or Boyce, (1465–1536), whose *Scotorum Historiae*
is said at least to have the merit of being written in a Latin style rather more
elegant than that of his predecessors, is only of academic interest to-day,
even to historians.

The best of these early writers, John Major, or Mair (d. 1550) who was
educated at Cambridge and Paris, where he remained as a lecturer at the
colleges of Montaigu and Navarre, before returning to Scotland to teach at
Glasgow University (where one of his pupils was John Knox), ending his
career as Provost of St Salvators College, St Andrews, was essentially a
medieval "Schoolman". Nevertheless he wrote in what Archbishop Spottiswoode called a "sorbonick and barbarous style". Major's patriotic
myth-making, however, is leavened by a certain Humanist approach to
high matters of state, and a readiness to express vigorously more forward-looking opinions on such matters as the relationship between kings
and their subjects, and the desirability of union between the English and
Scottish kingdoms. But Latin is still his chosen language.

As T. F. Henderson so succinctly put it, at that time, what there was of
"Scottish vernacular prose can scarce be termed literature".

J. H. Millar does his best to fill the vacuum by urging that the less complex society of the times, and consequently the less formalized written
laws, enabled some sort of vernacular raciness to find its way into the Acts
of the Scottish Parliament. I find little to induce me to make further search
in the light of such examples as Act 1424, May 26, c. 25 (12mo ed. c. 24),
which he uses to substantiate this claim:

> It is ordained that in all burrow townes of the realme and throuchfaires,
> whair commoun passages are, that there be ordained hostillares and recipters,
> havand stables and chalmers [rooms]. And that men find with them bread
> and aile, and all uther fude, alsweill to horse as men, for reasonable price,
> after the chaipes [established price] of the country.

Nor do I find much that is readable, let alone rewarding, in the pamphlet

* Hay's works were first published in 1847.

called *The Craft of Deyng* (Dying), dating probably from the late fifteenth century, the advisory climax of which is that:

> . . . ilk man in the house of deid suld do, efter his poware as Cryst did on the cross; furst, he prayd, and swa [so] suld we; syne criyed efter help, and swa suld we, with the hart, gif [if] we mycht nocht with the moucht [mouth]; and syne he yauld [yielded] his saull to his father, and swa suld we, gladly gyfand him . . .[14]

The introduction of printing into Scotland in 1507* gradually encouraged the development of prose, although many churchmen and scholars avoided the written use of Scots for almost a further century. In view of the fact that it has taken the Roman Catholic Church, whose servants or adherents all these men were, until the late twentieth century to sanction the celebration of Mass in spoken English, perhaps we cannot afford to be too censorious.

* By Andrew Myllar and Walter Chepman who, fortified by royal privilege, set up printing works at the foot of Black Friars Wynd, Edinburgh. The workmen were brought over from France.

CHAPTER TWO

The Sixteenth Century

I

The period during which Henryson, Dunbar and Douglas were writing is sometimes referred to as Scottish poetry's "Golden Age". It is certainly true to say that during their lifetime there was no English poet of comparable skill or stature, the only possible claimant being John Skelton, whose "ragged rhymes" have to some extent come back into favour in our own day. This "Golden Age" did not, of course, come to an end at the turn of the century, or even with Flodden, although the makers who reached maturity after that disaster wrote in a different manner from their predecessors.

In the later 1550s a Dalkeith notary, John Rolland, was the author of two poems, "The Sevin Sages" and "The Court of Venus". Neither in itself is of much importance or interest. "The Court of Venus", an old-fashioned allegory based on "The Palice of Honour", describes a conversation between Esperance (who approves of love) and Desperance (who does not); the arrest, trial and conviction by Venus of Desperance for treason to her; and the commuting of the ensuing death-sentence, resulting in his enlistment into her service under the name of Dalliance. In the course of all this, Rolland tells us that four poets flourished at the Scots court, and names them as the historian John Bellenden—scarcely a poet, except for some verses of introduction to his prose works; William Stewart, probably Lyndsay's Stewart of Lorne, author of one surviving poem, "This hinder nicht near by the hour of nine", preserved in the Bannatynne manuscript; Bishop Durie of Galloway, none of whose verse has survived; and—

    . . . gude David Lyndsay,
    In vulgar tongue he bure the bell that day
    To mak meter, richt cunning and expert . . .

Sir David Lyndsay of the Mount—the Mount is still "a conspicuous hill on the north side of the Howe of Fife, in the Vale of Eden, about three miles from Cupar" where "the old mansion stood on the south side of the hill, and overlooked a great part of the valley of the Eden"[1]—was born probably in 1486 and died in 1555. He may have been the Da. Lindesay listed among the incorporated students of St Salvators College, St Andrews for 1508–9; or he may have been the "one called Lyndesay" listed in the Exchequer Rolls for 1508 as holding a position in the royal stables. By the winter of 1511–12, he certainly held office in James IV's court, for in that year the Treasurer's accounts record a payment to him of £40. That he was early interested in dramatics is testified by a record of the provision to him in 1511 of two and a half ells of blue taffeta and six quarters of yellow taffeta, "to be a play coat for the play played in the king's and queen's presence in the Abbey of Holyrood".

James's marriage to Margaret Tudor, his English wife, did not break the Franco-Scottish alliance. Indeed, on French urging, James decided in 1513 to make war on England. While the king was in St Michael's Church, Linlithgow, praying for success in battle, a middle-aged man in a blue gown pushed through the assemblage of lords, leant on the King's desk, and warned him on the authority of the Virgin Mary neither to go to war, nor "meddle with no women nor use their counsel", or he would be confounded and brought to shame. Before the King could answer, the apparition disappeared. Lyndsay was standing nearby, yet could not apprehend the stranger. Both Robert Lyndsay of Pitscottie and George Buchanan relate the story, but only on Sir David Lyndsay's authority. The assumption usually made is that this poet with a fondness for plays and pageants, who shortly before had been appointed usher to the baby prince later to become James V, had staged the affair in the hope of preserving peace. In any event, the apparition failed in its purpose. James is said to have "dallied" with Lady Heron of Ford,* who may possibly have betrayed the intentions of the Scots army to Surrey. The Battle of Flodden took place on 9th September 1513, leaving dead on its field besides the King himself, one Archbishop, two bishops, two abbots, twelve earls, fourteen lords, five heirs to peerages, representatives of every distinguished family in Scotland and at least ten thousand of their troops.

Fortunately, Lyndsay did not go to Flodden. Instead, he amused the baby prince, as he was later to remind him in "The Complaynt":

How, as ane chapman bears his pack,
I bore thy Grace upon my back,
And sumtynes, stridlings on my neck,
Dansand with mony bend and beck.
The first syllabis that thou did mute
Was PA, DA LYN. Upon the lute   [Play, David Lyndsay
Then playit I twenty springs, perqueir,
Whilk wes gret piete for to hear.

---

* According to Pitscottie, a generation later. Other historians say she merely bargained the life of two Scots soldiers in her possession to persuade James not to raze Ford.

Lyndsay married Janet Douglas, a seamstress of the royal household, in 1522. In 1524, during the four-year period when Angus and the Douglas faction had control of the boy king, Lyndsay was out of favour, though apparently he continued to receive his pension. He was restored to the Court, however, after the escape of James and the return of Albany in 1528. In 1542, Lyndsay became Lyon King, a function he had in effect been carrying out for some years, on behalf of an elderly predecessor, Thomas Pettigrew.

In the interval between his restoration to official favour and the granting of the position of Lyon King at Arms, chief Herald of Scotland, Lyndsay had been employed on diplomatic missions which took him to Flanders. He had arranged a ceremony to celebrate the coronation of James's first wife, but instead, on her death in 1537, had had to write "The Deploratioun of the Deith of Quene Magdalene". In 1538, he caused to be prepared "a triumphal pageant" of welcome for Mary of Lorraine, daughter of the Duke of Guise, when she landed in the East Neuk of Fife in June 1538, to become James's second Queen.

Lyndsay was present in the Palace of Falkland when, after the shameful rout of Solway Moss—the culmination of a long series of disasters—James V died, leaving as heir to the throne the baby Mary, Queen of Scots. Further foreign visits followed, as Lyndsay returned honours conferred upon his late Royal master. In 1548, he undertook a visit to Denmark to negotiate trade and seek help from the Danes in defending the Scottish coast from English marauders, the first of the two objectives being achieved successfully. Towards the end of his life Lyndsay seems increasingly to have felt that church reform had assumed paramount political importance. In 1547, he even became one of those who promoted the call to John Knox to undertake public ministry, an action the full consequences of which the poet could not have foreseen, since he died early in 1555, so far as is known (nominally at least) still a Catholic.

It is perhaps hardly surprising that a writer so deeply engaged in public affairs should apparently have been more concerned with what he said than how he said it. Not for him the stately rhetoric of Henryson, the impassioned organ-sounds of Dunbar. In his best work, Lyndsay's virtues were his ability to catch the speech and appreciate the worries of common people. He may thus be regarded as Scotland's first radical poet, in the sense that he allied himself not so much with traditional courtly interests as with the qualities that go to make good governance in the interests of John the Common Weill (the personification of good government).

His language at its best avoids the aureate terms of his predecessors. In his ability to produce lines enshrining common sense so that they sound like proverbs, he anticipated Burns. Indeed, until the spread of Burns's reputation and ensuing popularity, "the Bible and Davie Lyndsay" were said to be the books most frequently found in Scotland's cottage homes.

Even as late as 1720, in his "Streams of Helicon", Alexander Pennecuick thus described an evening scene inside just such a cottage:

.My Aunt, whom nane dare say has no Grace,
Was reading on the *Pilgrim's Progress*:
The meikle Tasker, Davie Dallas,
Was telling Blads of William Wallace: [sheafs
My Mither bade her second son say,
What he'd by heart of Davie Lindsay.

The choice of reading matter no doubt reflected patriotic passion and religious ardour rather than literary taste, for as Pennecuick's contemporary, Allan Ramsay, put it:

Sir David's satires helped our nation
To carry on the reformation,
And gave the scarlet dame a box
Mair snell than all the pelts of Knox. [sharp

A century later, Sir Walter Scott, in Canto IV of *Marmion*, put the same point rather more deftly, praising:

The flash of that satiric rage,
Which, bursting on the early stage,
Branded the vices of his age,
  And broke the keys of Rome.

If that were entirely so, then it might be upon the memory of Lyndsay rather than that of Knox that blame for detaching Scotland from European civilization would have to be laid. But it is not really true.

Lyndsay certainly wanted reformation in the practice of the Catholic Church's religion, particularly with regard to its social aspects. There is no evidence whatever that he wanted the total overthrow of Catholicism.

Though he had something in his temperament of that haranguing preacher's disease said to be endemic in every Scot (fortunately, usually remaining more or less dormant!) he at no time incited violence or advocated bigotry. The distinction of approving violent tactics to help achieve allegedly desirable partisan ends belongs to Knox, Melville and their less celebrated heirs and successors. "The Keys of Rome" were, indeed, broken; but only to be replaced by new locks of which Lyndsay would hardly have been likely to approve.

His earliest extant poem, "The Dreme", dates from 1528, and is just over a thousand lines long. Couched in rime royal (*ab ab bcc*), it is superficially yet another example of medieval-style allegory, beginning with the usual state of sleepiness commonly preluding such poetic happenings, and continuing with a dream-voyage through hell, purgatory and limbo, via the firmament, to Paradise, with Remembrance as guide. In the second part of the poem, however, the poet urges Remembrance to tell him why Scotland is so poor, seeing that she has fish, "bestiall" on her mountains, deer, valleys of corn, and even recent finds of gold and precious stones. Though she lacks wine and spices, she has food and drink enow, and nowhere are there:

> More fairer people, nor of greater ingyne   [integrity
> Nor of more strength gret deedis til endure.

The answer he gets states the theme to which Lyndsay was to return again and again in his later work:

> Wanting of justice, policy and peace,
> Are cause of their unhappiness, allace!

While the poet is digesting this information, attributed to the fact that "the slothfoul hird dois slough and sleep", during which time wolf and fox "the sely sheep dounthryng", a "bousteous bern" comes over the brae, lean-faced and ragged, with a "pyikstaff" in his hand. He turns out to be none other than John the Common Weill, who proceeds to give a depressing account of Scottish affairs: murder and robbery in the Borders, laziness and inhospitality in the Highlands, ruthless profit-seeking in the Lowlands, simony, covetousness, pride and sensuality among the clergy, and selfishness among the nobles. So John decides to stay away from Scotland until she has a mature ruler, since: "Woe to the realm that hes owre young a King". Consoling himself with the saw that "eftir the nicht cumis the glaid morrow", John disappears, flying over firth and fell, leaving Remembrance to conduct the poet back to the cave of his dreaming. However, the firing of a ship's guns in a New Year salute, and the ensuing "youte and yell" of her sailors, wakes him up: whereupon he sits down to write his poem, finishing with "Ane Exhortatioun" to the King to use good governance, eschew lechery by marrying "ane lusty pleasand Queen", take counsel from his prudent Lords, and:

> . . . finally, remember thou mon dee,
> And suddenly pass off this mortal see.

Possibly because so many of the early Stuart kings had to endure the inhibiting limitations of minority rule and the consequent brawling of power-seeking Regents, there was a family tendency towards absolutism. Yet James V seems to have taken no offence at his DA LYN's preaching, though the poet's next piece, "The Complaynt", five hundred and ten lines in octosyllabic couplets written after the King had escaped from the constraints of the Angus faction, suggests that now Justice is restored to the land, all will be well, except among the unreformed clergy and with the needy writer, whose many services to his master are pointedly recalled. The polite request for due reward, however, is very different from the begging tone used by Dunbar in similar circumstances; for Lyndsay merely reminds James:

> For thou art but ane instrument
> To that gret King, Omnipotent:
> So, when pleases his Excellence,
> Thy Grace sall make me recompence;
> Or He sall cause me stand content
> Of quiet life, and sober rent.

Lyndsay got his reward, if not quite the title of Lord he perhaps hoped for; but this did not stop him preaching at his employer and benefactor. "The Testament and Complaynt of Our Sovereign Lord's Papyngo" was apparently written in 1538. The Prologue is in the stanza of Douglas's "Palice of Honour", nine lines of five feet rhyming *aab aab bcc*. The rest of the poem is in the heptastich Chaucerian stanza.

The maintaining of aviaries was a favourite recreation of the Stuart Kings, so the idea of a poet being employed to train the King's Papyngo (parrot) to speak and whistle would seem a perfectly valid device on which to build 1185 elaborate lines of preaching, not to say proverb-making:

> Who climbs to hicht, perforce his feet mon fail.

The poor Papyngo ignores this advice, climbs a tree and falls. Instead of going to her help, Lyndsay somewhat callously hides beneath a hawthorn and listens to her dying words, thus establishing a convention of dying animal testimonies popular throughout the Eighteenth-century Revival. She is a moral as well as a learned bird, however, so is now painfully aware that:

> Who sitteth most hie, sal find the sait moist slidde

—drawing parallels to her own plight from France, Rome, England, Greece, Troy, and (of course) the Scottish court.

Eager to administer the last rites, down come Pie (Canon Regular), Raven (Black Monk), and Kite (Holy Friar). After having to listen to a recital of clerical degeneracy, the Papyngo is shriven by the Kite. In her will, the dying bird leaves different parts of her body to various other birds, but her heart to the King. On her death, her executors ignore her wishes and eat her body, the Kite making off with her heart.

We need not expend much space on "The Complaint of Bagsche", an "auld hound" whose place has been usurped by the pup Bawtie, except to note that its octosyllabics, rhyming *ab ab bc bc*, are used to carry yet another sermon, and that the poem suggests a possible prototype for "The Twa Dogs" of Burns. Nor is there much poetic interest in "The Answer to the Kingis Flyting", in rime royal and also dating from 1536. The King's abuse-hurling is lost, but with surprising bluntness, Lyndsay tells his sovereign to stop fornicating "like ane restless ram," otherwise he will discover:

> . . . when that the well gois dry,
> Syne can nocht get agane sic stuff to buy.

By way of softening the blow, he adds a final touch of flattery:

> Now, Schir, fairweill, because I can nocht Flyte,
> And thocht I could, I were nocht til advance
> Agains your ornate metre to indite.

"The Deploratioun on the Deith of Quene Magdalene", written the following year, shows that when Lyndsay had to turn out an official aureate rime royal threnody, he could produce workmanlike stuff, éven if one is left with a suspicion that he is more upset over his own wasted pageantries than at the royal lady's demise. It is all "traytour Deith's" fault!

> Thou suld have heard the ornate Oratours,
>   Makand his Hieness salutatioun,
> Baith of the Clergy, Toun and Counsalours,
>   With mony notable narratioun;
>   Thou suld have seen his Coronatioun,
> In the fair Abbey of the Holy Rude,
> In presence of ane mirthful multitude.

> Sic banketting, sic awful tournaments,
>   On horse, and fute, that time whilk suld haif been;
> Sic Chapel Royal, with sic instruments,
>   And crafty musick, singing from the splene,   [heart
>   In this country, was never heard nor seen.
> Bot, all this greit solempnitie, and gam,   [game
> Turnit thou hes, In Requiem aeternam.

"The Justing Betwix James Watsoun and Jhone Barbour, Servitours to King James the Fyft" is a short, amusing account in heroic couplets of a mock-tournament between a "medicinar" and a "leech", said to be part of the celebrations accompanying James's second marriage in 1538.

The modern sex war may, or may not, have developed as a reaction to the distant and dignified worship of women (all, nevertheless, with a view to ultimate seduction) practised in the Court of Love tradition. Lyndsay's little piece of anti-womanizing, "Ane Supplicatioun Directed to the

King's Grace in Contemplatioun of Syde Taillis," a hundred and seventy-six lines in octosyllabic couplets, probably dates from about 1538. It urges that long dresses, trailing through dust and mud, sweeping clean "kirk and causey", are unhygenic, and that the wearing of veils helps women evade men's greetings. Doubtless Lyndsay was right, although writers of every age have criticized woman's fashions. The subject certainly inspired some of Lyndsay's most unbuttoned humour:

> I ken ane man, whilk swore greit aiths,   [oaths
> How he did lift ane Kittock's claiths,   [peasant-girl's
> And wald haif done, I wat nocht what,
> Bot soon remeid of lufe he gat;
> He thocht na shame to mak it witten,
> How her side tail was all beschitten;
> Of filth sic flewer strak his heart,   [flavour
> That he behovit for til depart.

The octosyllabic couplets of "Kitteis Confessioun", if indeed they be by Lyndsay—the piece was published in 1568 by Charteris "compylit (as is belevit) be Schir David Lyndesay of the Mount"—indicts auricular confession as a means of allowing the clergy to practice sexual voyeurism, and urges that confession should be made to God alone.

"The Tragedie of the Cardinall," in the Chaucerian heptastich, was written in 1547. Cardinal Beaton's ghost provides an apology for its former owner's life, and is used to warn his fellows to take example from his fate. Great care should always be taken in the appointment of clerics, we are told, only deserving people being chosen. It is a dull poem.

The same cannot be said of "The historie of ane nobil and vailyeand squyer William Meldrum, umwhyle Laird of Cleische and Bynnis," written about 1550. It is a racy tale in two parts, "The Testament" in the Chaucerian heptastich (except for the final stanza, which is an octosyllabic octave), the rest in octosyllabic rhyming couplets.

Meldrum was a noble squire, a distinguished soldier, and an ardent lover who fell in love with Marion Lawson, widow of John Haldane of Gleneagles, but whom he was unable to marry for lack of papal dispensation. While living with her at Strathearn, he heard that her lands around Boturich were being harried by the Macfarlanes; so he immediately set out for Loch Lomond, attacked and dislodged the Highlanders, but spared Macfarlane himself, as was this Squire's practice where defeated enemies were concerned:

> And sa this Squire amorous
> Seigit and wan the lady's house,
> And left therein a capitaine,
> Syne to Strathearn returnit again:

Where that he with his fair Lady,
Receivit was full pleasantly,
And to take rest did him convey,
Judge ye gif there was mirth and joy.
Howbeit the chalmer door was closit,   [room
They did bot kiss, as I supposit.
Gif uther thing was them between,
Let them discover that luifers been:
For I am nat in luve expert,
And never studyit in that art.

Not that much study was necessary, for a few lines later on the poet tells us:

. . . this Lady fair
Ane dochter to the Squire bare.

However, Meldrum was later attacked by a wicked knight, a rival in love, and so grievously wounded that he himself decides to turn "chirurgeon". Forced away from his lady by her relations, who make her marry another against her will, he spends his final days practising healing, until:

. . . at Struther, into Fife,
His soul with joy angelicall
Passed to the Heavin Imperial.

In the ensuing Testament, Meldrum decrees that no priest must be present at his funeral, but only a member of "Venus profession", and bids farewell to all the ladies who will regret his going, especially Marion, the "Star of Strathearn". It is in this part of the poem that Lyndsay comes nearer the "high style" than anywhere else in his surviving output:

Fareweill! ye lemant lamps of lustiness
    Of fair Scotland: adieu! my Ladies all.
During my youth, with ardent business,
    Ye knaw how I was in your service thrall.
    Ten thousand times adieu! above thame all,
Sterne of Strathern, my Lady Soverane,
For whom I shed my blude with mekill pain.

Yit, wald my Ladie luke at evin and morrow
    On my legend at length, scho wald not miss
How, for hir sake, I sufferit mekill sorrow.
    Yit, gife I micht, at this time get my wis,   [wish
    Of hir sweet mouth, dear God I had ane kiss.

I wis in vane! allace! we will disever.
I say na mair: sweet hart, adieu for ever!

"Squyer Meldrum" is a curious poem in that it blends so many elements from past conventions: knightly chivalry, the exaggerated feats of arms such as are found in *The Wallace* and possibly relate to an oral tradition; and eventually that success in adultery which was the intended end-product of all manoeuvrings at the Court of Love. On the other hand, it anticipates the horse-cantering measure applied to verse story-telling which, more than two centuries later, made *The Lady of the Lake* and *Marmion* so readable to their wider audiences.

"Squyer Meldrum" is still very readable to-day; more than can be said for Lyndsay's last poem, which he probably regarded as his most significant achievement, "Ane Dialogue betwix Experience and ane Courteour," completed in 1553 and printed the following year. Its 6333 lines are divided into seven sections, the octosyllabic and rime royal stanzas all having been employed by Lyndsay in other poems to more telling effect. Beginning with the medieval morning walk, and for Lyndsay a prolonged excursion into the aureate manner heavy with alliteration, the narrator meets:

Ane Ageit Man, whilk drew me near;
Whose beard wes weill three quarter lang;
His hair doun owre his schuders hang
The whilk as ony snaw were white.

This character, Experience, provides his Courtier-listener with a history of the world from Creation to Judgement Day. It is boring stuff, for by now the preacher in Lyndsay had quite taken over from the poet. The "Dialogue", indeed, is an angry, detailed but dull rant against the corruptions of the Roman Catholic Church, including the practice of worshipping images. It has been said that merely to describe what actually happened in the day-to-day life of the Scottish Church immediately before the Reformation would make a writer of the time appear to us to-day to be a major satirist. The real trouble is that Lyndsay, in his greatest work, his one surviving drama, had said it all before, and much more effectively. At least it may be claimed for "Ane Dialogue" that Lyndsay rightly diagnosed, in "The Epistal to the Reader" which forms the first of the seven sections (and, incidentally invites inspirational help from the Almighty over the heads of the muses, a request unfortunately not granted), the likely source of the upheaval which was to follow so soon after the poet's own death.

We have no King thee to present, alas!
Whilk to this country been ane careful case,
   And als our Queen, of Scotland Heritour,

She dwellith in France; I pray God saif her Grace.
It war too lang for thee to rin that race
    And for langar or that young tender Flour
Bring home til us ane King and Governour.
Alas, therefore, we may with sorrow sing
Whilk must so long remain without ane King!

Lyndsay's greatest achievement was undoubtedly his "morality" play, *Ane pleasant Satyre of the Thrie Estaitis*. An early version, which has not survived, was presented before the Court at Linlithgow at the Feast of Epiphany, 6th January 1540. Sir William Eure, Commissioner for settling Border disputes, saw it, and sent a synopsis of it to Thomas, Lord Cromwell.[2]

John Bellenden relates that after seeing the play, the King warned the Archbishop of Glasgow that if he and other prelates did not reform, the six proudest would be sent to England, and the rest dealt with as Henry did these. Sir James Melville of Halhill preserves the incident more vividly in his *Memoirs*, quoting James as saying: "The King of England burns, the King of Denmark beheads you: but I shall stick you with this same whinger," drawing his dagger, to the accompaniment of a scatter of frightened prelates.

A second performance followed on 7th June 1552, at Cupar, Fife, and a third before the Queen Regent, at the Greenside, on the lower slopes of the Calton Hill, Edinburgh, on 12th August 1554, before "an exceeding great number of people", according to Henrie Charteris.[3] The text of this version, which lasted from nine in the morning till six at night, was published by Robert Charteris in 1602. Doubtless the Court retired for refreshment, when the common people would be kept entertained by the various comic, and mostly coarse, interludes, which have nothing to do with the central play. Consequently, when Robert Kemp prepared his acting version for the Edinburgh International Festival of 1948, skilful pruning undoubtedly helped the by then four-hundred-year-old morality to achieve a new lease of life.*

In the first part of the play, Diligence heralds the approach of Rex Humanitas, King Humanity, who, though wild in youth, has now agreed to meet the personified virtues to discuss and make reformation. The Thrie Estates of the Realm—the Lords Spiritual, the Lords Temporal and the Burgesses—answer the summons, and the poor people arrive unbidden. The King, Rex Humanitas, appears with his courtiers, Wantonness and Placebo, eventually joined by a somewhat drunken Solace, who combine to cheer up their sovereign. They urge him to send for Dame Sensuality,

---

* Which it did, performances to capacity audiences being given at the Festival. It has subsequently been staged in St Andrew's Hall, Glasgow and at Glasgow University. A new adaptation by Tom Wright, less taut than Kemp's, was used for the Edinburgh Festival production of 1973.

arguing that since prelates have concubines, some as many as three, the King should not think lechery a sin. Lady Sensuality duly arrives, and thus announces herself:

Behauld my heid, behauld my gay attire,
Behauld my halse, lovesome and lily-white;
Behauld my visage flammand as the fire,
Behauld my paps, of portraiture perfyte!
To look on me, luvers has great delight;
Richt so has all the Kings of Christendom—
To them I have done pleasures infinite
And specially unto the Court of Rome.

The King at once falls in love with her, and conducts her to his chamber, while Wantonness persuades her lady, Hameliness, his "pleasure to fulfill". Good Counsel arrives, stating that he had had:

. . . residence
With high princes of great puissance
In England, Italy and France
And many other lands.
But out of Scotland, alas!
I have been banished long apace.

This time, however, he announces his intention to remain, although the King has fallen victim to Sensuality and evil counsellors.

Flatterie, Falsehood and Deceit gather together. There follows a richly comic scene as these old cronies meet up again, the colloquial language racily foreshadowing what was to become the prevailing conversational tone of so much of the best work of Ramsay, Fergusson and Burns. Flatterie has had a stormy passage, and proposes never again to put his life "in chance of waves". The three rascals decide to disguise themselves as clerics, Flatterie becoming a friar (since he cannot preach), Deceit, Discretion; and Falsehood, Sapience.

The ensuing dialogue is worth quoting at length,* because it demonstrates not only Lyndsay's satirical edge, but his ability to create popular comic characters, an ability that makes us the more regret his presumed lost other plays.

Flatterie: Was never seen sic wind and rain,
                   Nor of shipmen sic clitter-clatter.
              Some bade "Hail!" and some bade "Stand-by!"
                   Till all the rapes began to rattle,
              Was never wight sae fley't as I,

* I have used Kemp's acting text here to demonstrate its actability.

When all the sails played brittle-brattle!
To see the waves, it was a wonder,
And wind, that rave the sails in sunder!
Now am I scapit frae that affray;
What say ye, sirs, am I not gay?
    Ken ye not Flatterie, your ain fule,
That gaed to make this new array?
    Was I not here with you at Yule?
Yes, by my faith, I think on weel!
Where are my fellows that wad not fail?
    We should have come here for a cast!
Ho, Falsehood, ho!
(*Falsehood enters*)

Falsehood: Wa sair the Devil!
Wha's that that cries for me sae fast?

Flatterie: Why, Falsehood, brother, know thou not me,
I am thy brother, Flatterie!

Falsehood: Now let me brace thee in my arms,
When friend meets friend, the heart aye warms!

Flatterie: Where is Deceit, that limmer loon?   [rascal

Falsehood: I left him drinkand in the toun;
He will be here incontinent.

Flatterie: Now by the Haly Sacrament,
Thae tidings comforts all my heart!
He is richt crafty as ye ken,
And counsellor to the Merchant-men!
(*enter Deceit*)

Deceit: Bon jour, brother, with all my heart,
Here am I come to tak your part
    Baith into gude and evil!
I met Gude Counsel by the way,
Wha pat me in a felon fray
    I give him to the devil!
How came ye here, I pray you tell me?

Falsehood: Marry, to seek King Humanitie!

Deceit: Now, by the gude lady that me bare,
That same horse is my ain mare!
Sen we three seeks yon noble King,
Let us devise some subtle thing!
Also, I pray you as your brother,
That we, ilk ane, be true to other.
I pray to God, nor I be hangit,
But I sall die ere ye be wrangit!   [wronged

Falsehood: What is thy counsel that we do?

Deceit: Marry, sirs, this is my counsel, lo!

Frae time the King begin to stir him,
I dreid Gude Counsel may come near him,
And be we known to Lord Correction,
It will be our confusion.
Therefore, my dear brother, devise
To find some toy of the new guise.

Flatterie: Marry, I sall find a thousand wiles.
We maun turn our claiths, and change our styles
And disaguise us, that nae man ken us.
Has nae man clerk's cleathing to lend us?
And let us keep grave countenance,
As we were new come out of France.

Deceit: Now, by my saul, that is weel devysit!
Ye sall see me soon disgysit.

Falsehood: And sae sall I, man, by the Rood!
Now, some gude fellow, lend me a hood!
(*Flatterie helps Deceit and Falsehood to
disguise themselves*)

Deceit: Now am I buskit, and wha can spy?   [dressed
The devil stick me, if this be I!
If this be I, or not, I cannot weel say
Or has the Fiend of Fairy-folk borne me away?

Falsehood: What says thou of my gay garmoun?
Deceit: I say thou looks even like a loon.
Now, brother Flatterie, what do ye?
What kind of man shape ye to be?

Flatterie: Now, by my faith, my brother dear,
I will gang counterfeit a Friar!
Deceit: A friar? Whereto ye cannot preach?
Flatterie: What rack, if I can flatter and fleech?   [coax
Perchance I'll come to that honour,
To be the kinges confessor.
Puir friars are free at any feast
And marshallit aye amang the best!
(*Deceit has fetched a monk's cowl*)

Deceit: Here is thy gaining, all and some,
This is a cowl of Tullilum!

Flatterie: Wha has a breviary to lend me?
The fiend a saul I trow will ken me!

Falsehood: We maun do mair yet, by Saint James!
For we maun all three change our names.
Christen me, and I sall baptise thee.
(*There follows a mock ceremony*)

Deceit: By God and thereabout may it be!
How will thou call me, I pray thee tell!

Falsehood: I wat not how to call mysel!
Deceit: But yet aince name the bairn's name!
Falsehood: Discretion, Discretion in God's name!
             I need not now to care for thrift,
             But what sall be my Godbairn gift?
Falsehood: I give you all the devils of hell.
Deceit: Na, brother, hauld that to thysel!
             Now, sit doun! Let me baptise thee—
             I wat not what thy name should be.
Falsehood: But yet aince name the bairn's name!
Deceit: Sapience, Sapience, in God's name!
Flatterie: Brother Deceit, come baptise me.
Deceit: Then sit down lowly on thy knee!
Flatterie: Now brother, name the bairn's name.
Deceit: Devotion, in the devil's name.
             (*He splashes Flatterie*)
Flatterie: The deil receive thee, lurdan loon!   [stupid
             Thou has wat all my new shaven croun!
Deceit: Devotion, Sapience and Discretion—
             We three may rule this region.
             We sall find mony crafty things
             For to beguile a hundred kings!
             For thou (*to Falsehood*) can richt weel crack and clatter.
             And I sall feign, and thou (*to Flatterie*) sall flatter.
Flatterie: But I wald have, ere we depairtit,
             A drink to mak us better heartit.
Deceit: Weel said, by Him that herryit hell,
             I was even thinkan that mysel!

While the King lies down among the ladies, they sing "ane sang".*
Verity now enters. "Get up, thou sleepis all too lang, O Lord!" she cries.
Flatterie soon seizes the book she is carrying.

    What buik is that, harlot, into thy hand?
        Out, walloway! This is the New Testament,
    In English tongue, and printed in England.
        Heresay, heresay! Fire! Fire! Incontinent.

Verity is clapped into the stocks.
Chastity comes next upon the scene, complaining that she can find no
refuge with the clergy, the lords or the merchants. A tailor and a shoe-
maker offer her a drink—another comic moment this, the two men ironically being more interested in her womanliness than in her personified

---

* In the twentieth-century productions "To Luve unluvit is ane pain" by Alexander
Scott has been used.

role—until their wives arrive and drive Dame Chastity off, knocking their
husbands about in the process. This makes the husbands think priests lucky
not to have to make their women into wives. After a verbal brush with
Sensuality, Chastity ends up in the stocks beside Verity.

At this point, and just before the Realm is totally ruined, Divine Correction makes his appearance. The vices flee the land, stealing the King's treas-
ure-chest as they go; Virtue is restored; and Sensuality, chased from the
King's side, is received by Spirituality. Surrounded now by Verity,
Chastity and Gude Counsel, the King promises to amend his ways, and is
ordered by Divine Correction to summon the Thrie Estates in Parliament
to make the necessary reformation. Diligence proclaims the Parliament,
and uses the occasion also to announce the interval, urging:

> Go tak ane drink, and mak collatioun;
>   Ilk man drink to his manner, I you pray,
>   Tary nocht lang, it is late in the day;
> Let some drink ale, and some drink claret wine,
>   Be great Doctors of Physick I hear say   [By
> That michty drink comforts the dull ingyne!   [intelligence

Those who complain that, for all his reforming zeal and high moral tone,
Lyndsay had no hesitation in stooping to gross coarseness when he thought
that by doing so he might please the groundlings, can point to Diligence's
final stanza of exhortation to the ladies—omitted from the Kemp acting
version—the least offensive half of which urges:

> Let nocht your bladder burst, I pray you,
> For that war even eneuch to slay you:
> For yit there is to come, I say you,
>   The best part of our play.

In strictly dramatic terms, this claim is arguable. In the first part of the
play, where Lyndsay is concerned with depicting the moral sickness and
cure of the individual, personified by Rex Humanitas, there is not only
greater opportunity for comic character-drawing, but to a modern audience living in an open society, inevitably a higher degree of interest in the
state and fate of these characters than with the sickness and cure of the sixteenth-century Body Politic, with which the second part is mainly concerned.

Nevertheless, Part Two opens with a comic interlude between a Poor
Man and a Pardoner, the former complaining that he cannot see for what he
is paying his last groat. The Pardoner, Sir Robert Rome-Raker, explains:

> Pardoner: Ane thousand year I lay upon thy heid,
>   With *totiens quotiens*; now mak nae mair plead.

	Thou has receivit thy pardon now already.
Poor Man:	But I can see naething, sir, by our Lady!
Pardoner:	What craves the carle? Methinks thou art not wise!
Poor Man:	I crave my groat, or else my merchandise.
Pardoner:	I gave thee pardon for a thousand year!
Poor Man:	How sall I get that pardon? Let me hear!
Pardoner:	Stand still, and I sall tell thee the haill story!
	When thou art deid and gaes to Purgatory,
	Being condemned to pain a thousand year,
	Then sall thy pardon thee relieve but weir!
Poor Man:	Sall I get nothing for my groat till then?
Pardoner:	Thou sall not! I mak it to you plain!

(*Poor Man is now very angry*)

Poor Man:	Na? Then, gossip, give me my groat again!
	What say ye, master? Call ye this gude reason?
	That he should promise me a gude pardon?
	And here receive my money in this stead,
	Syne make me nae payment till I be deid?
	When I am deid, I wat, full sickerly,
	My silly saul will pass to Purgatory.
	Declare me this! Now God nor Belial bind thee,
	When I am there, curst carle, where sall I find thee?
	Not into heaven, but rather into hell! [coarse fellow
	When thou art there, thou cannot help thysel!
Pardoner:	Swith, stand aback! I trow this man be mangit! [frantic
	Thou gets not this groat, though thou should be hangit!
Poor Man:	Give me my groat, weel bound into my clout!
	Or, by God's breid, Robin sall bear a rout!

They fight, and are chased away by Diligence to make way for the Thrie Estates, though in Lyndsay's unpruned original the Pardoner also encounters one Wilkin, then parts a Soutar from his wife after each has kissed the other's backside.*

The Thrie Estates now make their formal entrance backwards, the visible sign of their political retrogression. Once they are seated, Divine Correction states it is their will that those who feel themselves oppressed should make due complaint. John the Common Weill, symbol of the welfare of the community as a whole and champion of the much less articulate and rather simple-minded Poor Man, alleges that the Thrie Estates are led by Flatterie, Falsehood and Deceit. Their disguises penetrated, these three find themselves in the stocks. Then, in ringing terms, John goes on to detail the abuses of the clergy; plurality of benefices and bribery and incompetence, to which the Poor Man adds lechery. Lyndsay allows the leaders of the

* Restored in Tom Wright's Edinburgh Festival adaptation of 1973.

clergy to reply with spirit though without benefit of argued defence.

Spirituality calls for John's creed to be examined, and at the behest of Correction, John recites his belief with simple native dignity.

> I believe in God that all has wrocht,
> And create every thing of nocht;
> And in his Son, our Lord Jesu,
> Incarnate of the Virgin true;
> Who under Pilate tholit passioun
> And deit for our salvatioun
> And on the third day rais again
> As holy Scripture showis plain . . .

The other two Estates, forming a majority, then agree to the necessary reforms. The spiritual leaders, male and female, are now publicly humiliated and stripped, courtly clothing being found under their habits, while John the Common Weill, as Kemp puts it, "is presented with a gay garment, a sort of Labour Peerage". Falsehood and Deceit are executed, amid great mock lamentation, Falsehood's speech from the gallows combining satire and comicality:

> Alas, mon I be hangit too?
> What meikle devil is this ado?
>   How came I to this, cummer?
> My gud maisters, ye Craftsmen,
> Want ye Falset, full weel I ken
>   Ye will all die for hunger . . . .
> Find me ane Wabster that is leal   [weaver
> Or ane Walker that will nocht steal!
>   Their craftiness I ken:
> Or ane Miller that has nae fault,
> That will steal neither meal nor malt,
>   Hauld them for holy men! . . .
> Adieu, Blacksmiths and Lorimers,
> Adieu, ye crafty Cordiners
>   That sells the shoon owre dear!   [shoes
> Amang craftsmen it is a wonder,
> To find them leal amang a hunder,
>   The truth I to you tell!
> Adieu, I may nae langer tarry,
> I maun pass to the King of Fairy,
>   Or else straichtway to hell!

With wryly ironic implication, Lyndsay lets Flatterie escape, boasting that he deserved:

> . . . by All Hallows,
> To have been marshalled with my fellows,
>   And heich abune them hangit!
> I made mair faultis nor my mates,
> I beguiled all the Thrie Estates
>   With my hypocrisy.

There, except for Diligence's final address to the audience, Kemp's version ends, though Lyndsay inserts an interlude entitled "The Sermon of Folly", which adds nothing to the force of the play's message, and distorts its dramatic shape. Diligence apologizes to the audience:

> Because we have been some part tedious,
> With matter rude, denude of eloquence,
> Likewise, perchance, to some men odious.

The minstrels are bidden strike up "ane brawl of France", while Diligence tells us he means to run:

> To the tavern, or ever I stent.
> I pray to God Omnipotent,
>   To send you all gude rest.

The variety and aptness of the metres and measures to the characters or situations to which they relate, and the ability to blend comedy with high seriousness of moral purpose, and irony with good humour, as well as the sense of what is effective in stage terms, mark out *The Thrie Estates* as a very considerable achievement, far ahead of anything comparable that had yet been written in England at that time. The use of colloquial speech and the contra-manipulations of the serious with the absurd provide stylistic pointers to what was to become the general tone—song apart—of the achievement of the eighteenth-century Scots Revival. The fact that the play still repeatedly works for audiences to-day disproves those who claim its twentieth-century success to be due to the skill of modern acting rather than the intrinsic merit of the text.

The Thrie Estates surely cannot have been Lyndsay's first or only play. The others have vanished, as has most of the work of the "ghosts" whose names he recalls in "The Testament and Complaynt of the Papyngo", ghosts as tantalizing as Dunbar's a generation before.

After paying due tribute to the solid reputations of "Chaucer, Gower and Lydgate laureate", to "Kennedy, with termis aureate" and to Dunbar himself "whilk language had at large", Lyndsay catalogues "Quintyn, Mersar, Rowle, Henderson, Hay and Holland", telling us that:

Thocht they be deid, their libels bene livand,
Whilk to rehearse maks readers to rejoice.

Of Quintyn, unless he be that Quintyn Shaw whom Kennedy, in his
"Flyting" with Dunbar, calls his "cousing Quintine", and therefore the
author of some "Adveyce to a Courtier" (much better as counsel than as
verse) nothing is known. Mersar is presumably also the "Merser" of
Dunbar's "Lament", one of several of the name mentioned in the Treasurer's Accounts, and though believed by the older poet to have "in luf so
lifly write", known now only as the author of *The Perrell of Paramours*,
which has plenty to say about love, but not with much liveliness. Bannatyne credits him with a further two pieces, one of which, "Of Lufe whay
Likis," is a kind of practical treatise in rime royal on "the way of a man
with a maid".

Gif mony luvars thy lady will pursue,   [If
   Swa at thou leif nocht in jolesy;   [See
Scho is the better swa that scho be true: [so
   Non wald her luve was scho nocht womanly.   [not
   Repair nocht til her ay openly,
Bot in all time be ready her to please,
Howbeit thy hairt thou think sometimes at weiss.   [opposed

Rowle is doubtless one or other of the two "Rowlis" referred to by
Dunbar. Sir Richard Holland, linked by Dunbar with Barbour, was a
priestly follower of the Douglases exiled to England for rebellion, but
unpardoned in 1482. He is the author of *The Howlat*, which T. F. Henderson calls the solitary example of "the engraftment of allegory on the old
alliterative romance stanza." It is a story of that visually dull bird the Owl
dressing himself out in borrowed plumage, and meeting the usual naked
fate of all such creatures, being left alone in the end to reflect:

I may be sample heireft   [hereafter
That pride yet never left
His feir but a fall.   [companion

Henderson, of course, is none other than Henryson. Sir Gilbert Hay is
the author of a tediously long and flat-footed epic *The Buke of the Conqueror, Alexander the Great*, as well as of some of our earliest surviving Scots
literary prose.

    Other minor makars more nearly Lyndsay's contemporaries include Sir
James Inglis, who died in 1531 and with him all his works; Kyd, called by
Lyndsay "cunning and practick, richt prudent", survived by courtesy of

Bannatyne through some advice-giving to the young king more notable for its obvious common sense than for its poetic craftsmanship; and an industrious Stewarte, who, Lyndsay tells us, "Full ornate workis daily does compile". Perhaps because of the regularity of this exercise more of Stewarte's work has survived. It includes a "Flyting betwix the Soutar and the Tailor", a fairly average abusive excursion into what was never a particularly edifying tradition, and some rather dry love poems, all of which, however, apparently took the industrious Bannatyne's fancy.

There are one or two late makars whose names and occasional pieces owe their continuing existence mainly or entirely to Bannatyne, among them an unidentifiable Balnaves; and the musician Sir John Fethy (1480?–c. 1570)—the "Sir" was a priestly title—who trained abroad, was a canon of the Chapel Royal in Stirling and Chantour (Precentor) there by 1545. For a short time master of the Aberdeen Sang Scule, in 1551 he was master of the choir school of Edinburgh, where he remained until 1568. Two of his love poems have survived, one of which has the haunting refrain:

Cauld, cauld cools the lufe
That kindles owre het.

No doubt he provided music for amorous verse, as he did for his one certainly attributable religious piece, "O God Abufe," reprinted with both words and music in *Music of Scotland 1500–1700*. We have it on the authority of Thomas Wode,[4] one-time vicar of St Andrews and a kind of musical counterpart to Bannatyne, that Fethy introduced to Scotland the new skill of five-fingered organ-playing.

There was also one Fleming, responsible for some jovially injunctive stanzas beginning "Be merry brethern", and forming an amusing exposé of the nuisance caused by wicked wives.

George Steil (?1510–1542) was apparently a specialist in cloth and tapestry, and groom of the chamber, a "fervent if untheologically-minded, Catholic" who, Knox tells us in his *History of the Reformation*, in James V's presence "dropped off his horse, and died without word . . . in open audience of many". He is known from the Maitland manuscript as the author of "The Ryng of the Roy Robert", a political piece of some spirit, and credited by Bannatyne with two love poems, one, the beautiful "Lantern of lufe and lady fair of hue";[5] and Sir John Moffat, whom Bannatyne allows to be the author of the lively "Brother, Bewar I rede you now", and who is sometimes given credit for the still livelier and much-anthologized tale of the husband and wife who swopped roles for a day, much to the husband's discomfiture, "The Wife of Auchtermuchty." Wedded bliss is also the theme of the sole surviving piece by another priestly ghost, Sir George Clapperton, Provost of Trinity Church, Edinburgh, in 1564 and sub-dean of the Chapel Royal, but who seems to have died a Protestant in 1574. Maitland's manuscript saves for us Clapperton's "Wae Worth Marriage".

In Bowdoun, on black Monunday
When all was gadderit to the play,
　　Baith men and women semblit there,
I heard ane sweet ane sich, and say—　　　　　　　　　　　　[sigh
　　"Wae worth marriage for evermair."　　　　　　　　　　[woe betide

It is very possible that Clapperton's words were also originally matched
to music.

The triumph of the Reformation did not immediately bring about the
end of the three centuries-old tradition of the Scots Makars. The events of
1560 did, however, encourage the introduction of alien influences which
gradually enticed writers to follow new directions. The later Makars favoured foreign forms, like the roundel and the sonnet. These were less
easily subjectable to that "change of mood and meaning" Kurt Wittig
rightly claims were imposed by the earlier Makars upon their basically
English models. Above all, however, the later Makars—James VI's Castalians, some of whom survived to grace Charles I's Court—were either
musicians, or closely associated with music-making. One of the most distinguished was Alexander Scott (c. 1515–1583). There is still a good deal of
speculation as to Scott's actual background. John MacQueen opts for 1515
as his likely year of birth.[6] Helena Mennie Shire,[7] on the other hand, thinks
1525, or thereabouts, a more probable year: but this seems mainly to be able
to support her argument that Scott would be about the age of fifteen in
June 1540 when Claude Chorel, clerk of the Palace and captain of the band
of the Knights of the Round Table of the King of the Bazoche, employed
Jehan de Laulnay, a Swiss player of the tambourine, and one, Alexander
Scott, a fife and drum player, for a *montre*, or general review, performed in
July of that year at the Palace of Justice in Paris. The King of the Bazoche
was the official leader of the association of law students. Pantomimes and
tableaux vivants were performed on these occasions, no doubt with much
the same splendour as their English counterparts, staged at the Inns of
Court, in London.

In 1548, Alexander Scott, "musician and organist", received a Canon's
position in the Augustinian Priory of Inchmahome, an island in the Lake
of Menteith, the Commendator of which had been Robert Erskine, succeeded after his death in battle in 1547 by John, his younger brother. It has
been established[8] that this Scott was appointed "for the decoir of our queir
in musik and playing", and that he was to be paid "alsweill in his absence
as presens." The prior, with Scott in attendance, then described as "per-
soun of Balmacellane" (parson of Balmaclellan, in the Stewartry of Kirkcudbright) were given licence to go to France by the Queen and the
Regent Arran on 23rd July. Balmaclellan was one of the benefices annexed
for the upkeep of the Chapel Royal, so its occupant would be likely to be a
musician. Thus between 1547 and 1561, by which year Scott had lost or

relinquished the benefices connected with the Chapel Royal both at Balmaclellan and at Stirling, we may feel reasonably sure that the canon and
organist of Inchmahome, servant of the Erskine family and perhaps also of
the Queen, the musician Alexander Scott and the poet of the same name,
were one and the same person.

On 21st November 1549, the Register of the Great Seal of Scotland
shows that the natural sons of Alexander Scott—John and Alexander—
prebendary of the Chapel Royal at Stirling, were legitimatized. In 1821
David Laing speculated that the poet was the younger of the two brothers,
the legitimatized Alexander junior. Most critics, including Professor
MacQueen, assume the poet to have been the father, possibly legitamizing
his children "when his wife left him", a desertion Bannatyne claims was
the immediate inspiration of Scott's song "To luve unluvit."

What does seem beyond doubt is that Scott was both musician and poet:
that "musick fyne", or part-song, to which his words were probably
usually written, has in some instances survived; that some of it is of French
origin, and none of it positively identifiable as his own original composition; and that the musical maker of the songs of love's opposites, the
player in courtly pageants, recovered from whatever misfortunes befell
him before, or around, the Reformation and lived to enjoy a substantial
pension from the Perthshire Augustinian house of Inchaffray, to acquire
lands in Fife and Perthshire, and to see his son, Alexander, and his daugh-
ter-in-law, Elizabeth Lindsey well set-up (though this son predeceased
him, leaving grandson Alexander, and the other son, John, to inherit the
poet's wealth after his death).

On the evidence surviving, like Burns after him, Scott seems to have
devised his songs for music, only for part-song rather than for monodic
folk-air. The surviving examples are certainly very beautiful. We, however, are mainly concerned with Scott, the poet, rather than Scott, the
composer or musical arranger.

"Scott, sweet-tung'd Scott", as Allan Ramsay called him, was primarily
a lyricist whose theme was usually love and its pangs. He is our most concentrated love poet before Burns, although the medieval love-game rather
than personal romantic experience sometimes inspired his muse. Even
when Scott's subject-matter is trite—and often it is!—his intricate and apt
choice of metres and stanza-forms, as well as the fresh, melodic directness of
his manner give his handful of surviving poems their immediate attract-
iveness, sung, spoken or read. Happily, the "lectori" stanza which he
appends to his "New Year Gift to the Queen Mary," with its unspeakable
alliteration and absurd use of old-fashioned aureate terms, is quite untypi-
cal of his best achievement.

Fresh, flugent, flurist, fragrant flour formois,
Lantern to lufe, of ladies lamp and lot,
Cherrie maist chaste, chief charbucle and chois,   [carbuncle

Smail sweet smaragde,* smelling but smit of smot,
> [small, sweet emerald, smelling neither of stain nor blot.

Noblest natour, nurice to nurtour, not
This dull indyte, dulce, double daisy dear,   [composition
Sent be thy simple servand Sanders Scott
Greeting grit God to grant thy Grace gude year.   [praying

Two respectable enough Scots versions of the Psalms apart, the only
other poem by Scott not about love out of his meagre total of thirty-six—
all of which survived unaltered by musicians only because Bannatyne transcribed them—is "The Justing and Debait up at the Drum betwix William
Adamsone and John Sym". It follows the subject-matter of Dunbar's
"Turnament" and Lyndsay's "Justing", but differs from these in that its
stanza-form is based on that of "Peblis to the Play" (in this case a double
stanza of eights and sixes plus a bob-wheel) and deploys peasant characters
for the exchange of jousters' dunts "Up at Dalkieth that day".

The link between this rustic buffoonery, perhaps harking back to the
Pantomimes of the Paris days, and Scott's songs, is the crude "Ballat maid
to the Derisioun and Scorne of Wantoun Wemen." It is so prurient an
exercise in defining sexual mechanics under guise of pretended moral purpose that "the scorne" gets turned back upon the writer by the reader, as
one of the less scatalogical stanzas perhaps demonstrates:

Licht wenches luve will fawin   [court
   Even like ane spaniel's lauchter,
To lat her wamb be clawin
   Be them, list geir betawcht hir;   [that goods be given her
   For conie ye may chawcht hir   [money . . . induce
To shed hir shanks in twane,   [open her legs
   And never speir whais awcht hir   [who has possessed her
I sall not said again.

The rhythmic economy and controlled verbal energy of Scott at his best
are well demonstrated in his famous "Roundel of Luve", a condensed but
superior version of Wyatt's "Abused Lover".

   Lo! what it is to lufe
   Learn ye, that list to prufe
Be me, I say, that no ways may   [by
   The grund of grief remufe,
Bot still decay, both nicht and day:
   Lo'. what it is to lufe.

---

* Since we know Mary to have been exceptionally tall, this line, as well as being
singularly inept poetically, seems hardly apt factually either.

Lufe is ane fervent fire,
    Kendillt without desire:
Short pleasour, lang displeasour,
    Repentance is the hire;   [price
Ane pure tressure without measour;
    Lufe is ane fervent fire.

To lufe and to be wise
    To rage with guid advice,
Now thus, now then, so goes the game,
    Incertain is the dice:
There is no man, I say, that can
    Both lufe and to be wise.

Flee always from the snare;
    Learn at me to beware;
It is ane pain and double train   [lure
    Of endless woe and care;
For to refrain that danger plain,
    Flee always from the snare.

There are many such pieces from his pen, reflecting a graceful and gentle
cynicism deployed in various intricately weaved forms of *rime couée*
(fashioned on the imperfect iambic tetrameter, a stanza form found in
Early Norman, and developed in sixteenth-century England). In some of
these songs, a passing note of defiance is struck, as in "In June the Gem":

Als guid luve comes as goes,
    Or rather better.

But in general, the prevailing mood is one of despondency, occasionally
even of bitterness, as in "Ye blindit lovers look", an outright attack on
sexual love. Like his medieval predecessors, Scott was only too well aware
both of love's pleasures and its pains.

Curiously enough, his most deeply felt stanzas seem to be those of "The
Lament of the Maister of Erskine," that former Commendator at Inchmahome and a young nobleman said to have been in love with the Queen-
Dowager, Mary of Lorraine, but who was killed at the Battle of Pinkie-
cleugh on 10th September 1547:

Adieu, my awin sweit thing,
My joy and comforting
My mirth and solaceing,
    Of erdly gloir!
Farewell, my lady bricht,

And my remembrance richt,
Farewell, and have guid nicht,
  I say no more.

The poem may have been written as a "Depairte" (of which "Auld Lang Syne" is the most famous example) on the occasion of the final meeting of the lovers. Scott had reason to be grateful to the Erskines.

Among Scott's more joyful pieces, "Up halesome hairt" is a particularly spirited example, with its celebration of the satisfaction of consummated love.

In oxters close we kiss, and cossis hairts,   [arms, exchange
  Brint in desire of amorous play and sport;   [burnt
Meittand our lustis spreitless we twa depairts,   [meeting
  Prolong with leisure, Lord, I Thee exhort,
  Sic time that we may both tak our comfort,
First, for to sleep, syne wauk without espyis.
I blame the cock, I plain the nicht is short;
Away I went, my watch the cushat cries
  Wishing all luvars leal to haif sic chance
  That they may haif us in remembrance.

If indeed, as has been conjectured, the even smoother-flowing "My hairt is heich above," is also by Scott, then it might seem that the poet did not wholly lack consolation for his wife's desertion:

The thing that may hir please
  My body sall fulfill;
Whatever her disease,
  It does my body ill.
My bird, my bonny ane,
  My tender babe venust
My luve, my life alane,
  My liking and my lust.

Scott's more versatile, if less narrowly intense, contemporary Alexander Montgomerie (?1540–?1610), the last of the great Scots Makars and the most versatile of the Castalians, was the younger son of Hugh Montgomerie of Hesilhead, Ayrshire, and a relation of the Montgomeries, Earls of Eglintoun. Through his mother, Lady Margaret Fraser, a great granddaughter of Sir John Stewart of Darnlay, Montgomerie enjoyed kinship with James VI.

Like many younger sons, Montgomerie seems to have become a soldier. Possibly he served abroad. He certainly had some experience of the Highlands, because he earned himself the nickname of "Eques Montanus", the highland trooper, a point not lost on his flyting adversary, Polwarth. There are various references to him as "Captain". It seems probable that while in Spain he abandoned the Calvinstic faith in which he had been brought up, and embraced Catholicism. Like most converts, he then adhered to the religion of his choice with fanatical enthusiasm. Indeed, it seems likely that his zeal for the old faith and his desire to support the Counter-Reformation led him to become involved in spying and intrigue in the Catholic cause, much of his activity being unavowed.

By 1579 he was already at the Scottish Court of the thirteen-year-old, but already cultured James, a monarch vacillating between the emotional demands arising from the position in which his imprisoned Catholic mother found herself, and the prevailing political Protestant pressures from his immediate circle of advisers.

At this time, however, the influence of Esmé Stuart, Sire d'Aubigny, the King's Catholic cousin, later to be made Duke of Lennox but already accused by the Protestants of teaching the King debauched French ways, was in the ascendant. Aubigny's ambition being to have Queen Mary and Catholicism restored, Montgomerie naturally found in him an ally and patron. Montgomerie soon became the leading poet at court, the King's "Beloved Sanders, maistre of our art," successor to Polwarth, reputedly ousted from popularity after the famous "flyting" pronounced in the royal presence.

By 1581, after involvement in the purchase of a ship for use in Jesuit intrigue Montgomerie was back at the Scottish Court, engaged in the "writing game" of the Castalians, led and encouraged by the King, and being chidden in Royal verse for acts of boastfulness about the prowess of a horse. For his part, Montgomerie's early verses deal much with the fanciful affairs of Cupid's court, and the laws of "Venus queen".

A year later, in August, the Protestant Lords headed by Ruthven staged the "Ruthven Raid" and seized the King, holding him in captivity until June 1583. Lennox retreated to France, and died soon afterwards. The only poet in the retinue of the imprisoned King seems to have been one William Murray, whose literary abilities were minimal.

After his escape, and the overthrow of the Ruthven supporters, the King surrounded himself with nobles carefully chosen to ensure a safer balance of Catholics. His household staff was reassembled, and Montgomerie once more given an honoured place, along with the musicians Robert and Thomas Hudson, the composer James Lauder, Christian Lindsay and "Old Scott and Robert Semphill". Younger men soon included Stewart of Baldynneis and William Fowler.

A flowing smoothness of style closely related to suitability for matching with music, was one of the main requirements of the Castalian manner, even sonnets being set to "musick fyne". The way to royal favour, Fowler tells us in a poem addressed to Robert Hudson, was at this time undoubtedly prowess in the making of verse:

If Ovid were to life restored
   to see which I behold,
he micht inlairge his pleasant tales
   of formis manifold
be this, which now into the Court   [by
   most pleasantly appears,
to see in penners and in pens
   transformed all our spears,
and into paper all our joiks,
   our daggs in horns of ink   [daggers
for knapstaves, seals and signatures
   to change ilk man does think . . .

For two years Montgomerie kept bright his favour with a supply of son-nets to the royal Apollo, and in 1583, the poet—by then also secretly *persona grata* with Philip of Spain—received a royal pension to be paid out of certain monies belonging to the See of Glasgow, but which had fallen into d'Aubigny's hands.

The following year there was legal trouble as to whether or not Montgomerie had fulfilled his financial obligations over the *Bonaventor*. In this year, too, Montgomerie began his long poem *The Cherrie and the Slae*, which was eventually to reflect in its final form (through the device of dream-vision), his anger at the deviousness of his royal patron, and his total dedication to Catholicism as against the religion then in the ascendant.

By 1585 there was a definite Kirk move to "cleanse" the King's presence of "undesirable Catholic influences". A poem by Montgomerie written in that year shows that he had already fallen from the King's good favour.

Nevertheless, under royal licence, Captain Montgomerie went abroad in 1586 to "Flanders, Spain and uthers beyond the sey". In the same year, a similar licence was granted to two notorious Catholic intriguers in Queen Mary's cause, Sir William Stewart of Houston (who had organized James's escape from the Ruthven Raiders), and Hew Barclay of Ladyland.

Whether in the service of the Master of Gray in the Low Countries, or as captain of a Scots barque carrying troops for the Netherlands but also a cargo of contraband, we do not know; but in either event, during June 1586, a ship apparently under Montgomerie's command was intercepted by an English vessel, and as a result of the encounter the poet ended up a Scots pirate in an English prison. There he stayed until 1589, by which time Queen Mary had been put to death at Fotheringay.

Help Prince, to whom, on whom not, I complain,
But on, not to, false Fortune, ay my foe . . .

The poet appealed. The fickle King, however, was too busy with the arrangements for his Danish marriage to bother about a poet in trouble,
and Montgomerie had to content himself with the support of the young
second Duke of Lennox. We do not know whether or not Lennox helped
financially, but Montgomerie was by now embroiled in lengthy court proceedings to try to secure his pension, which, though granted several years
before, was apparently never actually paid.

What had happened was that, for tangled political reasons too involved
to enter into here, William Erskine had been appointed Archbishop of
Glasgow against the King's nominee, a pliant "tulchan", Robert Montgomerie. Since the poet's pension was to derive from part of the revenues of
the Glasgow See, there was naturally resistance from the new incumbent.
James did his unsuccessful best to oust Erskine in favour of Archbishop
Betoun, the last Catholic occupant who, at the Reformation, had fled to
Rome with the muniments. Montgomerie meanwhile engaged in a series of
legal actions, which culminated in July 1593 with a decision by the Com-
missionary Court in favour of Erskine. By then, James had probably lost
interest in the whole matter. In any case, in 1592, on the information of a
Paisley minister, the Reverend Andro Knox, one George Ker was tortured
into "confessing" royal involvement and contact with Spain in what became known as the affair of the "Spanish blanks". This led to an outcry
against all Catholics, and the end of any hope for the return of Betoun.

Understandably, Montgomerie's bitterness was considerable, much of it
directed against the King. By 1595, Montgomerie apparently intended to
visit a newly-founded community of Scottish Benedictines in the monastery
of Arctanum, at Würzburg. But the final "second Armada" plot by King
Philip decided the poet against taking this safe, retreating step. Instead, he
became involved with Hew Barclay of Ladyland in a plot—codenamed
"Isle of Guyannna"—for capturing Ailsa Craig, in the Clyde, as a Catholic
stronghold to support an invasion. But once again the ubiquitous Reverend Mr Knox discovered and exposed the plot. James, now bent on
securing the English succession, could less easily afford to equivocate.

An English ship arrived off Ailsa Craig while some of the conspirators
were hunting on Arran, Montgomerie presumably among them. Hew
Barclay, left behind on the rocky island, drowned himself rather than be
taken. Montgomerie was summoned to present himself before the Privy
Council in July to explain his treason. He failed to appear, and was accordingly "put to the horn", or outlawed.

What happened to him then? Was he killed soon after, as an outlaw
might lawfully be by anyone? Did he reach the sanctuary of the Scottish
Benedictines, and there add to, and in the doing turn his major poem
The Cherrie and the Slae from a pleasant pastoral allegory into an accusation against the King's deviousness? Did he die in 1597, 1602, or survive
until 1611, all terminal dates suggested by various critics? Nobody
knows.

A Latin poem alleges that as Montgomerie lay dying the Calvinists decided to deny him burial rites, and only the King's personal intervention ensured a decent interment. The King himself, according to Dempster, experienced great grief—"magno regis dolore"—at his former master-poet's death, and produced a memorial sonnet which confirms the deplorable spite of Montgomerie's victorious religious opponents:

> What drowsy sleep doth syle your eyes, allace!   [seal
> Ye sacred brethren of Castalian band?
> And shall the prince of Poets in our land
> Go thus to grave unmourned in any case?
> No! Whet your pens, ye imps of heavenly grace,
> And tune me up your sweet, resounding strings,
> And mount him so on your immortal wings
> That ever he may live in every place.
> Remember on Montgomerie's flowand grace,
> His sugared style, his weighty words divine,
> And how he made the sacred Sisters nine
> Their mountain quit to follow on his trace,
> Though to his burial was refused the bell,
> The bell of fame shall aye his praises knell.

And so it did. Montgomerie's popularity for long rested securely, and almost entirely, upon *The Cherrie and the Slae*, which was probably begun early in his career and certainly completed towards the end of it. Its "114 quatorzains" contain many aphorisms, some of which quickly passed into common educated currency. It soon went through several editions, and was translated into Latin.

Although in conception it is medieval, it is not really an old-style allegory. Indeed, in its final form it appears to have been deliberately revised to make it carry religious and political overtones which could not safely have been sounded openly. The cherry has a long history as a symbol of the delectable, the "Cherry-Tree Carol" suggesting that the fruit was believed to be what today we would call the "pregnant whim" of Mary before Jesus was born. For Montgomerie, the cherry was thus the inaccessible but delicious heavenly fruit, the Christ-eucharist symbol, while the bitter black sloe, its thirst-quenching effect short-lived though easily accessible from a bush,* represented the Reformed religion.

The poet debates with himself whether to try to reach the cherry on the cliff, or be satisfied with the more easily accessible sloe. While Courage and Hope spur him on, Dread, Danger and Despair try to discourage him. Will, the original urger of the poet's earlier rashnesses, still cries for action. Reason, Wit, Skill and Wisdom have their say. Reason claims that the

---

* Given additional significance by the choice in 1563 of a "Burning Bush" as the symbol of Reformed religion, and still used by the Church of Scotland.

cherries can be reached, and Wit shows how the cliff on which the cherry-tree stands may be scaled. Suddenly, out of ripeness, the cherries fall of their own accord, and the poet eats, is refreshed, and thanks his Catholic God for His Love.

The poem differs from such earlier allegories as "The Romaunt of the Rose," Douglas's "Palice of Honour" or Lyndsay's "Dreme" in that no worldly falling asleep is described. The visionary quality is, so to say, inbuilt. Similarly, Courage, Dread and their companions are not so much medieval personifications as aspects of the poet's mood-reactions, contentions of his own inner voices.

Like so much Scottish poetry, the piece moves with the liveliness of a dance, albeit a prolonged one, and abounds in that colourful painting of Nature, including the play of light and colour on water which was a characteristic feature of the Scots tradition almost from its beginning, and has remained so with the Anglo-Scots poetry of the twentieth century. Not for nothing have most of the Scottish schools of painting been fundamentally colourist!

A fair sample of the vivid melodiousness of the poem is this description of a summer morning. The birds are singing and flying nimbly about the reclining poet who, looking upward, notices that:

The dew as diamonds did hing
Upon the tender twistis ying
    Owre-twinkling all the trees;
And ay where flours did flourish fair,
There suddenly I saw repair
    Ane swarm of sounding bees.
Some sweetly has the honey socht,
    Whill they were cloggit sore;
Some willingly the wax has wrocht,
    To keep it up in store.
        So heaping, with keeping,
            Into their hives they hide it,
        Precisely and wisely
            For winter they provide it.

To pen the pleasures of that park,
How every blossom, branch, and bark
    Against the sun did shine,
I leif to poets to compile
In stately verse and ornate style:
    It passes my ingine.
Bot as I muissit myne alane,
    I saw ane river rin
Out owre ane crag and rock of stane,

Syne lichtit in ane linn,
  With tumbling and rumbling
    Amang the rockis round,
  Devalling and falling
    Into that pit profound.

For all its easy melodiousness, a comparison between the original version of *The Cherrie and the Slae*, as published by Waldegrave in 1597, and the Wreitoun text of 1636 (the Hart first edition of the revised version being now lost), certainly does confirm a pointing of references which could be construed as condemnation of a double-dealing monarch who came down on what was, for the poet, the wrong side, and a passionate personal rejection by the poet of the bitter sloe of Protestantism.

Much of the music for which Montgomerie's words were written has been found, sometimes having to be reassembled from widely-scattered part-books. Not the least interesting suggestion made by Mrs Shire,[9] prompted by Ian Ross's[10] hint that the stanza form of *The Cherrie and the Slae*—in purely literary terms correctly enough described by T. F. Henderson as the addition "to a ten-line stave, very common in England from the beginning of the fourteenth century" of "a peculiar wheel borrowed from a stave of the old Latin Hymns"—might be related to music and dance, is that the poet's rhythm-sequence matches a tune, "The Nine Muses," itself unfortunately lost. "The Nine Muses" is known to have been a dance involving a change of pace, like the French *double-danse*. In 1568, Bannatyne noted that a poem of Maitland's in the same stanza-form went to the tune "The Bankis of Helicon". Kirkcaldy of Grange's ballad, written from the standpoint of one on Queen Mary's side, "Ane Ballat of ye Captane of the Castell", and dating from 1571, also in the same stanza-form, would almost certainly have been designed for derisive singing. In one of Thomas Wode's Part-Books, Andro Blackhall's tune "The Bankis of Helicon" shows the tenor part specifying *The Cherrie and the Slae*. Mrs Shire has stated that the yet unpublished[11] Taitt Manuscript contains a four-part setting of this tune matched to the first stanza of *The Cherrie*.

It would therefore seem possible that when first written, even Montgomerie's longest and most elaborately structured poem was designed for singing, its intricacy dictated at least in part, by the steps of a dance and its music.

There are those who feel that the love poem "The Bankis of Helicon" itself, Montgomerie's earlier and shorter poem in the same stanza-form, is an even defter performance. In a fairly similar form is couched the exquisite "Adieu to His Mistress", the beautiful music for which has also happily survived.[12] The last verse runs:

O lady, for thy constancy,
A faithful servant sall I be,

Thine honour to defend;
And I sall surely, for thy sake,
As doth the turtle for her make,
   Love to my lifis end.
No pain nor travail, fear nor dreid,
   Sall cause me to desist.
Then ay when ye this letter read,
Remember how we kiss'd;
   Embracing with lacing
      With other's tearis sweet,
   Sic blissing in kissing
      I quit till we twa meet.

Montgomerie was always inventive with his metres, doubtless influenced by his English contemporaries—possibly through Tottel's *Miscellany* of 1557—but also by Ronsard and the other poets of the Pléiade. At least seventy sonnets stand to Montgomerie's credit, some of them in Sydney form—*abba, abba//cd, cd, ee*—others in the Wyatt form—*abba, abba,//cdd, cee*. No known examples are written in the Surrey/Shakespeare form. However, some are to be found rhyming *abab, bcbc//cdcd, ee*, the form now known as Spenserian, although Montgomerie and other Scottish sonneteers, including King James himself, were apparently using this variant seven years before Spenser hit upon it.*

Unlike some of the "amateurs" among the Scots, Montgomerie handled all forms of the sonnet with firmness, octave and sestet often showing an appropriate modulation of thought, as in this example, "To His Mistress".

Bright amorous e'e where Love in ambush lies,
   Clear crystal tear distill'd at our depairt,
   Sweet secret sigh more piercing nor a dairt,
Inchanting voice, bewitcher of the wise,
White ivory hand whilk thrust my fingers prize:
   I challenge you, the causers of my smart,
   As homicides, and murtherers of my heart,
In Reason's court to suffer ane assise.
   Bot oh! I fear, yea rather wot I weil,
   To be repldg'd ye plainly will appeal
To Love, whom Reason never culd command.
   Bot since I can not better mine estate,
   Yit while I live, at least I sall regrate   [lament
Ane e'e, a tear, a sigh, a voice, a hand.

* While it is possible that Spenser knew James's work, if not Montgomerie's, it may be that both Spenser and the Scots writers devised this fairly obvious variant of a popular form quite independently of each other.

Other measures used by Montgomerie are: the rhymed alliterative staves of the old romances employed in "The Flyting of Montgomerie and Polwart," and "Ane Answer to ane Helandmanis Invective" (Montgomerie's early military connection with Argyll was a reproof flung at him in the invective of Polwarth's side of "The Flyting"); the sixteen-line stave in *rime couée*—*aaab, aaab, aaab, aaab,*—as in his "Address to the Sun"; the five-line stave with internal rhyme followed by the bob-wheel, taken from the alliterative romances; the English six-line *ab, ab, cc* stave which Gascoigne called the "Ballade"; and other variations of these, as well as what one of his contemporaries called his "cuttit and broken verse". In "The Flyting," played before King James with Montgomerie pronounced the winner, he uses the common rondeau in triple measure to match the particular kind of quick, small abuse he wishes to level:

Polwart ye peip
Like a mouse among thorns,
　Na cunning ye keep.
Polwart ye peip,
　Ye look like a sheep
And ye had twa horns.
　Polwart ye peip
Like a mouse amang thorns.

At one high point of Montgomerie's many-sided achievement stands his fine set of verses to an old Scots air, the "new" version of a very old song:

Hey! now the day dawis;
The jolly Cock craws
Now shroudis the shawis
　Throu Nature anon.
The thrustle-cock cryis
On lovers wha lyis;
Now skaillis the skyis   [empties
　The nicht is near gone.

At another, there is his curiously passionate poem "Margareit", addressed to his relative, Margaret Montgomerie, wife of Lord Robert Seton, which suggested to George Stevenson, editor of the supplementary volume of the Scottish Text Society edition of Montgomerie's work, that he was perhaps "something more than an impartial admirer". There are also religious sonnets and rhymed versions of the psalms. There is the beautiful poem of leave-taking, "A Lang Gudenicht," and that rather prurient old man's advice-giving, "An Admonition to Young Lassies."

Here and there, too, strong elements of folk superstition, and even of folk-poetry, burst through the courtier's smoothness, the well-ordered skill

of the man of letters, like this untitled fragment, which certainly has the
ring of earthy folk-balladry:

> Glad am I, glad am I,
> My mother is gone to Henislie.
> Steek the dure and catch me,
> Lay me doun and streche me,   [stretch
> Ding me, and dang me,   [pierce
> Ye, gif I cry, hang me—
> Ye, gif I die of the same,
> Bury me, bury, in Goddis name.

Later, Burns was certainly to make much of that particular aspect of
woman's nature. Other links between medieval superstition, the world of
"The Gyre-Carling" and its poetic re-creation in the eighteenth century,
are to be found in passages of "The Flyting"; such as this, on "Allhallow
E'en":

> In the hinder end of harvest, on Allhallow e'en,
> When our good nichbours rides, if I reid richt,
> Some bucklit on a bunweed and some on a bean,   [ragweed
> Ay trottand in troupis fra the twilicht;
> Some saddland a she-ape, all graithit into green,   [equipped
> Some hobbland on ane hemp-stalk, hovand on hicht;
> The King of the faeries with his court and the Elf-queen,
> With mony elritch incubus was ridand that nicht.

Or this "Witch's Curse", from the same poem:

> Be the heicht of the heavens, and be the howness of hell,   [depth
> Be the winds and the Weirds and the Charlemaine,   [Fates
> Be the Hornis, the Handstaff and the Kingis Ell,
> Be thunder, be fireflauchts, be drauth and be rain,   [lightning
> Be the poles, and the planets, and the signs all twell,
> Be the mokness at the morn—let mirkness remain—   [moistness
> Be the elements all that our craft can compel,
> Be the fiends infernal, and the furies in pain,
> For all the ghaists of the deid that dwellis there doon   [make
>   In Lethe and Styx the stinkand stands,
>   And Pluto that your court commands,
>   Receive this howlet aff our heads   [owl
>   In name of Mahoun.   [devil

Around Montgomerie there were, of course, the minor figures of the
King's Castalian band. The King himself had poetic pretentions, tutored,

perhaps, by Montgomerie. "The first verses that ever the king made", circulated when he was fifteen, already reveal his tortuous thinking on matters of policy; the trick of double-think which once led English Elizabeth to refer to him as "The false Scotch urchin":

Since thought is gree, think what thou will,
O troubled hart to ease thy paine.
Thought unrevealed can do no evil,
But words past out cummes not again.
Be careful aye for to invent
The way to get thy own intent.

The royal essay on "*Reulis and Cautelis* to be observit and eschewit in Scottish Poesie", written when he was eighteen, may possibly have been inspired by Gascoigne's "Instruction" published in 1575, when James was nine. The book of which the King's essay forms a part, "Essayes of a Prentise in the Divine Art of Poesie," deals extensively with such matters as rhyme and rhythm (or "flowing", as he called it), of the relationship between sound and memorability, and, since lyric verse was then meant actually to be sung, on the supreme importance of music, which he called the "vere twiche stane".

The verse part of the book includes a translation of Du Bartas's "Uranie", and a poem based on the death in banishment of his beloved cousin Lennox. James's "Poetical Exercise" includes further translations and a description of Lepanto, suggested by the victory over the Turks in 1571, couched in about a thousand dull lines and written when the royal author was sixteen. Later poems include a sonnet to the Swedish astronomer, Tycho Brahe, some love-poems to the Queen, and his best-known sonnet, that with which he prefaced the "Basilikon Doron," his essay on the craft of being a monarch written for the edification of his son, Prince Henry, who died before he had any opportunity of putting his father's teaching to practical use. The King was even bold enough to set out his own ideas on what constituted the perfect poet.

Ane rype ingyne, ane quick and walkned wit,
    With sommair reasons, suddenlie applyit,
For every purpose—using reasons fit,
    With skilfulness, where learning may be spyit,
    With pithie words for to express you by it
His full intention in his proper leid,
    The puritie whairof weill hes he tryit:
With memorie to keep what he does read,
With skilfulness and figures, whilks proceed
    From Rhetorique, with everlasting fame,
With others woundring, preassing with all speed

For to atteine to merit sic a name:
　All thir into the perfyte poet be.　　　　　　　　　　　　　[these
God grant I may obtain the laurell tree.

Sir Richard Maitland of Lethington (1496–1586), who, as Lord Lethington, became a judge in 1561, at about the same time lost his sight. To compensate for this loss, he began to compose verse. He was thus a late starter,
"commencing poet" (in Burns's phrase) only when he was sixty. His
sharp, satirical verse is drily wise rather than sensuous, but technically he
was certainly deft. "Againis the Theivis of Liddisdail" is the most frequently anthologized of his many pieces deploring the troubled state of the
early Reformation times (which, however, he rode out successfully, drawing his salary up to his death).

Of Liddisdale the common thievis
Sa pertlie stealis now and reivis,
　That nane may keep
　Horse, nolt, nor sheep,
Nor yit dar sleep for their mishiefis.

Other targets for his satire include the fairly obvious one of "The Folye
of ane Auld Manis Maryand ane Young Woman" and the fashionable
foibles of the young in "Satire on Toun Ladis".

Their collars, carcats, and hals beidis!　　　　　[necklaces, throat-beads
With velvet hats heicht on their heidis
　Coirdit with gold like ane younker　　　　　　　[young dandy
Bourdit about with goldin threidis,
　And all for newfangilnes of geir.

Their shoon of velvet and their muillis!　　　　　[embroidered slippers
In kirk they are not content of stoolis,
　The sermon when they sit to hear,
But carries cuschings, like vain fuillis,
　And all for newfangilnes of geir.

Maitland regretted the passing of the old, gay times of his youth, contrasting them sadly with the present:

And we hald nather Yule nor Pace　　　　　　　　　　[Easter
Bot seik our meat from place to place,
And we have neither luk nor grace,
　We gar our landis double pay,
Our tennants cry, "Alace! Alace!"
　That routh and pity is away.

Now we have mair, it is weill kend,
Nor our forebearis had to spend;
Bot for less at the yeiris end;
  And never hes ane mirrie day:
God will na riches to us send
  Swa lang as honour is away.

Inflation, it would seem, is not only a late twentieth-century affliction!
Above all, as might be expected of a wise and learned judge in
Maitland's circumstances his philosophy stresses the practicality of resigna-
tion:

When I have done consider
  This worldis vanity,
Sa brukill and sa slidder,   [brittle, slippery
  Sa full of misery;
  Then I remember me,
That here there is no rest;
  Therefore, apparently
To be mirrie is best.

William Fowler (1562–1612), who seems to have succeeded Montgomerie in the King's favour, was the son of a wealthy Edinburgh lawyer. He
studied at St Andrews and Paris. Fowler received the patronage of Francis
Stewart, Earl of Bothwell, the nephew of Mary's James Bothwell, and had
a successful career as a spy in England. He took charge of the masques in
honour of Prince Henry's christening, and from 1603, had a post in the
Queen's household.*
He translated the "Trionfi" of Petrarch, which was published in 1587;
turned out medieval psalms (almost as much a literary requirement of the
times as a poem to "Hugh MacDiarmid" in the twentieth-century's Scottish Renaissance); wrote treatises on memory, the mounting of masques
and the composing of letters. He also produced some excellent sonnets.
One, "Solitude", indicates the increasing Anglicization of style and spelling affected by these later makars. Amongst the best are "In Orknay," a
place which scarcely otherwise features in earlier Scots literature:

Ship-broken men whom stormy seas sore toss
Protests with oaths not to adventure more;
Bot all their perils, promises and loss
They quite forget when they come to the shore;
Even so, fair dame, whiles sadly I deplore
The shipwreck of my wits procured by you,

* So could scarcely have been a "Parson of Hawick", as some writers have suggested.

Your looks rekindleth love as of before,
And dois revive which I did disavow;
So all my former vows I disallow,
And buries in oblivion's grave, but groans;
Yea, I forgive, hereafter, even as now
My fears, my tears, my cares, my sobs, and moans,
In hope if anes I be to shipwreck driven,
Ye will me thole to anchor in your heaven.

The practice of translation—or rather re-creation—from the Italian (since poetry, strictly speaking, is not really translatable, as the worthy efforts of countless uncreative academics over many centuries demonstrate) was carried on by other minor poets, notably John Stewart of Baldynneis (c. 1550–c. 1605), younger son of Lord Innermeath. Stewart's abridged version of Ariosto's *Orlando Furioso* suffers from maddening over-alliteration, which makes much of it to-day almost unreadable in bulk, although he could produce now and again what Agnes Mure Mackenzie calls "a dreamy, plangent music", exemplified in his still anthologized lines on a fountain.[13]

Stewart, who could claim kinship with James VI, and was a distant cousin of Alexander Montgomerie, followed the regular course of seeking royal favour by in 1586 presenting the king, "brycht purpour Pean", as the poet called him, with his book of verse, *Rapsodies of the Author's Youthfull Braine*. Some of these pieces had been designed to console the young monarch while he was "in fascherie", held by the Ruthven Raiders. They include such counsel as:

Live still heirfoir in esperance alway;   [hope
Maist pleasour purchest is by price of pain.
Those that indures the winter's sharp assay
Sall see the seemly simmer shine again.

Stewart's Protestant anti-Catholic strain led to a rupture in his friendship with Montgomerie, whilst his too obvious association with a court favourite, the Master of Gray, ended all hopes of royal preferment when Gray himself fell from favour.

It is interesting to note, with Burns's "Mary Morrison" in mind, that Stewart's "His Fareweill to the muses" contains the lines:

Fareweill my toynles, trimbling strings,   [toneless
Fareweill, the source where poems springs.

Alexander Arbuthnot (1538–1583), who became Principal of King's College, Aberdeen, and was a distinguished scholar who had studied law in France before entering the church, was described by the historian Archbishop John Spottiswoode as being "pleasant and jocund, and in all sciences

expert, a good poet, philosopher, and lawyer, and in medecine skilful"
What at best can now be said for his poetry is that in an age decidedly anti-
feminist, he wrote "The Praises of Wemen," albeit lame-sounding compared with the dextrous manipulations of his contemporary, Scott:

> Wha dewly wald descern
>   The nature of gud wemen,
> Or wha wald wis or yairne
>   That cumly clan to ken,
> He hes greit need, I say indeed,
>   Of toungis ma than ten: [more
> That pleasant sort are all comfort
>   And mirriness to men.

Little need be said of Robert Sempill (1530–1595), who found himself
in Paris during the Massacre of St Bartholomew in 1572. He celebrated the
Regent Moray's death in his "Regentes Tragedy," and his pedestrian per-
sistence is enlivened only by an unsavoury bitterness in such others of his
pieces as "Sege of the Castel of Edinburgh" and "The Legend of the
Lymmaris Lyfe", the latter an attack on Archbishop Adamson.

He has been credited, on wholly insubstantial evidence, with the verse-
comedy *Philotus*, which draws heavily upon a novel by Barnabe Rich,*
and, either directly or through a translation, on an Italian comedy of the
Cinquecento, *Gli Ingannati*. In any case, the piece is now more usually
credited to that most agelessly prolific of all authors, Anon.

The Scots play re-tells the age-old story of the attempt of an old man,
Philotus, to secure by his riches the pretty daughter of Alberto, a friend
who tries to arrange the marriage, although the girl already has a secret
lover of her own age. A pedant unsuccessfully acts as would-be pander, but
to fool this old lecher and the father, Emilie's brother, Philerno, dressed up
as a girl, undertakes the marriage ceremony, with consequences which can
easily be imagined. However, the disguised young man, supposedly
Emilie, is put in charge of Philotus's own young daughter, Brisilla—
forcedly betrothed to the aged Alberto—until the day of the old man's
wedding. Philerno, disguised as Emilie, falls in love with Brisilla, and persuades her that he can transform himself into a man, so strongly does "she"
feel for their common plight, a soon-to-be-imposed maidenly subjection to
the lusts of old men. Naturally, Philerno has no difficulty in accomplishing
this feat. With the aid of a whore temporarily employed to fool Philotus,
both pairs of young lovers win through, and the two old men come to
accept the limitations of their years, and the fact that youth calls to youth, as
Philotus admits:

> Allace, I am forever schamit,
> To be thus in my eild defamit,   [age

* *Of Phylotus and Emilia*, the eighth in the series *Riche, his Farewell to Militaire Profession*.

My dochter is not to be blamit,
    For I had all the wyte: [blame
Auld men is twyse bairns, I persaif,   [twice
The wisest will in wowing raif,   [wooing
I for my labour will the laif,   [others
    Am driven to this despite.

This play, with its Italianate stock characters, is so slight, in spite of some sense of comic situation, that it is scarcely worth the acting, although it has been revived in modern times by Scottish student companies. Its survival in two copies, one printed by Robert Charteris, in Edinburgh in 1603, the other by his successor in business, Andro Hart, in 1612, has at least given us an amusing description, through the enticements of the Macrell or pander, of how a rich Scots lady passed the time of day towards the end of the sixteenth century. Here, we must be content with that period between the late morning, spent ordering about (and finding fault with) the servants, to the afternoon.

And now, when all thir warks is done,   [their
For your refresching efternone,
Gar bring into your chalmer sone,   [cause to be brought soon
    Sone dainty dische of meat;   into your room
Ane cup or twa with Muscadell,
Some other licht thing therewithal,
For raisins or for capers call,
    Gif that ye please to eat.

Till suppertime then may ye chois
Unto you garden to repose,
Or merrily to tak ane glois,
    Or tak ane buke and read on: [talk
Syne to your supper are ye brocht,
Til fair full far that has been socht,
And dainty dishes dearly bocht,
    That ladies loves to feed on.

The organs there into your hall,
With schalme and tymbrell sound they sall,
The Viole and the Lute withal,
    To gar you meat digest . . .

John Burell, an Edinburgh burgess, author of "The Passage of the Pilgremer," is worthy of mention if only because in his "Description of the Queens Majisties maist Honourable Entry into the Town of Edinburgh, upon the 19th day of May, 1590", he lists the instruments making up the band that led the ceremonial procession. These apparently included organs, oboes, harps, lutes, viols, virginals, girchons, trumpets and timbrels, together with:

> The seistar and the sumphion,
> With clarche, fife and clarion.

Such a combination must, indeed, have produced a very strange sound!

James Melville (1556–1614), nephew of Andrew Melville, the Presbyterian leader who many would claim played a more vigorous part even than Knox in killing the old Scots sense of delight in the arts, had one brief moment of poetic inspiration amid much religio-literary flatulence, a little poem "Robin at my Window".[14]

Passing quickly over John Napier of Merchiston (1550–1617), whose mathematical inventiveness, presented in 1614 to the world as *Mirifici Logarithmorum canonis constructio*, more than makes up for the sheer dullness of his rhymed "Revelation of Saint John" (1593), and Alexander, Earl of Glencairn (d. 1574), another Reformer whose satirical epistle from the Hermit of Loretto to his brethren the Grey Friars, would be quite forgotten had it not been quoted by Knox, we come to a near-ghost poet, and to a ghastly example of the disease that sapped the last strength from the old tradition of the Scots makars.

The near-ghost, poetically speaking, is Mark Alexander Boyd (1563–1601), soldier, traveller and physician to Henry IV of France. He was the author of some Latin verse deemed by classicists among the best to be found in that Amsterdam anthology of 1637, *Delitiae Poetarum Scotorum*, and the author of one fine surviving Scots sonnet in the Italian form, its use thus perfected in Scotland a generation before it was taken up in England.

> Fra bank to bank, fra wood to wood I rin
> Owrehailit with my feeble fantasie,   [overwhelmed
> Like til a leaf that fallis from a tree   [to
> Or til a reed owreblowin with the wind.
> Twa gods guides me: the ane of tham is blind.
> Yea, and a bairn brocht up in vanitie;
> The next a wife ingenerit of the sea,
> And lichter nor a dauphin with her fin.
>
> Unhappy is the man for evermair
> That tills the sand and sawis in the air;   [sows
> Bot twice unhappier is he, I lairn   [learn
> That feedis in his hairt a mad desire,
> And follows on a woman through the fire,
> Led by a blind and teachit by a bairn.

Finally, the "ghastly example" Alexander Hume (1560–1609), brother of that "Polwart", who involved himself in flyting with Montgomerie. Hume, who became minister of Logie, near Stirling, published in 1599 his *Hymnes or Sacred Songs where the richt use of Poetry may be Espied*. His preface gives further proof of his modesty and tolerance, for he declares: "In princes' Courts, in the houses of greate men, and at the assemblies of yong gentilmen and yong damosels, the chief pastime is to sing prophane sonnets, and vaine ballads of love, or to rehearse some fabulous faits of Palmerine, Amadis, or such like raveries." He himself celebrated the defeat of the Armada with leaden poetic feet, and provided some examples of the devotional verse he proposed should be substituted for the "profane sonnets". It is in praise of his grim, Calvinistic God:

That gave thy servant David king
    A scepter for a staff,
Syne made him sacred Psalms to sing,
    A hundreth and a halfe.

In similar lofty strains he attacks the king, the courtiers and the Privy Council. Even the humbler officials are not spared:

Some officers we see of naughty braine,
Meere ignorants, proud, vicious, and vaine,
Of learning, wit, and virtue all denude,
Maist blockish men, rash, riotous and rude.

Happily, in his younger days, before he had seen what Victorian evangelists liked euphemistically to call "the light," the warm light of a long Scottish summer day moved him to write his one great poem, "Of the Day Estivall." The slow passage of the sun across the sky is described with sensuously accurate observation:

The time sa tranquil is and still,
    That na where sall ye find—
Saif on ane high and barren hill—
    Ane air of peeping wind.

All trees and simples great and small,
    That balmy leaf do bear,
Nor they were painted on a wall*
    Nor mair they move or steir.

---

* Had Coleridge read Hume's poem, one wonders, before "The Ancient Mariner" was written?

Sa silent is the cessile air,
    That every cry and call,
The hills, and dales, and forest fair,
    Again repeats them all . . .

Whatever defence is put up by pro-Reformation critics like M. P. Ramsay[15] and Kurt Wittig,[16] such trends as the obvious narrowing of post-reformation Scottish humanism, the accompanying contempt for Catholic, and therefore Continental manners and letters, and the growing suspicion that beauty, having a sensuous and therefore a sexual connotation, must be damaging to the Reformed soul, had stopped up the well-springs of Scottish art-poetry long before King James proceeded to London in 1603. He took with him many of those who, had the Court remained in Scotland, might have countered a little the gathering gloom of that unctuous and self-righteous Presbyterianism even then hatching its pernicious doctrine of predestination.

The heavy-handed de-poetizing of older folk-poems and poems of courtly love practised by the three Wedderburn brothers of Dundee, ministers of the Kirk, further demonstrates the point. *Ane Compendious Book of Godlie Psalms and Spiritual Song collected out of sundrie partes of the Scriptures with sundrie other ballads changed out of prophane sangis for avoyding of sinne and harlotrie with the augmentation of sundrie gude and godlie Ballats not contend in the first edition*, was published in 1567.

Usually its title is understandably contracted to *The Gude and Godlie Ballats*. No first edition has survived. The absurdity of this attempt to de-secularize old folk-fragments is made plain by such clumsy adaptations as:

Johne, cum kiss me now,
Johne, cum kiss me now,
Johne, cum kiss me by and by
And mak no moir adow.

The Lord thy God I am,
That Johne dois thee call;
Johne representis man,
By grace celestial.

Where any of the poetry survives, as in "All my lufe, leave me not," the alterations made on the pre-Reformation originals are minimal.

Poetry simply cannot withstand the weight of dogma-carrying. Writing a generation or so after the Wedderburns, Hume did not even favour such attempts as theirs at compromise. For him, the category into which fell all writings that did not reflect Knox's unvarying Presbyterian "Trewth" was clearly defined:

O poets, pagans impudent,
  Why worship ye the planets seven?
The glore of God by you is spent
  On idols and the host of heaven,
Ye pride your pens men's ears to please
With fables and fictitious lees.   [lies

So ended poetry in the sixteenth century, and with it, apparently, the Scots tradition. But this, in fact, was not to prove so. The "fables and fictitious lees" merely went underground, to re-emerge a century later, when totalitarian religious bigotry at last began to lose ground.

II

In Scotland, as in most European countries, prose as a literary medium developed later than verse. As we have already seen, fifteenth-century Scots prose is scant indeed, and if any was written before that, then it has been lost.

The reasons for this early predominance of verse are not hard to find. Strange as it may seem to us now, to the medieval mind, verse seemed the appropriate medium for theology, history, science and the recording of current events. It was comparatively easy to memorize in a non-literate age. Prose in Scots, or for that matter English, was not regarded as a worthy vehicle for literature, those scholars who wrote for their fellows in the world at large using the international language of Latin if they wanted a sizeable audience: hence the choice of Latin—and sometimes strange Latin at that—by the historians Fordun, Boece and Major.

As a result of this situation, some of the earliest attempts at Scots prose take the form of translation from Latin or other languages. Murdoch Nisbet made a Scots version of Wycliff's version of the New Testament towards the end of the second decade of the sixteenth century, but it failed to make any headway against the steady surge of Anglicization on which the Reformers rode. Had Scots in fact become the language of the Protestant religion, and therefore stood a better chance of survival, here is how the familiar description of the Nativity might still have sounded:

And schephirids war in the sammin cuntre wakand and kepand the wackeingis of the nycht on thare flock. *9*. And, lo, the angel of the Lorde stude beside thame, and the cleirness of God schynit about thame; and thai dread with gret dreed. *10*. And the angel said to thame, Will ye nocht dreed, for, lo, I preche to you a gret joy, that salbe to all the pepile. *11*. For a salvatour is born this day to you, that is Crist the Lord, in the citee of David. *12*. And this is a tokin to you: Ye sall find a yonng child wrappit in clathis, and laid in a cribbe. *13*. And suddanlie thare was made with the angel a multitude of hevenlie knichthede loving God, and sayand, *14*. Glorie be in the hieast thingis to God, and in erd peace, to men of gude will.

The first Protestant treatise to appear in Scots, John Gow's *Richt Way to the Kingdom of Hevine* was truly international, made from a Danish rendering out of the German, and being published in Sweden in 1533. It is only marginally less boring than *Justification by Faith* (1548), the work of Henry Balnave (1502–1530).

The most important figure in the earlier part of the century was John Bellenden (or Ballantyne), Archdeacon of Moray (1495–1587?), who made Scots versions both of the first five books of Livy (1532) and of Boece's *Historia*, (1536), to which later he prefaced his own introductory verses. It is not easy to read with much tolerance these early translated histories because of their Latinized constructions and their credulity where facts and fancies are concerned.

The first sixteenth-century prose work of interest is therefore the anonymous *The Complaynt of Scotland*, printed and apparently published in Paris in 1549. Four copies survive, two of which are in the Harleian Collection. In the Harleian catalogue of 1743, an attribution of authorship was made; but between 1801 and 1872, some leaves of the Harleian copies disappeared. One of these lost leaves, seen by the antiquarian Pinkerton, was supposed to contain the attribution "Wedderburns Complaynte of Scotlande wyth ane Exhortatione to the thrie Estatis to be vigilante in the Deffens of their Public Weil". The author suggested by its modern editor, A.M. Stewart (Scottish Text Society, 1979) is Robert Wedderburn, the youngest of the three Dundee brothers, writing *c*. 1548–50. The *Complaynt* has also been attributed, on no real evidence at all, to Sir James Inglis and to Sir David Lyndsay.

The *Complaynt* is a strange work, partly original, partly a refurbished translation of the fifteenth-century Senecan *Le Quadrilogue Invectif* by Alain Chartier (1394–1439), with some additional indebtedness to a version of Ovid's "Epistles" by Saint Gelais, Bishop of Angoulême. Its purpose was to arouse patriotic Scots fervour.

The piece begins with an aureately elaborate dedication to Mary of Guise (the Queen Regent), well-laced with scriptural and classical allusions, in which her noble defence of her country against the "cruel woffis off ingland" is deemed to merit more praise than that accorded to the heroic ladies celebrated by Plutarch or Boccaccio.

> The immortal gloir that procedis be the richt line of vertu, fra your magnanime avansing the public weal of the affligit [afflicted] realme of Scotland, is abundantly dilatit, athort all cuntries; throucht the whilk the precius germ of your nobility bringis nocht furth alanerly [only] branchis and tender leyvis [leaves] of virtue; but als weil, it bringis salutiferre and hoilsum fruit of honour, whilk is ane immortal and supernatural medicyne, to cure and to gar

convallesse all the langorius, desolat, and affligit pepil, whilks are all maist disparit of mennis supple [help], and ready to be venquest and to becum randrit in the subjection and captivity of our mortal auld enemies, be rason that their cruel invasions appearis to be onremedabil.

This leads naturally to a survey of the sad state in which Scotland then found herself—a state which, in fact, had probably never been worse since the days of Bruce—enabling the writer to discourse upon what thus seemed to him to be the approaching end of the world.

Then follows a long interlude, the "Monolog Recreatif," which portrays a romanticized vision of a kind of idealized Scotland in times past, the most interesting section of this strange production.

Wearied by the labours of composing the first part of his book, his mind understandably "sopit" in sadness, he seeks recreation in the countryside.

Til eschaip [to escape] the evil accidents that suceedis fra the onnatural day's sleep, as caterris [catarrhs] hede crekes [headaches], and indigestion, I thoucht it necessair til excerse me with some active recreation, to hald my spreittis [spirits] walkand fra dullness. Then, to execute this purpose, I passed to the green hoilsum [wholesome] fieldis, situat maist commodiously fra distemprit air and corrputit infection, to resave the sweet fragrant smell of tendir girssis [grasses] and of hoilsum balmy flouris maist odoreferant: beside the foot of ane little montane, there ran ane fresch rivir as clear as beryl, whar I beheld the pretty fish wantounly stertland with their reid vermeil finnis, and their skalis like the bricht silver. On the tothir side of that rivir, there was ane green bank full of rammed [branchy] green trees, whar there was mony small birdis happand fra busk to tuist [from bush to bank], singand melodius reportis of natural music in accordis of mesure of dispasons prolations [continuous melody].

Thus, he spends his first day roaming the fields and the woods until dawn, a process which gives rise to the expected and conventional classical imagery, but also to an interesting description of the sights and sounds associated with the coming of the new day. Sound, indeed, plays a loud part in the imagination of the writer of the *Complaynt*, and the result reads rather like a prose version of a Gavin Douglas Prologue.

The green fieldis, for grite drought, drank up the drops of the fresh dew, whilk before had made dikis [ditches] and dailis very donc [damp]. Thereftir I heard the rumour of rammaschne fowlis [flocks of birds], and of beastis that made grite beir [noise], whilk passed beside burnis [streams] and boggis [marshes] on green bankis to seek their sustenation. Their brutal sound did resound to the hie skyis, whill [until] the deep hou [hollow] cavernis of cleuchis [hollows] and rotche [rocky] craggis answerit with ane hie note, of that saimyn sound as the beastis had blawen.

Next, the author betakes himself to the shore, where he sees a galasse, or warship, getting ready for action. He observes the cries and actions of the sailors, and describes the subsequent contest between this ship and another, though he is so much a man of peace that apparently he did not wait to see the outcome.

Back amongst the green fields again, he is able to join the shepherds, newly returned from loosing their flocks in the fields, over a substantial breakfast of milk, curds and whey, butter, cream and cheese. There then follows a lengthy rural entertainment. After a prologue, in which the "hie state and dignitie" of the pastoral calling is established by the senior shepherd, with many allusions to the famous members of antiquity who had plied the shepherd's trade, the time it affords for the study of natural science, astronomy and geography is discoursed upon at such great length that the wife of the speaker understandably describes the performance as a "tideous, melancholie orration". Fortunately for us, if not for the sheep, she suggests instead, some "joyous comonyng." The list of the enormous number of stories told and songs sung, though stated by the author to be only a selection, has provided us with a fascinating record of the titles of old tales and pieces of music, often tantalizing in that no other record of them exists.

The recital of all this, however, must have added up to one of the longest public performances ever to take place. No doubt to relieve his mental indigestion, the author next seeks refuge in a meadow lush with grasses, herbs and flowers, though now it is their medicinal properties which most interest him. Having resolved to return to the town and to his literary labours, exhaustion overcomes him. With his head on a pillow of grey stone, he falls asleep, and conveniently experiences a vision which provides him with the conclusion of his book.

The vision, heavily drawn from Chartier's work, though freely adapted—medieval visions were rarely exclusive to those they benefitted—introduces Dame Scotia and her three sons, Labour, the Nobles and Spirituality. Dame Scotia denounces England in vigorous terms. Labour, her youngest but disinherited son, representing the Commons, then utters his complaint against the nobles and clergy, more ruthless to him, he tells us, than even the English. He puts in a powerful plea for the nonsense of belief in "blue blood". Dame Scotia answers this son with some downright speaking on the gullability, intemperance and unruliness of ordinary people, concluding that virtue cannot be attained without education. The lady, however, then turns her attention to the shortcomings of the nobles and the gentry, rounding on them for their ostentatious extravagance. When the Dame comes to dealing with Spirituality, he is told that reform, not persecution, is the only sound way to cope with schism—perhaps a fore-runner of Sir Karl Popper's plea for "piecemeal social engineering", rather than Marxist slate-wiping, as a cure for the difficulties of any age.

With these various diagnoses, and an appeal to close ranks in the national interest, Dame Scotia's foresight and wisdom seem to desert her. She urges Spirituality to de-frock, put on "steil jakkis" and "coites of mail", then take the field against the old enemy, telling all her three children that they must lay aside internal strife and combine against England, since from her Franco-Scottish point of view:

> There is nocht twa nations under the firmament that are mair contrar and different fra uthers nor is Inglis men and Scottis men, whoubeit that they be within ane isle, and nychbours, and of ane language. For English men are subtil, and Scottish men are facile. Inglis men are ambitious of prosperity, and Scottis men are humane in prosperity. Inglis men are himil [humble] when they are subjeckit by force and violence, and Scottis men are furious when they are villently subjeckit. Inglis men are cruel when they get victory, and Scottis men are merciful when they get victory. And to conclude, it is onpossible that Scottis men and Inglis men can remain in concord under one monarch or one prince, because their natures and conditions are as indifferent as is the nature of sheep and wolvis.

The *Complaynt* is an extraordinary amalgam of common sense and nonsense, of quick humour and heavy pedantry; at one and the same time an exercise in a medieval convention already virtually dead by then, yet a striving after a more flexible new prose style for the needs of satire.

The man who developed that style much more effectively was John Knox (*c.* 1513–1572), born at Gifford, East Lothian and educated at the burgh school in Haddington, and then possibly at Glasgow University, where he is said to have studied under John Major, or more probably at the University of St Andrews. He became a priest, and as late as 1543 was still an ecclesiastical notary in his native district.

What apparently caused Knox to change sides was his growing belief in "election"—some might prefer to call it the development of an arrogance that eventually grew to megalomaniac proportions—and the arrival in Leith in 1545 of that youthful prophet of Reformation, George Wishart. Knox followed Wishart, and in 1547 after the burning of his leader and the reciprocal murder of Cardinal Beaton at St Andrews, Knox took refuge in the castle. When the Protestant defenders of the castle surrendered, Knox was sent as prisoner to the French galleys. Nineteen months later, he came to England as a Protestant chaplain during the brief reign of Edward VI, after whose death he once more fled to the Continent, becoming minister at Geneva, where he communed with Calvin, making occasional visits to Scotland.

In 1558, after the riot of St Giles's Day in Edinburgh, Knox returned to Scotland, and from Edinburgh, bent his energies so successfully towards overthrowing the Catholic Church in Scotland that by 1560, as he himself claimed, "the Papistes war so confounded that none within the Realme durst more avow the hearing or saying of messe". His triumph was shaken somewhat, however, by the arrival of Queen Mary the following year, and the tolerance of those Protestants who saw no reason why the Queen should not "have her ain messe". Though once again Knox's first reaction was flight from the Capital to England, where he visited his two sons by his first wife, he soon returned and, backed by Protestant nobles most of whom were probably more concerned with the profits of personal rapacity than by the problems of private conscience, ministered in Edinburgh until his death.

This is neither the place to comment upon Knox's praiseworthy attempt to set up a school in every Scottish parish,* albeit primarily for the propagation of his own version of "the Trewth", nor to attempt to analyse the impact of Knoxian Calvinism on the character, life-style and arts of the Scottish people down to the middle years of the twentieth century. Nevertheless, it is perhaps reasonable to reflect that however deplorable the events in Scotland between the capture of the Queen by the Protestant Lords in 1567 and the escape of the seventeen-year-old James VI from captivity in Stirling Castle following the Protestant-organized Raid of Ruthven, the young monarch's release, as J. H. Millar puts it, at least: ". . . secured the escape of Scotland from the imminence of an ecclesiastical tyranny compared with which the yoke of Rome had been almost beneficient, and which not the most strenuous efforts of later reformers could succeed in imposing outright upon a sullen and independent people."

Unpleasant to later taste as is much of Knox's polemical writing, and unfair and inaccurate as is often its argument, it is impossible not to be impressed by the balanced skill and rhythms of his rhetoric, whether he is manipulating forceful Scots or higher-flying English. Thomas Carlyle went so far as to insist that Knox was a "poet—one of the wild Saxon kind, full of deep religious melancholy that sounds like Cathedral music". Certainly, Knox's judgement relied heavily on his emotions.

His earlier polemical essays were attended by foreseeable consequences which, however, characteristically, he had failed to foresee. By attacking Queen Mary of England in "The Faythful Admonition unto the professours of Godis truthe in England" (1554), he secured his own banishment to Frankfurt, and deeply alarmed English Protestants. With the most famous of these tracts, the "First Blast of the Trumpet against the monstrous Regiment of Women" (1558), he infuriated her Protestant sister, Elizabeth, who by then had succeeded to the English throne.

The "First Blast" is a ludicrous production, its arguments dependent on special pleading, its Pauline dislike of women pathological wherever religion is concerned (though not so in the private life of its author who, at fifty-nine, was to marry a fifteen-year-old girl). It simply cannot be taken seriously. From Paul's dubious premise: "I suffer not a woman to teache, neither yet to usurpe authoritie above man. . . . Let women kepe silence in

* An intention thwarted by the reluctance of the heritors to meet the cost.

the congregation, for it is not permitted to them to speake, but to be subject, as this lawe sayeth", Knox prophecies the downfall of the authority of all women, including, of course, Queen Elizabeth.

> To promote a Woman to bear rule, superioritie, dominion, or empire above any Realme, Nation or Citie, is repugnant to Nature; contumelie to God, a thing most contrarious to his revealed will and approved ordinance; and finallie it is the subversion of good Order, of all equitie and justice. . . .
>
> And first, where that I affirm the empire of a Woman to be a thing repugnant to Nature, I mean not anlie that God, by the order of his creation, hath spoiled woman of authoritie and dominion, but also that man hath seen, proved and pronounced just causes why that it so should be. Man, I say, in many other cases blind, doth in this behalf see very clearlie. For the causes be so manifest that they cannot be hid. For who can deny but that it be repugneth to nature, that the blind shall be appointed to lead and conduct such as do see? That the weak, the sick, and impotent persons shall norishe and kepe the whole and strong? And finallie, that the foolish, mad, and phrenetike shall govern the discrete, and give counsel to such as be sober of mind? And such be all women, compared unto men in bearing of authoritie. For their sight in civil regiment [government] is but blindness; their strength, weakness; their counsel, foolishness; and judgement, phrenesie, if it be rightly considered.

This is sound and fury, perhaps signifying interest to the historian of the period, but of no greater value as literature than such other biased once-topical effusions as *A Letter to the Commonality of Scotland* (1559), or the treatise *Predestination* (1560), a monument to arrogance the theory of which was later to bring untold mental anguish to many innocent people. Knox's claim to literary fame thus rests entirely upon his main work, *The History of the Reformation of Religion within the Realme of Scotland* (c. 1556–7).*

It is a vigorous, colourful defence of the part he himself played in an event which was to have so profound and lasting an effect upon his countrymen. It avoids imagery, regarded by Calvin as the verbal equivalent of Popish idols, but neither bias nor invective. Its long rhetorical periods are carefully balanced, as if designed for pulpit delivery. Like most autobiographies it is, of course, essentially a work of self-justification, reflecting the narrative abilities of a man of iron determination and courage, narrow, obdurate and intolerant, in whose imagination the aureate colours of the Makars blended with the fierier hues of the Old Testament. What results is the creation of a highly personal style, even if one which the modern reader may be likely only to enjoy in limited quantity.

Two extracts must here serve to illustrate the way in which Knox's personality is imprinted on every page of his *History*. The first relates to the murder of Cardinal Beaton, in St Andrews in May 1546. William Kirk-

* Published 1586.

caldy of Grange, the younger—afterwards so revolted by the brutality of the proceedings that he eventually became one of Mary's staunchest adherents—and six other people gained entrance to Beaton's residence by engaging the porter in conversation about building work in progress. Meanwhile, some others, led by Norman Leslie, managed to get into the building under cover of this ruse before the porter could pull up the drawbridge. Defending himself, the porter had his head broken and his keys stolen. His body was then thrown over the Castle walls onto the foreshore.

The schout arises; the workmen, to the number of mo than a hundreth, ran off the wallis, and war without hurt put furth at the wicked [wicket] yett [gate]. William Kirkcaldy took the guard of the privy postern, fearing that the fox should have eschaped. Then go the rest to the gentilmenis chalmeris, and without violence done to any man, they put mo than fifty personis to the yett. The number that enterprised and did this was but sextein personis.

The Cardinal, awalkned with the schouttis, asked from his windo, "What ment that noise?". It was answered, "That Normand Leslye had taken his Castell." Which understand, he ran to the posterne; but perceaving the passage to be kept without, he returned quickly to his chalmer, took his twahanded sword, and gert [made] his chalmer-child cast kists [chests] and other impediments to the door.

In this meantime came John Leslye unto it, and biddis, open. The Cardinal askyne, "Who calls?" he answeris, "My name is Leslye." He redemandis, "Is that Normand?" The other says, "Nay, my name is John." "I will have Normand," sayis the Cardinal, "for he is my friend". "Content yourself with such as are here; for other shall ye get nane . . ."

In this meantime, whill they force at the door, the Cardinal hides a box of gold under coals that were laid in a secret corner. At length he asked, "Will ye save my life?" The said John answered, "It may be that we will". "Nay" sayis the Cardinal, "Swear unto me by Goddis wounds, and I will open unto you." Then answered the said John, "It that was said, is unsaid;" and so cried, "Fire, fire;" (for the door was verray stark); and so was brought ane chymlay full of burning coals. Which perceived, the Cardinal, or his chalmer-child (it is uncertain), opened the door, and the Cardinal sat doun in a chair and cried, "I am a priest; I am a priest; ye will not slay me."

The said John Leslye (according to his former vows) strook him anes or twice, and so did the said Peter. But James Melven (a man of nature most gentill and most modest) perceiving thame both in choler, withdrew them, and said, "This work and judgement of God ought to be done with greater gravity;" and presenting unto him the point of the sweard, said; "Repent thee of thy former wicked life, but especially of the schedding of the blood of that notable instrument of God, Maister George Wishart, which albeit the flame of fire consumed before men; yet cries it a vengeance upon thee, and we from God are sent to revenge it. For here, befoir my God, I protest, that nether the hetterent [hatred] of thy person, the luif of thy riches, nor the fear of any

trouble thou could have done to me in particular, moved nor moves me to
strike thee; but only because thou hast been, and remanes, ane obstinat enemy
against Christ Jesus and his holy Evangel." And so he stroke him twice or
thrice through with a stog sweard; and so he fell, never word heard out of his
mouth, but, "I am a priest, I am a priest; fy fy! all is gone."

The Provost and the townsfolk, attracted by the hubbub, gather outside,
and demand to see "my Lord Cardinal". They refused to disperse, crying
more angrily:

"We shall never depart till that we see him." And so was he brought to the
East blockhouse head and schawen dead ower the wall to the faithless multitude, which wold not believe before it saw how miserably lay David Beaton,
careful Cardinal. And so they departed, without *Requiem aeternam*, and *Requie-
scat in pace*, song for his saule.

Now, because the weather was hot . . . and his funerallis could not sud-
dendly be prepared, it was thought best, to keep him from stinking, to give
him great salt eneuch, a cope of lead, and a nuke in the boddome of the Sea-
touer (a place whare many of God's children had been empreasoned before)
to await what exequeis his brethern the Bishops wold prepare for him.

These things we wreat mearelie [merrily].

Here is one of Knox's own modest accounts of one of his interviews with
the Queen.

The Queen, in a vehement fume, began to cry out, That nevir Prince was
handilled as she was. "I have," said she, "borne with you in all your rigorous
manner of speaking, both against myself and against my unkles; yea, I have
socht your favor by all possibill means; I have offered unto you presence and
audience whensoevir it pleasit you to admonische me, and yit I cannot be quit
of you. I vow to God I sall be once revenged." And with these words, scar-
sely culd Marnock, hir secreit Chalmerboy, get napkins to hald hir eyes dry
for the tears, and the owling, beside womanly weaping, stayed hir speech.
The said John did patiently abide all the first fume, and at opportunity answered. "Trew it is, Madam, your Grace and I have been at divers controversies, into the whilk I nevir preceaved your Grace to be offendit at me. Bot
when it sall please God to deliver you frae that bondage of darkness and
errour in the which ye have bene nourisched, for the lack of trew doctrine,
your Majesty will find the liberty of my toung nothing offensive. Without
the preaching place, Madam, I think few have occasioun to be offendit at me;
and there, Madam, I am not master of myself, bot maun obey Him who commands me to speak plain, and to flater no flesche upon the face of the
earth" . . .

"What have ye to do", said she, "with my marriage? Or what are ye in this
Commonwealth?"

"A subject born within the same," said he, "Madam. And albeit I be neither Earl, Lord, nor Baron within it, yet hes God made me (how abject that evir I be in your eyes) a profitabile member within the same: Yea, Madam, to me it appertains no less to forwairn of sic things as may hurt it, if I forsee thame, than it doth to ony of the nobility, for both my vocatioun and conscience craves plainness of me; therefore, Madam, to yourself I say that whilk I spake in public place. Whensoevir that the nobility of this Realme sall consent, that ye be subject to an unlawful husband, they do als mekle as in thame lieth to renunce Christ, to banische his Treuth from thame, to betray the freedom of this Realme and perchance sall in the end do small comfort to yourself."

At these words, owling was hard and tears micht have been seen in gritter abundance than the matter required. John Erskine of Dun, a man of meek and gentle spirit, stude beside and entreated what he culd to mitigat hir anger, and gave unto hir many pleasing words of hir bewty, and her excellency, and how that all the princes of Europe wald be glad to seek hir favour. Bot all that was to cast oil in the flamming fire.

The said John stude still without ony alteratioun of countenance for a long season, until that the Queen gave place to sic inordinat passioun; and in the end he said, "Madam, in God's presence I speak, I nevir delyted in the weeping of ony of God's creatures; yea, I can scarcely abide the tears of my awin boys, wham my awin hand corrects, mekle less can I rejoice in your Majesty weeping: Bot seeing that I have offered you no just occasioun to be offendit, bot have spoken the Treuth, as my vocatioun craves of me, I maun sustain (albeit unwillingly) your Majesty's tears, rather than I dar hurt my conscience, or betray my Commonwealth, throw my silence."

Herewith was the Queen more offendit, and commandit the said John to pass furth of the cabinet, and to abide farther of his plessour in the chalmer.

Knox's greater than life-size arrogance is superb, his kinship with the teachings of Jesus less obvious. "Imagine", Cyril Connolly recently wrote, "what might have been the benefits of a tolerant Christianity!"[17] They were certainly benefits which Knox's dogmatism ensured Scotland was to enjoy less than most.

Unpleasantness of a different kind characterized George Buchanan (1506–82), born at Killearn, Stirlingshire, and educated at the Universities of Paris and St Andrews; the most distinguished of the Scottish Latinists, a humanist who was the wearer of a European reputation, and as the author of several Latin plays performed by his students at the College de Guyenne, a writer who helped shape the French drama of the *Grand Siècle*. At one time Montaigne's tutor, tutor to Queen Mary, and the author of a Latin epithalamium celebrating her marriage to Darnley, this distinguished author of high-minded Latin tracts not only deserted her after the Kirk o'Field affair, but in 1568, while Principal of St Leonard's College, St Andrews—and according to Sir James Melville by then "sleeprie and cairles"—journeyed to London to place before Queen Elizabeth a rhetorical and substantially dishonest Latin indictment (the *De Maria Scotorum Regina*, published in 1571) of the mistress in whose royal favour it had once suited him to revel and rhyme, and whose pension he had greedily accepted. He is at his most vividly journalistic in his account of the supposed circumstances of Queen Mary's visit to the wounded Bothwell in 1566.

> She heard of Bothwell's wounds, whereupon she flingeth away in haste like a mad woman, by great journeys in post, in the sharp time of winter, first to Melrose, then to Jedworth. There, though she heard news of his life, yet her affectioun, impatient of delay, could not temper itself, but neids she must bewray her outragious lust, and in an inconvenient time of the year, despising all discomodities of the way and weather, and all dangers of thieffis, she betook herself hedlong in hir journey, with sic a company as na man of any honest degree wald haif adventured his life and his goods amang them.

Agnes Mure Mackenzie has commented tartly that in this passage "there are ten categorical lies all of which Buchanan quite certainly knew were lies, for he was Moray's intimate hanger-on, and Moray was there." Of course she was already at Jedburgh for the Jeddart Assizes when news of Bothwell's injuries reached her. She simply rode the twenty-five miles to Hermitage to visit her Warden of the Middle Marches, which post Bothwell held; not only one of her officials, but the only man around her who had not betrayed this twenty-five-year-old Queen to further his own self-interests.

Queen Elizabeth can hardly have relished the anti-monarchical sentiments that followed in his *De jure Regni apud Scotus* (1579). Few of her subjects—or indeed, those of her successors—are likely to have read his twenty-volume *Rerum Scoticarum Historia*, which appeared in 1582, the year of his death and burial in Greyfriars' Churchyard, Edinburgh.

In 1570, the year he became tutor to James VI—some have blamed Buchanan for the pedantry that monarch was sometimes later to display—the author wrote two tracts in Scots, one *Ane Admonitioun to the true Lordis* attacking the Hamilton family, the other *Chamaeleon*,[18] revealing the "machiavellianisms" of Maitland of Lethington, both opponents of the rule of the Regent Moray, whom Buchanan supported. They are of purely historical rather than literary interest now, as is *The Pretended Conference*, an anonymous satirical tract dated 1569.

On the Catholic side, the most able controversialist was Ninian Winzet (1518–1592), a Renfrew man who probably attended Glasgow University before becoming a teacher in Linlithgow Grammar School, where he probably first debated with Knox in 1559, an exercise which may have contributed to his expulsion ten years later. In 1562 he produced "The Last Blast of the Trumpet of Godis Word aganis the usurpit auctorite of Johne Knox," a magnificent gesture on behalf of free speech which resulted in the seizure of the printer and the printing office, but the escape of the author to the Continent. In Queen Mary's service he visited England in 1571, and produced in 1582 a Latin counter-attack upon Buchanan's *De jure regni*, his services to the Catholic Church bringing him in the end the Abbacy of the Benedictine monastery at Ratisbon, Germany.

He could flyte as unfairly and viciously as Knox, though he resorted less regularly to this unsavoury native procedure. Like Quintine Kennedy (*c.* 1520–1564), Abbot of Crossraguel, Winzet neither lost heart before the Knoxian onslaught nor failed to admit the need for the removal of these abuses in his own church that had sparked off the Reformation. Unlike such minor writers of the so-called counter-reformation as James Tyrie, John Hay, Adam King, Nicol Burne (all of whom wrote in Scots), and Archbishop Hamilton (who wrote in Latin, and whose abuse of Knox in that tongue is said even to exceed the calumnial powers of the great Reformer himself, and who was eventually hanged in his vestments,) Winzet could occasionally strike off an eloquently moving strain, especially when puzzled as to why God should have allowed disaster to overwhelm his Church in Scotland. To his fellow-priests, he issued in *The First Tractat*, this vain rallying-call:

> Bot yit, O merciful God, what deidly sleep is this that hes oppressit you, that in sa gret uproar, tumult, and terrible clamour ye walkin not furth of your dream, and in sa gret danger of death, ye haif na regard of your awin lives nor others? Awalke! awalke! we say, and put to your hand stoutly to saif Peter's sheep: for He nother slepis nor slummeris wha beholdis all your doingis, and sees your thochts, but sall require the blude out of your handis of the smallest ane that sall perise through your negligence.

There is also a *Historie of Scotland* by John Leslie (1526–1596), who studied at Aberdeen and Paris and was one of the two Catholics named in 1560 by the Lords of the Congregation, to debate points of doctrine with Knox. He remained faithful to Mary, and was threatened with the rack for his alleged part in the plot to unite Mary and Norfolk, a fate he escaped by confessing and turning against her, an act he later justified by claiming to have believed that he would be of more use to her escaped and alive than dead. On the news of her execution in 1587 he retired to a Brussels monastery. His vernacular prose style, like Buchanan's, suffers from the constructional effects of a more regular use of Latin than Scots. He lacks the eye for vivid detail, the ear for a well-turned phrase, possessed both by Knox and by Leslie's rival and younger contemporary, Robert Lindsay of Pitscottie (?1532–1578).

Lindsay's *Historie and Cronicles of Scotland* is not only the most important work of its kind to that date written in Scots, but, together with selections from *The Complaynt* and from Knox's *Historie*, virtually the only sixteenth-century Scots prose which can still be read as literature with real pleasure. Lindsay was a kinsman of Sir David Lyndsay of the Mount. He seems to have been a tenant-farmer at Pitscottie, near Cupar, Fife. Beyond the recorded fact that his son, Christopher, married in 1592, and was then described as "lawful heir to the late Robert Lyndsay of Pitscottie," little else is known of his life.

Lindsay regarded his work as a continuation of Boece's *Historie*, already translated by John Bellenden, an overlap being provided in that Boece's eighteenth book, retranslated, becomes Lindsay's first chapter. Nor, apparently, did he intend the work for immediate publication, suggesting in his dedication to the Bishop of Caithness that it should not appear so long as Morton held power. It did not, in fact, come before the public until 1778.

Like Knox, Lindsay excels as a narrator with a vivid eye for detail, though of course, he is a rather cooler reporter, especially in that part of his story for which he must have received information at first, second or third hand from the descendants or friends of those who took part in the incidents described. He himself tells us that some of his information came from his cousin, Lord Lindsay of the Byres; Sir William Scott of Balwearie; Andrew Wood of Largo, the son, and Sir Andrew Wood of Largo, the grandson, of the famous Scots Admiral; John Major, who had retired to St Andrews, where he lived on until 1550; Sir William Bruce of Earlshall; and, of course, Sir David Lyndsay of the Mount, on whose authority the tale of the Linlithgow apparition was recounted.

Where Pitscottie had to rely on older authorities, his chronology is frequently vague and his facts erroneous. The section dealing with the period from 1565 to 1604 was added by another hand.

However, one does not read old historians for their accuracy, but for the flavour of their style. Lindsay of Pitscottie's images linger on in the reader's mind; as, for instance, when James II "more curious than became a King", stood too close to a cannon during the siege of Roxburgh Castle, as a result of which by "ane piece of ane misframed gunne, his thigh bone was dung in two": or that memorable interview between the Border reiver, Johnie Armstrong, and James V, when the reiver, about to be hanged, exclaimed: "I am bot ane foole to seik grace at ane graceless face." Most powerful of all, there is that clear description of the last words of James V, told to Lindsay by one who was present at the death-bed:

> Be [by] this the post came out of Lythtgow [Linlithgow] schawing to the king good tidings that the queen was deliverit. The king inquirit "whether it was man or woman". The messenger said "it was ane fair dochter." The king answerit and said: "Adew, fareweill, it come with ane lass, it will pass witht ane lass." And so he recommendit himself to the marcie of Almighty God, and spak ane little then from that time forth, bot turnit his back into his lordis and his face into the wall.
> At this time David Bettoun, Cardinal of Scotland, standing in presentis of the king, seeing him begin to fail of his strength and natural speech, held ane through of paper to his grace and causit him subscryve the samin, whair the

Cardinal wrait that plessit him for his awin particular weill, thinkand to have autoriety and prehemenence in the goverment of the country; bot we may know heirbe the kingis legacy was very short, for in this manner he depairtit, as I sall you tell. He turnit him back and luikit and beheld all his lordis about him, and gaif ane little smile and lauchter, syne kissit his hand and offerit the samin [same] to all his lordis round about him, and thirefter held up his handis to God and yieldit the spreit.[19]

Some sixteenth-century writers directed their talents neither to the blastings and trumpetings of religious dogma, nor to the colourful traceries of history, but simply to setting down in diary form the actual experiences of their own lives. Two outstanding examples of this kind of private literature have survived the clearing-out of lumber-rooms. One is the *Memorials* of Sir James Melville of Halhill (1535–1617), who became a page to Mary, Queen of Scots, when he was fourteen and she was still in France. When she returned to Scotland, Melville again settled at her court, and became a privy councillor and a gentleman of the bed-chamber. His diplomatic ability was recognized and used by Mary, as it was later used again by her son. To Melville we owe the observation that George Buchanan, that "man of notable qualities for his learning and knawlege of Latin", was also "of gud religion for a poet".

Even more attractive is his story of how Queen Elizabeth tried to force him to account some of her physical attributes and qualities higher than those of the Scots queen, Melville's employer. Towards the end of the interview, Elizabeth asked what kind of exercises Mary used. "I said, that the Queen was bot new com bak from the Highland hunting; and when she had leaser fra the affairs of hir country, she read upon gude bukis, the histories of divers countries and sometimes wald play upon lute and virginelis. She speirit gin she played well. I said, raisonably for a Queen."[20]

Sir James Melville writes with grace and charm. There is a less genial charm about the alert style of the Reverend James Melville (1556–1614), a son of the manse who was educated by his uncle, that most unrelenting of all the Reformers, Andrew Melville, Principal of the University of Glasgow in 1574. James himself became Professor of Oriental Languages in New College, St Andrews, but his outspoken utterances eventually led to his flight to England. Back in St Andrews again in 1585, Melville quarrelled with Bishop Adamson, and was told by the King that he would do well to confine his activities to his work for the University. James Melville's ministry at Anstruther West, and then at Kilrenny, ended when both Melvilles overplayed their hands while arguing in London with the King about Episcopacy. The diarist did not receive permission to return to Scotland until the year before his death.

Some critics have found his *Diary* a particularly delightful work of its kind. Much of it deals with religious controversies which, though once urgent and seemingly all-important, scarcely encouraged the production of literature. Still, his description of Knox's last appearance in a St Andrews pulpit captures something of the dying Reformer's indomitable strength:

> Being in St Androis he was verie weak. I saw him evrie day of his doctrine go hulie and fear [shaven] with a furring of martriks [marten fur] about his neck, a staff in the ane hand, and guid godlie Richart Ballanden, his servand holding up the uther oxter [armpit], from the Abbay to the paroche kirk; and be [by] the said Richart and another servant, lifted upe to the pulpit, whar he behovit to lean at his first entrie; bot on he haid done with his sermont, he was sa active and vigrous that he was lik to ding that pulpit in blads [break that pulpit in pieces] and fly out of it!

Those who read the *Autobiography and Diary* (which remained unpublished, incidentally, until 1829) to find that charm for which Victorian critics praised it, must search in the records of Melville's earlier entries; as, for instance, his description of his primary schooling, before he was sent south to Uncle Andrew.

> My father put my eldest and onlie brother, David, about a year and a half in age above me, and me togidder, to a kinsman and brother in the ministerie of his to scholl, a guid, learned, kind man, whom for thankfulness I name, Mr Wilyam Gray, minister at Logie, Montrose.
> He had a sister, a godlie and honest matron, rewlar of his hous, wha often rememberit me of my mother, and was a verie loving mother to us, indeed. There was a guid nomber of gentle and honest menis berns [children] of the country about weill treaned up baith in letters, godliness and exercise of honest geams [games]. There we learned to read the Catechism, Prayers and Scripture efter the reading thereof. We learned there the Rudiments of the Latin Grammair, with the vocables in Latin and French, also divers speeches in French, with the reading and right pronouncition of that toung . . .
> He [Gray] had a verie guid and profitable form of resolving the authors, he teatched gramaticallie, baith according to the Etymologie and Syntax;* bot as for me, the treuthe was, my ingyne and memorie was guid aneuche, but my judgment and understanding was as yet smored [smothered] and dark, sa that the thing whilk I gat was mair be rat ryme [learned parrot-fashion] nor knawledge.
> There also we had the air guid, and fields reasonable near; and be [by] our maister were teached to handle the bow for archerie, the glub [club] for goff [golf], the batons for fencing; also, to rin, to loope, to swoom, to warsill [wrestle] to preve pratteiks [to become practised], every ane haiffing his match and antagonist, baith in our lessons and play. A happie and golden time indeed. . . .

---

* By Sir Thomas More's friend William Lily (1468–1522), the widely travelled first headmaster of St Paul's School in London.

But that golden happiness was not to last. The middle section of Melville's book is largely concerned with religious controversies and those involved in them, all treated with a kind of gossipy garrulousness which gives what would otherwise be a pedestrian account of dead matter, a certain animated savour.

There only remains to be considered the prose work of King James. Mention has already been made of his *Reulis and Cautelis*, wherein he treats of rhyme, of the use of words, the virtues of alliteration, the necessity for variety, the importance of music and other common matters.

His *Demonologie* (1597) is a sorry reflection on the superstitions of times which felt the persecution of old women as witches to be a laudable and godly pursuit.

His *Basilikon Doran* (1599) retains scant literary value, though nothing James wrote is wholly without some interest. His liveliest piece, *A Counterblast to Tobacco* (1604), unlike the Scots *Reulis and Cautelis*, is in English, as was everything he wrote from London after the Union of the Crowns. It is a well-argued pamphlet, working up to a climax which, at least in the manner of utterance, savours a little of the temper of the Reformers, although its practical sentiments would now be supported by twentieth-century medical opinion.

> Have you not reason then to be ashamed and to forbeare this filthy noveltie, so basely grounded, so foolishly received, and so grossely mistaken in the right use thereof; in your abuse thereof sinning against God, harming your selves both in persons and goods, and raking also thereby the markes and notes of vanitie upon you; by the custome thereof making your selves to be wondered at by all forreine civill nations, and by all strangers that come among you, to be scorned and contemned? A custome loathsome to the eye, hatefull to the nose, harmefull to the braine, dangerous to the lungs, and in the black stinking, fume thereof, neerst resembling the horrible Stigion smoake of the pit that is bottomlesse.

No image could be more appropriate on which to take our leave of sixteenth-century Scottish prose.

CHAPTER THREE

The Seventeenth Century

The seventeenth century, with its long and bitter periods of religious strug-gle—family divided against family, maintaining attitudes of bigotry and intolerance—is not an age upon which Scots can reasonably look back with much pride. Indeed, it is one of the ironies of history that those issues which once seemed so important as to justify their defence with the sacri-fice of life itself should in time come to seem to later generations utterly irrelevant.

When the hard-riding Sir Robert Carey arrived at Holyrood, wild-eyed and sleepless, "be-blooded with great falls and bruises", in the early hours of the morning of 28th March 1603, to announce to King James VI of Scot-land that he was now also King James I of England, the dissensions created by the causes leading to, and the severe effects stemming from the Refor-mation, had already brought the Scotland of the Makars to an end. As James's royal coach shuggled its leisurely way south, his golf-clubs slung beneath it, the scene was set for what Lauchlan Maclean Watt called "the strife of mutual intolerance on the part of Episcopalian and Covenanter, through which, led by their gibbering family phantom of 'divine right', the Stuarts staggered out of their kingdom". In the process of their doing so, the sheer waste of ability, the blood spilled upon futilities, allowed little enough opportunity or time for the cultivation of literature.

While the Castalians, led by Montgomerie, who had graced James's Scottish Court, for the most part did not go with him to London, other Scots writers did. Some, like Alexander Craig (c. 1567–1627), author of *Poetical Recreations* and *Amorous Songs, Sonnets and Elegies*, are still remem-bered; not because their productions had much merit, but because they provided early examples of what was to become that all too familiarly un-pleasant spectacle, the "Scot-on-the-Make." Craig went so far as to sign himself "Scoto-Britane".

Others had genuine talent. The St Andrews-educated wealthy secretary to Anne of Denmark and later to Henrietta Maria, Sir Robert Ayton (1570–1638), descendant of an old Fife land-owning family sprung illegit-imately from the royal Stuart line, has been cavalierly treated by most his-torians of our national literature, usually being compared unfavourably to English Waller.

His Scots poems, dating from the 1580s, and written as part of a sequence with his fellow students William Alexander and Alexander Craig, reflect the influence of the work of Alexander Scott, though already Ayton's verse is notable in style for its tone of reasonable statement, a characteristic also of his English work.

Ayton was, indeed, in two senses a pivot poet, bridging the change-over from Scottish poetry in Scots to that in English; perhaps more importantly, moving away from the openness of the Elizabethan lyric to the new metaphysical manner, combining forceful language with the use of irony and paradox and the employment of elaborate intellectual conceits.

Like Marvell after him, Ayton wrote lines "To His Coy Mistress"; like his contemporary Donne, he produced "A Valediction". The influence of Donne is to be seen in Ayton's "Upon Platonick love; To Mistress Cicley Crofts, Maide of Honour", where he reaches the practical, if not particularly profound, conclusion that it would be wisest to achieve physical union first, leaving more exalted spiritual union to follow.

Possibly Ayton had neither the time nor the talent fully to develop either the sinewy argument or the brilliant imagery of his English-born Metaphysical contemporaries. Probably the reasonableness necessary in a good Royal Secretary matched his own even temperament. In any case, at least two of Ayton's lyrics to survive through the currency of anthologies, "Inconstancy Reproved" and "To An Inconstant Mistress", reflect emotional balance as well as polished craftsmanship. Courtier or not, the man was no fool, who, in "The Exercise of Affection", could proclaim to the seventeenth century:

Methinks a wise man's actions should be such
As always yield to reason's best advice,
Now for to love too little, or too much,
Are both extremes, and all extremes are vice.

Yet have I been a lover by report,
Yea, I have died for love as others do.
But praised be God, it was in such a sort,
That I revived within an hour or two.

Even without such claims to distinction as his handful of fine lyrics in English, or his Latin verses included in the *Delitiae*, Ayton, the last of the Castalians, would be of interest to us if only because the far from scholarly James Watson, in *A Choice Collection of Comic and Serious Scots Poems* (Part III, published in 1711), credited him, unsupported by any shred of evidence (though Ayton's claims seem very much stronger than anyone else's) with a poem beginning:

Should old acquaintance be forgot,
  And never thought upon,

The flames of love extinguished,
    And freely past and gone?
Is thy kind heart now grown so cold
    In that loving breast of thine,
That thou canst never once reflect
    On old-lang-syne?

Ayton was famous in his day for his songs; not for "musik fyne", as were his Castalian predecessors, but for monophonic songs such as Thomas Campion and other lute-song composers were providing in England. His "depairt" song "Then wilt thou go and leave me here" survives, complete with its music, in the lute-book of the Skenes of Hallyards. It appeared, slightly modified, in various printed music collections thereafter. The version printed in *Music of Scotland 1500–1700* strongly suggests the basis of a native Scots air. The words of this version may well have been "Englished" by the unmarried Ayton's nephew and first editor, and there is a tradition that it was associated with King James's mourning for the death of his Queen Anne. However, in a fascinating volume edited by Dr Kenneth Elliott, *Musa Jocosa Mihi, Twelve songs for voice and keyboard by Lawes, Wilson, Blagrave, Playford and Anon., to poems by Sir Robert Ayton* (London 1965), we find a tune, "Old lang syne", together with a conventional set of "answer" verses (both printed in Watson's *Choice Collection*, the anthology which was to provide the corner-stone to the Eighteenth-century Scots Revival). Dr Elliott took the tune from a seventeenth-century manuscript. It turns out to be the tune for which Burns later wrote "Auld Lang Syne", the most famous of all "depairt" songs, originally matched in Johnson's *Scots Musical Museum* (1796) against the tune to which the Burns words are now commonly sung. Through Ayton, therefore, Burns's song-cobbling has an ancestral link with the song-making of the Castalians, the junction-point being Ayton's bringing together of court-song and native air.

In some ways the most outwardly successful of the Jacobean group who were familiars at King James's London court was Sir William Alexander (1567–1640). Of Highland descent, he could trace his ancestors back to that Lord of the Isles who married a daughter of Robert II, the name MacAlastair being Anglicized to Alexander when the family received grants of the lands around Menstrie.*

The sonnets which Alexander published under the title of *Aurora* were probably written in his youth when, after leaving Glasgow University, he travelled on the Continent with the Earl of Argyle. The *Aurora* sonnets reflect the popular fashion for this form created by Wyatt and Surrey, though lacking the fire of the former at his best or the metrical skill of the latter.

---

* The castle in which the poet was born was later the birthplace of Sir Ralph Abercromby, the hero of Aboukir Bay.

Back at court, Alexander concentrated on his four "monarchicke" tragedies, *Darius, Croesus, The Alexandrean* and *Julius Caesar*. Certainly, parallels of imagery suggest that Shakespeare may have been his inspiration; but unfortunately, Alexander's muse was not suited to extended composition, and he had no flair for the dramatic. Thus Shakespeare's:

> And, like this insubstantial pageant faded,
> Leave not a rack behind—

from *The Tempest*, becomes, in *Darius*:

> Should this worldly pomp our wits enchant
> All fades, and scarcely leaves behind a token.

Again, Shakespeare's:

> Let me have men about me that are fat!—

becomes, in Alexander's hands:

> No corpulent sanguinians make me feare!

Still, not all his trafficking in ideas was one-way. Alexander wrote of the grandeur of Nature:

> Whose strange effects may well be felt, but cannot be exprest

thus anticipating Byron's awareness of what it is:

> To mingle with the Universe and feel
> What I can ne'er express, yet cannot all conceal.

And in the midst of all Alexander's somewhat prosy rhetoric in these plays about the "Falls of Princes" (as opposed to "sad stories of the death of kings"!), occasional passages of poetry are embedded:

> Our painted pleasures but apparel pain:
>   We spend our days in dread, our lives in dangers,
> Balls to the stars, and thralls to Fortune's reign,
>   Known unto all, yet to ourselves but strangers.

In a sense, poor Alexander might have been writing of the fate that lay in store for him. Honours a-plenty were heaped upon him, both by James and by Charles I. The poet played a small part in that most unfortunate of enterprises, the final stages of the colonization of Northern Ireland by indigent

Scots, an activity from which little but human misery has subsequently flared. A much more important benefaction to Alexander was the gift and grant of the Canadas, including Nova Scotia and Newfoundland.

The poet, who, seven years later had followed his unactable plays with an unreadable poem, *Doomsday* (1614), devised a scheme whereby Nova Scotia would be colonized by baronetcies, the new baronets to be enfeoffed on the esplanade of Edinburgh Castle. Unfortunately, the French conquest of Canada rendered the baronetcies worthless, and the Nova Scotia barons rounded upon Alexander in rage when they found that they could neither claim their six square miles of colonized territory, nor recover the one hundred and fifty pounds which they had paid Alexander.

However, honours continued to flow in. Alexander received a grant from King Charles to manufacture "turners" or "black farthings". These merely stroked inflation, and soon lost their face value. For this, he was execrated by the common people.

But he became Secretary of State for Scotland in 1630, then Lord Alexander of Tullibody, Viscount Stirling, an extraordinary judge of the Court of Session, and by 1633, Earl of Stirling and Viscount Canada in quickly succeeding years. All this meant that he incurred the jealousy of his fellow noblemen, and because his position inevitably made him a buffer between king and populace, he also incurred a further measure of public obloquy. There must thus have been a consolatory intention in the title he chose for his collected works, *Recreations of the Muses*, published in 1637.

For huge ambition such as his, however, lasting consolation there could be none. Three years later, he died in disillusioned poverty, one of the most hated men in Scotland. Of the many venomous contemporary notices of his death, perhaps the most succinct is to be found printed in *Senators of the College of Justice* by Brunton and Haig:

Here lies a fermer and a miller,
A poet and a psalm-book spillar,   [spoiler
A purchessour by hook and crook,
A forger of the service book,
A coffersmith who did much evil,
A friend of bishops and the devil,
A vain, ambitious flattering thing,
Late secretary for a king;
Some tragedies in verse he pen'd,
At last he made a tragic end.

Sir David Murray of Gorthy (fl. 1610–1630), a member of Prince Henry's household, wrote some pretty sonnets about love, and in 1611 "The Tragical Death of Sophonisba" in *ab ab bcc* stanzas, cloyed by a profusion of double rhymes.

One need not be too concerned over the work of the songwriter

William Murray of Dysart, presumed to be the writer of poems, along with pieces by other writers that took his fancy, which are bound up with poems by Secretary William Fowler among the Hawthornden Papers in the National Library of Scotland; or about that John Murray, allegedly kinsman to Sir David, whom Mrs Shire conjectures may have been the "Murray myne" apparently regarded by Montgomerie as a particularly promising disciple, praised by Sir William Alexander in a Castalian sonnet, and praised again by Sir Robert Ayton in a Latin epitaph. This Murray, it seems, died young in disgrace in 1615 after a brief, spectacular spell of royal favour. Mrs Shire attributes several otherwise anonymous Castalian sonnets and ditties to him.

A more skilful courtly practitioner was Robert Kerr, Earl of Ancrum (1578–1654), who, in his day, was so much the familiar of the literary men of London that his friend Drummond of Hawthornden dubbed him "the Muses Sanctuarye". Ancrum lived long enough to be made a gentleman of the bedchamber by Charles I, and to be granted his earldom in 1633. Although his son, the Earl of Lothian, deserted the royal cause, Ancrum remained faithful to the king. After the King's death Ancrum went to Amsterdam, where he died. Most of his work has been lost, and he is remembered now for one fine sonnet, preserved in the Drummond manuscript and addressed to Drummond, "In praise of a solitary life", suggesting that the courtier and the man of action, who once found himself forced to kill a wealthy but offensive boor, Charles Maxwell, in a duel not of the poet's choosing, envied Drummond, the scholar-poet, his quiet of mind:

Most happy state, that never tak'st Revenge
For injuries received, nor dost fear
The Court's great earthquake, the griev'd truth of change
Nor none of Falsehood's savoury lies dost hear
Nor knowest Hope's sweet disease, that charms our sense,
Nor its sad cure, dear-bought Experience.

Alexander's close friend, William Drummond of Hawthornden (1585–1649), though in sympathy a follower of the Whitehall group, spent most of his life in his beautiful castle, perched high upon a rock above the then unpolluted River Esk, near Roslin. His father was one of the king's gentlemen ushers, his mother a sister of William Fowler. He had been educated in France as well as at Edinburgh, and had read widely in French and Italian literature, in both of which he amassed a considerable library.

Like most poets active in 1613, he commemorated the death of Prince Henry, his piece being entitled "Tears on the death of Meliades". Another death a year or two later, that of the daughter of Cunningham of Barnes on the eve of the poet's marriage to her, deepened the depression of what was perhaps a naturally rather gloomy temperament, and kept him a retired bachelor into middle life. His *Poems, Amorous, Funereall, Divine, Pas-*

torall, in Sonnets, Songs, Sextains, Madrigals was published in 1616,* the year before King James paid a return visit to Scotland, an event celebrated by much bad versifying collected in the anthology *The Muses Welcome* (1618). Drummond's celebration is more notable for its loyal flattery than for its poetic quality:

> O virtue's pattern, glory of our times,
> Sent of past days to expiate the crimes,
> Great King, but better far than thou art great,
> Whom State not honours, but who honours State . . .

Still, it pleased well enough for him to be asked to provide *The Entertainment* for Charles's Scottish coronation in 1633.

The year 1618 was notable in that Ben Jonson visited Drummond, who kept notes of the conversations that occurred between them. Jonson, whose tour to Scotland inspired the mocking emulation of John Taylor, the Thames water-poet, could well have proved a more tiresome guest than his strict observance of the unities in his plays may have led his host to expect. At any rate, Drummond's notes were far from uncritical, and have provoked the wrath of many a Jonsonian since. The subject of most of these conversations was, of course, Ben himself, a topic Jonson seems to have found endlessly fascinating.

Drummond's collection of religious verse, *Flowers of Sion*, appeared in 1623. Apart from the lively display of macaronics known as *Polemo-Middinia inter Vitarvam et Nebernam*, one hundred and seventy hexameter lines in dog-Latin surviving through a "reprint" of 1684, but which may, or may not, be by Drummond at all†—his name was first attached to it in an edition of 1691—and which deals with a dispute over a right-of-way between the people of Tarvet and the people of Newbarns, Drummond published only one other collection during his lifetime. His collected prose works (of which more later) and poems came out in Edinburgh in 1711 edited by Bishop Sage and Thomas Ruddiman, and included many hitherto unpublished pieces.

From the prudent seclusion of Hawthornden, Drummond—who, in 1632, had married Elizabeth Logan, daughter of Sir Robert Logan of Restalrig—watched the struggle of Charles to assert his will over both his Scots and English subjects and the tragic outcome, as well as the rise and fall of Sir William Alexander and the sad eclipse of his friend Montrose. A royalist at heart, Drummond nevertheless saw fit to sign the National Covenant of 1638. But one can perhaps best appreciate his true position

---

* A shorter volume, known as the Haigh Hall edition, appeared, possibly in 1614, perhaps from the Edinburgh press of Andro Hart. The 1616 edition contains many revisions.

† Defoe, in his *Tour of the Whole Island of Great Britain* (1727), attributed the authorship to a pamphleteer, Samuel Colvill.

through the posthumous satire *A Character of the Anti-Covenanter*, or his short epitaph on the Parliamentarian John Pym, who died in December 1643:

When Pym last night descended into Hell,
Ere he his cups of Lethe did carouse,
What place is this (said he) I pray me tell?
To whom a Devil: 'This is the lower house.'

The execution of Charles plunged Drummond into a profound gloom, accentuated by the death of many of his close friends in 1649. On 4th December, Drummond himself died, his faith in humankind finally shattered, as one of his last sonnets, published in a London selection of his poems in 1656, shows:

Doth then the World go thus? Doth all thus move?
Is this the Justice which on Earth we find?
Is this that firm decree which all doth bind?
Are these your influences, Powers above?

The first collection of Drummond's poems traces his contentment with Hawthornden, that "sweet solitary place", his falling in love, impatience at the absence of the beloved, joy at the prospect of their union and the chilling devastation her unexpected death wrought upon him, so that he could declare:

I have nought left to wish: my hopes are dead;
And all with her beneath a marble laid.

He was a skilful and musical madrigalist, a delicate handler of Italianate trifles, some of the ideas and images (specialist scholars tell us) borrowed, but recreated, from French, Italian, English or, indeed, Scots sources; Marino, Despontes, Sidney, Fowler and Alexander, a matter of no real importance since Drummond's voice is so markedly his own:

Like the Idalian queen,
  Her hair about her eyne,
With neck and breast's ripe apples to be seen
  At first glance of the morn,
In Cyprus gardens gathering those faire flowers,
  Which of her blood were born,
I saw, but fainting saw, my paramours.

The Graces naked danc'd about the place,
  The winds and trees amazed

With silence on her gazed
The flowers did smile, like those upon her face,
And as their aspen stalks those fingers band
     (That she might read my case)
A hyacinth I wisht me in her hand.

In both his collections there are many fine sonnets, mostly in the Italian rhyme pattern, at least one of which anticipates—some might say equals—Milton's handling of that form, the frequently anthologized "For the Baptist":

The last and greatest Herald of Heaven's King,
Girt with rough skins, hies to the deserts wild,
Among that savage brood the woods forth bring,
Which he that Man more harmless found and mild:
His food was locusts, and what young doth spring,
With honey that from virgin hives distilled;
Parched body, hollow eyes, some uncouth thing
Made him appear, long since from Earth exiled.
Then burst he forth. "All ye, whose hopes rely
On God, with me amid these deserts mourn,
Repent, repent, and from old errors turn."
Who listened to his voice, obeyed his cry?
     Only the echoes which he made relent,
     Rung from their marble caves, "Repent, repent".

The most dashing of the Royalist poets was undoubtedly James Graham, Marquis of Montrose (1612–1650). Drummond did not live to see the sad end of his friend at the hands of the Argyle government. Like Drummond, Montrose had a tendency to employ conceits, sometimes reflected in verbal artificiality, and often classical in their allusion. Both this tendency, and a certain sense of gusty "overplay"—as we have seen, a recurring Scottish poetic phenomenon—are reflected in his lines written on the martyrdom of King Charles I:

Great, good, and just, could I but rate
My grief to thy too rigid fate,
I'd weep the world in such a strain
As it would once deluge again.
But since thy lovd-tongu'd blood demands supplies
More from Briareus' hands than Argus' eyes,
I'll tune thy elegies to trumpet sounds,
And write thy epitaph in blood and wounds.

And so he did: six spectacular victories, ending with defeat at

Philiphaugh; betrayal by Macleod of Assynt; and an execution to which, as a humiliating prelude his calm dignity turned against his gloating adversary, Argyle, himself to die with far less dignity after the Restoration. Unfortunately for Montrose, he did not follow the conclusion reached in "This World's a Tennis-Court":

'Tis strange to see how spiders oft do spin
   A trifling gin
To trap a gnat; and Man, with anxious care,
   Contrives a snare
For his own foot, and, whilst that wretched he
   Strives to be free,
In vain he toils; for who can 'scape a fall
When Heav'n writes *Mene Tekel* on the wall?

Adieu then, brain-sick pleasures, get you gone,
   Let me alone;
I'll drink o' th' brook and eat o' th' honey-comb
   In peace at home,
Not caring to be great, but good; for lo!
   Events do show
That outward gilding cannot serve to hide
   The ruins of a rotten inner side.

The reason he could not, in fact, rest "in peace at home" is made plain enough in the poem on which his fame rests most securely, "An Excellent New Ballad", usually known as "My dear and only love", in the first of the two parts of which the poet declares:

He either fears his fate too much,
   Or his deserts are small,
Who dares not put it to the touch
   To win or lose it all.

The Covenanting side also had its poets, though less accomplished than either Drummond or Montrose. The most able Covenanter poet was Sir William Mure of Rowallan (1594–1657), whose French-style castle was built in 1562 and extended by the poet, and whose great-uncle was the poet Montgomerie. Prior to 1617 he wrote in the Castalian manner, apparently with sung performances in mind. The Rowallan Music-Books begun by his father, and continued by the poet and his younger brother, contain not only native airs but part-songs by Morley, Wilbye, Weelkes and others from printed song-books. Then Mure recanted his talents and his graces and turned Protestant. Some of Mure's religious verse looks forward to the Augustan manner of the next century, as parts of "The true Crucifixe for true Catholics" (1629) shows:

> 'Tis most absurd, even in the last degree
> To think God's word and Spirit disagree,
> *This*, striving to restrain and stop the way,
> *That*, grounds to this impiety to lay.
> God's holy Spirit by no other means
> Doth work, but such as God Himself ordains.

He followed the event outside Whitehall with, in 1650, "The Cry of Blood and of a Broken Covenant" upon "our late soveraigne's most treacherous and inhuman murther", and left a version of the Psalms not without metrical merit. His best purely literary achievement is his lengthy version of *Dido and Aeneas* (1614), in three books of verse in *ab ab cc* stanza form, and one or two of his sonnets. Sometimes, as the conclusion to "Fancies Farewell" illustrates, the quality of the poetry only just sustains the burden of the moralizing:

> Look on thy labours: timously lament.
> Trees are hew'd down unwholesome fruits bring forth.
> Thy younger years, youth's sweet Aprile misspent,
> Strive to redeem with works of greater worth.
>   Look home, I say, make haste, O shun delay
>   Hoise sail while tide doth last: time posts away.

Fancy was also the theme, handled with an altogether lighter touch and a delightful dash of Scottish exuberance, by William Cleland (*c.* 1661–1689):[1]

> When I look before me,
>   Thee do I behold
> There's none that sees or knows me;
> All the world's a-gadding,
> Running madding;
>   None doth his station hold.
> He that is below envieth him that riseth,
> He that is above, him that's below dispiseth
> So every man his plot and counter-plot deviseth,
>   Hallo, my fancy, whither wilt thou go?
> Hallo, my fancy, hallo,
>   Stay, stay at home with me;
> I can thee no longer follow,
> For thou hast betrayed me;
>   It is too much for thee.

Stay, stay at home with me; leave off thy lofty soaring;
Stay thou at home with me, and on thy books be poring;
For he that goes abroad, lays little up in storing:
Thour't welcome home, my fancy, welcome home to me.

There is a suggestion of the dance about this piece, which may well have
been based on an older fragment. It is his best achievement.[2]

Cleland, the son of one in the service of the Marquis of Douglas and
therefore probably born in Dumfriesshire, was no more able to stay at
home with his books in those unhappy and divided times than was Montrose. After studying at St Andrews University, Cleland threw in his lot
with the Presbyterians, and at the age of eighteen became an officer in the
Covenanting army. He fought at Drumclog and at Bothwell Brig, where
squabbling Presbyterian divines brought defeat and disaster to their own
troops. He then took refuge in the Low Countries, returning to Scotland
again in 1685 to become involved in the hit-and-run skirmishes which
were regular occurances in the glens and on the moors of the South-west.
For a time he fought under Argyle, but again had to flee abroad, returning
in 1688. When the Covenanter Richard Cameron raised the Cameronian
Regiment, Cleland was made its first lieutenant-colonel, in which role he
took part in the campaigns leading to the success of what Burns called "the
Glorious Revolution" against James II and VII, but died on the field at
Dunkeld the following year.

Like other Lowland poets before him, including Dunbar, Cleland disliked the Highlanders, a dislike reflected in a kind of contemptuous dog-
gerel:

Their head, their neck, their legs and thighs,
Are influenced by the skies,
Without a clout to interrupt them;
They need not strip them when they whip them,
Nor loose their doublet when they're hang'd;
If they be miss'd, its sure they're 'wrang'd' . . .
Nought like religion they retain,
Of moral honesty they're clean.
In nothing they're accounted sharp,
Except in bag-pipe, and in harp.
For a misobliging word,
She'll durk her neighbour ov'r the boord,
And then she'll flee like fire from flint,
She'll scarcely ward the second dint.
If any ask her of her thrift,
Foresooth, her nain sell lives by thift.   [theft

Like Burns, he was aware of the inspirational force of his native landscape, although with Cleland the country muse was apt to hobble!

My feet ne'er filed that brooky hill
Where ancient poets drank their fill.
But these who have the Thames and Humber,
The Tees and Tyne, need not them cumber
To go so far to fetch a drink;
For I am very apt to think
There's als much vertue, sonce and pith
In Annan, or the water of Nith
Which quietly slips by Dumfries,
Als any water in all Greece.

Of the other still more minor bards supporting the Covenanting and Presbyterian causes, only Elizabeth Melville, Lady Cumrie, is worthy of passing mention, and that not an account of her amateur versifying, found in her "Godlie Dreame", but because we are told[2] that once, whilst in bed, "having great motion upon her," she prayed aloud "to a roomful of people for large three hours' time". Religious exercising of this exhausting kind was also an ability practised by Zachary Boyd (1585?–1653), who, having been educated at the Universities of Glasgow and St Andrews, taught at the Protestant College of Saumur, in France, until the Huguenot persecution of 1621 drove him back to Scotland. Minister of the Barony Church in Glasgow in 1623, and Rector of Glasgow University in 1634, 1635 and 1645, he railed so lengthily at Cromwell in Glasgow Cathedral during a Sunday service in 1650, that the dictator's secretary, Thurloe, requested permission to "pistol the scoundrel". Cromwell took more subtle revenge. He invited Boyd back to sup with him at his lodgings in the Saltmarket, then led the divine in prayer until three o'clock in the morning.

His poetic abilities were scarcely greater, though much more productive, than Lady Cumrie's. Boyd's *Zion's Flowers* (1644) rhymed a considerable part of the Old Testament, to that work's manifest disadvantage. Like Mure of Rowallan, he also made metrical assault upon the Psalms (in 1646), though the marginally less uninspired version by an Englishman, Francis Rous (1579–1659), was and still is preferred for popular use.

Boyd left £20,000 Scots and his library to Glasgow University on condition that they published his manuscripts. The University took the money, but put off publishing the verse for so long that in the end they were able to get by with the erection of a small bust of the poet instead.

Even in the religious "killing times", some poets survived without becoming involved in the physical struggle, mostly because they were able to travel abroad. Nevertheless, the burden of their best verse was their passion for their native land. Simeon Grahame (1576?–1614), whose prose *Anatomie of Humours* is said to have inspired Burton's *Anatomy of Melancholy*, published in 1604 *The passionate Sparke of a relenting mind*, a series of lengthy elegies of less interest than the companion pieces, "To the famous Isle of Glorious Brittaine," in *ab ab cc* stanzas, and "To Scotland his Soyle":

To thee, my Soyle (where first
   I did receive my breath)
These obsequeis I sing
   Before my swan-like death.
My love by nature bound,
   Which spotless love I spend,
From treasure of my hart
   To thee I recommend.
I care not Fortune's frown,
   Nor her unconstant Fate:
Let her dissembling smile,
   And triumph in deceate.   [deceit
Curs'd be the man which hoards
   His hopes up in her lap,
And curs'd be he that builds
   Upon her helpless hap.

We know very little about Grahame except that he was brought up in King James's fickle favour, lost it, and tried to recover it by outrageous flattery in the dedication of his book. We also have the somewhat dubious testimony of Sir Thomas Urquhart, in his *Jewel*, that Grahame spent a licentious youth which cooled to a pious old age, and that he was "a great traveller and very good scholar."

William Lithgow (1582–1661?), a native of Lanark, was an even greater traveller, claiming to have covered thirty-six thousand miles in nineteen years. Shetland, Switzerland, Bohemia, Palestine, Egypt, Tunis and Spain made up his astonishing itinerary. On his last journey he was apprehended at Málaga as a supposed spy and tortured, part of the process involving the removal of his ears; hence his subsequent nickname, "Lugless Will".

Not even Glaswegians will be much moved by this "Farewell to the Clyde":

Ten miles more up, thy well-built Glasgow stands,
   Our second metropole of spirituall glore;
A city deckt with people, fertile lands:
Where our great King gat Welcome, welcome's store;
   Whose Cathedrall and steeple threat the skies,
   And nine-archt bridge out ou'r thy bosom lies.

Lithgow was neither the first nor the last Scottish poet to attempt in verse what could better be done in prose. But his command of the *ab ab cc* stanza is well enough shown in his "Conflict between the Pilgrim and the

Muse". "Elegy", the final poem in his volume (which is entitled *The Pilgrims Farewell to his native country of Scotland*, and appeared from the Edinburgh Press of Andro Hart in 1618), has genuine feeling:

> So, dearest soyle, O deare, I sacrifice, now see,
> Even on the altar of mine hart a spotless love to thee.
>   And Scotland now farewell, farewell for many yeares;
> This echo of farewell brings out from me a world of tears.

Even more touching are his lines written about 1640 as he stood alone one night "in a creek of the Grecian Archipelago," dreading the attack of Turkish galliots:

> Would God I might but live
>   To see my native soil,
> Twice happy is my happy wish
>   To end this endless toil.
> Yet still would I record
>   The pleasant banks of Clyde,
> Where orchards, castles, towns and woods
>   Are planted side by side;
> And chiefly, Lanark, thou,
>   Thy country's lowest lamp,   [brightest
> In which the bruised body now
>   Did first receive the stamp.

Not, as Neil Munro has remarked, the "pure jewel of poetry, yet eloquent of the true *maladie du pays* which always makes the exiled Scot a poet of sorts."

Lithgow got his wish, and is buried in ruined St Kentigern, alongside several Covenanting martyrs and Lord Braxfield, the prototype of Stevenson's Weir of Hermiston. However, there is some doubt as to the precise year Lithgow arrived in this company. 1645 is the date usually given, but *The Gushing Teares of Godly Sorrow, containing the Causes, Conditions, and Remedies of Sinne*, published in 1640, was apparently followed by *Scotland's Paraenesis to her dread Sovereign King Charles the Second*, published anonymously in 1660 but bearing the hallmarks of Lithgow's style, and attributed to him by the printed catalogue of the Advocates' Library. If this attribution is correct, then clearly he must have survived to see and celebrate that Restoration the news of which caused Sir Thomas Urquhart to die from a fit of understandably immoderate laughter.

II

The move away from the Scots of the Makars begun by Montgomerie, who was both Makar and Castalian, was complete by the time Sir Robert Ayton, the last Castalian, died. Either he or the nephew who edited his work Englished Ayton's early poems, which had been first written in a thinned though still unmistakable Scots. Montrose, the last of the Cavalier poets whose associations were Carolingian rather than Jacobean, died in 1650. What happened to Scottish poetry during the half century or so between Montrose's execution and the publication of the first volume of Watson's *Choice Collection* in 1706?

There was the work of Robert Sempill (1595?–1669?), and of his son, Francis (c. 1616–1682). Robert was the son of Sir James Sempill of Beltrees, Renfrewshire—a pupil of George Buchanan and author of some anti-Catholic verses—and grandson of that "John Sempill the dancer", who married Marie Livingstone, one of the Queen's four Maries and who, according to Knox, was "surnamed the Lusty". Robert Sempill studied at Glasgow University, and probably served as a Cavalier officer under Charles I. He was certainly engaged in helping forward the promotion of the Restoration. Robert, not to be confused with the earlier Robert, author of the series of political pasquils known as the *Sempill Ballates*, is chiefly known to-day for "The Life and Death of Habbie Simson, the Piper of Kilbarchan." It is an unequal poem, but it carried forward in popularity the tradition of the mock elegy which Ramsay, Burns and others were to use a century later. It also firmed as a convenient vehicle for verse, the pace and content of which were largely colloquial or conversational, an old Scots stanza, basically a variant of *rime couée* already used by troubadours in the twelfth century; by the authors of some English miracle plays; by Lyndsay, Scott and others; and much favoured by all the poets of the Eighteenth-century Scots Revival. Ramsay dubbed it "Standard Habbie". In the hands of Sempill, Ramsay and even Burns, the stanza could not be made to carry the "high" strain with which Alexander Scott had infused it. The reasons for this will be discussed in the context of the Eighteenth-century Revival. In any case, Sempill's piece has nothing of the pointed vivacity of the best excursions into the *genre* by Burns or even Ramsay, as these typical stanzas from "Habbie Simson" show.

> Kilbarchan now may say alas!
> For she hath lost her game and grace,
> Both *Trixie* and *The Maiden Trace*,
>   But what remead?
> For no man can supply his place:
>   Hab Simsons dead . . .
>
> At fairs he play'd before the spear-men,
> All gaily graithed in their gear, man: [attired

Steel bonnets, jacks, and swords so clear then
  Like ony bead:
Now wha will play before such weir-men
  Sin' Habbie's dead? . . .

And at horse races many a day,
Before the black, the brown, the grey,
He gart his pipe when he did play,
  Baith skirl and skreed:
Now all such pastime's quite away
  Sin' Habbie's dead.

Habbie's nephew, a butler, was the subject of a similar performance, the "Epitaph on Sanny Briggs".

The attraction of the stanza is that the first line lends itself to the establishing of a visual scene, or the setting of a situation, while the last two lines enable a pointed, satirical or ridiculing comment to follow without destroying the unity of effect. It is not difficult to manage, and was thus eminently suitable for social use; verse written by gentlemen for their own or their friends' amusement.

One or two other Scots-writing named poets survive through single songs. John Hay, the tenth Lord Yester (1645–1713), wrote one sprightly song to the beautiful tune "Tweedside".

When Maggie and me were acquaint
  I carried my noddle fu' hie,
Nae lintwhite on all the gay plain,
  Nor goudspink sae bonny as she . . .

Yester's lively words, however, scarcely match the grave beauty of the old air—"Doune Tweedside", it is called in the Blaikie MS of 1692—so it is perhaps neither surprising that it was soon replaced by undistinguished English words which aim at the high vein, "What beauties does Flora disclose!" by Robert Crawford (1695–1732), nor that his words were chosen both for *The Scots Musical Museum* and for Thomson's *Select Airs*.

Happier in this respect is the best, though not quite the sole surviving song of Lady Grizel Baillie (1665–1746) the daughter of a Covenanter who helped her father to hide and then to escape to the safety of the Continent. Not only by her life-span does the authoress of the touching song "Werena my hert licht, I wad dee," bridge the seventeenth and eighteenth centuries (although the song was a work of her youth), but she also became a patron of James Thomson, thus evincing interest in native poetry whether written in Scots or English. She was, of course, destined to become the first of a long line of aristocratic female song-writers.

During the seventeenth century, there was also in circulation a body of

popular verse, now more or less anonymous, dealing with country occasions; a wedding, in "The Blythesome Bridal", or the age-old pleasures
of drinking, in "Todlen butt and todlen ben"; or good-natured dissension
between husband and wife, in "Get up and Bar the Door", the female protagonist surely a distant relation of "The Wife of Auchtermuchty".

The main flow of poetry in Scots, however, had nothing to do with
written art. It was the sung ballad, transmitted orally. So far as we can
judge by historical references contained in, or implied by them, ballads
flourished in Scotland probably from about the fourteenth to the end of the
seventeenth centuries. Frequently, with due allowance for artistic licence,
they related to actual happenings. Often they showed an interest in the fancied way of life of social classes above those of a particular minstrel. As in
earlier literate poetry, magic and "glamourie" found a frequent place in
balladry.

Ballads "were made for singing and no' for reading", the mother of
James Hogg, the Ettrick Shepherd, remarked to Walter Scott, complaining
that by writing them down he had "broken the charm". But the "charm"
had been broken by less sympathetic hands long before Scott came on the
scene. As David Daiches so succinctly puts it: "A literary language, arising
out of the different forms of the spoken language and transcending them,
reflects back on the spoken language and gives it a steady relationship to the
national culture". The literary language reflecting back to the spoken by
the end of the seventeenth century was English, the language of Alexander,
Drummond and Ayton.

By 1700, Scotland was probably worse off in material terms than she had
been since the days of Bruce. She had lost her navy, and both her confidence and her trade in the Darien *débâcle*, and the pattern of her agriculture
had been disrupted by civil war. Economically, it was claimed that in 1699
the available coinage in the country worked out at no more than the
equivalent of seventy-five pence per head of population.

Yet in some ways, it was the dark before a new dawn. After 1707, in
place of sustaining her lost political nationhood, bought out by English
bribes, Scotland re-asserted herself in literature. Part of that re-assertion
manifested itself through a revival of interest in the pre-Union past; in
the work of the Makars and in oral folk-song not hitherto systematically
recorded, but which in any case could no longer have continued to react
fruitfully to the changing cultural *mores* of post-Union social and economic conditions.

This, therefore, seems an appropriate moment to consider the oral culture out of which the ballads sprang; for in the closing decades of the seventeenth century they had still not been firmly caught in writing and
laid upon the page, to be touched-up by editors frequently neither scrupulous nor skilful.

Much speculation has been expended on the vexed question of how the
ballads came into being. Could there really have been a host of mute,

inglorious Miltons secluded in rural communities throughout the world providing, so to say, the basic 'matrix', from which later singers simply memorized the original, with human variations from generation to generation, much as late twentieth-century pop-groups take commercial hit-tunes one from the other and adapt them to their own "sound"?

Speculation of this sort arises out of applying the standards of a literate society—one in which large numbers of people can read and write—to the non-literate societies of former times. Here, we are not concerned with those international links which seem thematically to connect the ballads or folk-songs of many lands, perhaps mainly because their subject-matter deals with those basic dramatic human situations which are comparatively few in number, and to a lesser extent, through the constant interflow of migrants. The fact is that in Scotland most of society, including the majority of its lesser or "bonnet" lairds, were non-literate. In the ballad context in which the term is here applied, the word carries no pejorative overtones.

The only way to approach an understanding of the ballad heritage, which seems to have flourished most strongly among the sustained tensions of borderlands—either those of the physical marches between Scotland and England, or the linguistic divide separating the Lowland North-east of Scotland from the Gaelic-speaking Highland area—is to accept that the transmission of oral verse, whether a classical epic running to thousands of lines, a ballad of more modest proportions in couplets, or a ballad cast in the later form of stanzas of four lines (usually in octosyllabics, though sometimes alternating the old eight-feet lines with even lines of six feet, and using a wide variety of rhyming patterns) is to assume a totally different approach from that of the literate poet. The most wide-ranging of all ballad-collectors, the Bostonian Francis James Child (1825–1896), unfortunately died before he could produce his Introduction to what has become the standard British ballad anthology, the five volume *English and Scottish Ballads*—final editions as supervised by Child (1882–98,) in many cases including several variant "readings". He did, however, leave some notes, presumably intended to have been incorporated in the unwritten Introduction. One of them refers to Anna Gordon, Mrs Brown, who learned her huge store of balladry in and around Aberdeen about the middle of the eighteenth century, when the North-east was still largely non-literate. It shows Child's intention to "remark on the differences between Mrs Brown's earlier and later versions". This suggests his realization that every performance was, in a sense, a re-creation.

So far as Scotland is concerned, it has been left to David Buchan[3] in our own day to unravel the so-called "ballad enigma", and by providing an analysis in detail of North-east ballads as exhaustive as it is convincing, to make clear the processes of oral composition and transmission, originally part of the one process.

Clearly, some individual must have been the first to 'start' any particular ballad off, whether 'inspired' by an actual happening among the brawling local great folk, like "The Baron of Brackley", or by an event of wider historical fame, like "Mary Hamilton".* But thereafter, if the story was considered worth the telling, then it would have been re-created anew every time within a framework of architectonic "rules" learned by the minstrels along with the basic stories. It would, of course, be as pointless to try to discover how the first minstrel began to evolve these "rules" as to seek to establish the "rules" by which prehistoric man learned to decorate the walls of his cave-dwellings; irrelevant, too, in our present context, since nobody would ever contend that the conception of oral literature is Scottish in origin. The ability to create orally, to operate an unwritten structure-system adaptable to any story while preserving each story's essential individual features, has fallen away from literate man as surely as any other item of evolutionary apparatus no longer needed for survival.

As Dr Buchan puts it: "The process of traditional oral transmission is not, as the inflexibly literate would have it, merely a process of memorization by rote. To the literate mind, the process of transmission posits, firstly, a fixed text. It is conceived of as a largely visual process: the words are seen, then committed by repeated readings to memory, where they are perhaps retained by an art of visual imagination.† The non-literate person does not possess this kind of visual imagination: words for him cannot be translated into pictorial symbols, they exist as sound-groups; his faculty for imaginative retention is largely auditory. For basically the same reason, the lack of a capacity for literate visualization, he has no conception of a fixed text; the belief that a story and the words in which it is told must be the same or else the story is altered would be to him incomprehensible. He has none of the sophisticated literate mind's word-fixation; he makes no attempt to render the actual words of the story as he heard it, but he does make a strenuous effort to render the story itself exactly as he heard it. For him, the story's the thing."

This is why ballads are always active, self-contained dramas rather than comment upon past action. Active drama can be kept powerfully impersonal. Comment is by its nature subjective.

Buchan goes on to analyse the structure of the ballads, and demonstrates convincingly that they are usually basically built up of "scenes"—which often change with ruthless abruptness, and thus help sustain both performing pace and dramatic tension—each of which is a frame consisting of "a balancing pair of stanzas which flank a single stanza or a balance or a triad.

* Though there is no certainty that one of the Queen's "Four Maries" ever was executed for baby-murder, a similar event does seem to have befallen a Mary Hamilton at an early eighteenth-century Czar's court in Russia. The similarity of name and the traditional Marian associations, may have led to this misunderstanding.

† Nevertheless, at a late stage in the history of oral transmission, when non-literacy was merging into literacy, this was probably the method used.

Stanzaic structure may have binary, ternary or annular patternings. A similar balancing is achieved with the characters concerned, the three-character
ballad of hero, heroine and villain being the central norm even where subsidiary characters support them or react to their deeds. Narrative structure
is also carefully patterned. The range of rhyming words is limited, the non-
rhyming lines often carrying the story forward, while, for structuring reasons, more or less stock lines and phrases recur from ballad to ballad. The
secret of the talent to recreate orally thus lay in the youthful mastery of the
systems of patternings."

It would be as absurd as it would be unjust to seem to suggest for a
moment that a study as thorough and profound as Dr Buchan's can be adequately summed up in a few sentences. His book must be of permanent
value to those whose special field of literary interest is folklore, and to sociologists whose concern with balladry is that of the quarrier seeking to
unearth evidence of past attitudes or behaviour-patterns; work which is
being carried out on an extensive scale at Edinburgh University's School of
Scottish Studies.

Here, however, our interest must necessarily lie in the literary value of
the printed texts of the finest of the ballads to come down to us. It would
not only be impossible meaningfully to apply value-judgements of this
kind to such variants as the few 'genuine' surviving folk-singers may from
time to time come up with for academic collectors, but pointless, since
nobody in late twentieth-century Scotland can possibly be totally free of
the 'taint' of the printed, broadcast, filmed, or recorded word. Non-
literacy, as opposed to illiteracy, has gone from Scotland for good. The
value of these variant versions now being so painstakingly recorded, even
at this late stage of what is left of Scotland's oral tradition, is only likely to
be of significance to scholars. It is highly improbable that any hitherto un-
discovered masterpiece, judged simply by the power of the poetry, will be
forthcoming. We are thus left with fixed, no longer re-creatable texts. Yet
this is no mean heritage.

The ballads which spring most readily to the minds of most readers are
those associated with the Border tensions between Scotland and England.
Most of them have come down to us filtered through the sensibility of an
eighteenth-century editor, and without their original tunes. Because of its
comparatively later physical isolation, however, the North-east produced
a number of versions of ballads associated with Border or general Scottish
themes, if not from the first fully oral phase, at least from that period when
the oral tradition was in transition—a phase in which the singer no longer
re-composes, using the older "structural and formulaic patternings", but
half-recreates in looser fashion from partly memorized originals. Thus, in
David Buchan's *A Scottish Ballad Book*[4], an anthology derived wholly from
North-east sources (usually via Child or Gavin Greig[5]) there are to be
found versions of "Thomas the Rymer" and "Willie o'Douglas Dale",
clearly Border in thematic origin, alongside ballads arising out of the

Lowland/Highland tensions (bride-stealing in this area apparently being preferred to cattle-reiving) such as "Bonny John Seton" and "Bonny Baby Livingstone".

The ballads that deal with actual happenings, local or national, relate only vaguely to historical fact, by the very nature of the re-creative process. But they do relate positively to other factors: to the seasons, as in "The Battle of Otterburn":

It fell about the Lammas tide,
　When the muir-men win their hay—

or again, in "Edom o' Gordon":

It fell about the Martinmas
　When the wind blew shrill and cauld.—

or, in "Tam Lin":

About the middle of the night
　She heard the bridles ring.

This kind of instant season-setting or time-placing, practised by Henryson, was to become a characteristic also much favoured by Burns.

Precision of ballad imagery, however, is by no means confined to the farming round. What could be more vivid than the picture of the storm-sunken ship of Sir Patrick Spens, with its luckless cargo of aristocratic nobles and their ladies:

O laith, laith were our good Scots lords
　To weet their cork-heel'd shoon.
But lang or a' the play was play'd,
　They wat their hats aboon.

And mony was the feather-bed
　That flottered on the faem,
And mony was the gude lord's son
　That never mair cam hame.

Such terse images as those of the bare, drowned heads and the floating beds, have r ever been bettered by any literate Scots poet. Nor can one fail to be aware of the death-levelling implications. Not only common sailors stand in danger of drowning.

As has already been mentioned, another group of ballads was evolved around supernatural events, "Thomas the Rymer" and "Tam Lin" being the best known. Familiarity with the superstitious world of fairies, elves and the Devil, whether so designated or merely portrayed as an unnamed evil force, doubtless goes back far beyond anything revealed even in Gaelic literature. The reappearance of the three drowned sons of "The Wife of Usher's Well", and their return to the place of the spirits—precise in terms of the powers of magic, though geographically vague—typifies the extraordinary poetic force which imagery deep-rooted in communal beliefs matched to lines bared of unessentials, can produce.

Up then crew the red, red cock
  And up and crew the gray.
The eldest to the youngest said,
  " 'Tis time we were away."

The cock he hadna crow'd but ance,
  And clapped his wings at a',
When the youngest to the eldest said,
  "Brother, we must awa.

The cock doth crow, the day doth daw,
  The channerin worm doth chide
Gin we be missed out o' our place,
  A sair pain we maun bide."

Somewhere about:

. . . that braid, braid road
That winds about the fernie brae . . .

down which unwise True Thomas was taken by that "lady bright" whom he mistakenly supposed to be the "mighty Queen of Heaven", occurs the tersest drama of them all, that dialogue between "The Twa Corbies" (one male, the other female, according to the composer Francis George Scott), with its vivid picture of the often speedily realistic consequences of chivalry, the pitiless unconcern of the birds for the human tragedy implied, and their chilling conclusion.

O'er his white banes, when they are bare,
The wind sall blaw for evermair.

The third group of ballad-subjects relates to domestic tragedies; usually lovers got-at by mothers—Scottish balladry is full of doom-loaded matriarchy!—or by brothers more mindful of pride, or the importance attached to inter-family feuding, than to the happiness of their sisters. "Lady Maisry" is one such tale, in which sister, brother, mother and father all call the girl a whore:

"A whore, father, a whore, father?
　A whore I'll never be,
I'm but with child to an English lord
　Who promised to marry me."

Then in came an old woman,
　The lady's nurse was she,
And ere she could get out a word
　The tear blinded her ee.

"Your father's to the fire Janet,
　Your brother's to the whin,
All for to kindle a bold bonfire,
　To burn your body in!"

Tears blinded many an eye in balladry, but few with greater cause than the nurse's; for although she procured a boy to gallop to the noble lord who was the putative father, and he immediately galloped to the rescue, spurring on three horses in turn, he arrived too late:

And boots and spurs all as he was,
　Into the fire he lap,
Gat one kiss of her comely mouth,
　While her body gave a crack.

All that was left to him was to avenge her by killing her kinsfolk.

The facts of love, birth and death and revenge occur over and over again, unsentimentally and impersonally presented; horrible happenings which today would merit a paragraph or two in the sloppy prose of one of the less salubrious newspapers, honed by the heightened communal interest of comparatively isolated social groups and the fierce concentration of the oral architectonic process, to poetry as fine as anything in the language. What modern practitioner could dream up a more complex case of psychological illness than "Edward"?* What account of the tragic misunderstanding arising out of a mother's fixation on her son, could be more grippingly presented than "The Lass of Roch Royal"?

Naturally, not all ballads unfold themselves on this high level of well-formed literary quality. Semi-literacy weakened the oral structure, while

* Since the oldest known text was given to Bishop Thomas Percy (1729–1811)—whose *Reliques of Ancient Poetry*, published in 1765, did much to stimulate an interest in balladry—by Lord Hailes (1726–1792), it has sometimes been suggested that "Edward" is possibly a fake by this eminent legal luminary and author of *Canons of the Church of Scotland*. I find the theory that dull writers like Maçkenzie, Lady Wardlaw or Hailes, should suddenly erupt with a creative outburst of genius far finer in quality and linguistic consistency than anything else they produced, somewhat unconvincing.

chap-book printing settled memorizable versions, and often imperfect ones at that. The spread of literacy into even the remoter places led generally to the gradual fixing of texts, and in doing so, drove what was left of the oral-transition ballad tradition lower down the class structure, through the Bothy Ballads of the North-east in the nineteenth century (some of which have a certain rough poetic merit), to the sub-literate pop products of today, often dogmatically political in character, and almost always devoid of technically disciplined genuine feeling, and therefore of literary value.

From such modal tunes as have survived attached to the older ballads, almost all of them showing affinities with Gaelic airs—probably these tunes were always in shorter supply than the stories, tunes being less amenable to the full recreative process than words, and therefore used for several different ballads—we can see that the music shows a similar steady decline in quality, the tunes of the Bothy Ballads sometimes revealing the rhythmic and melodic influences of Lowland fiddle-music and suggesting the stylistic manner of early nineteenth-century popular songs. The so-called late twentieth-century folk-revival is, of course, musically almost entirely the debased by-product of a television sub-culture fostered by purely commercial interests.

Literacy and oral balladry cannot possibly survive together. The fate that befell the ballad after the end of the seventeenth century, given the changing economic and sociological conditions which developed out of the Union of 1707, was thus without doubt inevitable.

III

A distinguishing feature of seventeenth-century Scottish prose is that it is mostly the work of lawyers, divines or country gentlemen. Scotland at that time possessed no counterpart to London's professional men of letters. Because of this, much of what has come down to us takes the form of "private literature"; letters, diaries or journals which, not unnaturally, feature vignettes of leading characters of the times. Much also, unfortunately, is the merest rohdomontade, religious rhetoric as boring as it is absurd in its painful manipulation of language.

One reason for the flourishing of such more or less empty rhetoric was, of course, the religious controversy on methods of church government which rent the country asunder throughout most of the century, and visited it with all the distressful consequences of civil war. Another is the nature of the Scots temperament united to the natural traditions of the Scots tongue. The "high style" when applied to indignant, partisan prose, proved a sure recipe for clattering emptiness.

Sir George Mackenzie (1636–1691) was nicknamed "Bluidy Mackenzie" by the Covenanters because, as Lord Advocate, it was his duty to prosecute them for the rebels which, in terms of law, they were, having taken arms against their king. In fact, however, he not only endeavoured to alter court practice to the advantage of prisoners on trial, but also opposed the lamentable treatment of almost two thousand women tried for the former crime of witchcraft. His collected *Works* were published in 1816, and included in them, by way of a preface, is an eloquent but revealing defence of Scots speech:

> To me it appears undeniable that the *Scottish* Idiom of the *British* Tongue is more fit for Pleading than either the *English* Idiom or the *French* Tongue; for certainly a Pleader must use a brisk, smart and quick way of speaking; whereas the *English*, who are a grave nation, use a too slow and grave pronunciation, and the *French* a too soft and effiminate one. And therefore, I think the *English* is fit for haranguing, the *French* for Complementing but the *Scots* for pleading. Our *Pronunication* is like ourselves, fiery, abrupt, sprightly and bold . . . more fitted to the complexion of our people than the *English* accent is. . . .

This combination of the suitability for haranguing in English and the fiery, abrupt and sprightly Scots manner, led to the production of an endless series of sermons and tracts the only interesting aspects of which were titles such as *Aaron's Rod Blossoming*, the work of George Gillespie (1613–1648), minister of Wemyss and afterwards of Edinburgh; *The Scotch Presbyterian Eloquence*, by Patrick Walker (d. 1745); *The Poor Man's Cup of Water* by the post-Restoration Covenanter Robert McWard (1633?–1687); or, in a secular connection, *The Staggering State of the Scots Statesmen* by Drummond's friend, Sir John Scot of Scotstarvit (1585–1670). Small wonder that the Jacobite Latinist and medico, Dr Archibald Pitcairne (1652–1713), in his comedy *The Assembly*—the General Assembly of the Church of Scotland, which he had already satirized in Hudibrastic-like octosyllabics with *Babell*—should make one of his characters, a pious old lady, include among her sources of quotation the fanciful tract, *Eleven Points to bind up a Believer's Breeches*.

Since the issues between Covenanters and Episcopalians are without literary interest, and the merits of the controversialists' sermons—mere "matters of moonshine", Calderwood called them—so slight, the eloquence of these wordy divines may be passed over speedily.

Writing on behalf of moderate episcopacy were William Forbes (1585–1634), first Bishop of Edinburgh, whose *Considerationes modestae et pacificae* (published posthumously in 1658), was aimed at encouraging reconciliation through the old wide-ranging though diminishing Latin-reading audience, but had little effect: Patrick Forbes (1564–1635), Bishop of Aberdeen, whose *Commentarie upon the Revelation of St John* (1614) defended the lawfulness of the Reformed preacher's "calling"; and Patrick's son, John Forbes (1593–1648), who produced in 1645 *Instructiones Historico-Theologicae*, though little enough good his declared moderation did him either, since he was banished the country for refusing to sign either Covenant.

If it is the case (as claimed by J. H. Millar) that his unpublished diary, which I have not been able to see, does, indeed, contain a declaration that "the episcopacy, which I think lawful and agreeable to God's word, is not destructive of the presbyterie, nor inconsistent therewith", then it is clear why his moderation would incur the ire of men as immoderate in their utterance of dogmatic opinions as Alexander Henderson (c. 1583–1646), minister of Leuchars, the effects of whose historic moderatorship of the famous Glasgow Assembly of 1638 outlived both his sermons and his treatise *The Government and Order of the Church of Scotland* (1641); David Dickson (1583–1663), minister of Irvine and, especially after he became Professor of Divinity at Edinburgh, an expert in casuistry, as his once-popular *Therpeutica Sacra* (1652) shows; and the aptly-named Andrew Cant (1590–1664), of Pitsligo, Newbattle and Aberdeen, whose *Sermon on Zephaniah* iii.1, 2. with its absurd headings enclosing sub-headings, and its verbose, empty ranting, earned him from Robert Baillie the title of "ane super-excellent preacher", but from posterity the adaptation of his name to provide the English language with a new word for sententious hypocrisy.

Even more "super excellent", in Baillie's sense, was Samuel Rutherford (1600–1661), Professor of Humanity at Edinburgh University from 1623 until 1626, when he was dismissed for a pre-marital sexual indiscretion, and thereafter minister at Anwoth, until his failure to "conform" and the appearance of a book of Calvinistic criticism of Arminianism and other doctrines. Bishop Thomas Sydserf prosecuted him in 1636, and as a result Rutherford was exiled for eighteen months to Aberdeen; not a city particularly noted for the silence of its inhabitants, but where he was forbidden to open his preaching mouth. From then until the triumph of the Covenanting party, and Rutherford's consequent "promotion" to be Principal of the New (St Mary's) College at St Andrews, he passed his time writing unctuously and at great length to a troubled soul with an insatiable appetite for rhetoric, one Marion McNaught.

Unfortunately, Rutherford had become an early addict to the sexual imagery and seductive word-music of the *Song of Solomon*. These inspired him to devise word-play which, to a modern reader, seems as absurdly comical as it would no doubt be deeply revealing to a psychologist. One morning, Marion is told:

> You have been in the King's wine-cellar, where you were welcomed by the lord of the inn, upon condition that you walk in Love.

Yet another lady correspondent was informed that:

> It is part of the truth of your profession to drop words in the ears of your noble husband continually of eternity, judgement, death, hell, heaven, the

honourable profession

and "the sins of his father's house"; advice hardly calculated to improve any marriage. As well as employing a liberal sprinkling of terminology drawn from Scots law, Rutherford occasionally hits off a memorable, if still slightly comic, image: "Ye are going into a clean heaven and an undefiled city: take not filthy clatty hands and clatty feet with you."

Rutherford was the best known of the voteless Scottish Commissioners who attended the Westminster Assembly, summoned to meet in June 1643 as a Council created by Parliament to give advice on church matters. Although it resulted in the production of *The Confession of Faith*, and the *Longer* and *Shorter Catechisms*, still in Protestant Anglo-Saxon use, Rutherford would have been disappointed that that church polity the Scots desired did not materialize. In later life his pamphlet *Lex Rex*, postulating that the power to elect a king lay with the people, brought him into conflict with those who supported Charles II, and it was burnt publicly at Edinburgh Cross by the public hangman.

In spite of the application of so extreme a form of criticism to this one work, and surprising as it may seem so far as the others are concerned, Rutherford has never lacked defenders. One of his twentieth-century champions is Ronald D. S. Jack; who admits that: "The charms of Rutherford's letters are many, and the basis of this charm is in many cases non-literary."[6] To back up this claim, he quotes one of Rutherford's biographers, Robert Gilmour, who declares that this charm is produced by "a transcendent synthesizing force, based on the writer's mystical desire to see one Face, which is yet unseen": in other words, recourse to the religious let-out, which has periodically bedevilled Scottish literary criticism from Rutherford's day almost to our own.

The works of Henry Scougal (d. 1678), minister of Auchterless and later Professor of Divinity at King's College, Aberdeen, notably his *Life of God in the Soul of Man* (1677); the writings of Robert Leighton (1611–1684), minister at, then Principal of, Edinburgh University; the sermons of Robert Bruce (1559–1631); those of James Guthrie (1612–1666), who believed that to encourage schism was lawful for a defeated minority (an encouragement that was to prove nationally disastrous, and not only to the church in Scotland!), and others still more minor but too numerous even to mention, are only of interest to-day to theologians, if at all. So we may turn to two divines whose church histories are still not without general interest.

John Spottiswoode (1565–1639) became Archbishop of St Andrews in 1615. His *History of the Church of Scotland* (1655) was commissioned by no less a person than James VI, who instructed Spottiswoode, in a memorable phrase, to "speak the truth, man, and spare not". Spottiswoode commands a cool narrative style, and is neither pugnacious nor vindictive. It is a tribute to his restraint that he is thus able to describe the events which led to the deliberate destruction by the Reformers of much that was irreplaceable in Scotland's architectural and cultural heritage:

An Act was passed for demolishing cloisters and abbey churches such as were not yet pulled down; the execution whereof was, for the west parts, committed to the Earls of Arran, Argyle and Glencarne; for the north to Lord James; and for the in-countries to some barons that were held most zealous.

Thereupon ensued a pitiful vastation of churches and church buildings throughout all parts of the realm; for every one made bold to put to their hands, the meaner sort imitating the ensample of the greater and those who were in authority. No difference was made, but all the churches were either defaced or pulled to the ground. The holy vessels, and whatsoever else men could make gain of, as timber, lead and bells were put to sale. The very sepulchres of the dead were not spared. The registers of the church and biblioteques were cast into the fire. In a word, all was ruined, and what had escaped in the time of the first tumult, did now undergo the common calamity; which was so much the worse, that the violences committed at this time were coloured with the warrant of public authority.

David Calderwood (1575–1650), minister of Crailing, opposed King James VI's ideas in the practice of worship, and had to flee to Holland. He returned to Scotland upon the succession of Charles I. Calderwood's *History of Scotland*, published posthumously in 1678, lacks the calm judgement of Spottiswoode's. It makes up for this by the author's superior ability in dramatic presentation. Here is Calderwood's description of Knox's death, the vividness of which is curiously enhanced by the quaint, original spelling:

Upon Moonday, the 24th of November, he rose about nine or tenne houres, and yitt was not able to stand by himself; put on his hose and doublett, and satt in a chaire the space of halfe an houre, and then went to bed againe. Being asked by the good-man of Kinzeancleughe if he had anie paine, he answered, "no great paine, but suche as, I trust, sall put end to this battell"; and said to him, "I must leave the care of my wife and children to you, to whom you must be a husband in my rowme". After noone, he caused his wife read the 15th chapter of the First Epistle to the Corinthians; and when it was ended, he said, "Is not that a comfortable chapter?" A little after, he sayeth "I commend my soule, spirit, and bodie (pointing up his three fingers) into thy hands, O Lord".

After five houres, he sayeth to his wife, "Goe, read where I first cast my first anker": and so, she read the 17th chapter of the Gospell according to Johne, and after that, some sermons of Mr Calvin's upon Ephesians. About halfe houre to tenne, they went to the ordinar prayer, which being ended, Doctor Preston said unto him, "Sir, heard ye the prayer?" He answered, "I would to God that yee and all men heard them as I heard: I praise God for the heavenlie sound." Then Robert Campbell of Kinzeancleughe sitteth down before him on a stoole and incontinent he sayeth, "now it is come!"—for he had given a long sigh and sob. Then said Richard Bannatyne to him, "now, sir, the time yee have long called to God for, to witt, an end of your battell, is come; and seeing all naturall powers faile, give us some signe that yee remember upon the comfortable promises which yee have oft shewed unto us". He lifted up his one hand, and incontinent thereafter randered his spirit, about elleven houres at night.

In such a transitional age prose in Scots was almost non-existent, except for such trivialities as *The Rolment of Courtis* (1622) by Abacuck Bysset, or the *Grammatica Nova* (a tract on the essentiality of sound grammar) by Alexander Hume (1558–1631?). This latter work yields such pearls as:

In school materes, the least are not the least, because to erre in them is maest absurd. If the fundation be not sure, the maer gorgiouse the edifice, the grosser the falt.

By comparison with crabbed pedantry of this sort, Calderwood's English comes as near to the 'feel' of Scots as anything else of worth then being produced.

The *History of Scotland* by John Ross (1568–1646), minister of Carnock, relates acutely enough the troubles of the Kirk, but is of no more interest to-day than *The Red-Shankes Sermon* (1642) by his son, James. John Spalding (1609?–1700) produced *Memorialls of the Troubles in Scotland and England* (1624–1625) which, like the *History of Scots Affairs* (1637–1641) by James Gordon (1615?–1686)—a cartographer, as was also his father, Sir Robert Gordon of Straloch—provides a plenitude of more or less useless historical detail.

Three other historians must certainly be chronicled. They are Gilbert Burnet (1643–1715), Robert Wodrow (1679–1734) and Patrick Walker (1666–1745). Little enough they have in common, except that all of them are still occasionally quoted.

Though born in Edinburgh (his father was an advocate, his mother a sister of Archibald Johnston, Lord Warriston), holding the charge of Saltoun for a while, then becoming Professor of Divinity at Glasgow University, Burnet is now best remembered as Bishop of Salisbury, which office he was given the year after his arrival back in England with the Prince of Orange. A moderate who hated Episcopalian oppression as much as he disliked Covenanting stubbornness, he somewhat unfairly earned the dislike of both sides and, in the end, also that of King William.

Burnet's works include a *Vindication of the Authority, Constitution and Laws of the Church and State in Scotland* (1672), a *History of the Reformation* (1679–1714), two biographies, an essay on the biographer's art which is still not without interest, and his most important production, the *History of my Own Time*, published after his death. In it are to be found those vignettes which allow most of the prose of the time to become openly personal, and so to retain whatever general interest it may still possess. Here, for instance, is how Burnet deals with the fate of Montrose:

> At last he was betrayed . . . and was brought a prisoner to Edinburgh. He was carried through the streets with all the infamy that brutal men could contrive: And in a few days he was hanged on a very high gibbet: And his head and quarters were set up in divers places of the Kingdom. His behaviour under all that barbarous usuage was as great and firm to the last, looking on all that was done to him with a noble scorn, as the fury of his enemies was black and universally detested. This cruelty raised a horrour in all sober people against those who could insult over such a man in misfortunes. The triumphs that the preachers made on this occasion rendered them odious.

Burnet's portraits of Charles II and Lauderdale, the Covenanter who helped betray Charles I, turned conscience-stricken Royalist, was captured at the battle of Worcester in 1651 and imprisoned until the Restoration, when he became Secretary of State for Scotland, are masterly in their elegant conciseness. His account of the muddle and duplicity that resulted in the Massacre of Glencoe is presented with moving simplicity. He is also good on the shortcomings of the Presbyterian ministers who had "a very low measure of learning, and a narrow compass in it . . . little men, of a very indifferent size of capacity, and apt to fly out into great excesses of passion and indiscretion . . . apt to censure all who differed from them and to believe and report whatsoever they heard to their prejudice. . . ."

Patrick Walker (1666–1745) wrote lives of the Covenanters, Peden, Semple and Cameron. He has been described, with some justification, as "an inferior Bunyan." Certainly, his rough vigour brings alive the intolerable and intolerant self-righteous unction of the persecuted "remnant"; men like Alexander Peden, who prophesied sudden death for anyone who dared hold an opinion contradictory to his own. Indeed, Walker's clumsy attempts to whitewash these extremists merely served to underline their less praiseworthy characteristics.

Yet compared to the remaining divine yet to be described, Walker appears almost a scholarly moderate—Robert Wodrow (1679–1734), much of whose work is unpublished and likely to remain so, welcomed as a boy the "Glorious Revolution" of 1688, but produced his major published work, *The History of the Sufferings of the Church of Scotland from the Restoration to the Revolution* in 1721–1722, and probably also compiled his *Analecta, or materials for a history of remarkable providences* in the eighteenth century, though it first appeared under the imprint of the Maitland Club in 1842. In thought and literary style and in the choice of much of his subject-matter, however, Wodrow belongs to the century of his boyhood and youth. The influence of his *History* was out of all proportion to its merits. Subsidized by the Hanoverian Government, it became one of the most popular Scottish books of the early eighteenth century, affecting several later writers, including Crocket, who accepted several of its highly coloured myths as sober fact.

The second son of James Wodrow, Professor of Divinity at Glasgow University, Robert took an Arts degree there in 1691, and whilst studying theology in 1697 became University librarian. Licensed to preach by the Presbytery of Paisley, he was given the Parish of Eastwood by his relative, Sir John Maxwell of Pollok, a Lord of Session. Wodrow remained at Eastwood for the rest of his life. He was every bit as credulous as those belonging to that other category of seventeenth-century authors to whom we shall presently turn, the purveyors of authoritative text-books on witchcraft and magic. Wodrow was just as willing to accept anything discreditable to the anti-Covenanting clergy as he was to believe in absurd stories:

> I am weel assured that the Countess of Drumfreice, Stair's daughter, was under a very odd kind of distemper, and did frequently fly from the one end of the room to the other, whither by the effects of witchcraft upon her, in some way is a secret. The matter of fact is certain.

His vignettes of some of the Bishops created, or in some cases re-ordained, from Presbyterian orders, give a fair sample of his charitable charm.

> Mr Andrew Fairfoul got the archbishopric of Glasgow; a man of some learning and neat expression, but never to be taken either serious or sincere. He had been minister first at Leith, and this time was at Dunse, and in that country there was no small talking of his intrigues with a lady who shall be nameless. . . .
>
> Mr George Wishart is placed at the see of Edinburgh. He had been laid under Church censure by the old Covenanters, about the time of the encampment at Dunselaw, in the year 1639, and this probably recommended him now. This man could not refrain from profane swearing, even upon the street of Edinburgh. . . .
>
> Mr Robert Wallace, minister at Barnwell in the shire of Ayr, famous for his large stomach, got the bishopric of the Isles, though he understood not one word of the natives. He was a relation of the Chancellor's, and that was enough. . . .

The belief held by Sir George Mackenzie of Rosehaugh (1639–1691) in the practical use of Scots as a tongue for pleading has already been referred to. He was a man of remarkable ability who became King's Advocate shortly before the Revolution forced him into exile. He founded the Advocates' Library (since 1925 the National Library). He was the author of several *Moral Essays* on such school examination topics as "Solitude",

"Frugality" and "Gallantry". His *Memoirs of the Affairs of Scotland from the Restoration* was published posthumously, and is still valuable as an historian's source book. But his two most important productions are the romance, *Aretina*, (1660), the first prose work of its kind to be published in Scotland, and *Religio Stoici* (1663).

Though too interlaced with political and philosophical references to be successful as a romance, *Aretina* is not without interest. It tells of the successful heroic deeds of Megistus and Philarites against the traitor Sophander, chief minister of Egypt, who has been plotting against his sovereign with the King of Persia. There is also a love interest—Philarites gets his Aretina and Megistus his Agopeta as a suitable reward for loyalty—and some thinly disguised allegorical references to events in England between the death of Charles I and the Restoration. Mackenzie's description of the celebrations accompanying the latter event suggests that his stern Scots temperament did not perhaps allow him to put quite the same high price on freedom as Barbour and the author of the Declaration of Arbroath. His account of the return of Charles II, in the guise of Theopemptus, suggests some lack of understanding of the force with which the spirit of a suppressed people springs back when released from the constraint that had held them tightly down:

> At his Proclamations the people kindled innumerable bonfires, as if by them they intended to purge the air of these nations, which had been polluted with blasphemy against the gods, and rebellion against the king formerly: or else, as if they intended to bury in these graves and burn to ashes those cares, wherewith they had been formerly afflicted. Their flames mounted so high, that one might have thought that they intended to carry news of the solemnites to heaven, and the smoke covered the towns pend-ways, lest heaven should have discerned the extravagancies whereof the inhabitants were guilty: for gravity was banished as an enemy to their duty, and madnesse was judged true loyalty; the trumpets were echoed by the vociferations of the people, and those vociferations seemed to obey the summons of the trumpets; and bells likewise kept a part with the singing multitude, so that both bells and people did both sing and dance all at once; and the air no sooner received these news, but it dispersed them to all the corners of the city and ears of the citizens, it being no crime to be in this a talebearer; and the bullets did flee out of the cannons, as if they intended to meet him half way. Wine was sent in abundance to the earth, that it might drink his majestie's health also, and the glasses capreoled in the air, for joy to hear his name. Some danced through the fire, knowing that the wine had so much modified them, that they needed not fear burning; and others had bonfires kindled in their faces by the wine they had drunk.

Broadly speaking, the *Religio* is a plea for religious tolerance, directed against those extreme Covenanters who sought not only freedom to worship as they chose, but the power to impose their views on the people of England and Wales, who were to be denied a similar freedom of conscience.

Mackenzie's legal writings, notably the *Institutions* (1684) and the *Observations* (1686), were soon superseded in practical use by the classic *Institutions of the Law of Scotland* (1681) of his political opponent, James Dalrymple, Viscount Stair (1619–1695), notorious for his part in furthering the Massacre of Glencoe.

It might be said that in the matter of public unpopularity, the reputation of the one man vied with the other for supremacy. Yet Mackenzie's sobriquet was far less deserved than Stair's wordless obloquy; for Mackenzie, like all upholders of the law, had a clear duty to prosecute rebels, however sincerely they adhered to their cause.

Of writers whose main interest to us now lies in their recording of domestic events, few are more balanced than the learned and tolerant Robert Baillie (1599–1662), at first an Episcopalian priest, then tutor to the sons of the Earl of Eglinton, a Presbyterian incumbent of the charge of Kilwinning parish, a member of the Assembly of 1638, and joint Professor of Divinity at Glasgow University in 1642, of which establishment he became Principal after the Restoration, having been one of those sent to Holland in 1649 to invite Charles II to accept the Covenant along with the Crown of Scotland.

In Baillie's alertly written *Letters and Journals*, there is plenty of material relating to such matters as the procedures of the Westminster Assembly (to which Baillie was also a commissioner), the behaviour of the Covenanting Army at Duns Law (where Baillie had been an army chaplain), and the state of Scotland under Cromwell between 1655 and 1658—

exceeding quiet, but in a very uncomfortable condition; very many of the noblemen and gentlemen, what with imprisonments, banishments, farfaulters, fynes, as yet continuing without any releasement, and private debts from their former troubles, are wracked, or going to wrack.

True to his age he had his share of superstitions, but his writing is untinged by Wodrow's too frequently over-evident satisfaction in the practical outcome of the sad situations so absurdly diagnosed. Writes Baillie:

Sundrie heavie accidents have lately fallen out amongst us. Bailie Walkinshaw's most prettie boy of four or five years old, on a Sunday afternoon, fell down his stair, and spoke no more, but died. Thomas Brown, late bailie, having supped, lay down and died before midnight. Thomas Muir, our factor, at his breakfast weel, while he strecht out his hand to the cup, is suddenly overtaken with a palsie; spoke no more, but in a day or two dies. Thomas Robison, in Salcots, sitting at his own fire-side, is stabbed to death by a highlandman. . . In Glenluss parish, in John Campbell a webster's house, for two or three yeares a spirit did whiles cast stones, oft fire the house, and tut the webs in the looms, yet did never any considerable harme. . . There is much witcherie up and downe our lande; though the English be but too spareing to try it, yet some they execute.

Those with a taste for witches and fairies will find Scots credulity displayed at its most extreme in *Satan's Invisible World Discovered* (1685) by George Sinclair (1618–1687) or in *The Secret Commonwealth of Elves, Fauns and Fairies* (1691) a pseudo-scientific analysis of the fairy hierarchy by a worthy minister of Aberfoyle, Robert Kirk (1641–1692).

The source-book of Scottish demonology and the literary accompaniment to the revolting practice of trying and burning people in their hundreds as supposed witches, sometimes on the "evidence" of a mere child, or on no real evidence at all—the last witch to be burned in Scotland suffered at the stake in 1722—is *The Secret and True History of the Kirk of Scotland* by James Kirkton (d. 1699). Fear and magic, commonly associated in the minds of primitive peoples and harmlessly deployed in balladry and earlier Scottish literature, were fused into vicious cruelty by the fires of religious bigotry and the resulting social violence.

It is therefore with relief that one turns from the strange bigotries of these men to Andrew Fletcher of Saltoun (1653–1716), the scholar and politician who foresaw how inevitable the ultimate decline of Scotland would be following upon an incorporating union with England. He fought passionately, though unsuccessfully, to achieve federal union instead. Some of his political ideas seemed eccentric to thinkers in the upper strata of the settled society of Victorian times—for instance his belief that every young man should do two years' military service—while the twentieth century may raise its eyebrows at his propostion that a kind of modified slavery for people who will not work would help in the reorganization of Scottish agriculture. Yet what he was really advocating, in these and other notions, was merely that measure of discipline necessary if great ends are ever to be achieved—a doctrine abhorrent to Marxists in theory, but relentlessly and brutally pursued wherever the dogmas of Marxism have been implemented.

Fletcher, the political orator, the purveyor of effective spoken prose, knew he would be misinterpreted and miscalled. Such is the common, if frequently deserved, lot of politicians. To those who would attack him, he says, in *The Second Discourse*:

But they must pardon me if I tell them, that I regard not names but things; and that the misapplication of names has confounded everything. We are told there is not a slave in France; that when a slave sets foot upon French ground, he becomes immediately free: and I say that there is not a free man in France, because the King takes away any part of any man's property at his pleasure:

and that, let him do what he will to any man, there is no remedy . . . A slave
properly is one who is absolutely subjected to the will of another man without any remedy: and not one that is only subjected under certain limitations,
and upon certain accounts necessary for the good of the commonwealth,
though such an one may go under that name. And the confounding these two
conditions of men by a name common to both has, in my opinion, been none
of the least hardships put upon those who ought to be made servants. We are
all subjected to the laws: and the easier or harder conditions imposed by them
upon the several ranks of men in society make not the distinction that lies between a freeman and a slave.

Political speeches rarely make great literature. Fletcher's are no exception
to the general rule. Yet to later Scots who may have found themselves
regretting the long, slow weakening of so many of their traditions, and the
ever-increasing loss of the power of Scottish decision-making to the nume-
rically superior partner in the Union of 1707, the name of Fletcher of Saltoun has a special significance. Had his policies been adopted, Scotland
might have enjoyed both the benefits of union and the privileges of independent judgement in the affairs of the whole island.

Be that as it may, he is well remembered to-day for at least one sentence,
from his *Letter to the Marquis of Montrose* which, since it is usually misquoted,
is here given in full:

I knew a very wise man so much of Sir Chr—'s sentiment, that he believed
if a man were permitted to make all the ballads, he need not care who should
make the laws of a nation.

The traveller–poet Lithgow produced a prose work, *Anatomie of
Humours*, the main claim to fame of which, as we have noted, is that it is said
to have inspired Burton's *Anatomy of Melancholy*. A much more learned and
skilful eccentric was Sir Thomas Urquart of Cromarty (1611–1660), a
perpetually disorganized, belligerent pedant, as constantly in debt as he
was fascinated by the sheer sound of language. He produced a splendidly
robust version of the first two books of Rabelais in 1653. A third, published
posthumously in 1693, was completed by Pierre Anthony Motteux, a
Frenchman who had settled in England. I doubt if there are many who
could still read for pleasure such tortuous verbal oddities as Urquhart's virtually unintelligible *Trissotetras*, a work on trigonometry, or even his *Pan-
tochronochanon, a peculiar Promtuary of time*, in which he wordily weaves his
way through the medieval practice of tracing the descent of his ancestors
from Adam and Eve through one hundred and fifty generations. His *Logop-
andecteison*, part autobiographical, part outline of proposals for a universal
language, appeared in 1653.

Urquhart appeals to believers in the existence of a "Caledonian
Antisyzygy", since he perfectly exemplifies this alleged Scots tendency to

try to push extremes, so to say, beyond their own ends. Consequently, an Urquhart cult was one of the more theoretical aspects of that twentieth-century revival of poetry and letters dubbed by Denis Saurat *The Scottish Renaissance*. If any of those latter-day Urquhartians actually read in entirety their hero's original writings, the most likely candidate for their attention must surely have been his *Discovery of a Most Exquisite Jewel* (1652), in which he further propounds his theories for a universal language, but also lays about Presbyterianism with an engaging, round-bellied gusto. His most famous vignette, however, is his word-portrait of the "Admirable Crichton", James Crichton of Cluny (d. 1583).

Crichton—whose character inspired Harrison Ainsworth's novel *The Admirable Crichton* (1831), and provided Sir James Barrie, after a hint from Conan Doyle, with the idea of a play about the perfect butler, also called *The Admirable Crichton* (1902)—took degrees at St Andrews University, served in the French army, spoke ten languages, was skilled in philosophy, theology and astrology, had a public disputation with priests in Venice, and possessed a photographic memory.

Under the influence of Rabelais Urquhart, even in the *Jewel,* invents words that have unfortunately proved notably unmemorable, indulges in preposterous exaggeration, and generally mis-applies the techniques of satire to what is meant to be the depiction of the career of a romantic hero. Thus in a love affair that was to have a fatal termination, Urquhart describes the lady's "hirquitalliency at the elevation of the pole of his (Crichton's) microcosm", and of the hero's "luxuriousness to erect a gnomon on her horizontal dyal."

In the midst of these sexual acrobatics, the lady's Prince arrives at the palace by night in carnival dress. Instead of finding a compliant mistress, he is confronted instead by a somewhat ridiculous rival caught, so to say, just after the act:

The Admirable and ever-renowned Crichtoun, who at the Prince's first manning of the court taking the alarm, step'd from the shrine of Venus to the oracle of Pallas Armata; and by the help of the waiting gentlewoman, having apparelled himself with a paludamental vesture, after the antick fashion of the illustrious Romans, both for that he minded not to make himself then known, that to walk then in such like disguise was the anniversary custome of all that country, and that all, both gentlemen and others standing in that court, were in their mascaradal garments; with his sword in his hand, like a messenger from the gods, came down to relieve the page from the poste whereat he stood sentry; and when, as the light of the minor planets appeares not before the glorious rayes of Titan, he had obscured the irradiancy of Pomponacio with his more effulgent presence, and that under pretext of turning him to the page to desire him to stand behind him, as he did, he had exposed the full view of his left side, so far as the light of torches could make it perceivable to the lookers on, who being all *in cuerpo* carying swords in their hands, instead of cloaks about them, imagined really, by the badge or cognizance they saw neer his heart, that he was one of my ladie's chief domestick servants; he addressed his discourse to the Prince, and the nine gentlemen that were with him; neither of all whereof, as they were accoutred, was he able, either by the light of the tapers, or that of the moon, which was then but in the first week of its waxing, it being the Tuesday next to the first new moon that followed the purification day, to discern in any manner of way what they were; and for that he perceived by their unstedfast postures, that the influence of the grape had made them subjects to Bacchus, and that their extranean-like demeanour towards him, not without some amazement, did manifest his certainty of their not knowing him; he therefore, with another kind of intonation, that his speech might not bewray him, then that which waited upon his usual note of utterance, made a pithy panegyrick in praise of those that endeavured, by their good fellowship and Bacchanalian compagnionry, to cheer up their hearts with precious liquour, and renew the golden age; whence descending to a more particular application, he very much applauded the ten gentlemen, for their being pleased, out of their devotion to the Lyaean god, who had with great respect been bred and elevated amongst the nymphs, not to forget, amidst the most sacred plying of their symposiasms, that duty would have made him a patient, in as short space as the most diagrammatically-skilled hand could have been able to describe lines representative of the distance 'twixt the earth and the several kardagas, or horary expeditions of the sun's diurnal motion, from his æquinoxial horizontality to the top of his meridian hight, which, with the help of a ruler, by six draughts of a pen is quickly delineated, livered out six several thrusts against them; by vertue whereof he made such speedy work upon the respective segments of that debauch'd circumference, through the red-ink-marks which his streight-drawn stroaks imprinted, that being alonged from the center-point of his own courage, and with a thunder-bolt-like-swiftness of hand radiated upon their bodies, he discussed a whole quadrant of those ten, whereof four and twenty make the circle, and laying six of the most inraged of them on their backs, left, in the other four, but a sextant of the aforesaid ring, to avenge the death of their dismal associates. Of which quaternity, the Prince being most concerned in the effects of this disaster, as being the only cause thereof, though his intentions levelled at another issue, and like to burst with shame to see himself loadned on all sides with so much dishonour by the incomparable valour of one single man, did set forward at the sword's point, to essay if in his person so much lost credit might be recovered; and to that purpose coming within distance, was upon the advancing of a thrust in quart, when the most agil Crichtoun, pareing it in the same ward, smoothly glided along the Prince's sword, and being master of its feeble, was upon the very instant of making his Highness very low, and laying his honour in the dust, when one of the three courtiers whom fortune had favoured not to fall by the hand of Crichtoun, cryed aloud, "Hold, hold! kill not the Prince." At which words the courteous Crichtoun recoyling, and putting himself out of distance, the Prince pulled off his vizard, and throwing it away, shew his face so fully that the noble-hearted Crichtoun, being sensible of his mistake, and sory so many of the Prince's servants should have enforced him, in his own defence, to become the actor of their destruction, made unto the Prince a very low obeisance, and setting his left knee to the ground, as if he had been to receive the honour of knighthood, with his right hand presented him the hilt of his own conquering sword, with the point thereof towards his own breast, wishing his highness to excuse his not knowing him in that disguise, and to be pleased to pardon what unluckily had ensued upon the necessity of his defending himself, which, at such an exigent, might have befaln to any other that were not minded to abandon their lives to the indiscretion of others. The Prince, in the throne of whose judgement the rebellious vapours of the tun had installed Nemesis, and caused the irascible faculty shake off the soveraignty of reason, being without himself, and unable to restraine the impetuosity of the will's first motion, runs Crichtoun through the heart with his own sword, and kills him.

Mention should certainly be made of David Crawfurd (1665–1726), eighth Laird of Drumsoy, who went in for fantasy of another kind. He became Historiographer Royal for Scotland in 1705, and produced his *Memoirs of the Affairs of Scotland* (1706), which sets out Mary, Queen of Scot's side of the story of her confrontation with the Reformers. Though several editions appeared, the last in 1767, Malcolm Laing, in 1804, dismissed the author's claim to have edited a manuscript by a disinterested contemporary as "downright forgery".

Crawfurd wrote three novels, all couched in epistolary style. They were published in a single volume under the collective title *The Unfortunate Duchess* (1700). Although he made some attempt at lively characterization, tales of high life the characters of which have names like Daria, Timandra and Eriphele were already old-fashioned by the turn of the century. When one remembers that Congreve's incomparably wittier Restoration comedy *The Way of the World* failed to please in 1700 because it seemed too heavily mannered, Crawford's two comedies *Love at First Sight* and *Court-ship-à-la-Mode* (allegedly written in "ten forenoons") can be seen also to have been catering for a vanished generation. *Courtship-à-la-Mode*, however, could still perhaps be made to work in the theatre. Crawfurd does not deserve the total neglect that has been his fate, even if the verse of his *Ovidius Britannicus* (1703), in which abandoned or protesting lovers vent their interminable feelings in rhyming couplets, suggests more than anything else the conventionalized Italian opera libretti of the ensuing century.

I have kept to the end the one short prose work of the period which deservedly holds its place as literature, William Drummond's *A Cypress Grove* (1623). It first appeared in the company of his poems, *Flowers of Sion*. Neither his many tracts vainly urging a moderate and peaceful settlement of the religious disputes of the 1630s, nor his *History of Scotland from 1423 to*

1542, published in 1655, hold much of interest to us now. But this meditation on Death, though it owes something to Bacon, Sylvester, Lyly, de Mornay and others, digests these influences, and in turn may itself have influenced the *Religio Medici* (1642) and *Urn-burial* (1658) of Sir Thomas Browne, which it anticipates by a generation. Many critics have been tempted to compare Browne's more rugged eloquence with Drummond's quieter music; but the exercise is pointless. Having once listened, one cannot forget the sound of Drummond's:

> Death is the sad estranger of acquaintance, the eternal divorcer of marriage, the ravisher of children from their parents, the stealer of parents from the children, the interrer of fame, the sole cause of forgetfulness, by which the living talk of those gone away as of so many shadows, or fabulous Paladins. All strength by it is enfeebled, beauty turned in deformity and rottenness, honour in contempt, glory into baseness: it is the unreasonable breaker-off of all the actions of virtue; by which we enjoy no more the sweet pleasures on earth, neither contemplate the stately revolutions of the heavens. The sun perpetually setteth, stars never rise unto us. It in one moment depriveth us of what with so great toil and care in many years we have heaped together. By this are successions of lineages cut short, kingdoms left heirless and greatest states orphaned . . . By Death we are exiled from this fair city of the world; it is no more a world unto us, nor we anymore people into it. The ruins of fanes palaces, and other magnificent frames, yield a sad prospect to the soul: and how should it consider the wreck of such a wonderful masterpeice as the body without horror?

In the decades of the half-century following Drummond's own death, so much futile religious struggle, and such distorting hatreds, erupted over the formalistic details of an issue on which basically both sides must either have been right or wrong—the idea of any kind of supposedly omnipotent God concerning Himself with the Presbyterian versus the Episcopalian or Catholic approaches to the system of church government or procedure of worship being fundamentally ludicrous!—that perhaps it might not be unfair to quote Drummond's consolatory thoughts against the importance of the idea of Death; words that somehow reach across the divisions and the dissensions of warring sects to the increasingly accepted secularity of the later twentieth century.*

> If thou dost complain that there shall be a time in which thou shalt not be, why dost thou not too grieve that there was a time in the which thou wast not, and so that thou art not as old as that enlifening planet of time? For, not to have been a thousand years before this moment, is as much to be deplored as not to be a thousand after it, the effect of them both being one: that will be

* Hawthornden Press edition, 1914.

after us which long ere we were was. Our children's children have that same reason to murmur that they were not young men in our days, which we have, to complain that we shall not be old in theirs. The violets have their time though they empurple not the winter, and the roses keep their season, though they disclose not their beauty in the spring.

When *A Cypress Grove* was being written, the century of religious conflict had still a long way to go. Moderates like Drummond and, later, Leighton and Spottiswoode, could not make their compromising voices prevail over the clamour of the contest between Kirk and King, the rigours of the Cromwellian dictatorship, or the Resoration which was almost immediately followed by the persecution of the Covenanters. What Burns chose to call the "Glorious Revolution", in which James VII and II was defeated at the Battle of the Boyne and William of Orange and his Stuart Queen invited to mount the throne of the two Kingdoms, at first looked like victory for the Kirk. It was, however, a forced compromise the weakening effects of which were to be felt increasingly in the century that followed. Anger at the part England was believed to have played in bringing about the disastrous overthrow of the Scots colonizing scheme at Darien, on the swamp-infested isthmus of Panama, produced the threat of a separate choice of monarch to succeed Queen Anne; a threat which, had it materialized, would have undone the Union of the Crowns of 1603. This was a prospect England could not face. From the moment the threat began to assume the proportions of probability, plans for governmental union, which had been mooted in one form or another for more than half a century, became inevitable.

Here, we need not concern ourselves with the rights or wrongs of the incorporating Union of 1707; with the passions it aroused, the smouldering resentments it engendered, or the short and long-term material gains and losses that may have ensued from it. It did, however, induce a gradual return of interest in the poetry of the old Scots Makars, and, as if to assert the survival-power of the junior nation in the new partnership in non-political fields, shook awake another flourishing of the boughs, the period known to us now as the Eighteenth-century Revival.

CHAPTER FOUR

The Eighteenth Century

I

Throughout the seventeenth century, the Makars had been largely, though not totally, forgotten. Two English cataloguers, Nicholas Brigham (d. 1558)* and John Bale (1495–1563), intent upon producing a record of the literature of the two kingdoms, listed the writers Major, Boece, James I, Blind Harry, Douglas, Bellenden and Lyndsay, to which Dempster later added the names of Hume, Montgomerie, Polwarth, Semple and Scott. But a catalogued author is not necessarily one whose works are still read. In any case, neither Dunbar nor Henryson featured.

The earlier poems that lived on throughout the seventeenth century, and well into the eighteenth, were Barbour's *Bruce* and Blind Harry's *Wallace*, the works of Lyndsay and *The Cherrie and the Slae*. Patrick Gordon (1615–1650) had pronounced on the *Bruce* that "the old printed book, besydes the outworne barborous speiches, was so evill composed that I could bring it to no good method", and accordingly produced his own rhyming "Historie of Robert the Bruce" published at Dordrecht. It probably performed a similar popularizing function to Hamilton of Gilbertfield's abridged paraphrase of *Wallace*, with which for sheer absence of literary quality it certainly vies.

While Lyndsay still remained the poet of the people, Douglas was the scholar's man. David Hume of Godscroft (*c.* 1560–1630), the genealogist, said of Douglas's *Aeneid*:

> In his Prologues before every book where he hath his libertie, he sheweth a naturall and ample vein of poesie, so pure, pleasant and judicious, that I believe there is none that hath written before or since, but cometh short of him.

And in 1623, William L'isle, in *A Saxon Treatise concerning the Old and New Testament*,† recorded how he:

> . . . lighted in Virgil Scotished by the Reverend Gavin Douglas, Bishop of

* His *Illustrium Majoris Britanniae Scriptorum Summarium in Quinque Centurias Divisum* was published in 1548.

† Attributed to Aelfric.

Dunkell, and uncle to the Earle of Angus: the best translation of that Poet that ever I read: and though I found that dialect more hard than any of the former (as nearer the Saxon, because further from the Norman), yet with help of the Latine, I made shift to understand it, and read the booke more than once from the beginning to the end.

Indeed, it was as "a sort of exercise towards a knowledge of the Anglo-Saxon" that in 1691 a Bishop of Lincoln produced an edition of Drummond's macaronic "Polemo-Middinia", coupled with "Christis Kirk on the Green". But like the work of similar Anglo-Saxon studies of the time by scholarly divines, who considered Barbour, Wyntoun, Blind Harry, James I and Dunbar out of their native context, this merely served as a tenuous link through neglectful times; times during which, in James VI's words, poets no longer "writ of auld: lyke as the tyme is changit sensyne, sa is the ordour of Poesie changit.

The anthology which ushered in the Eighteenth-century Revival by establishing a direct link with the Makars★ who wrote before the Castalians‡ and the Cavaliers† (though some of their work was also included in it) was the *Choice Collection of Comic and Serious Scots Poems*, which came out in three parts in 1706, 1709 and 1711. The editor was James Watson (d. 1722).

Watson's father had managed to wrest from Andrew Anderson—the son of George Anderson, the first printer to set up in Glasgow—a printing monopoly granted by Charles II. But Watson senior was never able to make much use of what he had thus gained. The younger Watson not only experienced a good deal of trouble because of the rivalry of Anderson's widow, but found himself briefly in prison for having published an outspoken tract, "Scotland's Grievance respecting Darien." However, operating as a printer, first from Warriston's Close in the High Street of Edinburgh, then from Craig's Close, and selling his publication through his bookshop "next door to the Red Lion, opposite to the Luckenbooths" (which faced St Giles,) his anthology, "the first of its nature which has been published in our native Scots dialect", seems to have found ready purchasers. Doubtless it sublimated the strong current of political Jacobitism then running through Scottish life by carrying it harmlessly over into literature, much as the annual lucubrations performed in Burns's name every 25th January still reflect to some degree the sublimation of the Scot's thwarted sense of nationhood.

The anthology is a strange mixture, offering something for every taste. The poems in English include selections from the work of Montrose and Ayton, Cleland's "Halloo my Fancie" and Sir George Mackenzie's "Caelia's Country-house and Closet", the latter an artificial exercise in Augustan heroic couplets which achieves passing sincerity, however, in its

★ The Scots name for those poets called by the English "Scottish Chancerians".
† The poets at the Courts of Charles I and Charles II.
‡ The poetic friends of James I and VI.

tributes to Charles I and Montrose. For the kind of readership who liked their satire rough, Watson included Drummond's "Polemo-Middina" and a tasteless anonymous piece, "The Woman's Universe".

Since Watson's motives were undoubtedly patriotic, his aim being to counter the increasing Edinburgh tendency to accept anglicization, a large section of the anthology is taken up with Scots poems, often inaccurately ascribed or transcribed. Yet it contains pieces as diversified in mood as *The Cherrie and the Slae*, "Christis Kirk on the Green", "Lady Anne Bothwell's Balow", Semple's "Habbie Simson" and "Sanny Briggs" and that old "catalogue" song, "The Blythsome Bridal," with its jingling listing of the guests attending and the variety of Scots delicacies to be tasted at their celebrations:

There will be good lappered-milk kebucks
    and sowens, and farles, and baps,
And swats, and weel-scraped paunches,
    and brandie in stoups and in caps.
And there will be meal-kail and castocks,
    and skink to sup till you rive,
And rosts to rost on a brander,
    of flouks that was taken alive.

Scrapt haddocks, wilks, dulse and tangle,
    and a mill of good shising to prie,
When wearie with eating and drinking
    We'll rise up and dance till we die.
Fy, let us all to the briddel
    for there will be lilting there,
For Jockie's to be married to Maggie,
    the lass with the gauden hair.

As in the case of "Jocky said to Jenny", "Maggie's Tocher" and others of their dance-like kind dealing with the enjoyments of rustic celebrations, it is generally supposed that their anonymous authors came from a superior social class, and were recording what went on, so to speak, from outside, looking in. There is nothing really surprising about this. The ballad-makers frequently sang of what they fancied was the way of life of their social superiors. Only in the affluent societies of the late twentieth century has it become fashionable to deride the material comforts after which the deprived have striven for centuries.

The most significant piece in Watson's anthology, from the point of view of what it germinated, was undoubtedly "The Last Dying Words of Bonny Heck", a famous greyhound in Fife, by William Hamilton of Gilbertfield (1665?–1751), an army officer who retired, then lived as a country gentleman at his estate near Glasgow. It is couched in the "Standard Habbie" stanza, and reflects through the animal's viewpoint the Henrysonian fable tradition, though handled in a much less subtle fashion.

Without doubt, Watson the editor, and Hamilton the poet, inspired emulation in Allan Ramsay (1684–1758), born in Leadhills, Dumfriesshire. His father, overseer to the Hopes of Hopetoun, died when Ramsay was about a year old, leaving his mother, Alison Bower, a mining engineer's daughter from Derby, with two children, or one child and another about to be born. Soon after, she re-married a "bonnet-laird" called Andrew Crichton, by whom she had two more children. On her death in 1700, the fifteen-year-old future poet no longer had anything to keep him in Leadhills. He therefore followed the example of his elder brother, Robert, and went to Edinburgh, where he became apprenticed to a wigmaker in 1704. Industrious and level-headed, he soon turned bookseller, and in 1728 opened the first circulating library in Scotland. But for the machinations of the Kirk, aided by Walpole's Special Licensing Act of 1737, Ramsay would also have succeeded in establishing in Carruber's Close a regular theatre several decades before the anti-theatre prejudices of ministers of religion were put to rout by the Reverend Alexander ("Jupiter") Carlyle. Because Ramsay was of humble origin—indeed, almost the first Scots poet in the literate tradition to be so—and had the Scots desire to "get on in the world", he has often been dismissed, even by such pro-Scots critics as Wittig, as being more important as an editor than as a poet. He was, of course, very important in the former, if minor, capacity. Yet he was also a much better poet than is generally acknowledged. Like many an artistic practitioner, he wrote for money and was unwise enough unambiguously to say so.

> If happily you gain them to your side,
> Then bauldly mount your Pegasus and ride,
> Value yourself what only they desire,
> What does not take, commit it to the fire.

What 'took' in the divided society of his day—a society anxious, on the one hand, to keep up with English artistic customs and English commercial opportunities, yet on the other, fascinated by the achievement and tradition of those whom Ramsay himself called the "good old Bards" who, writing before 1600, "had not yet made Use of imported Trimmings upon our Cloaths"—was all too often smooth, social verse in the heroic couplets of the English Augustan writers. Some of his pieces in this borrowed style, like "Tartana, or the Plaid", are simply a weak imitation of Pope's manner. Others, like "The Rise and Fall of Stocks", amount to no more than versified journalism. But, contrary to the common belief of many Scots critics down the ages, an artist should be judged by his best work, not by his middling or his worst. Ramsay's best Scots writing achieves a taut and racy urban originality which the later, much greater but fundamentally non-urban achievement Burns was to build from similar materials, has unfairly overshadowed.

It must, of course, be admitted that the percentage of Ramsay's output possessing this quality is small in relation to the total corpus of his work. The best of what he achieved includes the supplementary stanzas he added to the obviously incomplete old poem "Christis Kirk on the Green", attributed to James I. Still better, however, are the "Familiar Epistles" Ramsay exchanged with William Hamilton of Gilbertfield. Hamilton's side of the exchange consists of little more than gentlemanly rhyming compliment. Thus he tells Ramsay:

> Of Poetry the haill Quintessence
> Thou hast suck'd up, left nae excrescence
> To petty Poets, or sic messens,
>   Tho round thy stool,
> They may pick crumbs, and lear some lessons
>   At *Ramsay's* school.

Ramsay's reply to the Third Epistle illustrates his down-to-earth Scots smeddum:

> That bang 'ster billy *Caesar July*,
> Wha at *Pharsalia* wan the tooly,
> Had better sped, had he mair hooly
>   Scamper'd thro' life,
> And 'midst his glories sheath'd his gooly,
>   And kiss'd his wife.
>
> Had he like you, as well he cou'd
> Upon burn banks the Muses woo'd,
> Retir'd betimes frae 'mang the crowd,
>   Wha'd been aboon him?
> The Senate's durks, and faction loud,
>   Had ne'er undone him.

Ramsay's easy-going attitude to the comforts of life is well set out in this "Answer to the Third Epistle":

> Tho I were Laird of tenscore acres,
> Nodding to jouks of hallenshakers,   [trembling attendants
>   at a great man's gate
> Yet crush'd wi' humdrums, which the weaker's
>   Contentment ruines,
> I'd rather roost wi' causey-rakers,   [street cleaners
>   And sup cauld sowens.   [boiled oatmeal eaten with milk or butter
>
> I think, my friend, as fowk can get

A doll of rost beef pypin het,   [share
And wi' red wine their wyson wet,   [gullet
  And cleathing clean.
And be nae sick, or drown'd in debt,
  They're no too mean.

Out of these exchanges evolved the later Epistles of Burns, more sharply pointed but deriving in form, tone and manner from Ramsay. In his day-to-day way of life, Ramsay was much the more fortunate, and made no attempt to disguise his delight in the good things his worldly success enabled him afford:

See that shining glass of claret.
  How invitingly it looks.
Take it aff and let's have mair o't,
  Pox on fighting, trade and books.

Let's have pleasure while we're able,
  Bring us in the meikle bowl,
Place't on middle of the table,
  And let wind and weather growl.

Equally hedonistic in his rendering into Scots of Horace's Ode "Vides ut alta stet nive candidum Soracte . . ." (Ramsay's poem begins "Look up to Pentland's tow'ring taps"):

Be sure ye dinna quit the grip
  Of ilka joy when ye are young,
Before auld age your vitals nip,
  And lay ye twafauld o'er a rung.

It is hardly surprising that a poet with such an open love of life should relish the social occasions provided by Maggy Johnston, who kept an ale-house a mile to the south of Edinburgh, and whose death Ramsay celebrated:

When we were wearied at the gowff
Then Maggy Johnston's was our howff;
Now a' our gamesters may sit dowff,
  Wi' hearts like lead;
Death wi' his rung rax'd her a yowff,
  And sae she died.

Maun we be forced thy skill to tine?
For which we will right sore repine;

Or hast thou left to bairns of thine
   The pawky knack
Of brewing ale amaist like wine,
   That gar'd us crack?

Even more Burnsian is his "Elegy on John Cowper, Kirk-Treasurer's Man, Anno 1714". This character was employed by the Kirk Treasurer as a kind of sexual spy in the days when the Church still did its best to dominate every aspect of private life. Those suspected of having intercourse outwith marriage were persecuted, and when caught, ridiculed in front of the congregation. Ramsay, the avowed Jacobite who found it convenient to be absent from Edinburgh while Prince Charles occupied Holyrood, doubtless had no clandestine dealings of this sort himself. But he still observed the ongoings of the Edinburgh members of the oldest profession with keen, ironic relish:

Fy upon Death, he was to blame
To whirle poor John to his lang hame:
But tho his arse be cauld, yet fame
   Wi' tout of trumpet,
Shall tell how Cowper's awfou name
   Cou'd flie a strumpet.

He kend the bawds and louns fou weil,
And where they us'd to rant and reel,
He paukily on them cou'd steal,
   And spoil their sport;
Aft did they wish the muckle Deil
   Might take him for't.

Not even the Kirk could prevent the practice of the oldest profession. In "Lucky Spence's Last Advice", a famous brothel keeper who had an establishment near Holyrood House, passes on her knowledge of the trade. Ramsay manages to catch the debauched, rapacious tone of the worldly-wise old whore as she tells the girls she will shortly be leaving:

When e'er ye meet a fool that's fou,
That ye're a maiden gar him trow,
Seem nice, but stick to him like glew;
   And whan set down,
Drive at the jango till he spew,
   Syne he'll sleep soun.

So much for her professional instruction. Once the clients are asleep, other things should be remembered:

Cleek a' ye can be hook or crook,
Ryp ilky poutch frae nook to nook;
Be sure to truff his pocket-book,
　　Saxty pounds Scots
Is nae deaf nits: in little bouk
　　Lie great bank-notes.

In other words, roll the sleeping drunk over and do a thorough job on his
clothes. Rarely has a prostitute been portrayed so vividly, yet without any
loss to the reader of the absurdity of the human comedy on both sides.

Best of all in point of characterization, however, is his "Last Speech of a
Wretched Miser", a poem which has suggested to various critics a parallel
with Scott's observations on the miserable end of the elder Dumbiedykes in
The Heart of Midlothian:

O gear! I held ye lang thegither;
For you I starved my guid auld mither,
And to Virginia sauld my brither,
　　And crush'd my wife;
But now I'm gown, I kenna whither,
　　To lease my life!

My life! my god! my spirit yearns,
Not in my kindred, wife or bairns—
Sic are but very laigh concerns
　　Compar'd with thee;
When now this mortal rottle warns
　　Me I maun die.

It to my heart goes like a gun,
To see my kin, my graceless son,
Like rooks already are begun
　　To thumb my gear,
And cash that hasna seen the sun
　　This fifty year.

There is nothing of the "high style" about this sort of conversational
writing. It derives in part from the colloquial manner of Lyndsay's "The
Thrie Estates", and to a lesser extent from the light-metred political satires
of the seventeenth century, most of which were mere gutter-journalism
versified. Like Lyndsay before him, Ramsay was good at making literature
out of low life. He was simply not capable of achieving anything like the
"high style". When he did aspire to it, he resorted to flaccid Augustan
English, as unable as those who came after him to resolve the dichotomy

which the events of 1603 and 1707 had inflicted on the Scots tradition. Yet he managed to achieve at least an acceptable measure of compromise in his Scots ballad-opera, "The Gentle Shepherd" (1725), which anticipated John Gay's *The Beggar's Opera* by three years.

No one today would claim "The Gentle Shepherd" to be a masterpiece of the first order. Its rustic verse dealing with a village wooing is modelled on English pastorals, and follows Ramsay's own less successful Scots experiments of the same kind. In "Richy and Sandy", Richard Steele and Alexander Pope, in the Theocritean disguise of shepherds, discuss the death of their friend Edie (Joseph Addison). Less ludicrous is "Patie and Roger", where the subjects of the shepherds' conversation is love.

Patie and Roger are, indeed, the names of the two young men who woo Peggy and Jenny respectively, in "The Gentle Shepherd," Roger turning out to be the son of the laird, Sir William Worthy, who returns from exile to his neglected house some few miles from Edinburgh, following the Restoration, during the "twenty hours" in which the piece is set.

Patie's advice to the plaintive Roger on how to get the girl of his choice illustrates the way in which Ramsay's easy colloquial handling of the iambic pentameter in rhyming couplets just manages to keep the piece from degenerating into sentimental Kailyard:

Daft gowk! Leave off that silly whindging way;
Seem careless, there's my hand ye'll win the day.
Hear how I serv'd my lass I love as weel
As you do Jenny, and with heart as leel.
Last morning I was gay and early out,
Upon a dyke I lean'd glowring about,
I saw my Meg come linkan o'er the lea;
I saw my Meg, but Meggy saw na me:
For yet the sun was wading thro' the mist,
And she was close upon me ere she wist;
Her coats were kilted, and did sweetly shaw
Her straight bare legs that whiter were than snaw;
Her cockernony snooded up fou sleek,
Her haffet-locks hang waving on her cheek:
Her cheek sae ruddy, and her een sae clear;
And O! her mouth's like ony hinny pear.
Neat, neat she was in bustine waistcoat clean,
As she cam skiffing o'er the dewy green
Blythesome, I cry'd "My bonny Meg, come here,
I ferly wherefore ye're sae soon asteer;
But I can guess, ye're gawn to gather dew:"
She scour'd awa, and said: "What's that to you?"
"Then fare ye weel, Meg Dorts, and e'ens ye like,"
I careless cry'd, and lap in o'er the dike.

I trow, when that she saw, within a crack,
She came with a right thievless errand back;
Misca'd me first,—then bade me hound my dog
To wear up three waff ewes stray'd on the bog.
I leugh, and saw did she; then with great haste
I clasp'd my arms about her neck and waist,
About her yielding waist, and took a fouth
Of sweetest kisses frae her glowing mouth.
While hard and fast I held her in my grips,
My very soul came lowping to my lips.
Sair, Sair she flet wi' me 'tween ilka smack;
But weel I kent she meant nae as she spake.
Dear Roger, when your jo puts on her gloom,
Do you sae too, and never fash your thumb.
Seem to forsake her, soon she'll change her mood;
Gae woo anither, and she'll gang clean wood.   [mad

Patie's advice to create a Robene and Makyne situation pays off, the lads win their lasses, and the final song—like the others in the ballad-opera written to a folk-air, in this case "Corn-riggs are bonny"—finds Peggy (to give the "Meg" in the scene just quoted her more formal title, as befits a girl betrothed to a shepherd who turns out to be a future laird) dispensing discreet and characteristically Ramsayan advice:

Let lasses of a silly mind
    Refuse what maist they're wanting;
Since we for yielding were design'd
    We chastly should be granting.
Then I'll comply, and marry Pate
    And syne my cockernonny   [snood, a hair-gathering band
He's free to touzel air or late,   [rumple
    Where corn-riggs are bonny.   [early

Burns, much less concerned with the Kirk's traditional domestic virtues of chastity and sex-only-within-marriage, was to make an infinitely greater song out of that tune and its title line. One feels that Peggy's Pate would undoubtedly end up like his father, Sir William, dispensing comforting platitudes in Augustan English:

Be ever vertuous, soon or late you'll find
Reward and satisfaction to your mind.
The maze of life sometimes looks dark and wild;
And oft when hopes are highest, we're beguil'd.
Aft, when we stand on brinks of dark despair,
Some happy turn with joy dispels our care.

As an arranger, Ramsay took older Scots songs and gentilified them. Almost always, the originals were probably much better than his newer versions, judging by "Bessy Bell and Mary Gray", "My Daddy Forbad", "Jenny Nettles" and "Auld Lang Syne", four where comparison is still possible. These were mostly prepared for inclusion in Ramsay's anthology *The Tea-Table Miscellany*, the four volumes of which appeared in 1724, 1725, 1727 and 1732, a lacing together of old songs, patched songs and new. As a means of popularizing Scots song, it was highly successful, titled ladies and those of their servants who could read being equally anxious to have sight of it. Ramsay only indicated tune-titles in his volumes, leaving Alexander Stuart to produce in 1726 his *Music for Allan Ramsay's Collection of Scots Songs*, published without texts, the melodies supported by feeble instrumental bass lines. William Thomson, a well-known singer of Scots songs in his day, produced his *Orpheus Caledonius* in London in 1725, a second version containing fifty songs—twice the original number— coming out in 1733 with firmer bass-lines, but without acknowlegment to Ramsay, the author or arranger of most of the words.

Alongside his work as a song-writer and song-cobbler, Ramsay also carried out important work as editor and popularizer of the poetry of the Makars, a task he consolidated with the publication of his *Evergreen*** anthology in 1724. Unlike Watson, who used broadsheets or printed texts for his sources, Ramsay had access to the Bannatyne Manuscript. He probably also had the assistance of Thomas Ruddiman (1674–1757), David Hume's predecessor as Keeper of the Advocates' Library, the author of a school text-book *Rudiments of the Latin-Tongue* (1714), long popular with Scots classics masters, and for a time printer and publisher of the journal *The Mercury*. Even so, Ramsay, though less guilty of 'modernizing' than Watson, could not resist an occasional touch of Augustan smoothing, and in any case seems to have been a somewhat careless copyist with an imperfect knowledge of Middle Scots.

In atrocious imitation Middle Scots, Ramsay set out his aims:

Thair Warkis I've publisht, neat, correct and fair,
Frae antique manuscripts, with utmost cair.
Thus to their fame, a monument we raise,
Quhilk sall endure quhyle Tymis telld out be days.

His actual achievement hardly matched up to the first of these claims, for he even inserted two poems of his own, "The Eagle and the Robin Redbreast", and an absurdly pseudo-Middle Scots poem, the "Vision", palming it off as by "Ar. Scot". Yet by providing a link between the originals and the editions of such better-trained scholars of the later eighteenth cen-

* Less popular than its companion anthology, *Evergreen* was reprinted in 1761, 1824, 1874 and 1875.

tury as Hailes and Pinkerton—who, however, were much less concerned with patriotic popularization than Ramsay—the anthology served a useful purpose. In the circumstances of the times, it is not too difficult to see why he unwrinkled Dunbar's:

> And first of all, with bow in hand ybent,
> Come dame Beautee, rycht as scho wald me schent:
> Syne folowit all his dameselis yfere. . .

to:

> And first of all with Bow in Hand ay bent
> Came Beauty's *Dame* right as scho wald me schent
> Syne followit all her Damosells in Feir . . .

even if one may not approve of such pointless bowdlerization as changing "By Chryste" to "By Claude", and "Christe's blude" to "the blude". As A. M. Kinghorn has pointed out[1] in connection with the song "The Generous Gentleman", set to the tune of "The Bonny Lass of Branksom" and published in *The Tea-Table Miscellany*, Ramsay's attacks of gentility were sporadic, a more or less honest third stanza being succeeded by a fourth stanza in which the disease is suddenly in evidence:

> Ae little coat and bodice white,
>   Was sum of a' her claithing;
> Even these o'er mickle; . . . mair delyte
>   She'd given cled wi' naithing . . .

> She leand upon a flowry brae,
>   By which a burny trotted;
> On her I glowr'd my soul away,
>   While on her sweets I doated.

> A thousand beauties of desert,
>   Before had scarce alarm'd me,
> Till this dear artless struck my heart
>   And bot designing, charm'd me . . .

She was not so artless as the poet supposed, however, for:

> Hurry'd by love, close to my heart,
>   I grasp'd this fund of blisses;
> Wha smil'd and said, "Without a priest,
>   Sir, hope for nought but kisses."

Truly, Ramsay's wife, Christian Ross, had nothing to fear from her virtuous husband, the enthusiastic member of the Easy Club of whom their still more famous son, Allan Ramsay the painter, was to write:

> . . . he was of middle stature, or somewhat less, but well shaped and active; and enjoyed perpetual good health except that in his later years he was, now and then troubled with the gravel. His disposition was cheerfull and benevolent; and, what is not often the lot of men with lively imaginations, he was blest with an equality of mind, free from impatience or anxiety, and little elevated or cast down, with anything prosperous or adverse that befell him.

The poet's curious mixture of talent, energy, enterprise and bland lapses of taste—for instance, Ayton's first hint of "old lang syne" becomes with Ramsay:

> Should auld acquaintance be forgot,
>   Tho' they return with scars?
> These are the noble hero's lot
>   Obtain'd in glorious wars.
> Welcome, my Varo, to my breast . . .

—are thus made plain.

Ramsay was no match to Burns when it came to prose letter-writing, though Ramsay uses an unbuttoned loosely-punctuated Scots containing hardly any sexual references, at least in the surviving seventy-seven examples. His letters were designed entirely to convey information to the addressees. Yet there is something endearing about the cheerful old poet, who, from his house on the Mound (now part of Ramsay Gardens, and looking down on Sir John Steele's statue of him in Princes Street), could write to his friend, Sir Alexander Dick, on 17th December 1741:

> . . . You are baith but young yet,—for me, I am ane auld fellow tired with hurry and noise, and now wad fain indulge my self in a calm retreat while wrapt in my virtue and chearfullness I can survey the vanitys of the vulgar Great with contempt. In a word, I am grown a stark staring philosopher, and believe me, whoever can purchase this same happyness, by the arts of good management and living cheap, makes one of the best bargains. But Lord pity the covetous the humdrums and discontent, this tranquillity can never be their portion. . .[2]

From his new shop in the Luckenbooths, using the sign of Ben Jonson and Drummond of Hawthornden, Ramsay issued a new edition of his poems in 1728, followed by *Thirty Fables* in 1730 (their tattling English couplets not remotely standing comparison either with the originals of La

Fontaine, or with what Henryson had done for Aesop), and in 1736, a volume of *Scots Proverbs*. Ultimately, it derived from *Scottish Proverbs* (1641) by David Ferguson (d. 1598) and John Ray's *A Collection of English Proverbs* (1670), both of which had already provided source-material for Ramsay's near-hand quarry, the *Complete Collection of Scottish Proverbs* (1721) by James Kelly, a minister about whom little is known. Kelly, however, systematically anglicized the traditional saws; Ramsay did his best to restore the Scots.

An edition of Ramsay's poems was published in London in 1731 and a Dublin edition followed in 1736. He died in his grand house, nicknamed "The Goose-pie" by the burghers of Edinburgh because of its peculiar shape, on 7th January 1758, and was buried in Greyfriars Churchyard.

During the first half of the eighteenth century, other enthusiasts for the preservation of the Scots tradition were grouped around Ramsay: friends, correspondents, or associates in Edinburgh club-life. Among these was the gifted Sir John Clerk of Pennecuik (1676–1755), at whose country seat Ramsay stayed each summer. Sir John was a pupil of the Italian composer and violinist, Arcangelo Corelli, and about 1698 Clerk composed five cantatas for solo voice (four to a Latin, one to an Italian text). Another outcome of his European travels was a book of memoirs. Ramsay's contemporary detractors claimed that Sir John had a hand in "The Gentle Shepherd", a claim that a textual analysis of the styles of the two men hardly supports. But Clerk, who on inheriting his title forsook the arts in favour of running his estate and playing a part in national affairs—he was one of the commissioners in the negotiations preceding the Union—could turn out neat verses, as his best-known song testifies:

Merry may the maid be
    That marries the miller;
For, foul day and fair day,
    He's ay bringing til her;
Has aye a penny in his purse,
    For dinner and for supper;
And, gin she please, a good fat cheese
    And lumps of yellow butter.

There were also the two Alexander Pennecuik's, often confused. Dr Alexander Pennecuik (1652–1722), a medical practitioner from Newhall and Romano, published in 1715 *A Geographical and Historical Description of the Shire of Tweeddale, with a Miscellany and Curious Collection of Select Scottish Poems*. The poems reappeared by themselves in 1762, the collected works with a biographical memoir in 1815. The doctor's style is somewhat wooden, and even his best excursion into verse, "Truth's Travels", an allegory, uneasily marries the colloquial style of Ramsay with the pseudo-Middle Scots of Ramsay's *Evergreen* imitations.

When kirk was skaeled and preaching done,   [dispersed
    And men and women baith hame,
Nae man call'd Truth to his disjeun,   [breakfast
    Albeit he was of noble fame.
    There was not ane that kept a craim,   [booth, shop
But they had bacon, beef and ale,
    Yet no acquaintance Truth could claim,
To wish him worth a dish of kail.

Except pastors or judges sought him,
    I trow his dinner was but cauld;
For advocats much skaith they wrought him,   [harm
    He maks their gowns so bare and auld.
    And merchant men, that bought and sauld,
For sundrie things could not abide him,
    And poor craftsmen, albeit they would,
They had no portion to provide him.

Truth has never been a particularly welcome guest anywhere, so the complaint is hardly an original one. In any case, the debt to Lyndsay (Flatterie's speech after escaping the gallows in *the Thrie Estates*) and to Dunbar's "To the Merchants of Edinburgh" (particularly with regard to the tone, and to the stressing of the octosyllabics, though Dunbar's seven-line stanza is subtler) are obvious.

The other Alexander Pennecuik (d. 1730), who was no relation to the doctor, is a somewhat obscure figure. He died in poverty, but was also buried in Greyfriars Church. He seems quite consciously to have striven to divert some of Ramsay's popularity towards himself by producing rival poems on similar themes. Thus, Ramsay's "Elegy on John Cowper, Kirk-Treasurer's Man" and "The Last Speech of a Wretched Miser" were followed by Pennecuik's "Elegy on Robert Forbes, Kirk-Treasurer's Man" and "The Picture of a Miser; written of George Heriot's Anniversary, 3rd June 1728". There are other instances.

Unlike "Honest Allan", Pennecuik lacked money, literary tact and religious tolerance. He was therefore the poet of the close-mouths of Edinburgh, uninhibited by the gentilifying influences which contact with upper-class society, common sense and self-interest led Ramsay to cultivate, though Pennecuik was equally prone to banality. In "The Presbyterian Pope", he offers us a dialogue between Meg, one of Lucky Spence's pupils, and the Kirk Treasurer himself. He is made to seem a sort of precursor of Hollie Willy, full of high-sounding sentiments, but willing enough to waive them in return for suitable favours. Thus compromised, the exchange goes:

Meg: The auldest trade that's in the nation,
       Aamaist as auld as the creation,

> Shou'd be made an incorporation,
>   I'm no in joke,
> That we may trade wi' reputation,
>   Like burgher fowk.
>
> Kirk Treasurer: It may be done. Meg, say nae mair.
>   I'm deacon, and I'll take the chair . . .

What a timeless Scottish ring that confidential retort has about it!

William Hamilton of Bangour (1704–1754)—not to be confused with Hamilton of Gilbertfield—belonged to the landed gentry. He was 'out' with the Jacobites in the '45, celebrated the defeat of Sir John Cope at Prestonpans with an Augustan victory ode—an event much better marked by the song "Hey, Johnnie Cope, are ye waulking yet" by the Haddington farmer Adam Skirving (1719–1803), who actually witnessed the unfortunate Cope's enforced retreat at the head of his cowardly army—shared the heather and the cave in hiding with the Gaelic poet John Roy Stewart, and was finally pardoned in 1749. Soon after succeeding to the estate, his health drove him abroad, where he died of consumption at Lyons. His *Poems on Several Occasions* appeared in 1748, prefaced by Adam Smith. The only piece still worthy of notice is his ballad "The Braes of Yarrow", which inspired Wordsworth, and which is still anthologized. Some of its more unfortunate stanzas and lines are now usually expunged, lines such as:

> And why yon melancholias weeds
> Hang on the bonnie birks of Yarrow.

Hamilton of Bangour probably assisted Ramsay with *The Tea Table Miscellany*, as did Robert Crawford (1695–1732), whose father owned the property of Drumsoy, in Renfrewshire, and whose brother, Thomas, was a diplomat in the service of the Scottish court. Crawford wrote the vapid lyric beginning "What beauties does Flora disclose!" to the glorious tune "Tweedside". His lines are still remembered because Burns used Crawford's words rather than the less sentimental (and admittedly, in the matter of pace, less suitable) words by Lord Yester, for the *Scots Musical Museum*. Crawford also wrote *"The Bush abune Traquair"*, later touched up, though not improved, by Principal J. C. Shairp (1819–1885), and "Doun the Burn Davie", similarly interfered with, though to much greater effect, by Burns.

The most fruitful influence exerted by Ramsay was on Alexander Ross (1699–1784), who was born at Kincardine O'Neil, on Deeside, and spent his days on the slopes of Kincardine as schoolmaster at Lochlea. His *Helenore, or the Fortunate Shepherdess* appeared in 1768, when the author was in his seventieth year. It has some vivid passages of scenic description couched in the Lallans of the North-east, and a love-story rudely punctuated by a raid of Highland caterans. The similarity between *The Gentle Shepherd* and *Helenore* does not favour the later arrival on a by then rapidly changing literary scene.

Much livelier are Ross's songs, "The Rock and the Wee Pickle Tow", "The Bridal O't" and "Wooed and Married and A'", which catch success-fully more than purely regional humour. The latter song in particular, is highly effective:

Wooed and married and a',
  Married and wooed and a';
The dandilly toast of the parish   [over-admired
  Is wooed and married and a'.
The wooers will now ride thinner,
  And by, when they wonted to ca';
'Tis needless to speer for the lassie
  That's wooed and married and a'.

The girss had na freedom of growing
  As lang as she wasna awa',
Nor in the town could there be stowing
  For wooers that wanted to ca'.
For drinking and dancing and brulyies,   [broils
  And boxing and shaking of fa's,
The town was for ever in tulyies;   [turmoils
  But now the lassie's awa'.

But had they but ken'd her as I did,
  Their errand it wad ha'e been sma';
She neither kent spinning nor carding,
  Nor brewing nor baking ava'. . .
But wooers ran all mad upon her,
  Because she was bonnie and braw,
And sae I dread will be seen on her,
  When she's byhand and awa'.   [decided

The practice of ballad-patching began to develop about the same time as the old songs were being collected. Because of the intricately-knit struc-tural pattern-making of the oral tradition, faking a ballad was much more difficult than cobbling the refrain of a lyric. The one who most successfully fooled her contemporaries with a ballad of her own making was the daughter of Sir Charles Halkett of Pitferran, Lady Elizabeth Halkett, who in 1696 married Henry Wardlaw of Pitreavie. Her "Hardyknute", which Watson first published, was alleged to have been discovered in a vault in Dunfermline. It passed through Ramsay's *Evergreen* anthology as a genuine ballad, and was only called into question after Bishop Thomas Percy

(1729–1811) had included it in his *Reliques of Ancient Poetry*. Neither in structure nor in language does it really ressemble an oral ballad, although it is a good enough period "adventure" poem. Because it has one stanza which bears a superficial resemblance to the content of a stanza in "Sir Patrick Spens", it has been suggested that Lady Wardlaw may have had a hand in re-shaping that ballad. Linguistically, the argument is not convincing. One has only to compare the artificially expressed plight of the widowed heroine after the Battle of Harlaw:

> On Norway's coast the widowed dame
>   May wash the rocks with tears—
> May lang look o'er the shipless seas
>   Before her mate appears.

—with the more realistic picture of the widows left behind after the shipwreck of Sir Patrick Spens:

> O lang, lang may the ladies stand
>   Wi' their gold kems in their hair,
> Waiting for their ain dear lords,
>   For they'll see them na mair.

The image in the "Hardyknute" stanza is an upper-class literary conceit. The image in the older ballad not only reflects the ballad-makers' practice of depicting life as they fancied it to exist among their social betters, but more genuinely suggests the distraction of a bereaved female.

Another ballad-manufacturer was David Mallet, or Malloch, as he was originally called in Perthshire before altering the name to the softer form once he had become a literary hack in London. Mallet's "The Excursion" is too imitative of Thomson to be of any real interest now, while his play *Mustapha* gathers the same dust as most of the other ponderously declaimed eighteenth-century verse-tragedies based on stories of antiquity. He is remembered now, if at all, only for "William and Margaret", which Percy thought: "One of the most beautiful ballads in our own or any other language." A thwarted passion so strong as to be able to cause death, if not much encountered in medical treatises, is nevertheless evident in the folklore of many lands, reflected both in "The Wife of Usher's Well" and in Bürger's "Leonora". Mallet may well have had some original fragment to work upon.

Alison Rutherford (1712–1794) of Fairnilee, Selkirkshire, grew up to become an Edinburgh beauty, and, in 1731, to marry Patrick Cockburn. As Mrs Cockburn, she flourished in the role of hostess, and wrote a series of entertaining, gossipy letters which make delightful reading. Probably during her youth she produced one version of "The Flowers of the Forest". Strange to relate, her song was inspired, not by the memory of Flodden, but by the financial failure of several Border lairds with whom her father was friendly. Her version is decidedly inferior to the more direct version by Jean Elliot (1727–1805), sister of Sir Gilbert Elliot of Minto (1722–1777). He himself was the author of a rather weak pastoral song, "My Sheep I neglected", which has somehow managed to survive through various song collections. Both Miss Elliot and Mrs Cockburn were one-song poetesses, who, after the custom of the time, pretended that their productions were by other hands, song-writing not being as lady-like a pursuit as sewing.

Only mention need be given to George Halket (d. 1756) for his still popular song "Logie o' Buchan", before passing on to Ramsay's most important successor before Burns, Robert Fergusson (1750–1774).

Fergusson's parents came from Aberdeenshire, where part of his boyhood was spent, although he was actually born opposite Edinburgh's Tron Kirk in a house in the Cap-and-Feather Close, destroyed in 1767 when the North Bridge was built. He attended the High School for three years, then went on a bursary to the Grammar School at Dundee for two years. This course eventually led him to St Andrews University, where, for a further four years he was a student of Divinity. Rarely can what must have seemed a boon at the time sown seeds of such disastrous consequences. Six years later, the young man who left St Andrews in 1767 because of the financial difficulties resulting from his father's death, developed religious mania.

Faced with the need to find employment, Fergusson turned first to his Aberdeenshire uncle, John Forbes, a farmer who held several factorships and, according to Thomas Sommers, one of the poet's earliest biographers, a man who enjoyed "affluent" circumstances. Successful men of business are rarely sympathetic to impecunious, aspiring poets. After some sort of humiliating scene, Fergusson walked the hundred or so miles to Edinburgh, an effort which exhausted his delicate constitution.

There, once recovered, he got himself a job as a writer or copyist in the office of the Commissary Clerk, a dull position he held down for the rest of his short working life. His lively temperament soon produced a cluster of friends about him. His earliest surviving poems were three songs to Scots airs. They were written for one of these new-found friends, the castrato Tenducci, to sing in Dr Arne's opera *Artaxerxes* when it was being staged in Edinburgh. They are couched in the vapid fashionable English manner of the time:

O where shall I wander my lover to find
And with sweet discourses indulge my fond mind?
Once more I must view her before I depart,
And with mild embraces enliven my heart.

Fergusson's heart does not seem to have been much enlivened by any woman's embraces, mild or otherwise, so far as we can deduce from his work. But fortunately, something happened to turn the aspiring poet's interest from English to Scots, though the linguistic dichotomy of a spoken language apparently socially in decline set against a written language powerfully in the ascendent kept him still sporadically attached to what was considered by the upper classes to be the politer tongue.

It may have been a reading of some of Ramsay's vernacular poems, or it may have been the sheer raciness of the Scots-sounding day-to-day city life into which he increasingly plunged, that brought about Fergusson's linguistic conversion. In any case, "The Daft Days" by Robert Fergusson appeared in the January, 1772 number of Walter Ruddiman's *Weekly Magazine, or Edinburgh Amusement*, which had been founded in 1768 to encourage native talent in a way that the long-established *Scots Magazine*, with its strong London ties, had for long failed to do.

Fergusson's poems had an altogether livelier ring than anything the *Weekly Magazine* had hitherto printed. "The Daft Days" showed the pointing of a sprightlier creative intelligence than "Honest Allan" had ever been able to deploy; and it drew its strength from the sights and sounds and smells of urban life.

> Auld Reekie! thou'rt the canty hole,   [lively
> A bield for mony caldrife soul,   [shelter, chilly
> Wha snugly at thine ingle loll,
>   Baith warm and couth;
> While round they gar the bicker roll   [wooden drinking-cup
>   To weet their mouth.
>
> When merry Yule-day comes, I trow
> You'll scantlins find a hungry mou;
> Sma' are our cares, our stamacks fou
>   O' gusty gear,
> And kickshaws, strangers to our view,   [novelties
>   Sin Fairn-year.   [last-year

As was perhaps understandable in a poet brilliantly demonstrating the possibilities of what was clearly already a culture under seige, a defensive note of provincialism occasionally creeps in; a note quite foreign to the Makars, with their European contacts, but echoed by Burns in "The Jolly Beggars" and the "Address to a Haggis", and by MacDiarmid in "Crowdieknowe."

> Fidlers, your pins in temper fix,
> And roset weel your fiddle-sticks,
> And banish vile Italian tricks
>   From out your *quorum*,
> Nor *fortes* wi' *pianos* mix,
>   Gie's *Tulloch Gorum*.

For nought can cheer the heart sae weil
As can a canty Highland reel;
It even vivifies the heel
   To skip and dance:
Lifeless is he wha canna feel
   Its influence.

Ruddiman became the young poet's patron. According to Alexander Balloch Grossart, who edited an edition of Fergusson's poems in 1857, to which he prefaced a "Life"* claiming to have used original source-material subsequently lost or destroyed, Walter Ruddiman's sister, Janet, declared that her brother had made the young poet "regular payments for his poems as they appeared from week to week, and from 1771–72 the poet had a gift of two suits of clothes—one for week-days and one for Sundays."

There followed in March the "Elegy on the Death of Scots Music", in June "The King's Birth-Day in Edinburgh", in October "Caller Oysters" and "Braid Claith", and in November "To The Tron-Kirk Bell".

Enthusiastic readers were not slow to suggest that the mantle of Ramsay had found a new wearer—"Is Allan risen frae the deid?" one reader from Berwick, who signed himself J S, inquired in 1772, drawing from the poet a modest rhyming disclaimer, "Answer to Mr J S's Epistle".

In Fergusson's day, the building of the New Town had only recently begun. Though George Square was under construction, and in October, 1772 the barge "Marty" of Carron arrived at the eastern end of the Forth and Clyde Canal carrying oak for Sir Laurence Dundas's fine new house in St Andrew's Square,† the good folk of Edinburgh were still mostly crammed into its towering Old Town lands down the spine of the Royal Mile. Propinquity made life a social affair, what with turnpyke stairs, narrow wynds and closes, the unsavoury but necessary habit of crying "Gardyloo' at sundown from upper windows then tipping domestic slops down into the open street, and a gregarious tavern life, lack of room making home entertaining virtually an impossibility. Fergusson no doubt enjoyed himself as freely as most of his contemporaries, especially after he had been elected a member of the convivial Cape Club, with the title "Sir Precenter", in October 1772. Also under such fancied ennobling were "Sir Brimstone" (Alexander Runciman, whose sketch of the poet, made on the back of his "petition" for entry, is possibly more lifelike than the romanticized portrait in the National Portrait Gallery, Edinburgh); "Sir Thumb" (Alexander Nasmyth, painter of the famous portrait of Burns, now housed in the same collection); "Sir Scrape-Greystiel" (David Herd, the editor and folk-song collector, who had been Fergusson's proposer); "Sir Old-Wife" (Stephen Clarke, Burns's musical collaborator in the *Scots Musical*

* Subsequently augmented to a *Life* in the *Famous Scots* series, published in 1898.

† Now the headquarters of the Royal Bank of Scotland.

Museum); "Sir Tumult" (James Balfour, a well-known singer); and "Sir Sluggard" (Deacon Brodie, a respected citizen by day, but a house-breaker by night, eventually to be hanged on a gibbet of his own designing in his magisterial capacity, and later to become the prototype for Stevenson's *Dr Jeykll and Mr Hyde*). Other members included Henry Raeburn, later genuinely knighted; the actor William Woods; the manager of the Theatre Royal, Stephen Kemble; barbers, saddlers, advocates, shipowners, naval officers and Thomas Sommers, who held the sinecure of H.M. Glazier for Scotland, but saw enough of Fergusson to make him a biographer with an eye for physical detail:

His complexion [was] fair; but rather pale. His eyes full, black and piercing. His nose long, his lips thin, his teeth well set and white. His shoulders narrow and his limbs long, but more sinewy than fleshy.

Another who knew him, and who claimed that he had "almost nightly enjoyed his company" says that "in stature Fergusson was about five feet nine, slender and handsome. His face never exhibited the least trace of red, but was perfectly and uniformly pale, or rather yellow. He had all the appearance of a person in delicate health. His forehead was elevated, and his whole countenance open and pleasing. He wore his own fair brown hair* with a long massive curl along each side of the head, and terminating in a queue, dressed with a black silk ribband. His dress was never very good, but often much faded, and the white thread stockings which he generally wore in preference to the more common kind of grey worsted, he often permitted to become considerably soiled before changing them." Alexander Campbell adds: "His countenance was somewhat effeminate, but redeemed by the animation imparted to it by his large black eyes."

The Cape Club usually met every evening about seven o'clock and dispersed before the hour when the "noisy ten-hour drum of the City Gaird," or "black banditti", as Fergusson called this inadequate police force, heralded the descent of the "impure ablution from the garrets", though now and again they would carouse until eleven or so. Fergusson was apparently much in demand as a singer, and was renowned not only for his ready wit but for his practical jokes.

Then, suddenly, Fergusson one day told Woods that he was on his way to denounce to Lord Kames "one of the miscreants who had crucified our Saviour". The poet stopped writing, burned his manuscripts, and sank into a religious mania. He made a sally in connection with an election into "one of the eastern counties" early in 1774, caught a chill, and appeared among his friends of the Cape Club no more. Early in July they raised a fund for his benefit. There was rumour of his recovery. But by the end of July, he had been "seized with a very dangerous sickness."

* A lock, found in the Chambers' copy of the 1807 edition of Fergusson's poems, is preserved in the National Library, Edinburgh.

One September evening, he recovered sufficiently to go out and drink with a friend. Falling "from a stair-case", however, he sustained concussion. He soon became violent and was removed, raving, to the city bedlam, where he was found by a visitor "lying with his clothes on, stretched upon a bed of loose straw."

He died on 16th October 1774, "in the cells", as the official record puts it, not quite twenty-four years old. Dr Chalmers Davidson has conjectured that the poet probably suffered from "a manic depressive psychosis", but that "given modern care and treatment Fergusson would have recovered", perhaps to survive "another fifteen years without a relapse."[3] He could thus have been at the height of his powers when Robert Burns came to Edinburgh in 1786.

As it was, using a Scots that was certainly not pure Edinburgh (any more than Burns's Scots was pure Ayrshire) but employing such North-east turns of phrase as "Hyne awa" for "far away", "nae" rather than "not" after a verb, "skelf" for "Shelf", and so on, and often following Ramsay's habit of spelling Scots as if it was English—"creature" is on one occasion made to rhyme with "nature", when what the poet must clearly have heard in his mind's ear was "craitur" and "naitur"—and anticipating Burns and, more especially Byron, with such fantastic rhymes as "capernoity"/"banditti", "fash us"/"Parnassus", "duddies"/"proud is", and "gart lich"/"heart-ache", Fergusson enshrined in his best poems the spirit of the ordinary people of Edinburgh. Upwards of five hundred copies of *Poems by Robert Fergusson* were published in Edinburgh at two shillings and six pence by Drummond and Elliot early in 1773, perhaps at the expense of the Ruddimans. While it is unlikely that Grossart's report of the fantastic success of the volume is accurate, the poet apparently made twice what Burns secured from his Kilmarnock edition. But there was no similar outpouring of eulogizing reviews. Fergusson's initial appeal had been to the general reader, who no doubt appreciated what Sydney Goodsir Smith has called his "personal kind of utterance", his directness of approach, rather than to the literati.

Although Fergusson never wholly relinquished his interest in Englishing—for instance, he produced three decidedly feeble songs, "Where winding Forth adorns the vale", "No repose can I discover" and "Amidst a rosy bank of flowers" for *A Collection of Scots Songs adapted for a Voice and Harpsichord* printed and sold by Neil Stewart "at his shop, Millars Square Opposite to the Tron Church" in 1772—his main concerns were with urban people, and scenes from the vantage-point of one who participated in their pleasures and tribulations.

He celebrated the delights of the produce of the Forth in "Caller Oysters".

Whan big as burns the gutters rin,
Gin ye hae catcht a droukit skin,

To *Luckie Middlemist's* loup in,
      And sit fu' snug
O'er oysters and a dram o' gin,
      Or haddock lug.

the pleasures of "Hallow-Fair"; the gay social parade at "Leith Races",
with its overtones of "Christ's Kirk" and "Peebles to the Play"; the inescapable annoyance of "The Tron-Kirk Bell":

Your noisy tongue, there's nae abideint,
Like scaulding wife's, there is nae guideint:
When I'm 'bout ony bus'ness eident,
      It's sair to thole;   [put up with
To deave me, than, ye tak a pride in't
      Wi' senseless knoll.   [hillock

O! war I provost o' the town,
I swear by a' the powers aboon,
I'd bring ye wi' a reeshle down;   [rustle
      Nor shud you think
(Sae sair I'd crack and clour your crown)
      Again to clink.

Sometimes, as happens with many poets, a prose report in *Ruddiman's
Weekly* touched off a poem. Thus, in the issue of 10th September 1772,
commenting on the collapse of the Ayr bank of Douglas and Heron, a
writer opines:

The scarcity of money . . . is not entirely owing to the late failures; for, if
we consider the great balances which England annually draws from us, for
broad-cloths, silks, grain groceries etc., and many other articles, there will be
found, in a great measure, the cause of our want of money. If . . . our nobility
and gentry would stay more at home, and improve their estates . . . in place
of spending their fortunes in London; and if all ranks would join in encouraging our own manufactures, particularly Scots broad-cloth, we might soon
expect to see plenty of money in the country.

Could it be chance that Fergusson's poem for 15th October was called
"Braid Claith"?

Braid Claith lends fock an unco heese,   [gives people a lift of spirit
Makes mony kail-worms butter-flies,
Gies mony a doctor his degrees
      For little skaith: [harm

In short, you may do what you please
Wi' gude Braid Claith.

During 1773, a language controversy raged in the pages of *Ruddiman's*. Someone calling himself "Anthropos" summed up the case against Scots by saying:

Though my heart beats as warm with a partiality for old Caledonia as that of any man, yet I cannot see any diminution that its ancient glory would suffer by giving up a dialect which we all disdain to write in, for a language, in point of beauty and energy, the first perhaps in the world.

A rival retorted that it might be

more judicious in us to . . . retain these words and phrases to help enrich our mother language, rather than by rejecting them, oblige ourselves to have recourse to a tedious circumlocution . . . which might have been avoided, by retaining such particular words as have no exact synonyms in the English language.

Plainly, the ding-and-dang dichotomy was hard at work among the *Magazine's* readers. In September of that year, in "The Election", Fergusson made his stance plain:

"Whar's Johnny gaun," cries neebor Bess,
  "That he's sae gayly bodin   [supplied
Wi' new kam'd wig, weel syndet face,   [washed
  Silk hose, for hamely hodin?"   [homely, rough, grey material
"Our Johnny's nae sma' drink you'll guess,
  He's trig as ony muir-cock,
An' forth to mak a Deacon, lass;
  He downa speak to poor fock."

Again, as John W. Oliver pointed out, "when a controversy was raging over the Mortmain Bill, which, had it become law, would have adversely affected the return from such charitable foundations as Heriot's Hospital and George Watson's Hospital,"[4] Fergusson came up with a racy dialogue called "The Ghaists: A Kirkyard Eclogue", in which Watson and Heriot discuss things much as Burns's Auld and New Brigs, in "The Brigs of Ayr", were later to do.

Burns's most obvious direct debt to Fergusson is, of course, his portrait of the country smallholder drawn in "The Cottar's Saturday Night". With Burns's uneasy alternation between colloquial Scots and Augustan English, and his hysterical (not to say hypocritical!) outburst about seduced Jenny, the hint for which is also to be found in the older poem, Burns scarcely matches the unified, homely dignity of Fergusson's "The Farmer's Ingle".

Peace to the husbandman and a' his tribe,
  Whase care fills a' our wants from year to year;
Lang may his sock and couter turn the gleyb, [ploughshare, strip of land
  And bauks o' corn bend down wi' laden ear.
May Scotia's simmers ay look gay and green,
  Her yellow har'sts frae scowry blasts decreed;   [scouring
May a' her tenants sit fu' snug and bien,
  Frae the hard grip of ails and poortith freed,   [poverty
And a lang lasting train o' peacefu' hours succeed.

But Fergusson's masterpiece is undoubtedly "Auld Reekie", which, as it comes down to us, some critics have suggested is merely the first part of what was to have been a longer poem. Yet it is an entity as it stands, tracing the passing of an Edinburgh day from the moment when:

. . . morn, with bonny purpie-smiles,
Kisses the air-cock o' St Giles;
Rakin their een, the servant lasses
Early begin their lies and clashes . . .

to:

. . . Night, that's cunzied chief for fun,   [known
Is wi' her usual rites begun;
Thro' ilka gate the torches blaze,
And globes send out their blinking rays.
The usefu' cadie plies in street   [message
To bide the profits o' his feet;
For by thir lads Auld Reekie's fock   [these
Ken but a sample o' the stock
O' thieves that nightly wad oppress,
And make baith goods and gear the less.

Here are the sights, smells, sounds and daily ongoings of this smoky old town Fergusson affectionately dubbed "Auld Reekie", the phrase which titles his poem, and Burns later addressed as "Edina, Scotia's darling seat"! Evocatively, Fergusson fills in his urban imagery with the kind of local detail he knows so well:

Gillespie's snuff should prime the nose
Of her that to the market goes,
If they wad like to shun the smells,
That buoy up frae markest cells;   [darkest
Whare waves o' paunches sav'ry scent

To nostrils gi'e great discontent.
Now wha in Albion could expect
O' cleanliness sic great neglect?
Nae Hottentot that daily lairs   [lies
'Mang tripe, or ither clarty wares,
Hath ever yet conceiv'd, or seen
Beyond the Line, sic scenes unclean.

There are deft portraits of the drunken dandy, or "macaroni" as he was
then called, fallen insensible in the street where slop-pails had already been
emptied:

Whan feet in dirty gutters plash,
And fock to wale their fitstaps fash;   [pick their steps carefully
At night the macaroni drunk,
In pools or gutters aftimes sunk:
Hegh! what a fright he now appears,
Whan he his corpse dejected rears!
Look at that head, and think if there
The *pomet* slaister'd up his hair!
The cheeks observe, where now cou'd shine
The scancing glories o' carmine?
Ah, legs! in vain the silk-worm there
Display'd to view her eidant care;   [eager
For stink, instead of perfumes, grow,
And clarty odours fragrant flow.

What Burns owed to Fergusson for the idea of this trick of ironic contrast, also used in "To a Louse", needs no stressing.
    Then there is Fergusson's unforgettable picture of the "staff" of such es-
tablishments as Lucky Spence's, which Ramsay had pictured from the complacent male aspect. In "Auld Reekie", we are shown the other side of this
particular social coin:

Near some lamp-post, wi' dowy face,
Wi' heavy een, and sour grimace,
Stands she that beauty lang had kend,
Whoredom her trade, and vice her end.
But see wharenow she wuns her bread,
By that which Nature ne'er decreed;
And sings sad music to the lugs
'Mang burachs o' damn'd whores and rogues.   [gatherings

By the time Ramsay reached the age of twenty-four, he was still a wigmaker. Had Burns died in his twenty-fourth year, he might have been

remembered for "Poor Mailie's Elegy" and a handful of songs. In the light
of these comparisons, what Fergusson did achieve in so short a space of time
seems doubly remarkable. He handled both "Standard Habbie" and the
octosyllabic rhyming couplet with ease and fluency. When writing in
Scots, while he may now and then have let pass an occasional unpressurized
stanza or passage, his more ardent intelligence kept him well clear of those
cliché-soaked swamps of banality into which Ramsay so often and so
blythly fell, apparently unaware of what had happened to him.

When writing in English, Fergusson remained an imitative versifier, one
of his last poems in what was for him the lesser tongue still containing lines
like:

Oh exercise! thou healing power,
The toiling rustic's chiefest dower.

As Burns well knew, that was not quite how an agricultural labourer of
1774 would have regarded his working conditions.

Much has been made of the fact that Fergusson wrote so few songs, since
he was both a singer and also friendly with musicians as widely different in
character and talent as Stephen Clarke and Tenducci. Of Fergusson's two
Scots songs, "My Ain Kind Deary, O!" might be better remembered if
Burns had not infused into broadly similar sentiments a more touching tenderness, a warmer passion. Sang Fergusson:

Will ye gang o'er the lee-rigg,
  My ain kind deary, O!
And cuddle there sae kindly,
  Wi' me, my kind deary O!

At thornie-dike and birken tree
  We'll daff, and ne'er be weary O;
They'll scug ill een frae you and me,   [screen
  Mine ain kind deary, O!

Nae herds wi' kent, or colly there, [shepherd's pole used for leaping ditches
  Shall ever come to fear ye O;
But lav'rocks, whistling in the air
  Shall woo, like me, their deary, O!

While others herd their lambs and ewes,
  And toil for warld's gear, my jo,
Upon the lee my pleasure grows
  Wi' you, my kind deary O!

Burns, in his interleaved copy of the *Scots Musical Museum*, recorded a folk-version which may also have been known to Fergusson, the second half of the eight-line stanza of which goes:

Altho' the night were ne'er sae wat,
    And I were ne'er sae weary, O,
I'll rowe thee o'er the lea-rig,
    My ain kind dearie O.

Fergusson's fellow Cape Club "knight", David Herd—whose *Ancient and Modern Scottish Songs (1776)* is one of the most important eighteenth-century folk-song source books—collected yet another version:

Tho' the night were ne'er sae dark,
    And I were ne'er sa weary,
I'd meet thee on the ley-rig
    My ain kind deary.

The idea contained in the first line, as William Montgomerie has pointed out, survived into a ballad known to the nineteenth-century collector, Peter Buchan, in a piece entitled "The Ware-Horse". More importantly, it appeared in Burns's song "The Lea-Rig", of which the first two stanzas show how much more pointedly than anyone else he could make use of folk-material. With Fergusson, Herd and Buchan, we get a picture of a pastoral cuddling-session (with Buchan—"Then row me up and row me doon"—perhaps a hint of something more energetic): but with Burns, we are made aware, by direct statement rather than through moralizings over "Warld's gear", of the tired return from the new-ploughed field of man and beast, and the importance put upon the love-relationship in the limited context of the realities of agricultural life:

When o'er the hill the eastern star
    Tells bughtin' time is near, my jo;
And owsen frae the furrow'd field
    Return sae dowf and weary O;
Down by the burn, where scented birks
    Wi' dew are hangin' clear, my jo,
I'll meet thee on the lea-rig,
    My ain kind dearie O.

At mid-night hour, in mirkest glen,
    I'd rove, and ne'er be eerie O,
If thro' that glen I gaed to thee,
    My ain kind dearie O.
Altho' the night were ne'er sae wild,
    And I were ne'er sae weary O,

I'll meet thee on the lea-rig,
  My ain kind dearie O.

Burns's handling is incomparably the surest. But song-making and song-repairing only became his main preoccupation comparatively late in his creative life. Fergusson, though clearly also in touch with the same folk-sources that Burns was later to exploit, simply had insufficient time granted to him to become the accomplished song-maker his two Scots examples suggest he might possibly have done.

W. E. Henley, in an essay in his Burns Centenary Edition, perhaps sums up the nature of Fergusson's achievement better than most:

"He had intelligence and an eye, a right touch of humour, the gifts of observation and style together with a true feeling for country and city alike; and his work . . . with its easy expressiveness, its vivid and unshrinking realism, and a merit in the matter of character and situation . . . is nothing less than memorable. . . .

Fergusson was essentially an Edinburgh product. . . . The old Scots capital, gay, squalid, drunken, lettered, venerable, lives in his verses."

It would be an overstatement to suggest that had Ramsay and Fergusson not preceded him, Burns would not have been a poet. Quite certainly, he would have been a very different kind of poet. There are some artists who are innovators, albeit within the framework of that inevitable continuity which binds together human affairs. Others take forms fashioned by their predecessors and adapt them to their own characteristic uses. Burns in literature, like his contemporary Mozart in music, belonged to the second category.

In the purely formal sense, Burns was no innovator. He took up traditional themes—the mock elegy, the duologue, the meditations of living or dying animals, the folk-song in need of mending—and well-used forms, like "standard Habbie", the more complicated *Cherrie and the Slae* stanza, and the octosyllabic couplet. These he infused with a greater strength and a wider range of feeling than Ramsay could muster or Fergusson was granted enough of life to master.

Like Fergusson's ancestors, Burns's father came from the North-east, William Burnes (1721–84)—the poet was the first to drop the "e" from the spelling of the family name—was running a small market garden at Alloway, near Ayr, when the poet was born in a two-roomed thatched cottage on 25th January 1759. The poet's mother, Agnes Broun (1732–1820), had seven children in all. The poet was the eldest. He himself recalled her ability to tell stories, while his sister noted that their mother "possesed a fine musical ear, and sang well".

When the future poet was seven, his father found that the market garden could no longer support his growing family, so he set up home in the farm of Mount Oliphant, a few miles away. It was while the family was at Mount Oliphant that Burns got much of his schooling, the father having the traditional Scots respect for education. Limited though it was by circumstances, it was still more extensive than that afforded to the average rural Scots boy of Burns's time.

By Whitsun 1777, William Burnes managed to free himself from the unprofitability of this farm just in time to escape ruin, moving to Lochlea, midway between Tarbolton and Mauchline. By then, Burns had started to labour with his father in the fields, and had gained his first insight into the burdens of the agricultural worker: a life which he himself said combined "the cheerless gloom of a hermit with the ceaseless toil of a galley-slave." He had also probably done that damage to his heart which was to result in his early death.

The adolescent Burns attended a young man's debating society and a dancing class in Tarbolton, the latter "in absolute defiance" of his stern, Calvinistic father's wishes. So long as he lived, however, the old man managed to hold in check the ardently expanding temperament of his most gifted son. But in February 1784, worn older than his years, William Burnes died, after victoriously concluding a long drawn-out dispute with his landlord which went the length of the Court of Session. Robert and his brother Gilbert then became partners in the farm of Mossgiel, which they rented from the Ayr lawyer Gavin Hamilton when it became obvious that their father was unlikely to live much longer.

Gilbert Burns remained at Mossgiel during the remainder of his brother's days, though he was only able to weather one particularly severe crisis with the aid of a loan from Robert. But the poet spent less and less time over farm concerns and more and more on literature and the lasses. In the series of great satires which he produced during 1786, he thundered against the hypocrisy of the extreme narrow "Auld Licht" sect of the Kirk, using their purely local squabbles to reflect his humanity and concern for universal values. He also started a series of ardent philanderings. Over the years, Burns's pre-marital and extra-marital affairs resulted in a fairly numerous brood of illegitimate children; but also in the warmest, richest, most tender and most sensuous love-songs that any poet has given to the world.

His seduction of Jean Armour, a Mauchline mason's daughter, and the repudiation of him which her outraged parents insisted upon, threw him into an emotional tangle which it is now impossible to sort out with any certainty. He may well have married her by declaration—valid under Scots Law until 1939—before her parents moved her to Paisley, away from him. At any rate, his entanglement with "Highland" Mary Campbell, whom he invited (in verse) to flee with him to Jamaica—that unsavoury haven of eighteenth-century Scots in trouble!—ended with her mysterious death at Greenock in 1786. Jean Armour thereafter bore twins, and Robert rode off to Edinburgh to be lionized, the triumph of his "Kilmarnock Poems", published earlier that year, having made him a celebrity, the so-called "ploughman poet" without whom a smart party in the capital was not considered complete. In Edinburgh, he had his affair with Agnes

("Clarinda") Maclehose, summed up so poignantly in the song "Ae fond kiss". There, too, he met the engraver James Johnson, then planning to publish his *Scots Musical Museum* as a permanent repository for Scots folk-songs. Fortunately, Johnson invited Burns's aid. Burns soon became virtually editor of the *Museum*, and during the last ten years of his life, "Tam o' Shanter" apart, he poured all his rich genius into the moulds of song-writing and song-repairing prepared for him by Johnson and, later, by another editor, the dilettante clerk, George Thomson, with his *Select Scottish Airs*.

But after a while, Edinburgh grew tired of Burns and left him with the problem of earning a living unsolved. In April 1788—after having seduced her once again, and wrapped his intentions and actions in further epistolary mystifications to his friends—Burns suddenly acknowledged his marriage to Jean Armour. From June 1788 until November 1791, he farmed Ellisland in Dumfriesshire, latterly holding at the same time an Excise appointment. Thereafter, until his death in July 1796, Burns lived in Dumfries, working as an officer in the Dumfries Port Division of the Excise. He died, not as his unctuous nineteenth-century biographers tried to make out, from excesses either of wine or of women, but from some form of endocarditis, established at Lochlea when the boy had to perform the labours of a man.

Burns's literary background[5] encompassed not only the work of Ramsay, Fergusson and the others, but also that of the older Makars as reprinted by Watson and Ramsay, and the prose and verse of the near-contemporary English school of Pope, Collins, Gray, Shenstone, and the Scot, Thomson. Burns also tells of the influence of another unidentified book:

> The Collection of Songs was my vade mecum. I pored over them, driving my cart or walking to labor, song by song, verse by verse; carefully noting the true tender or sublime from affectation and fustian. I am convinced I owe much to this for my critic-craft such as it is.

Burns also had a grounding in Shakespeare and Milton, and a knowledge of the Bible, together with some of the numerous concordances and interpretative commentaries then popular. The English poets may have alerted his sensibilities, although they also inspired from time to time most unfortunate emulation. Fortunately, the Bible did not have the disastrously disruptive effect it had on Fergusson. One of the symptoms of the heart disease caused in Burns by an excess of physical strain in boyhood produced in him a morbid anxiety often reflected in his letters. It also found expression in "Winter: A Dirge", such fragments as "Remorse", and more effectively, in that other dirge which mirrors the age-old acceptance of their lot by generation after generation of labourers who were tied to the land, "Man was made to mourn".

> O Death! the poor man's dearest friend,
> The kindest and the best!

Welcome the hour my aged limbs
   Are laid with thee at rest!
The great, the wealthy fear thy blow,
   From pomp and pleasure torn,
But oh! a blest relief for those
   That weary-laden mourn!

Burns tells us in his famous autobiographical letter to Dr John Moore that it was the combination of love and poetry which induced him first to commit "The sin of RHYME".

You know our country custom of coupling a man and woman together as Partners in the labors of Harvest.—In my fifteenth autumn, my Partner was a bewitching creature who just counted an autumn less. My scarcity of English denies me the power of doing her justice in that language; but you know the Scotch idiom. She was a bonie, sweet, sonsie lass. In short, she altogether un-wittingly to herself, initiated me in a certain delicious Passion, which in spite of acid Disappointment, gin-horse Prudence and bookworm Philosophy, I hold to be the first of human joys, our dearest pleasure here below. How she caught the contagion I can't say; you medical folks talk much of infection by breathing the same air, the touch, &c. but I never expressly told her that I loved her. Indeed I did not well know myself, why I liked so much to loiter behind with her, when returning in the evening from our labors; why the tones of her voice made my heartstrings thrill like an Eolian harp; and par-ticularly, why my pulse beat such a furious ratann when I looked and fingered over her hand, to pick out the nettle-stings and thistles. Among her other love-inspiring qualifications, she sung sweetly; and 'twas her favorite reel to which I attempted giving an embodied vehicle in rhyme.—I was not so presumtive as to imagine that I could make verses like printed ones, com-posed by men who had Greek and Latin; but my girl sung a song which was said to be composed by a small country laird's son, on one of his father's maids, with whom he was in love; and I saw no reason why I might not rhyme as well as he, for excepting smearing sheep and casting peats, his father living in the moors, he had no more Scholar-craft than I had:[6]

The names of the girls with whom he had made love, or the women too far above his station for physical contact but whom he "used" emotionally to rouse himself to song, are scattered through the Burns story. The com-bination of love and poetry, the two main outlets for his exuberance, was to lead him into many a difficulty, and leave him with frequent pangs of remorse. Yet in his poetic oddysey, "The Vision", he saw clearly that the creative, the hedonistic impulses, are closely related, deriving from the one source.

I saw thy pulse's maddening play,
Wild-send thee Pleasure's devious way,

Misled by Fancy's meteor-ray,
  By passion driven.
But yet the light that led astray
  Was light from Heaven.

It was frequently sexual passion which inspired Burns, the song-writer. It was passion of another sort which set him thundering off upon the series of satires against the hypocrisies of behaviour and belief among the reactionary "Auld Licht" followers of the Church, and compassion for the underdog which resulted in "The Jolly Beggars". Associated with these poems of his early manhood are the verse-epistles which memorably enshrine common sense maxims so that they ring with the clear inevitability of proverbs.

Only once in his lifetime had Burns the chance to present to the public a completely new book of verse the contents of which he had fully revised and polished. *Poems, Chiefly in the Scottish Dialect* appeared from the Kilmarnock press of John Wilson on 31st July 1786 at a cost of three shillings the copy. Six hundred and twelve copies were printed, and the edition was sold out just over a month after publication.

Two Edinburgh editions of his poems were also produced during his lifetime. The first was printed by William Smellie and published by William Creech, by subscription "for the sole benefit of the author", on 21st April 1787. A second printing of this edition—three thousand copies in all, costing three shillings to subscribers and six to others—had a famous misprint in the "Address to a Haggis", "skinking" becoming "stinking".

A few days later, advised by Henry Mackenzie, Burns disposed of the property of his poems for one hundred guineas. Creech then put out the second Edinburgh Edition on 18th February 1793, in two volumes, "greatly enlarged with new poems." Included in the fifty extra pages was the one major sustained creative effort of Burns's post-Edinburgh years, "Tam o' Shanter". This edition was re-issued in 1794.

From the Kilmarnock Edition, Burns probably cleared just over £50, and about £855 from the first Edinburgh Edition, together with the proceeds from the sale of the copyright. This meant that so as far as the second Edinburgh Edition was concerned, Burns received only a few complimentary copies from Creech.

Burns wanted no money for the song-writing work he did for Johnson and Thomson. As he told Thomson: "As to my remuneration, you may think my Songs either *above* or *below* price, for they shall absolutely be the one or the other. In the honest enthusiasm with which I embark in your undertaking, to talk of money, wages, fee, hire, and etc., would be downright Sodomy of Soul!" Towards the end of his short life Burns, fancying he was being dunned by a tailor, begged Thomson to send him £12, which that editor immediately did.

As a by-product of his song-writing, Burns made a collection of bawdy song-versions, some no doubt original, others perhaps touched up by the poet, although Professor Egerer has recently conjectured that only six of the pieces in what came to be known after Burns's death as *The Merry Muses of Caledonia* are actually by Burns.

As he himself made plain, the pattern of Burns's creative endeavour and achievement began with song, went on to lead him to produce poems on themes by Fergusson, almost always packing greater emotional force in lesser bulk and exhibiting a lither linguistic fluency, then burst out into the great satires against that Calvinistic repression which had more or less held Scotland in joyless thrall since the Reformation, making leisure and pleasure, especially sexual pleasure, seem guilty things.

At this stage in his career, Burns's ardent nature had involved him in his own sexual difficulties, as it was to do almost to the end of his life. His "critic-craft" had led him to consider whether or not he had by then enough manuscripts in his desk to make up a volume which could stand comparison with books by more regularly educated urban writers—Burns was always a little self-conscious about his lack of a more extensive orthodox education, which perhaps explains his fondness for scattering French phrases through letters written to people he was particularly anxious to impress.

He was also recurrently uncertain in which direction his gifts lay. At least at the time he was writing his best work, dealing with the basic strengths, needs and weaknesses of humankind universal in their significance, whether urban or rural in setting, he knew that Scots was his true *métier*. But the inherited dichotomy first awakened by his education, and widened by his visit to Edinburgh, was stimulated there by such friends as Dr Hugh Blair (1718–1800)—who, in 1787, successfully urged him not to include "The Jolly Beggars" in his collection—and Dr John Moore (1729–1802), who became interested in Burns after the poet's "mother-confessor" friend Mrs Dunlop had sent him a copy of the Kilmarnock Edition. Thereafter, Moore tried to persuade Burns to abandon Scots in favour of Thomsonian English nature-verse, "only livelier". The fact that the texts of poems from the Kilmarnock volume were to some extent Englished for the Edinburgh editions—the "ing" ending in most case replacing the Scots "an" or "in" (both a corruption from the Middle Scots "and",) "o'er" being used instead of "owre"—suggests either that Burns's urban connections from 1786 onwards made him realize that the Scots language was thinning as a spoken tongue, or that he himself had simply become less interested in Scots for its own sake than he had been when first confined to what he called his rural "shades". The fact that the later songs are in a very much thinner Scots than either the earlier songs or the majority of poems in the Kilmarnock volume, could be advanced to support both theories.

In his autobiographical letter to Moore—that "honest narrative" whose purpose seems as much to have been to reinforce the writer's self-assurance on the rightness of the stand he had taken by the traditions of Scots as to amuse or inform his Edinburgh friend and patron—Burns claims that the "great misfortune" of his life was "never to have AN AIM". This may have been so in a material sense, although had he lived, there is evidence to suggest that he would soon have risen much higher in the Excise. He believed his other misfortune to be too great an addiction to what he called "a certain fashionable failing", which led to much tutting by old women of both sexes in the nineteenth century though, so far as is known, no complaints from those on whom the poet actually exercised it. These two characteristics combined to make a poet of this man who, his dry old friend John Syme of Dumfries said, had eyes that were "coals of living fire"; whom the Duchess of Gordon confessed was the only man who had ever "carried her off her feet" (presumably she was speaking metaphorically!); and of whom another upper-class and therefore physically unobtainable woman—the close friend of Burns's last years, Maria Riddell—was to aver that she knew of no man "ever gifted with a larger portion of the *vivenda vis animi*".

The poems in direct emulation of Fergusson include "Scotch Drink", stimulated by the earlier poet's "Caller Water"; "The Twa Dogs", inspired by "The Mutual Complaint of Plainstanes and Causey"; "The Holy Fair", touched off, perhaps by "Hallow Fair"; and "The Cottar's Saturday Night", which alone among those and other possible pattern-pairings, leaves Fergusson the sounder of the stronger and more genuine strain.

Over and over again Burns acknowledged the influence of his ". . . elder brother in misfortune, by far my elder brother in the muse"—verbally repaying a far greater debt than had actually been incurred. Thus, in answering William Simson, a schoolmaster in Ochiltree who indulged in the then currently fashionable practice of penning verse-epistles—as also did Lapraik and Sillar, countrymen better educated than most of their kind, pleasant company for young farmer Burns, and whose poetic abilities he therefore exaggerated—the poet indicated the direction in which his "absence of aim" was already leading him;

My senses wad be in a creel,
Should I but dare a hope to speel,
Wi' Allan, or wi' Gilbertfield,
    The braes o' fame;
Or Fergusson, the writer-chiel,
    A deathless name.

The special force of his debt to Fergusson is underlined by the next stanza, bracketed in parenthesis:

O Fergusson! thy glorious parts
Ill suited laws dry, musty arts!
My curse upon your whunstane hearts,
   Ye E'nbrugh gentry!
The tythe o' what ye waste at cartes
   Wad stow'd his pantry!

Then comes Burns's statement of his own poetic aim:

Ramsay an' famous Fergusson
Gied Forth an' Tay a lift aboon;
Yarrow and Tweed, to monie a tune
   Owre Scotland rings;
While Irvine, Lugar, Ayr an' Doon
   Naebody sings.

The Illissus, Tiber, Thames, an' Seine
Glide sweet in monie a tunefu' line:
But, Willie, set your fit to mine,
   An' cock your crest;
We'll gar our streams an' burnies shine
   Up wi' the best!

In a later stanza, Burns sets out something of his method of composition, echoing Andrew Fletcher of Saltoun's remark in his *Letter to the Marquis of Montrose* on the relative significance of law-making as against ballad-making:

The muse, nae poet ever fand her
Till by himsel he learn'd tae wander,
Adown some trottin burn's meander,
   An' no think lang:
O sweet to stray, an' pensive ponder
   A heart-felt sang!

The warly race may drudge an' drive
Hog-shouther, jundie, stretch, an' strive;   [jostle
Let me fair Nature's face descrive,
   And I, wi' pleasure,
Shall let the busy, grumbling hive
   Bum owre their treasure.

But these were times when the weary moil of farming made the effort of concentrating on writing at the day's end a heavy task, as Burns explained in his second "Epistle to J. Lapraik":

Forjesket sair, with weary legs,   [jarred with fatigue
Rattlin' the corn out-owre the rigs,   [ridges
Or dealing thro' amang the naigs   [distributing the horses' food
   Their ten-hours' bite,
My awkwart Muse sair pleads and begs
   I would na write.

The tapetless, ramfeezl'd hizzie,   [feckless, worn-out, lass
She's saft at best an' something lazy:
Quo' she, "Ye ken we've been sae busy
   This month an' mair,
That trowth, my head is grown right dizzie,
   An' something sair."

Her dowff excuses pat me mad;   [dull
"Conscience", says I, "ye thowless jade!   [lazy
I'll write, an' that a hearty blaud,
   This verra night;
So dinna ye affront your trade,
   But rhyme it right . . ."

Sae I got paper in a blink,   [twinkling
An' down gaed stumpie in the ink: [his worn-down pen
Quoth I, "Before I sleep a wink,
   I vow I'll close it;
An' if you winna mak it clink,   [rhyme
   By Jove, I'll prose it!"

Apart from marvellously communicating the sense of that physical
fatigue he determindly mastered, Burns makes it plain that he expected his
muse to "rhyme it right" even if, as in the "Epistle to James Smith", the
poet declares:

Some rhyme a neibor's name to lash;
Some rhyme (vain thought!) for needfu' cash;
Some rhyme to court the countra clash,   [country
   An' raise a din:
For me, an aim I never fash;   [bother about
   I rhyme for fun . . .

An anxious e'e I never throws
Behint my lug, or by my nose;
I jouk beneath Misfortune's blows
   As weel's I may;

Sworn foe to Sorrow, Care and Prose,
  I rhyme away.

Rhyming for Fun, his "cronie dear", as the third Hizzie in "The Vision", that highly successful poem which traces the poet's development, was thus his motive: theraputic relaxation, we might more pompously put it to-day. But this business of exchanging gossipy, Scots verse-epistles—albeit switching into English when Sorrow and Care, or other personified aspects of seriousness are implied—was only part of the story. Without, indeed, bothering about the possible consequences, Burns was taking deadly and effective aim with the precise intention not only of "a neebor's name to lash", but of attacking the prying, canting hypocrisy of the Auld Licht faction of the Kirk, and of establishing the fact that sex and death, the universal levellers, make social pretentions, and injustice based upon them, alike absurd.

It is not necessary to consider Burns's 'hits' on these targets in any strictly chronological order, because in one form or another, and with varying degrees of intensity, he kept up his fire throughout his life, if not latterly in verse, then in the excellently ordered and always lively prose of his letters. Without a doubt, however, it was the Kirk's officious concern with his youthful sexual ongoings which first brought that institution into the range of his poetic sights. But sexual prying was only one aspect of the hypocritical, Calvinistic interference by which the Church then still obtruded into almost every side of private lives. Almost all its abuses of human dignity quickly became targets for Burns's satirical raillery.

There was "Holy Willie's Prayer", inspired, Burns tells us, by "a rather oldish bachelor elder in the parish of Mauchline, and much and justly famed for the polemical chattering which ends in tippling orthodoxy, and for that spiritualized bawdry which refines to liquorish devotion", as Burns informed Robert Riddell of Glenriddell in the handwritten preface to a copy of the poem. This prototype was William Fisher (1737–1809), a narrow-minded bigot who himself fell from grace in October 1790, accused by the Reverend "Daddy" Auld of drunkenness. Twenty years after Fisher had frozen to death in a ditch on a snowy night in February 1809, he was alleged by Allan Cunningham to have been guilty of having pilfered from an alms box, an accusation also made in 1790 by Burns in "The Kirk's Alarm":

Holy Will, Holy Will, there was wit i' your scull,
  When ye pilfered the alms o' the poor;
The timmer is scant when ye're ta'en for a saunt,
  Holy Will! ye should swing in a rape for an hour.

Burns's jangling mockery of these insignificant religious, or quasi-religious, persons whom he so much disliked, is severe enough. But in

"Holy Willie's Prayer", Burns takes the doctrine of predestination, whereby the elect are assured of heaven and the rest are damned regardless of merit or conduct, shaking it derisively into pieces. The drunken Ayrshire pilferer who clothed himself in an extra thickness of pretended sanctimoniousness becomes a universal symbol for an attack upon hypocrisy itself; a satirical poem which can have few equals for the power and economy of its thrust in European literature. The "Standard Habbie" is manipulated with a telling force and fluency never before achieved by any of those who had handled it; indeed, not even previously by Burns himself.

Gavin Hamilton, Burns's genial Ayr lawyer friend, had been censured for irregularity in church attendance. He is merely a useful pretext for Burns's attack. It is the system which had crippled the Scots spirit for generations that Burns is out to bring down. Cries Holy Willie:

> O Thou, who in the heavens does dwell,
> Who, as it pleases best Thysel,
> Sends ane to heaven, an' ten to hell,
>   A' for thy glory,
> And no for any gude or ill
>   They've done afore Thee!

> I bless and praise Thy matchless might,
> When thousands Thou hast left in night,
> That I am here afore Thy sight,
>   For gifts and grace
> A burning and a shining light
>   To a' this place.

Already, the picture of oozing unctiousness is masterly. The deadly self-revelation continues with a rationalization of Holy Willie's own sins:

> O L—d! yestreen, Thou kens, wi' Meg—
> Thy pardon I sincerely beg,
> O! may't ne'er be a livin' plague
>   To my dishonour,
> An' I'll ne'er lift a lawless leg
>   Again upon her . . .

> Maybe Thou lets this fleshly thorn
> Buffet Thy servant e'en and morn,
> Lest he owre proud and high shou'd turn,
>   That he's sae gifted:
> If sae, Thy han' maun e'en be borne,
>   Until Thou lift it.

Then the old hypocrite burst out in fury against Gavin Hamilton who "drinks and swears, an' plays at cartes", calling upon his Christian Lord:

Curse Thou his basket and his store,
  Kail an' potatoes.

—not the least absurd point being the juxtaposition of the high-minded with the mundane, through which Burns often achieved pointed effect.

But there was worse to come from the same source. Religious hypocrisy was once again the target for attack in the double ballad stanzas with internal rhyming which are used in the "Address to the Unco Guid". This time, the poet reminds those who are not by temperament subject to temptation, that they have little enough to boast of in avoiding it. Once again, glancing ironic contrasts flash out with a more lasting deadliness than the scorn from the poet's remarkable eyes:

Ye high, exalted, virtuous dames,
  Tied up in godly laces,
Before ye gie poor Frailty names,
  Suppose a change o' cases;
A dear-lov'd lad, convenience snug,
  A treach'rous inclination;
But, let me whisper i' your lug,
  Ye're aiblins nae temptation.   [perhaps

Moving into English for his serious conclusion, Burns pronounces his typical proverb-like wisdom in language which has proved memorable, even to the less literate:

Then gently scan your brother man,
  Still gentler sister woman:
Tho' they may gang a kennin wrang,
  To step aside is human,
One point must still be greatly dark,
  The moving *Why* they do it;
An just as lamely can ye mark,
  How far perhaps they rue it.

In the tradition of "Christis Kirk" and its kind is "The Holy Fair," which launches into that immediate scene-setting we have already encountered as Henryson practised it:

Upon a simmer Sunday morn,
  When Nature's face is fair,

> I walkèd forth to view the corn,
>   An' snuff the caller air.
> The rising sun owre Galston muirs,
>   Wi' glorious light was glintin';
> The hares were hirplin' down the furrs,
>   The lav'rocks they were chantin'
>   Fu' sweet that day.

But this was no medieval fair where the sole purpose was rustic jollity. True, the people streaming in from all directions for the celebration were not so very different from their earlier counterparts. You can almost smell the horse-leather, hear the rustle of the dresses:

> Here farmers gash, in ridin' graith,   [gear
>   Gaed hoddin' by their cottars:
> There swankies young, in braw braid-claith,
>   Are springin' owre the gutters.
> The lasses, skelpin' barefit, thrang,
>   In silks an' scarlets glitter;
> Wi' sweet-milk cheese in mony a whang,
>   An' farls, bak'd wi' butter,   [oatcakes
>   Fu' crump that day.   [crisp

Apart from food and drink, there is preaching: rival ministers of differing doctrinal prejudice roaring their messages at the scarce-heeding crowd, whose members sat boozing and flirting as the holy men thundered:

> But now the L—d's ain trumpet touts,
>   Till a' the hills are rairin'
> And echoes back-return the shouts;
>   Black Russell is na sparin':
> His piercin' words, like Highlan' swords,
>   Divide the joints an' marrow;
> His talk o' Hell, whare devils dwell,
>   Our vera sauls does harrow.
>   Wi' fright that day!

As at all these country festivals, however, for the young and nubile the ending is more or less the same:

> How mony hearts this day converts,
>   O' sinners and o' lasses!
> Their hearts o' stane, gin night, are gane,
>   As saft as ony flesh is:
> There's some are fou' o' love divine;

There's some are fou' o' brandy;
An' mony jobs that day begin
   May end in houghmagandie   [sexual intercourse
      Some ither day.

The familiar association of evangelical fervour with fervour of a more immediate physical kind Burns later elaborated more explicitly in one of his *Merry Muses* pieces, "Godly Girzie":

The night it was a holy night,
   The day had been a holy day;
Kilmarnock gleamed wi' candlelight,
   As Girzie hameward took her way.
A man o' sin, ill may he thrive!
   And never holy-meeting see!
Wi' godly Girzie met belyve,
   Amang the Craigie hills sae hie.

The chiel was wight, the chiel was stark,   [mighty, bare
   He wad na wait to chap na ca',
And she was faint wi' holy wark,   [work
   She had na pith to sae him na.
But ay she glowr'd up to the moon,
   And ay she sigh'd most piteously—
"I trust my heart's in heaven aboon
   Wheree'r your sinful p—e be."   [pintle

Small wonder that the narrower churchmen fulminated against Burns: men like the poet's former 'victim', Dr William Peebles of Ayr, who produced his *Burnsmania* in 1811, when the poet was no longer around to deal with him. When Burns lashed out at the nonsense of Auld Licht preachers, he vindicated his deeply held view that of all nonsense, "religious nonsense is the most nonsensical"*:

But I gae mad at their grimaces,
Their sighin', cantin', grace-proud faces,
Their three-mile prayers an' half-mile graces,
   Their raxin conscience
Whose greed, revenge an' pride disgraces.
   Waur nor their nonsense.

What, it may be asked, was Burns's attitude to religion itself, until recently so basic an ingredient in the fierce stratae of the Scots character? In the "Epistle to John M'Math" (a moderate minister) Burns apostrophizes:

* He did not have the opportunity of acquaintance with their pseudo-religious nonsense of Marxism!

All hail Religion! maid divine!
Pardon a muse sae mean as mine,
Who in her rough imperfect line
    Thus daurs to name thee;
To stigmatise false friends of thine
    Can ne'er defame thee.

He could opine that:

An atheist-laugh's a poor exchange
For Deity offended.

Yet in "The Jolly Beggars", he could assert with apparently equal conviction:

Courts for cowards were erected,
Churches built to please the priest.

In a letter to Robert Muir, dated 7th March 1788, the poet meditates:

The close of life, indeed, to a reasoning eye is,
                        ". . . dark
As was chaos, ere the infant sun
Was roll'd together, or had try'd his beams
Athwart the gloom profound."

But the honest man has nothing to fear. If we lie down in the grave, the whole man a piece of broke machinery, to moulder with the clods of the valley—be it so; at least there is an end of pain, care, woes and wants: if that part of us called Mind, does survive the apparent destruction of the man— away with old-wife prejudices and tales! Every age and every nation has had a different set of stories . . .

Even as late as December 1794—just eighteen months before his death—Burns is still questioning orthodoxy;

What a transient business is life! Very lately I was a boy; but t'other day I was a young man; and I already begin to feel the rigid fibre and stiffening joints of Old Age coming fast o'er my frame. With all my follies of youth, and I fear, a few vices of manhood, still I congratulate myself on having had in early days religion strongly impressed on my mind. I have nothing to say to anybody, as to which Sect they belong, or what Creed they believe in; but I look on the Man who is firmly persuaded of Infinite Wisdom and Goodness superintending and directing every circumstance that can happen in his lot— I felicitate such a man as having a solid foundation for his mental enjoyment;

a firm prop and sure stay, in the hour of difficulty, trouble and distress; and a
never-failing anchor of hope, when he looks beyond the grave.

"Hope", be it noted; not "faith". That, as Thomas Crawford has
remarked, is not "either orthodox or atheistic."[7]

The side of Burns that yearned towards a settled religious observance is
reflected in "The Cottar's Saturday Night", a somewhat overpraised picture of a severe countryman, into which is injected by the poet an hysterical
autobiographical episode. This poem forms the most substantial piece as
regards length and ambition of aim in the Kilmarnock volume. With it,
Burns succeeded in reaching the wider "peasant" public who did not care
overmuch if the poetry was at times rather poor so long as it reflected their
manners, their way of life and their simple undeviating view of religion. It
would not be too much to say that with "The Cottar's Saturday Night",
Burns ousted Lyndsay from his previously held position of "National
Bard".

As we have already seen, Burns's model was Fergusson's "The Farmer's
Ingle". The ground-plan of both poems is similar. Burns, however, felt
compelled to fill out his framework with pseudo-philosophical reflection,
while Fergusson was content to record what he saw. Burns also employed
the strict Spenserian stanza of Shenstone's "The School-mistress"—
ababbcbcc—whereas Fergusson rhymed *ababcdcdd*.

Burns gets off to a bad start with an absurd opening stanza addressed to
his friend Robert Aitken ("Orator Bob"), a prosperous Ayr lawyer,
suggesting that he would have been happier in a peasant's dwelling than in
his comfortable and convenient town home:

To you I sing, in simple Scottish lays,
  The lowly train in life's sequester'd scene;
    The native feelings strong, the guileless ways;
  What Aiken in a cottage would have been;
  Ah! tho' his worth unknown, far happier there, I ween.

The echo of Thomas Gray's village Hampdens and mute inglorious Miltons is obvious. (Possibly these dreadful lines were an afterthought). Gray
also lurks in the background of the second stanza, though by now Burns has
settled into his attention-arresting, scene-setting manners, and the brush-
strokes are brisk:

November chill blaws loud wi' angry sugh;
  The short'ning winter day is near a close;
The miry beasts retreating frae the pleugh;
  The black'ning trains o' craws to their repose:
  The toil-worn Cottar frae his labour goes—
This night his weekly moil is at an end,
  Collects his spades, his mattocks and his hoes,

Hoping the morn in ease and rest to spend,
And weary, o'er the moor, his course does hameward bend.

The poet describes the Cottar's children running to meet him, the arrival
of the elder bairns who have been helping in the field, and the appearance
of Jenny, "woman grown", who hands over "her sair-won penny-fee".
Burns's linguistic dichotomy bursts out anew as he attempts to establish the
worth of those who lead the simple domestic cottage life for the benefit of
these gentler readers who will never have to experience it:

The parents partial eye their hopeful years;
Anticipation forward points the view;
The mother, wi' her needle and her shears
Gars auld claes look amaist as weel's the new;
The father mixes a' wi' admonition due.

This picture of the thrifty mother making do and mending, and of the
father, after the manner of his Scots kind, assuming the role of household
God-on-earth, is certainly valid. The first two lines are one of Burns's
many attempts to persuade his muse, Coila, as he actually puts it in the
second Duan of "The Vision":

. . . To paint with Thomson's landscape glow;
Or wake the bosom-melting throe,
    With Shenstone's art;
Or pour, with Gray, the moving flow,
    Warm on the heart.

At this point in "The Cottar's Saturday Night", a "neibor lad" comes in
to woo Jenny, and mother gets into a terrible tiz lest he should be some
"wild, worthless rake". Fair enough. Peasant women were doubtless being
seduced in their hundreds by young men of means. It is not without significance that the Kilmarnock poems appeared in the same year as Mozart's
opera *The Marriage of Figaro* (based on a play by Beaumarchais), which
deals with a nobleman who is already regretting abolishing the *droit de seig-
neur*, or feudal privilege whereby the lord had the right to spend the first
night of her marriage with every new bride on his estate, ostensibly so that
the quality of the human "stock" might be kept up! But whereas Fergusson
merely makes this the passing subject of after-supper conversation:

How Jack woo'd Jenny here to be his bride,
And there how Marion, for a bastard son,
    Upo' the cutty-stool was forced to ride,
    The waefu' scald o' our Mess John to bide.

—Burns, who had himself endured the "cutty-stool" for his seduction of his mother's servant, Elizabeth Paton, had also seduced Jean Armour, and had felt the "waefu' scald" of "Daddy" Auld, bursts out into eighteenth-century grease-paint rhetoric:

> Is there, in human form, that bears a heart,
>   A wretch! a villain! lost to love and truth!
> That can, with studied, sly, ensnaring art,
>   Betray sweet Jenny's unsuspecting youth?
> Curse on his perjur'd arts! dissembling, smooth!
>   Are honour, virtue, conscience, all exil'd?
>   Is there no pity, no relenting ruth,
> Points to the parents fondling o'er their child?
> Then paints the ruin'd maid, and their distraction wild.

The poet's brother, Gilbert, relates how Burns once commented upon the solemn impression the words "Let us worship God" made on him. It is not the description of the Cottar's meal—a variant upon a common Scots theme, though handled with greater fluency than most others of its catalogue kind—but the description of the ensuing family prayers which makes this poem memorable, despite all its faults and idiomatic inconsistencies:

> The cheerfu' supper done, wi' serious face
>   They, round the ingle, form a circle wide;
> The sire turns o'er, wi' patriachal grace,
>   The big ha'-bible, ance his father's pride: [large hall bible
>   His bonnet rev'rently is laid aside,
> His lyart haffets wearing thin and bare;   [grey side-locks
>   Those strains that once did sweet in Zion glide,
> He wales a portion with judicious care;   [chooses
> And "Let us worship God!" he says with solemn air.

Burns caught and fixed the rustic customs and manners of agrarian Scotland—customs and manners which had probably remained unchanged for centuries—just before they began to crumble before the technological and social pressures arising from the Industrial Revolution. In the stanza just quoted, he captures the enduring dignity that sustained so many generations of poor but hard-working Scots in their simple religious faith, picturing the daily better side of what so often appeared as overweening pride or bad-tempered intolerance among those extremists who unfortunately make up most of recorded history.

At the same time, however, Burns was able to look forward to social reform, even if, during his final years, he was misled into over-enthusiasm for the French Revolution, as were many other more widely travelled if less volatile idealists. In any case, Burns never attempted to disguise the compelling force of his own emotions. He wrote to James Smith:

O ye douce folk that live by rule,
Grave, tideless-blooded, calm an' cool,
Compar'd wi' you—O fool! fool! fool!
    How much unlike!
Your hearts are just a standing pool,
    Your lives, a dyke! . . .

Ye are sae grave, nae doubt ye're wise;
Nae ferly tho' ye do despise
The hairum-scairum, ram-stam boys,
    The rattling squad:
I see ye upward cast your eyes—
    Ye ken the road!

Once again, as with Mozart, it is impossible to imagine Burns an old man, although his attitudes towards the abstract concept of freedom and, as his songs show, human relationships, went on deepening right up to his premature death.

His major youthful tribute to the vitality of those "hairum-scairum, ram-stam boys" he so admired in his twenties, is his cantata, "The Jolly Beggars". Probably originally called "Love and Liberty", it remained unpublished until 1799, when Stewart and Meikle of Glasgow brought it out as part of a chapbook.

Modelled in a general way on what Daiches calls a "long line of songs and poems in goliardic vein which goes far back into the Middle Ages", but more immediately on a short piece, "Merry Beggars", in *The Tea-Table Miscellany*, and another anonymous poem, "The Happy Beggar", Burns celebrates the fancied freedom that men and women might be supposed by idealists to enjoy as a result of being thrall to no responsibilities save their own impulses and loyalties. The cantata is said to have been inspired by a visit to Poosie Nansie's tavern in Mauchline which Burns made with his two friends and fellow adventurers in sexual exploits, Smith and Richmond. After "witnessing much jollity" amongst a company who by day appeared as miserable beggars but by night felt monarchs of all they surveyed, Burns left, expressing much amusement, especially at the antics of an old, maimed soldier. Because each of the vigorously drawn characters is given only one song to sing (to a named air), and the passages marked "recitativo" bear no musical instructions, the work is difficult to perform. Unaccompanied folk-performances lack gusto. The nineteenth-century versions of Sir Henry Bishop and John More Smieton lack guts. The version by Cedric Thorpe Davie, using the convention of having a chamber ensemble and four singers who act out all the parts—the soldier who had served with Eliott at Gibraltar, his doxy, the disillusioned professional fool, the widow of a recently-executed Highland cateran, a fiddler, and a tinkler—and which is rounded off with a rousing *quod libet*, is much the most effective.

Burns gives each of the characters images and rhythms exactly suited to his individual situation, while the Bard (as the younger Burns was fond of calling himself) reserves for himself a toast to women:

Their tricks an' craft hae put me daft,
   They've ta'en me in, an' a' that;
But clear your deck's, an' here's the Sex!
   I like the jads for a' that.   [loose women

For a' that, and a' that,
   An' twice as muckle's a' that;
My dearest bluid, to do them guid,
   They're welcome till't for a' that.

In response to thunderous applause, the Bard sums up the philosophy of the piece, supported by the others in chorus. In the sweaty, smelling atmosphere of Poosie Nansie's, these people whom society has rejected, hail what seems to them an ideal life, in which social, religious and moral conventions simply do not exist (forgetting, as Kokoschka was later to remark, "that free will is mere sophistry"[8]):

Life is all a variorum,
   We regard not how it goes;
Let them cant about decorum,
   Who have character to lose.

A fig for those by law protected!
   Liberty's a glorious feast!
Courts for cowards were erected,
   Churches built to please the priest.

Henley called "The Jolly Beggars", "humanity caught in the act". Burns caught other humans too, in other acts. In "The Twa Dogs", for example, Caesar, a rich man's dog, and Luath, a farmer's "gash an' faithfu' tyke", discuss in octosyllabic couplets their respective master's ways of life, having first of all in the old realistic Scots animal tradition, done their introductory nosing and snuffing before they "set them down upon their arse."

Caesar is inclined to pity the lot of poor folk. Luath, like Henryson's Country Mouse, paints the pleasing side of rural life and the joys of communal festivals, making chance reference to politicians who travel to Parliament in London. At the mention of travel, the pace of the lines quickens, and before the reader is fully aware of what has happened, Caesar has dropped his loyal serving-mask of gentility, and launched into contemptuous condemnation of the habits of some of those who belong to his master's social class:

> There, at Vienna, or Versailles,
> He rives his father's auld entails;
> Or by Madrid, he takes the rout,
> To thrum guitars an' fecht wi' nowt;   [fight bullocks
> Or down Italian vista startles
> Whore-hunting amang groves o' myrtles:
> Then bouses drumlie German-water,   [drinks, muddy
> To mak himsel' look fair an' fitter,
> An' clear the consequential sorrows,
> Love-gifts of Carnival signoras.

Caesar's thoughts about the absurdity of assumptions arising out of the accident of birth are expressed openly by Burns in "A Man's A Man For A' That."

> Ye see yon birkie ca'd "a lord,"   [lively, smart person
>   Wha struts, and stares, and a' that
> Though hundreds worship at his word,
>   He's but a coof for a' that: [fool
> For a' that, and a' that,
>   His ribband, star and a' that;
> The man of independent mind
>   He looks and laughs at a' that.

The man of independent mind who wrote these radical lines was to fall under the violent spell of the French Revolution, but unlike Wordsworth, not to live long enough to experience the inevitable disillusion.* That same man of independent mind could also look and be content with an ironic laugh, as he watched a louse making its way up to the top of a lady's bonnet, reminding us of her basic humanity by the familiarity of first-name address:

> O Jenny, dinna toss your head,
> An' set your beauties a' abroad!
> Ye little ken what curse'd speed
>   The blastie's makin' . . .

Where sex itself was concerned, lady and maidservant at least had the artificial distinctions of rank and dress laid aside:

* Though to resent French expansionism in "Does Haughty Gaul Invasion Threat?"

O, I hae tint my rosy cheek,
  Likewise my waste sae sma';
O wae gae by the sodger lown,   [soldier
  The sodger did it a' . . .

Now I maun thole the scornfu' sneer
  O' mony a saucy quine;   [women
When, curse upon her godly face!
  Her c——t's as merry's mine.

Our dame hauds up her wanton tail,
  As due as she gaes lie;
An' yet misca's a young thing,
  The trade if she but try! . . .

The direct relationship between humans and animals was the theme of
several of Burns's finest poems. The warm fellow-feeling which once
existed between farmer and horse (though not between modern farmer and
tractor!) is reflected in "The Auld Farmer's New-Year Morning Salutation to his Auld Mare, Maggie, On Giving her the Accustomed Ripp of
Corn to Hansel in the New Year". It is a realistic relationship, mixed with
gratitude for the beast's long years of service, and rising to an emotion
echoed in not dissimilar human terms in the song "John Anderson, My Jo".
Burns assures his old mare:

We've worn to crazy years thegither;
We'll toyte about wi' ane anither;
Wi' tentie care I'll flit thy tether,   [heedful, move
  To some hain'd rig,   [reserved ridge
Whaur ye may nobly rax your leather,   [stretch
  Wi' sma fatigue.

More famous, deeper in its human implications, but marred a little by
linguistic dichotomy, is "To a Mouse, On Turning Her Up on Her Nest
With the Plough, November 1785". The opening picture is again vividly
direct:

Wee sleeket, cowrin' tim'rous beastie,
O, what a panic's in thy breastie,
Thou need na start awa' sae hasty,
  Wi' bickerin' brattle!   [crashing noise
I wad be laith to rin an' chase thee,
  Wi' murderin' pattle!   [plough-spade

Only the honest strength of the poet's feeling for the oneness of all things in Nature gets him through the linguistic stress of the next stanza:

I'm truly sorry man's dominion
Has broken nature's social union,
An' justifies that ill opinion,
    Which makes thee startle
At me, thy poor, earth-corn companion,
    And fellow-mortal!

The mouse, of course, does not have the poet's sentience. So the poem
ends with two of Burns's most touching stanzas. The man who felt he
lacked an aim in life really lacked that sense of security necessary even for
an eighteenth-century poet if he was to develop his gift to the full.

But Mousie, thou art no thy lane,
In proving foresight may be vain;
The best-laid schemes o' mice an' men
    Gang aft agley,
An' lea us nought but grief an' pain,
    For promis'd joy.

Still thou art blest, compar'd wi' me!
The present only toucheth thee:
But och! I backward cast my e'ee,
    On prospects drear!
An' forward, tho' I canna see,
    I guess an' fear!

Retrospectively, in the light of what was to be his own life-experience,
we can see that few poets have packed so much justified apprehension into
so taut a stanza.

Those who maintain that after the Edinburgh period Burns's story is one
of creative decline, do him an injustice. For one thing, there was still "Tam
o' Shanter" to come, and the great bulk of his song-work.

"Tam o' Shanter" is surely one of the finest narrative poems ever written. According to Gilbert Burns, the poet asked his friend, the antiquary
Francis Grose, to include a drawing of Alloway Kirk in the second volume
of Grose's *Antiquities of Scotland*, and Grose agreed, provided Burns would
give him something to print with it. Writing to Grose in June 1790, Burns
gave the antiquarian three prose witch-stories. The second turned out to be
the tale of "Tam o' Shanter", the poetic version of which, couched in
rhyming octosyllabic couplets, first appeared in the *Edinburgh Magazine* for
March 1791, and a little later the same month came out again in the *Edinburgh Herald*. The following month it appeared in Grose's book. Lockhart
and Cunningham put it about that the poem was written in a single day. Its

subtle nuances of tempo, pace and tone suggest that it had, indeed, been given, as Burns put it to Mrs Dunlop in a letter of 11th April 1791, "a finishing polish that I despair of ever excelling."

After a mock-philosophical prologue, we are introduced to Tam o' Shanter and his crony, Souter Johny, drinking together in an Ayr tavern. Tam is magnificently drunk:

Kings may be blest, but Tam was glorious,
O'er a' the ills o' life victorious!

Because Burns retains the objectivity of the narrator throughout, and does not allow his own emotions to become directly involved (as he did with the Jenny episode in "The Cottar's Saturday Night") even the switch from Scots to English in a moment of high seriousness is contained:

But pleasures are like poppies spread,
You seize the flow'r, its bloom is shed;
Or like the snowfall in the river
A moment white—then melts for ever;
Or like the borealis race,
That flit ere you can point theie place;
Or like the rainbow's lovely form
Evanishing amid the storm.
Nae man can tether Time nor Tide;
The hour approaches Tam maun ride . . . .

Edwin Muir once used the first eight lines of this passage[9] to illustrate his thesis that since Scots disintegrated as a homogeneous language capable of expressing life at all levels, Scots writers have more and more tended to feel in Scots but think in English. Be that as it may—and we later shall be considering these matters in relation to the Scottish Renaissance Movement—Burns gave plenty of evidence that he could feel and think in Scots, as the satires show. David Daiches, seeking to correct Muir, suggests that the lines are "written in a deliberately 'fancy' English . . . a form of expression which will set the sternness of objective fact against the warm, cosy and self-deluding view of the half-intoxicated Tam": an ingenious theory which the switch to English in "To a Mouse" perhaps helps to bear out. But are these lines "fancy" English? Apart from the archaic word "evanishing", which is oddly effective in its context, they come nearest in feeling to the "high style" of an earlier age than anything else Burns wrote, and echo the poet's apprehension of the mutability of all things mortal, just as do the concluding stanzas of "To a Mouse" in a more personal way. Human transience turned the eighteenth-century mind to the Bible, and the Bible automatically meant expression in English to post-Reformation Scots.

From the moment Tam steps out of the warm pub interior into the snowy night, and mounts his horse, Maggie, passing Kirk-Alloway, where the "bleeze" of the witches' celebrations lure him to watch their eerie proceedings, calling out "weel done, Cutty-sark", so that "out the hellish legion sallied"; until by crossing the arch of the bridge over the Doon, Tam escapes, Maggie's tail being all that the foremost witch could grab, we are whirled forward by the effortlessness of the narration, sustained by the amused detachment. In the end, Burns provides a mock-moral by way of a coda:

Now, wha this tale o' truth shall read,
Each man and mother's son, take heed:
Whene'er to drink you are inclin'd,
   Or Cutty-sarks rin in your mind,   [short shifts
Think! ye may buy the joys o'er dear,
Remember Tam o' Shanter's mare.

The final form of the description of the eerie paraphernalia surrounding the witches' orgy came during revision. Until 1793, this section ended with a swipe at unpopular professional people;

Three lawyer's tongues, turned inside out,
Wi' lies seamed like a beggar's clout;
Three Priests' hearts, rotten black as muck,
Lay stinking, vile, in every neuk.

Burns's friend the Professor of Universal History at Edinburgh University did the poet a favour when he suggested, and Burns agreed, that the passage would end more effectively with the sinister generalization:

Wi' mair of horrible and awfu'
Which even to name wad be unlawfu'.

This passage no doubt owes something to "Macbeth", as well as perhaps to some lines by Ramsay in "Three Bonnets." Any poet writing at white heat, and summing up a tradition, uses older undertones and heightens and recasts them for his own purposes. The pursuit of such references is an arid and pointless business, except perhaps to seekers after Ph.Ds.
More importantly, William Montgomerie has drawn attention to the fact that Auld Nick is to be found "significantly in the Kirk, though in opposition to it. He is a creature of the historical past, like his warlocks and witches, like the dead.

Coffins stood round like open presses,
That shew'd the dead in their last dresses;

And by some devilish cantraip sleight
Each in his cauld hand held a light.

He is part of the human personality suppressed by Calvinism, Burns the
poet and fornicator, the creator of music, the inspirer of dancing (the Kirk
for centuries discouraged dancing), summing up in himself all the elements
in the Scotsman that the Kirk, unable to destroy them, for they are essential
parts in our nature, has suppressed. He is 'a touzie tyke', the animal in us."[10]

Clearly, there is here a link, however tenuous, with the attitude to Calvinist repression which inspired the great satires of the earlier years.

"Go on", Tytler encouraged Burns: "write more tales in the same
style—you will eclipse Prior, La Fontaine; for with equal wit, equal power
of numbers and equal naïveté of expression, you have a bolder and more
vigorious imagination."

"Your approbation, Sir", replied Burns, "has given me such additional
spirits to persevere in this species of poetic composition, that I am already
revolving two or three stories in my fancy."

Alas! these "floating ideas" were never to be given the "embodied
form" Burns told Tytler he was seeking for them; not, as is sometimes
suggested, because of a decline in Burns's ability to sustain his creative
drive, but because by then he had become almost wholly absorbed in the
exacting task of song-writing for Johnson and Thomson.

By involving Burns in *The Scots Musical Museum* (from the second
volume onwards), Johnson, who met the poet in 1786 in Edinburgh, un-
wittingly ensured that his collection would become the standard contemporary work of its kind. In all, Burns probably contributed about one
hundred and sixty songs of his own, mending and patching many others.
The musical editorship, held by Stephen Clarke and later by his son, William, provided the airs with a lightly figured bass.

Johnson rarely argued with Burns on points of taste. In this respect he
was unlike Thomson, to whom Burns was introduced by letter through
Alexander Cunningham in 1792. Thomson employed, among others,
Haydn (who valued his settings on the grounds that they would keep his
name alive in Scotland!), Beethoven (who frequently had to set airs without ever seeing the words), Weber and Hummel to arrange the music.
Select Scottish Airs may to-day be an occasionally revived musical curiosity;
yet its six volumes, published between 1793 and 1841, evoked from Burns
about a hundred and fourteen songs.

In a letter to Thomson, dated September 1793, Burns put on record his
method of song-composition:

. . . Until I am compleat master of a tune, in my own singing, (such as it is) I
never can compose for it. My way is: I consider the poetic Sentiment, correspondent to my idea of the musical expression; then chuse my theme; begin
one Stanza; when that is composed, which is generally the most difficult part

of the business, I walk out, sit down now and then, look out for objects in Nature around me that are in unison or harmony with the cogitations of my fancy and workings of my bosom; humming every now and then the air with the verses I have framed: when I feel my Muse beginning to jade, I retire to the solitary fireside of my study, and there commit my effusions to paper; swinging, at intervals, on the hind-legs of my elbow-chair, by way of calling forth my own critical strictures as my pen goes on.

The range of Burns's song-work is so considerable that in a sense this particular division of his poetic labours illustrates the depth of his feeling better than almost any other. There are political songs, like "Is There For Honest Poverty?", and "When Guildford Good our Pilot Stood"; patriotic songs like "Scots Wha Hae", the nearest thing to a Scottish National Anthem, but which could hardly become so because of the absurdity—obvious even to some Scots—of, on the one hand allegedly wishing to "lay the proud usurper low", whilst on the other, still wishing to pocket the financial benefits of English-dominated rule; Jacobite songs, like "It was a' for our rightfu' king", that capture perfectly "the Gael's last gallant battle, greatly lost":

Now a' is done that men can do,
   And a' is done in vain:
My Love and Native Land farewell.
   For I maun cross the main,
     My dear;
   For I maun cross the main.

—drinking songs like "O Willie brew'd a peck o' maut", with the honest abandon of the chorus, so different from the Christmas-card jollity of contemporary English drinking songs:

We are na fou, we're nae that fou,
   But jist a drappie in our e'e;   [little drop
The cock may craw, the day may daw,
   And aye we'll taste the barley bree.

Above all, however, it is in his songs dealing with the relationship between men and women that Burns excels. In one of his bawdy songs, the "Ode to Spring", he satirizes the Augustan pastoral classical apparatus superbly:

When maukin bucks, at early f . . . s,   [male hares
   In dewy grass are seen, Sir;
And birds and boughs, take off their mows,
   Among the leaves sae green, Sir;

Latona's sun looks liquorish on
　　Dame Nature's grand impètus,
Till his p —— go rise, then westward flies
　　To r—ger Madame Thetis.

The scatalogical versions of "Green Grow the Rushes O'", "John Anderson, my Jo" and "Duncan Gray"* to be found in "The Merry Muses" suggest the kind of crude but insignificant originals Burns may often have had to work from. But whether re-writing crude old originals—and, unlike Ramsay, improving them—or creating afresh, Burns ranged over the anatomy of love, from a girl's fears at her first wooing in "I am my mammy's ae bairn", through the young man's ache in the presence of many beautiful women, but not the one he loves in "Mary Morrison", to the celebration of sexual satisfaction in "Corn Rigs" and the contentment of old age in "John Anderson".

Above all, Burns provided, in "Auld Lang Syne", the valedictory song, often sung inaccurately but nevertheless sung, at countless gatherings the world over as a thanksgiving for friendships enjoyed and an affirmation of the intention to keep them in repair.

In a survey such as this, it is clearly not possible to touch upon every aspect of the genius of Scotland's greatest poet. His large humanity, his exuberant vitality and his more pointed and fuller use of forms, rhythms and subjects provided for him by his predecessors through several preceding generations, meant that his premature death virtually marked the end of an era.

His work has been translated into as many languages as has that of Shakespeare, but unlike the "Swan of Avon", Burns has his national memory widely toasted annually at birthday celebrations. Though he speaks to us with a more "modern" voice than either Dunbar or Henryson, and though he understood and reflected in his poems and songs far more that is fundamental to the national character, the language dichotomy he had to cope with, and the weakening sense of Scottish nationhood in the 1780s and 1790s, placed him under conditions and in circumstances where the choices open to him were circumscribed. Consequently, his greatness is a vernacular, a colloquial greatness, with, in world terms, the drawbacks such a limitation necessarily implies.

In Scotland, therefore, Burns had few real successors in the tradition he capped and finalized, and those who did seek to emulate him mostly confined themselves to songs. The new status which he had given to Lallans, or the vernacular (sometimes wrongly called "Doric" by non-classicists) resulted in a plentiful crop of imitators whose rural hiccoughings sprouted like fungus in the seams of country newspapers for more than a century,

* Most disgracefully given false emphasis at the expense of Burns's published songs in that inadequate and inaccurate anthology *The Penguin Book of Scottish Verse*, ed. Tom Scott, London, 1970.

and were solemnly collected in various anthologies, the most fatuous of which must surely have been Edwards' many-volumed *Modern Scottish Poets,* in which the rhymsters are painstakingly categorized by trade.

James Beattie (1735–1803) was neither much of a poet nor much of a philosopher—he was unwise enough to take on David Hume—and his best work is in English. Occasionally, a verse-letter in Scots, "To Mr Alexander Ross", gets itself anthologized, but it is really sub-Ramsay stuff, as might be expected of a Scot who belonged to that misguided eighteenth-century band publicly concerned to rid their speech of Scotticisms. William Julius Mickle (1734–1788), a Langholm man, probably wrote "There's nae luck aboot the hoose", which has survived, as well as a rather cold English translation of Camoens' "Lusiad" (which nevertheless assured Mickle popularity in Portugal when he went there as naval secretary) and an imitation ballad, "Cumnor Hall", which caught the attention of the young Walter Scott and is said to have suggested to him the theme of *Kenilworth.* Burns gave John Ewen (1741–1821), a Montrose man, credit for the popular song "O Weel may the Boatie Row", although it may have been based on an older fragment. Alexander, Duke of Gordon (1743–1827), husband of Burns's admiring Duchess, who raised the Gordon Highlanders, gave his native airt (direction) "There's cauld kail in Aberdeen", a reel-song. Hector MacNeill (1746–1818) mistook the purposes of poetry so far as to try to cure the social disasters of the hour aggravated by excessive drinking, through verse exhortations: "Scotland's Skaith" in 1795 and "The Woes o' War" in 1796. In spite of his efforts Scotland still has one of the highest rates of alcoholism in Europe. More successfully, he wrote a number of light and pleasing lyrics, the best being "My Boy Tammie" (derived from a fragment collected by David Herd), "I Lo'ed ne'er a Laddie" and "Come under my Pladdie".

Elizabeth Hamilton (1758–1816) celebrated domesticity without sentimentalism in "My Ain Fireside". Mrs Grant of Carron (1745–1814) sent "Roy's Wife of Aldivalloch" humorously shrugging off to strathspey measure the experience of being jilted. James ("Balloon") Tytler (1747–1805) who, as Burns put it, "projected a balloon"—he actually made an ascent in a Montgolfier fire-balloon—was an "obscure, tippling, but extraordinary body . . . a mortal who, though he drudges about Edinburgh as a common printer, with leaky shoes, a sky-lighted hat, and knee-buckles as unlike as George-by-the-Grace-of-God and Solomon-the-son-of-David; yet that same unknown drunken mortal is author and compiler of three-fourths of Elliot's pompous "Encyclopaedia Britannica", which he composed at half-a-guinea a week." He also composed "The Bonnie Brucket Lass", the humorously original "I ha'e laid a herring in saut", and gave Burns some help with *The Scots Musical Museum* before accidentally drowning in a clay-pit near Salem.

The two most important of Burns's successors, though they survived into the nineteenth century, mostly wrote in the latter decades of the eighteenth. John Mayne (1759–1836), born the same year as Burns, gave the greater poet more than a hint or two for his "Halloween", Mayne's poem of the same name being less consciously a museum of archaisms as is the not very successful Burns poem. Mayne also beat Burns in depth and sincerity in the song "Logan Water", which both men re-worked from an older song. Mayne's "The Siller Gun" commemorates a Dumfriesshire custom. To Glaswegians, he is remembered because of his "Standard Habbie" but vivid picture of the eighteenth-century city just before its industrial despoilation:

> Clean-keepit streets! so lang and braid,
> The distant objects seem to fade;
> And then, for shelter or for shade
>   Frae sun or shower,
> Piazzas lend their friendly aid
>   At ony hour.

> Wond'ring, we see new streets extending,
> New squares wi' public buildings blending,
> Brigs, stately brigs, in arches bending
>   Across the Clyde,
> And turrets, kirks and spires ascending
>   In lofty pride.

Robert Tannahill (1774–1811), the unhappy Paisley poet who drowned himself in a canal, sang sweetly and sentimentally, mostly to "new" Scottish airs composed for his verses by R. A. Smith (1780–1829), the editor of *The Scottish Minstrel* which, after the *Museum*, is the best collection of its somewhat later kind. One Tannahill song became so popular that, indeed, when a Paisley teacher of what is known now as 'religious instruction' inquired of her class who Jesse was, the answer came "Please Sir, 'Jessie, the Flower o' Dunblane'".

There are good lyric things in Tannahill, like "The Midges dance aboon the Burn", "Gloomy winter's noo awa", "O, are Ye sleepin Maggie" and "Thou bonnie Wood o' Craigielea". But whereas Burns's love songs never lost sight of the basic physical man-woman relationship, Tannahill becomes romantically obsessed with Nature's surrounding stage-properties—the "howlet's cry", the "lightnin's gleam athwart the lift" and the linn "roarin o'er the warlock craigie." As Robert Dewar somewhat tartly remarks: ". . . when a poet makes a habit of losing the lady of his song in description of the scenes devised for meeting her (however attractive his songs may still be in their own fashion) we can be sure he is no Burns".[11]

Because of her friendship with Scott and the nineteenth-century ambience of her dramatic productions, the long-living Joanna Baillie

(1762–1851) is associated in the minds of those who give her a thought with the nineteenth century. Yet Burns was still alive when she wrote her spirited version of "Woo'd and Married and A'", "The Weary Pund o' Tow" and her narrative piece "Tam o' the Linn". Burns went so far as to declare her substantially original version of "Saw ye Johnie Comin'?", "unparalleled . . . for genuine humour in the verses and lively originality in the air." In "A Scottish Song", she could add her own note, wholly unaided by echoes from the common stock:

The gowan glitters on the sward,   [daisy
  The lav'rock's in the sky,   [lark
And Collie on my plaid keeps ward,
  And time is passing by.
    Oh no! sad an' slow
And lengthen'd on the ground,
  The shadow of our trysting bush,
It wears so slowly round.

Burns's only real rival in continuing song-popularity, albeit with a more limited range, has proved to be Carolina Oliphant, Baroness Nairne (1766–1845). While she certainly does not possess either Burns's depth or passion, the devotion of her house to the lost cause of Jacobitism enabled her to produce the most touchingly heart-felt of all non-Gaelic laments for that which had gone, and gone forever, in "Will ye no come back again?". Because of a disastrous quirk in the native temperament, which enables Scots to profess sentimental devotion to one cause while giving practical support to another, often diametrically opposed, this song has long been used to sublimate regret, not merely for an unrestorable monarchical house, but for that "auld sang" the ending of which Lord Seafield proclaimed so contemptuously to the last Scottish Parliament in 1707. Lady Nairne has also to her credit not only such other melodiously memorable expressions of regret for the times that are no more as "The Rowan Tree", "The Auld Hoose" and "The Land o' the Leal", but the social picturesqueness of "Caller Herrin", with its updated treatment of the seventeenth-century custom of street-crying by those with foods to sell, the harmless martial swing of "The Hundred Pipers", and the graceful wit of "The Laird o' Cockpen".

Leaving aside Hogg, who properly belongs elsewhere, it remains only to chronicle some minor figures who warmed momentary life with a song or two out of the embers of old traditions that changing times had dampened down. Burns's admirer Sir Alexander Boswell (1775–1822), son of James Boswell, was a man of outstanding abilities who set up a private printing press at Auchinleck. He hit off the humorous lyrics "Jenny's Bawbee" and "Jenny Dang the Weaver", as well as "The East Neuk o' Fife", a matrimonial argument which domesticizes the ancient tradition of flyting:

Auld gudeman, ye're a drucken, drucken carle;
A' the lang day ye're winkin', drinkin', gapin', gruntin'
O' sottish loons, ye're the pink and pearl, pink and pearl,
Ill-far'd, doited ne'er-do-weel.

This matrimonial duel, like all flytings, necessarily remains unresolved. Not so his real-life duel with James Stuart of Dunearn, a Writer to the Signet, over a political squib, in which unfortunately Boswell was killed.

Allan Cunningham (1784–1842) helped in the making of Cromek's so-called *Remains of Nithsdale and Galloway Song*, published in 1810. "Hame, Hame, Hame" and "The Wee, Wee German Lairdie" represent respectively the sentimental and the contemptuously humorous approaches to Jacobitism. Significantly, it was his English song, "A Wet Sheet and a Flowing Sea", that won him most fame.

Under the expansive spread of the Burns tree are also to be found such diverse occasional shoots as "Lucy's Flittin" by Scott's friend and amanuensis William Laidlaw (1790–1845), "The Mitherless Bairn", by the weaver poet William Thom (1789–1848), "O Why Left I My Hame?" by Robert Gilfillan (1798–1850), and the by no means ineffectual Galloway ballad of "Aiken Drum" by William Nicholson (d. 1849). William Watt (1793–1859) is as good a figure as any on which to leave these post-Burnsians, not so much for his vigorous if romantic account of "The Tinkler's Waddin'", but because of "Kate Dalrymple", a distant relation of Burns's Mrs Willie Wabster. Watt's comic masterpiece swaggers its seemingly endless stepping-out of rhymes to "Dalrymple", through a vigorous reel tune. Like several of Lady Nairne's pieces, "Kate Dalrymple" has a continuing currency otherwise only granted to many of the songs of Burns.

Scots verse continued to be written throughout the nineteenth century; but its practitioners lost hold of the poet's most vital possession, objectivity, and so floundered aimlessly between marshes of sentimentality, puddles of self-conscious rural "wut", and the conventional painted-glass shadows cast by Victorian pietism.

II

In eighteenth-century England there was a reaction against the turbulence that had troubled the country during most of the seventeenth century. This reaction led to a period of cultural and economic stability, which was to remain more or less unruffled until its placid surface was broken by the shock-waves of the French Revolution. In society, the ordered scheme of things formalized by Newton allowed men to believe that those who made or maintained money created their own peculiar good. Poetry, therefore, must be the fruit of idleness, and so need make no claims on social conscience.

In such a purely rational scheme of things, the heroic couplet became the popular vehicle for mainly urban expression, man surveying man, usually with a full measure of complacent satisfaction.

In the hands of a writer like Pope, the heroic couplet, as used in "The Rape of the Lock", could be an instrument of subtle and destructive delicacy. In the hands of Allan Ramsay, and even of Robert Burns, it could turn into a clumsy weapon for the expression of an alien, self-conscious awkwardness.

Nearly all the Scots poets of the eighteenth century made use of the heroic couplet, presumably to show the world that they could match English Chesterfieldian refinement with the best of the writing fraternity of south Britain. Only a small number of poets relied on English as their sole medium. Of those who did, one alone scored a major success; and he made his home in England.

James Thomson (1700–1748), son of the minister of Ednam, Roxburghshire, was educated in the local school at Southdean (to which village his father was "called"), at Jedburgh, and at Edinburgh University. There, he studied for the ministry. But the Professor of Divinity objected to the style of one of his sermons as being too flowery in expression and too imaginative—a properly Presbyterian objection—whereupon Thomson decided to abandon all idea of entering the Church and seek literary fame in London. He arrived there in 1725 with a draft of the poem, "Winter", in his luggage. Through the influence of Mallet, Thomson became tutor to Lord Binning, son of the Earl of Haddington, and was introduced to Pope, Arbuthnot, Gray and their circle. His work as tutor continued with a continental tour, in which he accompanied Charles Talbot, son of the Lord Chancellor. As a result, there followed the poet's appointment to the sinecure Secretaryship of Briefs, a post he lost in 1737 by a characteristic piece of laziness, simply forgetting to apply for its renewal to Talbot's successor. However, the Prince of Wales granted him a pension of £100 the following year. His appointment as Surveyor-General of the Leeward Islands left him with a further £300 per annum, even after he had paid a deputy who knew something about surveying to do the job for him.

Comparatively rich and famous, Thomson now retired to a villa near Richmond, where he devoted his time to writing, cultivating his garden and entertaining his friends; a genial, kindly bachelor whose unrequited love for Elizabeth Young had confirmed him in his withdrawn ways, and whose early death was much lamented.

English critics commonly claim that Thomson was not really a Scottish poet at all, but merely an offshoot of English Augustanism; a kind of poetic link-man between the Age of Reason and the ensuing Age of Sensibility. This seems a highly partial view.

Scotland experienced no fully-fledged Augustan age. The religious tur-moils of the seventeenth century, followed almost immediately by the traumatic shock of the Union and the ensuing departure of the leaders of fashion and taste for London, threw her back upon her native traditions. No doubt because of the smallness of Scottish cities and towns and their inevitably close links with the surrounding countryside, these traditions in-corporated a greater preoccupation with Nature than featured in their English counterparts. Thomson, brought up in the rolling Scottish Border country was no doubt imbued there with an early love of Nature. He car-ried the influence of his Scots upbringing south with him.

It is true that he was much influenced by the Newtonian conception of order and God's Laws; by Milton, whose blank verse he modified, not always seccessfully, to suit his own and his age's requirements; and by Shaftesbury's *Characteristics* and other writings which set out to vindicate "the ways of God to man", discarding the moral sanction of authority as the motivating force towards the achievement of goodness, preferring instead to substitute the voice of conscience and the love of God.

Though Shaftesbury's views opposed those of Hobbes and Locke, they were nevertheless taken up to some extent by Hutcheson and the Scottish School of Philosophers.

What Thomson did, therefore, was to create a taste for acute poetic ob-servation of Nature and set it within the philosophic and moralizing intel-lectual framework of the English Augustans. Unlike such contemporaries as Johnson and Pope, what we admire about his work to-day is not such philosophic lines as these, from his "Poem Sacred to the Memory of Sir Isaac Newton":

O unprofuse magnificence divine!
O wisdom truly perfect! thus to call
From a few causes such a scheme of things,
Effects so various, beautiful and great,
A universe complete! And O beloved
Of Heaven! whose well-purged penetrating eye
The mystic veil transpiercing, inly scanned
The rising, moving, wide-established frame—

a sentiment sounded again, though more musically, in the Hymn with which *The Seasons* concludes:

These, as they change, Almighty Father, these
Are but the varied God. The rolling year
Is full of Thee . . .

Mysterious round! what skill, what force divine,
Deep-felt in these appear! a simple train

Yet so delightful mixed, with such kind art,
Such beauty, and benificence combined.
Shade unperceived, so softening into shade,
And all so forming an harmonious whole
That, as they still succeed, they ravish still.

The idea of the "harmonious whole" retains an oddly childlike appeal. For my own part, in pre-adolescent days I used to read *The Seasons* annually, deriving from it a reassuring pleasure. The four books which comprise it appeared separately, in the order "Winter" (1726), "Summer" (1727), "Spring" (1728) and "Autumn" (1730), the latter part of the first collected volume.

What we may still enjoy in Thomson is his countryman's lore, the same lore lovingly noted by Henryson before him: for instance, the description by Thomson of the hesitancy of newly arrived Spring:

As yet the trembling year is unconfirmed,
And Winter oft at eve resumes the breeze,
Chills to pale morn, and bids his driving sleets
Deform the day delightless; so that scarce
The bittern knows his time with bill engulfed
To shake the sounding marsh; or from the shore
The plovers when to scatter o'er the heath,
And sing their wild notes to the listening waste.

There are good things, too, in each of the other three books, like this example of another hesitating weather-change, this time from "Winter":

With broadened nostrils to the sky upturned,
The conscious heifer snuffs the stormy gale,
Even as the matron, at her nightly task,
When pensive labour draws the flaxen thread,
The wasted taper and the crackling flame
Foretell the blast. But chief the plumy race,
The tenants of the sky, its changes speak.
Retiring from the downs, where all day long
They picked their scanty fare, a blackening train
Of clamorous rooks thick-urge their weary flight
And seek the closing shelter of the grove.
Assidious, in his bower, the wailing owl
Plies his sad song.

You have to take Thomson all of a piece, and put up with Latinizations like "umbrageous multitude of leaves" which often border on comicality, and the use of terms like "finny race" for fish, "feathered eddy" for swallows setting out on migration, and so on. These are simply the

Augustan equivalent of the "termis aureate" of the Makars, and devised for exactly the same purpose: an attempt to create heightened dignity. More irritating are Thomson's frequent recourses to apostrophe, personal reflection, moralizing, invocation and quasi-rhetorical questions which imply the poet's own answers. For all that, *The Seasons* is a fine poem, its varied nuances of observation not again to be sounded in English literature until Wordsworth, though never wholly absent from Scottish poetry.

Liberty, published in 1735 and dedicated to the poet's "lamented Talbot", need not detain us long. Its Miltonian strains rove fancifully in pursuit of the personified progress of that lady through ancient and modern Italy, Greece, Rome, Britain, and two thousand three hundred and eighty-four lines of turgid blank verse. Its culminating moment is a paean to the progress of the arts and industry in Britain. Thomson considered it his masterpiece. Dr Johnson gave up attempting to read it.

Much more rewarding is "The Castle of Indolence" (1748), two Cantos of verses couched in the Spenserian stanza and occasionally employing Thomson's idea of Spenserian language. In murmurous, sleepy tones which some critics have seen as presaging the mood-music of Tennyson's "The Lotus Eaters", the first canto describes the haunts of Indolence:

Was nought around but images of rest:
Sleep-soothing groves, and quiet lawns between;
And flowery beds that slumberous influence kest,
From poppies breathed; and beds of pleasant green,
Where never yet was creeping creature seen.
Meantime unnumbered glittering streamlets played,
And hurlèd everywhere their waters sheen;
That, as they bickered through the sunny glade,
Though restless still themselves, a lulling murmur made . . .
A pleasing land of drowsyhed it was:
Of dreams that wave before the half-shut eye;
And of gay castles in the clouds that pass,
For ever flushing round a summer sky:
There eke the soft delights, that witchingly
Instil a wanton sweetness through the breast,
And the calm pleasures always hovered nigh;
But whate'er smacked of noyance, or unrest,
Was far, far off expelled from this delicious nest.

However, in the second canto, this "delicious nest" is assailed by Sir Industry, who overthrows the Castle of Indolence, and enables Thomson to dissertate with approval upon:

Whatever arts and industry can frame,
Whatever finished agriculture knows . . .

In collaboration with Mallet, Thomson provided the text for *Alfred: A Masque*, staged to music by Thomas Augustine Arne in Cliveden House, near Maidenhead, at the command of the Prince of Wales, on 1st August 1737. For the last scene, Thomson provided the words of "Rule Britannia" which, declared Robert Southey, "will be the political hymn of this country as long as she maintains her political power", a statement that was to be borne out by fact.

Thomson's efforts at drama unsupported by music were less successful. *Agamemnon* was produced in 1738 and *Edward and Eleonora* published in 1739, when it ran into trouble with the censor. *Tancred and Sigismundo* followed in 1745, and *Coriolanus* in 1748, to be staged the following year.

The taste for stilted declamation by heroic characters pasted together out of the legends of antiquity did not survive the age that brought it forth. Indeed, Thomson's reputation as a "straight" dramatist now rests on what is commonly supposed to be one of the worst lines of verse ever written in English. It comes from his first tragedy, *Sophonisba*, and runs:

"Oh! Sophonisba, Sophonisba, oh!"—

which was soon parodied into:

"Oh! Jemmy Thomson, Jemmy Thomson, oh!"

It cannot be too often repeated that what ultimately matters about a writer is his best work, not his lapses. As Douglas Grant puts it, Thomson "sensibly affected the whole temperament of poetry, and could often claim as his own those praises which are lavished on his successors. His genius is only fully recognized when we attempt to imagine what would have been the course of English poetry and sensibility had he not written. We are for ever meeting the shadow of his presence as we read, or look out upon Nature."[12] Indeed we are; and furthermore, it is a curiously Scottish presence.

The dramatic success which eluded Thomson was visited briefly upon John Home (1722–1808), son of a Leith town clerk, who entered the ministry after graduating at Edinburgh University. He fought on the Hanoverian side during the '45, and became a Jacobite prisoner in Doune Castle. His pastoral career at Athelstaneford, East Lothian, came to a voluntary end after the Church courts moved against him following the presentation of his play *Douglas* on an Edinburgh stage in 1756. It was received with immense enthusiasm, a voice from the gallery shouting through the first-night applause, "Whaur's your Wullie Shakespeare now?". Not even success at London's Covent Garden in the following year made any answer to that rhetorical question necessary. For Garrick, who had initially rejected the play, as he had rejected the author's first attempt, *Agis*, was soon proved right. The blank verse of *Douglas* is stiff and stilted, much of it banal. An example of it at its best is the first speech of the hero, a passage for long a favourite with Victorian parlour elocutionists:

My name is Norval: on the Grampian hills
My father feeds his flocks; a frugal swain,
Whose constant cares were to increase his store,
And keep his only son, myself, at home.
For I had heard of battles, and I long'd
To follow to the field some warlike Lord:
And heaven soon granted what my Sire deny'd.

Nominally at least, heaven appeared to become considerably involved, because the "high-flyers" of the Church, who thought theatrical performances immoral and tried to impose a ban on clerical attendance, were defeated by the determined defiance of that formidable figure, the Reverend Alexander "Jupiter" Carlyle.

Home became private secretary to the Earl of Bute, and thereafter tutor to the Prince of Wales. On his accession to the throne as George III, the dramatist was granted an annual pension of £300. No doubt this compensated in some measure for the varying degrees of failure experienced by his later pseudo-Shakespearian dramas, now taken up by Garrick, *The Siege of Aquileia* (1760), *The Fatal Discovery* (1769), *Alonzo* (1773) and *Alfred* (1778). His *History of the Rebellion of 1745* (1801) is of some interest where it relates to his personal experiences. He spent his last days in the midst of Edinburgh's brilliant circle of talkers, the historian Principal Robertson at the centre of these northern New Athenians. Today, Home is remembered mostly for the amusing lines he produced when a heavy duty was imposed on claret:

Bold and erect the Caledonian stood,
Old was his mutton and his claret good;
Let him drink port, the English statesman cried—
He drank the poison, and his spirit died.

A more immediate contemporary of Thomson's was Robert Blair (1699–1746), son of an Edinburgh clergyman. The poet also became a minister, and was actually Home's predecessor at Athelstaneford. Blair's lugubrious blank verse poem *The Grave* (1743) owes much to Young's *Night Thoughts*, the first part of which had appeared the previous year. Blair could produce a telling single line now and then, but lacked Young's sustaining power, sporadic even though that was.

It is often difficult for us to understand the enthusiasm of a past age that could applaud Blair's morbid meditations. The case of William Falconer

(1732–1769), son of an Edinburgh barber, is easier to understand. His poem *The Shipwreck* was the outcome of his own experience. For all its heaviness of movement, the detailed describing of ship's-business had not been attempted before:

A lowering squall obscures the southern sky,
Before whose sweeping breath the waters fly;
Its weight the topsails can no more sustain—
Reef topsails, reef! the master calls again.
The halyards and top bow-lines soon are gone,
To clue lines and reef tackles next they run:
The shivering sails descend; the yards are square:
Then quick aloft the ready crew repair:
The weather earings and the lee they past,
The reefs enrolled and every point made fast . . .

Before the storm breaks, Palemon, the purser and son of the owner, sent to sea to cure him of his passion for the daughter of Albert, the captain, recounts his love story to Arion, the second mate. The shipwreck and its aftermath are portrayed with vivid realism, in spite of the inappropriateness of the formal heroic couplet for the depiction of violent formlessness.

Burns had a high regard for the poem, recommending it to Mrs Dunlop and, on 25th July 1790, answering her query as to the fate of the author:

Falconer, the poor unfortunate Author of the Shipwreck, that glorious Poem which you so much admire, is no more. After weathering that dreadful catastrophe he so feelingly describes in his Poem, and after weathering many hard gales of Fortune, he went to the bottom with the Aurora frigate! . . . He was one of those daring adventurous spirits which old Caledonia beyond any other nation is remarkable for producing.

The eighteenth century's attempt to revive the medieval use of verse as a medium for conveying information because of its easier memorability failed, as revivalist endeavours out of context usually do. Social conditions and literary techniques had both irrevocably changed. While we need not concern ourselves here with the sillier English verse-treatises on a wide variety of subjects, we must note John Armstrong (1709?–1779), son of a Roxburghshire minister, who took his medical degree in Edinburgh and practised in London. Friendly with Thomson, Armstrong is said to have contributed the four stanzas at the end of the first part of "The Castle of Indolence". On his own, he produced *The Economy of Love* in 1736, which led an apothecary of the time to observe: "How, in the name of heaven, could he ever expect that a woman would let him enter her house again, after that?"[13]

"That" was, in fact, a practical sex manual intended for the helpful instruction of married couples. Having for the first time removed the beloved's clothes, the young man is told:

> . . . Then when her lovely limbs,
> Oft lovely deem'd, far lovelier now beheld,
> Thro' all your trembling joints increase the flame;
> Forthwith discover to her dazzled sight
> The stately novelty, and to her hand
> Usher the new acquaintance. She perhaps
> Averse, will coldly chide, and half afraid,
> Blushing, half pleas'd, the tumid wonder view.

Armstrong's main claim to fame,—if such be the proper word—is his equally gross misuse of the Thomsonian periphrasis in *The Art of Preserving Health* (1744), though again the work was primarily intended to be of practical use.

So, too, were innumerable other "instructive" poems of the period. In a Scottish context, one that has at least the merit of being funny is James Arbuckle's *Glotha*, written while he was a student at Glasgow University. Arbuckle, a friend of Allan Ramsay, became a schoolmaster in Northern Ireland, dying at thirty-four. His lines on "Golf on Glasgow Green, 1721" might not have frightened Armstrong's ladies. It is doubtful if they would have been particularly helpful to their menfolk either.

> In winter, too, when hoary frosts o'erspread
> The verdant turf, and naked lay the mead,
> The vig'rous youth commence the sportive war,
> And, arm'd with lead, their jointed clubs prepare
> The timber curve to leathern orbs apply,
> Compact, elastic, to pervade the sky;
> These to the distant hole direct they drive;
> They claim the stakes who hither first arrive.
> Intent his ball the eager gamester eyes,
> His muscle strains, and various postures tries,
> Th' impelling blow to strike with greater force,
> And shape the motive orb's projectile course.
> If with due strength the weighty engine fall,
> Discharged obliquely, and impinge the ball,
> It winding mounts aloft, and sings in air;
> And wondering crowds the gamesters skill declare.
> But when some hapless wayward stroke descends,
> Whose force the ball in running quickly spends,
> The foes triumph, the club is cursed in vain,
> Spectators scoff and even allies complain.

Thus still success is followed with applause;
But ah! how few espouse a vanquish'd cause.

Another of Thomson's friends was David Malloch or Mallet
(1700–1765), who hailed from Perthshire, a descendant of one the fierce
MacGregors whose persistent banditry led to the proscribing of their name
in 1603 and their subsequent adoption of Malloch, derived from the Gaelic
Mollachd, "Accursed", in its stead. Malloch Anglicized his name after John
Dennis instigated the prank of referring to him as "Moloch". It was an
appropriate enough joke, for Mallet accepted £1000 under the will of the
Duchess of Marlborough to write a biography of her husband, the Duke.
The author pocketed the money, reported continuing assiduity in the pro-
gress of his work, but never wrote a word. His ballad "William and Mar-
garet" was founded on the seduction of a daughter of Professor Gregory of
St Andrews by Sir William Sharpe of Strathryum, nephew of the notorious Archbishop Sharp. His play *Mustapha* (1739), satirizing Walpole in
order to please Prince Frederick, like his other dramas *Eurydice* (1731) and
Elvira (1763), and his poem *The Excursion* (1728) have been forgotten.
What has not been forgotten is that this janitor from the High School of
Edinburgh who became tutor to the Duke of Montrose, sold his vituperous
journalistic talents to Bolingbroke, for whom he vilified the dead Alexander Pope. Mallet further compromised his integrity by arousing dishonest mob fury against Admiral Byng through a letter published over the
signature "A plain Man" in return for a state pension.

An interesting follower of Thomson was the anonymous author of
Albania, a poem also couched in the imitation Miltonic style of the period.
First published in 1737 by T. Cooper in London, and dedicated by the editor to General Wade, only one copy of the original edition survived. It
came into the possession of Beattie, and was seen by Leyden during a
northern tour. Leyden then reissued it in 1803, along with Wilson's *Clyde*
and some earlier poems by Hume and Fowler, under the title *Scottish Descriptive Poems*. In two hundred and ninety-six lines the poet—claimed by
the original editor to have been "a Scots clergyman"—demonstrates by his
use of Gaelic names and epithets that he was probably himself a Highlander.

Another image in this ardent survey in verse of Scotland's legendary past
and physical present, "Loved Albania, hardy nurse of men", may have
been at the back of Scott's mind when he wrote:

O Caledonia! stern and wild,
Meet nurse for a poetic child!

But the most interesting aspect of *Albania* is its author's representation of
such local phenomena as the belief that over the mountainy solitude of the
Highlands, fairy hunters ride:

There oft is heard at midnight, or at noon,
Beginning faint, but rising still more loud
And nearer, voice of hunters and of hounds,
And horns hoarse-winded, blowing far and keen;
Forthwith the hubbub multiplies, the gale
Labours with wilder shrieks, and rifer din
Of hot pursuit—the broken cry of deer
Mangled by throttling dogs, the shouts of men,
And hoofs thick-beating on the hollow hill.
Sudden the grazing heifer in the vale
Starts at the noise, and both the herdsman's ears
Tingle with inward dread. Aghast he eyes
The mountain's height and all the ridges round,
Yet not one trace of living wight discerns;
Nor knows, o'erawed, and trembling as he stands,
To what or whom he owes his idle fear,
To ghost, to witch, to fairy, or to fiend,
But wonders, and no end of wondering finds.

That Highland world of hot pursuit and throttling dogs, to say nothing of the awareness of inexplicable fears, was a far cry from the gentle purl of Thomson's Thames-side ambience, and looks forward to the grim faerie world of Hogg.

John Wilson (1720–1789), the son of a Lanarkshire farmer, wrote a tragedy, *Earl Douglas*, in imitation of Home's *succès d'estime*, and a once-popular poem in rhyming couplets, *Clyde*, both published in 1764. By then the father of nine children, and in order to become a master in the grammar school of Greenock, he had to sign an undertaking to abandon "the profane and unprofitable art of poetry-making". Though *Clyde* makes pleasant reading, the loss to Scotland was not great.

The poem, which invites comparison with Denham's *Cooper's Hill* and Pope's *Windsor Forest*, is marred by false periphrases, mis-applied classical allusions, and what an admiring contemporary critic called "a number of moral sentiments, judiciously interspersed."

William Wilkie (1721–1772) of Dalmenny, an eccentrically mannered farmer who struggled through university to reach a pulpit of his own at Ratho, become Professor of Natural Philosophy at St Andrews, and secure the admiration of David Hume for a poem of epic proportions on the siege of Thebes, *Epigoniad* (1757), and some dull *Moral Fables in Verse* (1768), would be quite forgotten but for the philosopher's surprising outburst in the defence of his friend. Smollett, at that time editor of the *Critical Review*, had drawn attention to faults in Wilkie's prosody. Hume retorted furiously, pointing out what he considered to be the work's merits, and excusing such failures as it might have as being due "entirely from the author's being a Scotchman, who had never been out of his own country."

Tobias Smollett (1721–1771), though primarily a novelist, is still remembered as a poet for the indignant patriotism which inspired his "The Tears of Scotland", following the butchery of Culloden in 1746, and for his "Ode to Leven Water", which first appeared in *Humphry Clinker* (1771).

Of other classicists, the most famous in his own day was undoubtedly James Beattie (1735–1803), as a poet never quite able to match form and content. His "Hermit" has the rhythm of a gregarious drinking song. This ludicrous effect could hardly have been the poet's intention. His most popular piece, "The Minstrel", uneasily drifts through Spenserian stanzas, bereft of the music and dignity with which the inventor of that form could fill it out. Beattie did, however, possess a thin-coloured talent for nature-painting which still allows "The Minstrel" to retain a certain watery charm:

> But who the melodies of morn can tell?—
>   The wild brook babbling down the mountain side;
> The lowing herd; the sheepfold's simple bell;
>   The pipe of early shepherd dim descried
>   In the lone valley; echoing far and wide,
> The clamorous horn along the cliffs above;
>   The hollow murmur of the ocean-tide;
>   The hum of bees; the linnet's lay of love;
> And the full choir that wakes the universal grove.
>
> The cottage curs at early pilgrim bark;
>   Crowned with her pail the tripping milkmaid sings;
> The whistling ploughman stalks afield; and hark!
>   Down the rough slope the ponderous waggon rings.
>   Through rustling corn the hare astonished springs;
> Slow tolls the village clock the drowsy hour;
>   The partridge bursts away on whirring wings;
> Deep mourns the turtle in sequestered bower,
> And shrill lark carols clear from her aërial tower.

Beattie, who vainly attempted to refute Hume's scepticism, and was taken in by "Ossian" Macpherson, nevertheless became Professor of Moral Philosophy at the University of Aberdeen and induced Dr Johnson to proclaim: "We all love Beattie. Mrs Thrale says if ever she has another husband she will have him."

The blind clergyman Dr Thomas Blacklock (1721–1791), a native of Annan, perversely insisted on writing neo-classical descriptive verse, and would probably be forgotten but for his part in persuading Burns to abandon his intention to flee to the West Indies when his amorous involvements caught up with him in 1786. The name of John Lapraik (1727–1807), a laird ruined by the failure of the Ayr bank who turned farmer, miller and pub-owner at Muirkirk, survives partly because Burns wrote "honest-hearted auld Lapraik" three verse-epistles, and partly because Burns sufficiently admired Lapraik's song "When I upon thy Bosom lean" (which conjures up an image of some physical discomfort for the object of his attentions!) to print it in the *Museum*. Lyrics celebrating married love are not over plentiful.

Michael Bruce (1746–1767), born in the weaving village of Kinnesswood, Kinrossshire, was the son of a pious Burgher elder. Young Bruce got himself to Edinburgh University, came down at nineteen to teach near Alloa, and two years later was dead of consumption, having foreseen his own end in his sadly melodious "Elegy for Spring":

Now Spring returns, but not to me returns
   The vernal joys my better years have known,
Dim in my breast life's dying taper burns,
   And all the joys of life with health are flown!

When that taper had guttered out, Bruce's college friend, John Logan (1748–1788), was entrusted with the task of bringing out the dead man's poems. Logan, a known sermon-plagiarist, produced a volume of sorts, but claimed authorship of the "Ode to the Cuckoo" in his own volume, published eleven years later. The "Cuckoo" is a slight enough piece; but it sounds a clear pair of notes, contrasting the bird with no sorrow in its song, "no winter in thy year", and the poet, aware of impending dissolution:

Alas! sweet bird! not so my fate,
   Dark scowling skies I see,
Fast gathering round, and fraught with woe
   And wintry years to me.

Of necessity, Logan had to omit this "autobiographical" stanza when he laid claim to Bruce's work.

Bruce and Logan both had a hand in several of the most famous of the Church of Scotland's paraphrases, although Logan's share was probably no more than that of a polisher. Generation after generation of Scots have probably thrilled to Bruce's resounding paraphrase words:

No strife shall rage, nor hostile feuds
   disturb those peaceful years;
To ploughshares men shall bend their swords
   to pruning-forks their spears.

No longer hosts encount'ring hosts
   shall crowds of slain deplore;

They hang the trumpet in the hall,
and study war no more.

The classical English tradition, though it neither ousted nor even matched that of Scots, lingered long, among its northern autumnal fruits being *The Course of Time*, a vast didactic blank verse poem by Robert Pollock (1789–1827), which came out the year of his death, went through eighty editions in Scotland, and more than a hundred and sixty in America. Had he lived, he would have surpassed even Sir Walter Scott's earnings on a single long poem.

His moralizing seems exactly fitted to the receptive mould of Victorian pietism. But the popularity of this "Milton in Scots hodden", as Lauchlan MacLean Watt called him, is not likely to revive in an age turned against fanciful genealogy and stained-glass sentimentality. I have always been amused by his not wholly unjust description of the race of critics, which is to be found in the eighth of the poem's ten books.

> . . . some, but few
> Were worthy men, and earned renown which had
> Immortal roots; but most were weak and vile.
> And, as a cloudy swarm of summer flies,
> With angry hum and slender lance, beset
> The sides of some huge animal, so did
> They buzz about the illustrious man, and fain,
> With his immortal honour, down the stream
> Of Fame would have descended: but alas!
> The hand of Time drove them away. They were,
> Indeed, a simple race of men, who had
> One only art, which taught them still to say
> Whate'er was done might have been better done;
> And with this art, not ill to learn, they made
> A shift to live . . .

There was Roxburghshire-born John Leyden (1775–1811). In many ways he was at heart a romantic in his enthusiasm for Gothic poetry and ballad-collecting, and helped Scott with *The Minstrelsy of the Scottish Border*. But Leyden also had a passion for Arabic and Persian, which led him to become a judge in India, and so to visit Java, where he caught a fatal virulent fever. Yet he was a classicist in his own writings, the most sustained of which is his *Scenes of Infancy* (1803). The form and the content sometimes contrast rather oddly:

> The woodland's sombre shade that peasants fear,
> The haunted mountain streams that murmur'd near,
> The antique tomb-stone and the churchyard green,
> Seem'd to unite me with the world unseen:

Oft when the eastern moon rose darkly red,
I heard the viewless paces of the dead,
Heard in the breeze the wandering spirits sigh,
Or airy skirts unseen, that rustled by.

Here, the feeling is romantic and nineteenth century, the mode of expression that of the eighteenth century, as, more characteristically, both usually were with Leyden.

Teviot, farewell! for now thy silver tide
Commix'd with Tweed's pellucid stream shall glide;
But all thy green and pastoral beauties fail
To match the softness of thy parting vale.

Great learning often damps down poetic fires. Scott, however, thought sufficiently highly of his dead friends to write a laudatory memoir of him in the *Edinburgh Annual Register* of 1811, and to commemorate him in Canto IV of *The Lord of the Isles*:

Quenched is his lamp of varied lore,
That loved the light of song to pour;
A distant and a deadly shore
   Holds Leyden's cold remains.

The final poet whose work must here be considered belongs in the company of the Scottish classicists only insofar as he looked for his inspiration primarily to the ancients of the Celtic rather than the Greco-Roman world. James Macpherson (1736–1796) was born at Ruthven, Invernesshire. After studying at Marischal College, Aberdeen, he took to school-mastering. His early poem *The Highlander* (1758), in English heroic couplets, has little to commend it, though it shows that Macpherson had a desire to achieve a Scottish patriotic epic before he assumed the mantle of Ossian. Meeting John Home, the author of *Douglas*, at Moffat where Macpherson was then tutoring, he was persuaded by the playwright to publish some translations from the Gaelic. These appeared in Edinburgh in 1760 as *Fragments of Ancient Poetry Collected in the Highlands of Scotland and translated from the Gaelic or Erse language*. The Edinburgh literati, Dr Hugh Blair, Professor Adam Fergusson and Principal William Robertson in particular, to say nothing of Beattie, were wildly enthusiastic about this production. The preface contained the claim that a major epic in Gaelic existed which, given money and encouragement, Macpherson could recover. The money was raised and, accompanied by several Gaelic scholars, Macpherson made an exploratory tour, the results of which appeared as *Fingal*, published with fifteen smaller poems in 1762, and *Temora*, an epic in eight books which came before the public the following year.

The authenticity of Macpherson's translations was quickly challenged by Dr Johnson (part of the purpose of whose Scottish visit was to gain further evidence in support of his scepticism), David Hume (after a brief period of support for Macpherson) and Malcolm Laing. A resounding controversy broke out, and reverbrated throughout Scottish and English literary circles for more than a century. Challenged to produce his Gaelic originals, Macpherson failed to do so during his lifetime. Unfortunately, when the Highland Society eventually made them available in 1807, the manuscripts had been revised, transcribed for publication, and then destroyed.

Numerous later scholars investigated the mystery, notably Alexander Macbain in 1885[14] and L. C. Stern[15] in 1893. The facts seem to be that Macpherson did possess some fragments in Gaelic, though not necessarily of third-century origin; that much of the English material is of his own invention, blending or confusing the Ulster and Fenian heroic cycles, and devising names like Selma for which there is no Gaelic original; that Macpherson's Gaelic is "unnaturally strained" and unidiomatic; that the Gaelic versions of 1807 represent only about half the English versions; and that the *Temora* of 1763 is quite different from the 1807 Gaelic version.

Macpherson made money out of his work, and no doubt as a result of his poetic fame, is reported to have been paid £3,000 for his *Original Papers, containing the Secret History of Great Britain from the Restoration to the Accession of the House of Hanover; to which are prefixed Extracts from the Life of James II, as written by himself* (1775). As a public defender of Lord North's government, Macpherson received a handsome salary, and was also well-paid as the London agent of Mohammed Ali, Nabob of Arcot. In 1780 Macpherson entered Parliament. He died at his estate, Belville, Inverness, a rich man, and was buried at his own expense in Westminster Abbey.

It is easy to dismiss Macpherson as a literary forger whose "translations" undoubtedly abound in Homeric and Miltonic overtones. It is certainly the case that the inflated poetic prose in which they are couched is not at all to the taste of the late twentieth century. A brief extract will allow readers to form their own judgement:

> Now I behold the chiefs, in the pride of their former deeds! Their souls are kindled at the battles of old, and the actions of other times. Their eyes are like flames of fire, and roll in search of the foes of the land. Their mighty hands are on their swords. And lightning pours from their sides of steel. They come like streams from the mountains; each rushes roaring from his hill. Bright are the chiefs of battle, in the armour of their fathers. Gloomy and dark their heroes follow like the gathering of the rainy clouds behind the red meteors of heaven. The sounds of crashing arms ascend. The grey dogs howl between. Unequally bursts the song of battle. And rocking Cromla echoes round. On Lena's dusky heath they stand, like mist that shades the hills of autumn: when broken and dark it settles high and lifts its head to heaven!
>
> "Hail," said Cuthullin, "sons of the narrow vales! hail, ye hunters of the

deer! Another sport is drawing near: it is like the dark rolling of that wave on the coast! Shall we fight, ye sons of war! or yield green Inisfail to Lochlin! O Connal, speak thou first of men! thou breaker of the shields! thou hast often fought with Lochlin: wilt thou lift thy father's spear.

"Cuthullin!" calm the chief replied, "the spear of Connal is keen. It delights to shine in battle, and to mix with the blood of thousands. But though my head is bent on war, my heart is for the peace of Erin. Behold, thou first in Cormac's war, the sable fleet of Swaran. His masts are as numerous on our coast as reeds in the lake of Lego. His ships are like forests clothed with mist, when the trees yield by turns to the squally wind. Many are his chiefs in battle. Connal is for peace! Fingal would shun his arm, the first of mortal men! Fingal who scatters the mighty, as stormy winds the heath, when the streams roar through echoing Cona, and night settles with all her clouds on the hill!"

"Fly, thou chief of peace," said Calmar, the son of Matha; "fly, Connal, to thy silent hills, where the spear of battle never shone! Pursue the dark-brown deer of Cromla: and stop with thine arrows the bounding roes of Lena. But blue-eyed son of Semo, Cuthullin, ruler of the war, scatter thou the sons of Lochlin! and roar through the ranks of their pride. Let no vessel of the kingdom of snow bound on the dark-rolling waves of Inistore. O ye dark winds of Erin rise! roar ye whirlwinds of the heath! Amidst the tempest let me die, torn in a cloud by angry ghosts of men; amidst the tempest let Calmar die, if ever chase was sport to him, so much as the battle of shields."

Whatever may be later reactions to his Gael-mongering, no amount of high-toned purist condemnation gets over the fact that Macpherson's influence on Europe was immense. Herder and Goethe were among his German admirers, and Cesaroth's Italian translation of *The Works of Ossian* (as the collected 1775 volume was called) became one of Napoleon's favourite books. The cloudy heroes of this so-called Celtic Homer not only turned men's attention to the force of Nature in lonely places, but did much to institute that renaissance of wonder which provided the foundation of the Romantic movement. Composers as widely different in outlook as Mehul, Pavesi, Gade and Ippolitov-Ivanov used Ossianic ideas for operas or symphonic works, and Scotland became established in the European mind as a major source of romance and heroic myth. Macpherson thus prepared the way for that triumphal progress along which Sir Walter Scott (who did not himself believe the Ossian poems to be genuine) was later to carry the romanticized fame of Scotland's story to every corner of civilized Europe.

III

Eighteenth-century Scottish prose falls mainly into three categories: philosophical, theological and historical writing: 'private' autobiographical literature and biography; and fiction.

By far the greatest writer in the first category was David Hume (1711–1776). He was the second son of Joseph Hume, laird of Ninewells, a small estate in Berwickshire. Born in Edinburgh and educated at Edinburgh University, David Hume, who had been intended for the law, left without taking a degree. He then spent three years reading voraciously at home. After a brief period in a Bristol counting-house, he went to Rheims and La Flèche, in France, where he produced his first major work, *A Treatise on Human Nature*. The first two volumes were published in 1739, the concluding volume coming out the following year. Hume believed—rightly, as it happened—that he had hit upon a new philosophical system, or "Scheme of Thought", as he called it. The *Treatise* formed the grounding for much of his later writings.

It fell on deaf ears at first; perhaps hardly surprisingly, since its author was refusing to take for granted the rationality of the existence of the external world, and had dared critically to examine the concepts of substance and cause. No review appeared for seven months after the book was published, and the one review then forthcoming was frivolous and uncomprehending; so Hume published an anonymous abstract of the *Treatise*. However, his sceptical philosophy, the foundations of which were laid in this work, conceived in adolescence, dealt a death-blow to all previous rationalistic metaphysics and ethics. It stimulated Kant to stir from his "dogmatic slumbers"; it was elaborated, rather than advanced upon, by such later philosophers as J. S. Mill; it provided Jeremy Bentham with much of the inspiration behind his doctrine of Utilitarianism; and it established the ancestry of Logical Positivism in our own century.

It is not, however, our task in a history of Scottish literature to concern ourselves, other than superficially, with the philosophical significance of Hume's achievement. He followed up his early work with *Essays Moral and Political* in 1741 and 1742 respectively, and in 1748 with his *Philosophical Essays Concerning Human Understanding*, less fundamental than the *Treatise* though more famous, and containing the essay on "Miracles" which effectively cut away whatever logical or scientific props theology had previously claimed upheld it. Hume himself considered his *Inquiry concerning the Principles of Morals*, published in 1751–1752—virtually a re-cast of Book 3 of the *Treatise*—to be his best work. While it was being written, he was also preparing his *Dialogues concerning Natural Religion* which, according to the terms of his will, was published posthumously.

It takes the form of an interlocution between Demea, who maintains that the existence of God is capable of *a priori* proof; Cleanthes, a Lockeian deist maintaining that the proof of God's existence was *a posteriori*, or from evidence of design; and Philo, who upholds Hume's view that argument from reason or experience cannot transcend experience itself, and that therefore no kind of proof of God's existence is possible.

In 1745, in the midst of all this activity, Hume applied for, but failed to get, the chair of Moral Philosophy at the University of Edinburgh; instead, he undertook a well-paid but tedious engagement as private tutor to a young nobleman, the Marquis of Annandale, ending when the philosopher had to resort to legal action to secure arrears of salary. In 1747, in the position of Judge-Advocate-General, he accompanied General St Clair on the disastrous military expedition to the Brittany coast, and later on diplomatic missions to Vienna and Turin.

In 1752, Hume became librarian to the Faculty of Advocates, and in the same year published his *Political Discourses*, following this work in 1753 with *Essays and Treatises on Various Subjects*; subjects which included Commerce, Money, Interest and the Balance of Trade. These helped to establish the relation between economic facts and other aspects of social life, and by applying historical method, could be said to have gone some way towards laying the foundations of economic science. Librarians in those days were poorly paid. Although his job must have allowed him ample opportunity for research, Hume's salary was only £40 per annum, so in 1757, the year in which his *Natural History of Religion* was published, he resigned.

His travels abroad had given him time and opportunity to assemble material for a *History of England* in five volumes, the first two volumes of which came out in 1754 and 1756, the work being completed in 1762.

Hume undoubtedly revolutionized the approach to the writing of history, in that his work is a first attempt at comprehensively treating historic facts, regarding sociology and literature as of importance in a nation's life. He did not, of course, have access to the information available to later historians. But the main defect of this work is simply that it deteriorates in quality as it advances in length. Because he believed the political divisions of his own day to originate with the early seventeenth century, Hume begins his work with James I and VI. Its judgements on the disputed issues of the period are generally regarded as fair. But initially, this volume met with a poor reception from the public, and Hume's disappointment resulted in the beginnings of his hatred of things English, and his belief that there existed in London a conspiracy to eradicate Scottishness. In Volume II, Hume brought his account up to the Revolution of 1688. He then decided to work backwards, giving freer reign to his Tory beliefs, but distorting the possibilities of any reasonable overall form. Nevertheless, after its slow commercial start, the work not only sold so well that it ran through many editions (giving Hume revisionary opportunities to remove what he called "plaguy prejudices of Whiggism"), but actually earned its author more money than any previous literary production.

In 1763, Hume was chosen to accompany the Earl of Hertford, the British Ambassador, to Paris, where Hume became Secretary to the Embassy. While his later works had sold well and Hume was now by no means a poor man, his popularity at home was affected by the hue and cry crystallized later by such unsuccessful attempts to refute his sceptical religious views as the *Essay on the Nature and Immortality of Truth* by James

Beattie, Professor of Moral Philosophy at Aberdeen University, and the *Dissertation on Miracles* by George Campbell (1719–1796), Principal of Marischal College. In France, he was received with the respect due to an eminent man of letters as well as that to which he was entitled by virtue of his official position. In the Ambassador's wake he met Voltaire, Diderot, d'Alembert and Rousseau, the latter, however, treating Hume with the same vicious ingratitude meted out to all who sought to help that many-talented but unhappy prince of sentimentalists. Hume, against all advice, imported the stateless philosopher—exiled from Switzerland and France—to England, and established him in Staffordshire, equipping him with both a mistress and a dog for company. Rousseau nevertheless believed Hume to be plotting his ridicule, and as a result of the public quarrel which ensued Hume was forced in self-defence to publish the correspondence, which clearly showed that Rousseau, said to be the only man ever to hate Hume personally, was mad.

From 1767 to 1769 he was Under-Secretary of State. London seemed cold and unreceptive after France, and left Hume not only with his permanent dislike of the English, but also a grievance against their capital city, where he seems best to have enjoyed the society of his fellow-countrymen, the novelist Tobias Smollett, a man of "great urbanity of conversation" and "polished and agreeable manners", and the autobiographer Dr Alexander ("Jupiter") Carlyle.

Nevertheless, Hume seems in general to have been possessed of a balanced and equable temperament. On his return to his native city in 1769, he had built for himself a house in a then unnamed street linking Princes Street with St Andrews Square. His friend Nancy Orde chalked "St David's Street" on the walls of his house. The street has been so named ever since.

Hume contracted cancer of the bowels, and realized that he was fatally ill. He went on cheerfully making corrections for future editions of his works, and shortly before his death on 29th August, put to shame the inquisitive James Boswell, who paid a call expressly to find out how a sceptical philosopher faced death. Robert Adam designed Hume's monument in Calton Cemetery.

His real monument is, of course, his work. Enough has been said to indicate the scope of its subject matter and the variety of its influence. Hume believed in clarity of expression, and in an age when rhetorical pomposity was still generally favoured by some Scots lawyers and divines, he held that the true purpose of language was communication. In a letter to his cousin, the playwright John Home, Hume says: "Of all the vices of language, the least excusable is the want of perspicuity; for, as words were instituted by men merely for conveying their ideas to each other, the employing of words without meaning is a palpable abuse, which departs from the very original purpose and intention of language."

Hume's political writings assume a greater degree of the influence of reason on men, and on the formulation of the policies of political parties, than in fact exists. Thus, in his essay "The Science of Politics", he observes:

> Those who attack or defend a minister in such a government as ours, where the utmost liberty is allowed, always carry matters to an extreme, and exaggerate his merit or demerit with regard to the public. His enemies are sure to charge him with the greatest enormities, both in domestic and foreign management; and there is no meanness or crime, of which, in their account, he is not capable . . . On the other hand, the partisans of the minister make his panegyric run as high as the accusation against him, and celebrate his wise, steady, and moderate conduct in every part of his administration.

Hume concludes:*

> There are enow of zealots on both sides, who kindle up the passions of their partisans, and, under pretence of public good, pursue the interests of their particular faction. For my part, I shall always be more fond of promoting moderation than zeal; though perhaps the surest way of promoting moderation in every party is to measure our zeal for the public. Let us therefore try, if it be possible . . . to draw a lesson of moderation with regard to the parties into which our country is at present divided; at the same time, that we allow not this moderation to abate the industry and passion, with which every individual is bound to pursue the good of his country.

Moderation was not a term which the contemporary defenders of orthodox religion would have readily applied to Hume. His elegant demolition of many of their beliefs, including the defence of religion through reason, may best be illustrated by a quotation from the famous essay "Of Miracles". There is no mistaking the drift of what is intended here:

> What we have said of miracles, may be applied without any variation to prophecies; and, indeed, all prophecies are real miracles, and as such, only can be admitted as proofs of any revelation. If it did not exceed the capacity of human nature to foretell future events, it would be absurd to employ any prophecy as an argument for a divine mission or authority from heaven. So that, upon the whole, we may conclude, that the *Christian Religion* not only was at first attended with miracles, but even at this day cannot be believed by any reasonable person without one. Mere reason is insufficient to convince us of its veracity: and whoever is moved by *Faith* to assent to it, is conscious of a continued miracle in his own person, which subverts all the principles of his understanding, and gives him a determination to believe what is most contrary to custom and experience. Our most holy religion is founded on *Faith*, not on reason; and it is a sure method of exposing it to put it to such a trial as it is by no means fitted to endure . . . Thus, suppose all authors, in all languages, agree, that, from the 1st of January, 1600, there was a total darkness over the

---

* For the sake of clarity, in these abbreviated quotations I have reversed the order in which the passages appear in the original.

whole earth for eight days: suppose that the tradition of this extraordinary event is still strong and lively among the people: that all travellers who return from foreign countries bring us accounts of the same tradition, without the least variation or contradiction: it is evident that our present philosophers, instead of doubting the fact, ought to receive it as certain, and ought to search for the causes whence it might be derived. The decay, corruption, and dissolution of nature, is an event rendered probable by so many analogies, that any phenomenon, which seems to have a tendency towards that catastrophe, comes within the reach of human testimony, if that testimony be very extensive and uniform.

But suppose that all the historians who treat of England should agree, that on the first of January, 1600, Queen Elizabeth died; that both before and after her death, she was seen by her physicians and the whole court, as is usual with persons of her rank; that her successor was acknowledged and proclaimed by the Parliament; and that, after being interred for a month, she again appeared, resumed the throne, and governed England for three years; I must confess that I should be surprised at the concurrence of so many odd circumstances, but should not have the least inclination to believe so miraculous an event. I should not doubt of her pretended death, and of those other public circumstances that followed it: I should only assert it to have been pretended, and that it neither was, nor possibly could be, real. You would in vain object to me the difficulty, and almost impossibility of deceiving the world in an affair of such consequence; the wisdom and solid judgment of that renowned Queen; with the little or no advantage which she could reap from so poor an artifice: all this might astonish me; but I would still reply, that the knavery and folly of men are such common phenomena, that I should rather believe the most extraordinary events to arise from their concurrence, than admit of so signal a violation of the laws of nature.

But should this miracle be ascribed to any new system of religion; men, in all ages, have been so much imposed on by ridiculous stories of that kind, that this very circumstance would be a full proof of a cheat, and sufficient, with all men of sense, not only to make them reject the fact, but even reject it without further examination. Though the being to whom the miracle is ascribed, be in this case Almighty, it does not, upon that account, become a whit more probable; since it is impossible for us to know the attributes or actions of such a Being, otherwise than from the experience which we have of his productions in the usual course of nature. This still reduces us to past observation, and obliges us to compare the instances of the violation of truth in the testimony of men, with those of the violation of the laws of nature by miracles, in order to judge which of them is most likely and probable. As the violations of truth are more common in the testimony concerning religious miracles than in that concerning any other matter of fact; this must diminish very much the authority of the former testimony, and make us form a general resolution never to lend any attention to it, with whatever specious pretence it may be covered.

Against this sort of argument, the eloquence of Dr Hugh Blair (1718–1800), five volumes of whose sermons were published in Edinburgh and London between 1777 and 1801, was of no avail. His work was later to be dismissed by Gosse as "Blair's bucket of warm water". The man would scarcely be worth even the mentioning were it not that, as minister of the High Kirk of St Giles and then as Professor of Rhetoric at Edinburgh University, Blair exercised enormous influence, was extremely popular, and even won the admiration of Burns, whom he befriended, and to whom he gave singularly bad advice on what to hold back from publication. Burns, however, though grateful for the support of such a pillar of the moderate establishment, described Blair as "an astonishing proof of what industry and application can do". Sir Leslie Stephen was later unkindly to depict him "mouthing his sham rhetoric".

The university at which Blair declaimed, as well as its sister establishment at Glasgow, had others equally renowned for "eloquence", including Colin Maclaurin (1698–1746), the mathematician, whom Dugald Stewart (1753–1828) tells us could "adorn the most abstracted subjects" with it; the anatomist Alexander Monro (1697–1767); and, of course, the philosophers of the Scottish School: Francis Hutcheson (1694–1746), whose principal works, the *Inquiry into the Original of our Ideas of Beauty and Virtue* (1725), the Essay on the *Nature and Conduct of the Passions* (1728) and *System of Moral Philosophy* (1755), much influenced by Shaftesbury's benevolent notions, are as little likely to promote literary interest today as the *Works* of Thomas Reid (1710–1796), Professor of Moral Philosophy at Aberdeen, later Adam Smith's successor in the same subject at Glasgow. By questioning Hume's total scepticism, in his *Inquiry into the Human Mind* (1764) and *Essays on the Intellectual Powers of Man* (1785), Reid did his best to confront scepticism with "common sense", seeking to establish that the "ultimate elements of experience" are not simply unrelated sense perceptions. He maintained, in fact, that the unit of knowledge was not an isolated impression, but a judgement containing reference both to a permanent subject and a permanent world of thought. By "common sense", Reid meant those principles "common to the understanding of all men", and the indispensable precedent to an act of judgment by anyone. Once again, philosophic rightness or wrongness is not our concern. Reid's style, with its lapses into old-fashioned rhetoric—"Admired Philosophy! daughter of light! parent of wisdom and knowledge!"—makes it fairly certain that his works are now unlikely to be read other than by students of philosophy.

The same judgement might well have been passed upon Hume's friend, Adam Smith (1722–1790), if his reputation had to rest upon his *Theory of Moral Sentiments* (1759), based upon the extraordinary proposition that: "We either approve or disapprove of the conduct of another man, according as we feel that, when we bring his case home to ourselves we either can or cannot entirely sympathize with the sentiments and motives which directed it. And, in the same manner, we either approve or disapprove of our own conduct, according as we feel that, when we place ourselves in the situation of another man, and view it, as it were, with his eyes and from his station, we either can or cannot entirely enter into and sympathize with the sentiments and motives which influenced him." Leaving aside the mental gymnastics involved, the style is such as would hardly encourage the seeker after literature.

Smith, however, proved, like many Scots, to be a late developer. Born in Kirkcaldy, Fife, the son of a customs controller, he became a pupil of Hutcheson at Glasgow University before winning a Snell exhibition to Balliol College, Oxford in 1740. After spending two years in Kirkcaldy with his widowed mother—the father had died when his son was three—Smith, patronized by Lord Kames, settled in Edinburgh and gave a freelance course of lectures on rhetoric and *belles lettres*.

The profundity of these no doubt played some part in his appointment to the chair of logic at Glasgow University in 1751, from which he moved to that of moral philosophy a year later.

In 1763, having been made a doctor of law by Glasgow, he resigned and spent eighteen months in Switzerland and France as tutor to the young Duke of Buccleuch, meeting d'Alembert, Helvetius, de la Rochefoucauld and, most importantly, Quesnay, whose system of political economy Smith described as: "with all its imperfections, the nearest approximation to truth that had yet been published on the principles of science." At Toulouse, he probably began his great work, *Inquiry Into the Nature and Causes of the Wealth of Nations*, which appeared in 1776, causing his friend Hume to burst out: "*Euge! belle!* dear Mr Smith, I am much pleased with your performance, and the perusal of it has taken from me a great state of anxiety. It was a work of so much expectation, by yourself, by your friends, and by the public, that I trembled for its appearance, but am now much relieved. . . . It has depth, and solidity, and acuteness, and is so much illustrated by curious facts that it must at last attract the public attention."

It did. Displaying a wide and keen-sighted observation of social facts and using them to draw significant conclusions rather than resorting to abstractions or generalized principles, it discredited the European economic policies of the past, had a practical influence on economic practice for the next half century, and provided a guide to the future organization of social and economic reconstruction, necessarily tentative since theoretical, but a contribution of sufficiently lasting value two centuries later still to be necessary reading for students of a subject more than any influenced by constant change.

Once again, however, our concern is not with any judgement upon Smith, the political economist, but with Smith, the prose-writer. He lacks his friend Hume's elegance of style. Smith's sentences are shorter and more direct (allegedly due to his practice of pacing his room while dictating). But he is eminently readable, as this passage, not without continuing practical relevance, shows:

> People of the same trade seldom meet together even for merriment and diversion but the conversation ends in a conspiracy to raise prices. It is impossible, indeed, to prevent such meetings by any law which either could be executed, or would be consistent with liberty and justice. But though the law cannot hinder people of the same trade from sometimes assembling together, it ought to do nothing to facilitate such assemblies, much less to render them necessary.
>
> A regulation which obliges all those of the same trade in a particular town to enter their names and places of abode in a public register, facilitates such assemblies. It connects individuals who might never otherwise be known to one another, and gives every man of the trade a direction where to find every other man of it. A regulation which enables those of the same trade to tax themselves in order to provide for their poor, their sick, their widows and orphans, by giving them a common interest to manage, may also render such assemblies necessary.

Unlike Hume, Smith lacked personal charm, was an indistinct speaker and notorious for his absent-mindedness. Nevertheless, he belonged to the Select Society, founded in 1754 by the portrait painter Allan Ramsay—son of the poet—and which met to discuss the issues of the day in the Advocates' Library every Friday.

The only other historian in that brilliant Edinburgh company whom it is necessary to mention is William Robertson (1721–1793), the second edition of whose collected *Works*, edited by Dugald Stewart, appeared in Edinburgh in 1820.* A son of the manse, Robertson was born at Borthwick. He ministered first at Gladsmuir, and later at Lady Yester's, in Edinburgh, and then in Old Greyfriars. Principal of Edinburgh University in 1762, and Moderator of the General Assembly of the Church of Scotland in 1763, a year in which he was also appointed Historiographer for Scotland, Robertson was even more renowned than Hume for the agreeableness of his disposition.

His literary reputation, which was considerable, was based on his *History of Scotland During the Reign of Queen Mary and of King James VI Till His Accession to the Crown of England* (1759), a *History of the Reign of the Emperor Charles V* (1769) which netted him the then huge profit of £4,500, the *History of America* (1777), and finally an *Historical Disquisition* (1791).

As with Hume, later evidence has invalidated many of Robertson's then no doubt justifiably generalized conclusions. Like Hume, too, Robertson, in his *History of Scotland*, though in a more orderly manner, helped to place the writing of our history in a context of informed objectivity, as he himself explained:

---

* The first, edited by Alexander Stewart, had come out in 1818.

The transactions in Mary's reign gave rise to two parties, which were animated against each other with the fiercest political hatred, embittered by religious zeal. Each of these produced historians of considerable merit, who adopted all their sentiments, and defended all their actions. Truth, however, was not the sole object of these authors. Blinded by prejudices, and heated by the part which they themselves had acted in the scenes they describe, they write an apology for a faction rather than the history of their country. Historians have followed these guides almost implicitly, and have repeated their errors and misrepresentations. But as the same passions which influenced parties in that age have descended to their posterity; as almost every event in Mary's reign has become the object of doubt or dispute; the eager spirit of the controversy soon discovered that without some evidence more authentic and more impartial than that of historians, none of the points in question could be decided with certainty. Records have therefore been searched, original papers have been produced, and publick archives, as well as the repositories of private men, have been ransacked by the zeal and curiosity of writers of different parties. . . But many important papers have escaped the notice of those industrious collectors, and after all they have produced to light, much still remained in darkness, unobserved or unpublished. It was my duty to search for these, and I found this unpleasant task attended with considerable utility.

Although Dr Johnson, on whose weighty prose periods so many lesser eighteenth-century writers modelled their style, complained that Robertson's works had too many "fine passages", his narrative flows easily. In religion a moderate, he shows no great enthusiasm for the excesses of the Reformation, but usually strives to give a balanced viewpoint where matters of historical controversy are concerned. Here, for example, is his summing-up of the character of Queen Elizabeth:

Foreigners often accuse the English of indifference and disrespect towards their Princes. But without reason; no people are more grateful than they to those Monarchs who merit their gratitude. The names of Edward III and Henry V are mentioned by the English of this age, with the same warmth, as they were by those, who shared in the blessings and splendour of their reigns. The memory of Elizabeth is still adored in England. And the historians of that kingdom, after celebrating her love of her people; her sagacity in discerning their true interest; her steadfastness in pursuing it; her wisdom in the choice of her Ministers; the glory she acquired by arms; the tranquillity she secured to her subjects; and the increase of fame, of riches, and of commerce, which were the fruits of all these; justly rank her among the most illustrious Princes. Even the defects in her character, they observe, were not of a kind pernicious to her people. Her excessive frugality was not accompanied with the love of hoarding; and though it prevented some great undertakings, and rendered the success of others imcompleat, it introduced economy into her administration, and exempted the nation from many burdens, which a Monarch, more profuse, or more enterprizing, must have imposed. Her slowness in rewarding her servants sometimes discouraged useful merit; but it prevented the undeserving from acquiring power and wealth, to which they had no title. Her extreme jealousy of those princes, who pretended to dispute her right to the Crown, led her to take such precautions, as tended no less to the public safety, than to her own; and to count the affections of her people, as the firmest support to her throne. Such is the picture the English draw of this great Queen.

Whoever undertakes to write the History of Scotland finds himself obliged, frequently, to view her in a very different and in a less amiable light. Her authority in that kingdom, during the greater part of her reign, was little inferior to that which she possessed in her own. But this authority, acquired at first by a service of great importance to the nation she exercised in a manner extremely pernicious to its happiness. By her industry in fomenting the rage of two contending factions; by supplying the one with partial aid; by feeding the other with false hopes; by balancing their power so artfully, that each of them was able to distress, and neither of them to subdue the other; she rendered Scotland long the seat of discord, confusion and bloodshed: and her craft and intrigues, effecting what the valour of her ancestors could not accomplish, reduced that kingdom to a state of dependance on England. The maxims of policy, often little consonant to those of her morality, may, perhaps, justify this conduct. But no apology can be offered for her behaviour to Queen Mary; a scene of dissimulation without necessity; and of severity beyond example. In almost all other actions, Elizabeth is the object of our highest admiration; in this, we must allow that she not only laid aside the magnanimity, which became a Queen, but the feelings, natural to a woman.

Few historians can expect to write of ages other than their own and command the attention of later generations. Principal Robertson is not of their number. No one would now read his books from cover to cover, if only because to do so would inevitably be to absorb much out-of-date or factually inaccurate information. But he could well be resuscitated by anthologists. His tense account in his *History of America* of the agonizing and uncertain hours of darkness before the sighting of America by Columbus, for example, is a gripping piece of narration such as neither Defoe nor Scott could have bettered.

Three Scots out of many who left interesting accounts of foreign exploration should at least be noted. James ("Abyssinian") Bruce (1730–1794), born at Kinnaird House, Stirlingshire, was a wine merchant in London for some years, but later set out in 1768 from Cairo to reach Abyssinia by the Nile, Asswan and the Red Sea. His *Travels and Discoveries of the Source of the Nile* (1790) revealed much about Abyssinia now known to be true, but which was regarded as fabrication by his contemporaries. Although after his return to Scotland Bruce dressed himself up in Abyssinian costume, his Scots common sense and his homesickness both frequently asserted themselves when he finally reached the object of his arduous explorations. He began by recording the plain facts.

On Monday the 5th of November, the day after my arrival at Geesh, the weather perfectly clear, cloudless, and nearly calm, in all respects well adapted to observation, being extremely anxious to ascertain, beyond the power of controversy, the precise spot on the globe that this fountain had so long occupied unknown, I pitched my tent on the north edge of the cliff, immediately above the priest's house, having verified the instrument with all the care possible, both at the zenith and horizon. With a brass quadrant of three feet radius, by one meridan altitude of the sun's upper limb, all necessary equations and deductions considered, I determined the latitude of the place of observation to be 10° 59′ 11″; and, by another observation of the same kind made on the 6th, 10° 59′ 8″; after which, by a medium of thirty-three observations of stars, the largest and nearest, the first vertical, I found the latitude to be 10° 59′ 10″; a mean of which being 10° 59′ 9½″, say 10° 59′ 10″; and if we should be so unnecessarily scrupulous as to add 15″ for the measured distance the place of the tent was south of the altar, then we shall have 10° 59′ 25″ in round numbers, for the exact latitude of the principal fountain of the Nile, though the Jesuits have supposed it 12° N. by a random guess; but this being nearly the latitude of Gondar, the capital from which they set out, shews plainly they knew not the precise latitude of either of these places. . . .

The night of the 4th, that very night of my arrival, melancholy reflections upon my present state, the doubtfulness of my return in safety, were I permitted to make the attempt, and the fears that even this would be refused, according to the rule observed in Abyssinia with all travellers who have once entered the kingdom; the consciousness of the pain that I was then occasioning to many worthy individuals, expecting daily that information concerning my situation which it was not in my power to give them; some other thoughts, perhaps, still nearer the heart than those, crowded upon my mind, and forbade all approach of sleep.

I was, at that very moment, in possession of what had, for many years, been the principal object of my ambition and wishes: indifference, which, from the usual infirmity of human nature, follows, at least for a time, complete enjoyment, had taken place of it. The marsh, and the fountains, upon comparison with the rise of many of our rivers, became now a trifling object in my sight. I remembered that magnificent scene in my own native country, where the Tweed, Clyde, and Annan, rise in one hill; three rivers, as I now thought, not inferior to the Nile in beauty, preferable to it in the cultivation of those countries through which they flow; superior, vastly superior to it in the virtues and qualities of the inhabitants, and in the beauty of its flocks crowding its pastures in peace, without fear of violence from man or beast. I had seen the rise of the Rhine and Rhone, and the more magnificent sources of the

Soane; I began, in my sorrow, to treat the inquiry about the source of the Nile as a violent effort of a distempered fancy:—

> What's Hecuba to him, or he to Hecuba,
> That he should weep for her?—

Grief, or despondency, now rolling upon me like a torrent; relaxed, not refreshed, by unquiet and imperfect sleep, I started from my bed in the utmost agony; I went to the door of my tent; every thing was still; the Nile, at whose head I stood, was not capable either to promote or to interrupt my slumbers, but the coolness and serenity of the night braced my nerves, and chased away those phantoms that, while in bed, had oppressed and tormented me.

The book as a whole is still extremely readable.

Sir Alexander Mackenzie (1753–1820), a Stornoway-born traveller with a Canadian river named after him, became the first white man to cross North America from coast to coast. He recorded his experiences, somewhat drily, in his *Voyage through the Continent of North America to the Frozen and Pacific Oceans* (1801).

Mungo Park (1771–1806), a native of Selkirk, explored the Niger, in Africa, and published his *Travels in the Interior of Africa* in 1799, achieving instant popularity through its ludicity of style and wealth of incident.

The supreme eighteenth-century writer of biography, autobiography and domestic travel was, however, undoubtedly James Boswell (1740–1795), the son of Lord Auchinleck, an Ayrshire laird and distinguished judge who disapproved of his son's youthful fecklessness and failure to apply himself to the family profession with sufficient obvious seriousness.

Boswell was educated at Edinburgh High School, and at the Universities of Edinburgh, Glasgow and Utrecht (where he studied law). He was admitted to the Scottish Bar in 1766. His official publications began with an anonymous *Ode to Tragedy*, which appeared in 1761. He met Dr Johnson in a London bookshop on 16th May 1763, and won his friendship. Later that year Boswell made a continental tour, meeting Rousseau and Voltaire, and getting himself introduced to the Corsican patriot Paoli. Boswell's *An Account of Corsica* (1768) scored an immediate success. In 1769 he married his cousin, Margaret Montgomerie, by whom he had seven children, and soon afterwards began his period of close association with Johnson, whose conversation he began to record. In 1773 Boswell was elected a member of the club to which Johnson, Reynolds, Burke and Goldsmith belonged. In the same year, Boswell persuaded Johnson to accompany him to the Hebrides, where the doctor hoped to secure evidence to disprove the genuineness of Macpherson's Ossian productions. *A Journal of a Tour of the Hebrides* (1785)* was Boswell's account of the adventure, Johnson having chronicled his

* Though due to the loss for a time of the original manuscript it did not appear in its complete form until 1936.

story in the less gossipy but much more solid *Journey to the Western Isles of Scotland* in 1775.

In 1782, Boswell succeeded to his father's estate. He got no further in satisfying his political ambitions than securing the Recordship of Carlisle, which he only retained for a year. After the death of his wife, whom he had latterly neglected, in 1789, he himself succumbed increasingly to his life-long tendancies towards drunkenness and dissipation. Before he died, however, he was able to enjoy the success of his *Life of Samuel Johnson*, which first appeared in 1791, a second edition being needed two years later. With Lockhart's *Life of Scott*, Boswell's *Johnson* is unquestionably one of the two greatest biographies written in English.

Boswell's *Letters* appeared in 1924 and his *Notebooks 1776–1777* in 1925. But the great mass of his diaries turned up, mostly at Malahide Castle, Ireland, the seat of his great-grandson. They have appeared in a remarkable series which includes *Boswell's London Journal* (1950), *Boswell in Holland 1763–4* (1952), *Boswell on the Grand Tour* (1955–6) and *Boswell in Search of a Wife 1766–9* (1957). And there is more, much more one gathers, to come.

What is one to make of this inspired gossip with a photographic memory, a notebook at the ready, and a prose style as piquant as it is entirely candid? That he was lascivious, vain, a seeker after notoriety, almost unsnubbable, unfaithful to his wife, curious about his neighbours beyond the bounds of courtesy or even decency, a man whose conscience pained him when he erred but failed to help him sustain his personal remorse or his age's notions of social virtue? "Bozzy" was all these things. Taken together, they enabled him to become a writer of genius, whether arranging the facts of the life of his great hero, Johnson, and even recording crushing retorts unflattering to their recipient, or easing the Boswellian restlessness by writing lengthy yet fascinating diaries, as a less talented man of vanity might frequently contrive to admire his own reflection whenever he encountered a mirror.

In some respects the most moving moment which Johnson and Boswell experienced during their Hebridean tour was their arrival on Iona. Wrote Boswell:

We continued to coast along Mull, and passed by Nuns' Island, which, it is said, belonged to the nuns of Icolmkill, and from which, we were told, the stone for the buildings there was taken. As we sailed along by moon-light, in a sea somewhat rough, and often between black and gloomy rocks, Dr Johnson said, "*If this be not roving among the Hebrides nothing is.*"—The repetition of words which he had so often previously used, made a strong impression on my imagination; and by a natural course of thinking, led me to consider how our present adventures would appear to me at a future period.

I have often experienced, that scenes through which a man has passed, improve by lying in the memory: they grow mellow. *Acti labores sunt jucundi.* This may be owing to comparing them with present listless ease. Even harsh scenes acquire a softness by length of time. . . .

After a tedious sail, which, by our following various turnings of the coast of Mull, was extended to about forty miles, it gave us no small pleasure to perceive a light in the village of Icolmkill, in which all the inhabitants live, close to where the ancient buildings stand. As we approached the shore, the tower of the cathedral, just discernible in the air, was a picturesque object.

When we had landed upon the sacred place, which, as long as I can remember, I had thought on with veneration, Dr Johnson and I cordially embraced.

The richness with which Boswell brings before the reader the difficulties of travel, his veneration for his somewhat ponderously erudite hero, and his own vanity scarcely need comment. Boswell's instincts as a reporter were constantly at work. There is, his naïvely serious vein, that incredible account of his visit to the dying Hume, already referred to. Hume survived the encounter with good-humoured dignity, Boswell with the puzzlement of a yellow-press journalist whose scoop story has gone unexpectedly sour on him:

On Sunday forenoon the 7th of July 1776, being too late for Church, I went to see Mr David Hume, who was returned from London and Bath, just a dying. I found him alone, in a reclining posture in his drawing-room. He was lean, ghastly, and quite of an earthy appearance. He was drest in a suit of grey cloth with white metal buttons, and a kind of scratch wig. He was quite different from the plump figure which he used to present. He had before him Dr Campbell's *Philosophy of Rhetorick*. He seemed to be placid and even cheerful. He said he was just approaching to his end. I think these were his words. I know not how I contrived to get the subject of Immortality introduced. He said he never had entertained any belief in Religion since he began to read Locke and Clarke. I asked him if he was not religious when he was young. He said he was, and he used to read the *Whole Duty of Man*; that he made an abstract from the Catalogue of vices at the end of it, and examined himself by this, leaving out Murder and Theft and such vices as he had no chance of committing, having no inclination to commit them. This, he said, was strange Work; for instance, to try if, notwithstanding his excelling his school-fellows, he had no pride or vanity. He smiled in ridicule of this as absurd and contrary to fixed principles and necessary consequences, not adverting that Religious discipline does not mean to extinguish, but to moderate, the passions; and certainly an excess of pride or vanity is dangerous and generally hurtful. He then said flatly that the Morality of every Religion was bad, and, I really thought, was not jocular when he said "that when he heard a man was religious, he concluded he was a rascal, though he had known some instances of very good men being religious." This was just an extravagant reverse of the common remark as to Infidels. I had a strong curiosity to be satisfied if he persisted in disbelieving a future state even when he had death before his eyes. I was persuaded from what he now said, and from his manner of saying it, that he did persist. I asked him if it was not possible that there might be a future state. He answered It was possible that a piece of coal put upon the fire would not burn; and he added that it was a most unreasonable fancy that he should exist for ever. That immortality, if it were at all, must be general; that a great proportion of the human race has hardly any intellectual qualities; that a great proportion dies in infancy before being possessed of reason; yet all these must be immortal; that a Porter who gets drunk by ten o'clock with gin must be immortal; that the trash of every age must be preserved, and that new Universes must be created to contain such infinite numbers. This appeared to me an unphilosophical objection, and I said, "Mr Hume, you know Spirit does not take up space". . . .

I asked him if the thought of Annihilation never gave him any uneasiness. He said not the least; no more than the thought that he had not been, as Lucretius observes. "Well," said I, "Mr. Hume, I hope to triumph over you when I meet you in a future state; and remember you are not to pretend that you was joking with all this Infidelity." "No, No," said he, "But I shall have been so long there before you come that it will be nothing new." In this style of good-humour and levity did I conduct the conversation. Perhaps it was wrong on so aweful a subject. But as nobody was present, I thought it could have no bad effect. I however felt a degree of horrour, mixed with a sort of wild, strange, hurrying recollection of My excellent Mother's pious instructions, of Dr Johnson's noble lessons, and of my religious sentiments and affections during the course of my life. I was like a man in sudden danger eagerly seeking his defensive arms; and I could not but be assailed by momentary doubts while I had actually before me a man of such strong abilities and extensive inquiry dying in the persuasion of being annihilated.

With equal innocence, a younger Boswell could discuss with himself the effects of his encounter in 1763 with Louisa, a London society prostitute:

THURSDAY 20 JANUARY. I rose very disconsolate, having rested very ill by the poisonous infection raging in my veins and anxiety and vexation boiling in my breast. I could scarcely credit my own senses. What! thought I, can this beautiful, this sensible, and this agreeable woman be so sadly defiled? Can corruption lodge beneath so fair a form? Can she who professed delicacy of sentiment and sincere regard for me, use me so very basely and so very cruelly? . . .

Am I, who have had safe and elegant intrigues with fine women, become the dupe of a strumpet? Am I now to be laid up for many weeks to suffer extreme pain and full confinement, and to be debarred all the comforts and pleasures of life? And then must I have my poor pocket drained by the unavoidable expense of it? And shall I no more (for a long time at least) take my walk, healthful and spirited, round the Park before breakfast, view the brilliant Guards on the Parade, and enjoy all my pleasing amusements? And then am I prevented from making love to Lady Mirabel, or any other woman of fashion? O dear, O dear! What a cursed thing this is! What a miserable creature am I!

Private literature in the form of journals and diaries is, as we have seen, no new feature in the Scottish tradition. No other diarist, however, has been so frank, so engagingly ingenuous and so prolific as Boswell. His great work of biography apart—and much of its merit results from the reporting abilities of its author and his tireless recording discipline!—Boswell's self-revelations do not benefit from sustained study. No other Scot has left us as rich a common-place book for casual dipping: no other author has left so fully documented an account of a life made interesting because of a zest for words which transformed even trivia into colourful detail.

Alexander Carlyle (1722–1805), nicknamed "Jupiter" because of his imposing demeanour, was not the one to tolerate trivia; but he, too, possessed a vivid talent for reportage, expecially when applied to character-sketches. Son of the minister of Cummertrees, Dumfriesshire, after the manner of the times, he followed study at Edinburgh and Glasgow Universities with a period abroad, in his case at Leyden University, Holland. He became minister at Inveresk, near Edinburgh, and excelled not only as a clerical "politician", a man of so great connection that his support of his brother clergyman John Home, when attacked for writing the play of *Douglas*, forced the narrower brethren to weaken their opposition to the theatre, a frequenter of literary company in both London and Edinburgh, and a famous enjoyer of club life. With the brilliant company of those intellectuals who glorified the capital during the latter half of the eighteenth century, oysters from the Forth in good supply, and French claret eighteen shillings the dozen, there cannot have been much to attract men like Carlyle south.

Two Swiftian pamphlets appeared during his life-time; one, the ironically titled *An argument to prove that the Tragedy of "Douglas" ought to be publicly burnt by the Hands of the Hangman* (1757), and two years later another rather less pungent effort, *Plain reasons for removing a certain great man from his Majesty's presence and Council for ever.* His autobiographical *Memoirs*, left in manuscript, were not published until 1860, when they were edited by Hill Burton. It is a fascinating book, as is shown by this brief account of a Scot who fled his country after a duel, joined the Indian Army, and eventually became a distinguished Persian scholar, Alexander Dow:

Dow was a Scotch adventurer, who had been bred at the school of Dunbar, his father being in the Customs there, and had run away from his apprenticeship at Eyemouth and found his way to the East Indies, where, having a turn for languages, which had been fostered by his education, he soon became such a master of the native tongue as to accelerate his preferment in the

Army, for he soon had the command of a regiment of Sepoys. He was a sensible and knowing man of very agreeable manners and of a mild and gentle disposition. As he was telling us that night, that, when he had the charge of the Great Mogul, with two regiments under his command at Delhi, he was tempted to dethrone the monarch and mount the throne in his stead, which he said he could easily have done. When I asked him what prevented him from yielding to that temptation, he gave me this memorable answer, that it was reflecting on what his old schoolfellows at Dunbar would think of him for being guilty of such an action.

Interesting too, though lacking Carlyle's sharp edge of enjoyment in all he did or wrote about, is *My Own Life and Times* by the long-lived Dr James Sommerville (1741–1830), minister of Jedburgh.

We must turn to the novel, noting, however, that one of the two outstanding Scottish novelists of the period, Henry Mackenzie (1745–1831), left a posthumous volume of fascinating interest, unpublished until 1927, *Anecdotes and Egotisms*. Unfortunately, it was not apparently intended for the general reader, and some of its entries are couched in note form. Yet it remains a valuable account of Edinburgh customs and society in the heyday of its "Athens of the North" phase, which roughly coincided with the beginnings of the building of Craig's New Town in 1768.

Before we may properly take account of Mackenzie's novels, it is necessary to trace the development in Scotland of what was virtually a new form, and consider the work of Tobias Smollett (1721–1771), the Dunbartonshire counterpart of England's Henry Fielding.

Story-telling goes back to the beginnings of civilization, early traditional stories often having magical properties associated with them. In time, primitive story-telling became formalized into *fabliaux* and romances of various sorts, including such categories as the beast fable, the fertility tale and the *roman d'aventure*. Many of these tales were couched in verse, it being easier for a largely non-literate society to enjoy and remember fiction in this form.

The prose novel, however, is a relatively late arrival on the literary scene. It differs from all earlier forms of tale-telling—even such comparatively late tales as Mackenzie's *Aretina*—in two essential ways: the narration should have continuity of story-line, rather than be merely a loosely-threaded series of diverting episodes; and the characterization must be realistic.

The English Elizabethan writer Thomas Nashe (1567–1601) produced a tale almost sickening in the brutality of its realism with *The Unfortunate Traveller, or the Life of Jack Wilton* (1594). It has the distinction of being the first picaresque novel to be written in English. The picaroon is a rogue type to be found as long ago as in the *Satyricon*. But it was a Spaniard, Mateo Alemán, who, in his *Guzmán de Alfarache* (1599), founded the picaresque tradition through which a real or imaginary rogue gives his autobiography in prose.

Based on this Spanish example, and other early Spanish picaresques, Nashe tells a tale of everyday contemporary low-life and rascality far removed from either John Lyly's *Euphues* (1579), with its artificial classicism and phraseology of evasion, or even Sir Philip Sydney's *Arcadia* (1593), also a highly stylized story about, and intended for the diversion of, aristocratic readers.

With some success, Nashe strove towards the end of unity and characterization. We need not concern ourselves here with *Thomas of Reading* or *Jack of Newbury*, two of the novels with which the Norwich silk-weaver Thomas Delohey (1543?–1600) did much to achieve continuous narration, writing of middle-class citizens rather than courtiers or rogues. Nor need we more than note the influence of John Bunyan (1628–1688) and his allegory *The Pilgrim's Progress* (1678). In spite of its narrative fluency, it was rather the dogmatic intolerance of its virtuous characters which ensured its popularity for more than two centuries, even among readers to whom the concept of prose fiction was positively sinful.

The father of the novel in English is really Daniel Defoe (1660?–1731), son of a Cripplegate, London, butcher. Defoe is also, as it happens, the founder of modern journalism. Although he was not only not a Scot, but in fact a spy who came to Scotland under the name of "Alexander Goldsmith" in 1706 to help further English interests in procuring incorporating Union between Scotland and England, his two-volume novel, the parts of which both appeared in 1719 under the eventual title of *Robinson Crusoe*, was based upon the real-life adventures of a sailor from Largo, Fife, Alexander Selkirk.

While it does not deal with picaresque characters such as those who feature in Defoe's other novels, *Moll Flanders* and *Roxana*, in *Robinson Crusoe* the narrative is told in the first person, and the author does not indulge in much elaboration of style. There is, however, much realistic detail; as, for instance, in the description of the accoutrements Crusoe managed to salvage from the ship and the ingenious uses to which he put them. There is also a strong sense of incident, heightened by the author's artifice in pretending from time to time not wholly to believe in the truth of what he is under an "obligation" to relate.

In England, Defoe was followed by Samuel Richardson (1689–1761). With *Pamela* (1740), the sentimental tale of a chaste maid-servant, a certain slightly puritanical strain discernible in Defoe's writings (though not in his life-style) is consciously developed. Female virtue, in the form of successfully avoided seduction by people of superior class, though sensitively portrayed from a womanly viewpoint, is nevertheless made to seem positively priggish. Character-drawing is stronger in the later *Clarissa* (1748). In Richardson's portrait of that too-good-to-be-true Christian gentleman, *Sir Charles Grandison* (1754), the novelist still remained hampered by his insistence that virtue must not only triumph but must always be seen to receive a handsome reward.

The stylistically robust and more worldly Henry Fielding (1707–1754) began his career with a take-off of Richardson's pretentiousness, *Shamela* (1741). *Joseph Andrews* (1742) was likewise initially conceived in a spirit of ridicule, but its author went on to create a magnificent portrait of bewildered innocence in Parson Adams. By the time Fielding came to write down his history of the foundling *Tom Jones* (1749), he had achieved a racy manner of handling incident and a ripe ability to portray vividly a wider range of characters than any English prose writer before him.

Smollett and Fielding certainly have common characteristics. It is what was not common that matters most. While Fielding was undoubtedly able to draw in depth a wider range of characters than the Scot, Smollett did remember, and frequently put to good use, many of the traits of his nation and his fellow-countrymen. He is thus not only the first Scottish novelist in any real sense of the term, but in *Humphry Clinker* at least, the author of a masterpiece.

Life, however, was not particularly kind to Smollett, and a long succession of disappointments, combined with years of arduous journalistic hack work, undermined his health and led him to adopt a certain misanthropic bitterness. His popularity as a writer was eclipsed by that of Fielding. Through Smollett's early death, he missed inheriting his grandfather's Dunbartonshire estate of Bonhill by four weeks, as a result of which it went to his sister, Mrs Telfer.

After leaving Dumbarton Grammar School, Smollett proceeded to Glasgow University, then served as an apprentice doctor-apothecary. In 1739 he travelled to London, hopeful that his tragedy *The Regicide* might be staged. It was not accepted; so, disappointed, he joined the naval expedition to Carthagena in 1741, serving on H M S *Chichester* as a ship's surgeon, an experience which gave him an insight into how the lower orders lived. Back in London, his attempts to build up a medical practice were only moderately successful. Although further attempts to get *The Regicide* staged also failed, now, however, he decided that literature was his bent. His first novel, *Roderick Random*, appeared in 1748, and was well received. It was followed by *Peregine Pickle* in 1751, *Ferdinand, Count Fathom* in 1753, *Sir Launcelot Greaves* in 1762, and by *Humphry Clinker* in 1771.

His other works include the satire, *The Adventures of an Atom* (1769), translations of Lessage's *Gil Blas* (1749)—the tale of another Spanish picaroon—Cervantes' *Don Quixote* (1755), a thirty-eight volume edition of the works of Voltaire (1761–1774), a *History of England*, and the work which led Sterne to dub him Smelfungus, the caustic, thoroughly entertaining *Travels through France and Italy* (1766).

The pattern of Smollett's earlier novels was more or less similar in outline. The ingredients are neatly defined by Harrison R. Steers as "a mixture of wayside encounters, night adventures at inns, coffee-house quarrels, puerile practical jokes, *chroniques scandaleuses*, politicians' levées, gambling, cudgel-fighting, occasional duels, trivial amours, influence-peddling, for-tune-hunting, stories of abandoned women, debtors' prisons, excursions into criticism, coxcombry, arrogant egotism, and late repentance, all held together by a frail thread of plot, and ending in a happy settlement of all the unheroic hero's problems by a very landslide of wealth, with social resur-rection and marriage to a charming and inflexibly constant young lady who is virginal to the deepest recesses of her thought.''[16]

In fact, with the exception of the landslides of wealth and the deeply vir-ginal ladies, Smollett's ingredients are such as might be found reported in the pages of any less salubrious late-twentieth-century Sabbath newspaper; cheek by jowl, the vile and the vicious, the senseless and the sentimental, formless as life itself. What is undeniable is that because of his charac-terization, and the vitality with which his anti-heroes face up to their vari-ously changing fortunes and situations, Smollett does manage to achieve a cohesive form.

Ostensibly at least, when Smollett wrote he was inspired by moral pur-pose. His picaroons were not just to be high-spirited, reprovable rascals, but—as their creator fancied he himself was—the victims of an unjust so-ciety. In his preface to *Roderick Random*, Smollett defined his intention:

> The reader gratifies his curiosity in pursuing the adventures of a person in whose favour he is prepossessed; he espouses his cause, he sympathises with him in distress; his indignation is heated against the authors of his calamity; the humane passions are inflamed; the contrast between dejected virtue and insulting vice appears with greater aggravation; and every impression having a double force on the imagination, the memory retains the circumstance, and the heart improves by the example.

It would probably be true to assert that novelists whose works survive the fashions of their own time achieve success or failure in proportion to the degree of absorption in scene and character they allow to obliterate their message-carrying intentions. Happily, Smollett generally forgot his high purpose, if not so easily his social grudge, as he became involved in his story-telling. He wrote almost at the end of what had been a long-lasting taste for the picaresque, and at a time when 'sentiment' had begun to soften earlier harshness. Thus, the 'refining' influence of young women not only links Smollett with the novel of sentiment, that later strain of eighteenth-century fiction which developed from the softer side of Richardson's characterization (and from much eighteenth-century philosophy, culminating with the sentimentalism of Rousseau) providing an example to those lesser Victorian writers who placed their worshipable women on pedestals beyond the touch of sex.

Roderick Random is, in fact, autobiographical, the story of a young man come to London to make his mark on life. Not fundamentally a bad char-acter, he is, however, prepared to swashbuckle his way out of whatever

difficulties may lie in his path. He encounters gamesters, seamen, prostitutes, highwaymen, sharks of all sorts, politicians urgent with dishonest
promises, sponges and bailiffs. After wasting much of his inheritance, he
embarks on a series of ill-considered adventures to retrieve his losses. The
adventures fail, and so would he, did not the heroine, somewhat surprisingly, drag him up out of the morass of his foolishness and redeem him by
her affection and fortune.

There are magnificent 'set-pieces' in the book, some drawn from
Smollett's own naval observation, in particular Roderick's experiences
afloat after being shanghied by a press-gang. In this respect, David Hannay
comments that Smollett: ". . . helped to make his generation understand
what a hateful cruel thing military inefficiency is, and how surely the
wretched personal squabbles of leaders mean death and useless suffering to
the men who are so unhappy as to be placed at their mercy."[17]

There is also the interpolated story of the downward drift, through
seduction to prostitution and attempted suicide of Miss Williams, luckier
than most of her kind in that she becomes a virtuous Mrs Strap.

The linking strength of the book, however, lies in the interplay between
the conflict of the racial antipathies of the Englishmen, Captain Oakum
and Crampley; Dr Mackshane, the Irish surgeon; Dr Morgan, the Welshman; and Roderick, the Scot. There is also rugged character-drawing of a
kind to become familiar in Smollett's later work (as in Fielding's) in
Roderick's rough but kindly and reliable patron, uncle Jim Bowling, and
Strap, his valet, a kind of devoted philosopher-counsellor cast in the Figaro
mould.

Peregrine Pickle also makes use of Smollett's seagoing experiences, but
although the lineaments of the characters are oddly similar, they are more
finely drawn. Commodore Trunnion is a fiercer Bowling, Emilia, a
warmer-blooded Narcissa, Pipes a humbler Strap, Lady Vane a socially
superior Miss Williams. Peregrine himself is another Roderick-like figure,
but with the advantages of more money and a year of University idling:
Peregrine's vainglorious coxcombing is cut short when Commodore
Hawser Trunnion sends him off on the Grand Tour to complete his education. Between his naval service and the writing of this novel, Smollett,
himself an enthusiastic traveller, had several times undertaken the Grand
Tour, and in *Peregrine Pickle* we are treated to some delightful sketches of
other people engaged in the same pursuit: a French marquis; an Italian
count; a German baron; and an English painter, Pallett. One of the many
vigorously funny incidents with which this book is packed is the reaction
by the representatives of these different nationalities to a revolting "feast
after the manner of the antients", given by an eccentric doctor, using a
recipe-book completed in the latter part of the third century by the gourmet Marcus Gabius Apicius.

The Grand Tour over, Peregrine inherits £30,000 from Trunnion, and
sets off in pursuit of Emilia. His methods, to say the least of it, are somewhat

rough and ready, and he is rebuffed. He then plunges into a life of immorality, from which emerges "The Memoirs of a Lady of Quality", apparently written by a dissipated real-life "lady of fortune"—a Roxana-like creature—and simply bought from her and inserted into the book. Peregrine meanwhile runs through his fortune in London, and ends up in the Fleet, the prison where debtors were lodged.

Helped by his friend Godfrey Gauntlet, who has discovered that Peregrine's good offices facilitated Gauntlet's marriage to Sophy, and by the unexpected prospering of a foreign trade venture written off for lost, Peregrine tries again, eventually assisted by the fact that not only has Emilia inherited £10,000 from a favourite uncle, but that Mr Pickle senior has died, leaving Peregrine heir to a considerable estate. The rest can be imagined.

The first part of *Peregrine Pickle* is much livelier than what follows after the hero—for such Smollett eventually calls him—returns from the Continent, but the book is nevertheless greatly enjoyable as a whole. Incidentally, in Chapter 87, Pickle's attempts to turn a beggar-girl of sixteen into a lady of fashion, an attempt spoiled by her persistent swearing, anticipates Eliza Doolittle in *Pygmalion*.

Ferdinand, Count Fathom and *Sir Launcelot Greaves*, are both the products of Smollett's two decades of unremitting journalistic hack-work in a London hostile to Scots because of memories of the '45 and the unpopular ministry of Lord Bute. Fathom, however, contains Smollett's definition of what a work of prose fiction should be:

> A novel is a large diffused picture, comprehending the characters of life, disposed in different groups, and exhibited in various attitudes, for the purposes of an uniform plan, and general occurrence, to which every individual figure is subservient. But this plan cannot be executed with propriety, probability or success, without a principal personage to attract the attention, write the incidents, unwind the clue of the labyrinth, and at last close the scene, by virtue of his own importance.

Unlike his title-bearing predecessors, Fathom begins and ends a villain. The book seems to have been influenced by Otway's play *The Orphan*, the heroine in both carrying the unusual name of Monimia. The scenes of Fathom's adventure during the storm in a forest near Paris, and the English church in which Monimia is reunited with her lover, Renaldo, suggest stage settings. *Fathom* also differs from its predecessors in that for the first time Smollett leaves his characters in the doldrums from time to time, and digresses in his own person. But there is a fascinating account of Fathom's stage-coach journey from Deal to London, touching upon such changeless matters as the nature of the countryside, English humour, and the stupidity of officials.

This novel was not well received. Smollett waited five years before embarking on *Sir Launcelot Greaves*, which opens, without any moralizing preamble, with a chance encounter of the leading characters, Fillet, Captain Crowe, Tom Clarke and Ferret before a friendly fire in the Black Lion Inn at Weston, near Sutton-on-Trent. The arrival of Sir Launcelot incites them to press his acquaintance, Tom Clarke, to tell the knight's story, a picaresque adventure ending in the happy union of Sir Launcelot and his Aurelia.

The weakness of the novel is Smollett's too close and quite un-English imitation of Cervantes's *Don Quixote*. The novel's strengths are the mellowing of the humour, and the manner in which the influence of the by now more popular Fielding led Smollett to emulate the English writer's detachment, leisurely richness of style, ability to handle burlesque, and skill in portraying English life.

These mature qualities were to be fully deployed only once, in *Humphry Clinker*, the more remarkable an achievement in that Smollett was already worn out with over-work, his final foreign trip to France and Italy from 1763 to 1765 having restored him only a limited amount of energy for active life. This he employed in his *Travels Through France and Italy*. It shows a man of ready enthusiasm, one not afraid to acknowledge the limitations of his tastes, and with a vivid appreciation for colourful people and their situations. Its merits fully justify the praise it was to receive from a later journalizing traveller, Arnold Bennett, who called it "a fine *splenetic* book, thoroughly interesting. The kind of book that a few men might, and probably do, cherish as a masterpiece too special in its flavour to please the crowd. It gives the impression of a sound, sincere personality, not very cultured in the arts, but immensely well informed, and breathing a hard, comfortable common sense at every pore." Bennett adds: "One leaves this book in thankfulness that one is not an eighteenth-century traveller."[18]

Once the *Travels* were out of the way, Smollett, who had moved to Bath for the sake of his declining health, experienced a desire to visit his native country again. He had gone to Aberdeen in 1750 to receive a medical degree, and was made Guild Brother of Edinburgh during another visit in 1753 and a Freeman of the Capital in 1759. Now, he felt the need for what he seems to have forseen would be a farewell visit.

Accordingly, he began his last Scottish tour on 1st April 1766, spending in all about seven months away from Bath. In Glasgow, he met his old friend, the recipient of Burns's "autobiographical letter" and many others, Stirling-born Dr John Moore (1729–1802), author of *A View of Society and Manners in France, Switzerland, and Germany* (1799), to which a volume on Italy was added in 1781. Indeed, in *Humphry Clinker*, Jerry Melford reports that in Glasgow, he and the others "had the good fortune to be received in the house of Mr Moore, an eminent surgeon . . . a merry, facetious companion, sensible and shrewd. . . ."

Of Moore's three novels, *Zeluco* (1786) is set in southern Italy, brings a thoroughly bad villain to an appropriately just end, and so was relatively popular in the nineteenth century. *Edward* (1796), in W. L. Renwick's words, is "a transference into English society of Marivaux's *Vie de Marianne* with . . . a hero in place of a heroine"[19]. *Mordaunt* (1800), however, includes a fascinating account by means of the letter tradition, of society in various parts of Europe during the last decade of the eighteenth century. The wisdom and humanity of a man who had studied at Glasgow University in the days of Hutcheson and Smith, served as an army surgeon, and done the Grand Tour with the Duke of Hamilton, is reflected in cool and compassionate prose. The views of the hero (and presumably of Moore) on the descent of the French Revolution from misdirected idealism to the butchery of power-drunk dictatorship is a recording of first-hand experience. From a constructional point of view, unfortunately, the latter half of the book becomes an examination of the social niceties which eventually lead to the hero's marriage. Jane Austen was to do this much better, and by means of dialogue rather than letter-narrating. Still, *Mordaunt* is an enjoyable novel.

Moore, the friend of William and John Hunter, and the father of Sir John Moore of Coruna, had first met Smollett in Paris in 1750, and, as we have seen, shared his enthusiasm for travel. The renewal of their old friendship must have made Smollett happy.

From Cameron, the family seat by Loch Lomond, Smollett paid his only visit to the Highlands, and visited Islay, Jura, Mull and Iona. His return journey to Bath took him through Lanark and Dumfries.

This tour provided the inspiration for *The Expedition of Humphry Clinker*. The book, however, took Smollett several years to complete; restless years, when he knew that he had not long to live. After David Hume, then Under-Secretary of State, had failed to secure for Smollett a consulship at Nice or Leghorn, the novelist set out for Italy late in 1768, living at Lucca and Pisa before he finally settled in a villa two miles from Leghorn, by the slopes of Monte Nero. There, Smollett's last book was finished; and there he died on 17th September 1771, three months and a day after *Humphry Clinker* had been published.

It too is couched in letter form, then still regarded as a suitable medium for travel books, but although Chambers claimed that *Humphry Clinker* was regarded by Smollett's relations as "only a history, fictiously coloured, of his northern tour in search of health", it is a much more complex masterpiece. Smollett chose for his travelling family neither Scots, whom the English still distrusted and disliked, nor French, since the author himself disliked that race, but Welsh; people wholly acceptable to English readers and liked by Smollett, yet with enough of a difference in outlook to make their epistolary comments credible. Matthew Bramble, while an imaginary invalid with something of Smollett's nature in him, is certainly not an autobiographical likeness. Bramble's experiences left him enriched with a "considerable stock of health". Smollett recorded that at that time, he himself often retired to bed feeling so ill that he "fervently wished" he "might be dead before morning". The characterization comes out in the tone of the letters which Bramble and the members of his family and their entourage send back home: Bramble himself, the man of the world, mellowed by age and experience; sister Tabitha, whose letters, abounding in malapropisms, reveal the greedy, selfish nature which no doubt contributed to her spinsterly condition; teenage niece Lydia Melford, good-natured and impressionable, with a touch of romanticism in her nature; Jerry, her brother, full of the self-assurance of an Oxford undergraduate; Clinker, the comedy-creating character who ostensibly enters the family as a ragged servant but turns out to be the product of a youthful *amour* of Bramble's; and Lieutenant Obadiah Lismahago, not only one of the most original and funniest realistic fictional creations in eighteenth-century British literature, but a wonderful portrayal of Scots weaknesses still all too apparent in the national character.

It matters little that Lismahago's prototype was probably met in that gathering-place of London Scots, the British Coffee House. His remarkable life and adventures were chronicled in the *Memoirs of Major Robert Stobo, of the Virginia Regiment* (1800). It matters no more that he is both the supposed prototype of Scott's Captain Dugald Dalgetty in *A Legend of Montrose*, or the central figure in his own right in Sir Gilbert Parker's one-time Canadian best-seller, *Seats of the Mighty* (1900).

About a third of *Humphry Clinker* relates to Scottish scenery and manners, the rest to English fashions and foibles. The range and diversity of incident and character is considerable, and, as with most of Smollett's characters, we get to know them through their limitations rather than their virtues.

As a sample of the engaging nature of the narration and the character-contrasts often achieved in a single letter, here is part of one of Bramble's letters to Dr Lewis, describing a discussion with Lismahago:

> His manner is as harsh as his countenance; but his peculiar turn of thinking, and his pack of knowledge, made up of the remnants of rarities, rendered his conversation desirable, in spite of his pedantry and ungracious address. I have often met with a crab-apple in a hedge, which I have been tempted to eat for its flavour, even while I was disgusted by its austerity. The spirit of contradiction is naturally so strong in Lismahago, that I believe in my conscience that he has rummaged, and read, and studied with indefatigable attention, in order to qualify himself to refute established maxims, and thus raise trophies for the gratification of polemical pride. Such is the asperity of his self-conceit, that he will not even acquiesce in a transient compliment made to his own individual in particular, or to his country in general.
>
> When I observed that he must have read a vast number of books to be able to discourse on such a variety of subjects, he declared he had read little or nothing, and asked how he should find books among the woods of America, where he had spent the greatest part of his life. My nephew remarking, that

the Scotch in general were famous for their learning, he denied the imputation, and defied him to prove it from their works. "The Scotch", said he, "have a slight tincture of letters, with which they make a parade among people who are more illiterate than themselves; but they may be said to float on the surface of science, and they have made very small advances in the useful arts." "At least", cried Tabby, "all the world allows that the Scotch behaved gloriously in fighting and conquering the savages of America." "I can assure you, madam, you have been misinformed", replied the lieutenant; "in that continent the Scotch did nothing more than their duty; nor was there one corps in his Majesty's service that distinguished itself more than another. Those who affected to extol the Scotch for superior merit, were no friends to that nation. . . .

Smollett belonged to a category whose members were to achieve well-rewarded success in the nineteenth century, the London Scot; but Smollett's success did not come up to his expectations, and had to be bought at the cost of years of health-breaking hack-work. Unlike many later examples of the breed, his love of his homeland never left him. Thus, his novels give the curious impression of someone outside looking in on English (and, to a much lesser degree, Scottish) foibles; they feature the travels and the eventual deserved happy homecoming of the virtuous; and deal much with gatherings of the public, such as a restless exile would be particularly liked to turn to, and manifest a curious interest in prisons. Observing this mass of life around him, whether at sea or on land, Smollett selected and pointed his view of the human comedy by contrasting physical appearances and manners, and incongruities of behaviour, customs, or surroundings. His sense of the absurd and his gusto for life at all levels justifies Thackeray's verdict that Smollett had, indeed, "the keenest perceptive faculty and described what he saw with wonderful relish and delightful broad humour."

Gusto is hardly a term likely to be associated with Henry Mackenzie (1745–1831), the only other Scottish novelist of the century whose reputation has in some measure survived, even although his novels had ceased to be much read before his own death.

Born in Edinburgh, the son of a doctor, he was educated at Edinburgh High School and studied law at the University there. He practised law in the Scottish court, helped found the Royal Society of Edinburgh in 1783, and in 1799, was appointed Comptroller of Exchequer of Taxes of Scotland, a post he held until his death. He became the editor of, and so a regular contributor to, the periodicals *The Mirror* (1779–80), and the almost equally short-lived *Lounger* (1785–7),—the last of a long line of magazines featuring literary, moral and social comment, of which *The Spectator* was the most distinguished. Indeed, he was dubbed "the Northern Addison" by his literary friends in the capital.

The cult of sentimentalism displayed by this high-minded yet, as may be seen from the *Anecdotes and Egoisms*, sometimes caustic man, was no more of a paradox than its middle and upper-class popularity in a century that thought of itself as "The Age of Reason". Sentiment, of course, has always existed in art, as in honest human relationships. Its corruption into the debased coinage of deliberately cultivated sentimentality—the flaunting for the sake of effect of exploited emotion—may possibly have been a kind of secular reflection of the century's emotional, evangelical, religious revivalism. An unnatural reticence about sex and, among the married, about the first intimations of its natural outcome; an exaggerated dramatization of virtue with a view to public reward; fainting on the slightest pretext; the unhealthy romanticizing of the "interesting" illness of consumption; a deluge of tears, poured copiously at every opportunity.

Sterne and Goldsmith, among great writers, both deployed a fair measure of sentimentality, though always under control. Lesser writers like Mrs Radcliffe, Mrs Robinson and Fanny Burney were much more prone to let it run away with itself. These English ladies are not our concern here. In any case, Henry Mackenzie's first novel, *The Man of Feeling* (1771), is object lesson enough on what happens to a talent when its possessor forces it into a fashionable mould.

As a novelist, Mackenzie's gift was largely imitative. He owes something in the matters of style and punctuation to Sterne and a great deal for his characterization to Smollett. His tearful unceasing pity, braced neither with the force of detached indignation nor the political desire (or ability) to nurture practical reform, becomes wearisome.

In *The Man of Feeling*, the hero, young Harley, encounters a series of pathetic creatures discarded by an acquisitive and thrusting society. Though they have made their sad way out of Smollett's ambience, the low-life world, their gentleness is sometimes touching. Yet whether it is the girl broken by a forced marriage, the discharged old beggarly soldier, the ruined tenant farmer or the seduced rich man's plaything-turned-prostitute, all usually end up by joining Harley in a shower of shared tears. No wonder that when this unheroic hero, for whom life is always too rough, discovers that the pure Miss Walton, whom he fancied to be beyond his matrimonial reach, really does love him, he drops dead! It is just possible that Harley represented to Mackenzie his own awareness of "the pity of it all", a late eighteenth-century legal man's powerlessness to attack in any meaningful way what must have seemed totally intractable social problems. Even so, what Harley conveys is self-pity, rather than pity for the social misfits vignetted.

The Man of the World (1773), intended as a balancing study from the other side, has its sentimentality somewhat tempered, but the crude literary contriving is just as obvious. *Julia de Roubigne* (1777) is in many ways his most polished effort, even if the polish is on plating rather than sterling metal. Couched in the by then old-fashioned form of letters—though later to be used again successfully by Scott—the book tells of how Julia, believing her

unofficially betrothed young man to have married another abroad, weds a
rich nobleman out of gratitude to her father. But the former lover returns
from the West Indies to claim Julia's hand in marriage, having meantime
made his fortune. Montauban, the husband, learns of a perfectly innocent,
if damp-eyed, farewell meeting between his wife and this former suitor
before the lover leaves to go into permanent exile in France. Immediately
placing a wrong contruction on the incident, instead of first making a few
commonsense enquiries, Montauban poisons Julia. On discovering, too
late, her innocence, he then poisons himself. The world could not be said to
have been much the poorer for this double loss. Indeed, one cannot but
note that, to use Mackenzie's own expression, "those tender regrets which
the better part of our nature feels have something in them to blunt the edge
of that pain they inflict, and confer on the votaries of sorrow a sensation
that borders on pleasure." In plain words, Mackenzie's characters rather
enjoyed their misery.

Undoubtedly, Mackenzie's social perceptions were keener than those of
many of his contemporaries. He did not approve of the British conquest of
India, the slave trade, press-ganging, land monopoly and political favour-
itism, all causes then still generally tolerated. And some of his essays—
notably his *Lounger* welcome to Burns, the "heaven-taught ploughman",
and his much warmer welcome to the work of the author of *Waverley*—
show a firmness of handling absent from his fiction.

But then he was really a man of letters rather than a creative writer; a
journalist, not a novelist. He was also a transitional figure. As Scott himself
wrote of Mackenzie: "He has, we believe, shot game of every description
which Scotland contains (deer and probably grouse excepted), on the very
grounds at present occupied by the extensive and splendid streets of the
New Town of Edinburgh; has sought for hares and wild ducks where there
are now palaces, churches, and assembly rooms; and has witnessed more
revolutions as surprising as this extraordinary change of local circumstances."[20]

CHAPTER FIVE

The Nineteenth Century

I

So far as Scottish literature is concerned, the first half of the nineteenth century is dominated by the achievement and personality of Sir Walter Scott. There are those who would wish to add the name of George Noel Gordon (1788–1824), sixth Lord Byron, who was half-Scots by birth and partly so by education. But the mature Byron involved himself primarily with English traditions. Scott, on the other hand, not only drew his inspiration from the history, scenery and folk-culture of his native land, but peopled European interest in "Ossian's" cloudy myth-land with the characters of flesh-and-blood historical romance.

Walter Scott (1771–1832) was born in Edinburgh, the son of a lawyer. Before his second birthday, an attack of poliomyelitis had lamed him for life, frustrating a later-recounted wish (shared, on occasion, by his predecessor Burns) to become a soldier. From Edinburgh High School Scott proceeded to the University, and in 1786 entered his father's office as an apprentice writer to the signet, the Edinburgh title for a solicitor. Two years later he decided to become an advocate, so there followed a further period at Edinburgh University. In 1792, he was admitted to the Scottish Bar. In 1799, he was appointed Sheriff-Depute of Selkirk, a position worth £300 per annum, and in 1806, he became also Clerk of Session in Edinburgh, which brought him a further assured £800. Of Border extraction on both sides of his family, Scott's emotional involvement with Border history appears first to have been stimulated during recuperation from a student illness when reading was his only recreation. It was to be an involvement which lasted throughout his life.

His first love was the daughter of a Kelso tradesman, his second, Williamina Belsches, who in 1796 married instead the banker later to become Sir William Forbes. The break with Miss Belsches seems to have left Scott with a sense of pain that he remembered for many years. On the rebound, he married Charlotte Carpenter in Carlisle, a union which perhaps soon cooled into friendship. At any rate, he wrote to Lady Abercorn on 21st January 1810: "Mrs Scott's match and mine was of our own making and proceeded from the most sincere affection on both sides which has rather increased than diminished during twelve years' marriage. But it was something short of love in all its fervour which I suspect people only feel once in their lives. Folks who have been nearly drowned in bathing rarely returning a second time out of their depth."[1]

When not required to be at his Edinburgh home in Castle Street, he lived, first at Ashestiel, and then on the site of Cartley Hole, which he bought from a Dr Douglas in 1812 for £4,000 and began to transform into the romance in stone that became Abbotsford, "a place to dream of, not to tell", as he himself described it. Soon, he was hugely enjoying the life of a Border laird, constantly adding to the bounds of his property, and mixing with the élite of the day.

He had begun his literary career with translations of Bürger's "Leonore" and "Der Wilde Jäger" in 1796. A meeting with the English Gothic horror-novelist "Monk" Lewis (1775–1818) seems first to have aroused Scott's interest in collecting ballads, an interest which resulted in the *Minstrelsy of the Scottish Borders*, the first edition of which was published in Kelso in 1802.*

Following the success of this anthology, for which he rode many rough miles to collect ballads from country people of all degrees and social stations—a labour in which he had the assistance of Leyden, Charles Kirkpatrick Sharpe (1781–1851) and others—Scott next spent some years in editing—notably, the romance *Sir Tristem* (1804), and the great editions of Dryden (1808) and Swift (1814)—and in writing the first of his ballad epics *The Lay of the Last Minstrel* (1805), *Ballads and Lyrical Pieces* (1806), *Marmion* (1808), *The Vision of Don Roderick* (1811) and, most profitable of all, *The Lady of the Lake* (1810). *Rokeby* (1813), for which he received £3,000, sold less well, but was followed by *The Bridal of Treirmain* (1813), *The Lord of the Isles* (1815), *The Field of Waterloo* (1815), and *Harold the Dauntless* (1817).

The first of his novels, *Waverley*, appeared anonymously in 1814. It was followed by *Guy Mannering* in 1815 and *The Antiquary* in 1816. Perhaps fearing that the much-applauded "author of Waverley" might glut his own market, Scott's next series of novels came out as component parts of *Tales of My Landlord*, allegedly communicated by Jedediah Cleishbotham, schoolmaster and parish clerk of Gandercleugh, and written up by his assistant, Peter Pattieson, from material orally supplied by the landlord of the Gandercleugh Inn. *The Black Dwarf* and *Old Mortality* both appeared in 1816, *The Heart of Midlothian* in 1818, *The Bride of Lammermoor* and *A Legend of Montrose* in 1819. The "Author of Waverley" had meanwhile produced *Rob Roy* in 1817, and there then followed a long list of successes: *Ivanhoe* (1819); *The Monastery* and *The Abbott* (1820), the year in which Scott was made a baronet: *Lives of the Novelists, Kenilworth* and *The Pirate* (1821); *Peveril of the Peak, Quentin Durward* and *St Ronan's Well* (1823); and *Redgauntlet* (1824). Other "personae" that were facets of Scott himself pro-

* Another edition, together with a third volume, all with additions by Scott himself, as well as several reprints, came out during the next decade.

duced the *Tales of the Crusaders—The Betrothed, The Talisman* (1825)—
Chronicles of the Canongate—The Highland Widow, The Two Drovers and *The
Surgeon's Daughter* (1827); *The Fair Maid of Perth* (1828)—and the final
Landlord tales, *Count Robert of Paris* and *Castle Dangerous* (1831). Add to that
The Letters of Malachi Malagrowther (1826), a defence of Scotland's right to
print her own bank notes at a time when it was threatened by the English
desire for conformity; *Woodstock* (1825); the *Life of Napoleon Buonaparte*
(1827); that charming history-book for the young, *Tales of a Grandfather*
(1827/28/29); *Anne of Geierstein* (1829); a vast quantity of miscellaneous
prose-work in the form of articles and reviews; the noble, posthumously published *Journal*, and one is left marvelling at Scott's industry and
inventiveness, and baffled at how adequately to do it justice in a survey
such as this.

The stimulus to Scott's feverish industry was at first his land-hunger,
which drove him to acquire more and more territory around Abbotsford.
After the financial crash of 1826, he was driven on by his determination to
make as sure as he possibly could that no creditors would be left unpaid
through any lack of effort on his part.

Like Burns before him, Scott had to deal with the dichotomy which has
faced all Scottish writers since 1707. On the one hand Scott's appreciation
of the romantic past led him to steep his imaginative faculties and his antiquarian talents in the heroic or anti-heroic drama of Scotland's history. On
the other, his inherently common-sense nature made him support the industrial changes that came with the Union, and which he realized were inevitable. The gratifying of his desire to be a laird, a possessor of that land
which in the old Scotland was the symbol of power, brought about his
undoing, for he constantly needed more and more money to finance his
acquisitions. Imprudently, in 1802 he lent his old schoolfriend, the Kelso
printer James Ballantyne, £500 to set himself up in Edinburgh. To avoid
the embarrassment of further borrowing, Scott invested an inheritance of
£5,000 in Ballantyne's business in 1805. Thus he was drawn into business
affairs he never fully understood. By 1809, when James's brother, John, was
set up as publisher, Scott in effect controlled both businesses.

Because of the pernicious system whereby bills of credit were accepted
by one firm against the debt of another, and transferred like actual currency, it would in these days have been difficult enough for an astute financier to be sure at any moment where the affairs of firms like the
Ballantynes' stood. Scott was no financier. In June 1826, the year of Lady
Scott's death, the failure of the London publishing house of Hurst and
Robinson brought down the publishing house of Constable. Archibald
Constable (1774–1827), called by Lord Cockburn "the most spirited bookseller that ever appeared in Scotland" and by Scott "a prince of booksel-
lers", had come to the aid of the Ballantynes during an earlier financial
crisis in 1813, when the profits of the printing-house were being used to
shore up the publishing firm. Following this shake-up the Ballantynes'

publishing house went out of business in 1817. James remained with the printing business, but Constable was effectively in command. The failure of Constable in 1826 brought down Ballantyne, and Scott felt morally responsible for the general ruin. He drove his pen the harder, and by the time of his death, worn-out and broken by a paralytic stroke, he had paid off more than £60,000 of the final debt, the balance being cleared by his executors through the sale of copyrights.

It is obviously impossible to attempt a detailed book-by-book account of Scott's huge output in the present context. It is, however, necessary to consider Scott's achievement by categories, and to attempt some assessment of their overall significance in the course of Scottish literature.

The *Minstrelsy*, Scott's first major contribution, was divided into three sections; Historical Ballads, allegedly founded on actual events; Romantic Ballads; and Imitations of the Ancient Ballads, many of which were by Scott himself. He declared his motives in making his collection at the end of the Introduction, where he hoped that: "By such efforts, feeble as they are, I may contribute somewhat to the history of my native country; the peculiar features of whose manners and character are daily melting and dissolving into those of her sister and ally. And trivial as may appear such a offering to the manes of a kingdom once proud and independent, I hang it upon her altar with a mixture of feelings, which I shall not attempt to describe."

It is important to appreciate Scott's attitude to handling ballad material. His aim was not to pin down upon paper an actual text taken from a possibly corrupt oral source with all its imperfections still upon it, as the field-workers of the School of Scottish Studies are to-day assiduously, and properly, taping the last gleanings of a by now all but spent harvest. Scott set out to produce the best composite text he could from the variety of versions available to him. Indeed, as Charles G. Zug III puts it: "Since he was only interested in producing a *single*, finished text, Scott was apparently very careless about saving the often incomplete variants which served as the basis for his finished products."[2] There is thus today a lack of original texts, especially for the historical ballads. But, as Zug says, this "lack of materials is the direct result of editorial work, and there is absolutely no evidence to commit Scott of forging spurious traditional ballads for the *Minstrelsy*."

"Kinmont Willie" is a case in point, the only known text being the one printed in the *Minstrelsy*, the subject, Sir Walter Scott of Branxholm, an ancestral kinsman of the poet. The probability is that the basic ballad was a product of one of those ballad-collecting "raids" into Liddisdale made in conjunction with Robert Shortreed, and that Scott simply polished and added a line or a stanza here and there, in his usual manner.

The most famous of the Romantic Ballads is undoubtedly "Sir Patrick Spens". Here, Scott seems to have made only minor changes in rhythms. It seems that the "gurly sea" and "the King's daughter of Norroway" came to Scott through Leyden, who alleged that he had had them "from a woman in Kelso".[3]

On the other hand, "The Gay Goshawk" and "The Dowie Dens of Yarrow", to name but two, contain much of Scott, particularly the latter. Thomas Crawford, in considering Scott's contribution to "The Wife of Usher's Well", pertinently asks: "But who shall say who was responsible—Scott or his source—for the magnificent . . . 'the channerin worm doth chide'?"[4]

In some ways the finest of all the Border ballads is "The Twa Corbies". Its career into captivity was a chequered one. Scott had it from C. K. Sharpe,[5] who said he had received it from Jean Erskine, daughter of Lord Alva, "who, I think said that she had written it down from the recitation of an old woman at Alva." Another, rougher version was published by Child, taken from *Albyn's Anthology* (1818), whence it had come from Thomas Shortreed of Jedburgh, who noted it from his mother's singing. Scott's version is immeasurably superior, leading M. J. C. Hodgart to claim that "no one but a purist could object to this reshaping by Scott, since the result is a ballad by any standards and is good poetry."[6] "Good poetry" was, in fact, precisely what Scott was always out to achieve.

Crawford perhaps sums up the merits of these splendidly vivid pieces, which he calls "some of the finest poems of the Romantic Revival", when he says: "The ballads that [Scott] pieced together are sometimes characterized by self-identification with his own freebooting ancestors: when this occurs, a form of heroic action-poetry is generated that looks forward to the battle scenes in the lays and the novels. At other times, they exhibit a tension between reality and romance that seems fundamental to Scott and made him, much later, at one and the same time a romantic and an anti-romantic novelist."[7]

The leap from editor of the *Minstrelsy* to the creator of original epic-ballads—for such is what all Scott's long poems are in essence—was, so to say, sprung from the second edition of the anthology, in which Scott's original contribution in the third section increased from three poems to seven. We have Lockhart's[8] authority for it that *The Lay of the Last Minstrel* was first conceived as a ballad, but grew into a longer poem as its author came under the influence of English medieval romances. The Border legend of Gilpin Horner having been suggested to him as a fitting subject by the Countess of Dalkeith, Scott began work on it in 1802. At first he used the Coleridgian "Christabel" measure, varied, once he had fully embarked upon his extended scheme, with the octosyllabic couplet he was later so often to favour and which, as he himself declared, is a measure derived from the English medieval romances. The *Lay* has in common with all Scott's epic-ballads a major emphasis on story-telling, and an unabashed use of the clichés of common speech to hurry along the narrative between the strongly visualized sights and sounds of the built-in set-pieces.

For this, his first major original work, Scott was concerned not only with the backcloth of history—more will be said about the strands of that backcloth in connection with his novels—but also with his own largely imagined characters set in the context of the manners of a particular period. It is quite clear from Scott's own references, in connection with both poems and novels, that by "manners" he means the social conditions and communal behaviour of people in earlier times. What he declared in his Preface to the *Lay* is indicative of the plan he was later to adopt for the novels:

> The Poem . . . is intended to illustrate the customs and manners which anciently prevailed on the Borders of England and Scotland. The inhabitants living in a state partly pastoral and partly warlike, and combining habits of constant depredation with the influence of a rude spirit of chivalry, were often engaged in scenes highly susceptible of poetical ornament. As the description of scenery and manners was more the object of the Author than a combined and regular narrative, the plan of the Ancient Metrical Romance was adopted, which allows greater latitude . . . than would be consistent with the dignity of a regular Poem.

Scott repeats his interest in manners in connection with *Marmion*, when, in a letter dated 26th April 1808, he says: "My plan . . . has always been . . . to exhibit ancient costume, diction and manners."

If the *Lay* is uneven, as many of its critics have suggested, this is perhaps because Scott deliberately allowed "manners" to divert his usual impetuous narrative flow. Perhaps for this very reason, the *Lay* contains isolated memorable things; for instance, mocked though it be, "Breathes there the man"; the sounding of a kind of re-animated "high style" in ballad context in "Rosabelle"; and the powerful translation of the "Dies Irae" at the close of the poem:

> That day of wrath, that dreadful day,
> When heaven and earth shall pass away,
> What power shall be the sinner's stay?
> How shall he meet that dreadful day?
>
> When, shrivelling like a parched scroll,
> The flaming heavens together roll;
> When louder yet, and yet more dread,
> Swells the high trump that wakes the dead!
>
> Oh! on that day, that wrathful day,
> When man to judgment wakes from day,
> Be THOU the trembling sinner's stay,
> Though heaven and earth shall pass away!

These lines remind us that behind Episcopalian, tolerant (though

basically anti-Catholic) Scott hovered not only the Presbyterian God of
Burns, but the medieval God of Dunbar.

Marmion, subtitled "A Tale of Flodden Field", has much less time than its
predecessor for incidentals, and so makes greater use of Scott's favourite
octosyllabic couplet in various groupings, interrupted by six-syllabled
lines of three stresses, which create a characteristic surging effect, as has
been said, like the riding and breaking of a wave. Unfortunately, this light-
horse canter of a measure, as it may also be described, came increasingly
easily to Scott, and resulted in a facility that sometimes produced the effect
of surface monotony.

Once again, however, the set-piece scenes in *Marmion* give the impression of having been pre-visualized in much the same way as the scenes
from the novels, the choice of the ancient story-telling medium of verse
seeming almost a secondary consideration. Indeed, the battle-scene at Flodden relies for its effect more on what is told than on the swift manner of the
telling.

> But as they left the dark'ning heath,
> More desperate grew the strife of death.
> The English shafts in volleys hail'd,
> In headlong charge their horse assail'd;
> Front, flank, and rear, the squadrons sweep
> To break the Scottish circle deep
>   That fought around their King.
> But yet, though thick the shafts as snow,
> Though charging knights like whirlwinds go,
>   Unbroken was the ring;
> The stubborn spear-men still made good
> Their dark impenetrable wood,
> Each stepping where his comrade stood,
>   The instant that he fell.
> No thought was there of dastard flight;
> Link'd in the serried phalanx tight,
> Groom fought like noble, squire like knight,
>   As fearlessly and well;
> Till utter darkness closed her wing
> O'er their thin host and wounded King.
> Then skilful Surrey's sage commands
> Led back from strife his shatter'd bands;
>   And from the charge they drew,
> As mountain-waves, from wasted lands,
>   Sweep back to ocean blue.
> Then did their loss his foemen know;
> Their King, their Lords, their mightiest low,
> They melted from the field as snow,

When streams are swoln and south winds blow,
    Dissolves in silent dew.
Tweed's echoes heard the ceaseless plash,
    While many a broken band,
Disorder'd, through her currents dash,
    To gain the Scottish land. . . .

The Lady of the Lake was justly regarded in Scott's own day as the most successful of his epic ballads, and it still is. Scott's awareness of the effect of light and shade upon scenery, a feature of both his earlier epic ballads—and perhaps influenced by his friend Anne Grant's rather stilted poem *The Highlander* (1802)—is here applied with such telling effect to the Trossachs that, on its curiousity arousing account, he has been dubbed "the father of Scottish tourism".

The accidentally unhorsed King James V, roaming the country in the guise of Fitz-James, climbs to the top of a mound:

The broom's tough roots his ladder made,
The hazel saplings lent their aid;
And thus an airy point he won,
Where, gleaming with the setting sun
One burnish'd sheet of living gold,
Loch Katrine lay beneath him roll'd,
In all her length far winding lay,
With promontory, creek and bay,
And islands that, empurpled bright,
Floated amid the livelier light,
And mountains that like giants stand,
To sentinel enchanted land.

The barrier of Gaelic that for so long had separated Highlands and Lowlands was already receding in Scott's times. To the Romantic mind, the old Highland ways were an irresistible attraction. In his Introduction to the poem, Scott says:

The ancient manners, the habits and customs of the aboriginal race by whom the Highlands of Scotland were inhabited, had always appeared to me peculiarly adapted to poetry. The change in their manners, too, had taken place almost within my own time, or at least I had learned many particulars concerning the ancient state of the Highlands from the old men of the last generation. I had always thought the old Scottish Gael highly adapted for poetical composition.

The story, centring round the supposed habit of the monarch to move among his subjects incognito, is told with the same vigour, with less padding and fewer inversions for the sake of a rhyme, though with a greater reliance on octosyllabic couplets, than its two predecessors.

Rokeby followed in 1812, the year in which Scott acquired the first tract of what was to become the estate of Abbotsford. This poem was the product of Scott's friendship with John Bacon Sawrey Morritt (1772?–1843), squire of Rokeby, Yorkshire, and a classical scholar. It was less well received by the public than its predecessors, however; so Scott, aware of the superiority of Byron's rising genius, took, as he put it, those "steps by which I declined as a poet to figure as a novelist." While it is true to say that the scenic effects in Rokeby wear something of a pasted-on look, the plot of this Cromwellian verse-tale is more credible than that of the more celebrated earlier epic-ballads.

But Scott's "declension" to novelist was to be a gradual one. Another epic ballad, *The Lord of the Isles*, appeared in 1815. It still retains its own energy of action, and manages some well-observed passages of scenic description by one who then saw himself as:

> . . . a lonely gleaner I,
> Through fields time-wasted on sad inquest bound,
> Where happier bards of yore have riper harvest found.

The same cannot be said for the somewhat mechanically contrived *The Vision of Don Roderick* (1811) in Spenserian stanzas, still less for *The Bridal of Triermain* or *Harold the Dauntless*. *The Field of Waterloo* (1815) has been justly eclipsed by Byron's *Childe Harold*; yet the melancholy rhetoric of the first two stanzas of the concluding section of Scott's poem are moving, reflecting, as they do, the resigned sadness inherent in the poet's nature:

> Stern tide of human Time! that know'st not rest,
> But, sweeping from the cradle to the tomb,
> Bear'st ever downward on thy dusky breast
> Successive generations to their doom;
> While thy capacious stream has equal room
> For the gay bark where Pleasure's streamers sport,
> And for the prison-ship of guilt and gloom,
> The fisher-skiff, and barge that bears a court,
> Still wafting onward all to one dark silent port. . . .

Poems are to be found in many of the novels, some of them perfect in their distillation of ballad-simplicity, like Madge Wildfire's song in *The Heart of Midlothian*, "Proud Maisie":

> Proud Maisie is in the wood,
>   Walking so early;
> Sweet Robin sits on the bush,

Singing so rarely.

"Tell me, though bonny bird,
  When shall I marry me?"
"When six braw gentlemen
  Kirkward shall carry ye."

"Who makes the bridal bed,
  Birdie, say truly?"
"The grey-headed sexton
  That delves the grave duly."

"The glow-worm o'er grave and stone
  Shall light thee steady.
The owl from the steeple sing,
  Welcome, proud lady."

Scott, who wrote rapidly all his life, made only one small emendation in the manuscript of that particular poem.

There is the superb polish of David Gellatly's song from *Waverley*, "Young men will love thee more fair and more fast"; the moving lament for the mutability of all things, "Why sit'st thou by that ruin'd hall?", from *The Antiquary*; and the swaggering bravura of "Bonny Dundee", from *Woodstock*, written while Scott, on learning of his financial crash, erroneously believed for a few hours that he had escaped its worst consequences:

To the Lords of Convention 'twas Clavers who spoke,
'Ere the King's crown shall fall there are crowns to be broke;
So let each Cavalier who loves honour and me
Come follow the bonnet of Bonny Dundee,
Come fill up my cup, come fill up my can,
Come saddle your horses and call up your men;
Come ope the West Port and let me gang free,
And it's room for the bonnets of Bonny Dundee.

Unlike Burns, Scott did not compose his lyrics with a tune in his mind's ear. His songs thus have to rely on their own word-music. Perhaps for this very reason, the Scott lyric, even at its most accomplished, often achieves its effects at a kind of surface level. Yet the range of experience he encompassed is considerable; so considerable, in fact, as to make him a poet of much more rewarding consequence than many critics have allowed.

In his most highly personal moments, Scott, the poet, always keeps his emotions under classical restraint:

The sun upon the Weirdlaw Hill
  In Ettrick's vale is sinking sweet;

The westland wind is hush and still,
 The lake lies sleeping at my feet.
Yet not the landscape to mine eye
 Bears those bright hues that once it bore;
Though evening, with her richest dye,
 Flames o'er the hills of Ettrick's shore.

It was Scott, the novelist, who was later to analyse human motivation from behind the quasi-impersonal cover of the guise of narrator, and who therefore in prose penetrated more deeply the outward *chiaroscuro* of daily life.

Much of the lively background and the bitterness with which Scottish writing was associated during the earlier half of the nineteenth century arose out of the association of literature and politics as reflected through the Whig *Edinburgh Review*, founded in 1802, and whose most distinguished associate was Francis Jeffrey (1773–1850), its editor almost from its founding until 1829, when he mounted the bench as Lord Jeffrey. Its Tory rival was *Blackwood's* founded in 1817 by William Blackwood (1776–1834) as *Edinburgh's Monthly Magazine*, changing its name with the seventh number to that which it still carries,* although this became abbreviated to "Maga", since the broad-tongued proprietor with the shaggy eyebrows and the fierce, grey eyes usually referred to it as "ma Maaga". Although Scott disliked *Blackwood's*, nearly all the other figures who surrounded or followed Scott on the Scottish literary scene were involved with one or the other of the two magazines.

Poetically, the most important was James Hogg (1770–1835), known as "The Ettrick Shepherd". The son of a Border farmer, his early days were spent herding cows until he was old enough to be entrusted with a flock of sheep. His mother possessed an inexhaustible stock of ballads and folklore, which she imparted to her son. His sheep-knowledge was to be put to good use in his text-book, *The Shepherd's Guide: being a practical treatise on the diseases of sheep* (1807), a work that was to prove of service to hill farmers for several decades. His folk-lore, mixed up with the fashionable culture of the day which he strove to acquire by self-education, was to provide him with the raw material for a considerable if uneven crop of novels, stories and poems.

Hogg entered the service of a friend of Scott, and so met the poet. In this way, Hogg came to assist Scott in the collecting of material for the *Border Minstrelsy*. On a visit to Edinburgh in 1801, Hogg published his earliest original pieces, *Scottish Pastorals, Poems and Songs*, which he followed up with *The Mountain Bard* (1807). With the profit of £300 which he made out of *The Shepherd's Guide*, he set up his own sheep-farm in Dumfriesshire, a venture which ended in bankruptcy. In 1810, Hogg settled in Edinburgh in order to support himself with his pen. In this year *The Forest Minstrel* appeared. He also founded a journal, *The Spy*, which

* Until December 1980, when it ceased publication.

only survived for a single year. In 1813, however, he published *The Queen's Wake*, which revealed the full extent of his poetic powers, and won him a place on Blackwood's staff, as a result of which he became a friend of Wordsworth and Byron, as well as of many of his lesser Scottish contemporaries. There then followed a series of somewhat vapid poems in the Scott-inspired manner of the day: *The Pilgrims of the Sun* (1815), *Mador of the Moor* (1816) and *Queen Hynde* (1826).

Another publication, *The Jacobite Relics of Scotland* (First Series, 1819, Second Series 1821), contained a few of those pieces by which Hogg is best known today, including "Bonnie Prince Charlie", "M'Lean's Welcome" and "Charlie is my Darling." Yet another, *The Poetic Mirror* (1816), established a taste for parody and light verse that was to provoke emulation throughout most of the century.

Both in his prose-work and in his poetry, Hogg provides one more example of the disastrous effects of the Scottish dichotomy stemming from the political events of 1560, 1603 and 1707. Understandably, he admired Scott, whose intellectual and social position perhaps led the greater writer to misunderstand the lesser. Hogg's talent was not for polite Regency verse or fashionable fictioning, but for the uninhibited expression of those folk-forces nurtured by his mother. He inhabited the "kingdom of the mountain and the fairy"—which, he once told Scott, "is a far higher one than yours" (meaning the school of chivalry, or polite manners). Hogg's natural element was that old Scottish pagan world of the supernatural, and the dark legends surrounding the early men of the reformed religion who routed these older superstitions to make way for their own grimmer mythology. Both these traditions still co-existed at the beginning of the nineteenth century; both had their roots deep in the soil of the Scots character.

Scott's epic ballads, as Louis Simpson puts it, "created a fashion for Scottish scenes and characters, but he had relegated the vernacular to second place and falsified those traditions which are embodied in the vernacular";[9] a limited view which does not, of course, relate to Scott's impact as a whole, or take sufficient account of the social and economic pressures relentlessly operating against the traditions "embodied in the vernacular". The practical effect of Scott's influence on Hogg was to make the Ettrick Shepherd uncertain whether to obey his own folk-inspired impulses, or set himself out to go after the more modern Scott-worshipping audience. He compromised, often unsuccessfully, by trying to please everybody.

At his worst he writes dull, dead, English pastiches. In *The Pilgrims of the Sun*, for instance, he imitates the style of Pope or Dryden:

Thus tis ordained—these grosser regions yield
Souls, thick as blossoms of the vernal field,
Which after death, in relative degree,
Fairer or darker as their minds may be,
To other worlds are led. . . .

Mador of the Moor is couched in strained Spenserian stanzas, its subject deriving from the story of *The Lady of the Lake*. In Hogg's poem the heroine is seduced and abandoned by Mador, a minstrel, whom she follows to court, only to discover that he is the king.

Queen Hynde is written in the English octosyllabics of Scott, handled with an absence of technical skill which necessitates numerous inversions and other syntactical perversions. The story deals with the fate of a young queen besieged by King Eric of Norway. He wishes to marry her so that he may gain Scotland. To Queen Hynde's rescue comes none other than St Columba, who agrees to bring across the rightful heir, Prince Eiden, from Ireland.

Not only was Hogg uneasy over his linguistic position in these and in many of his shorter poems. He was also quite unable to hold the reader's interest when he tried to relate a long verse-tale. *The Queen's Wake*, though ostensibly a long poem, is, in fact, nothing of the sort. Its framework, in English octosyllabics, imagined an idealized version of the celebrations which took place when Mary, Queen of Scots arrived at Holyrood in August 1561, and, according to Knox, "a cumpanie of maist honest men, with instruments of musick, gave their salutation at her chalmer windo: the melodie, as she alleged, lyked her weil, and she willed the same to be continued sum nychts efter with grit diligence."[10]

According to Hogg's poem, the Earl of Argyle summons together seventeen bards. Fortunately, all of them do not perform within Hogg's pages. Of the thirteen who do, the efforts of the favoured one, like those of Beckmeister, the official favourite in *Die Meistersinger*, go unappreciated. Another, the Ettrick bard, is Hogg himself. He sings of David, who leads his seven sons to rescue maidens kidnapped by fairies. In his role as narrator Hogg describes himself as:

> Poor wight! he never weened how hard
> For Poverty to earn regard!
> Dejection o'er his visage ran,
> His coat was bare, his colour wan,
> His forest doublet darned and torn,
> His shepherd plaid all rent and worn . . .
> The bard on Ettrick's mountain green
> In nature's bosom nursed had been . . .
> When o'er her mellow notes he ran,
> And his wild mountain chant began,
> Then first was noted in his eye
> A gleam of native energy.

On the third night, the first vote in the final leet is awarded, not to Rizzio, the Queen's favourite, but to Gardyn, who sang a ballad, "Young Kennedy"; a horror-tale in the "Monk" Lewis manner, which tells how Kennedy, a highlander, seduces Matilda, then, on her father being found dead, marries her, only to be pursued on his bridal night, and forever after, by the ghost of the father-in-law he had strangled.

The Ettrick Shepherd himself gets the second vote, and a nameless youth, who then withdraws, the third. Gardyn wins the final contest, and to console the Shepherd, Queen Mary offers him a cottage and an endless store of Scottish songs. Somewhat ungraciously, the bard asks instead for a harp. A magical one "framed by wizard of the wild" comes his way, having passed from its magical manufacturer through the hands of Hamilton of Bangour, Ramsay, Langhorne (a forgotten poet some of whose lines were identified by the boy Scott for Burns at their only meeting), Logan and Scott himself, who presents the shepherd with the harp.

The Queen's Wake makes fairly interesting reading, in spite of such howlers as:

No more the watch-fires gleam to the blast,
McKinnon and friends arrive at last. . . .

from "The Abbot McKinnon". Its diversity of stanza-forms and rhyme-schemes ensure a pleasant variety. Yet its main importance is that two of the "songs", neither of which won "prizes", happen to be among Hogg's very best poems; "Bonny Kilmeny", sung by the thirteenth bard; and the eight bard's piece, "The Witch of Fife." In spite of its unplaced position, Hogg himself tells us—in that exercise in bad taste *The Domestic Manners of Sir Walter Scott*, which shows why Hogg's limitations and pretensions sometimes encouraged risibility—that "The Witch of Fife" was "the most happy and splendid piece of humorous ballad poetry" he had written.

It is, indeed, a superb piece, unmarred even by the phoney archaic spelling Hogg employs. A husband questions his wife about her nocturnal ongoings, and learns that she is a witch who by night goes hunting, drinking the Bishop of Carlisle's wine, and lighting on "Lommond height". While the husband at first thinks these ongoings mean that she must be false to God and untrue to him, the thought of the free wine makes him eager to join his wife and her supernatural friends. He asks her for the necessary "word", which she refuses to give him on eminently reasonable grounds:

O fy! fy! my leil auld man,
    That word I darena tell;
It would turn this world all upside down,
    And make it worse then hell.

For all the lasses in the land
    Wald munt the wynd and fly;

And the men wald doff their doublets syde,
     And after them wad play.

But the "cunning auld man" spies on her, overhears the word, says it,
flies out through the chimney and lands in the vaults of the Bishop of Carlisle. There, unfortunately, he becomes too drunk to fly home, and is
caught and about to be burnt, a fate which would have overtaken him had
not Scott suggested the present ending whereby his wife, in the shape of a
bird, flies in from Fife, puts "ane reide cap" on his head, and says "ane
word intil his lug". Whereupon:

He drew his breath, and he said the word,
     And he said it with muckle glee,
Then set his fit on the burnying pile,
     And away to the aire flew he.

Till aince he clerit the swirlyng reike,
     He lukit beth ferit and sad;
But whan he won to the lycht blue aire,
     He lauchit as he'd been mad.

His armis war spred, and his heide was hiche,
     And his feite stack out behynde,
And the laibies of the auld manis cote   [skirts
     War wauffing in the wynde . . .   [flapping

He lukit back to the Carlisle men
     As he borit the norlan sky;
He noddit his heide, and gae ane grin,
     But he nevir said good-bye . . .

May everlike man in the land of Fife
     Read what the drinkeris dree;   [endure
And nevir curse his puir auld wife,
     Rychte wicked altho scho be.

With its easy mixture of Scots and English, the poem draws its supernatural framework from folk-lore and ballad sources; yet its amusing
counterpointing of these with the human failings of the husband is Hogg's
own devising. Although the final stanza has Burnsian overtones, in pace,
wit and tautness, I would place "The Witch of Fife" in the same category
as "Tam o' Shanter", and not very far below it.

     "Bonny Kilmeny", on the other hand, has no such human streak run-
ning through it. Its tetrameters are compounded of disyllabic and trisylla-
bic feet, and once again, the Scots is heavily diluted:

Bonny Kilmeny gaed up the glen;
But it wasna to meet Duneira's men,
Nor the rosy monk of the isle to see,
For Kilmeny was pure as pure could be.
It was only to hear the Yorlin sing,   [yellow-hammer
And pu' the cress-flower round the spring;
The scarlet hypp and the hyndberrye,
And the nut that hung frae the hazel-tree . . .

But Kilmeny encountered the spirits, who transported her to a "land of
light", from which vantage-point, in true medieval manner, she overlooks
such historical happenings as the war between England and France in the
symbolic form of a tussle between a lion and an eagle. Seven years later,
Kilmeny awakens from the trance into which she has been cast, and
returns for a month and a day, before vanishing again to "the greenwood",
this time for ever. "Thomas the Rhymer" and "Tam Lin" are the best
known of several ballads which deal with mortals similarly affected. It is, of
course, quite possible that Hogg, through his mother, was in touch with
some of the sources from which both these ballads were themselves composed. Unlike the old balladists, who could set their scene with a terse
phrase or line, Hogg left the topography of his otherworld vague, and this
is the most common criticism levelled against "Kilmeny". Yet in spite of
the undoubted diffuseness thus created, "Bonny Kilmeny" is still a remark-
ably beautiful and original poem.

Hogg also produced one or two good individual poems in the ballad
manner, among them "The Pedlar" from *The Mountain Bard*, one of the
best in his melodramatic vein. The subject is the haunting of the Thirlestane
millers by "Rob Riddle" in the form of a human pedlar wearing a "muckle
green pack", until Rob's death at the hands of one of them is avenged.
"Ringan and May", which first appeared in *Blackwood's* in 1825, is a love
tale which combines subtle female characterization with a fine climax of
lyricism. "The Monitors", published in *Blackwood's* in 1831, shows the poet
in his later, more subjective manner, voicing a sentiment similar to that in
Burns's "To a Mouse", less tautly if with a braver flourish of courage.

The poet's wide popularity in his own day was based on the song
"Donald Macdonald", as well as on his Jacobite favourites. Readers of anthologies, besides the shortened version of "Kilmenny", often reproduced,
will be familiar with the racing vocables of "Lock the Door, Lariston",
and the strange ongoings which took place in "The Village of Balmaqu-
happle". Children of many generations have chanted Hogg's "Boy's
Song" and "The Skylark". These alone should have earned him that gratitude which enabled him to live and work during the last twenty years of his
life at Altrive, a cottage on an estate owned by the Duke of Buccleuch.

In 1814–15, Hogg invited contributions for a new anthology he proposed to put together. Among those asked were Southey, Wordsworth, Byron and Scott. Scott refused to help this "joint-stock adventure in authorship". Byron did agree to contribute, but like most of the others similarly invited, failed to do so. So Hogg, as he relates in his *Autobiography*, finished off imitations of the popular poets of the day "in three weeks, except in a very small proportion; and in less than three months it was submitted to the public".

The parodies are amusing enough, though most of them imitate only the more superficial stylistic characteristics of their subjects. Much the most successful is Hogg's take-off of Wordsworth's characteristic elevation of simple things into epiphanies of high moral significance. It is cast in the pedestrian iambic plodding that the greatest of the Lakers could so easily fall into:

> A pair
> Of breeches, to his philosophic eye,
> Were not what unto other folk they seem,
> Mere simple breeches; but in them he saw
> The symbol of the soul—mysterious high
> Hieroglyphics! such as Egypt's priest
> Adored upon the holy Pyramid,
> Vainly imagined tomb of monarchs old,
> But raised by wise philosophy, and to spread
> Knowledge of dim concealment . . .

John Gibson Lockhart (1794–1854), the biographer and son-in-law of Scott, is dealt with more fully in connection with his prose achievements. In the rhyming department, he produced a considerable quantity of verse that appeared in the pages of *Blackwood's*. He would be hard put to it who could find much beyond fashionable smoothness in *Napoleon* (1821), or, for that matter, in the imitation Byronic *Don Juan* stanzas of *The Mad Banker of Amsterdam*. Even the *Ancient Spanish Ballads* (1823), collected from the pages of the magazine, never warm into poetry for more than an occasional stanza, whatever may be their merits as translations. One of his best poems is his vivid sketch of a well-known Glasgow character, Captain Paton; a piece which would have been better still had Lockhart not used the archaic "mo" for "more" simply to get a rhyme for "wo" (as he spells it). Here, however, is Paton in the midst of his accustomed pleasures:

> Now and then upon a Sunday he invited me to dine,
> On a herring and a mutton chop, which his maid dressed very fine;
> There was also a little Malmsey and a bottle of Bordeaux,
> Which between me and the Captain passed nimbly to and fro.
> Oh! I ne'er shall take pot-luck with Captain Paton no mo!

Or if a bowl was mentioned, the Captain he would ring,
And bid Nelly run to the West Port and a stoup of water bring.
Then he would mix the genuine stuff as they made it long ago
With limes that on his property in Trinidad did grow.
    Oh! we ne'er shall see the like of Captain Paton's punch no mo!

"When youthful faith has fled", Lockhart's heart-felt lines occasioned by the death of his wife, Sophia Scott, were sent by the poet to Carlyle when he, too, had newly suffered bereavement. Its conclusion only just manages to avoid that dogmatic pietism which was to provide so many bad nineteenth-century versifiers with a let-out for genuine poetic resolution:

Yet, 'tis an old belief
    That on some solemn shore
Beyond the sphere of grief
    Dear friends shall meet once more—

Beyond the sphere of Time,
    And Sin, and Fate's control,
Serene in changeless prime
    Of Body and of Soul.

That creed I fain would keep,
    That hope I'll not forgo;
Eternal be the sleep
    Unless to waken so.

John Wilson (1785–1854) was another *Blackwood's* man, better known under the pseudonym of "Christopher North". The son of a wealthy Paisley manufacturer, Wilson passed from Paisley Grammar School to Glasgow University, and thence to Magdalen College, Oxford, where he won the Newdigate Prize for Poetry (that kiss of death upon genuine poetic talent!), but distinguished himself most notably as an athlete. Inheriting a fortune of £50,000, he settled at Elleray, in the Lake District, where he became friendly with Wordsworth, Coleridge, Southey and De Quincey. His vapid English poem *The Isle of Palms* (1812), followed by *The City of the Plague* (1816), gained him enough of a contemporary literary reputation for him to be welcomed by the Blackwood group when he lost part of his fortune. In 1820, though possessing no real qualifications, he became Professor of Moral Philosophy at the University of Edinburgh. Never much of a philosopher, his striking peculiarity of expression, overflowing high spirits and leonine head enabled him to exercise a more stimulating influence on his students than his intellectual powers would appear to have justified. Any serious notion that Wilson may have been the author of the beautiful but anonymous "Canadian Boat Song" is, on stylistic grounds, only a little less absurd than the counter-theory that it may have been by Lockhart.

The Glaswegian Thomas Campbell (1777–1844) became Lord Rector of Glasgow University three times over, on one occasion defeating Scott himself. Campbell's early poem *The Pleasure of Hope* (1799) has at least given to the language the thought that:

'Tis distance lends enchantment to the view
And robes the mountains in its azure hue.

His gusty ballads "Lord Ullin's Daughter" and "Hohenlinden" are familiar to every schoolboy, while his sea-song "Ye Mariners of England" has justly enjoyed a wider currency. He himself set most store on his now forgotten longer poems, *Gertrude of Wyoming* (1808), *O'Connor's Child* (1809), and *Theodoric* (1824), catering for a now vanished taste for what were really novels in verse. Campbell thought up the aphorism, often wrongly attributed to Byron, "Now Barabbas was a publisher", wrote the charming poem "Freedom and Love", and at least one touching lyric, "Florine", in which Age resigns itself to the fact that Youth calls to Youth:

Could I bring back lost youth again
    And be what I have been,
I'd court you in a gallant strain,
    My young and fair Florine.

But mine's the chilling age that chides
    Devoted rapture's glow,
And Love—that conquers all besides—
    Finds Time a conquering foe.

Farewell! we're severed by our fate
    As far as night from noon;
You came into the world too late,
    And I depart so soon.

Of those who sought to continue the epic-ballad manner of Scott, the most industrious was William Motherwell (1797–1835), another product of Glasgow University. The introduction to his *Minstrelsy, Ancient and Modern* (1827) shows that he certainly knew what he was about in the field of balladry, and may even have had some inkling of the functioning of the oral recreative process. Unfortunately, however, his "original" imitations were leaden-footed, while his Scots poems mostly succumbed to the pull of that sickening sentimentality so common a by-product of Victorian pietism. Even his best piece in his native tongue, "Jeanie Morrison", abundantly exemplifies his prevailing fault:

I wonder, Jeanie, often yet,
    When sitting on that bink,   [bench
Cheek touchin' cheek, loof lock'd in loof   [palm
    What our wee heads could think?
When baith bent down owre ae braid page,
    Wi' ae buik on our knee,
Thy lips were on thy lesson, but
    My lesson was in thee.

Yet the nadir of sentimental double-think was reached in a poem by Alexander Rodger (1784–1846), a tradesman turned journalist, from Mid-Calder, in Midlothian:

Behave yoursel' before folk,
Behave yoursel' before folk,
And dinna be sae rude to me,
    As kiss me sae afore folk.

It wouldna gie me meikle pain,
Gin we were seen and heard by nane,
To tak a kiss, or grant you ane,
    But gudesakes! no before folk . . .

Rodger's "Robin Tamson's Smiddy", another excursion into couthy, amorous domesticity, has its admirers of whom I am not one. Certainly, his political and economic satires have more *virr*,* although for the most part they relate to the abuses they assail in rather too journalistic a fashion to survive as literature.

Nor can I summon much enthusiasm for most of the work of the Aberdeen-born weaver poet William Thom (1798–1848), whose pieces "The Mitherless Bairns" and "The Blind Boy's Pranks" survive in anthologies. Thom himself enjoyed for a few years a passing popularity in London literary circles. But he was basically a victim of the decline which overtook handloom cotton-weaving as linen supplanted it, yet without enough education or talent to escape the grip of poverty by the exertions of his pen. Separated from his wife, his first "companion" died leaving him with several "mitherless bairns", while his second common-law "wife" added to his family and bravely endured the miseries attendant upon his decline through tuberculosis and drink.

In the improbably titled "Whispers for the Unwashed", he achieves a certain brief nobleness of protest, despite the Burnsian echoes:

The nobler spider weaves alone,
And feels the little web his own,
* An untranslatable word for a combination of energy and common sense.

His house, his fortress, foul or fair,
No factory whipper swaggers there,
Should ruffian wasp or flaunting fly
Touch his lov'd lair, 'tis touch and die!
Supreme in rags, ye weave, in tears,
The shining robe your murderer wears;
Till worn, at last, to very "waste",
A hole to die in, at the best;
And dead, the session saints begrudge ye
The twa-three deals in death to lodge ye;
They grudge the grave wherein to drap ye,
An' grudge the very much to hap ye.

His satire against the Established Kirk's lack of concern for those who, like the poet, saw hope in Chartism, finds vigorous expression in "Sit Siccar on Yer Seat, Sawtan":

Ken ye carls howkin' out,
Wha darena howk within,
    Holy wark gies yer sark,
    Yer siller, an' yer sheen.
Gae wark a fyke to feed the kirk,
Although ye starve yer kin,
    An ye'll be lauchin' lairdies yet,
    Youplin' in yer yairdies yet,
    Heich ayont the moon.

Unfortunately, Thom could not sustain this level for very long.

The non-satirical work of both Rodger and Thom, along with that of Robert Gilfillan (1798–1850) and William Miller (1810–1872), was gathered into *Whistle Binkie; a Collection of Songs for the Social Circle* (1846). The "Whistle Binkie" group met regularly in a Glasgow tavern. Never has the Scots tongue been reduced to so sickly a plight as in the pages of their anthology. Alone amongst their products, Miller's well-known nursery song "Wee Willie Winkie" has a certain limited vitality. Virility is the quality totally lacking in the verses of all the other members of the group, except perhaps occasionally in the work of James Ballantine (1808–1877), whose "Gaberlunzie's Wallet" at least nods politely to the vanished glories of the Scots tongue.

Amongst English-writing poets, William Edmonstone Aytoun (1813–1865), also a "Blackwood" man, blended Scott-like historicism with rhetorical sentimentality in such pieces as "The Execution of Montrose" from his *Lays of the Scottish Cavaliers*, a strain also sounded by James Hyslop (1798–1827) in "The Cameronian's Dream", and by Henry Glassford Bell (1805–1874) in "The Execution of Mary, Queen of Scots", both

once popular with that mercifully vanished party performer, the elocu-
tionist.

Aytoun, however, achieved more lasting fame in other directions.
Talented Alexander Smith (1830–1867), Kilmarnock-born pattern-
designer turned poet and essayist, was an original handler of sensuous
imagery, as is testified by his much anthologized poem "Glasgow", from
City Poems (1857). But he was unwise enough to produce a turgidly uneven
long poem, *A Life Drama* (1853), in which passages of genuine feeling and
sensitive imagery are ludicrously punctuated by lines which alternate between rhetorical posturing and bathetical collapse. As a result, Smith and
his English friends Bailey and Dobell, were dubbed the "Spasmodics", and
Aytoun mercilessly, though wittily, parodied them in *Firmillian, a Spasmo-
dic Tragedy* (1854). Here too, passages of mock-grandeur are interspersed
with lines of flat mockery, like:

Firmillian, Firmillian,
What have you done with Lilian.

Aytoun's gift for satire found happier expression in *The Book of Ballads
Edited by Bon Gaultier* (1855), in which he collaborated with Sir Theodore
Martin (1816–1909), the friend of his youth and a fellow *Maga* contributor.
Martin lived to write the *Life of the Prince Consort* (1874–1880), *Queen Vic-
toria as I Knew Her* (1908) and to become Lord Rector of St Andrews Uni-
versity. But in his less exalted days Martin joined Aytoun in parodying
Lockhart's *Spanish Ballads*, imitating every kind of poetic form and subject
popular during the mid-century, including the cult of the East. Using a traditional ballad stanza-form, they even had a tilt at the monarch herself in
"The Queen in France: an Ancient Scottish Ballad." Modelled on "Sir
Patrick Spens", the wit is trenchant, not only in its take-off of the manner-
isms of balladry, but in its juxtaposition of medieval ceremony and the die-
tary preferences of a particularly stolid British queen. Here is how the piece
ends:

Three days had come, three days had gone,
    The fourth began to fa',
When our gude Queen to the Frenchman said,
    "It's time I was awa!

O, bonny are the fields o' France,
    And softly drops the rain;
But my bairnies are in Windsor Tower,
    And greeting a' their lane.

Now ye maun come to me, Sir King,
    As I hae come to ye;

And a benison upon your heid
  For a' your courtesie!

Ye maun come, and bring your ladye fere;
  Ye sall na say me no;
And ye'll mind, we have aye a bed to spare
  For that gawsy chield Guizot!"

Now he has ta'en her lily-white hand,
  And put it to his lip,
And he has ta'en her to the strand
  And left her in the ship.

"Will ye come back, sweet bird?" he cried,
  "Will ye come kindly here,
When the lift is blue, and the lavrocks sing,
  In the spring-time o' the year?"

"It's I would blithely come, my Lord,
  To see ye in the spring;
It's I would blithely venture back
  But for ae little thing.

It isna that the winds are rude,
  Or that the waters rise,
But I love the roasted beef at hame,
  And no thae puddock pies."

In Scotland's mid-century, most of what was being produced was a hic-cuping re-tasting of long since digested vernacular flavours, a windily blown-up imitation of the English Romantic high-style, or witty parody and light verse. To the light verse category, Charles, Lord Neaves (1800–1876)—an Edinburgh judge who, in his youth, had been another Blackwood man—contributed *Songs and Verses, Social and Scientific*. It in-cluded a hilarious parody to the strathspey lilt of "Roy's Wife of Aldival-loch" by Mrs Grant of Carron (1745–1814). Part of the parody runs:

Stuart Mill on Mind and Matter,
  All our old Beliefs would shatter:
    Stuart Mill exerts his skill
  To make an end of Mind and Matter.

The self-same tale I've surely heard
  Employed before, our faith to batter:

Has David Hume again appeared,
  To run amuck at Mind and Matter?

It diverted the aged Thomas Carlyle at the dinner celebrating his inaugur-
ation as Lord Rector of Edinburgh University.

Scarcely less good is the "Lyric for Saturday Night", with its refrain-
theme, "Let us all be unhappy on Sunday".

Though Thomas Babington Macaulay, first Lord Macaulay
(1800–1859), politician, historian and poet and son of a West Indian merchant, was a full-blooded Scot, he was born in England. Apart from
contributing to the *Edinburgh Review* articles later collected as *Critical and
Historical Essays* (1843), and twice representing Edinburgh in Parliament,
his activities related mainly to England and to the Indian interests of the
British Empire. The *Lays of Ancient Rome* (1842), however, of which
"How Horatius Kept the Bridge" is widely known, show strongly the influence of the Scots ballad tradition. Like Thomas Carlyle (1795–1881), it
is for his prose that Macaulay is remembered now. Carlyle's lines
"Today", suitably admonitory for so grimly Scottish a sage, end:

Here hath been dawning
  Another blue Day;
Think wilt thou let it
  Slip useless away?

As with Thomas Campbell, Allan Cunningham's best claim to fame is
an English sea-song, "A wet sheet and a flowing sea". He asserted that
when he was six, he had heard Burns read "Tam o' Shanter" in the Cunningham home at Dalswinton, Dumfriesshire. After apprenticeship as a
stone-mason, Cunningham became friendly with Scott and Hogg on the
strength of his contributions to Cromek's *Remains of Nithsdale and Galloway
Song* (1810). He went to London, where he became a Parliamentary reporter, and subsequently assistant to Chantrey, the sculptor. Cunningham's
The Songs of Scotland, Ancient and Modern (1825) is, to put it mildly, less than
frank in its faking, although his *Life of Sir David Wilkie* (1843) is regarded as
an honest source-biography. Cunningham's poem of exile "Hame! Hame!
Hame!" and his version of "My Ain Countree" are frequently anthologized. His dramatic poem *Sir Marmaduke Maxwell* (1822), of which "A
wet sheet and a flowing sea" is the First Mariner's Song, and his romantic
verse-tale *The Legend of Richard Faulder*, both couched in high-style English,
have not survived the taste of their age.

Hogg's employer, and later Scott's amanuensis, William Laidlaw, Sir
Alexander Boswell, Robert Tannahill and William Watt have already
been mentioned, their roots being in the eighteenth-century tradition,
although Watt's feat of rhyming in "Kate Dalrymple" went unchallenged
until his slightly younger Glasgow-born contemporary, George Outram

(1805–1856) deployed his rhyming skill on "The Annuity", in *Lyrics, Legal and Miscellaneous* (1874). A member of the Scottish bar, Outram became editor and part-time proprietor of the *Glasgow Herald*. The publisher of that paper still carries his name.

William Tennant (1784–1848) deserves more attention. Born a cripple at Anstruther, Fife, he studied languages in his spare time, became a schoolmaster at Lasswade, Midlothian, then classics master at Dollar Academy. In 1835, still on his crutches, he accepted the chair of Oriental Languages at the University of St Andrews. His linguistic erudition was reflected in his *Syriac and Chaldee Grammar*, his unsuccessful dramatic ambitions in two Shakespearean plays, *Cardinal Beaton* (1823) and *John Baliol* (1825), and his high poetic aim in *The Thane of Fife* (1822). *Papistry Storm'd* (1827), dedicated to Sir David Lyndsay and couched in stanza forms derived from the older poet, is a mock epic in Scots effectively depicting the mob violence which destroyed St Andrews Cathedral; an interesting and surprising performance from a writer brought up an Anti-Burgher.

What keeps Tennant's name alive is his mock-heroic poem in *ottava rima* (*abababcc*) *Anster Fair*, published in 1812. It is an elaborate variant on the old Scots theme describing country folk from the surrounding district flocking in to the local centre of attraction to celebrate a festival. Tennant's people, however, were by no means rustic Jocks and Jennys. Nor did his celebrants all arrive in conventional landward manner:

> Nor only was the land with crowds opprest,
>   That trample forward to th' expected fair;
> The harness'd ocean had no peace or rest,
>   So many keels her barmy bosom tear:
> For, into view, now sailing from the west,
>   With streamers idling in the bluish air,
> Appear the printed pleasure-boats unleaky,
>   Charg'd with a precious freight, the good folks of Auld Reekie,
>
> They come, the cream and flower of all the Scots,
>   The children of politeness, science, wit,
> Exulting in their bench'd and gawdy boats,
>   Wherein some joking and some puking sit;
> Proudly the pageantry of carvels floats,
>   As if the salt sea frisk'd to carry it;
> The gales vie emulous their sales to wag,
>   And dally as in love with each long glided flag,
>
> Upon the benches seated, I descry
>   Her gentry; knights, and lairds, and long-nail'd fops;
> Her advocates and signet-writers shy;
>   Her gen'rous merchants, faithful to their shops;
> Her lean-cheek'd tetchy critics who, O fy!

Hard-retching, spue upon the sails and ropes;
Her lovely ladies, with their lips like rubies;
Her fiddlers, fuddlers, fools, bards, blockheads, blackguards, boobies . . .

The stanza-form, the mood of light satirical burlesque, and the up-dated eighteenth-century tone are all essentially Byronic, in the manner of *Don Juan*. Yet Byron's masterpiece was still a decade away. Indeed, the first part of *Childe Harold's Pilgrimage*, which makes serious use of the Spenserian stanza, only appeared in 1812. *Anster Fair* was widely and favourably reviewed, the notices including a eulogy in the *Quarterly Review*, which carried several quotations. It is difficult to believe that Byron did not read that issue of the *Quarterly Review*. It therefore seems reasonable to suppose that the amusing, though limited, burlesque manner of Tennant at least played some part in suggesting to the greater poet an appropriate stanza-form for the wittiest and most wide-ranging satirical burlesque in verse ever written.

William Nicholson (1783–1849), a Galloway poet who suffered from bad sight, spent his life wandering the countryside singing his own ballads, and finally dying of exposure beside a dyke. His weirdly humourous ballad of "Aiken Drum" keeps his name alive in the South-west, as "O gin I were where Gadie rins" does for John Imlach (1799–1846) in the North-east. Imlach, an Aberdonian, became a piano-tuner in London, dying in Jamaica.

Hugh Macdonald (1817–1860), a Glasgow journalist, has left interesting sociological material in his once-popular guidebooks *Days at the Coast* and *Rambles around Glasgow*. A fountain on the Braes of Gleniffer, near Paisley, carries his lines:

The bonnie wee well on the breist o' the brae,
Where the hare steals to drink in the gloamin' say grey,
Where the wild moorland birds dip their nebs and tak' wing
And the lark weets his whistle ere mountin' to sing.

He produced neither better nor worse Scots verse than dozens of others whose work is still occasionally to be found in anthologies. They include Thomas Castairs Latto (b. 1818)—"When we were at the Schule"; John Campbell Shairp (1819–1885)—"The Bush Aboon Traquair"; John Thomson of Hawick (1827–1888)—"Hogmanay" and "Hairst"; John Usher (1809–1896)—"The Channel-Stane", a poem about curling; the sentimental "Surfaceman", alias Alexander Anderson (1845–1909)—"The Bairnies cuddle doon at nicht"; and the prolific but pedestrian "Hugh Haliburton", schoolmaster J. Logie Robertson (1846–1922), whose pawky "imitations" of Horace, though once extremely popular and successful at a certain linguistic level, must have convinced true-poetry-lovers that the end for Scots as a vehicle for literature had indeed come.

Of those who wrote in English in the middle and later half of the century, Thomas Tod Stoddart (1810–1880), the head of a Border family, produced two volumes, *Angling Songs* (1839) and *Songs of the Seasons* (1881). From the earlier book a splendid fishing song has survived:

> A birr! A whirr! a salmon's on,
>   A goodly fish! A thumper!
> Bring up, bring up, the ready gaff,
> And if we land him, we will quaff,
> Another glorious bumper!
>   Hark! 'tis the music of the reel,
> The strong, the quick, the steady;
>   The line darts from the active wheel;
>   Have all things right and ready.

Sheriff Alexander Nicolson (1827–1893), like Thomas Pattison (1828–1865), strove to capture in English the yearning quality of the poetry of the exiled Gael. Neither managed to breathe much life into their verse. The vociferous John Stuart Blackie (1809–1895) was, in his day, a colourful academic at the University of Edinburgh, though no poet, as a glance through his *Lays of the Highlands and Islands* (1872) or his *Songs of Religion and Life* (1876) will confirm.

The once-popular preacher turned man-of-letters, George Macdonald (1824–1905), a native of Huntly, Aberdeenshire, whether verse-writing in Scots or English, allowed the pietistic let-out—using the God of Christianity as if He were still universally believed in as a substitute for a genuine inferred poetic resolution, much as the Greek device of the *deus ex machina* was used as an easy avoidance for a credible solution to novels and opera-plots—to mar almost everything he did.

Robert Buchanan (1841–1901), born in Staffordshire but brought up in Glasgow, settled in London in 1860. That the empty swagger and consistent insincerity of his verses once led him to be dubbed "The Scottish Browning" now seems astonishing. His *Idylls and Legends of Inverburn* (1865) and *London Poems* (1866) are hollow, posturing stuff. However, in 1871 he wrote a derogatory article, "The Fleshly School of Poetry", against his betters, the Pre-Raphaelites, for the *Contemporary Review*. This provoked a libel action, which he won, and, more importantly, Gilbert's and Sullivan's comic opera *Patience* (1881). Douglas Young remarked that when preparing his fascinating compendium, *Scottish Verse 1851–1951*, he learned that Buchanan, "a big man in London journalism . . . had issued a *Poetical Works* in 534 octavo pages, double-columned (1884)." Yet Young was "surprised to find nothing worth printing, except a stanza of *The Wedding of Shon Maclean*, to which nothing is added by the rest of the piece." He goes on to point out that, like his contemporary Tennysonian, the ninth Lord Southesk, "Buchanan never seems to give birth to more than a small idea, and then suffocates it with poeticizing." The favoured stanza goes:

To the wedding of Shon Maclean,
  Twenty pipers together
Came in the wind and the rain
  Playing across the heather;
Backward their ribbons flew,
Blast upon blast they blew,
Each clad in tartan new,
  Bonnet and blackcock feathers:
And every piper was fou,
  Twenty pipers together!

It would be difficult to disagree with Young's verdict.

Buchanan's young Kirkintilloch friend David Gray (1838–1861), a Keatsian dreamer, left Glasgow University to lead a literary life in London, but spent his first night in Hyde Park, caught consumption, and soon came home again to die. His Thomsonian river-celebration, *The Luggie*, has some original sensuous imagery, while one or two of the sonnets he wrote as he wasted towards death have a moving simplicity. Had he lived, he might well have found the discipline successfully to order his undoubted talent.

The first "modern" poet to breach the cosy conventionalities of mid-nineteenth-century Scottish literature was James Thomson (1834–1884). He was born in the squalid surroundings of Port Glasgow. His mother, Sarah Kennedy, was a Galloway woman and a devout follower of the secessionist Edward Irving. The poet's father was a ship's officer who contracted paralysis when his son was six. Two years later the family moved to London, where the father lapsed into religious mania and hopeless invalidism.

When the poet was eight, his mother died, and he was put to learn in the Royal Caledonian Asylum. He left to become an army schoolmaster, and while stationed at Cork, became friendly with Charles Bradlaugh and fell in love with Matilda Weller, the daughter of a sergeant. Her death three years later was, for him, a traumatic experience, which no doubt played a part in making him determinedly wear inside-out the Calvinistic mental coat he had been supplied with in extreme youth.

He contributed regularly to the *National Reformer* until 1874, and for a brief period thereafter to a house magazine called *Cope's Tobacco Plant*. For a time he was secretary of a mining company, and in their service visited Colorado; he was an even less successful business man than that "gawcie Greenock man", John Galt. In 1873, Thomson went to Spain to join the Carlist Army as war correspondent for the *New York World*; but he was out of sympathy with the Carlists, and forwarded so few despatches to his own employers that they were soon out of sympathy with him.

Back in London, though befriended by Charles Kingsley, George Mere-
dith and a few others, Thomson sank into despairing alcoholism, until a
massive bout of drinking led to his death in University Hospital. He was
buried in Highgate Cemetary, with a locket containing a strand of Matilda
Weller's yellow hair on his breast.

Thomson, a good scholar, was widely read, but particularly admired
Leopardi, that prince among pessimists. His translation of Leopardi's *Dialogues* is a genuine piece of re-creation. Thomson's admiration for Shelley
and Novalis is testified by the pseudonym he used, "Bysshe Vanolis"
("B.V."), the second word an anagram on the German writer's name. In
philosophy, Schopenhauer won his strong admiration.

Thomson is virtually a one-poem man. *Weddah and Om-el-Borain* gathers
the same dust as *Lalla Rookh* and *Gertrude of Wyoming*. His *Idylls of Cockenzie*
are even feebler than John Davidson's *Fleet Street Eclogues*, with which they
invite comparison, causing William Power aptly to remark that they "illustrate the Nemesis of the Scottish poet who deserts Clydesdale or the
Carse of Gowrie for the bricky chaos of London."[11]

One or two small trifles are neatly done, and "To Our Ladies of Death"
might have been more highly regarded were it not surpassed by "The City
of Dreadful Night". Into it Thomson poured the essence of his despair,
outdoing even Leopardi, and polishing the finished product till, within its
terms of reference, it could not be bettered:

Why break the seals of mute despair unbidden,
And wail life's discords into careless ears? . . .

Because a cold rage seizes one at whiles
  To show the bitter, old, and wrinkled truth . . .
Because it gives some sense of power and passion
In helpless impotence, to try to fashion
Our woe in living words, howe'er uncouth.

Thomson's words were not uncouth. The magnitude and grandeur of his
despair makes most of his late twentieth-century fellow despairers sound
like petulant whimperers. Thomson lamented:

The sense that every struggle brings defeat
  Because Fate holds no prize to crown success;
That all the oracles are dumb or cheat
  Because they have no secret to express;
That none can pierce the vast black veil uncertain
  Because there is no light beyond the curtain;
That all is vanity and nothingness . . .

While this message may be acceptable enough to readers in the twentieth century, many of his contemporaries were shocked:

My Brother, my poor Brother, it is thus;
   This life itself holds nothing good for us,
But it ends soon and nevermore can be
   And we knew nothing of it ere our birth,
And shall learn nothing when consigned to earth!
   I ponder these thoughts, and they comfort me.

He was paralleled in pessimism by John Davidson (1857–1909), the son of a minister at Barrhead, Renfrewshire, who moved soon after the future poet's birth to Greenock. The two poets shared not only the common backgrounds of youthful subjection to religious extremism in an industrialized environment, but also a family history of mental unbalance—Davidson's brother tried to kill their mother with a carving knife he had secreted under his bed.

After leaving Greenock's Highlanders' Academy, Davidson went to Edinburgh University. Between 1877 and 1889, he held various teaching posts in Glasgow, Paisley, Greenock and Crieff, before going to London to live by his pen. There, he became a *Yellow Book* contributor, and gained the friendship of Yeats—who, however, found Davidson's "blood and guts" influence on the Rhymers' Club disrupting—Gosse, Beerbohm, and Sir William Rothenstein. Davidson received a Civil List pension in 1906, and in 1908 a gift of £250 from George Bernard Shaw to enable him to write a poetic masterpiece. His verse-plays *Smith* (1888), *An Unhistorical Romance* (1889) and *Scaramouch in Naxos* (1889), are an odd blend of misdirected energy, fashionable cliché, and flashes of poetic talent embedded in sheer unreadability. He could never earn enough money adequately to maintain himself, as he poured out his series of unprofitable volumes of poems, beginning with *In a Music Hall* (1891) and ending with *Fleet Street and Other Poems* (1909), the manuscript of which was posted to his publisher shortly before its author drowned himself near Penzance, poverty-stricken and under the mistaken belief that he was suffering from cancer. His collected poems appeared in two volumes, edited by Andrew Turnbull, in 1974.[12] In some ways, his best achievement is contained in *God and Mammon*, a trilogy only the first two parts of which were written. In these, like Thomson, he, too, shows himself to have been an inverted Calvinist, although influenced not by Schopenhauer but by Nietzsche. Nevertheless, there is certain forceful grandeur behind the rhetoric with which he makes one of his characters urge the need for mankind to accept the full responsibility of being human:

Mammon: We ourselves are fate;
          We are the universe; we are all that is:

Outside of us nothing that is not us
Can be at all. No room! The universe
Is full of us, the matter of the stars;
The all-pervading ether seen as light,
Elaborate purity of rainbows; heard
As music, woven of elemental sounds;
And smelt in perfume, the poetry of flowers
Exhaled from sex, which in all plants and beasts
Secretes and sows the ethereal universe.
Seen in the light, in music heard, and smelt
In subtle odour of a thousand flowers,
In us the ether consciously becomes
Imagination, thought, religion, art.
We are the ether, we are the universe,
We are eternity: not sense, not spirit,
But matter; but the whole become self-conscious.
Whatever Heaven there is, whatever Hell,
Here now we have it; and I cannot wait
On God, the nothing, and his damned event
That mocked the world for sixty centuries;
Nor will I linger eating out my heart
While this new proxy of divinity
Your specious evolution, blunders on
From tedious age to age. I'll carve the world
In my own image, I, the first of men
To comprehend the greatness of mankind;
I'll melt the earth and cast it in my mould,
The form and beauty of the universe.

Even Shaw's gift was of no avail for, as the playwright wrote to me long after: "Davidson was so overwhelmed by this endowment that he resolved to give me a great surprise and make an immense sum of money for me by writing, not the Lucretian poem, but a popular historical melodrama. He forgot that if he could not do this for himself, he could not do it for me. The melodrama was quite useless commercially: no manager would touch it. He had thrown away his big chance; and instead of asking me for another £250, which I would have given him, he drowned himself . . . It was a tragi-comedy and a great pity."[13]

Davidson produced too much, and apparently did little revising. *God and Mammon* apart, his handful of best poems are those most regularly anthologized—"Romney March", "Thirty Bob a Week" (the workaday Cockney clerk's language of which influenced both Eliot and MacDiarmid, although the poem is over-long), "The Runnable Stag" and the moving epitaph he provided for himself in *The Testament of John Davidson* (1908).

My feet are heavy now, but on I go,
   My head erect beneath the tragic years,
The way is steep, but I would have it so;
   And dusty, but I lay the dust with tears,
Though none can see me weep: alone I climb
The rugged path that leads me out of time.

The good things in many other pieces are flawed by slipshod workmanship or by an obvious attempt to force his imagination.

In their revelations of, or revellings in, despair, Thomson and Davidson look forward to the twentieth century. With the exception of Robert Louis Stevenson (1850–1894)—and, even then, primarily in his role as novelist—the others all looked back.

In spite of an obvious preoccupation with style for its own sake, there are delightful things in Stevenson's *A Child's Garden of Verses* (1885), and an honesty of expression, if not always of factuality, about such other delicately turned pieces as "In the Highlands", "To S.R. Crockett" and the much quoted "Requiem", all now to be found in his *Collected Poems* (1951). Of course the music is often set to escapist magic, as in the familiar lines:

I will make my kitchen, and you shall keep your room,
Where white flows the river and bright blows the broom,
And you shall wash your linen and keep your body white
In rainfall at morning and dewfall at night.

Even in a poem titled "Romance", the prospect of a woman washing herself "white" in "dewfall at night" is prettily ridiculous, due allowance being made for the absence of running water, hot or cold. At least it is poeticizing for its own sake with an infinitely more skilful touch than most other nineteenth-century practitioners could command.

Some of his poems in what, borrowing Burns's word, Stevenson called Lallans, helped to keep the language alive and a little above its general ruck of vernacular sentimentality, although they are too often couched in "Standard Habbie" and reflect a parochialism which did not otherwise usually inhibit Stevenson. "A Mile and a Bittock" describes the old "Scotch convoy" system, where friends see each other home, walking backwards and forwards for the sake of the talk, and so indefinitely delaying the actual parting. It has its share of Stevenson's clean out-door imagery:

A wind got up frae affa the sea,
It blew the stars as clear's could be,
It blew in the e'en o' a' the three,
   And the müne was shining clearly!

"A Lowden Sabbath Morn", with its picture of the verbose minister and his nodding congregation, appears to be set on a parochial path towards the Kailyard, yet veers off into gentle irony:

> Wi' sappy unction, hoo he burkes   [saturated, dodges
> The hopes o' men that trust his works,
> Expounds the fau'ts o' ither kirks,
>> And shaws the best o' them
> No muckle better than mere Turks
>> When a's confessed o' them.

> Bethankit! what a bonny creed!
> What mair would ony Christian need?—
> The braw words rumm'le ower his heid,
>> Nor steer the sleeper;
> And in their restin' graves, the deid,
>> Sleep aye the deeper.

Andrew Lang (1844–1912), Stevenson's "dear Andrew with the brindled hair", was another Scottish writer who never quite seemed fully to realize his potential as a poet. Born at Selkirk, the son of the county sheriff-clerk, he passed through Edinburgh Academy and St Andrews and Glasgow University to become a Fellow of Merton. But he opted for the life of a journalist in London in 1875. *Ballades and Lyrics of Old France* (1872) and *Ballades in Blue China* (1880) helped inaugurate a revival of interest in old French lyric metres, which were to be turned elegantly, if emptily, by most of the *fin de siècle Yellow Book* rhymers of the '90s. Lang's widow brought together her husband's *Collected Poems* (1923) in four volumes; not, even so, complete.

His best things, though few, are admirably graceful. Fortunately, it is only a man's best things that ultimately matter. We can forget the embarrassing heartiness of his tomboy verses on golf and cricket. The sense of sadness for the lost possibilities of vanished youth inspired poems like "Cleveden Church" and "Twilight on Tweed", while his "Almae Matres", contrasting the "feel" of St Andrews and Oxford, leaves us with memorable portraits of both cities. St Andrews, however, remained foremost in Lang's affections:

> *St Andrews by the Northern Sea,*
>> *A haunted town it is to me!*
> A little city, worn and grey,
>> The grey North Ocean girds it round,
> And oe'r the rocks, and up the bay,
>> The long sea-rollers surge and sound,
> And still the thin and biting spray

    Drives down the melancholy street,
And still endure, and still decay,
    Towers that the salt winds vainly beat.
Ghost-like and shadowy they stand
Dim mirrored in the wet sea-sand.

One or two poets who survived well into the twentieth century, and by virtue of the breadth of their choice of themes or the honesty of their emotional treatment of them have tenuous links with the Scottish Rennaisance movement, nevertheless produced most of their best work before the dividing cataclysm of the 1914–18 war.

J. Pittendrigh MacGillivray (1856–1939), a fine sculptor, produced two books, the beautifully printed but jingoistic *Pro Patria* (1915), and the even more lavish-looking *Bog-Myrtle and Peat Reek* (1922). In this second volume, "Glances" makes use of the old Scots theme of the girl pretending to be indignant at the attention she attracts, "Abasshyd" is a pre-MacDiarmid attempt at incorporating Middle Scots words into a modern texture, and "Mercy o' Gode" echoes distantly the old Scots world of the fearful supernatural.

Violet Jacob (1863–1946) had a freshness of approach and a touch of Angus colour in her best lyrics, like Tam o' the Kirk", "The Wild Geese" and "Baltic Street", though she, too, made her contribution to the jingoistic versifying inspired by the First World War. Her fellow poetess Marion Angus (1866–1946), apt to get lost among the whimsy of a suburban elfland no longer believed in by anyone by the time she was writing, is represented in every Scottish anthology with her portrayal of Queen Mary's womanly struggle against the bullying Knox, "Alas! Poor Queen". A note of unsentimental regret for the what-might-have-been that must trouble many women who never marry, is movingly caught in several of the lyrics to be found in her *Selected Poems*,[14] notably in "Mary's Song" and "Think Lang".

Within the loose time-bracket of the late-nineteenth and early-twentieth centuries, mention should be made of a further collection of names encountered in period anthologies, and once highly regarded. None of them rise much beyond the level of competent versifying, except occasionally, and then usually only in a single poem. There is Sir James Noel Paton (1821–1902), much more successful as a Scottish Pre-Raphaelite painter than as a poet, a distinction he shared with William Bell Scott (1811–1890), Rossetti's friend; Roger Quin (1850–1925), a Dumfriesshire-born travelling tinker who in summer slept out-of-doors and earned a sort of living with concertina and flute, but in winter lived in a Glasgow model lodging house, and whose sonnet "To a Skylark singing above Barnhill Poorhouse", though aping the English Romantic style, is still sometimes to be seen; Lord Alfred Douglas (1870–1945), a skilful sonneteer more famous for the part he played in the sad downfall of Oscar Wilde than for either his

Sonnets (1909) or his *Collected Satires* (1927); and the two novelists, John Buchan, Lord Tweedsmuir (1875–1940) and Neil Munro (1864–1930), neither of whom achieved anything noteworthy in the poetic department. Will H. Ogilvie (1869–1963), a Border squire, might be said to belong to a slightly higher category in that "Hugh MacDiarmid" put "Ho! for the blades of Harden" into his *Golden Treasury of Scottish Verse*. Aberdonians take pleasure in some of the poems of Charles Murray (1864–1941) to be found in *Hamewith* (1900), notably "The Whistle", which gives off a strong whiff of the decayed cabbage-patch. But the 1914–18 war seems to have jolted Murray out of his backward-looking attitudes. "Gin I was God" mildly anticipates MacDiarmid, while "Dockens Afore his Peers" in an Exemption Court reveals an outlook very different from the fashionable mood of join-up jingoism reflected by most other Scots writers at that time. Kailyardism and rural irrelevancies mar virtually everything W. D. Cocker (1882–1970) produced, except perhaps his comic piece "The Flood", to be found in his *Scots and English Poems* (1932). Yet David Rorie (1867–1946), in the title piece of *The Pawky Duke*, and one or two others, shows a defter touch.

The shock and surge of the First World War removed not only some of the finest minds of a new generation—including several Scottish poets, most notably, Ewart Alan Mackintosh (1893–1916), "In Memorium, Private D. Sutherland"; and Aberdeen-born C. H. Sorley (1895–1915), "The Song of the Ungirt Runner"—but the whole worn-out nineteenth-century convention of poetry as a game to be played with archaic words no longer used in speech and concerned exclusively with harmless subject-matter isolated from the rawness of the life of those ordinary people whose problems and concerns the war had exposed for all to see. Retrospectively, Thomson and Davidson now seem to have been indicating, however tentatively, the mood—if neither the manner nor the widened range—of the kind of poetry the post-war years were to nurture.

II

The impact of Scott's novels on nineteenth-century literature was even greater than that of his poetry, although the aims and methods employed in the creation of his epic ballads were merely adapted to the needs of fiction. Scott was always interested in manners as a reflection of the way of life of a particular society. He was an erudite antiquary with an immense amount of reading behind him, yet acutely aware of the irrevocable events of Scottish history which, in the eighteenth century, altered the course of Scotland's future: the Union of 1707, which lost Scotland her Parliament, the power of decision-making, and those settled cultural conditions which usually only exist in an entire nation; and the Jacobite rising of 1745, which put paid for ever to the traditions of chivalry and personal heroic feats-of-arms, traditions that had survived in one form or another from the Middle Ages. Henceforth, the Union with England and the pursuit of business were to be what really mattered; but that vanished, heroic past which had shaped the very lineaments of the Scottish character, aroused in Scott, and in his Scottish readers, a passionate nostalgia.

The man whose imagination fed on the great Scottish confrontations, Scots against English, Catholics against Protestants, Patriots against Unionists, Jacobites against Hanoverians, was also the first Chairman of the Edinburgh Gas Company. The romantic dreamer, whose need for money made him force himself to write too much too fast, and who ruined himself financially in pursuit of his ambition to become an old-style landed proprietor, nevertheless heated internally the walls of his orchard and installed air-pressure bells and gas lighting in his Gothic mansion by the Tweed, which he filled with a huge assortment of relics dismembered from history.

Once he had covered most of the ground contested by the traditional Scottish historical conflicts, and the need for money remained more pressing than ever, Scott turned to English history and to medieval subjects— *Kenilworth, Woodstock* and those colourful if somewhat stagey stories, *Ivanhoe* and *The Talisman. Quentin Durward*, which anticipated Dumas at his own French game, was written with a view to enhancing Continental sales. His one more or less "contemporary" novel, *St Ronan's Well*, gives the impression of rarely penetrating much beneath the surface. In fact, it took the fundamental already-decided conflicts of Scotland to keep him in close and constant touch with his sources of inspiration, whether in verse or in prose.

At his best or at his most prosey, common to all his novels is the new way in which Scott made creative use of history. He believed that while history could provide the author with the stimulus of a starting point, events too well known or about which no authentic background material could be established would be better left alone. As examples of subjects not to be tackled, he instanced the Armada, or a poem about Nelson by a landsman, as illustrations of the too well known. King Alfred was a subject about whom too much seemed to Scott conjectural. His practice in the great Scottish novels was to establish a series of generalized historical backcloths complete with minor figures—Highland social conditions just before 1715 in *Rob Roy*, the Porteous affair after 1707 in *The Heart of Midlothian*, and the consequence for Jacobite hopes after the shattering defeat at Culloden in *Redgauntlet*—then set in the foreground the main characters, mostly of his own creation, but sometimes incorporating aspects of actual people, though not usually placed precisely in their real-life context. In *Ivanhoe*, Reizor remarks: "There are several historical characters, the principal one being Richard I. But Richard's actions described in the novel are not to be found in any historical documents and Scott doesn't seem to be much worried about it. He showed Richard as seen by him through the pages of genuine documents. By making Richard visit Friar Tuck's hut, and set up a

merry feast there, Scott reproduces Richard's character, welcoming all the
unexpected things in life and utterly consistent with the knight's tradition
of 'seeking adventure'. In addition, Scott made use of the old ballads with
an analogous motif that were widely spread not only in England and Scotland but also all over Europe, Africa and Asia, and echoed in *The Lady of
the Lake* and in Lermontov's *Ismail-Bei*. As depicted in the novel, Richard's
character is even truer to life than it would have been had the author
known the real person."[15] And so it is, one feels, with the Scottish figures,
Balfour of Burley, Claverhouse, Montrose, even James VI in *The Fortunes
of Nigel*.

To assist him in creating this impression, Scott frequently made use of
remarks or turns of phrase which had stuck in his capacious memory,
though again not always in the same form of words, or from the same
mouths as those from which in real life they had issued. In *Waverley*, Evan
Dhu's famous speech during his trial for treason, in which he offers to go
back to the Highlands and return with six of his MacIvor kind willing to
undergo death if only their chief might go free, and who rebukes the new-
world legal men who doubt his word because they must "ken neither the
heart of a highlander or the heart of a gentleman", is an echo of the reply of
the Covenanter Bailie of Jerviswoode, when offered his life if he turned
King's evidence. Said Bailie: "They who can make such a proposal to me
know neither me or my country". Again, in *The Heart of Midlothian*, David
Deans remarks: "Ye're a silly callant, Reuben, with your bits of argument," echoing a remark in Walker's *Life of Peden*: "Ye're a vain man,
James, with your bits of paper and drops of blood." *Old Mortality* abounds
in overtones of Covenanting writings. In *Ivanhoe*, the Jewess Rebecca,
rebuking the guards at her trial with: ". . . It suits not a maiden to be disturbed by such rude grooms", is clearly echoing Queen Mary's famous
remark just before her execution.

Such instances are numerous. For those who think the unweaving of a
great artist's web of magic into constituent strands of sufficient importance,
a modest though scholarly start has been made by James Anderson.[16]

Scott's attitude to such pedantry was simple enough: "Were accuracy of
any consequence in a fictitious narrative . . . we may charitably suggest
that he [the author] was writing a romance and not a history."[17] Yet the
justification of Scott's methods, as Anderson points out, is that, in the
event, "the Waverley novels are an epitome, not merely of one man's personal experience, but of the records of several nations over many centuries."

The value of Scott's antiquarian and historical knowledge was that even
where the re-use of a phrase or a custom strictly speaking was an anach-
ronism, he could usually give it a turn to make it add to the sense of realistic
detail, a faculty upon which Scott set much store, and which his vast reading had so pre-eminently fitted him to employ, no doubt often subcon-
sciously.

He certainly believed in the value of the historical novel, both as a means of keeping alive a knowledge of tradition among those who never read history, and as an added stimulus to those who did.[18] Outwardly, he was adamant that "scenes in which our ancestors thought deeply, acted fiercely, and died desparately, are to us tales to divert the tedium of a winter's evening".[19] If he had really believed this to be true, then it could reasonably be asserted that Scott was a serious writer almost in spite of himself.

The form of many of the great Scottish novels is broadly similar. A Lowland Scot, or an Englishman, goes north at a time when national or regional feelings are exacerbated; finds himself involved by chance with the prevailing Scottish cause; never quite totally compromises himself, and in the end, returns safely to the modern world of civilization, leaving some of his sympathies behind him. So it is in *Waverley*, the first novel of all and, in point of plot construction, in some respects "better wrought" (as Stevenson remarked) than any of the others.

From the moment he moved on from the business of translating, collecting and fashioning ballads, Scott's intention had been to produce, "a tale of chivalry, which was to be in the style of *The Castle of Otranto*, with plenty of Border characters, and supernatural incident". First attempts, made around 1799, were *Thomas the Rhymer* and *The Lord of Ennerdale*, both of which were soon abandoned. Instead, the "manners which anciently prevailed on the borders of England and Scotland" were celebrated in verse in *The Lay of the Last Minstrel*.

By 1805, the year of the next prose attempt, Scott had become interested in his "early recollections of the Highland scenery and customs". He had known "many of the old warriors of 1745", and, as he tells us in the preface to *Waverley*, had consequently conceived the idea that "the ancient traditions and high spirit of a people, who, living in a civilized age and country retained so strong a tincture of manners belonging to an earlier period of society, must afford a subject favourable for romance." A romance was begun and the seventh chapter reached, before the manuscript was laid aside after Ballantyne had accorded it only lukewarm enthusiasm. In the meantime, Scott undertook to write a conclusion to Joseph Strutt's *Queen-Hoo Hall*, a story written to "illustrate the manners, customs and language of the people of England" during the reign of Henry IV. The book was poorly received, and the lesson Scott learned was that for fictional purposes, one could not use "language too ancient or indulge in antiquarian knowledge too liberally displayed" if the general reading public was to understand a tale. When he came to write his crusading novels, Scott therefore made no serious attempt to re-create the language of the fourteenth century, contenting himself with such period effect as could be got by the use of a kind of quasi-Elizabethan dialogue. It worked. *Ivanhoe* was for long Scott's most popular novel.

But to return to *Waverley*. In the autumn of 1813, with a good run of salmon on the Tweed and guests at Abbotsford eager to fish, Scott climbed

up into a garret to find his tackle. In a corner of an old escritoire, he came
upon the lost chapters. As he told Morritt in a letter[20], he then carried the
manuscript downstairs to see what could be made of it and, as John Buchan
puts it, "thereby entered into his true kingdom".[21]

Scott is often so anxious fully to set the scene, that the opening chapters
of his novels seem tedious to a reader in an age less leisurely than his own. It
is almost as if his inspiration only warmed out of application as the characters shaped themselves from the tip of his pen. The early chapters of
Waverley, however, have an autobiographical interest, in that Edward
Waverley appears to reflect one side of Scott's own nature—strong good
sense contrasting with poetic sensitivity. In a way, all the slightly detached
male lead-characters, like Waverley and Francis Osbaldistone in *Rob Roy*,
are not so much heroes as symbols of the inevitable triumph of modern
commerce and common sense over the blood and sweat and glamour of
romance. Waverley, in the end, does not marry the glamorous but com-
mittedly Jacobite Flora MacIvor, settling—perhaps as Scott himself had
settled—for a more prosaic second best, Rose Bradwardine. Similarly,
Osbaldistone is apparently able to marry Di Vernon (according to the Epi-
logue) only after she has renounced her former adherence to the lost cause
of the Stuarts.

Waverley became the first instalment of what turned out to be an extended plan to portray Scottish manners and social change throughout the
eighteenth century. As Scott himself reminded his readers in his original
preface to *The Antiquary*: "*Waverley* embraced the age of our fathers, *Guy
Mannering* that of our youth and *The Antiquary* refers to the last years of the
eighteenth century."

Written in the space of six weeks, *Guy Mannering* has a plot—if such it
can be called—based upon the conventional "missing heir" theme of
countless ballads. There is perhaps a touch of the tight-lipped side of
Scott—the reverse of his outgoing energy and abundant good spirits—
about Colonel Mannering. Julia, his daughter, is a typical, cold Scott heroine. Psychologists may well suggest that Scott's *penchant* for reserved
high-born heroines, and his inability, or unwillingness, to deal convincingly with sexual passion, were subconscious projections of his own relations with his wife. It may be so. In any case, in *Guy Mannering*, the centre
of interest lies not so much in the story itself as in the counterpointing of
characters out of the old Scotland with those whose associations are
strongly with the new. The gypsy Meg Merrilies, Dandie
Dinmont—"wise like a wise dog, with a limit to his intelligence but none
to his fidelity"[22]—like the decayed Bertram family with whom the Man-
nerings become involved, to say nothing of MacMorlan, Mrs MacCand-
lish, Dominie Simpson and Councillor Pleydell (one of Scott's many
successful portraits of old-fashioned-dry-as-dust lawyers) are all part of the
vanishing Scotland. Indeed, the Bertram fortunes are only restored
through the good offices of Mannering, the visiting Englishman.

In *Guy Mannering*, what is important is the richness and humanity of the character-drawing. Even early in the first quarter of the nineteenth century, Scott could not validly use Scots for anything other than dialogue, and then usually only for those in humble situations or in other contexts oblivious to the pressures of political, social and economic change affecting the spoken use of the Scots tongue. But it is a mark of his development that in the Scottish novels from *Waverley* to *The Heart of Midlothian*, the amount of dialogue increases, and the richness of the spoken Scots is as noteworthy as its colloquial aptness.

Nominally, *The Antiquary* has for its hero the somewhat colourless Englishman Lovel, who conveniently turns out to be the lost heir of Glenallan. The real hero, of course, is the antiquary himself, Jonathan Oldbuck, a Whig of German extraction, and a pedant who nevertheless savours enough of the temper of his era to realize that the past now belongs to historians and antiquarians like himself, and certainly not to the pompous and stupid Sir Arthur Wardour, still trying to live it, ridiculously preoccupied with his meaningless pedigree. His daughter, Isabella, is a stilted heroine, even by Scott's standards. But to offset her, there are the Mucklebackits, Griselda Oldbuck, and gossipy Mrs Mailsetter in the Post Office. (With his comic characters, at any rate, Scott never quite outgrew the Restoration trick of giving them names suggestive of their occupations or oddities.) Above all, there is Edie Ochiltree, whose willingness to accept whatever comes, and whose patient radicalism stems more mildly from the same folk-sources as Burns's "Jolly Beggars". Confronted with the storm which is one of the set-pieces in the book, and in which the Wardours and Edie are cut off by the sea, their fundamental attitudes are revealed:

> "Good man", said Sir Arthur, "can you think of nothing—of no help—I'll make you rich—I'll give you a farm—I'll—" "Our riches will soon be equal", said the beggar, looking out upon the strife of the waters—"they are sae already; for I have nae land, and you would give your fair bounds and barony for a square yard of rock that would be dry for twa' hours."

Latter-day Marxist critics who accuse Scott of the "disease" of gentility, choose to forget his profound understanding of the national character that rises to a simple and solid dignity in such incidents as Saunders Mucklebackit, stricken with tearless sobbing as his drowned son's coffin leaves the house, but next day back at the mending of his boat:

> "What would you have me do," he asks, "unless I wanted to see four children starve because one is drowned? It's weel wi' you gentles, that can sit in the hoose wi' handkerchiefs to your een when ye lose a friend; but the likes o' us maun to our work again if our hearts were beating as hard as any hammer. . . . Yet what needs one to be angry at her, that has neither soul nor

sense?—Though I am no that muckle better myself. She's but a rickle o' auld
rotten deals nailed thegither, and warped wi' the wind and the sea—and I am
a dour carle battered by winds and foul weather at sea and land till I am
almost as senseless as hersell. She maun be mended though again' the morning
tide—that's a thing o' necessity!"

At whatever social level Scott is operating, always the heroical left-overs
from a more romantic Scotland get brought back to face the ongoing demands of the contemporary scene. This is especially true of *Old Mortality*.
Although the troubles of the Covenanters were already far in the past by
Scott's day, the incessant squabbles within the Church throughout the
eighteenth century helped to perpetuate a false respect for the defence of
fanaticism allied to an almost legendary view of the actions of those who
opposed them. Scott's view of the Covenanting conflict was a fair one.
Henry Morton, the common-sense tolerant hero, after the manner of so
many Scott heroes, finds himself drawn into the impassioned affairs of the
Covenanters by a series of accidents. The characters on both sides are
sketched with skill and balance. On the Covenanting side, the portrait of
Balfour of Burley—a bitter man fired with the perennial energy of totally
committed fanaticism—is amongst the most powerful Scott ever drew.
Around him is the host of clergymen, ranging in bigotry from the ranting
madman, Habbakuk Muckleworth, to the worldly opportunist, Pound-
text. Among the common folk, there is Mause Headrigg, her wits stuffed
with misapplied biblical quotations, and torn between what are, to her, the
heroic demands of religious extremism, and maternal affection for her son,
Cuddie, who is forever trying to bridle her tongue in the interests of unromantic safety.

On the Government side, the aristocratic and assured arrogance of Claverhouse, "Bonny Dundee", is supported by Cornet Grahame, his dashing
nephew; by Bothwell, proud of his royal descent; and by the gentle Lord
Evandale, who represents the moderate viewpoint on the Government side
much as Bessie Maclure does for the Covenanters.

Nowhere, not even in *The Heart of Midlothian*, did Scott better the sharpness of his narrative technique, or the speed and economy of his presentation of the action. Nowhere is his Scots dialogue more sensitive to the
nuances of the reactions and interactions of ordinary folk. Nowhere did
Scott so successfully capture the conflict of passions in a tragic social event
of epic proportions, which was to influence critically the fate of the Stuarts,
and thus the shaping of the new Scotland. While making full allowance for
the sincerity of Covenanting fervour and the heady exultation it produced,
nowhere does Scott come down so tellingly on the side of moderation
against the futility of extremism.

Morton's attempts to get the squabbling ministers either to accept the
terms offered them by the Government, or cease their dissention,
Claverhouse's brooded outburst to Morton on the subject of death, and

Cuddie Headrigg's alterations with his mother just before he is due to appear before the Privy Council to answer for his presence on the field of Bothwell Brig, are but three of the high points in a story at once moving and gripping.

Much to his surprise, Scott was accused of bias in *Old Mortality* by a Presbyterian historian, M'Crie. Scott defended himself with dignity in the *Quarterly Review*, and the man of moderation had no difficulty in winning the argument.

Rob Roy again presents the confrontation of old and new, Rob Roy representing the one, Bailie Nicol Jarvie the other. David Daiches[23] has suggested that the Bailie, like Oldbuck and Pleydell, represents in one way or another the kind of compromise which in theory, if not in real life, most satisfied Scott.

To some extent *Rob Roy* repeats the message of *Waverley*, though set in an earlier period and ending just before the rising of 1715. It presents, however, a more detailed and accurate picture of the eighteenth-century Lowland character in opposition to that of the Highlander. The good Bailie's remonstrance with Andrew Fairservice, gardener at Osbaldistone Hall, when Fairservice had complained of the Union, illustrates the temper that prevails over the adventures of Rob himself, and the femininity—warmer than usual for Scott—of Rob's wife, Helen. Says the Bailie:

> "Whisht, sir!—Whisht! It's ill-scraped tongues like yours, that make mischief atween neighbours and nations. There's naething sae gude on this side o'time but it might hae been better, and that might be said o' the Union. Nane were keener against it than the Glasgow folk, wi their rabblings and their risings, and their mobs, as they ca' them now-a-days. But it's an ill wind that blaws naebody gude—Let ilka ane roose the ford as they find it.—I say, let Glasgow flourish! whilk is judiciously and elegantly putten round the town's arms by way of byword. Now, since St Mungo catched herrings in the Clyde, what was ever like to gar us flourish like the sugar and tobacco-trade? Will onybody tell me that, and grumble at the treaty that opened us a road west-awa' yonder?"

Many critics, among them the writers Landor, Fitzgerald and John Buchan, have placed *The Heart of Midlothian* at the summit of Scott's achievement. While it neither deals with a conflict so fundamental to the prejudice in the Scottish character as does *Old Mortality*, nor possesses so tight-knit a structure of high national drama as does *Waverley*, nor surges so insistently forward with the strange intensity of narrower passion, as *The Bride of Lammermoor* was later to do, as a fictional canvas *The Heart of Midlothian* is conceived on a larger scale than anything else Scott ever wrote.

The murder of the unfortunate Captain Porteous by an Edinburgh mob provides the historical starting point. But the theme of the novel is nothing less than the nature of Justice itself, examined through a wide range of contending opposites: town life against country; the law of man against the

Covenanters' sincere if mistaken view of the law of God; English against Scots law; and so on. Conflict is cleverly portrayed operating subjectively in the consciences of several of the leading characters, notably in that of David Deans, accepting that one daughter cannot be asked to lie to save another; in that of Jeanie herself, who has to try to answer the question "jesting Pilate" evaded; and in that of Reuben Butler, forced to become minister in attendance to the Porteous mob, his humanitarian urgings disregarded.

The variety of the characters is immense; Effie, that kind of beautiful woman to be found in the lower orders of Scottish society, yet with enough natural intelligence to enable her to take her place among the aristocracy without in any way losing our belief in her credibility; sister Jeanie, less good-looking but imbued with unshakeable honesty, as well as homely domestic virtues which, together, enable her to act with heroism when the unhappy Effie—the giver-in to illicit sexual temptation—is threatened with the legal consequences of Jeanie's truth-telling; the remote presence of the Queen alongside the larger-than-life symbolic impartiality of the Duke of Argyll, a feudal figure stranded in a modern context; the scrupulousness of David Deans's personal Puritanism, tempered with a tolerance not always to be found in his real-life prototypes; and the host of characters who fill in the teeming Edinburgh and London city scenes; gossipy Saddletrees, and Mrs Howden, Peter Plumdamas and Mrs Damahoy; the madwoman Madge Wildfire, and the underworld characters Meg Murdockson and Daddy Ratcliffe, set within the networks of underworld crime which flourish wherever people live crowded together, regardless of nationality.

With the possible exception of Effie's lover, not a single character is weakly drawn. Scene after scene is vividly and richly imagined; the great assembled crowd outside the Tolbooth, when the disciplined tautness and the threatening tension are wonderfully captured; the eerie meeting with Staunton at Mushat's Cairn; Jeanie's journey to the Court in London, begun against the comedy provided by the ineptness of Dumbiedyke's wooing and carried to its impressive conclusion through a series of episodes which some have thought picturesque, but which contemporary accounts confirm are quite in keeping with the kind of experience travellers in the early eighteenth century were only too likely to encounter; Jeanie's return and reunion with her father; then, her heroic moment past, her acceptance of the lot of a conventional country wife. Those who feel Jeanie turned Mrs Butler to be a kind of let-down, misunderstand not only Scott's anti-romantic purpose, but the fundamental requirement of resolution, to be found satisfied even in Greek tragedy.

If the book has a flaw, then it is surely the perfunctory treatment in the closing section of the dramatically unnecessary death of Sir George Staunton at the hands of his own son. We can hardly avoid being startled at its ignored and, in the context, irrelevant implications, which there is no longer opportunity to develop.

Fortunately, it is a minor blemish. In *The Heart of Midlothian*, Scott caught and fixed through the widest imaginable social range, the contrast in manners, the political and religious tensions, the very "feel" of what it was to be alive in Edinburgh during the reign of Queen Anne: in fact, nothing less than a microcosm of Scotland in the first decade of the eighteenth century. Poor, real-life Helen Walker of Irongay, who walked to London to save her sister's life and was only celebrated in a broadsheet ballad, supplied Scott with the story's counterpointing historical germ-idea. His huge absorption of folk material enabled him to flesh it. Since here at least the continuous involvement of his creative imagination triumphed over his antiquarian tendency to want to qualify or supplement every passing fact, the result is a story that grips the attention, thoroughly integrating the actions of the principal characters with their social, natural and historical backgrounds: in short, by any standards, a major masterpiece.

The Gowrie Conspiracy, together with a tragedy in the private life of a family of rank in the late seventeenth century, played the main part in the shaping of *The Bride of Lammermoor*, written in such pain that Scott claimed afterwards to be unable to remember how it had come to be conceived. It is a powerful distillation of popular superstition, "a story enacted beneath a brooding cloud, and pervaded by an evil fate".[24] In it, Scott achieved a quality of concentrated intensity only matched in "Wandering Willie's Tale" from *Redgauntlet*.

Superstitions also play their part in this tale, the last of the great Scottish novels, much of the raw background derived from *Satan's Invisible World Discovered*, which Scott had previously edited. However, the working out of superstitions is incidental to the true purpose of the novel.

Sir Harry Redgauntlet suffered for his part in the rising of 1745. His widow becomes guardian of their children, to the exclusion of her proscribed brother-in-law, Edward—an even more fanatical Jacobite than Sir Harry had been. The widow becomes obsessed with the fact that Hugh may seize the children and instil into them that Jacobitism which had lost her her husband. Hugh does succeed in capturing his niece, Lilias, but must also have her brother, Darsie, so that he can be brought up a Catholic and groomed to play his part in the projected third rising of 1765. Darsie, however, is out of sympathy with the ridiculous romantic role with which he is to be saddled, but is only saved by the total collapse of the conspiracy.

At a remote Solway inn, the conspirators assemble. Almost all those present, including Charles Edward Stuart himself, have no real enthusiasm for the matter they are met to discuss, feeling the cause already irretrievably lost. Only Redgauntlet is obliviously convinced of impending success. Slowly the meeting begins to disintegrate, as the realities of the present catch up with the dream of the past. Then in walks the Hanoverian General Campbell, and quietly tells them that if they all disperse, nothing will be held against them.

"Is this real?" asked Redgauntlet. "Can you mean this?—Am I—are all, are any of these gentlemen at liberty, without interruption, to embark in yonder brig which, I see, is now again approaching the shore?"

"You sir—all—any of the gentlemen present," said the General,—"all whom the vessel can contain, are at liberty to embark uninterrupted by me; but I advise none to go off who have not powerful reasons, unconnected with the present meeting, for this will be remembered against no one".

"Then, gentlemen," said Redgauntlet, clasping his hands together as the words burst from him, "the cause is lost forever".

Space does not permit detailed consideration of the English historical novels, of which *Woodstock* is the finest, or of the Crusading tales. There are also many pleasures to be found in the lesser Scottish novels, particularly in *A Legend of Montrose* and *The Fortunes of Nigel*, and in the one novel set in Scotland's Norse-influenced islands, in which for once the Scots are the "baddies", *The Pirate*. Nor is there need to dwell upon Scott's obvious failures, such as *Peveril of the Peak*, or upon the novels of the final years, when his will fought against the exhaustion of his body and mind to keep his pen productive for the honour of his family name and the benefit of his creditors.

In recent decades, Sir Walter Scott's reputation has been belittled by many lesser writers and critics. He has been accused of ignoring the issues of his own day, although, as we have seen, he upheld the contemporary ethos much more successfully than he could ever have done had he deployed his talents on the pseudo-Regency Edinburgh manners of those who flocked to see a kilt-clad George IV when he came to Scotland's Capital on a visit stage-managed by Scott in 1822. Scott's detractors have sought to impugn his middle-class origins, and to decry his business ineptitude, the snobbishness of some of his values, and the rigidity of his Toryism, particularly at the end of his life over the issue of Reform.

Such carping chatter, even if in small part true, is ultimately irrelevant in the face of the overwhelming fact that, having regard to the bulk, the variety and the quality of his achievement—not to mention the effect it has had, and continues to have, in shoring up the national identity—the creative imagination of Sir Walter Scott is still the first literary asset Scotland possesses.

Of his host of English imitators, all of whom lacked his extensive historical knowledge, the name of W. Harrison Ainsworth alone survives, but only through one novel, *The Tower of London*. Balzac and Pushkin acknowledged their debt to Scott, while Stendhal, writing to Balzac, called him simply "our father".

In Scotland, Scott's only successor in the historical field was Sir Thomas Dick Lauder (1784–1848), whose *The Wolf of Badenoch* (1827) is a vigorous enough tale. Unfortunately it suffers from Lauder's inability to cope with medieval speech, a difficulty he did not have to face in his exciting factual account of *The Great Floods in Morayshire* (1830).

Thereafter, the tradition of the historical romance in Scotland passed to Stevenson, Crockett and, finally, Neil Munro. But before tracing its later stages, we must turn to another novelist who did write of one aspect of the manners of his own day.

John Galt (1779–1839), born at Irvine, Ayrshire, was the son of a sea captain. The family moved to Greenock when the future novelist was ten. As a young man, Galt spent some time with a business firm before going to London, where he studied law at Lincoln's Inn. Two years travel abroad followed, during which he met Byron in Greece, an encounter which eventually resulted in his *Life of Byron* (1830), widely read when it first appeared. Galt's first published work was an epic-poem, *The Battle of Largs*, later suppressed—Galt was no poet, as a volume of his verse published in 1954* shows. This was followed by two travel volumes and a life of Wolsey. Galt's first real success was *The Ayrshire Legatees* (1821), which originally appeared in *Blackwood's*. His best book, *Annals of the Parish* (1821), was followed by *The Provost* (1822), *The Steamboat* (1822), *Sir Andrew Wylie* (1822), *The Entail* (1822), and in the following year *Ringan Gilhaize* (1823), which re-tells the events of Scott's *Old Mortality*, but from the Covenanting viewpoint. *The Last of the Lairds* came out in 1826. One final success, *The Member: An Autobiography*, rounded off the Scots series in 1832, depicting with kindly irony the deplorable parliamentary career of Archibald Jobbry just before the Reform Act of 1832.

In 1825, he went to Canada as Secretary of a land company, founding the town of Guelph in 1827, and having the town of Galt named after him. Back in London, he felt cheated (with some justification) out of the reward of a position in Canada commensurate with the efforts he had expended on behalf of British interests in North America. *Lawrie Todd* (1830), an uneven novel, commemorated these Canadian experiences.

Galt's *Autobiography* (1833)† is a shrewd and fascinating self-study. He

* *Poems of John Galt: A Selection*, edited by G. H. Needler, Toronto, 1954. Galt never abandoned his hopes of being remembered as a poet. After leaving Canada he produced a second volume, *Poems,* in 1833, and almost his last literary act was to correct the proofs of *The Demon of Destiny and Other Poems* which appeared after his death in 1839. His numerous wholly unsuccessful dramas are also mostly in verse. Although a *Complete Poems of John Galt* has been prepared for publication at the time of writing, no further service will be done to his memory if it appears. He was simply a skilful and diligent rhymster, as lacking in poetic "lift" as he was in knowledge of the practical necessities of the theatre.

† Galt's divided personality showed itself not only in literature but also in his life. In one mood, he needed travel and action to achieve satisfaction. His tortuous attempts to found overseas companies that would defeat the Napoleonic blockade ended in failure, but his work, undertaken initially on behalf of Canadian settlers who had lost money and possessions in the American War, and then on behalf of the Canada Company, resulted in him founding the city of Guelph. His dismissal from his Canadian post—partly the result of a clash of personality between Galt and the Governor of the Province, Sir Peregrine Maitland, and partly because of some lack of tact on Galt's part in dealing with the luke-warm

returned to Greenock in the year of its publication, and soon afterwards died, worn out with prodigious journalistic efforts, and the production of a list of "pot-boiler" novels so bad that it is difficult to believe they are by the same author as *Annals of the Parish*. Two volumes of excellent short stories in his best vernacular vein were collected from various periodicals long after his death, and published as *The Howdie and Other Tales* (1923) and *A Rich Man and Other Stories* (1925), both edited by William Roughead.

Galt has remained a sadly underestimated writer. Like Scott, he was aware of the inevitability of social change as a consequence of the Industrial Revolution. His concern, however, was not with the vanished heroic Scotland of pre-Jacobite days, but with the manners and modes of speech of small-town life which resisted the invasion of Anglifying influences longer than the cities; indeed, until the coming of the railway, a decade or so after Galt's death.

Galt usually adopts the posture of narrator, indulging in a good deal of ironic self-revelation in the telling of his tales. He exploits to the utmost the richness of the Scots still commonly in use among all classes in provincial towns long after it had begun to descend the social scale in Glasgow and Edinburgh. Above all, he is expert at contrasting the ways of the provincial world, where his best novels and stories have their origin, with the sophistication and manipulations of the wider world of business and politics in London. In a sense, therefore, his achievement provides a kind of domestic complement to Scott's. Yet, by and large, Galt's novels remain essentially a Scottish taste, for the same reason as do the poems of Fergusson. Both are inherently so affectionately involved with the nuances of the Scots tongue that much of their best work is not only untranslatable, but is only of limited interest to that outside majority of readers who have scant patience with what they are pleased to regard as "dialect" writing.

A passage from *The Provost* shows Galt at his pointed best:

On a Saturday night, as I was on the eve of stepping into my bed, (I shall

---

authorities at home—seems to have been a traumatic experience from which he never wholly recovered, although his three sons were later all to achieve distinction in the development of Canada after their father's death.

In the practical phases of his life, he was apt to regard literature as an unworthy pursuit. After the Canadian disaster, he fell under constant pressure to journalize for a living, and to over-produce. Apart from the fine stories collected by Roughead, only *The Member* (1832), a witty satire on political cynicism, deserves to be placed alongside the group of great novels written for Blackwood in the 1820s.

Even Galt's *Autobiography* stresses his divided approach. While it provides a justification for his practical ambitions and achievements, literature is reserved for its sequel of 1834, *The Literary Life and Miscellanies*. It should perhaps be remembered that although Galt applied his own standards of personal reserve to his treatment of Byron's life, and so avoided much that is now of considerable interest, Galt's *Life of Byron*, which became a run-away best-seller, is otherwise fair and well-written. *Lawrie Todd*, the story of a successful Scots settler, is more highly regarded in Canada than in Scotland, where it shares oblivion with Galt's unconvincing historical novels *Rothelan* (1824) and *Southennan* (1830).

never forget it—Mrs Pawkie was already in, and as sound as a door-nail—and I was just crooking my mouth to blow out the candle), I heard a rap. As our bedroom window was over the door, I looked out. It was a dark night; but I could see by a glaik of light from a neighbour's window, that there was a man with a cocked hat at the door. "What's your will?" said I to him, as I looked out at him in my night-cap. He made no other answer, but that he was one of His Majesty's officers, and had business with the justice.

I did not like this Englification and voice of claim and authority; however, I drew on my stockings and breeks again, and taking my wife's flannel coaty about my shoulders—for I was then troubled with rheumatiz—I went down, and, opening the door, let in the Lieutenant.

"I come," said he, "to show you my warrant and commission, and to acquaint you that, having information of several able-bodied seamen being in the town, I mean to make a search for them."

I really did not well know what to say at the moment. I begged him, for the love of peace and quietness, to defer his work till the next morning; but he said he must obey his orders, and he was sorry that it was his duty to be on so disagreeable a service,—with many other things that showed something like a sense of compassion that could not have been hoped for in the Captain of a pressgang.

When he had said this, he then went away, saying,—for he saw my tribulation,—that it would be as well for me to be prepared in case of any riot. This was the worst news of all; but what could I do? I thereupon went again to Mrs Pawkie, and shaking her awake, told her what was going on, and a terrified woman she was. I then dressed myself with all possible expedition, and went to the town-clerk's, and we sent for the town-officers, and then adjourned to the council-chamber to wait the issue of what might betide.

In my absence, Mrs Pawkie rose out of her bed, and by some wonderful instinct collecting all the bairns, went with them to the minister's house, as to a place of refuge and sanctuary.

Shortly after we had been in the council-room, I opened the window and looked out; but all was still: the town was lying in the defencelessness of sleep, and nothing was heard but the clicking of the town-clock in the steeple over our heads. By-and-by, however, a sough and pattering of feet was heard approaching; and shortly after, in looking out, we saw the press-gang, headed by their officers, with cutlasses by their side, and great club-sticks in their hands. They said nothing; but the sound of their feet and the silent stones of the causey was as the noise of a dreadful engine. They passed, and went on; and all that were with me in the council stood at the windows and listened. In the course of a minute or two after, two lasses, with a callan, that had been out, came flying and wailing, giving the alarm to the town. Then we heard the driving of the bludgeons on the doors, and the outcries of terrified women; and presently after we saw the poor chased sailors running in their shirts, with their clothes in their hands, as if they had been felons and blackguards caught in guilt, and flying from the hands of justice.

The town was awakened with the din as with the cry of fire; and lights came starting forward, as it were, to the windows. The women were out with lamentations and vows of vengeance. I was in a state of horror unspeakable. Then came some three or four of the pressgang with a struggling sailor in their clutches, with nothing but his trousers on—his shirt riven from his back in the fury. Syne came the rest of the gang and their officers, scattered as it were with a tempest of mud and stones, pursued and battered by a troop of desperate women and weans, whose fathers and brothers were in jeopardy. And these were followed by the wailing wife of the pressed man, with her five bairns, clammering in their agony to heaven against the King and Government for the outrage. I could not listen to the fearful justice of their outcry, but sat down in a corner of the council-chamber with my fingers in my ears.

In a little while a shout of triumph rose from the mob, and we heard them returning, and I felt, as it were, relieved; but the sound of their voices became hoarse and terrible as they drew near, and, in a moment, I heard the jingle of twenty broken windows rattle in the street. My heart misgave me; and, indeed, it was my own windows. They left not one pane unbroken; and nothing kept them from demolishing the house to the groundstone but the exaltations of Major Pipe, who, on hearing the uproar, was up and out, and did all in his power to arrest the fury of the tumult. It seems the mob had taken it into their heads that I had signed what they called the press-warrants; and on driving the gang out of the town, and rescuing the man, they came to revenge themselves on me and mine,—which is the cause that made me say it was a miraculous instinct that led Mrs Pawkie to take the family to Mr Pittle's; for, had they been in the house, it is not to be told what the consequences might have been.

This glimpse of the good Provost's canniness is true to a certain aspect of the Scots character, but the passage also indicates Galt's worst fault: the overstressing of comic pawkiness, which has the effect of holding the Scot up to ridicule to amuse English readers, a practice assiduously cultivated by Barrie and others, culminating in the profitable caricatures of "Scoatch Coamics" such as Sir Harry Lauder and Will Fyffe. His other fault is an inability to construct. Even in *The Entail*, that tale of grim Scottish acquisitiveness over several generations, the episodic nature of Galt's construction is obvious.

In his great novels—those that I have listed—Galt avoids the dangers of over-indulging in sentimentality more successfully than his closest imitator, David Macbeth Moir (1798–1851), a Musselburgh-born doctor of medicine who contributed to *Blackwood's* under the signature of Δ (Delta). A much more prolific though marginally better versifier than Galt, Moir's *Autobiography of Mansie Waugh* also explores the humour of small-town Scottish life, though with a more evident awareness of the kind of Scots "peculiarities" likely to be good for an English laugh. But to point the focus inwards rather than outwards has its dangers. Although *Mansie Waugh* is, in its way, a minor masterpiece, it clearly indicates the direction which the writers of the Kailyard or cabbage-patch school were soon to follow.

This danger is avoided by Thomas Hamilton (1789–1842), whose early years were spent in the army. His *Youth and Manhood of Cyril Thornton* (1827) deals with people who move in higher social circumstances than Galt's Laird Grippy. Although the influence of Lockhart sometimes gives an edge of malice to Hamilton's style, his re-creation of the customs and manners of Glasgow around the turn of the new century make this a novel justifying its late twentieth-century reissue.

Scott's older contemporary, Elizabeth Hamilton (1758–1816), author of the song "My Ain Fireside", produced a novel for the first time exhibiting the squalid side of the life of the small tenant-farmer, in *The Cottagers of Glenbervie* (1808). The comparatively short-lived Mary Brunton (1778–1818)—before her marriage, a Balfour from Orkney—was an admirer of the historian William Robertson's resounding periods. She wrote two "improving" novels, *Self-Control* (1811) and *Discipline* (1814), the second half of the latter a not unsuccessful attempt to portray Highland manners, but wholly outclassed by *Waverley*. In the preface to *Discipline*, in which Ellen Percy, the grand-daughter of one "doomed to starve upon a curacy in revenge for his contaminating the blood of the Percy's by an un-equal alliance", tells her story, the authoress warns us of what we are in for:

> The appetite for fiction is indeed universal, and has unfortunately been made the occasion of conveying poison of every description to the youthful mind. Why must the anti-dote be confined to such forms as are sure to be re-jected by those who need it the most? There is high authority for using fable as the vehicle of important, even solemn, truth; and to this purpose it is here applied without hesitation.

Indeed it is! Ellen, early left without a mother, is brought up by an indul-gent father who favours the matrimonial approaches of a grave Mr Mait-land. But Ellen is interested in the gay Lord Frederick de Burgh, who almost succeeds in seducing her, and in carrying her off to Scotland. He fails to keep the Scottish rendezvous, however, on learning that Ellen's father has lost all his money. In the end, Ellen savours the Perthshire High-lands as the guest of Henry Graham, who turns out to be none other than Maitland, and the Laird of Glen Eredine, near Aberfoyle, whom she duly marries.

Although the moralizing is heavy-handed, and the character of Miss Mortimer reflects the embodiment of the Calvinistic anti-pleasure prin-ciple at its most unctuous, there are some deft sketches of manners. Here, for instance, is a glimpse of the young Ellen out to "dangle" Maitland for the fun of it:

The Countess of ——'s ball was fixed upon as the occasion of my first appearance. What meditation did it not cost me, to decide upon the style of my costume for that eventful evening! How did my preference fluctuate between the gorgeous and the simple, the airy and the magnificent! The balance was cast in favour of the latter, by the possession of my mother's jewels, which my father ordered to be reset for me, with superb additions. "He could afford it," he said, "as well as Lady —— or any of her company, and he saw no reason why I should not be as fine as the proudest of them." My heart bounded with delight, when I at last saw the brilliants flash in my dark hair, mark the contour of my neck, and circle a waist slender as the form of a sylph. All that flattery had told, and vanity believed, seemed now to gain confirmation; yet, still some doubts allayed my self-conceit, till it received its consummation from the cold, the stately Mr Maitland. I overheard Miss Arnold whisper to him, as I entered the drawing-room where he and a large party were waiting to escort me, "look, what lovely diamonds Mr Percy has given Ellen." "They would have been better bestowed elsewhere," returned Mr Maitland; "nobody that looks at Miss Percy will observe them."

Though certain that this compliment was not meant for my ear, I had the hardihood to acknowledge it, by saying, "Thank you Sir; I shall put that into my memorandum book, and preserve it like a Queen Anne's farthing, not much worth in itself, but precious, because she never made but one."

"The farthing was never meant for circulation," returned he dryly, "but it unluckily fell into the hands of a child, who could not keep it to herself."

The word "child" was particularly offensive on this first night of my womanhood; and, in the intoxication of my spirits, I should have made some very impertinent rejoinder, if I had not been prevented by Miss Mortimer. "What, Ellen!" said she, "Quarrelling with Mr Maitland for compliments! Is it not enough to satisfy you, that he who is so seldom seen in places of that sort accompanies you to the ball to-night?

"Oh! pray," returned I, "since Mr Maitland has so few *bienseances* to spare, allow him to dispose of them as he pleases. His attendance to-night is meant as a compliment to my father."

"Do not make me pay a whole evening's comfort for what is only a farthing's worth, you know," said Maitland good humouredly, "but leave off trying to be disagreeable and witty. Nay, do not frown now; your face will not have time to recover itself. I see the carriage is at the door."

Even Brunton's best novel, *Emmeline* (1819), suffered the misfortune of being eclipsed by the work of another, this time a novel from the pen of another woman.

Susan Edmonstone Ferrier (1782–1854) was the youngest of the ten children born to a Court of Session colleague of Scott's. She has been called

the Scottish counterpart of Ireland's Maria Edgeworth and England's Jane
Austen, but the English comparison cannot be sustained. Like Jane Austen,
Miss Ferrier managed to find out a great deal about how men think and
behave, particularly in their relationships with women. But she lacks her
English contemporary's range and narrative impartiality, and is much
more ready to insert moral homilies for their own sake, unfortunately a
common Scots failing. Ferrier is at her best when dealing with the middle
and lower strata of society, describing the absurd affectations of the would-
be genteel, and filling out the daily details of middle-class life. *Marriage*
(1818), *The Inheritance* (1824) and *Destiny* (1831) all have their stock of
richly drawn characters, their racy humours, and their darts of animosity.
Here, for instance, from *The Inheritance*, is Mrs Major Waddell in action,
a lady whose formidable kind is still to be found determinedly in our midst:

"Bless me, Major!" exclaimed the lady in a tone of alarm," is it possible
that you have been walking? And the roads are quite wet! Why did you not
tell me you were going out, and I would have ordered the carriage for you,
and have gone with you, although I believe it is the etiquette for a married
lady to be at home for some time;" then observing a spot of mud on his boot,
"And you have got your feet quite wet; for Heaven's sake, Major, do go and
change your boots directly! I see they are quite wet!"

"The Major looked delighted at this proof of conjugal tenderness, but protested that his feet were quite dry, holding up a foot in appeal to the company.

"Now, how can you say so, Major, when I see they are quite damp? Do, I
entreat you, put them off; it makes me perfectly wretched to think of your
sitting with wet feet; you know you have plenty of boots. I made him get a
dozen pairs when we were at York, that I might be quite sure of his always
having dry feet. Do, my love, let Cæsar help you off with these for any
sake!—for my sake, Major. I ask it as a personal favour."

This was irresistible; the Major prepared to take the suspected feet out of
company with a sort of vague, mixed feeling floating in his brain, which, if it
had been put into words, would have been thus rendered—

"What a happy dog am I to be so tenderly beloved by such a charming
girl; and yet what a confounded deal of trouble it is to be obliged to change
one's boots every time my wife sees a spot of mud on them!"

"Now, you won't be long, Major?" cried the lady, as the Major went off,
attended by Cæsar. "The Major is so imprudent, and takes so little care of
himself, he really makes me quite wretched; but how do you think he looks?"

At that moment the Major entered, with a very red face and a pair of new
boots, evidently too tight.

"You see what it is to be under orders," said he, pointing to his toes, and
trying to smile in the midst of his anguish.

"It's lucky for you, Major, I'm sure, that you are for I don't believe there
ever was anybody on earth so careless of themselves as you are. What do you

think of his handing Lady Fairacre to her carriage yesterday in the midst of the rain, and without his hat, too? But I hope you changed your stockings as well as your boots, Major?"

"I assure you, upon my honour, my dear, neither of them were the least wet."

"Oh! now, Major, you know if you haven't changed your stockings I shall be completely wretched," cried the lady, all panting with emotion. "Good gracious! To think of your keeping on your wet stockings—I never knew anything like it!"

"I assure you, my dear Bell,"—began the Major.

"Oh! now, my dearest Major, if you have the least regard for me, I beseech you put off your stockings this instant. Oh! I am certain you've got cold already—how hot you are," taking his hand; "and don't you think his colour very high? Now I'm quite wretched about you."

In vain did the poor Major vow and protest as to the state of his stockings—it was all in vain; the lady's apprehensions were not to be allayed, and again he had to limp away to pull off boots which the united exertions of himself and Cæsar had with difficulty got on.

"I really think my wife will be for keeping me in a bandbox," said he, with a sort of sardonic smile, the offspring of flattered vanity and personal suffering.

The claims of Scott's son-in-law, John Gibson Lockhart (1794–1854) the son of a minister of Cambusnethan, have been variously berated, by no one more severely than Saintsbury, who proclaimed: "Lockhart had every faculty for writing novels except the faculty of novel-writing".[25] While it is true that his greatest talents lay in other directions, at least he attempted to probe behind the darker side of human nature. Inordinately proud of his ancestry, handsome, but cold and reserved except to his intimate friends, his attempts to flesh fictional characters with consistent credibility are marred by a curious stiffness at one emotional extreme, or raw melodrama at the other.

Valerius (1821) tells the story of a Roman Briton who falls in love with a Roman girl, Athanasia, whom he then discovers to be a Christian. She is threatened with martyrdom, but is rescued by her lover and brought to Britain. A sub-plot deals with the intentions of the father of Valerius's cousin to force the youth to marry the beautiful Rubellia, whose addiction to witchcraft is discovered just in time. The portrayal of Sixtos's tutor, Xenophrastes the Stoic, produces some forced humour, and Lockhart fails to evoke any kind of sustained period atmosphere. Yet Valerius's sideways glimpse of Rubellia's profile, as a young man lies in the arena pierced through by a sword and only awaiting Caesar's signal for the final finishing thrust, is uncomfortably memorable:

Rubellia laid her hand upon my elbow, whispering "Look, look, now look" in a voice of low, steady impatience. I did look, but not to the arena. No, it was upon the beautiful features of that woman's face that I looked, and truly, it seemed to me as if they presented a spectacle almost as fearful. I saw those rich lips parted, those dark eyes extended, those smooth cheeks suffused with a steadfast blush, that lovely bosom swelled and glowing; and I hated Rubellia, for I knew not before how utterly beauty can be brutalized by the throbbings of a cruel heart. But I looked round to escape from the sight of her;—and hundreds of females that I saw fixed with equal earnestness on the same horrors, taught me, even at the moment, to think with more charity on the pitiless gaze of one.

One wonders what Lockhart would have made of female behaviour at twentieth-century boxing matches or wrestling contests.

Reginald Dalton (1823) aimed at portraying undergraduate life in early nineteenth-century Oxford, but in spite of some charm and a sketch of Lockhart's father, suffers from obvious exaggerations.

Matthew Wald (1824), his last novel, blends religious fanaticism with melodramatic crime. The plot and the many sub-plots are extremely involved. Matthew—a surgeon under training who has taken the post of tutor in the household of Sir Claud Barr, a reformed baronet now an invalid—hears the story of how Perling Joan, seduced by Sir Claud in youth, dies under the wheels of the carriage which is bringing home the baronet and his bride. Matthew qualifies, and marries Perling Joan's daughter, Joanne, having found out that the love of his youth, Katherine, is now Lady Lascelyne. Matthew discovers in a locked casket letters showing that Sir Claud had, in fact, married Perling Joan, making Joanne heiress to half the Barr estate. Matthew becomes a Member of Parliament, learns that Katherine is unhappy, is found innocently comforting her by Joanne, who misreads the situation and dies of grief, so Matthew forces Lascelyne to a sword-fight, his Lordship soon lying "spitted through the heart". Back rushes Matthew to tell Katherine that now she is free.

> I held out the red blade before me—the drops had not all baked yet—one or two fell upon the floor.
> "Speak, Matthew, What is this? Speak. Ha! God of mercy, there is blood upon that sword!"
> "Ay, blood, my cousin, blood."
> "My husband! My Lascelyne!"
> I heard no more. Heavens and earth that I should write this down. One shriek—one, just one. Fainted? Swooned? Dead! Oh dead! I remember no more.

Matthew goes mad but, as we learn from the postscript, a later letter from one young man to another, recovers and lives into old age. This postscript reveals Lockhart's imperfectly realized purpose, a purpose foreshadowing

Stevenson *Dr Jekyll and Mr Hyde*: "That man . . . who was, whenever any of us met him in society, the soul of the party—that this man should have been in reality, the habitual victim of the darkest and most melancholy reflections, was undoubtedly a thing not likely to be suspected by observers so young and thoughtless as we both were when first we knew Mr Wald."

The "darkest and most melancholy reflections" also colour Lockhart's best novel, *Adam Blair* (1824), the only one of the four to be reprinted during the present century. It was based on a true story preserved in the *Fasti Ecclesiae Scoticanae*. Blair, minister of Cross-Meikle in the latter part of the eighteenth century, loses his wife and agrees to have Mrs Charlotte Bell, a former friend of his wife's, come to the manse to look after the family. Charlotte and Adam are attracted. Charlotte is summoned by the brutal agent Strahan to return to his master and her husband, Captain Campbell. Adam cannot forget her, and in response to an unhappy letter from Charlotte, rushes to her at her husband's castle. Charlotte pours out her woes, and with joyless, compelling passion, they make love. Adam then flees from her, conscience-stricken, and in his own eyes unfit for his charge. Eventually however, the old minister, who had once shocked the community of which he was the figurehead, is reinstated. The novel is lacking in contrast, and tears gush almost as readily from Lockhart's pen as from Mackenzie's. Much of the story is carried forward by somewhat ponderous narrative rather than by dialogue. As a result, the characters lack that spontaneous warmth of conviction, both in their lineaments and in their reactions to the situations which confront them, which make Scott's finest characters so memorable.

Yet both *Adam Blair* and *Matthew Wald* are serious attempts to deal with the dark religion-inspired ills that for long afflicted the Scottish psyche. They fail in their realization for reasons that are literary, yet for all that are still worth reading.

Somewhat surprisingly, it was left to another of Scott's friends, James Hogg (whose poetry has already been discussed) to portray with success the results of arrogance in the guise of Christianity pushed to its dogmatic Scottish extreme in *The Private Memoirs and Confessions of a Justified Sinner* (1824).

The source of Hogg's story was no doubt the pseudo-historic outpourings of the fanatical Robert Wodrow, imaginatively fused with folk-legend passed on to Hogg by his mother. As we have already seen, the devil has for many centuries been a feared familiar to ordinary Scots, even though regarded unquestionably as the embodiment of evil.

Out of whatever mixture of distorted religious traditions and folk-lore *The Confessions* may have sprung, the story is a psychological masterpiece of the first order. It is presented from three aspects. First, we are given the author-as-editor version of the story. From this we learn that George Colwan married Robina Orde and gave birth to two sons, the second of whom Colwan rejects, suspecting him to have been fathered by his wife's religious adviser, the Rev. Robert Wringhim. The young men grow up quite apart, and are always in conflict when they meet. Then the elder, liberal brother is murdered, and the younger disappears when he is suspected of fratricide. The mirror shifts, and we see the events of the story through the eyes of the younger brother, a Colwan in reality but known as Robert Wringhim. Finally, the "editor" tells us how he came into possession of the memoirs, and how Wringhim died. A drover sees two people moving round and round a hay-rick. When he goes to investigate, he finds only one man. It is Wringhim, hanged.

Outwardly, the book appears to present simply the story of what happens when a person becomes obsessed with the belief that he is a member of the Elect, and as such, "justified"; one who cannot be tempted and who can do no wrong. But this is not just an idle tale of bigotry; for Wringhim finds himself companioned by Gil-Martin, a figure of evil. Gil-Martin leads Wringhim nearer and nearer to destruction, much as the agent of Mephistopheles leads Faust, though without the young man ever signing away his soul or apparently even being aware that he is being argued logically towards a point at which he must commit two "justified" murders, and in the end, still believing himself to be godly and "saved", take his own life.

Many critics have argued about the significance of Gil-Martin. André Gide, one of the modern editors of the novel, thinks that this Devil may only be "the exteriorized development of our own desires, of our pride, of our most secret thoughts". Throughout, the ambiguity of the Gil-Martin symbolism creates a feeling of supernatural horror which puts the book on the same abiding plane of psychological interest as other distinguished European variants of the Faust legend by Marlowe, Goethe and Mann. With Hogg's version, however, Scots aware of their traditions are left wondering additionally about aspects of the national character.

Daiches thinks that the "power and economy of the tale is in the end dissipated in crude melodrama".[26] But supernatural situations are by their very nature unresolvable and readers must judge for themselves whether or not Hogg could really have made a fitter ending.

It is, however, true that in general Hogg rarely possessed enough self-critical ability to save him from diluting his good things. By way of preparation for what was to be his masterpiece, Hogg in 1822 produced a long work, The Three Perils of Man, subtitled "War, Women and Witchcraft", and called by the author a "Border Romance". It is an enormously rich and imaginative raid upon the store of folk-lore and balladry which Hogg learned at his mother's knee, spiced with his own brand of diablerie. In the matter of form, it sprawls. Few would deny that the book is over-long, mainly because the tales told by those incarcerated during the siege of Roxburgh Castle, hold up the basic action. It is an altogether more powerful achievement, however, than its successor, The Three Perils of Women, which followed the year after, and in which Hogg showed how ill-qualified he was to write a novel of manners. But then Hogg never felt wholly sure in which direction any of his talents lay. He was, in fact, the only prose writer who seemed to have direct intuitive access to the old world of balladry. His *Brownie of Bodsbeck* (1817) reflects the popular view of the alleged truth of Claverhouse's atrocities.

All his more adventurous prose enterprises were rewarded with only luke-warm enthusiasm by the Edinburgh readers of his day. It was his rural tales and his ghost stories that brought him popularity. Mocked both by Wilson and Lockhart, his fellow contributors to *Blackwood's*, and not always taken wholly seriously by Scott, he became dismayed, complaining, "I am grown to have no confidence whatever in my own taste or discernment in what is to be well or ill taken by the world or individuals. Indeed it appears that were I to make my calculations by inverse proportion I would be oftener right than I am."

A novelist who reminds us of Smollett's earlier knowledge of seafaring ways is Glasgow-born Michael Scott (1789–1835), whose *Tom Cringle's Log* (1833) drew upon his own experiences sailing to and from Jamaica, where he set up in business. It is every bit as vivacious as Captain Marryatt's English novels. Scott's *The Cruise of the "Midge"* (1836) is also well written, though giving something of an impression of "second time round;" which it probably was, since both first appeared in *Blackwood's*.

There was no lack of novelists during the second half of the century, though few are still read today. Some of them are, quite simply, unreadable. Into this category comes Alexander Smith's one novel, *Alfred Hagart's Household*, popular in its day. The dialogue is couched in language which no real-life Hagart would ever have uttered, the narration fulsome and overblown. Robert Buchanan's *The Shadow of the Sword* (1876) and *God and the Man* (1881), offer hearty pietism and a swaggering straining after effect at the expense of sincerity as obvious defects.

Into the category of work popular in its day also comes the considerable output of George John Whyte-Melville (1821–1878), the Fife-born novelist who spent his youth as an army officer and his later years in the active pursuit of field sports, from which, as the result of a hunting accident, he died. Admirers of Surtees might perhaps still take pleasure in his sporting novels, but the only novel to survive as literature is *The Queen's Maries* (1862), which deals with a subject of continuing fascination in a charming, if rather facile, fashion.

Lockhart's nephew, Laurence William Lockhart (1831–1882), war correspondent to *The Times* during the Franco-German war, had one success *Fair to See* (1871), which pulls gentle humour at Scottish customs, and includes a vivid account of such institutions as the Clyde Steamer, Highland Games and an Edinburgh Assembly. Lawrence Oliphant (1829–1888), born at Capetown, where his father was Attorney-General, achieved distinction through his travel-books, notably *Journey to Katmandu* (1852). His novel *Altidora Peto* (1883) loses itself in so-called scientific mysteries, than which nothing dates more quickly. His *Episodes in a Life of Adventure* (1887) is a racy if less objective account of his career than the study, *Laurence Oliphant*, written by his cousin, Mrs Oliphant.

With Mrs Margaret Oliphant (1828–1897), indeed, we come to the category of later nineteenth-century Scottish writers whose best achievement is no more deserving of neglect than were our finest Victorian buildings or Victorian *objets d'art* and design work during the first two-thirds of the twentieth century.

Born at Wallyford, near Musselburgh, the daughter of James Wilson, she married her cousin Francis Wilson Oliphant, a stained-glass artist, but by 1859, found herself a widow with three young children to maintain by her pen, in addition to brothers and a nephew. All her sons died while still dependent on her, while the nephew died almost as soon as she had finished educating him. She therefore became an indefatigable pen-pusher. Much of her work first appeared in *Blackwood's*, and inevitably a great deal of it was the outcome of too-hasty over-production. But her grasp of character-delineation was based on her own experience, and her depiction of the manners of her age was anything but superficial. Above all, her humour makes frequent little ironic darts.

Mrs Margaret Maitland (1849) first won her a name. Her English novels forming *The Chronicles of Carlingford* (1861–6) were much praised by critics when they first appeared, and justly so. Indeed, one of them *Miss Marjoribanks* (1866), is without doubt a masterpiece, filling in the gap in English literature between Jane Austen and George Eliot, on whose *Middlemarch* Mrs Oliphant seems to have exercised some influence. Lucilla, the heroine, returns home to her widowed father, Dr Marjoribanks (pronounced Marchbanks), and proceeds not only to organize his life, but to transform Carlingford Society with her as its undisputed queen. Dr Marjoribanks is typical of the Scottish medico settled in England, happy in the softer social climate of that country, preserving "a respect for *talent* in every development, as is natural to his nation". His daughter is no consumptive Victorian heroine subject to the vapours, but the possessor of what Q. D. Leavis describes as "large Scotch bones . . . moral solidity, and that characteristic Scotch complacency, based on the consciousness of undeniable superiority, which makes her able to ignore other people's so-called sense of humour."[27] The novel is thus in part a study of the impact of Scottishness on English provincial life.

What constituted Scottishness gives point to Mrs Oliphants many excellent short stories. Life had taught her that the inferior (often, understandably, males in her case) are left uncompensated. She did not fudge her endings for sentimentality's sake.

Her best Scots novels also deserve to be revived, among them *Mrs Margaret Maitland* and the admirable *Kirsteen* (1890), a study of a poor but arrogant Douglas laird, his weak wife and their fourteen children, each sent into the world with only their clothes to make their own way. My own choice among the novels, however, would be *Effie Ogilvie* (1886), a novel set in Dumfriesshire. Here, Victorian middle-class virtues are admirably portrayed. The dour Ogilvie, unwilling to be fashed with such women's business as who might, or might not, be a suitable husband for his daughter, is well contrasted with his position-seeking wife, and Effie, their daughter. In her, the spirit of rebellion against the hypocrisy of keeping up "appearances" almost, but not quite, triumphs.

Effie loves her boyhood friend, Ronald Sutherland, an officer in the 111th, serving in India. Ambitious Mama, however, forces her into an engagement with an unprepossessing tycoon, Fred Dirom, whose sisters, incidentally, are bitchily portrayed in all their genteel insipidity. When the Dirom fortune is brought down in what Fred's sisters politely call a "Great Smash", Mrs Ogilvie abruptly changes her tune. Here she is at it:

When Effie got near home, still full of agitation from this strange little opening and closing of she knew not what—some secret page in her own history, inscribed with a record she had known nothing of—she met her stepmother, who was returning very alert and business-like from a walk.

"What have you been saying to Ronald?" said Mrs Ogilvie, "to make him look so grave? I saw him turn the corner, and I thought he had seen a ghost, poor lad; but afterwards it proved to be only you. You should not be so severe: for he has liked you long, though you knew nothing about it; and it must have been very hard upon him, poor fellow, to find that he had come home just too late, and that you had been snapped up, as a person may say, under his very nose."

This was so strange an address that it took away Effie's breath. She gave her step-mother a look half stupified, half horrified. "I don't know what you mean," she said.

"Well, Effie, my dear, you must just learn; and I don't think you will find it very difficult, if you will give your attention to it. I have been wanting to speak to you for two or three days, and your father too. You must not trouble about Fred Dirom any more. I have never been quite satisfied in my own mind that your heart was in it, if he had not been so pressing and pushing, and, as we all thought, such a good match. But you see it turns out that's not the case, Effie. I got a letter yesterday from my cousin John; and it's all true about Dirom's firm. They are just going down hill as fast as can be, and probably by this time they've failed. Though you don't know about business, you know what that means. It is just the end of all things; and to hold the young man to his promise in such circumstances would be out of the question. We are quite agreed upon that, both your father and me. So, my dear Effie, you are free. It mightn't have become you to take steps; so your father and me— we have acted for you; and now you are free."

Effie stopped short in the road, and stared at the speaker aghast. If her heart gave a little leap to hear that word, it was merely an instinctive movement, and meant nothing. Her mind was full of consternation. She was confounded by the suddenness, by the strangeness of the communication.

Free! What did it mean, and why was it? Free! She repeated the word to herself after a while, still looking at her step-mother. It was but a single little word. It meant—what? The world seemed to go round and round with Effie, the dim November skies, the gray of the wintry afternoon, the red shaft of the setting sun beyond—all whirled about her. "Free!" She repeated it as an infant repeats a foreign word without knowing what it means.

"Now, Effie," said Mrs Ogilvie, "don't let us have any pretences: that is all I ask of you. Just face the thing honestly, and don't let us have any make-believe. If you tell me that you are deep in love with Fred Dirom and can't give him up, I will just not believe you. All I will think is that you are a little cutty, and have no heart at all. I was very glad you should make such a good match; but I could see all along your heart was not in it. And whatever he might say, I made no doubt but you would be thankful. So let us have none of your little deceptions here."

"I don't think I understand," said Effie, striving to speak. "I think I must have lost my senses or my hearing, or something. What was it you were saying? They say people call things by wrong names sometimes, and can't help it. Perhaps they hear wrong, too. What is it that you mean?"

"You know perfectly well what I mean," said Mrs Ogilvie, with some exasperation; "I have just written breaking off your marriage—is that plain enough? I've done it under your father's orders. It was he that accepted and I'm thinking it's he that has a right to refuse—It's all broken off—I cannot speak any plainer. Now, do you understand what I say?"

Effie had grown very pale—she shivered as if with cold—her lips quivered when she began to speak.

"And that is," she said, "because he has failed—because he is not a good match now, but a poor man—is that what it is?"

"If you like to put it in that broad way. Of course he is not in a condition to marry any longer. It is the kindest thing we can do—"

"Give me your letter," said Effie, holding out her hand. There was something threatening, something dangerous, about the girl, which made Mrs Ogilvie scream out.

Like most nineteenth-century Scottish novelists, Mrs Oliphant sometimes verges on sentimentality—which was, after all, a saleable commodity—yet she never quite lets her feet get trapped in its morass. She is characteristically unsentimental about the fate of the quick-rich Diroms, a fate common enough among the *nouveaux riches* in her age, and determinedly ambivalent about a happy-ever-after ending:

The Diroms disappeared from Allanbury as if they had never been there, and were heard of no more: though not without leaving disastrous traces, at least in one heart and life.

But it may be that Effie's wounds are not mortal after all. And one day

Captain Sutherland must come home—
And who knows?

Mrs Oliphant's *Annals of a Publishing House* (1897), the history of
Blackwood's, is essential reading for anyone interested in the literary scene
in nineteenth-century Edinburgh, its portraits of Lockhart and Wilson
especially sharp. Her *Autobiography*[28] is a human document of moving can-
dour, though inevitably lacking the high peaks of public interest which
makes Scott's *Journal* so compelling.

The twentieth century's total neglect of late nineteenth-century fiction
is hard to understand. While I would put in no strong plea for George
Macdonald (1824–1905), whose tendency to sermonize usually nullifies the
virtues of his Scots dialogue, *Lilith* (1895) re-creates a world where myth
can produce wisdom unattached to symbolism, at least until the somewhat
feeble transformation-through-redemption resolution at the end of the
book. Its horror scenes, particularly the grotesque dance of the clothed
skeletons, justify Auden's remark that "*Lilith* is equal if not superior to the
best of Poe".

Most of the myth-wisdom is distilled by the mysterious, ageless Mr
Raven. He tells the narrator and subject of the strange adventure:

"In this world never trust a person who has once deceived you—Above
all, never do anything such a one may ask you to do."
"I will try to remember," I answered; "—but I may forget!"
"Then some evil that is good for you will follow."
"And if I remember?"
"Some evil that is not good for you will follow."
The old man seemed to sink to the ground, and immediately I saw the
raven several yards from him, flying low and fast.

Lilith powerfully influenced the *Voyage to Arcturus* of David Lindsay, and
seems to occupy somewhat similar literary territory to that recently disclosed in *The Lord of the Rings* by the English writer J. R. R. Tolkien.

Macdonald's *Phantastes* (1858), much influenced by the shadows of
German Romanticism in general and by Novalis in particular, is a less suc-
cessful excursion into the world of Fairy, which nevertheless caused C. S.
Lewis to feel that on reading it, he had crossed "a great frontier".

Robert Falconer (1868) shows Macdonald—the son of a farmer from
Aberdeenshire who was a descendent of a survivor from the Massacre of
Glencoe—at his best in creating Scots character. Except in his tales for
children, *The Princess and the Goblin* (1872) and *The Princess and the Curdie*
(1883), pietism and its resultant sentimental collapse mar all he did. The best
of him—and some of the far from best!—was brought together in C. S.
Lewis's *George Macdonald: An Anthology* (1946).

Total oblivion has engulfed William Black (1841–1898), the Glasgow-born novelist who studied art, then practised journalism in London. His best books are *A Daughter of Heth* (1871), a tale about the impact a French girl made upon the manse-centred society of the West of Scotland, and *A Princess of Thule* (1873), much of which is set in the Outer Hebrides, reflecting and contrasting the "sophisticated" urban life of the "incomers" with that of the islanders, mildly foreshadowing Neil M. Gunn.

Black fell a victim of his own success—his complete works in twenty-six volumes appeared four years before his death—increasingly indulging in contrived theatrical effects, both in his handling of scenic description (particularly sunsets) and character-drawing. At his best, however, like Mrs Oliphant, he catches the atmosphere of a period that is becoming increasingly interesting to us now that its outwardly non-permissive complacency cannot any longer exert any practical influence upon our lives.

One of the curious facts of the nineteenth-century Scottish novel is its reluctance to allow itself be urbanized. As we have seen, Scott continually contrasted his acceptance of the new Scotland of commerce and technological development with his awareness of the need to shore up the fragments of our historic past, if the sense of nationhood was to survive. Yet although we are conscious of the existence of the steamboat and of a vague industrial presence somewhere in the background of Galt's novels and stories, the transformation which followed James Watt's perfection of the harnessing of steampower is nowhere directly reflected in Scottish fiction. In the novels of Brunton, Oliphant, and Black, mysterious "smashes" occur, causing the *nouveaux riches* suddenly to lose their fortunes. Their daughters, in consequence, cease to be desirable matrimonial game, either for the youthful scions of the aristocracy, or young men of their own class and kind. To fail, in middle-class Victorian society, was regarded as disgraceful and dishonourable.

As in the Bulika of Macdonald's *Lilith*, "poverty was an offence! Deformity and sickness were taxed; and no legislation of their princes was more heartily approved of than that which tended to make poverty subserve wealth."

The fact that the central belt of hitherto agrarian Scotland, within two generations, had been turned into a vast industrial machine, robbing the earth of its ancient minerals to provide the Empire with cheap manufactured goods and the captains of industry with fortunes based on the exploitation of cheap labour, much of it produced by the Irish potato-famines, could hardly be guessed at in the novels of the period. Since the simplest way for middle and upper-class consciences to soothe themselves was either to pretend that slums did not exist, or that the plight of only the "undeserving" poor was not susceptible to the condescending dispensation of charity, it is hardly surprising that Scotland produced no *Shirley*, no *Oliver Twist*.

The contemporary image of Scotland presented by later nineteenth-century novelists is thus primarily a rural one, the dominating influence that of the minister. To some extent the crippling grasp of the church on the imagination and on society which Hume, Burns and others had prized loose in the eighteenth century, was able to close tight again because of an infusion of new theological strength. The Disruption of 1843 brought out many of the best minds of the Church of Scotland, led by Thomas Chalmers (1780–1847), over questions concerning patronage and the relations between Church and State. On a lesser and more peaceful scale, it was to be the agony of the Reformation and the Covenanting troubles all over again with, as on these earlier occasions, the descendants of the Free Kirk reformers growing narrower and narrower in their dogmas, until science and social change began gradually to dislodge religion itself from the built-in position it had held for so long in all walks of Scottish life.

With the minor exception of an interesting novel by Sarah Tytler (1827–1914), *St Mungo's City*, which presents some vivid detail of the working of Glasgow's textile industry, no novelist cared to look closely at the human basis on which the growing middle-class prosperity of most of the characters in the novels of Oliphant and Black depended. Instead, there was a surge of escapism, in two directions. One led straight into the hypocritical but profitable climate of the village garden, the hand of the minister never far from the welcoming gate. The other pursued the ghost of Scott into the colourful historic past; a static past, however, about which his latter-day disciples saw fit to romance without displaying his awareness that the unromantic industrial present was here to stay.

Since the leading purveyor of romantic fiction was for long regarded as the third glittering stone in Scotland's literary crown—along with Burns and Scott—and since he is still unquestionably, and rightly, regarded as a great writer, even if his reputation has been filed down and re-set in a less prominent position, let us begin with a novelist whom ill-health helped turn into an escapist.

Robert Louis Balfour Stevenson (1850–1894)—pronounced Lewis—was born in Edinburgh. Both his father and grandfather were lighthouse builders. It was first intended that the boy should follow the family tradition, but a lung weakness made a career so strenuous impossible. After passing through the Academy and University of his native city, he therefore studied law, being called to the Scottish Bar in 1875. By then, he had already decided that his main interest lay with literature, and he had begun to contribute to various periodicals of the day. His first book, *An Island Voyage* (1878), describes a journey through France by canoe, while a later overland trip is charmingly and amusingly recounted in *Travels with a Donkey in the Cevennes* (1879). In France, he met and fell in love with Fanny Osbourne, separated from her husband, ten years Stevenson's senior, and the mother of a son, Lloyd Osbourne, with whom Stevenson later collaborated in the farcical tale *The Wrong Box* (1889) and the lurid story *The Wrecker* (1892). In 1879, a penniless Stevenson sailed to America on an emigrant ship, and in July 1880 married the now-divorced Mrs Osbourne in California. These first days together in a desolate mining camp formed the theme of *The Silverado Squatters* (1883). In Edinburgh again, the climate proved too much for his health, so they moved to Davos, where he remained till 1881, the year of *Virginibus Puerisque*.

Once more in Scotland for the summer months, Stevenson began writing *The Sea-Cook*, soon to be re-named *Treasure Island* (1883), which first appeared as a magazine serial. Wintering in Davos built up his health, but even in summer, the Scottish winds proved too much for his delicate lungs. So he moved to Switzerland, and then to the Riviera, where he wrote another boys' story, *The Black Arrow* (1888), and the greater part of *A Child's Garden of Verse* (1885). From 1884 to 1887 he lived mostly in Bournemouth. *Kidnapped* appeared in 1886, though its successor, *Catriona*;* was not published until 1893. By then, Stevenson had left Europe for good. He sailed from London for New York in August 1887.

After a voyage on the *Casco*, which took the Stevensons to Honolulu, where *The Master of Ballantrae* was finished, its author never again left the waters of the Pacific. He landed in Samoa around October 1889, and, except for a visit to Sydney, Australia, where in 1890, following a visit to the leper settlement of Molokai, he published the indignant *Father Damien: an Open Letter to the Rev Dr Hyde of Honolulu*, Stevenson spent the last four years of his life there, interesting himself energetically in local affairs, writing his *Island Nights' Entertainment* (1893), *The Ebb Tide* (1894), and beginning *St Ives* (completed by Quiller-Couch) and his unfinished masterpiece, *Weir of Hermiston*.

Talking gaily on the verandah of his house at Vailima on 3rd December 1894, just after he had fetched a bottle of wine from his cellar, he suffered an apopleptic stroke, and died a few hours later. His body was borne by six Samoans, who had come to regard their "Tusitala", or teller of tales, as their chief, to the summit of the almost inaccessible mountain of Vaea, where he lies with the Pacific at his feet.

Stevenson became a popular writer with the appearance of his boys' tale *Treasure Island*. It is by any standards a masterly piece of story-telling, cleverly constructed, vividly drawn, and grasping the reader's attention from beginning to end. It does seem to be claiming a lot for it, though, when Daiches, taking an adult viewpoint, asserts that: ". . . what we admire is not always what we approve of; energy of personality belongs to Long John Silver and not to any conventional hero; and the virtuous are saved in the end almost contemptuously by luck and an irresponsible boy who does not quite know what he is doing. Thus even in a boys' story Stevenson showed something of that interest in ambiguities which he inherited from his Calvinist forebears. . ."

The trick of making the virtuous triumph in this manner is one beloved of innumerable authors—for instance, W. S. Gilbert, who had no Calvinist ancestors!—simply as a useful suspense-stretcher.

The Black Arrow, Stevenson's next boys' story, is less compelling, though

* Originally titled in America *David Balfour*.

far from being the piece of mere "tushery" he himself thought it, inventing the word to define the false jargon usually to be found in historical novels set in medieval times. Like everything Stevenson wrote, it is eminently readable, yet it does not create that sense of atmosphere which makes the reader feel like a participant, and which is one of the qualities raising *Kidnapped* somewhat beyond the level of expert fabling for the young.

Of course, the desire to provide adventure at boys' level was no doubt the prime intention in *Kidnapped*: the aftermath of Jacobitism and the affair of the Red Fox simply the historical spring-board for the chase over Kinlochrannoch, the excitement of the incident of Breck and Balfour on the rock with the searching redcoats everywhere beneath, the fight in the round house aboard the brig *Covenant*, the secret signs, the wicked uncle and the duping of David Balfour aboard the rascally Captain Hoseason's ship at Queensferry. All this, at one level, is kids' stuff. At least it is supremely good of its kind, the action fast-moving, the historical detail accurate enough to satisfy even Scott's requirements, and the evocation of Scottish scenery sharply drawn. Balfour is a Scott-like hero, drawn into northern loyalties of which he does not approve; forced all but to compromise himself in their cause, yet in the end to come down on the side of modernism, leaving part of his affections with the lost cause.

The tension that holds the book together is provided by the constant clash of loyalties, an age-old Scottish dilemma: that of the young Whig David Balfour for his romantic Jacobite friend, Alan Breck; that of the clansmen for Breck himself; that of Macpherson to his clan; that of Breck for the King over the water; and that of the people of a country living under English troops for the cause they still believed in. Breck and Balfour are both moderately well drawn in the context of their adventures, and so is the Scrooge-like, eccentric miserly Uncle Ebenezer. The style throughout is mellifluous, Stevenson's instinctive ability to balance vocables within a period, and periods within a sentence, honed to suit the demands of fast action. The book thus to some extent escapes the charge of being "mannered"—the style counting far more than the content—commonly applied to his earlier books, and to *Catriona*, which suffers not only from less vigorous action, but from its author's inability almost to the end of his life to create convincingly the character of a young woman.

It is difficult to believe that *Treasure Island*, *Kidnapped* and *Catriona* will lose their appeal for children; or that Stevenson's other tales and travel-books will cease to give pleasure to those who, in an age largely given over to sloppy journalism and the clichéd dialoguing of television soap-opera, still take delight in fastidious expression.

Yet Stevenson's reputation as a great writer rests not on these things, but on four or five other works: *Dr Jekyll and Mr Hyde* (1886), that macabre tale based on the double day-and-night life of the notorious Deacon Brodie, and an excursion into the darker reaches of the Calvinist psyche; the fine Scots study in the exercise of the powers of darkness that is "Thrawn Janet" (from *The Merry Men* 1889), a miniature forerunner to Stevenson's master-piece *Weir of Hermiston*; another story, the powerfully told "The Beach of Falesa", from *Island Nights' Entertainment*; and his two late novels, *The Master of Ballantrae* (1889) and the posthumously published *Weir of Hermiston*.

On the face of it, *The Master of Ballantrae* is yet another exercise in the swashbuckling vein of his earlier Scottish romances. Yet it is more than that; more even than the "pure hard crystal", the "work of ineffable and exquisite art" Henry James[29] pronounced it to be. For all its inequalities, and its thoroughly unsatisfactory ending—a fault to which its author ad-mitted—it marks Stevenson's first success in the creating of character for its own sake, rather than the provision of characters who depend upon the action that involves them to give them their dimensions. The Durie bro-thers are interesting for what they are rather than for what they do. Alison Graeme, later Mrs Henry Durie, is in many ways Stevenson's first reason-ably convincing woman. There is the cleverly handled device of triple nar-rative. Stevenson edits the papers of the loyal Land Steward but dry-as-dust Epraim Mackellar—himself to become the most rounded character in the book—then has the Chevalier Burke (modelled on Thackeray's Barry Lyndon) fill in Mackellar with the Master's Indian experiences, thereby enabling Stevenson to get "into India and out of it again upon a foot of fairy lightness", as he himself put it[30] and also to vary the charac-ter-perspectives; then finally, Mackellar's paraphrases, duly correcting as he goes along, of the reports of Mountain and Secundra Das. The fact that all three narrators are biased in different ways provides a kind of verisimil-tude with the confusion of daily life, which rarely allows three people who have witnessed even the same single incident to report it in terms that exactly correspond.

Good though the best things in *The Master of Ballantrae* are, not least being their evocation of Scottish scenery and weather, *Weir of Hermiston* is an enormous leap forward. Based on the life-story of the "hanging judge", Lord Braxfield, *Weir*'s confrontation with his more sensitive but weaker son after a courtroom scene in which a man is condemned to be hanged, is one of the great moments in Scottish fiction:

My lord, after hanging up his cloak and hat, turned round in the lighted entry, and made him an imperative and silent gesture with his thumb, and with the strange instinct of obedience, Archie followed him into the house. . . .

The lamp was shaded, the fire trimmed to a nicety, the table covered deep with orderly documents, the backs of law books made a frame upon all sides that was only broken by the window and the doors.

For a moment Hermiston warmed his hands at the fire, presenting his back to Archie; then suddenly disclosed on him the terrors of the Hanging Face.

"What's this I hear of ye?" he asked.

There was no answer possible to Archie.

"I'll have to tell ye, then," pursued Hermiston. "It seems ye've been skirling against the father that begot ye, and one of his Maijesty's Judges in this land; and that in the public street, and while an order of the Court was being executit. Forbye which, it would appear that ye've been airing your opeenions in a Coallege Debatin' Society"; he paused a moment: and then, with extraordinary bitterness, added: "Ye damned eediot."

"I had meant to tell you," stammered Archie. "I see you are well informed."

"Muckle obleeged to ye," said his lordship, and took his usual seat. "And so you disapprove of Caapital Punishment?" he added.

"I am sorry, sir, I do," said Archie.

"I am sorry, too," said his lordship. "And now, if you please, we shall approach this business with a little more parteecularity. I hear that at the hanging of Duncan Jopp—and, man! ye had a fine client there—in the middle of all the riff-raff of the ceety, ye thought fit to cry out, "This is a damned murder, and my gorge rises at the man that haangit him.""

"No, sir, these were not my words," cried Archie.

"What were yer words, then?" asked the Judge.

"I believe I said, "I denounce it as a murder!" said the son. "I beg your pardon—a God-defying murder. I have no wish to conceal the truth," he added, and looked his father for a moment in the face.

"God, it would only need that of it next!" cried Hermiston. "There was nothing about your gorge rising, then?"

"That was afterwards, my lord, as I was leaving the Speculative. I said I had been to see the miserable creature hanged, and my gorge rose at it."

"Did ye, though?" said Hermiston. "And I suppose ye knew who haangit him?"

"I was present at the trial, I ought to tell you that, I ought to explain. I ask your pardon beforehand for any expression that may seem undutiful. The position in which I stand is wretched," said the unhappy hero, now fairly face to face with the business he had chosen. "I have been reading some of your cases. I was present while Jopp was tried. It was a hideous business. Father, it was a hideous thing! Grant he was vile, why should you hunt him with a vileness equal to his own? It was done with glee—that is the word—you did it with glee; and I looked on, God help me! with horror."

"You're a young gentleman that doesna approve of Caapital Punishment," said Hermiston. "Weel, I'm an auld man that does. I was glad to get Jopp haangit, and what for would I pretend I wasna? You're all for honesty, it seems; you couldn't even steik your mouth on the public street. What for should I steik mines upon the bench, the King's officer, bearing the sword, a dreid to evil-doers, as I was from the beginning, and as I will be to the end! Mair than enough of it! Heedious! I never gave twa thoughts to heediousness, I have no call to be bonny. I'm a man that gets through with my day's business, and let that suffice."

The ring of sarcasm had died out of his voice as he went on; the plain words became invested with some of the dignity of the Justice-seat.

"It would be telling you if you could say as much," the speaker resumed. "But ye cannot. Ye've been reading some of my cases, ye say. But it was not for the law in them, it was to spy out your faither's nakedness, a fine employment in a son. You're splairging; you're running at lairge in life like a wild nowt. It's impossible you should think any longer of coming to the Bar. You're not fit for it; no splairger is. And another thing: son of mines or no son of mines, you have flung fylement in public on one of the Senators of the Coallege of Justice, and I would make it my business to see that you were never admitted there yourself. There is a kind of a decency to be observit. Then comes the next of it—what am I to do with ye next? Ye'll have to find some kind of a trade, for I'll never support ye in idleset. What do ye fancy ye'll be fit for? The pulpit? Na, they could never get diveenity into that blockhead. Him that the law of man whammles is no likely to do mauckle better by the law of God. What would ye make of hell? Wouldna your gorge rise at that? Na, there's no room for splaigers under the fower quarters of John Calvin. What else is there? Speak up. Have ye got nothing of your own?"

"Father, let me go to the Peninsula," said Archie. "That's all I'm fit for— to fight."

"All? quo' he!" returned the Judge. "And it would be enough too, if I thought it. But I'll never trust ye so near the French, you that's so Frenchifeed."

"You do me injustice there, sir," said Archie. "I am loyal; I will not boast; but any interest I may have ever felt in the French—"

"Have ye been so loyal to me?" interrupted his father.

There came no reply.

"I think not," continued Hermiston. "And I would send no man to be a servant to the King, God bless him! that has proved such a shauchling son to his own faither. You can splairge here on Edinburgh street, and where's the hairm? It doesna play buff on me! And if there were twenty thousand eediots like yourself, sorrow a Duncan Jopp would hang the fewer. But there's no splairging possible in a camp; and if you were to go to it, you would find out for yourself whether Lord Well'n'ton approves of caapital punishment or not. You a sodger!" he cried, with a sudden burst of scorn. "Ye auld wife, the sodgers would bray at ye like cuddies!"

As at the drawing of a curtain, Archie was aware of some illogicality in his position, and stood abashed. He had a strong impression, besides, of the essential valour of the old gentleman before him, how conveyed it would be hard to say.

"Well, have ye no other proposeetion?" said my lord again.

"You have taken this so calmly, sir, that I cannot but stand ashamed." began Archie.

"I'm nearer voamiting, though, than you would fancy," said my lord.

The blood rose to Archie's brow.

"I beg your pardon, I should have said that you had accepted my affront . . ." I admit it was an affront; I did not think to apologise, but I do, I ask your pardon; it will not be so again, I pass you my word of honour. . . . I should have said that I admired your magnanimity with—this—offender," Archie concluded with a gulp.

"I have no other son, ye see," said Hermiston. "A bonny one I have gotten! But I must just do the best I can wi' him, and what am I to do? If ye had been younger, I would have wheepit ye for this rideeculous exhibeetion. The way it is, I have just to grin and bear. But one thing is to be clearly understood. As a faither, I must grin and bear it; but if I had been the Lord Advocate instead of the Lord Justice-Clerk, son or no son, Mr Erchibald Weir would have been in a jyle the night."

Archie was now dominated. Lord Hermiston was coarse and cruel; and yet the son was aware of a bloomless nobility, an ungracious abnegation of the man's self in the man's office. At every word, this sense of the greatness of Lord Hermiston's spirit struck more home; and along with it that of his own impotence, who had struck—and perhaps basely struck—at his own father, and not reached so far as to have even nettled him.

"I place myself in your hands without reserve," he said.

"That's the first sensible word I've had of ye the night," said Hermiston. "I can tell ye, that would have been the end of it, the one way or the other; but it's better ye should come there yourself, than what I would have had to hirstle ye. Weel, by my way of it—and my way is the best—there's just the one thing it's possible that ye might be with decency, and that's a laird. Ye'll be out of hairm's way at the least of it. If ye have to rowt, ye can rowt amang the kye; and the maist feck of the caapital punishment ye'll like to come across'll be guddling trouts. Now, I'm for no idle lairdies; every man has to work, if it's only at peddling ballants; to work, or to be wheeped, or to be haangit. If I set ye down at Hermiston, I'll have to see you work that place the way it has never been workit yet; ye must ken about the sheep like a herd; ye must be my grieve there, and I'll see that I gain by ye. Is that understood?"

"I will do my best." said Archie.

"Well, then, I'll send Kirstie word the morn, and ye can go yourself the day after," said Hermiston. "And just try to be less of an eediot!" he concluded, with a freezing smile, and turned immediately to the papers on his desk.

The central characters apart, the complete success of the two Kirsties, aunt and niece, the free and frequent handling of Scots and the telling economy of the writing combine to make the unfinished torso indisputably a masterpiece. Only the character of Archie's false friend, Frank Innes, is perhaps a trifle glib. But such people do exist.

Here, at last, the Stevenson whose wit and charm won him early and continuous popularity on both sides of the Atlantic, touched the well-springs of Scots character as no one had quite done before him. *Weir of Hermiston* tells itself almost with a ballad-like intensity.

With a puzzled girl weeping on his shoulder, Archie Weir's reflective words were the last Stevenson wrote, an hour or two before he died: "It seemed unprovoked, a wilful convulsion of brute nature".

There are two versions of how the book might have ended, one given by Stevenson's stepdaughter and amanuensis, Mrs Strong; the other by Sydney Lysaght, a visitor with whom Stevenson discussed his intentions in the spring of 1894. According to Lysaght, Archie's friend, Frank Innes, seduces Kirstie, and is murdered by Archie at the Weaver's Stone. Others are suspected, and brought to trial before Hermiston, the Lord Justice-Clerk. It becomes plain that the evidence points to Archie as the murderer, and the father orders the son's arrest. Kirstie's four blood-brothers plan revenge on Archie by taking justice into their own hands. The elder Kirstie, however, at last learns the truth from her niece, so the brothers, with some supporters, help Archie break jail, and arrange for Archie and Kirstie to escape to America. But Old Hermiston, thinking that by doing his duty he has brought his own son to the front of the gallows, dies.

Would Stevenson have fudged it, as he did the ending of *The Master of Ballantrae*, and as these notes suggest he might have done again? Like Schubert's "Unfinished" Symphony, Stevenson's *Weir of Hermiston* is better accepted for the rugged, unforgettable fragment it is. Imaginatively, it implies its own completeness.

Escapism of a milder variety was practised in prose, and to some extent also in verse, by William Sharp (1855–1914), the son of a Paisley merchant and a product of Glasgow Academy and Glasgow University. After an abortive start in life in a lawyer's office, he turned to journalism, becoming art critic of the *Glasgow Herald*. While on a visit to Rome in 1890, he "produced" a lady called "Fiona Macleod", whose biography he eventually provided for *Who's Who*. Before "she" had achieved such fortuitous eminence, the lady had had visions of old Celtic paganism, and had set them down in jewel-studded prose: *Pharais, a Romance of the Isles* (1893), *The Mountain Lovers* (1895), *The Washer of the Ford* (1896), probably the best of them, *Winged Destiny* (1904), and *The Immortal Hour* (1908), which Rutland Boughton made into an opera, the "Fairy Song" from which retains its popularity. The prose style resembles that of an up-dated "Ossian" Macpherson, the pagan creatures that people the books so absurdly naïve that it is small wonder they disappeared forever into their clouds and mountains without trace.

1890 was, of course, the official opening of the "Naughty Nineties", when even Yeats went a-fairy-mongering. But the most conspicuous Scot in the *fin de siècle* decade had no truck with fairies.

Being written at about the same time as Stevenson's novels, John Davidson's fiction, though in essence the obverse of Kailyardism, suffers from the same fault of basic careless under-revision as his poetry. In his prose, his fondness for extravagant, ironic humour is given freer rein than in the poems or, with the exception of *Scaramouch in Naxos*, the dramas.

The North Wall (1885) dates from his spell as a clerk in a Glasgow thread factory, between periods of study, and satirizes the Spasmodics' romantic belief that only an extraordinary, shocking experience provides a valid basis for art. Yet he himself was as "spasmodical" as any of them, his successes greater only because he wrote more, and because his impossible desire to establish a scientific philosophy which rejected the traditions of the past forced him to attempt more serious thinking than either Smith or the English Spasmodics Bailey and Dobell attempted. *The North Wall* was republished in England as "A Practical Novelist" in *The Great Men* (1891), along with some other short stories.

His first novelette develops the theme of the story-teller who contrives his own situations. Maxwell Lee, the hero, explains: "I am going to create a novel. Practical joking is the new novel in its infancy. The end of every thought is an action. We stand upon the threshold of that age, and I am destined to open the door." It is an original and diverting tale, already suffering, however, from Davidson's prevailing defect as a writer of fiction—an inability to avoid making each of his thinking characters sound unmistakably like the "voice" of John Davidson.

The Career of Ninian Jamieson appeared in (1890). It, too, has its touches of wry humour, as when Jamieson, the Provost of Mintern, alleged discoverer of a new process of making diamonds, and an example of what J. Benjamin Townsend[31] calls one of Davidson's "madcap heroes each with an *idée fixe*", meets up in a train with the equally capricious Hugh Smith. He has changed his name to Cosmo Mortimer, believing this to be a "great" name, and the bearing of such nomenclature essential to the achievement of "greatness". Unaware that he is talking to Provost Jamieson, whose exploits are reported in the newspaper that Smith/Mortimer is reading, his travelling companion is asked:

"Do you know this Ninian Jamieson? . . ."

"I know him well."

"You do! Then," said the little man, pointing to the newspaper "how can you reconcile the fact of his being a great man with the fact that he is a provost? . . . Sir, there is something incompatible between greatness and the provostship of a Scottish burgh. Take my word for it, men are born to be provosts just as they are born to be great; and just as great men are born with great names, so those men who are intended for provosts are born with names that have the true municipal ring."

Off that perhaps comes a distant whiff of Galt, and clearly, Davidson had read in Stevenson's essay on "The English Admirals" that: "most men of high destiny have high-sounding names". The adventures which follow in Davidson's story savour rather of Peacock. Jamieson attempts to will himself King of Scotland, only to be rescued from the inevitable bankruptcy and disgrace by the heroine, Marjory, who marries him on being informed that, in despair, he has burned the papers providing evidence that he is the direct Stuart descendant. His fellow fantasist and supporter, Smith/Mortimer, steals away from the embracing lovers, muttering: "It is this love that spoils greatness and eccentricity".

Laura Ruthven's Widowhood (1892), written in collaboration with C. J. Wills, reflects a well-known variant of the Scots dichotomy. Its hero, Alexander Murdoch, alias the "Englishman" Leonard Brandon, finds his early acting career hampered by his Scottish name and accent, and alters his life accordingly. Written so soon after Davidson's own arrival in London, it may well have an autobiographical element in it.

Baptist Lake (1894) satirizes extravagant gestures, whether by aesthetes or by aristocrats, and the artificiality of the popular rural fiction of the Nineties. In Mrs Tiplady, banished "Master Baptist's" barwoman accomplice, who extracts more and more money than she hands over from Baptist's father, Sir Henry Lake, Davidson creates his most rounded character. There is an amusing play of contrast between the Scots accent of Baptist's landlady, Mrs Macalister, and Mrs Tiplady's maid, Florrie; as when Florrie, come to deliver a Sunday invitation, remarks to the pious Mrs Macalister on the fineness of the weather:

> "Yes", said Mrs Macalister, who when she liked, could speak what she called English, "it is fyne. But I wonduh sometymes if God is not afryed to send sech lovelly weathuh to tempt people into bryekingg His Holy Dye!"
> "Ow bootiful!" exclaimed Florrie, "You talk like a duchess and a harch-bishop all in one, you do."
> "If some people," retorted Mrs Macalister, "would think maur of their own speakingg and less of others, they might learun in course of tyme that aitch belongs to some words and not to others. . . ."

A Full and True Account of the Wonderful Mission of Earl Lavender Which Lasted One Night and One Day: With a History of the Pursuit of Earl Lavender and Lord Brumm by Mrs Scawler and Maud Emblem (1895), to give the book its fulsome title, shows Davidson as the uneasy participator in the very *fin de siècle* decadence his story satirizes. The "madcap" impoverished hero's true name, like that of his henchman, is J. Smith. The two become, respectively, Earl Lavender, the prophet of the new doctrine of Evolution, and Lord Brumm, a Leporello-like follower who enjoys his master's ability to coax unpaid-for food and accommodation out of people in the name of Evolution, the new religion, yet is continually fearful of the more probable common-sense consequences. The fantasy abounds in wry and alert turns of phrase, but in the satirical flagellation scenes the description of the practice of this sexual perversion is just a little too lingering for the author's humorous detachment to be successfully sustained. The references to whipping in Davidson's other novels and tales (notably in "The Schoolboy's Tragedy") confirm this ambivalence. The book carries as frontispiece a birching scene by Aubrey Beardsley. It also bears a quotation from Gower's "Confessio Amantis"—

. . . I undertoke
. . . to make a boke
Which stant between ernest and game—

a difficult stance for a minor writer to sustain.

Miss Armstrong's and Other Circumstances (1896) and *The Pilgrimage of Strongsoul* (1897) are mostly reprints of earlier stories. The title-story of the final prose work goes back to 1890, where the impact of *The Pilgrim's Progress* on a churchman's son is sensitively if somewhat whimsically described.

Davidson's fiction is healthier and more forward-looking than Barrie's or Maclaren's. Davidson's many passages of Scots dialogue are authentic, and indeed few of his novels fail to reveal the nationality of the author. Yet his failure to stand outside himself consistently, the overall weakness of his plots, the artificial absurdity of some of his scenes, and the recurring expression of his teutonic belief in hero-worship (not to say the mating of the fittest man with fittest woman) must militate against the likelihood of any serious revival of his novels. Yet, though flawed, they have their interest. While their links with the *fin de siècle* brittle picaresqueness of Beerbohm, Wells and Chesterton is obvious enough, at least in the humorous purpose of Davidson's satire he seems also to point forward to the more successful socially orientated satire of Orwell, Aldous Huxley (like Davidson a poor creator of character) and Evelyn Waugh.

The two novelists most influenced by Stevenson were Neil Munro (1864–1930) and John Buchan, first Baron Tweedsmuir (1875–1940). Munro, a Highlander brought up within hail of Inverary Castle, dealt largely with the lesser affairs of Highland history, as in his tale *The Lost Pibroch* (1896), the gracefully written *John Splendid* (1898), *Gilian the Dreamer* (1899) and *Doom Castle* (1901). He had the ability to keep a romantic story on the move, though with an altogether more slender technical equipment than that at Stevenson's command. Munro was even worse than Stevenson at creating female characters, Munro's women being verbal wraiths. As a result, his presentation of Highland society as a whole is unbalanced.

His major success was scored with his Para Handy tales, beginning with *The Vital Spark* (1906). In these stories, as in *The Daft Days* (1907) and *Ayrshire Idylls* (1912), we are once more invited to applaud the tradition of the simple Scot as a figure of fun.

Buchan's range was wider, but he lacked Munro's artistic conscience. A new book a year and cheap reprints of earlier works were a life-long part of his budgeting.

His novels fall into several categories. He became a historical novelist with *John Burnet of Barns* (1898), a tale set firmly in the Border country of its author's upbringing, lovingly described and featured. In Stevensonian style, it tells of the wanderings of a youthful seventeenth-century hero caught up with Covenanters and gypsies. Burnet himself is modelled on Alan Breck Stewart, the book, even down to some of the chapter-headings—"How I ride to the South", "I Fall in with Strange Friends", "Of the Fight in the Moss of Biggar",—mainly on *Catriona*.

Later historical novels included *The Path of the King* (1921) which tells of the "tragically fated" Lovells, and another novel probing history's shadows, *Midwinter* (1923). Set in Oxfordshire, it is an interesting attempt to fill in the "missing" years in Boswell's knowledge of Johnson's life, 1745–1746. *Witch Wood* (1927), Buchan's own favourite, is a study of religious intolerance and extravagance, in which Montrose makes an appearance.

Buchan achieved wide popular acclaim, however, with his adventure stories or "shockers", as he called them. The best-known are the tales involving the escapades of Richard Hannay. These include *The Thirty-Nine Steps* (1915), where the chase across Kinlochrannoch in *Kidnapped* is emulated, *Greenmantle* (1916), *Mr Standfast* (1919) and *The Island of Sheep* (1936).

Another common-sense hero, Dickson McCunn, presents himself in *Huntingtower* (1922) and tramps over hills and through adventures in places as far apart as Glasgow's Gorbals and the imaginary central European county of Evallonia, before bowing out in *The House of the Four Winds* (1934).

In some ways the most interesting of Buchan's heros is Edward Leithen, whose full-length fictional appearance (after a try-out in a short story) was in the Highland poaching tale *John Macnab* (1925). Leithen survived to reflect something of Buchan's own emotional reserve in his final novel, *Sick Heart River*, where the now knighted but dying man gains courage over his fear of a crippling death, forgetting his plight by helping the Hare Indians.

Because of their fluency and sheer readability, the flaws in Buchan's novels seem especially exasperating. Few of his characters are wholly convincing, and many are positively grotesque. They are regularly involved in adventure for adventure's sake, as if life were a protracted affair of dangerous sport. Worst of all, they often appear to uphold values which are trivial, if not downright objectionable outside the boundaries of romancing. Too often, Buchan's approach to fiction is that of a confident fellow in a decidedly exclusive gentleman's club yarning over a post-prandial drink to a group of fellow-members.

Yet for Buchan, a barrister who became politician, statesman, and finally, Governor General of Canada, writing was only one facet of a long and successful life. His autobiography *Memory Hold-the-Door* (1940) lets in a fascinating slant of light upon the public man, if little on the private man

of the shadows whose habitual reserve, even in high places, seemed to
many of his contempories merely a Scottish characteristic. For all his vast
output I have no doubt that two in particular of his several biographical
studies—*Montrose* (1928) and *Sir Walter Scott* (1932)—stylish in presentation, warm and perceptive in their sympathies, make up the really significant part of his contribution to our literature.

Probably there is never likely to be an end to the writing of historical
novels. With Buchan, however, the last connection between the *genre* and
anything that might reasonably be considered as literature, was severed.
What has followed since has been, in more than the Stevensonian sense,
the merest slap-dash commercial tushery.

Those who chose to avoid history and seek their escape through the cabbage-patch, rather than face the realities of industrial Scotland, indulged in
both tushery and mushery. Their high priest was Sir William Robertson
Nicoll, C. H. (1851–1923), like Buchan a son of the manse, but essentially
an exploiter of the talents of others. After a spell as a Free Church minister,
first at Dufftown, Banffshire, and then at Kelso, in the Borders, Nicoll
went to London and, at the age of thirty-five, launched himself into a
journalistic career. Before long, he was editing a monthly theological journal, the *Expositor*, and in 1886 he produced the first number of the *British
Weekly*, a publication intended to be a beacon of enlightenment to the
faithful of the Free Kirk. Dogma, whether that of Catholicism, the Free
Kirk, or Karl Marx, has to be fostered on a carefully chosen diet if those
who have a vested interest in its survival are to achieve their ends. It was in
both the commercial and the religious interests of Nicoll to provide pabu-
lum which would keep alive the myth of the Scotland of kindly villages
inhabited by drooling sentimentalists begotten on a prayer of sweetened
water, and presided over by the hovering father-figure of the local minister.

Four writers upheld the cult of Kailyard fiction, the cult which Nicoll
cultivated so assiduously and profitably. The first to get herself established
on the scene was an Edinburgh-born farmer's daughter, who wrote under
her married name, Annie S. Swan (1859–1943). Her early novels were tales
of middle-class manners, in the tradition of Mrs Oliphant: notably
Aldersyde (1883) and *Carlowrie* (1884). Soon, however, she turned to the
harmless production of stereotyped material for Nicoll's publications, and
later, also for others.

Nicoll's next recruit was the Reverend John Watson D. D. (1850–1907),
born at Manningtree, Essex, the son of a Scottish civil servant, and educated
at Stirling High School and Edinburgh University. Although he was
intended to be a lawyer, he eventually studied divinity, and was in due
course given the charge of the Free Kirk at Logiealmond, Perthshire,
which provided the basis for the village of "Drumtochty" in the stories he
wrote under the pseudonym of "Ian Maclaren". Before he took to the pen,
he had held a church in Glasgow and had moved to the fashionable and

wealthy Liverpool church at Sefton Park, a developing suburb of that sea-port, which housed a large Scots colony.

Nicoll talked Watson into "commencing author", and within a year of the first Drumtochty sketch appearing in the *British Weekly*, a collection of them had been loosely put together in book form under the title *Beside the Bonnie Brier Bush* (1894), to be followed by *The Days of Auld Lang Syne* (1895), *Kate Carnegie and Those Ministers* (1897) and several others. Two lecture tours of America followed, one of which netted Watson a hand-some profit of over £7,000. Meanwhile, he retained his charge. On a third American tour, he contracted a throat infection and died, it is said, from overwork.

In Maclaren's work, cap-touching rustics indulge in lengthy exchanges in Scots on topics of the utmost triviality, supposedly showing the shrewd-ness and pawkiness attributed to that peculiar Scots commodity, "wut". The stories are foolish, the style abominable. The sad fact is that the literary labours of this sincere and energetic churchman are simply not worth serious study.

Nor is most of what was produced by that other Nicoll Kailyarder, Samuel Rutherford Crockett (1860–1914), who was born at Little Duchrae, Kirkcudbrightshire, the bastard son of a Galloway farmer. After attending Edinburgh University and then New College, he became Free Church minister at Penicuik, Midlothian. His book of sketches *The Stickit Minister* (1893)—one who has passed his examinations, but fails to get a "call" to a charge—was well received. These tales show clearly that, unlike Watson, Crockett did have some talent for writing. He dedicated the book to Stevenson, who had encouraged Crockett, and Stevenson ac-knowledged the dedication with one of the loveliest of all his poems, that beginning:

Blows the wind to-day, and the sun and the rain are flying . . .

For that, Crockett might almost be forgiven *The Lilac Sunbonnet* (1894), a whimsical love-story which is as sickly as it is totally incredible, and which marks the lowest sinking point reached by any widely read Scottish novel-ist believed by many to be a serious practitioner.

Crockett would scarcely be worth mentioning but for another novel produced in the same year, *The Raiders*, a tale of smugglers on the Solway Coast firmly in the Stevenson vein. Its dialogue has an awkwardness which the greater writer would never have permitted, and it indulges in senti-mental turns of phrase more fitted for, if anywhere, the pulpit than a work of literature. Still, it survives, even if mc t of its readers now are probably schoolboys.

The success of these two books induced Crockett to give up his church and follow the career of letters. More than forty books followed, but only *The Men of the Moss Haggs* (1895) keeps even its title above the Kailyard quicksands of sentimentality.

By far the most able Kailyarder, also born in 1860, was Sir James Matthew Barrie, O.M. (1860–1937). The ninth child of a handloom weaver, he was born at Kirriemuir, the "Thrums" of his novels, and educated at Glasgow Academy, Dumfries Academy and Edinburgh University. Even as a boy he was determined to be a writer, and from his first job on the staff of the *Nottingham Journal* to his comparatively unsuccessful last play, *The Boy David* (1936), reputation, honour, and—in due course—wealth, came his way.

Yet what is one to say of novels which, basically, are merely a skilful extension of the sketch-fabric devised for publication in popular periodicals? *Auld Licht Idylls* (1888) combines the Kailyard practice of trite domestic Scots dialogue with the whimsy, the make-believe fantasy of evasion, that was to become Barrie's stock-in-trade. "The Courting of T'nowhead's Bell" is generally regarded not only as the best thing in the book, but (at least by Roger Lancelyn Green) as good enough to stand as one of only two stories in the anthology of Barrie's *Plays and Stories* which he edited in 1962.[32]

Sam'l and Sanders are after the same local beauty. When all her family turn up together at church one Sunday, both men realize that Bell would be alone at the farm.

It was at the end of the psalm which preceded the sermon that Sanders Elshioner, who sat near the door, lowered his head until it was no higher than the pews, and in that attitude, looking almost like a four-footed animal, slipped out of the church. In their eagerness to be at the sermon many of the congregation did not notice him, and those who did put the matter by in their minds for future investigation. Sam'l, however, could not take it so coolly. From his seat in the gallery he saw Sanders disappear, and his mind misgave him. With the true lover's instinct he understood it all. Sanders had been struck by the fine turnout in the T'nowhead pew. Bell was alone at the farm. What an opportunity to work one's way up to a proposal. T'nowhead was so overrun with children that such a chance seldom occurred, except on a Sabbath. Sanders, doubtless, was off to propose, and he, Sam'l, was left behind.

The suspense was terrible. Sam'l and Sanders had both known all along that Bell would take the first of the two who asked her. Even those who thought her proud admitted that she was modest. Bitterly the weaver repented having waited so long. Now it was too late. In ten minutes Sanders would at be T'nowhead; in an hour all would be over. Sam'l rose to his feet in a daze. His mother pulled him down by the coat-tail, and his father shook him, thinking he was walking in his sleep. He tottered past them, however, hurried up the aisle, which was so narrow that Dan'l Ross could only reach his seat by walking sideways, and was gone before the minister could do more than stop in the middle of a whirl and gape in horror after him.

A number of the congregation felt that day the advantage of sitting in the laft. What was a mystery to those downstairs was revealed to them. From the gallery windows they had a fine open view to the south; and as Sam'l took the common, which was a short cut through a steep ascent, to T'nowhead, he was never out of their line of vision. Sanders was not to be seen, but they guessed rightly the reason why. Thinking he had ample time, he had gone round by the main road to save his boots—perhaps a little scared by what was coming. Sam'l's design was to forestall him by taking the shorter path over the burn and up the commonty.

It was a race for a wife, and several onlookers in the gallery braved the minister's displeasure to see who won. Those who favoured Sam'l's suit exultingly saw him leap the stream, while the friends of Sanders fixed their eyes on the top of the common where it ran into the road. Sanders must come into sight there, and the one who reached this point first would get Bell.

As Auld Lichts do not walk abroad on the Sabbath, Sanders would probably not be delayed. The chances were in his favour. Had it been any other day in the week Sam'l might have run. So some of the congregation in the gallery were thinking, when suddenly they saw him bend low and then take to his heels. He had caught sight of Sanders's head bobbing over the hedge that separated the road from the common, and feared that Sanders might see him. The congregation who could crane their necks sufficiently saw a black object, which they guessed to be the carter's hat, crawling along the hedge-top. For a moment it was motionless, and then it shot ahead. The rivals had seen each other. It was now a hot race. Sam'l, dissembling no longer, clattered up the Common, becoming smaller and smaller to the onlookers as he neared the top. More than one person in the gallery almost rose to their feet in their excitement. Sam'l had it. No, Sanders was in front. Then the two figures disappeared from view. They seemed to run into each other at the top of the brae, and no one could say who was first. The congregation looked at one another. Some of them perspired. But the minister held on his course.

Sam'l had just been in time to cut Sanders out. It was the weaver's saving that Sanders saw this when his rival turned the corner; for Sam'l was sadly blown. Sanders took in the situation and gave in at once. The last hundred yards of the distance he covered at his leisure, and when he arrived at his destination he did not go in. It was a fine afternoon for the time of year, and he went round to have a look at the pig, about which T'nowhead was a little sinfully puffed up.

"Ay," said Sanders, digging his fingers critically into the grunting animal; "quite so."

"Grumph," said the pig, getting reluctantly to his feet.

"Ou ay; yes," said Sanders thoughtfully.

Then he sat down on the edge of the sty, and looked long and silently at an empty bucket. But whether his thoughts were of T'nowhead's Bell, whom he had lost for ever, or of the food the farmer fed his pig on, is not known.

"Lord preserve's! Are ye no at the kirk?" cried Bell, nearly dropping the baby as Sam'l broke into the room.

"Bell!" cried Sam'l.

Then T'nowhead's Bell knew that her houb had come.

"Sam'l," she faltered.

"Will ye hae's, Bell?" demanded Sam'l, glaring at her sheepishly.

"Ay," answered Bell.

Sam'l fell into a chair.

"Bring's a drink o' water, Bell," he said.

But Bell thought the occasion required milk, and there was none in the kitchen. She went out to the byre, still with the baby in her arms, and saw Sanders Elshioner sitting gloomily on the pigsty.

"Weel, Bell," said Sanders.

"I thocht ye'd been at the kirk, Sanders," said Bell.

Then there was a silence between them.

"Has Sam'l spiered ye, Bell?" asked Sanders stolidly.

"Ay," said Bell again, and this time there was a tear in her eye. Sanders was little better than an "orra man", and Sam'l was a weaver, and yet—But it was too late now. Sanders gave the pig a vicious poke with a stick and, when it had ceased to grunt, Bell was back in the kitchen. She had forgotten about the milk, however, and Sam'l only got water after all.

This is sorry enough caricature. Yet what follows is worse. Sam'l rues his engagement, and talks Sanders into marrying Bell instead.

A Window in Thrums (1889), based on the recollections of Barrie's mother, Margaret Ogilvy, of bygone Kirriemuir characters, no doubt stimulated Maclaren's Drumtochty reminiscences, and others of their kind. The stories of Thrums are better written. *Sentimental Tommy* (1896) is a study of the boyhood of a literary genius—guess who?—while *Tommy and Grizel* (1900) recounts the circumstances of the hero's failure to achieve maturity, and the consequent breakdown of his marriage. Barrie's own marriage, by then in difficulties, ended in divorce in 1909.

Nor is there much to be said for *The Little Minister* (1891), in which clever characterization does not compensate for an absurdly improbable plot, although when dramatized, it eventually reaped the author £80,000. Surprisingly, perhaps, it also won an encomium from the ailing, home-sick Stevenson, although he was aware of Barrie's faults, telling Henry James: "But Barrie is a beauty, the *Little Minister* and the *Window in Thrums* eh! stuff in that young man; but he must see and not be too funny. Genius in him, but there's a journalist at his elbow—there's the risk!"

The fey ghost story, "Farewell, Miss Julie Logan" (1931) is an attempt at the macabre rendered ridiculous by the negative character of the teller, the Reverend Adam Festeen, and by the absurdity of the fatal words that made him drop the beautiful phantasy of his thwarted sexuality in the river:

She said: "Kiss me first, Adam, in case you have to drop me." I kissed her. "Hold me closer." she said, "lest by some dread undoing you should let me slip." I held her closer. "Adam dear," she said, "it is this, I am a Papist." At that awful word I dropped her in the burn."

Worst of all, however, was *Margaret Ogilvy and Her Son* (1896), like all the others deftly written, and so appealing to popular taste on both sides of the Atlantic that it sold by the thousand. Not everyone who had succumbed in youth to a mother-fixation complex would care to avenge himself on his parent immediately after her death by portraying her as a sentimental son-driver towards the great goal of success, and the wearerout of a dutiful daughter too decent to stand up for herself. Barrie could, and did.

It was inevitable that the reaction to all this slop, when it came, would be sharp and bitter. The critic J. H. Millar launched his anti-Kailyard attack in W. H. Henley's *New Review*, Volume 12 (May–June 1895), and followed it up at length and in more permanent form, in the concluding pages of his *Literary History of Scotland* (1903).

With more lasting effect, the bastard son of another farmer, this time from Ochiltree in Ayrshire, parodied the whole Kailyard cult. George Douglas Brown (1869–1902) left Ayr Academy to proceed to Glasgow University, and thence to Oxford, where he went to Balliol on a Snell Exhibition in 1891. His first major venture was a forthright essay on Burns, published in *Blackwood's*. *The House with the Green Shutters*, initially conceived as a long short story, first appeared in Britain and America in 1901.

The setting is Barbie, an alternative Drumtochty, where, instead of being sweet, everyone is unpleasant. As Walter Raleigh first pointed out, Barbie is as much a caricature of Scottish village life as any Kailyard village. Barbie is dominated, not by the minister, but by John Gourlay, a ruthless, forceful grain merchant and contractor. His green-shuttered house overlooks the village, and is the symbol of his domination.

Wilson, a Barbie man who has gained commercial experience in the wider world, returns to his native place and, being cleverer than Gourlay, soon begins to filch his business. The resulting rivalry is sharpened by Gourlay's insults. When Gourlay hears that Wilson's son is being sent to the University, nothing will do but that young John Gourlay, ill-fitted for higher education, must go too.

At Edinburgh, young John loses the place, is sent down for drunkenness. Drunk again, he confronts his father in a powerful scene reminiscent of the confrontation of Archie Weir and Lord Hermiston. Young Gourlay strikes his father with a poker. His father hits the fender in falling, and this is blamed for the accident. John's drinking problem increases. Finally, he poisons himself, leaving his mother and his consumptive sister to find enough dregs in the bottle to finish off their own lives.

There are some grounds for believing that the story might originally have been conceived as satire, if Brown's friend Andrew Melrose, in his somewhat sketchy introduction to the memorial edition of 1923, is to be believed. If that be so, then once under way, the book must have taken control of its author, for the narrative drive is strong and sustained, the "feel" of the gossipy side of life in a country town surprisingly telling, and the use made of the "bodies" of Barbie as a kind of "Greek Chorus" original and effective.

The character of old Gourlay may, indeed, be somewhat overdrawn; yet it embodies enough of the dour refuse of the Calvinistic spirit gone sour to make him credible. Given such an embodiment of the crudest kind of worthy success, the weakly young Gourlay is a pitifully true phenomenon.

It is, indeed, Brown's sense of pity for his victims that raises *The House with the Green Shutters* from its position as an interesting historical landmark to a great novel. Brown's anger, in the end, is turned not against the worthless target of the Free Kirk's fictional confectioners, but against that terrible human distortion for which their intolerant ministration over the centuries bore not a little responsibility.

There is nothing calculating about Brown's solitary masterpiece; no revelation of the author holding his fellow-countrymen up to ridicule for forgivable failings the literary exposure of which makes profits. For all its author's tendency to explain characters rather than let them unfold themselves, in *The House with the Green Shutters*, Brown successfully laid the guilty Knoxian ghost that Hogg and Lockhart had manfully tackled before him. In 1902, Douglas suffered a stroke of some kind, and died on 28th August, leaving behind only the tantalizing title of what might have been his next novel: *The Incompatibles*.

There is one outstanding novel which derives from Brown's book. It could well have carried such a title. It sets out to show, how, step by step, a man may use his fellows in a small community to achieve a dominant hold over them; psychologically, a very Scottish interest. The book is, in fact, named after its own anti-hero, Gillespie Strang.

Gillespie was the work of J. MacDougal Hay (1881–1919), almost an exact contemporary of Brown. Hay was born at Tarbert, Loch Fyne, in Argyll, the son of a steamship agent. After being schooled in Tarbert, he took an Arts degree at Glasgow University, and became a schoolmaster at Ullapool, where he developed a severe illness, probably rheumatic fever. The effects of this illness on his health led him to decide to give up schoolmastering and enter the Church. He therefore returned to Glasgow University, maintaining himself at Divinity Hall by free-lance journalism. After serving his time as a probationer at Morven, Agryll, he became assistant minister of Elderslie, Renfrewshire, the birthplace of Sir William Wallace. That same year, Hay married Catherine Campbell, the daughter of another minister. Their only son was to be George Campbell Hay, the poet.

Ministering at Elderslie involved repeatedly climbing up and down tenement stairs, which was not the best mode of life for a man weakened by rheumatic fever. It seems probable that *Gillespie* was begun in 1907, written for the most part late at night and apparently worked over several times. It was first published in 1914, widely acclaimed, then swept aside amid the ensuing tumult of war. Another novel, *Barnacles*, followed two years later. Part bitter-sweet kailyard, part horrifically melodramatic, its dialogue is more contrived than that of *Gillespie*, and it lacks the earlier novel's structural assurance.

Hay's third book, *Their Dead Sons*, was a volume of poems. It is couched in free verse not taut enough to hold the pieces together, but with a suggestion of Gaelic rhythms. Finally, a sermon commemorating the dead of the years of carnage was published a few weeks before the author's own death, on 10th December. According to Robert Kemp, who prefaced the reissued edition of *Gillespie* (1963), Hay had been thinking of giving up the ministry in order to devote all his time to writing, one project being a novel with a background of the Church of Scotland of his time, to be called *The Martyr*.

While it might be claimed that *Gillespie* could not have existed in its present form without the example of *The House with the Green Shutters*, which had appeared six years before Hay began writing, this is not to say that the later novel is in any sense mere pastiche. There are, however, several obvious surface parallels. The anti-hero of Barbie is old Gourlay, while the anti-hero of Hay's book is almost always referred to by his Christian name beginning with G, Gillespie. The rise and fall of Gillespie Strang, the trapper of rabbits whose ruthless determination leads him to become shop-owner, farmer, fleet-owner and local tycoon, but also trapped him into destroying his wife and two sons, takes place in Brieston. Brieston is easily identified as Tarbert, since there are references to a nearby place where there is a mental home, as there is at Lochgilphead, and to West Loch Brieston. A ladder is associated with Gourlay's death. A fall from a ladder marks the beginning of the murderous madness of Gillespie's younger son, Eaghon Strang, while a blow from a hammer plays a part in that fall.

Gillespie is in some ways a more poetical novel than Brown's, but at the cost of unnecessary length and some sacrifice of dramatic tautness. Yet its main characters are drawn with unforgettable firmness: Mrs Galbraith, the widow of a husband she had ceased to love, and whom Gillespie dispossesses; Lonend, a weaker counterpart to Gillespie, but whose smaller meanness was rewarded with less lavish wordly success: Mrs Strang, Lonend's daughter, married to Gillespie as a necessary stage in his commercial advancement, and whose misery drives her to drink, whoredom and disintegration; Iain, Gillespie's eldest son, broken and lost at sea because his father refused to pay the cost of making their steamer, *The Sudden Jerk*, seaworthy; Eaghon, the younger son and the final instrument of the tragedy's resolution, a boy meant by nature for learning, reflecting something of what Hay tells us he himself "felt and experienced as a boy at school". The novel also has its unforgettable set pieces, the firing of the fishing fleet by the radical conspirators once it had fallen into Gillespie's power, and the disintegration of Eaghon's sanity as he realizes the full enormity of his father's contemptuous neglect of his mother.

For a minister of the Church of Scotland to produce as "strong" a book as *Gillespie* in 1914 was a doubly astonishing achievement. In point of credibility and richness of human detail, it is a fuller, more compassionate masterpiece than *The House with the Green Shutters*.

Whether or not Hay could have surpassed *Gillespie* had he lived is pointless conjecture. The self-made world of the ruthless kailyard tycoon whom few dared oppose, except at their peril, was swept away, along with other lingering nineteenth-century attitudes and much else besides, by the war of 1914–18. The end of that war, and not 1901, really marks the beginning of twentieth-century Scottish literature.

III

The Scots habit of creating private literature continued to flourish during much of the nineteenth century. Scott opened his *Journal* in Edinburgh on 20th November 1825, with the words: "I have all my life regretted that I did not keep a regular Journal. I have myself lost recollections of much that was interesting, and I have deprived my family and the public of some curious information, by not carrying this resolution into effect."

Thereafter, however, his resolution made him confide his most heartfelt thoughts in the "handsome locked volume such as might serve for a lady's album" which he had aquired for the purpose: the death of his wife; the events leading up to the financial disaster of 1826; and the joys and losses, the struggles and the sorrows of the last years of striving to honour his debts; down, in fact, to the voyage to Italy in a final, futile search for health, and the unfinished last entry from Rome on 16th April 1832: "We slept reasonably, but on the next morning. . . ."

If Scott had no other claim to fame, his *Journal*, augmented perhaps by his *Letters*, would sustain for us the lineaments of one who was not only a great artist, but also a great man; a combination of qualities by no means common.

Much curious and diverting information was preserved for posterity by Henry Thomas Cockburn, who rose to the bench as Lord Cockburn (1779–1854). He was one of the leaders of the Whig party in Scotland in what were for it the dispiriting times immediately before the passing of the Reform Act in 1832. Occasionally, political prejudice mars some of his many confidently drawn portraits of his Tory contemporaries. His *Memorials of His Time*, which appeared in 1856, and the *Journal* published in 1874, together form one of the most delightfully vivid and well-observed autobiographies in Scottish literature.

He himself probably regarded his *Life of Francis Jeffrey* (1852) as his most important work, but time has dealt less kindly than Cockburn with Francis

Jeffrey (1773–1850), most of whose considerable critical talents were expended on his editorship of the second *Edinburgh Review*,* prior to his elevation to the bench in 1834. Although he totally failed to appreciate the merits of the writers of the English Romantic Revival, he did gather around him liberal-minded contributors, like the personally somewhat disagreeable Scot of Cumbrian extraction, Henry Peter Brougham, first Baron Brougham and Vaux (1778–1868), an Edinburgh-born lawyer who moved from the Scottish to the English bar, defended Queen Caroline with successful distinction when she was accused of adultery, took a leading part in founding London University, and wrote copiously on history and philosophy, his main works being his *Historical Sketches of Statesmen who Flourished in the Time of George III* (1843), and his *Autobiography*, written when he was eighty-three: and the English clergyman and wit, Sydney Smith (1771–1845), whose aphorisms are justly remembered wherever wit is honoured.

The ferocity with which the rival political factions attacked each other in their factional magazines is now of more interest to historians and sociologists than to students of literature. Even the sting of the *Translation from an Ancient Chaldee Manuscript* (1817), which once pained and agitated literate Edinburgh, has long since been blunted. This scurrilous attack, in biblical language and using the biblical devices of numbered paragraphs, was an all-out onslaught on the Whigs delivered by *Blackwood's*. Hogg claimed to have thought out the idea: Wilson and Lockhart were certainly involved in its creation. Fortunately, Lockhart laid aside his journalistic tendency to dip his pen in gall and so often be unfair in literary judgement and vicious in political comment, when he came to write *Peter's Letters to his Kinsfolk* (1819), a series of delightful sketches of Scottish society told in letter-form, the vignettes etched with a lighter hand than Cockburn's.

John Wilson (1785–1854) wrote *Lights and Shadows of Scottish Life* (1822), a kirkly forewarning of what was soon to come out of the kailyard, scarcely bettered by his mawkish novel, *The Trials of Margaret Lyndsay* (1823). He would be little more than a catalogued name today were it not for his *Noctes Ambrosianae* (1822–35). Here again, much of the wit, doubtless once pungent enough, seems to have lost its savour, while the lunges at political or critical targets of the day are often now irrelevantly tedious. It is, however, still a rewarding bedside book to take up at random, and enjoy the caricatured but vernacularly resounding portrait of the Shepherd (or the "Boar", as Hogg is habitually called), the vivid descriptions of Highland scenery and Lowland eating and drinking habits, and the many portraits and vignettes, including the hilariously funny account of sea-bathing at the then newly fashionable watering place of Portobello. The sheer gusto that was Wilson's most endearing characteristic seems to be reflected in the best of the *Noctes*, and in nothing else that he wrote. Millar's suggestion that "at

* The short-lived original *Edinburgh Review* of 1755 failed to survive the year of its inception.

his best he was like Rabelais and Diderot rolled into one" is not wide of the critical mark.

In the category of autobiography, Anne Grant (1755–1838) is remembered for her *Letters from the Mountains* (1806), keenly observed portrayals of Highland life as seen through the eyes of the daughter of the barrack-master at Fort Augustus and the wife of a military chaplain who later had a charge at Laggan. She is, of course, much more widely appreciated through her song "The Bluebells of Scotland", though not all who enjoy it are aware of its authorship.

She should not be confused with Elizabeth Grant (1797–1883), daughter of Sir James Grant, seventh Laird of Rothiemurchus. Miss Grant married a Colonel Henry Smith, but in later life preferred to be known as Elizabeth Grant of Rothiemurchus. Her eminently readable *Memoirs of a Highland Lady* was not published until 1897, when it was edited by her niece, Lady Strachey. Here for instance, is part of her description of a Highland church session in 1809:

The minister gave out the psalm; he put a very small dirty volume up to one eye, for he was near-sighted, and read as many lines of the old version of the rhythmical paraphrase (we may call it) of the Psalms of David as he thought fit, drawling them out in a sort of sing-song. He stooped over the pulpit to hand his little book to the precentor, who then rose and calling out aloud the tune—"St George's tune," "Auld Aberdeen," "Hondred an' fifteen," etc.—began himself a recitative of the first line on the key-note, then taken up and repeated by the congregation; line by line, he continued in the same fashion, thus doubling the length of the *exercise*, for really to some it was no play—serious severe screaming quite beyond the natural pitch of the voice, a wandering search after the air by many who never caught it, a flourish of difficult execution and plenty of the *tremolo* lately come into fashion. The dogs seized this occasion to bark (for they always came to the kirk with the family), and the babies to cry. When the minister could bear the din no longer he popped up again, again leaned over, touched the precentor's head, and instantly all sound ceased. The long prayer began, everybody stood up while the minister asked for us such blessings as he thought best. . . . The prayer over, the sermon began; that was the time for making observations. "Charity" and "Solomon's Lillies," soon required no further attention. Few save our own people sat around; old grey-headed rough-visaged men that had known my grandfather and great-grandfather, black, red, and fair hair, belonging to such as were in the prime of life, younger men, lads, boys—all in the tartan. The plaid as a wrap, the plaid as a drapery, with kilt to match on some, blue trews on others, blue jackets on all. The women were plaided too, an outside shawl was seen on none, though the wives wore a large handkerchief under the plaid, and looked picturesquely matronly in their very white high caps. . . . The wives were all in homespun, home-dyed, linsey-woolsey gowns, covered to the chin by the modest kerchief worn outside the gown.

The girls who could afford it had a Sabbath day's gown of like manufacture and very bright colour, but the throat was more exposed, and generally ornamented with a string of beads, often amber; some had to be content with the best blue flannel petticoat and a clean white jacket, their ordinary and most· becoming dress, and few of these had either shoes or stockings; but they all wore the plaid, and they folded it round them very gracefully.

They had a custom in the Spring of washing their beautiful hair with a decoction of the young buds of the birch trees. I do not know it if improved or hurt the hair, but it agreeably scented the kirk, which at other times was wont to be overpowered by the combined odours of snuff and peat reek, for the men snuffed immensely during the delivery of the English sermon; they fed their noses with quills fastened by strings to the lids of their mulls, spooning up the snuff in quantities and without waste. The old women snuffed too, and groaned a great deal, to express their mental sufferings, their grief for all the backslidings supposed to be thundered at from the pulpit; lapses from faith was their grand self-accusation, lapses from virtue were alas! little commented on; temperance and chastity were not in the Highland code of morality . . .

One major work belongs to this period: Lockhart's *Life of Scott* (1838). As Scott's son-in-law, Lockhart was in a unique position to discharge his task, a task which he defined in a letter to Will Laidlaw:

My sole object is to do him justice, or rather, to let him do himself justice, by so contriving it that he shall be, as far as possible, from first to last his own biographer. . . . A stern sense of duty—that kind of sense of it which is combined with the feeling of his actual presence in a severe state of elevation above all petty terrestrial and temporary views—will induce me to touch the few darker points in his life and character as freely as the others which were so predominant. . . .

The common charges against Lockhart are, that he telescoped letters without saying when or why; that he was unduly severe on Constable and the Ballantynes and over-lenient to Cadell—who had once written to Constable of Scott: "Let us stick to him, let us dig on and on at that inestimable quarry—and as sure as I now write to you we shall do well."— and that he falsified the famous "Be a good man" dying speech.

The telescoped letters would not be considered so heinous an offence by the standards of Lockhart's day as now, and in any case are not really material to the overall quality of the book. Lockhart's particular irritation with Constable is understandable, in that he was much closer in personal dealings, and more similar in temperament, to Scott than the distant and openly cynical Cadell. No one else can now prove or disprove what were Scott's last words:

On Monday he remained in bed, and seemed extremely feeble; but after breakfast on Tuesday the 17th he appeared revived somewhat, and was again wheeled about on the turf. Presently he fell asleep in his chair, and after dozing for perhaps half an hour, started awake, and shaking the plaids we had put about him from off his shoulders, said—"This is sad idleness. I shall forget what I have been thinking of, if I don't set it down now. Take me into my own room, and fetch the keys of my desk." He repeated this so earnestly that we could not refuse; his daughters went into his study, opened his writing-desk, and laid paper and pens in the usual order, and I then moved him through the hall and into the spot where he had always been accustomed to work. When the chair was placed at the desk, and he found himself in the old position, he smiled and thanked us, and said—"Now give me my pen and leave me for a little to myself." Sophia put the pen into his hand, and he endeavoured to close his fingers upon it, but they refused their office—it dropped on the paper. He sank back among his pillows, silent tears rolling down his cheeks; but composing himself by and by, motioned to me to wheel him out of doors again. Laidlaw met us at the porch, and took his turn of the chair. Sir Walter, after a little while, again dropt into slumber. When he was awaking, Laidlaw said to me—"Sir Walter has had a little repose." "No, Willie," said he—"no repose for Sir Walter but in the grave." The tears again rushed from his eyes. "Friends", said he, "don't let me expose myself—get me of to bed—that's the only place."

As I was dressing on the morning of Monday the 17th of September, Nicholson came into my room, and told me that his master had awoke in a state of composure and consciousness, and wished to see me immediately. I found him entirely himself, though in the last extreme of feebleness. His eye was clear and calm—every trace of the wild fire of delirium extinguished. "Lockhart," he said, "I may have but a minute to speak to you. My dear, be a good man—be virtuous—be religious—be a good man. Nothing else will give you any comfort when you come to lie here."—He paused, and I said—"Shall I send for Sophia and Anne?"—"No," said he "don't disturb them. Poor souls! I know they were up all night—God bless you all."—With this he sunk into a very tranquil sleep, and, indeed, he scarcely afterwards gave any sign of consciousness, except for an instant on the arrival of his sons. They, on learning that the scene was about to close obtained anew leave of absence from their posts, and both reached Abbotsford on the 19th. About half past one P.M., on the 21st of September, Sir Walter breathed his last, in the presence of all his children. It was a beautiful day—so warm that every window was wide open—and so perfectly still, that the sound of all others most delicious to his ear, the gentle ripple of the Tweed over its pebbles, was distinctly audible as we knelt around the bed, and his eldest son kissed and closed his eyes.

Lord Cockburn, although dubious as to the wisdom of Lockhart's unvarnished honesty, gives as his verdict of the book: "It is Scott to the life;

at least as much so as any man can be exhibited to the public by words. . . . The plain dress, the guttural, burred voice, the lame walk, the thoughtful, heavy face with its mantling smile, the honest, hearty manner, the joyous laugh, the sing-song recitation, the graphic story—they are all before me a hundred times a day."

Andrew Lang justified Lockhart's absence of "discretion"—a form of romantic dishonesty which hopelessly vitiates his *Life of Burns*—on the grounds that "Burns he never knew in the flesh, nor loved as a friend. But he would not show Scott—whom he loved and revered—other than as the whole man he was in his complexity of faults and heroic virtues."

Like Saintsbury, I have no hesitation in placing Lockhart's *Life of Scott* alongside Boswell's *Johnson* as one of the two great biographies in our literature. Scholars may have unearthed more detailed information than Lockhart possessed, or chose to reveal. John Buchan has certainly provided a much more concise later portrait of great merit. But in Lockhart's pages, the Edinburgh of Scott's day, and the life that revolved around him at Abbotsford, come alive as nowhere else. We are there with the man.

When one turns to the writings of that sea captain's son of Scandanavian descent, Hugh Miller (1802–1856), the man is almost too much with us. Miller, a Cromarty stone-mason, taught himself geology and became no mean expert in the subject, as *The Old Red Sandstone* (1841) and *The Testimony of the Rocks* (1857) amply demonstrate. Like so many of his self-educated kind, however, his piety assumed a narrow crabbedness which shows in recurring petulances when he encounters anyone whose religious views vary by a hair's breadth from his own. As a result, his forceful and effective prose, seen to by far its best advantage in *My Schools and Schoolmasters* (1852), is elsewhere too often marred by a rough arrogance of attitude. Overwork during his later years led to mental derangement and his suicide by shooting.

William Edmonstoune Aytoun's verse has already been mentioned. He contributed many of the still re-published *Tales From Blackwood*, among his best being "The Glenmutchkin Railway" and "Dreepdaily", the former a satirical prospectus no less accurate in its deadly parody than when it was first conceived, the latter a take-off of Scottish political toadyism.

Alexander Smith's *A Summer in Skye* (1865) is surely one of the most luminous Scottish travel-books ever written. It has rarely been out of print since it was first published, and its memorable descriptions of Stirling, Glasgow, Loch Coruisk and many other places, are frequently anthologized. No less vivid are the best things in his collection of essays, *Dreamthorpe* (1863), in spite of a touch here and there of Stevensonian preciousness. I doubt if anyone reading his account of a public hanging, "A Lark's Flight", is likely readily to forget it. His picture of Edinburgh under winter snow has a vivid directness which makes one the more regret the posturing which undid him as a poet.

Passing rapidly over the scores of minor mid-Victorian historians, philosophers and divines who wrote copiously for their day and age, only Edmund Bannerman Ramsay (1793–1872), Dean of Edinburgh, need be singled out for his still widely read and pointedly racy *Reminiscences of Scottish Life and Character* (1858). It is not, after all, his fault that the work has inspired countless feeble imitations.

I doubt if many now read the *Researches in South Africa* (1817–1874), the *Narrative of an Expedition to the Zambesi* (1865), or the *Last Journals* (1875) of David Livingstone (1813–1873), though tourist lip-service is still paid to his Blantyre birthplace. James Augustus Grant (1827–1892) has been rediscovered in recent years, *A Walk Across Africa* (1864) being demonstrated, as a result, to be a lively and well-told account of the expedition to discover the source of the Nile.

It is the fate of most philosophers that they are likely to be refuted, their work becoming of merely academic interest to later students; unless, as in the case of Hume, their demonstrations are so seminal that other branches of thought and learning must thereafter forever be affected, or their writing on more general topics continue to give pleasure as literature in its own right. It was the fate of historians, until comparatively recent times, to have had to operate without the apparatus of scientific scholarship, the cohorts of researchers available to twentieth-century practitioners. In consequence, unless, like Lyndsay of Pitscottie, they were possessed of information at near hand, or, like William Robertson, equipped with a peculiar ability to recreate past circumstances so vividly as to enable something of their writing to survive because of its sheer readability, then they, too, are inevitably superseded in the attentions of later generations of readers.

Two nineteenth-century Scottish historians stand out from the run of their kind in both these ways: Thomas Carlyle (1795–1881) and Lord Macaulay (1800–1859).

Carlyle was born at Ecclefechan, Dumfriesshire, the son of a puritanical stone mason and a conventionally pious mother. Schooled at Annan, he went to Edinburgh University when he was fifteen. There, he completed an Arts course, and began to study for the ministry. A crisis of belief made him abandon this course and take up teaching in Kirkcaldy, where he became friendly with the preacher Edward Irving, also a native of Annandale. Irving was later to rise to remarkable heights of preaching fame, then fall to disgrace and early death as a result of his belief in the validity of so-called prophetic "voices" amongst his worshippers.

In 1819, Carlyle returned to Edinburgh and spent some time abortively studying law, which he abandoned in exasperation in 1822 to become a private tutor. He was already forming ambitions to shape for himself some sort of literary career, which he embarked upon with a life of Schiller for the *London Magazine* in 1823, following this up with essays on Nelson, Montaigne, Montesquieu and others for the *Edinburgh Encyclopaedia*. He also translated Goethe's *Wilhelm Meister*, an achievement which won him the acquaintance of Hazlitt, Coleridge, Campbell, and other famous writers of the day, most of whom he reacted to with caustic epistolary comments, as he did in later life to Dickens, Thackeray and Tennyson.

In 1820 he married the daughter of a Haddington doctor, Jane Baillie Welsh. After some trying years at her bleak farm of Craigenputtock, where they were befriended by Jeffrey, who put work his way, the Carlyles settled in Cheyne Row, Chelsea. There they remained for the rest of their lives. Carlyle outlived his witty, unhappy wife by fifteen years.

They were, in some respects, an ill-suited pair, he, of rugged working-class origin, she with her middle-class upbringing and her ready talent for minute and often tart observation, much of it preserved in her *Letters and Memorials* (1883), *New Letters and Memorials* (1903) and other volumes. She had been a pupil of Irving's and a much sought-after local beauty, but Carlyle's rough-cut personality eventually came to dominate her mind. Whether it be true that her ultimate unhappiness stemmed from inadequate physical satisfaction—Jane is supposed to have told their physician, Sir Richard Quain, that on their wedding night, Carlyle "lay there, jiggling like", until she suddenly burst out laughing and he got "out of bed with one scornful word 'Woman!' and went into the next room" never to return to her bed again—or whether, as Carlyle's defenders have alleged, Jane was frigid, is little enough matter now. Yet the fusion of their curious relationship certainly sharpened Jane's own letter-writing talent, the more so as, until nearly the end of her life, Carlyle apparently was so absorbed in his own work, his chronic constipation and his neurotic dyspepsia (never, significantly, experienced in company, but always when broodingly alone) that he failed even to notice his wife's absence of fulfilment.

He himself is one of the strangest, most powerful characters Scottish literature has produced. Rejecting his parent's simple Calvinistic piety, he embraced Hume's scepticism, until walking down Leith Walk, Edinburgh in his twenty-eighth year during the summer of 1822, he suddenly experienced a "conversion". He ceased to accept the "Everlasting No" (*das ewige nein*) to life, and instead adopted the "Everlasting Yea". Unfortunately, at no time did Carlyle adequately define his new spiritual convictions. He certainly disbelieved in resurrection, and abolished in his mind any idea of hell. He claimed to believe in a "particular providence", and asserted that right, as "the eternal symbol of might", must triumph, since the world had been made by God. Art he always distrusted, and eventually claimed to despise. Work was his personal solution for most of the world's ills. "What the deuce is Carlyle's religion, or has he any?" once asked Erasmus Darwin,[33] understandably. So far as Darwin's question can be answered retrospectively, a variation of pantheism based on awe "at the dynamic forces both contained in man, and manifest in the universe around him", might be as good a definition as any.

Carlyle's achievement falls into two main categories—his significance as a social prophet, and his work as an historian. In addition, there is the less monumental but more appealing side of him, as represented by the "Encyclopedia" essays, and, of particular interest to Scots, the essays on Burns and Scott, as well as his memoirs on his father and his wife, and of course his correspondence.

Towards Burns, Carlyle was sympathetically patronizing, since he was already inclining to the view that poetry—even that of his early hero, Goethe—was mere triviality, and that action was what really counted. In *Past and Present* (1843), Carlyle was to lament the state of a society that made George III "head charioteer of the Destinies of England" and Robert Burns a gauger of ale in Dumfries; a piece of word-play the implications of which are so absurd as to baffle comment. It is not, therefore, surprising to find him attacking Scott for being content to write stories for the multitude to read and enjoy, Carlyle complaining that "the great mystery of existence was not great to him; did not drive him into rocky solitude to wrestle with it for an answer, to be answered or to perish.[34]

Carlyle's life was one weary wrestling: with dyspepsia, apparently psychosomatic in origin; with angry indignation at the state of society in his day; and with the psychological damage inflicted on him by his Calvinistic inheritance.

His first major work, and some would say his finest non-historic piece of writing, *Sartor Resartus*, was written at Craigenputtock, and published two years after completion, in 1833. *Sartor Resartus* is an imaginary biography of Herr Teufelsdröckh (Devil's Dung). Carlyle's fascinated contempt for bodily functions is noteworthy, and a familiar by-product of Scottish Calvinism. Teufelsdröckh is, of course, Carlyle himself.

Teufelsdröckh is Professor of Things in General at The University of Weissnichtwo (Know-not-Where), and author of a book on the Philosophy of Clothes, put out by Stillschweigen (Silence) and Company. The first part of the book describes, with heavy humour, Teufelsdröckh's career; the second deals with the hero's childhood and youth, much of it embodying Carlylean autobiography; the third is an attack upon various aspects of British life.

It is so confused a piece of work that it is all but unreadable today. Its mixture of autobiography and social fable is structurally unsatisfactory, and the solution proposed for the readjustment of society—a universal copying of the author's own journey from "No" to "Yea" via "The Centre of Indifference"—neither clear nor practical.

The book is nevertheless important, for two reasons: because it begins to canalize Carlyle's moral indignation against social injustice; and, because it is the first work in which his highly individual prose style is fully developed. Old Testament rhetoric, the traditional rant of the Scots preachers, the influence of the German Romantics, in particular of Jean-Paul Richter, no doubt helped to formulate it. What ultimately propelled it through all its forceful convolutions to telling effect was, however, the sheer moral force of Carlyle's anger at injustice. Words are jerked out of their conventional usage. Parts of speech are taken by the neck and shaken. Johnsonian balance—what the narrator in Mrs Gaskell's *Cranford* called the "rolling three-piled sentence"—is shattered in a new, an inescapable involuntary urgency.

We need here neither be concerned in detail with the accuracy of Carlyle's views on sociology or history. Yet they cannot quite be passed by. In Carlyle's earlier writings, his main target was *laissez-faire*, as reflected in what he called Mechanism, Mammonism, Dilettantism, and Benthamism. He realized that the great mass of the people would not for ever put up with the oppression of starvation:

> There is a deep-lying struggle in the whole fabric of society; a boundless grinding collision of the New with the Old. The French Revolution, as is now visible enough, was not the parent of this mighty movement, but its offspring. . . . Political freedom is hitherto the object of these efforts; but they will not and cannot stop there. It is towards a higher freedom from oppression by his fellow-mortal, that man dimly aims.

In his *Journal*, he suggested that political economists would do well to examine the basic facts about human conditions; why, for instance the wages of some were seven or eight thousand times those of others: "What do these highly beneficial individuals *do* to society for their wages?—*Kill Partridges*. Can this last? No, by the soul that is in man it cannot, and will not, and shall not."

The leaving of all to market forces, and the ensuing rush for cash, which was a product of *laissez-faire*, he wrote to a friend, had removed from the manufacturer in a sequestered spot dependent on water for his energy, the sense of responsibility for the community of workers he had gathered around him.

> This is now quite changed. The manufacturers are transferred to great towns where a man may assemble 500 workmen one week and dismiss the next, without having any further connection with them than to receive a week's work for a week's wage, nor any further solicitude about their future fate than if they were so many shuttles.

Carlyle, like Karl Marx and every other self-styled prophet and sage, found it markedly easier to analyze social evils than to pronounce remedies that would not lead to the creation of still greater social evils. Both Marx and Carlyle drew strength from what was, in effect, the Hegelian dialectic (though Carlyle had probably never heard of it as such); both believed that nothing truly creative out of the past could be lost; both shared the view (wrongly, it transpired) that the present (1840-ish) rotten state of society signified the imminence of early transformation; both believed in historicism, that doctrine which postulates an evolutionary interpretation of history, repudiated so devastatingly in the philosophy of Sir Karl Popper[35] and in practical terms by the events of the past century.

Thereafter, their prophetic views followed different directions. Marx believed in economic determinism, propounding the theory that the increasing injustice of bourgeois society would result in the eventual destruction of capitalism and the creation of a system of perfect social justice based on working-class values. Carlyle, on the other hand, came to believe that Benthamist Radicalism—the greatest happiness of the greatest number—could be enlightened by *Aufklärung*, "The Spiritual", and that a New Aristocracy must be found so that mass voting "given under the influence of beer and balderdash" would not merely produce a new kind of social wrongness.

Carlyle's progress from indignant work reformer to believer in the need for the hero and a governing class was made through *On Heroes and Hero-Worship* (1841)—the only set of Carlyle's four immensely successful series of public lectures to be preserved—*Past and Present* and *Latter-Day Pamphlets* (1850); and so to that sad product of his old age, *Shooting Niagra: and After?*, with its strident racialism, and its insistence that the only hope for Britain lay in "the noble Few, who we always trust will be born to us, generation after generation; and on whom and whose living of a noble and valiantly cosmic life amidst the worst impediments and hugest anarchies, the whole of our hope depends."

If, then, in the end, the situation of Carlyle as prophet now seems to justify Arthur Hugh Clough's remark: "Carlyle has led us out into the desert, and he has left us there", what justification is there for reading him today? Apart from his miscellaneous writings, the greatest of the three histories: not *Oliver Cromwell's Letters and Speeches with Elucidations* (1845), which, in its day, provided a necessary balance of approach to the Protector's achievements and shortcomings, but today seems merely eccentrically sycophantic: not that final piece of special pleading in six mammoth volumes, *Frederick the Great* (1858–1865), although the battle scenes are recreated with a vividness which reveals something of Carlyle's Freudian interest in violence: but in the first and finest of his histories, that on the *French Revolution* (1837).

Today, we can see that his treatment of characters with whom he had little sympathy, like Robespierre and Saint-Just, is inaccurate, his view of Mirabeau's unfulfilled potential, in the light of modern scholarship, exaggerated. We can also see that his before-and-after perspective of the economic and industrial background to the Revolution is decidedly inadequate. Yet, in the end, the book is still readable, and compellingly so, because, as his compatriot John Stuart Mill said, the sub-title of the book should not be "A History", but "A Poem". There are unforgettable things in it, made the more so by the sense of involvement Carlyle achieves through using the present tense; the taking of the Bastille; the march of the women on Versailles; the murder of Marat by Charlotte Corday; and the manner in which Carlyle contrasts the departure of Maria Theresa's beautiful daughter from Vienna on her way to become the French king's bride, with the sad end of her story before a crowd in a very different mood. What academic historian would ever have thought of pointing such a contrast?

Two Processions, or Royal Progresses, three-and-twenty years apart, have often struck us with a strange feeling of contrast. The first is of a beautiful Archduchess and Dauphiness, quitting her Mother's City, at the age of Fifteen; towards hopes such as no other Daughter of Eve then had: "On the morrow," says Weber an eye-witness, "the Dauphiness left Vienna. The whole city crowded out; at first with a sorrow which was silent. She appeared: you saw her sunk back into her carriage; her face bathed in tears; hiding her eyes now with her handkerchief, now with her hands; several times putting out her head to see yet again this Palace of her Fathers, whither she was to return no more. She motioned her regret, her gratitude to the good Nation, which was crowding here to bid her farewell. Then arose not only tears; but piercing cries, on all sides. Men and women alike abandoned themselves to such expression of their sorrow. It was an audible sound of wail, in the streets and avenues of Vienna. The last Courier that followed her disappeared, and the crowd melted away."

The young imperial Maiden of Fifteen has now become a worn discrowned Widow of Thirty-eight; grey before her time: this is the last Procession: "Few minutes after the Trial ended, the drums were beating to arms in all Sections; at sunrise the armed force was on foot, cannons getting placed at the extremities of the Bridges, in the Squares, Crossways, all along from the Palais de Justice to the Place de la Révolution. By ten o'clock, numerous patrols were circulating in the Streets; thirty thousand foot and horse drawn up under arms. At eleven, Marie-Antoinette was brought out. She had on an undress of *piqué blanc*: she was led to the place of execution, in the same manner as an ordinary criminal; bound, on a Cart; accompanied by a Constitutional Priest in Lay dress; escorted by numerous detachments of infantry and cavalry. These, and the double row of troops all along her road, she appeared to regard with indifference. On her countenance there was visible neither abashment nor pride. To the cries of *Vive la République* and *Down with Tyranny*, which attended her all the way, she seemed to pay no heed. She spoke little to her Confessor. The tricolor Streamers on the housetops occupied her attention, in the Streets du Roule and Saint-Honoré; she also noticed the Inscriptions on the house-fronts. On reaching the Place de la Révolution, her looks turned towards the *Jardin National*, whilom Tuileries; her face at that moment gave signs of lively emotion. She mounted the Scaffold with courage enough; at a quarter past Twelve, her head fell; the Executioner showed it to the people, amid universal long-continued cries of *Vive la République*."

In the end, whatever he is about, Carlyle fascinates us because he is himself; the establisher of a liberated prose; the seer who foresaw that social injustice must change, but could not anticipate that one injustice is inevitably replaced by another; the prophet who saw, and stated, that it is upon a basis of force that modern societies rest, however highminded the theorizing of their philosophers.

Macaulay, in many ways diametrically opposed to Carlyle in politics as in historical approach, had also the gift of imposing narrative conviction. Although fully of Scottish blood, Macaulay's Scottish connection never got much beyond his important contributions to *The Edinburgh Review*—notably, a famous essay on Milton, albeit one he later rightly claimed "contained scarcely a paragraph such as his natural judgement approved"—and at the end of his life, in 1850, representing Edinburgh in Parliament, shortly before his health began finally to fail.

He personified Carlyle's belief that only action counted, by being himself a man of action. He first entered Parliament as member for Calne in 1830, and was soon in the thick of the Reform struggle. Indeed, he spoke so eloquently on behalf of the Reform Bill that Sir Robert Peel declared portions of his speech to be "as beautiful as anything I have ever heard or read". Macaulay went to India in 1834, as a member of the Supreme Council. When he returned to England in 1838, he began his monumental *History of England* (1845–1855), a work of compelling and lucid narrative power, albeit vitiated by his exuberant misrepresentation of facts in the Whig interest when the occasion suited. More than one hundred and fifty thousand copies of this work were sold in these islands. It was pirated several times in America and translated into eleven languages.

Macaulay's description of another execution—the bungled killing of Monmouth following that unfortunate nobleman's unsuccessful rising—gives some idea of his flowing readability.

The hour drew near; all hope was over; and Monmouth had passed from pusillanimous fear to the apathy of despair. His children were brought to his room that he might take leave of them, and were followed by his wife. He spoke to her kindly, but without emotion. Though she was a woman of great strength of mind, and had little cause to love him, her misery was such that none of the bystanders could refrain from weeping. He alone was unmoved.

It was ten o'clock. The coach of the Lieutenant of the Tower was ready. Monmouth requested his spiritual advisers to accompany him to the place of execution; and they consented: but they told him that, in their judgment, he was about to die in a perilous state of mind, and that, if they attended him, it would be their duty to exhort him to the last. As he passed along the ranks of the guards he saluted them with a smile, and mounted the scaffold with a firm tread. Tower Hill was covered up to the chimney tops with an innumerable multitude of gazers, who, in awful silence, broken only by sighs and the noise of weeping, listened for the last accents of the darling of the people. "I shall say little," he began. "I come here, not to speak, but to die. I die a Protestant of the Church of England." The Bishops interrupted him, and told him that, unless he acknowledged resistance to be sinful, he was no member of their church. He went on to speak of his Henrietta. She was, he said, a young lady of virtue and honour. He loved her to the last, and he could not die without giving utterance to his feelings. The Bishops again interfered and begged him not to use such language. Some altercation followed. The divines have been accused of dealing harshly with the dying man. But they appear to have only discharged what, in their view, was a sacred duty. Monmouth knew their principles, and, if he wished to avoid their importunity, should have dispensed with their attendance. Their general arguments against resistance had no effect on him. But when they reminded him of the ruin which he had brought on his brave and loving followers, of the blood which had been shed, of the souls which had been sent unprepared to the great account, he was touched, and said, in a softened voice, "I do own that. I am sorry that it ever happened." They prayed with him long and fervently; and he joined in their petitions till they invoked a blessing on the King. He remained silent. "Sir," said one of the Bishops, "do you not pray for the King with us?" Monmouth paused some time, and, after an internal struggle, exclaimed "Amen." But it was in vain that the prelates implored him to address to the soldiers and to the people a few words on the duty of obedience to the government. "I will make no speeches," he exclaimed. "Only ten words, my Lord." He turned away, called his servant, and put into the man's hand a toothpick case, the last token of ill starred love. "Give it," he said "to that person." He then accosted John Ketch the executioner, a wretch who had butchered many brave and noble victims, and whose name has, during a century and a half, been vulgarly given to all who have succeeded him in his odious office. "Here," said the Duke, "are six guineas for you. Do not hack me as you did my Lord Russell. I have heard that you struck him three or four times. My servant will give you some more gold if you do the work well." He then undressed, felt the edge of the axe, expressed some fear that it was not sharp enough, and laid his head on the block. The divines in the meantime continued to ejaculate with great energy; "God accept your repentance! God accept your imperfect repentance!"

The hangman addressed himself to his office. But he had been disconcerted by what the Duke had said. The first blow inflicted only a slight wound. The Duke struggled, rose from the block, and looked reproachfully at the executioner. The head sank down once more. The stroke was repeated again and again; but still the neck was not severed, and the body continued to move. Yells of rage and horror rose from the crowd. Ketch flung down the axe with a curse. "I cannot do it," he said; "my heart fails me." "Take up the axe, man," cried the sheriff. "Fling him over the rails," roared the mob. At length the axe was taken up. Two more blows extinguished the last remains of life; but a knife was used to separate the head from the shoulders. The crowd was wrought up to such an ecstasy of rage that the executioner was in danger of being torn in pieces, and was conveyed away under a strong guard.

In the meantime many handkerchiefs were dipped in the Duke's blood; for by a large part of the multitude he was regarded as a martyr who had died for the Protestant religion.

Stevenson devoted some thought to the tactics which it is necessary for a writer to deploy if he is to achieve "the short study". In a sense, the great histories of Carlyle and Macaulay live today because of the vividness of the many "short studies" they contain. Yet, as Stevenson noted, the effects of those two writers were achieved by different means, neither without the stresses of distortion: "The two English masters of the style, Macaulay and Carlyle, largely exemplify its dangers. Carlyle, indeed, had so much more depth and knowledge of the heart, his portraits of mankind are felt and rendered with so much more poetic comprehension, and he had a fire in his belly so much more hotly burning than the patent reading lamp by which Macaulay studied, that it seems at first sight hardly fair to bracket them together. But the 'point of view' was imposed by Carlyle on the men he judged of in his writings with an austerity not only cruel but almost stupid. They are too often broken outright on the Procrustean bed; they are probably always disfigured. The rhetorical artifice of Macaulay is easily spied; it will take longer to appreciate the moral bias of Carlyle."

The remaining non-fictional prose-writers of the nineteenth century were mostly essayists.

James Thomson (B.V.) published one prose collection, *Essays and Phantasies* (1881), which deserves to be kept in print. Echoes of De Quincey, Swift and Carlyle are not hard to find; yet there is also a penetrating personal irony which keeps the prose alive:

> Immortality! Why, the most of us don't know what to do with this one little personal life, and might well wonder how we came to be promoted to the dignity thereof; the claim to immortality is the claim to be trusted with millions of pounds because one has shown himself unfit to be trusted with sixpence.

Or again, about women:

> I ardently love and admire the sex, but I am bound to say that I never knew a woman with even the most elementary idea of truth and justice. . . . The best woman would overthrow the equilibrium of the universe for the sake of her lover, her child or her husband.

More or less contemporaneous was John Brown (1810–1882), a Biggar man who became a general medical practitioner in Edinburgh, and whose essays—among the best of which are "Rab and his Friends", a touching study of Scott's child-friend "Pet Marjorie", "On Dogs" and "The Enter-tainer"—were collected along with his papers on art, medical history and biography, in *Horae Subsecivae* (1882). Brown had something of Lamb's humour and tenderness, and also deserves not to be forgotten.

Mention has already been made of the winning charm of Stevenson's *An Inland Voyage* (1878) and, more especially, *Travels with a Donkey in the Cevennes* (1879). By far his most polished non-fictional prose is to be found in *Virginibus Puerisque* (1881), its title "to maidens and boys" taken from Horace, and used as a text for gracefully expressed sound common sense, which would do much to ease the hurt of youth, if youth were a condition capable of rational remedy. *Familiar Studies of Men and Books* (1882), like *Memories and Portraits* (1887), deals mainly with literary concerns. His re-view of a book by Principal Shairp on Burns shows Stevenson to have been the forerunner of those twentieth-century critics who were to correct the malicious pietism of their predecessors, and administer a well-deserved trouncing in the doing:

> If you are so sensibly pained by the misconduct of your subject, and so paternally delighted with his virtues, you will always be an excellent gentle-man, but a somewhat questionable biographer. Indeed, we can only be sorry and surprised that Principal Shairp should have chosen a theme so uncongen-ial. When we find a man writing on Burns, who likes neither *Holy Willie*, nor the *Beggars*, nor the *Ordination*, nothing is adequate to the situation but the old cry of Geronte: "Que diable allait-il faire dans cette galère?"

Although Stevenson enthusiastically championed Whitman and Thoreau when both writers enjoyed scant popularity on this side of the Atlantic, he thought Villon a "bad fellow", though he admired the aban-don of the Frenchman's verse.

Among masses of fugitive journalism, that "droopy aristocrat of letters",[36] Andrew Lang, wrote a delightful history of *St Andrews*. Though inevitably superseded in the mere matter of fact, it has considerable charm of style, and is a tribute to the depth of his love for the place. His *History of Scotland* (1900–7) is also still worth reading for the vividness of much of the historical portraiture. *Letters to Dead Authors*—Flaccus, Rabelais, Fielding among them—and *Books and Bookmen*, both of which appeared in 1886, reflect the now vanished craft of the man-of-letters as essayist, elegantly and regularly filling in his appropriate word-length of space with readable, if sometimes almost frivolous, material. His Homer translation, however, is far from negligible and more readable than many a later version. Younger readers remember Lang with gratitude for his series of *Fairy Books*, called by the names of the different colours of their jackets.

Two writers who lived well into the twentieth century left autobi-ographies of interest to Scottish readers. John Joy Bell (1871–1934) created that once-popular character *Wee MacGreegor* (1902), a venture in Scots comicality several times repeated, the original of which sold more than a quarter of a million copies, and was even thought worth pirating in America. It has nothing to do with literature, but his volume of reminiscences *I Remember* (1932) recreates the sights and sounds of a nineteenth-century Glasgow childhood, while *Do You Remember?* (1934) contains, among other pleasantries, a vigorous account of the whale industry when, briefly, it had a Scottish base. Yet Bell's powers as an evoker of *le temps perdu* are surpassed in liveliness, breadth of matter and zest in the telling by Neil Munro's *The Brave Days* (1931), a volume of posthumously published reminiscences which includes a heart-rending account of the insensitive baiting of that sadly comical poetaster, William McGonagall; some interesting observations on the novelist William Black; and a strange account of a London visit to John Davidson—who, incidentally, had once been one of Bell's schoolteachers—to try to persuade the irascible poet of evolution to address a Burns Supper.

As in previous centuries, nineteenth-century Scottish drama was by far the least impressive aspect of the national literature. Only one dramatist is worthy of serious notice, Sir James Matthew Barrie, O.M.

Barrie's novels have already been discussed. His plays, for the most part, won him considerable success. When he died in 1934, he left £173,000, a very considerable sum for those days.

The first obvious point about Barrie, the playwright, is that he could exercise a command over the language of the theatre such as he never possessed in handling it in its more inert fictional guise. The second is that in his best plays, his characters come alive and sustain credible being within the terms of reference provided by the dramatist. He was also an expert stitcher-up of plots in an era when audiences were unwilling to accept any show of the ragged seams of real life, as they do so readily today.

All that said, why, then, is it that plays once so enormously popular, with one exception—that spiritual autobiography in children's terms, *Peter Pan* or *The Boy Who Never Grew Up* (1904)—should now seem so unsatisfyingly artificial?

Quality Street (1901), set in the period of the Napoleonic wars—its title actually that of a street in Leith—deals with two spinster sisters, one of whom has a romance with a handsome army Captain. The Captain, however, fails to "declare himself", so Miss Phoebe dons spectacles, a muslin cap and the attitudes then thought becoming to an old maid. Some years later, back comes the Captain, who invites Miss Phoebe to a ball. Instead, he is fobbed off with her "niece", who turns out (of course) to be none other than Miss Phoebe herself. Delighted with this deception, this time the Captain makes a suitable "declaration".

The Admirable Crichton (1902) amusingly portrays the super-butler who, when family and domestic staff are wrecked on an island, becomes a virtual dictator by virtue of his inherent abilities, only to revert to butlerdom once a rescue has been achieved.

Barrie's sense of late Victorian and Edwardian class structure, and the limiting dimensions which made it up, shows out strongly in most of his plays, although often the implication, as in this play, is that he comes down on the side of common-sense domestics. From the moment its exposition is complete, the plot is entirely predictable; yet a certain charm of phrase and plenty of well-turned wit keep it above surface through an occasional revival.

Peter Pan has been subjected to Freudian analysis and various other forms of destructive dissection. The wholly unintended sexual overtones of some of its stage directions produce an easy laugh in our more sophisticated age. Of course it has its horrible implications when the play is related to the psychological disability from which its author undoubtedly suffered. On the level of children's entertainment, however, the manner in which it successfully chimes in with a passing phase in the development even of a normal healthy child, is sufficiently attested by its constant revival.

Whimsy in a play about children is one thing. Whimsy projected upon adult situations is quite another matter, though whether more or less boring than late twentieth-century preoccupation with environmental sordidness and sexual mechanics is a matter for the individual to decide. In *A Kiss for Cinderella* (1916), Barrie tried hard to re-mix the successful recipe of Peter Pan. The ingredients simply do not cohere. *What Every Woman Knows* (1908) propounds the theory that behind every successful man is a staunch little woman. Most sickly of all is the Hebridean island-inspired *Mary Rose* (1920), which deals with the disillusionment of a "disappeared" mother-ghost who returns to see how her children are faring, only to discover that her son, now a grown man and a soldier, feels no connection with her at all. It has some psychological interest, however, if considered as a kind of obverse *Peter Pan*, a demonstration of the havoc a person with a mind which refuses to develop can have on the lives of others.

Dear Brutus (1917) explores with ease and wit the theme that everyone carries within him (or her) self the seeds of his (or her) destiny, and given a second shot at life, would come up with basically similar answers. But the whimsy surrounding Lob and his wood, which touches off the fantasy, bring what is regarded as one of Barrie's better plays very near to unacceptability.

Of the rest, *Shall We Join the Ladies?* (1921), an unconcluded murder story, promises well, but is dramatically pointless in the condition which Barrie left it. *The Boy David* (1936), an ill-advised excursion from his old age into religious drama, mawkish and unsuccessful from its first performance, indulges in unconvincing transvestism in the title role.

So the Barrie magic that once packed London's West End theatres, and brought eagerly to his roles many of the leading actors and actresses of the day, now seems sadly faded. At least it is indisputable that, apart (in a limited sense) from Sir David Lyndsay, Barrie is virtually the first Scot to understand and master practical theatre-craft. It could therefore be said that he is effectively the father of that still far from healthy literary stripling, twentieth-century Scottish drama.

CHAPTER SIX

The Scottish Renaissance . . .

I

Divisions between fashions and changes of mood and feeling in the arts rarely coincide tidily with the years on which the centuries turn. The beginnings of twentieth-century literature, most of which has been associated in some form or other with the Scottish Renaissance movement, really date from the years immediately following the First World War.

As we have seen, there had been earlier signs that a change was on the way. Murray, an "establishment" figure, appeared to have had some of his previously predictable rural attitudes disturbed by the war. Pittendrigh MacGillivray (1856–1938)—whose "Mercy o' Gode", like Murray's "Gin I was God", mildly anticipates MacDiarmid—and Lewis Spence (1874–1953), had both experimented with verse couched in a deliberately revived "antique" Scots. MacGillivray's love song "Abasshyd" begins:

I toke hyr heid atween my hondes
   And kyste hyr dusky hair;
I lyghtly touchte hyr luvely cheek,
   Syn kyste hyr mouth so rare.

A lityll flame cam up hyr neck
   To tell hyr herte had fyre;
But, sum aschamte, wyth eyen cast down,
   Hyr mynde restrainte desyre . . .

This, though pleasant enough, is little more than a nostalgic hark-back to the lost sound of Middle Scots.

Spence, a Broughty Ferry man who spent much of his working life as a journalist on *The Scotsman* and the London-based *British Weekly*, was one of the founders of the Scottish National Party, the first to contest a parliamentary seat (North Midlothian, in January 1929, when he lost his deposit) and the author of many useful works on early civilizations and mythologies. These include *The Gods of Mexico* (1923), in the former category, and in the latter, *An Encyclopedia of Occultism* (1920), *The Magic Arts in Celtic*

Britain (1945) and *The History and Origins of Druidism* (1950). His *Collected Poems* appeared in 1953.

As early as 1910, when Spence returned to Scotland, he began making tentative experiments in fortifying the Scots tongue with an infusion of older Scots phrases and syntax in an attempt to create what in 1929 he called "gentleman's Scots". Like those of MacGillivray, Spence's experiments were romantic and backward-looking in subject-matter, as is demonstrated by his sonnet "Portrait of Mary Stuart, Holyrood", with its Montgomerie-like octave:

> Wauken be nicht, and bydand on some boon,
>   Glamour of saul, or spirituall grace,
>   I haf seen sancts and angells in the face,
> And like a fere of seraphy the moon;
> But in nae mirk nor sun-apparelled noon
>   Nor pleasance of the planets in their place
>   Or luve devine haf seen sae pure a trace
> As in yon shadow of the Scottis crown . . .

There seems little doubt that the young C. M. Grieve (Hugh Mac-Diarmid) knew and approved of these gentle experiments with language. That Grieve succeeded, through the application of genius, where Spence, who had only the thinnest of poetic talents to apply to the task, failed, was to be the occasion of bitterness on Spence's part towards the end of his life.[1]

Christopher Murray Grieve (b. 1892) was born at Langholm, Dumfries-shire, the son of a postman. A voracious reader, he was educated at Langholm Academy—where his English master was the distinguished Scottish song-composer Francis George Scott, later to set so magnificently some of his former pupil's lyrics—Broughton Junior Students' Centre and Edinburgh University. But the death of his father ended Grieve's training as a teacher, and he turned, apparently with relief, to journalism. Between 1915 and 1918, he served in the R.A.M.C. in Greece, Italy and France. In 1918 he married Margaret Skinner and settled in Montrose as chief reporter of the *Montrose Review*. He made his literary début in 1920 as editor of the anthology *Northern Numbers*, modelled on Edward Marsh's Georgian anthologies. Three volumes appeared, the last in 1922, by which time the more backward-looking poets Murray, Buchan and Munro, had been largely replaced by Marion Angus, Helen B. Cruickshank, Alexander Gray, William Jeffrey and William Soutar. Grieve's own poem "Cattle Show", later reprinted in *Stony Limits* (1934) and since much anthologized, first appeared in one of these volumes, as did a number of other English poems already revealing his good Scots "coorseness" ("Consummation"); his view of the world from God's standpoint ("Within that Week"); and his philosophical approach to poetry and science ("Science and Poetry").

Above all, these early pieces show a flair for language and for rhythm.

The contents of the three anthologies, chosen by the invited authors themselves, was of a sufficient quality to prompt several reviewers to ask themselves if a "Scottish Renaissance" was taking place. At that time Grieve was still using his own name, writing in English, and predicting in 1921 that, henceforth among Scottish writers, "the majority will write in English—for the simple reasons (1) that they will reach a larger public (2) that the English language is an immensely superior medium of expression."[2] He was then opposing the formation of a Vernacular Circle of the London Burns Club, whose "revival of Doric" ambitions probably reached no further than that covered by the MacGillivray-Spence experiments.

A few months later, after he had founded his *Scottish Chapbook*, the first number of which appeared from his Montrose address in August 1922, Grieve had experienced a change of heart, for he announced his editorial intention of encouraging new work, whether "in English, Gaelic or Braid Scots". A semi-dramatic prose piece, "Nisbet, an Interlude in Post-War Glasgow", begun in that first issue, introduced the name of Hugh Mac-Diarmid to the public. *Nisbet* is unremarkable, except for its Spenglerian expression of belief in the exhaustion of Western European and American civilization and the view that Dostoevsky heralded the advent of a renewal, which the writer believed would come from Russia.

Readers of the *Dunfermline Press* on 30th September 1922 who had sufficient discernment might have wondered at a remarkable but anonymous lyric, "The Watergaw", later published in *Sangschaw* (1925). Though not perhaps the finest of MacDiarmid's lyrics, it is a splendid poem, showing dependence on little that had gone before, an ability to unlock the vivid potential of old Scots words, and a sure stylistic and rhythmic touch. Like most MacDiarmid lyrics, it offers superficial difficulties to those unfamiliar with Scots, and in any case, like many of the shorter lyrics, sounds richer in the mind's ear than when read aloud.

MacDiarmid lyrics then began to appear in subsequent issues of *Scottish Chapbook*. They differed from the work of the "preservationist" Scots writers within the exhausted old tradition not only by their skilful understanding of the hidden image-making power of words from Middle Scots and their disregard of the boundaries of the dialects into which Scots had finally become fragmented on the cutting-edge of the dichotomizing process during the eighteenth century, but also in their wide-ranging choice of subject matter, their use of cosmic imagery, their re-connection with European literary movements and thought, and their concentrated lyric force.

One of the finest lyrics in *Sangschaw* is "The Eemis Stane", in which the cold world at harvest time is compared to a teetering stone swaying in the sky, while the poet's memories fall like wind-driven snow, so thickly that he cannot read the words cut into the stone, even if the moss of fame and the lichens of history had not obscured them.

I' the how–dumb–deid o' the cauld hairst nicht
The warl' like an eemis stane
Wags i' the lift;
An' my eerie memories fa'
Like a yowdendrift.

Like a yowdendrift so's I couldna read
The words cut oot i' the stane
Had the fug o' fame
An' history's hazelraw
No' yirdit thaim.

Four of the key words in that poem must have been wholly strange, even to readers in 1925. Yet their power and their rightness are unquestionable. The movement of the poem is subtle, delicate and utterly economic, the Middle Scots trick of repeating the last line of one stanza to give the next momentum for a fresh yet unifying departure, masterly. Well, indeed, might David Daiches remark: "Criticism stands powerless before this miracle of verbal choice and placing."[3]

MacDiarmid's links with the past were forged not only through his unsealing of the silenced Scots image-words of our ancestors, but sometimes also through echoes of folk-song; simply, as in "Focherty", with its comic deflation of boss-power (even God's); or—also from *Pennywheep* (1926)—more subtly as in "Empty Vessel", the first stanza of which—

I met ayont the cairney
    A lass wi' tousie hair
Singin' till a bairnie
    That was nae langer there . . .

—echoes, deepens and transforms "Jenny Nettles", collected by David Herd in *Ancient and Modern Songs* (1769):

I met ayont the Kairney
    Jenny Nettles, Jenny Nettles,
Singing till her bairney,
    Robin Rattle's bastard . . .

Sometimes the link is through the juxtaposition of memories of childhood games or names with serious concerns, as in the pieces making up "Au Clair de la Lune", where the earth is a spinning top and the moon a tattered old "craw o' a body". What Kenneth Buthlay calls "cosmic conceits, if that is the word for them"[4] get mixed up with childhood memories to form archetypal images, which Buthlay aptly likens to the Jungian "collective unconscious of the race":

Men see their warld turned tapsalteerie,   [head-over-heels
Drookit in a licht owre eerie,   [drenched
Or sent birlin' like a peerie—   [spinning
Syne it turns a' they've kent till then
To shapes they can nae langer ken.*

When *Sangschaw* appeared, most of the lovers of preservationist "Doric" were appalled and bewildered; but a few of the discerning realized that in MacDiarmid Scotland had produced a poet of the quality of Burns and Dunbar. Francis George Scott maintained that even in 1925, Scots was only one of several "lines" with which the poet was experimenting, "Hugh M'Diarmid" (as it was at first spelled) one of several pseudonyms he was using to cover his tracks, and that the critical success of *Sangschaw* took no one more by surprise that Grieve himself. The "success" may have proved surprising, but I suspect that Scott gave his old pupil less credit for a sense of direction than at that time he deserved.

At any rate, the new poet quickly followed up his advantage. In *Pennywheep*, some of the lyrics are slighter, the Scots image-words less potent in their power. But the recurring way of the Scots countryman of looking nature straight in the eye is particularly memorable in "Scunner", with its frank acceptance of the pleasures of sexual love combined with a refusal to romanticize its physical connection:

Your body derns
In its graces again
As the dreich grun' does
In the gowden grain,
And oot o' the daith
O' pride you rise
Wi' beauty yet
For a hauf-disguise.

The skinklan' stars
Are but distant dirt
Tho' fer owre near
You are still—whiles—girt
Wi the bonnie licht
You bood ha'e tint   [should
—And I lo'e Love
Wi' a scunner in't.

Pennywheep also contains three longer poems. "Gairmscoile" hits back at

* A Drunk Man Looks at the Thistle.

the critics of MacDiarmid's Scots experiments, linking primitive sex and language as having—

> . . . keys to senses lockit to us yet
> —Coorse words that shamble thro' oor minds like stots,
> Syne turn on's muckle e'en wi' doonsin' emerauds lit.   [dazzling

His preoccupation with the "datchie sesames and names for nameless things"—a preoccupation later to prove over-mastering—then leads him to salute Wergeland, the standard-bearer of the Landsmaal language-movement in Norway.

"Sea Serpent" considers the possibility of human awareness of life achieving once again the freshness it is presumed to have had when newly minted (a parallel with Muir's "lost Eden" theory) and bursts out into a paean of rich and meaningful Scots such as had not been sounded since the time of Dunbar. "Bombinations of a Chimera" is a set of variations on the theme that Evil must, in the long run, be good:

> Sin' God has cherished us
> Wi' carefu' cruelty . . .

—a kind of poet-to-God confrontation over a paradox which Burns understood, but was content to resolve more gently:

> Then at the balance let's be mute,
> We never can adjust it . . .*

These poems prepared the way for MacDiarmid's longest and finest masterpiece, *A Drunk Man Looks at the Thistle* (1926), one of the most inventive poetic achievements of the twentieth century. Using the convenient disguise of drunkenness, though of that limited degree which made Burns's "Tam o' Shanter" be "O'er a' the ills of life victorious", MacDiarmid produces a series of satirical interludes which question a wide range of traditionally accepted Scottish values, interspersed with lyrics in some cases reaching more deeply into the recesses of the human spirit than those in the two previous collections. His belief in Gregory Smith's "Caledonian Antisyzygy"— what Smith called "the sudden jostling of contraries . . . the polar twins of the Scottish Muse"—enabled MacDiarmid to contain within what is basically a dramatic monologue a searching examination into nothing less than the whole process of creativity. A poem of such length necessitates peaks and valleys, provocations and resolutions, contrasts between the uniting of man and the infinite by Yggdrasil and the littleness of Scottish trivialities:

* "Address to the Unco Guid".

The munelicht ebbs and flows and wi't my thocht,
Noo movin' mellow and noo lourd and rough.
I ken what I am like in Life and Daith,
But Life and Daith for no man are enough . . .
And O to think that there are members o'
St Andrew's Societies sleepin' soon',
Wha to the papers wrote afore they bedded
On regimental buttons or buckled shoon. . . .   [shoes

All literatures have their examples of writers who push to the end of
extremes. It was really a personal antisyzygy—our old friend the Scottish
dichotomy in fancier clothes—that drove MacDiarmid to cry:

I'll ha'e nae hauf-way hoose, but aye be whaur
Extremes meet—its the only way I ken
To dodge the curst conceit o' bein' richt
That damns the vast majority o' men . . .

—and was eventually to "damn" MacDiarmid himself by leading him to
believe that all his own work was beyond criticism.

This rhapsodic poem that ranges through time, eternity, and the shabby
little prejudices which provincial Scotland made use of to prop up its
national ego—"The Warld and Life and Daith, Heaven, Hell ana'", as the
poet himself puts it—ends appropriately with an earthly deflation. Francis
George Scott claimed that he received a telegram from MacDiarmid, and
hurried to Montrose. There, he found the poet "surrounded by innumerable bits of paper about six inches long on which lay the material from
which the poem was to be made." According to Scott, he and his former
pupil sat down together with a bottle of whisky and spent the night picking
and choosing, till they "got the thing in order". Scott went on: "Early in
the morning, in the wee sma hours, with most of the whisky done, Chris
said: 'But how do we end it?', and I said 'How about repeating—

O, I ha'e Silence left,

adding:

'And weel ye micht',
Sae Jean'll say, 'efter sic an nicht!'"

It is the case that small sections of "a complete poem in over 600 lines",
using the same key-symbols of thistle and rose, moon and woman, whisky
and sea-serpent, appeared in the Glasgow Herald during February 1926. But
the title certainly came from Scott. There are those who believe that the
poem reveals so strong a sense of structure that Scott's story must be non-

sense. They should remember that MacDiarmid himself did not deny it during Scott's lifetime, either at the time of the recorded broadcast interview in which Scott first made his statement, or later, when it appeared in print. That MacDiarmid's sense of structure was perhaps less assured than his less critical admirers would like to believe is suggested by the fact that for his first *Collected Poems* (1962), the poet himself broke up his masterpiece into a series of separately titled short poems, an error of judgement subsequently rectified in later editions.

By 1926, MacDiarmid was indisputably at the head of a new movement in Scottish letters of which he was the principal figure. He was striving to bring about what he called quite openly in the promotion material for *Scottish Chapbook* "a Scottish Literary Revival": and in the April 1924 issue of the *Revue Anglo-Americaine*, Denis Saurat's essay "Le groupe de la Renaissance Ecossaise" gave the movement the title which subsequently stuck to it. To the over-literal mind, it seems a grandiose absurdity to compare a new movement in tiny Scotland's literature to the great awakening of the human spirit throughout fourteenth-century Europe after the long night of the Dark Ages. No such comparison was ever intended. Prefixed by the word "Scottish", Saurat's title implies its own limiting accuracy.

MacDiarmid's vision of freedom led him early in his career into the seemingly incompatible worlds of Scottish Nationalism and International Communism. One of the founders of the Scottish National Party (1928), he was in 1938, after four years as a member, expelled from the Communist Party for this deviation. Although he re-joined in 1956, after the Russian invasion of Hungary, when more politically realistic members were resigning in disgust, his belief that "the future belongs to Communism" soon led him to seize the ever-handy Scottish mantle of the preacher (albeit flyped [pulled] inside-out!) and increasingly use his verse as a political pulpit.

It is open to question whether MacDiarmid is not so much a Communist as simply a psychological rebel. In "Talking with Five Thousand People in Edinburgh"—"You've added a nothing", quipped F. G. Scott, when I first showed him the poem in *Poetry Scotland*: "Chris never talked to five thousand people in his life!"—MacDiarmid reveals himself as an individualist rooted in his personal idealism:

I stand to my position, do what I can,
And will never be turned into "a strong silenced man",
For I am corn and not chaff, and will neither
Be blown away by the wind, nor burst with the flail,
   But will abide them both
   And in the end prevail.

For I am like Zamyatin. I must be a Bolshevik
Before the Revolution, but I'll cease to be one quick

When Communism comes to rule the roost. . . .

To Circumjack Cencrastus (1930)* is similar in structure to its predecessor, though much looser. In spite of such good things as "The Mavis of Pabal", which signals his interest in Gaelic, and "A Moment in Eternity", taken from his early *Annals of the Five Senses* (1923), it reveals the beginnings of the disintegration of that sense of seemingly inevitable style which helps to make the first three books so exciting. The implied symbolism of sea with serpent is scarcely ever remembered by the poet, who now increasingly complains or attacks destructively.

As MacDiarmid began to lay aside Scots in favour of English, abandoning the idealistic, perfectionist technique of a major lyric poet for the impossible role of the creator of a poetry synthesizing total experience, the good things became fewer and fewer, and written mostly in English. An exception is "Milkwort and Bog-Cotton", which appeared in *Scots Unbound* (1932). According to Valda Grieve it was conceived in a pub and first set down on lavatory paper, that being all that could be procured when the poet suddenly called for something on which to write.

In too many of the later poems, vast tracts of quotation-saturated argument intrude, much of it reflected—some of it even borrowed without acknowledgment and chopped up into lines—from articles or books by other authors sympathetic to MacDiarmid's viewpoint. The interest in language has become intellectual; the subtle ear has lost its intuitive critical cunning.

Part of this poetic disintegration may be a reflection of what was happening to MacDiarmid's own life. In 1929, he left Montrose for London, where he became acting editor of Compton Mackenzie's critical radio review *Vox*, an under-capitalized publication catering for what proved to be a non-existent taste. It failed after three months. A spell as a publicity officer in Liverpool was followed by a brief return to Edinburgh. Soon MacDiarmid was in London again, "to accept responsibility for his broken marriage". He was divorced in 1932, and soon afterwards remarried.

Exactly why he moved away from Scots to English has never been fully explained. He himself was to suggest[5] that it resulted from the crisis in his personal life, that blocked the lyric springs from which the first three books had welled. There was also the fact of a severe break-down in the mid-thirties.

The theories of Major C. H. Douglas's Social Credit, which attracted MacDiarmid as they also attracted Pound, had found reflection in *Cencrastus*. The *First Hymn to Lenin* (1931) and the *Second Hymn to Lenin* (1932) marked MacDiarmid's adoption of Lenin as a kind of Gothicized Christ-substitute for the non-sectarian God and Christ used as symbols of unattainable perfection in the earlier collections.

Yet they are transitional books. The *First Hymn to Lenin* is still mostly in

* "Get the better of the curly snake", the allusions being to a path near Langholm and Jamieson's *Dictionary*.

Scots, and includes "The Seamless Garment", with its conclusion:

> And as for me in my fricative work
>   I ken fu' weel
> Sic an integrity's what I maun ha'e,
>   Indivisible, real,
> Woven owre close for the point o' a pin
>   Onywhere to win in.

Unfortunately, "fricative work" was to become increasingly an end in itself.

The poems in *Second Hymn*, mainly in English, contain that beautiful cosmically experienced epiphany, "O Ease My Spirit", and its frequent companion-piece in recitals and anthologies, "Lo! A Child is Born". The lyric impulse had not yet been relegated to the digressionary indulgence it later became.

Mixed up among these good things are chunks of loosely fitting propaganda for Douglasite Social Credit and for Communism. In the practical circumstances MacDiarmid was then having to endure, the fury and the bitterness are understandable, though in one poem, "Poetry and Propaganda", he admits:

> In short, any utterance that is not pure
> Propaganda is impure propaganda for sure.

As Buthlay pertinently remarks: ". . . it may be agreed that Coleridge's Ancient Mariner is propaganda, but it is not propaganda on behalf of a Society for the Prevention of Cruelty to Albatrosses."[6] The phrases "in short" and "for sure", which do no work and are there simply to fill out feet in one case and provide a rhyme in the other, are indicative of MacDiarmid's growing impatience with rhyme.

Meanwhile, a brief spell in Longniddry had been followed by the poet's departure to the island of Whalsay, in Shetland. A decade of poverty, a break-down in health, and the bitterness of undeserved neglect now followed. In 1936, he was presented with a public testimonial signed by several hundred writers got together by the essayist William Power, the poet's "very good friend" of the dedication to the *First Hymn to Lenin*. By now, MacDiarmid was an embittered loner, no longer willing gratefully to accept a helping hand from writers whose best work came nowhere near the standard of his own, as most of those concerned would themselves have admitted. In such a position of partially self-imposed siege, the seeds of megalomania find fruitful soil, producing a weed damaging to the source of their nourishment, as much of MacDiarmid's prose testifies.

Almost at the end of the Shetland stay, finding it increasingly difficult to get his work accepted anywhere, MacDiarmid founded another periodical, *The Voice of Scotland* (1938-39), which twice resumed publication: from 1945 to 1949, when it provided a platform for the younger Scots poets known as the Lallans Makars, and from 1955 to 1958. MacDiarmid remained on Whalsay until 1941. During most of the war of 1939-45 he lived in Glasgow, at first doing heavy manual work in a factory, then transferring to estuarial duties with the Merchant Navy. After a peace-time spell in Glasgow and a brief stay near Strathaven, he moved to a small cottage outside Biggar, Lanarkshire, where he finally settled.

In 1944, R. Crombie Saunders brought out a selection of MacDiarmid's poems in Maclellan's *Poetry Scotland* series, while another anthology, *Speaking for Scotland* (the poet's own choice) appeared in America in 1946. Both did much to spread his reputation.

Recognition began to come from the outside world at last. Scholars from many countries on both sides of the Iron Curtain acclaimed him. At the same time, tardy public appreciation of that part of MacDiarmid's work which entitles him to a place alongside Burns and Dunbar also developed in the post-1946 years.

It is neither possible nor necessary here to go into much detail about MacDiarmid's later work. *A Kist of Whistles* (1947) contained some poems which clearly belonged to the Shetland period, like "The Wreck of the Swan" (marred because the poet does not know when to stop), and some written still earlier. Two of the finest of MacDiarmid's later poems in English first appeared in *Poetry Scotland I*: "Two Religions", with its pantheistic fall-back on "The old loveliness of earth that both affirms and heals"; and "The Glass of Pure Water", a moving and typically surprising comparison between the importance of the constituents of water and "the essence of human life." The speech-rhythms are natural, and the imagery vivid. The piece stays on MacDiarmid's highest English level up to the line: "To still all sound save that talking to God." There is then a propaganda sermon upon the text "all Government is a monopoly of violence", especially those governments immersed in the "pollution and fog" of Capitalism.

The poems in *A Lap of Honour* (1967) supplement the so-called *Collected Poems* of 1962, while *A Clyack Sheaf* (1969) also contains pieces that had clearly earlier appeared elsewhere, in whole or in part. But the most important presentations of late MacDiarmid are undoubtedly *In Memorian James Joyce* (1955)—grandiosely sub-titled "A Vision of World Language"—and *The Kind of Poetry I Want* (1961).

Edwin Morgan has put the case for these late works as successfully as anyone, in "Poetry and Knowledge in MacDiarmid's Later Work"[7] quoting from the James Joyce poem, where MacDiarmid speaks of his search for:

The point where science and art can meet,
For there are two kinds of knowledge,

Knowing about things and knowing things,
Scientific data and realization.
And I seek their perfect fusion in my work.

Can such a fusion be found? I think not. The later MacDiarmid allows
his fascination for information and knowledge from any and every discipline to absorb his muse. Experts in these disciplines have not always been
impressed with the accuracy of the observations, or the uses to which they
have been put, although Morgan argues that this does not matter.

In marshalling his welter of information, MacDiarmid deploys vast catalogues which must become meaningless, even boring, to the majority of his
readers who will not have had access to the sources from which they are
taken. Often, it is true, these arid lists of technicalities serve to release contrasting passages of lyric beauty. Of architechtonic structure or shape,
however, there is none. Morgan does not really deal with this point.
Indeed, he moves round it quite openly by declaring: "As zoologists may
argue whether a colony is an organism, critics may hesitate to say that the
kind of *poetry* MacDiarmid wants is a kind of *poem*. A movement towards a
more "open" conception of poetry than has prevailed in the modern
period is however gaining ground, and I see no reason why we should deny
ourselves, for love of architectonics, the ingredient and emergent pleasures
of a poetry in evolution."

Emotion's fusing force, the poet's speculative powers which were once
the main-spring of his linguistic surprises, and even control of rhythm,
have all been sacrificed for a poetry of "fact". Admittedly, MacDiarmid's
material is often concerned with important issues, and therefore potentially
of greater consequence than that used by many of his contemporaries. But,
to quote Buthlay again: "If every age gets the poetry it deserves, perhaps
there is something appropriate about the poet in our own time becoming a
sort of sub-editor in an intellectual news agency, spotting the most interesting items and arranging them in unexpected sequences that shock the
torpid reader into attention." Yet "surely we are right to protest against, or
at least regret, the loss of these subtler qualities in the handling of language
that used to make the poet's words so quotable."

The poet's uncritical belief in his own infallibility may have arisen as a
protective rationale for the loss of his lyric impulse, or as a by-product of
his years of poverty and neglect, just as his Anglophobia was no doubt
strengthened by the unhappiness of the London days. But it has helped shut
the covers of the works of his later years to all but a handful of devoted disciples.

Even so, judged by the range, strength and quantity of the best of his
achievement[8]—all that will ultimately matter—MacDiarmid is unquestionably a great poet; the equal of Burns and Dunbar in his country;
the peer of Eliot, Pound and Wallace Stevens in his century.

The Scottish Renaissance which he identified and inspired had only one significant poet among its early followers, William Soutar (1898–1943).

The son of a Perth carpenter, Soutar began to decline in health while he was still at Edinburgh University, where he matriculated as a medical student, after wartime service in the Royal Navy. He soon transferred to the Arts faculty, however, and met Grieve. But illness crept relentlessly up on Soutar, and during his final year at the University he was already gripped by the paralysis which, for the last fourteen years of his life, kept him a bedridden but courageous invalid confined to a single room. While he appreciated MacDiarmid's early achievement and celebrated it in his own nationalistically over-emphatic extended poem "The Auld Tree", Soutar was always aware of the intellectual dangers MacDiarmid braved by crying "Not Burns, but Dunbar", and by saturating himself in the currents of world literature. In "The Thistle Looks at a Drunk Man", Soutar wrote:

But hamely fare wis no for him:
He laidl'd ower his gutsy rim
A' kinds o meat tae stap each whim
   Kitlin his void: [tickling his emptiness
Rocher and Blok and Joyce (Nim! Nim!)
Mallarmé, Freud.

Most of Soutar's early published collections were in English: *Gleanings by an Undergraduate* (1923), *Conflict* (1931), *The Solitary Way* (1934) and *Brief Words* (1935). These were followed by *A Handful of Earth* (1936), *In the Time of Tyrants* (1939), *But the Earth Abideth* (1943), and the posthumously published *The Expectant Silence* (1944). His English influences were Blake, Lawrence, Owen and the Ballad. There was a Georgian literariness about the contents of most of the earlier volumes, an absence of edge to the epigrams in *Brief Words*. In *A Handful of Earth*, Soutar sought to adumbrate his belief that "the contemplation of a single leaf can become a skylight through which the mind may stare on reality." In almost all his poems in English, a prim sententiousness, not helped by the tripping hymn stanza he so often used, results in a lifelessness absent from his best Scots verse. Only occasionally, as in "Revelation", from *But the Earth Abideth*, does the sensitive smouldering take fire, and blaze up into poetry, the impact here strengthened by the fact that the poem sounds like a grim parody of a Scottish Paraphrase:

Machines of death from east to west
   Drive through the darkened sky;
Machines of death from west to east
   Through the same darkness fly.

They pass; and on the foredoomed towns

Loosen their slaughtering load:
They see no faces in the stones:
   They hear no cries of blood.

They leave a ruin; and they meet
   A ruin at return:
The mourners in the alien street
   At their own doorways mourn.

Soutar himself maintained: "English is *not* natural to me; and I use it consciously even in conversation; it is always something of an effort for me to
find my words; and not uncommonly I labour as if I were speaking a
foreign language."[9]
This is exactly how many of the English poems sound. Not so his Scots,
so natural in his "off-taking" satirical vein, as in "The Philosophic Taed":

There was a taed wha thocht sae lang
On sanctity and sin;
On what was richt, and what was wrang,
And what was in atween—
That he gat naething düne.

The wind micht blaw, the snaw micht snaw,
He didna mind a wheet;
Nor kent the derk'nin frae the daw,
The wulfire frae the weet;
Nor fuggage frae his feet.

His wife and weans frae time to time,
As they gaed by the cratur,
Wud haut to hae a gowk at him
And shak their pows, or natter;
"He's no like growin better."

It maun be twenty year or mair
Sin thocht's been a' his trade;
And naebody can tell for shair
Whether this unco taed
Is dead, or thinks he's dead.

Soutar is equally his natural self in his comic "Whigmaleeries"[10], his
humorous bairn-rhymes, and in his Scots lyrics. *Seeds in the Wind* (1933,
enlarged and revised 1943) contains child's-eye poems in Scots of an innocent, amused naturalness, sometimes sounding folk-overtones no other
poet has equalled:

Dinna gang oot the nicht;
Dinna gang oot the nicht:
Laich was the müne as I cam owre the muir;
Laich was the lauchin though nane was there:
Somebody nippit me,
Somebody trippit me;
Somebody grippit me roun' an' aroun':
I ken it was Bawsy Broon:
I'm shair it was Bawsy Broon.

If one were to seek out Bawsy Broon's poetic ancestry, Hogg would doubtless be found somewhere in her lineage. But she is far removed from the exquisite lyrics that are the best things in *Poems in Scots* (1935): "The Tryst," with its resigned sublimation of unfulfillable physical desire; or the acceptance by the poet of his own impending fate, and his identification of it with the fate of all that is mortal, in "Song":

Whaur yon broken brig hings owre;
Whaur yon water maks nae soun';
Babylon blaws by in stour:
Gang doun wi' a sang, gang doun.

Deep, owre deep for onie drouth:
Wan eneuch an ye wud droun;
Saut, or seelfu', for the mouth;
Gang doun wi' a sang, gang doun.

Babylon blaws by in stour
Whaur yon water maks nae soun':
Darkness is your only door;
Gang doun wi' a sang, gang doun.

Had that door not cast its opening shadow so soon upon Soutar's life, his ironic humour, his sense of the ridiculous, and the seeming inevitability of his Scots, could scarcely have failed to enrich the development of the Scottish Renaissance, perhaps saving it from some of its "plastic" follies in the next generation.

But that second, more impersonal, world war—which deeply distressed the helpless, dying poet—intervened. It was part of a response to the desire for "personalism", felt especially by the people of small nations, that brought what Eric Linklater called the "second-wind" Scottish Renaissance poets into prominence.

There was one personal link between this new group and Soutar. That irrepressible Admirable Crichton of the Scottish Renaissance, Douglas

Young (1913–1973) visited the invalid poet in his room at Perth in 1939. To Soutar, the youthful scholar, poet, wit and nationalist politician was "an exceedingly tall fellow with a shovel-beard—his leanness, longness and fringiness gave one the initial impression of a B.B.C. announcer who had partially metamorphosed into an aerial: a fluent talker with a lectorial style."[11]

Young, a Fifer who became a lecturer in Greek at St Andrews University, but whost nationalist convictions against "English" conscription (which he would have been excused in any case, on grounds of weak sight) led to his trial and imprisonment in Edinburgh's Saughton Jail used his "lectorial style" to exhort his contemporaries in the use of Lallans. Yet there is a classical restraint as well as an intellectual control about his own verse. There is also a dry Scots wit, to be seen deployed in pieces like "Ice-flumes Owregie their Lades", or the often-quoted "Last Lauch":

The Minister said it wad dee,
    the cypress buss I plantit.   [bush
But the buss grew til a tree,   [to
    naething dauntit.

It's growan, stark and heich,   [high
    derk and straucht and sinister,
kirkyairdie-like and dreich.   [dreary
    But whaur's the Minister?

The influence of the ballad and the terse economy of the Greek Anthology are combined in his description of love:

Gie aa, and aa comes back
    Wi mair nor aa.
Hain ocht, and ye'll hae nocht,   [keep back anything
    Aa flees awa.

He was sometimes also unexpectedly successful in his poems about the concerns of country folk, giving what looks like becoming a mere Kailyard exercise a sharp psychological twist, as in "Sabbath i the Mearns" from *Auntran Blads* (1943) and "The Shepherd's Dochter" from *Selected Poems* (1950). These volumes and *A Braird o Thristles* (1947) include some vigorous Scots versions of Gaelic poems by Sorley Maclean and George Campbell Hay, to whom *Auntran Blads* is dedicated.

The most remarkable Scots poet after MacDiarmid is Sydney Goodsir Smith (1915–1975), who spent the first years of his life in New Zealand. He came to Edinburgh when his father, Professor (later Sir Sydney) Smith, took up the chair of Forensic Medicine at the city's older University. Goodsir Smith himself briefly studied medicine at Edinburgh before embarking on an arts degree at Oxford. For him, Scots was an acquired accomplishment.

His ebullient good-nature and ready wit so filled out his conversation that the impact of his personality perhaps resulted in an over-favourable initial assessment of his early books, *Skail Wind* (1941) and *The Wanderer* (1943). His first successes are to be found in *The Deevil's Waltz* (1946), with its brief threnody, "Largo", symbolizing the decline of Scotland through the image of the single fishing-boat setting out from the harbour at dawn, and in the modernized echoes of Dunbar and Burns, not to say MacDiarmid, which dance in company through the title poem:

> We kenna hert, we kenna heid,
> The Deivil's thirled baith quick and deid,
> Jehovah snores and Christ hissel
> Loups i the airms o Jezebel.

His masterpiece, *Under the Eildon Tree* (1948), revealed a thoroughly individual voice. Using the myth of Thomas the Rhymer as a binding agent, the poet celebrates and laments his own passions and the loves of some of the world's, and classical mythology's, great lovers—Orpheus and Eurydice, Dido and Aeneas, Burns and Highland Mary—in twenty-four "Elegies", each of which is basically a variation on the theme of love as experienced by the poet, whether with the "White Goddess" herself or "Sandra, the cou o' the auld Black Bull". Its mingling of comic exuberance and melancholy, its assimilated Poundian technique of references, and its irrepressible energy, place it fairly and squarely alongside *A Drunk Man Looks at the Thistle* as one of the two finest longer Scots masterpieces of the twentieth century.

> I got her in the Black Bull
> (The Black Bull o Norroway),
> Gin I mind richt, in Leith Street,   [if, remember
> Doun the stair at the corner forenent   [over against
> The Fun Fair and Museum o Monstrosities,
>   The Tyke-faced Loun, the Cunyiar's Den
>   And siclike.
> I tine her name the nou, and cognomen for that—   [forget
> Aiblins it was Deirdre, Ariadne, Calliope,   [perhaps
> Gaby, Jacquette, Katerina, Sandra,
>   Or sunkots; exotic, I expeck.
> A wee bit piece
>   O' what our faithers maist unaptlie,
>   But romanticallie designatit "Fluff".
> My certie! Nae muckle of Fluff
>   About the hures o Reekie!

Dour as stane, the like stane
As biggit the unconquerable citie   [built
Whar they pullulate,
      Infestan
The wynds and closes, squares
And public promenads
      —The bonnie craturies!
      —But til our winter's tale . . .

Gone is the awkward thickness of Scots, the air of manipulated artificiality, which characterized the earlier books.

Smith's ear for the handling of strict forms was always apt to be self-
indulgent: but there are fine lyrics, mostly on his favourite subject of love,
in the later volumes, notably *So Late Into the Night* (1952) and *Figs and
Thistles* (1959). At a time when most poets have concentrated on gaining
the maximum value out of the image, Smith's best lyrics are the more remarkable in that like all his poetry they rely basically on statement. He is
fundamentally concerned, as Wittig puts it, "with life as it is."[12] His use of
imagery is sparse, and much of it is commonplace. It is as the poet of blowsy
Auld Reekie's wynds and closes and the gangrels (wandering folk,) who
hang about them, that Smith really excels. Though nothing else ever quite
equalled *Under the Eildon Tree*, his conspicuous successes include "The
Grace o God and the Meth Drinker" (1959) and *Kynd Kittock's Land* (1965).
He is essentially a natural urban poet:

I loe ma luve in a lamplit bar   [love
Braw on a wuiden stool,
Her knees cocked up and her neb doun   [nose
Slorpan a pint o yill.   [guzzling, ale

His nearest counterpart is Robert Garioch Sutherland (b. 1909), known
as a writer by his first two names. An Edinburgh man with a fluent command of Scots, Garioch often manages to achieve a remarkable affinity of
spirit with his much-admired predecessor as laureate of Auld Reekie,
Robert Fergusson.

Garioch's muse is high-spirited and fundamentally comic. It is best represented in his *Selected Poems* (1966). *The Masque of Edinburgh* (1933 and 1954),
a dramatic fantasy, and his later Edinburgh sonnets, poke fun at various
forms of Scottish hypocrisy, ranging from pet-worshipping at the expense
of humans to the foibles of the city baillies. Describing a Saturday-night
argument about a religious play, Garioch's wry schoolmasterly comment,
while sharply-pointed, is essentially kindly:

It seemed discussion wad last oot the nicht,
hadna the poliss, sent by Mrs Grundy

pitten us oot at twalve. And they were richt!
Wha daur debait religion on a Sunday?

There are graver undertones, and sharper satire, in some of the later poems
of *The Big Music* (1971) and *Doktor Faust in Rose Street* (1973).

Alexander Scott (b. 1920), the youngest of the "second wind" Lallans
Makars* and an Aberdonian, educated at the Academy and University of
his native city, was a distinguished soldier who became the first lecturer in
Scottish Literature to be appointed (1948) to any Scottish University. By
1971, he headed the newly formed Department of Scottish Literature in
the University of Glasgow. As a lecturer, he has trained many of those who
have subsequently, and for the first time, introduced Scottish literature systematically into the curricula of Scottish schools. His biography of Soutar,
Still Life (1958), is likely to remain the standard work on its subject, combining the virtues of clarity in narration and sympathetic acumen in its appreciation of the poet's work.

It is with Scott the poet, however, that we are here concerned. From his
collections *The Latest in Elegies* (1949), *Selected Poems* (1950), *Mouth Music*
(1954), *Cantrips* (1968), *Greek Fire* (1971) and *Double Agent* (1972), his
Selected Poems 1943–1974 (1975) is drawn. Like Garioch, Scott is a native
speaker of the language, and uses it with the forthright directness which has
characterized so much of our literature. Like Smith, he tends to be a poet of
statement, although in such early and much-anthologized poems as "Haar
in Princes Street" and "Scrievin" there are memorable images. Nor does
his work lack the native sardonic humour, as in "Hollywood in Hades":

Jayne Mansfield, strippit mortal stark
  O' aa her orra duddies—   [worthless rags
For thae that sail in Charon's barque
  Keep nocht aside their bodies—
Comes dandily daffan til Hades' dark,
  A sicht to connach studies.   [destroy

Yet Pluto, coorse as King Farouk,
  Gies only ae bit glower—
She's naukit, ilka sonsie neuk,
  But he's seen aa afore—
And turns to tell the t'ither spook,
  "Marilyn, move outowre!".†

* As a *Glasgow Herald* controversy on the validity of Scots as a suitable vehicle for poetry
in the mid-twentieth century led to their being styled, although in fact Burns wrote of
"gude braid Lallans".

† Jayne Mansfield, a film star more noted for her physical attributes than the intellectual
qualities of her acting, was decapitated in a car accident in 1967. "Marilyn" is, of course,
Marilyn Monroe, onetime sex-symbol and wife of playwright Arthur Miller.

Scott has a wider effective range of themes than Young, Smith or Garioch, and possesses a corresponding command of a variety of forms, taking in love-poems, satires, elegies, epigrams, and even space-exploration. His English poems move from the brief atmospheric lyrics in the Hellenic sequence *Greek Fire* (1971) to the controlled anger of measured lamentation in "Ballade of Beauties."

It seems to me possible that Scott's Lallans may come to be regarded as a kind of generally understandable norm for the late twentieth century. Goodsir Smith's Scots was never spoken by anyone; but then the success of his best work was not dependent upon his handling of naturalistic language. Scott's was, and is. He uses it at its best—sound, sight and image matching—in the extended poem "Heart of Stone", which celebrates that "teuch toun, whaur even the strand maks siller", his native Aberdeen, with the glittering evocativeness that shows him to be, amongst other things, very much a poet of place. Although one of a series of several poems written for use against television film, it avoids the usual trap in such circumstances of padding valid images out to allow the lumbering camera-eye to catch up with the faster-moving mind's-eye of the poet:

But neither auld mistaks nor new mishanters
Can steerach the fine fettle o ferlie stane,
The adamant face that nocht can fyle,
Nae rain, nae reek,
Fowr-square til aa the elements, fine or foul,
She stares back straucht at the skimmeran scaud o the sun
Or bares her brou til the bite o the brashy gale,
Riven frae raw rock, and rocky-ruited,
A breem bield o steive biggins,
A hard hauld, a sterk steid
Whaur bonnie fechters bolden at ilka ferlie,
The city streets a warld o wild stramash
Frae clintie seas or bens as coorse as brine
For fowk sae fit to daur the dunt o storms
Wi faces stobbed by the stang o saut
Or callered by country winds
In a teuch toun whaur even the strand maks siller,
The sweel o the same saut tide
Clanjamfries crans and kirks by thrang causeys
Whaur cushat's croudle mells wi sea-maw's skirl,
And hirplan hame half-drouned wi the weicht o herrin
The trauchled trawler waffs in her wake
A flaffer o wings—a flash o faem-white feathers—
As the sea-maw spires i the stane-gray lift
Owre sworlan swaws o the stane-gray sea
And sclents til the sea-gray toun, the hert o stane.

There are several other writers whose work in Scots is either much smaller in quantity, or, in general, inferior in quality to their work in English. George Campbell Hay (b. 1915) comes into the former category. His admirably taut "Still Gyte, Man?" and his Scots re-creation of the dialogue sonnet of Angiolieri, beginning "'Beckie, my luve!'—'What is't, ye twa-faced tod?'" are but two examples of his multi-lingual versatility. As it happens, the best Scots poem of Hay's is MacDiarmid's version from Hay's own Gaelic, "The Auld Hunter". There are delicate overtones of Highland-English speech rhythms in "The Old Fisherman" from *Wind on Loch Fyne* (1948)—where the phrase "my dancing days for fishing are over" is an echo of an expression used by one of the characters in the novel by the poet's father, *Gillespie*—and a musical lilt to "The Kerry Shore" which made it, like "The Old Fisherman", apt material for setting by Francis George Scott.

Another Scots poet who deserves comment is Alastair Mackie (b. 1925). Like Alexander Scott, Mackie is an Aberdonian, and therefore brought up in the only part of Scotland where Scots of any richness (as opposed to the broken-down *patois* of Glasgow) is still spoken. *Clytach* (1972) contains twenty-eight poems, ranging from "Drappit", where a relegated footballer watches from the touchline his successor succeed where he has failed, and he becomes a pathetic symbol of the relativity of success, to an expression of the cosmic view in the early manner of MacDiarmid (though using free verse) in "In Absentia", and from the space-age angle in "The Cosmonaut". There is no denying Mackie's intellectual energy, wide range of interests and verbal skill. His habit of spelling phonetically according to Aberdeenshire pronounciation—the systematic spelling arrangements suggested by the Lallans Makars has been cheerfully disregarded by most subsequent practitioners!—though patriotically understandable, puts an unnecessary difficulty in the way of the average reader familiar with Lowland Scots, such as keeps that local prose masterpiece of manners *Johnnie Gibb of Gushetneuk* (1871) by William Alexander (1826–1894) a strictly regional pleasure.

Another doubt arises. Mackie's slim volume is accompanied by a "Word Leet/Glossary" containing over five hundred words. These include terms like "apen-furth" (open air), "laggans of the air" (horizon) and "indevallin" (incessant); terms scarcely likely to be heard on the tongues of many late-twentieth-century Aberdonians. In an age when the word "lift" is now only used in daily life as Glasgwegian for "hoist", it is perhaps questionable if even the lyric genius of a MacDiarmid could achieve again such linguistic revivifications as were still miraculously possible in the 1920s.

Other younger writers actively concerned with the continuing creative use of Scots include Duncan Glen (b. 1933). As with Donald Campbell (b. 1940) and Roderick Watson (b. 1943), who uses both Scots and English, it is too early to assess what lasting quality their work may possess.

Two older Scottish poets writing in English, but who consistently eschewed the modish, remaining entirely true to their own personal vision, are Andrew Young (1885–1971) and Edwin Muir (1887–1959).

Young was born at Elgin. Two years later his family moved to Edinburgh, where he attended the Royal High School and the University. He was ordained a minister of the United Free Church of Scotland, serving first at Berwick-upon-Tweed, and then at Temple, Midlothian. Shortly after the 1914–18 war, during which time Young spent several periods in France with the Y.M.C.A., he decided to leave Scotland. He moved to Hove, where he took charge of the English Presbyterian Church. In due course, he "went over" to the Church of England, becoming curate at Plaistow, West Sussex, in 1939, and Vicar of Stonegate in 1941, where he remained until 1959. Edinburgh University gave him an honorary degree in 1951, and the following year he received the Queen's Medal for Poetry.

Young was a naturalist and author of two botanical studies. A shrewd and accurate observation of Nature's moods and creatures provides the mainspring of his poetry. His reserved temperament and his economy of expression both proclaim his Scottishness, although his mysticism links him with the English poets Traherne and Vaughan, and his innocent simplicity of verbal approach to Clare, Edward Thomas, Hardy and Blunden.

A poet who writes imaginatively of Nature is never really in or out of fashion. He is simply there, like Nature itself, when we choose to turn to him for quiet refreshment. "Sudden Thaw" illustrates the gently self-generating quality of his imagery:

When day dawned with unusual light,
Hedges in snow stood half their height
And in the white-paved village street
Children are walking without feet.

But now by their own breath kept warm
Muck-heaps are naked at the farm
And even through the shrinking snow
Dead bents and thistles start to grow.

Muir, though also a keen-eyed manipulator of nature-imagery, and ultimately also an accepter of Christian mysticism, had a wider-ranging mind. He was the son of a Deerness, Orkney, farmer, educated in the "capital" of the islands, Kirkwall. The family moved to Glasgow when Muir was fourteen. There, amongst other jobs, he found work as a clerk in a beer-bottling factory, and later in a factory where maggoty bones were brought from all over Scotland to be reduced to charcoal and grease. A more depressing environment for an embyro poet could scarcely be imagined.

In Glasgow, Muir's elder brother, Willie, died painfully of consumption. Soon after, another elder brother, Johnnie, died even more painfully of a tumour on the brain. It is scarcely surprising that the clean, hard brightness of the wind-swept Orkney landscape should have seemed a lost Eden compared to Glasgow and its environs, where, Muir wrote: "The slums seemed to be everywhere around me, a great spreading swamp into which I might sink for good".

This, happily, he did not do. His escape route led him, through his belief in Socialism, to a London job on the staff of Orage's advanced-thinking periodical *New Age*, marriage in 1919, then several post-war years of free-lance writing in various European countries.

Thereafter, whilst living at St Andrews, Muir and his wife, Willa, made several translations of books by important German writers. His later years were spent mainly in the service of the British Council in Edinburgh, at Prague—where he was a distressed witness of the Communist coup of 1948—and in Rome. A spell as warden of Newbattle Abbey College, near Edinburgh, and a year at Harvard preceeded his final retirement to a village near Cambridge, where he died.

Although during his Roman stay Muir seems totally to have accepted Christianity, most of his poetry was written against the background of his awareness that religion no longer provided the generally accepted assumptions it did in previous centuries, and that no generally agreed substitute had been discovered. Muir therefore created his own background, the world of myth and symbol.

Even in his earliest collection, *First Poems* (1925), with its Georgian atmosphere and poetic diction (later revised in the few poems allowed to survive), the poet's distinctive thoughtfulness is apparent.

The Narrow Place (1943), his sixth collection, shows a notable advance in range of subject-matter and sharpened technical skill. All his words are now made to work. Here is to be found "Scotland 1941" and "Robert the Bruce", two frequently anthologized pieces. Yet Muir is not at his best in his poems relating to Scotland. He had little sympathy with the ideals of the Scottish Renaissance, and by doubting the validity of Scots as a fully expressive modern medium, touched off, in *Scott and Scotland* (1932), a long-drawn-out "flyting" with MacDiarmid which remained entirely one-sided, not even MacDiarmid's vicious personal insults drawing any protest from Muir.

His poem "The River", with its physical images of natural order invaded, and its symbolism of the river of history flowing towards no known end, is more characteristic:

> The stream
> Runs on into the day of time and Europe,
> Past the familiar walls and friendly roads,
> Now thronged with dumb migrations, gods and altars
> That travel towards no destination. Then
> The disciplined soldiers come to conquer nothing

March upon emptiness and do not know
Why all is dead and life has hidden itself.
The enormous winding frontier walls fall down
Leaving anonymous stone and vacant grass.

Muir's constant personal need for an ordered background did not allow him to contemplate any implication of meaningless casualness as finality: so, the poem concludes:

The stream flows on into what land, what peace,
Far past the other side of the burning world?

Muir's later collections *The Voyage* (1946), *The Labyrinth* (1949) and *One Foot in Eden* (1956), finally brought together with his earlier work in *Collected Poems* (1960), reveal his continuing preoccupation with the world of myth and dream. There is a gentle movement about many of the poems, a spare and considered tone, and a quiet and subtle imagery which gives his best work undemonstrative individuality. Yet there is also a feeling of remoteness about it, as if the reader was observing sensitive feelings laid out behind glass. Indeed, his work has been criticized by David Wright[13] for being allegedly lacking in rhythmic and linguistic vitality, though these are mere fashionable qualities, and a similar charge could be laid with equal justice at the door of many poets, including Wordsworth. The basic weakness, such as it is, lies elsewhere.

Muir's symbolism—in particular, that relating to a supposed lost innocent Eden—is often merely escapist. That much-admired later poem "The Horses", which visualizes apocalyptically a possible outcome of our accelerating technology, has the animals seen:

As fabulous steeds set on an ancient shield
Or illustrations in a book knights.

—the method of their arrival:

Dropped in some wilderness of the broken world,
Yet new as if they had come from their own Eden.

Here, we have both the book-thought image—as remote from physical experience as some of the more extravagant words burnished and positioned by Wallace Stevens—as well as the re-use of the "perfect" Eden symbol, in this case an Eden reserved for horses.

It has been suggested that the poet may have meant to imply that the innocence of the horses was pre-natal, new-born foals being commonly described as having been "dropped". But this interpretation strengthens the objection, since an Eden of innocence open only to the unborn would appear to imply a total rejection of any kind of life-principle.

Thus, despite their refined qualities, too often Muir's exquisitely fashioned lines, with their undemonstrative music and subtle rhythms, *feel* cold; as if they owed their origin to literature and not directly to life. Muir's poetry, for all its accuracy of observation, is strangely lacking in sensuousness. There is never mud on the boots of his muse. Undoubtedly, there are many who do not share these reservations. Muir is the kind of poet whose work either inspires intense enthusiasm, or little more than admiration for its unfailing technical skill.

Two other poets stand apart from the "movements" which prevailed in the post-Second World War decades: George Bruce (b. 1909) and Ruthven Todd (b. 1914).

Todd was basically a "30s" man, much influenced by the Auden school and *New Verse*. Born in Edinburgh, the exiled years of his adult life found reflection in some of his earliest poems, such as "Personal History". He is at his best where his conversational style gains tautness from the tension of such subject matter as the impact of war on the life of ordinary Londoners, and the brittleness of human love set against a backdrop of sudden violence. *The Acreage of the Heart* (1943) is his most successful collection. Later verse includes a fine love poem, "A Narrow Sanctuary", written after his departure for America, and an effective return to the theme of man's brittleness, contrasting pre-history and the present, in "Broken Arrowheads at Chilmark, Martha's Vineyard". Too many of the poems in his collected volume *Garland For a Winter Solstice* (1962) rely on literary or painterly springboards.

George Bruce (b. 1909), on the other hand, has steadily widened his horizons since the appearance of his first book, *Sea Talk* (1944), which dealt largely with his personal reaction to the fishing community of Fraserburgh, in which he was born, and the landscape of the North-east. He learned his spare and economical technique from Pound in his "Mauberley" period, and to some extent from Eliot, particularly in the matter of cadence. Yet the tone and timbre of the Scottish use Bruce makes of these techniques is entirely individual, relating to the durable qualities of rock, sea and element among which he grew up. Comparing even the limited graciousness of climate which allowed Gothic spires to flourish in wind-swept Balbec and Finistère with the granite knuckle-thrusts of headland among which the Buchan fisherman has his being, Bruce exclaims:

To defend life thus and so to grace it
What art! but you, my friend, know nothing of this,
Merely the fog, more often the east wind
That scours the sand from the shore,
Bequeathing it to the sheep pasture,
Whipping the dust from the fields,
Disclosing the stone ribs of earth . . .

Bruce is a poet of place against which "the hero" is the ordinary man going about his difficult business on sea or land. *Collected Poems* (1970) reveals a more cosmopolitan range of subject-matter, a broadening of tone, and an extension of metrical technique. Nothing, however, quite surpasses "A Gateway to the Sea", a stately elegy upon the changelessness of change. The "gateway" leads in a purely physical sense to ruined St Andrews Cathedral, which has accommodated both splendours and gossip:

... Caesar's politics
And he who was drunk last night:
Rings, diamants, snuff boxes, warships.
Also the less worthy garments of worthy men.

It leads, too, to that point in time and apprehended experience when Past and Present merge:

The European sun knew those streets
"O Jesu parvule; Christus Victus, Christus Victor,"
The bells singing from their towers, the waters
Whispering to the waters, the air tolling
To the air—the faith, the faith ...
All this was long ago. The lights
Are out, the town is sunk in sleep ...

The New Apocalyptic movement, to which most of the English-writing Scottish Renaissance poets at one time belonged, was almost entirely Celtic in origin. Its high priests were Henry Treece, a Welshman whose novels of early Britain were later to bring imaginatively alive the severities under which the inhabitants of these islands once lived out their brief and brutish lives; and J. F. Hendry, a dour Clydeside Scot. After writing two volumes of verse, *The Blackbird of Ospo* (1945), a collection of short stories mostly arising out of his experiences in Yugoslavia, and a novel based on his Scottish childhood, *Fernie Brae* (1947), Hendry became a Canadian academic.

Apocalyptisim was stimulated by stream-of-consciousness techniques; in prose by Joyce, in verse by Dylan Thomas. What lent it its relevant urgency was the contrasting impersonalism of the war. Romanticism and a return to a belief in the importance of the individual also played some part in the revival of interest in Scots, the language of a small nation. Both the upsurge of Apocalyticism and the return to Scots were understandable reactions to the ineffectualness in practical terms of England's political poetry of the '30s, and to the all-engulfing events of 1939–45.

D. H. Lawrence, in *Apocalypse*, provided the movement with its credo:

The rider on the white horse! Who is he, then? . . . He is the royal me, he is my very self and his horse is the whole MANA of a man. He is my very me, my sacred ego . . . And he rides forth, like the sun, with arrows, to conquest, but not with the sword, for the sword implies judgment, and this is my *dynamic* or potent self.

The rejection of "judgment" meant that no standards could readily be applied to Apocalyptic work, since, according to G. S. Fraser in *The White Horseman* (1941), one of the movement's anthologies,* it derived "from Surrealism . . . one might even call it a dialectical development of it: the next stage forward", in so far as, Fraser claimed, it was meant to allow that "the intellect and its activity in willed action" was "part of the living completeness of man."

But "willed action" without "judgment" produced an excess of romantic confusion, as Robert Conquest pointed out:[14]

In the 1940s the mistake was made of giving the Id, a sound player in the percussion side under a strict conductor, too much of a say in the doings of the orchestra as a whole. As it turned out, it could only manage the simpler part of melody and rhythm, and was completely out of its depth with harmony and orchestration.

Four of the Scots members of the New Apocalypse survived to pick up the sword of judgment and apply it to their early work. Tom Scott (b. 1918) renounced all his war-time English verse, and became a passionate pro-Lallans propagandist. His "Brand the Builder" catches something of the enduring strength-through-unawareness of an ordinary, uncomprehending man. G. S. Fraser (b. 1915) never forsook clarity of meaning, and in *Home Town Elegy* (1944) and *The Traveller Has Regrets* (1948), evocatively caught the bitter-sweet of young love, the pang of wartime exile, the regret for departure:

The traveller has regrets
For the receding shore
That with its many nets
Has caught, not to restore,
The white lights in the bay,
The blue lights on the hill,
Though night with many stars
May travel with him still,
But night has nought to say,
Only a colour and shape
Changing like cloth shaking,

*The others were: *New Apocalypse* (1940), *The Crown and the Sickle* (1944) and *A New Romantic Anthology* (1949).

A dancer with a cape
Whose dance is heart-breaking,
Night with its many stars
Can warn travellers
There's only time to kill
And nothing much to say:
But the blue lights on the hill,
The white lights in the bay
Told us the meal was laid
And that the bed was made
And that we could not stay

Norman MacCaig (b. 1910) began his poetic career as the most apocalyptic of all the White Horseman's Scottish followers with *Far Cry* (1943)
and *The Inward Eye* (1946), lunging and plunging on images that bucked
his verses wherever they willed:

I brought you elephants and volcano tops
and a eucalyptus tree on a coral island,
I had them in baskets. You looked with surprise
and went away to pick weeds out of the garden . . .

—in the circumstances a very reasonable reaction on the part of the lady to
whom the lines were addressed.

After an interval of nine years, MacCaig published *Riding Lights* (1955).
This showed that he had applied a new discipline to his technique, and also
immersed himself in metaphysics, throwing at first the shadow of Donne:

I who had nowhere else to go now do
Such journeys (here) as lie from me to you,
And think them nothing; which Time thinks them too.

In *The Sinai Sort* (1957) and *A Common Grace* (1960), the metaphysical
preoccupation has been tuned to a highly personal use, and provides a connecting link in the poet's development through the volumes of the '60s,
leading up to *Selected Poems* (1971). In MacCaig's later work, the metaphysics too easily become a sleight-of-hand trick of turning words when the
poet has nothing particular to say.

Metaphysics, though a very Scottish preoccupation, do not by themselves shape a poet, and it is the combination of that intellectual toughness
of strand they provide matched with the vigorous colours of MacCaig's
imagery in his middle and best period that has resulted in him producing
some of the finest poetry in English in our native literature.

Although born and educated in Edinburgh, MacCaig's West Highland
ancestry has exercised a strong pull upon his imagination, so that, poeti-

cally speaking, the crofts, the mountains and the seascapes of Sutherland-
shire are now recognizably "MacCaig country", providing the starting-
point for many of his best poems. Some of the mature poems still enshrine
the Apocalyptic "royal me"; "Summer Farm", for instance which illustrates both the accurate sensuousness of MacCaig's imagery and the thread-
ing tautness:

Straws like tame lightnings lie about the grass
And hang zigzag on hedges. Green as glass
The water in the horse-trough shines.
Nine ducks go wobbling by in two straight lines.

A hen stares at nothing with one eye,
Then picks it up. Out of an empty sky
A swallow falls and, flickering through
The barn, dives up again into the dizzy blue.

I lie, not thinking, in the cool, soft grass,
Afraid of where a thought might take me—as
This grasshopper with plated face
Unfolds his legs and finds himself a space.

Self under self, a pile of selves I stand
Threaded on time, and with metaphysic hand
Lift the farm like a lid and see
Farm within farm, and in the centre, me.

With *Measures* (1965), he began to experiment with free verse, though
never wholly abandoning the rhyming stanza-forms in which so much of
his richest work is couched. He also broadened the range of his subject-
matter, resulting in an extension of his sympathies, as in "Assisi" from *Surroundings* (1966)—one of the fruits of an Italian sojourn—or the reportage
sequence in *Rings on a Tree* (1968), with which he fixes the impact on him
of an American visit:

A fortnight is long enough
to live on a roller-coaster.
Princes Street, Edinburgh, even in the most rushed
of rush hours, you will be
a glade in a wood, I'll wrap myself
in your cool rusticity, I'll
foretell the weather, I'll be
a hick in the sticks.

The sun goes up on Edinburgh.

Manhattan goes up on the sun.
Her buildings overtop Arthur's Seat
and are out of date as soon as
a newspaper. Last year's artist is
a caveman. Tomorrow's best seller
has still to be born.

I plunge through constellations
and basements. My brain spins up there,
I pass it on its way down. I can't see
for the skyscraper in my eye, there's a traffic jam
in my ears. My hands are tacky
with steering my bolting self
through unlikelihoods and impossibilities.
Flags and circuses orbit
my head, I am haloed but not saintly—
poor Faust in 42nd Street.
The tugs in the East River butt
rafts of freight trucks through
my veins. I look at my watch
and its face is Times Square
glittering and crawling with invitations.

Two weeks on a roller-coaster
is long enough. I remember
all islands are not called Coney.

I think, Tomorrow my head will be
higher than my feet, my brain
will come home, I'll be able
to catch up on myself—and, tilting my halo,
I walk out into
exploding precincts and street-bursts.

An Apocalyptic who never openly associated himself with the movement, but whose influences were clearly Hopkins, Joyce and (especially)
Dylan Thomas, is W. S. Graham (b. 1918). Like Joyce and Thomas, his
preoccupation has always been primarily with the word itself. In *Cage
Without Grievance* (1939) and *2nd Poems* (1945), the sub-conscious stream,
although its imagery has obviously floated up out of his Clydeside upbringing, carries too many superfluous adjectives. Even in the best of the
early poems, where lyricism was applied like paint from a knife to his sense
of the brevity and uncertainty of life, the end result was often (as with so
much New Apocalypse verse) a blown-up, unyielding textual confusion:

Many dig deeper in joy and are shared with
A profit clasped in a furious swan-necked prow
To sail against sport of the monumental loss
That jibles with no great nobility its cause.
That I can gather, this parched offering
Of a day hut out of wrong weeping.

Apart from revealing his continued fascination for place-names from Clydeside, the imagery of his later poems draws its strength from the sea. A Melville allusion supplies the title for *The White Threshold* (1949), and the richly evocative manipulation of sea-imagery is further strengthened in *The Nightfishing* (1955). Both these collections are marked out by increasing lucidity, although the poet's lonely preoccupation with the little deaths that are life's failures of communication as prelude to physical death, remains:

I bent to the lamp. I cupped
My hand to the glass chimney.
Yet it was a stranger's breath
From out of my mouth that
Shed the light.

After fifteen years, the appearance of *Malcolm Mooney's Land* (1970) suggests that in his two preceeding collections he had drawn the full richness from his obsession with the basic elements of word and sea, although he never quite managed to break out of his sense of isolation and of the difficulties of communication which are the central themes of this book.

It fell to the editorial lot of the present writer (b. 1918) to try to bring into Scottish focus both the work of the native writers of the New Apocalypse and of the "second wind" Scots-writing-poets; through *Poetry Scotland*, four issues of which appeared between 1943–1949,[15] and in *Modern Scottish Poetry: An Anthology of the Scottish Renaissance*.[16]

Having moved through an apprenticeship in Apocalypticism and in Lallans, whatever seems to me tentatively worth preserving of my own poetry is to be found in *Selected Poems: 1942–1972*[17] (1973), *The Run From Life:* (1975)[18] and *Walking Without An Overcoat* (1977).[19] Reviewing the first of these, and referring to the titles of the original collections, Alexander Scott writes "of the new colloquial ease and force and brevity in 'Epitaph for a Farmer,' a new economy of evocation in 'Travellers' Tales,' a new tact in the witty melancholy of 'At Hans Christian Andersen's Birthplace,' and there and elsewhere he is able to resist the temptation to give deeper significance to moments of insight by tagging on to them conclusions which are perhaps philosophical but are certainly otiose. In 'School Prizegiving,' dramatization is complete, with thought and feeling embodied in action, and in 'Picking Apples' and 'Early Morning Fisher' (from *One Later Day*, 1961) the controlled sensuousness of the style is at once vivid and vibrant.

"With *This Business of Living* (1969) he begins to move away from set forms. 'A Ballad of Orpheus', a subtle exploration of the ambiguities of love, cunningly plays the paradoxes of its freely-moving emotions against the restrictions of the iambic quatrain, and 'At the Mouth of the Ardyne,' his first poem in free verse, wastes not a word in its stunning sequence of images evoking brutality and guilt.

The water rubs against itself,
glancing many faces at me.
One winces as the dropped fly
tears its tension. Then it heals.

Being torn doesn't matter.
The water just goes on saying
all that water has to say,
What the dead come back to.

Then a scar opens.
Something of water is ripped-out,
a struggle with swung air.
I batter it on a loaf of stone.

The water turns passing faces,
Innumerable pieces of silver.
I wash my hands, pack up, and
go home wishing I hadn't come.

Later, I eat my guilt.

"Other free-verse poems, from *Comings and Goings* (1971) are no less impressive. The satirical wit of 'The Vacant Chair,' the beautifully balanced emotional control in the 'Elegy' on his father, the wry humour of 'A Change of Fashion,' the fine combination of pity and self-depreciation in 'Feeling Small'—these demonstrate a range of subject-matter and feeling which shows a praiseworthy openness to new experiences and an equally admirable ability to find new ways to express them."[20]

Metaphysics plays little part in the work of Sydney Tremayne (b. 1912), whose senses of place and person enable him project childhood memories with gentle humour, and convey in well-shaped formal stanzas the evocative quality of a Scottish scene. His best work, produced over quarter of a century, is to be found in *Selected and New Poems* (1973).

Another poet of place with both a human and humorous touch is Edwin Morgan (b. 1920), a Glaswegian much influenced by Whitman. While his free verse often enables him to achieve broad paragraphs of rising feeling, it can sometimes degenerate into a series of jerky invocative statements, rather in the manner of a *Daily Express* leader in the hey-day of Beaverbrook. *The Second Life* (1968) contains much that reveals his strong sense of compassion for the disadvantaged, as in "Snack Bar", "Glasgow Green" (where the imagery of localized personal frustration is widened to take in the universal predicament) or in the less diffuse "King Billy", which deals with the burial of a:

. . , gang-leader in the bad times
of idleness and boredom, lost in better days.

"Starlings in George Square" is both a humorous example of his skill in word-play, and a serious reflection of the unnaturalness of the urban life towards which the birds are so strangely drawn.

From Glasgow to Saturn (1973) shows a considerable extension both of subject matter and of technique. The Whitmanesque rhetoric gives place to shorter lines, tauter rhythms. Not all the experimentation is successful. The handling of sonnet form in "Glasgow Sonnets" is often forced and clumsy, Sonnet vii, incidentally, echoing that hostility to the work of "environmentalists, ecologists and conservationists" previously hinted at, inaccurately, in "The Flowers of Scotland", a curious visual insensitivity in one so markedly a poet of place. "The Fifth Gospel" seems simply a piece of undergraduate bad taste, while some of the scientific word-play pieces have little more to offer than jokey novelty value. But there is an evocative "London" sequence, several moving poems on local themes, "Death in Duke Street" among them, stimulated by painful experience rather than study-bound mind-teasing, and some cool and delicate lyricism, as in the first section of "For Bonfires":

The leaves are gathered, the trees are dying
for a time.
A seagull cries through white smoke in the garden fires
that fill the heavy air.
All day heavy air
is burning, a moody dog
sniffs and circles the swish of the rake.
In streaks of ash, the gardener drifting
ghostly beats his hands a cloud
of breath to the red sun.

Morgan also carries on, with distinction, the native tradition of re-creative translation,* not the least of his successes being his vigorous Scots version of Mayakovsky, *Wi' the Haill Voice* (1972), brilliantly capturing the Russian poet's leaps between the impassioned clouds of rhetoric and the earth of the colloquial.

* Also featured in the best work of Sir Alexander Gray (1882–1968).

Iain Crichton Smith (b. 1928) who writes poetry, prose and plays in both English and Gaelic, is a Lewisman. He spent some years teaching in urban Dumbarton before moving to Oban, Argyll. He is therefore aware of urban as well as rural relevancies. Often, however, his themes are taken from the rent tapestry of Highland history—Culloden; Dr Johnson in the Highlands; the joyless repression of the Free Church; the Clearances. A just resentment of the narrowness of some aspects of Highland life and Smith's special compassion for the old, are illustrated in "Old Woman", as is his technique of the gently sounding but precisely placed statement:

Your thorned back
heavily under the creel
you steadily stamped the rising daffodil.

Your set mouth
forgives no-one, not even God's justice
perpetually drowning law with grace.

Your cold eyes
watched your drunken husband come
unsteadily from Sodom home.

Your grained hands
dandled full and sinful cradles.
You built for your children stone walls.

Your yellow hair
burned slowly in a scarf of grey
wildly falling like the mountain spray.

Finally, you're alone
among the unforgiving brass,
the slow silence, the sinful glass.

Who never learned,
not even aging, to forgive
our poor journey and our common grave,

while the free daffodils
wave in the valley and on the hills
the deer look down with their instinctive skills,

and the huge seas
in which your brothers drowned sing slow
over the headland and the peevish crow.

His *Selected Poems* (1970) contains the best of his earlier volumes, including "Deer on the High Hills", a "meditation" which owes something to Wallace Stevens but nonetheless successfully captures Highland visual characteristics. Though no collection by this poet is ever without interest, much of his later work has been uneven, the limping line and the forced metaphysical speculativeness unrelated to outstanding imagery, suggesting over-productiveness. Yet it has included two important re-creations: the one, a superb version of Duncan Ban Macintyre's *Ben Dorain* (1969), and a mellifluous rendering of Sorley Maclean's *Poems to Eimhir* (1971), the greatest Gaelic poets of the eighteenth and the twentieth centuries thus being made available for the first time to non-Gaelic-speaking readers with what must surely be a fair measure of the imaginative force of the originals.

Up in Orkney, George Mackay Brown (b. 1921) has caught more alertly than any other writer the overtones of the social customs of the island people, the deeply rooted significance of their myths, and the impact of the physical character of the wind-swept land in which they live. Influenced to some extent in his earlier poetry by Muir, as in "Saint Magnus on Egilsay", the later work in *Poems New and Selected* (1971) confirms his individuality, the skill with which he can bring to life Orkney characters and characteristics in a manner truly local yet wider by implication, and the way in which he weaves Orcadian history and myth into a thoroughly contemporary present. Thus, "Wedding", through its echoes of local tradition and religion, turns into a simple universal symbol of one of life's basic experiences:

With a great working of elbows
The fiddlers ranted
　—*Joy to Ingrid and Magnus!*

With much boasting and burning
The whisky circled
　—*Wealth to Ingrid and Magnus!*

With deep clearings of the throat
The minister intoned
　—*Thirdly, Ingrid and Magnus . . .*

Ingrid and Magnus stared together
When midnight struck
At a white unbroken bed.

In a survey as extended as this, it is obviously necessary in some arbitrary way to limit the ground that should be covered as the moment of writing is approached. So far, I have dealt only with poets whose work seems to me likely to be represented in any future competent anthology of the Scottish Renaissance. Others who might well have been added would include the short-lived Burns Singer (1928–1964), whose *Collected Poems* first appeared in 1970; Tom Buchan (b. 1931), whose best things are to be found in his *Dolphins at Cochin* (1969); or that late developer, Alastair Maclean (b. 1926), who, in *From the Wilderness* and elsewhere, can create an intensity almost desperate in its solitariness. Like Douglas Dunn (b. 1942), Maclean now dissociates himself from Scottish concerns. Much of Dunn's work reads like under-pressurized Larkin. George Macbeth (b. 1932) has associated himself largely with contemporary English experimentation, and would therefore have less claim for inclusion in a Scottish context than the equally cosmopolitan Alan Jackson (b. 1938) who, when not diluting his style in the manner of the Liverpool poets for the benefit of a "live" audience, can satirically synthesize the close kinship between the brutal and the comic in modern life, as in "Person":

i have no thum
i am a little
deformed
i don't wear gloves
but i suffer very much
from the insolence
of those who are thumbed,
and find in that
their distinction.

Among the youngest poets of all is a woman, Liz Lochhead (b. 1947), whose highly personal *Memo for Spring* (1972) seems to suggest more promise than most.[21]

As Herbert Read once pointed out apropos an earlier time, in an age of transition, such as is the final quarter of the twentieth century, charlatans flourish and are sometimes hard to distinguish from the pioneers of new ground likely to prove fruitful. There is certainly no lack of experimentation in contemporary Scottish verse. It includes some Scottish purveying of concrete verse. To the present writer at least, this seems unlikely to be of lasting interest or significance, since the overtones of poetry must ripple outwards, not attempt to turn impossibly back upon themselves.

II

The most colourful figure to become involved with the Scottish Renaissance is Compton Mackenzie (1883–1974), a remote descendant of John Mackenzie of Kintoul. Mackenzie's father, the actor Edward Compton, had decided to drop the Scottish surname for professional reasons, and the future author was born in West Hartlepool, County Durham. His education was English—St Paul's School, London, leading to Magdalen College, Oxford. Mackenzie's intellectual abilities were formidable. He began Latin at the age of four, and Greek when he was nine.

During the First World War he served in the Dardanelles Expedition and later became Director of the Aegean Intelligence Service. In 1932 he was successfully prosecuted, and fined one hundred pounds, for a technical violation of the Official Secrets Act, a prosecution which greatly enhanced public appreciation of his own war record.

Mackenzie's first ambition was to write plays, but he achieved no more success with *The Gentleman in Gray* (Edinburgh, 1907), or *Columbine* (Nottingham, 1912) than with his derivatively Georgian *Poems* (1907) or his *Kensington Rhymes* (1912). So, as he himself put it, he "abandoned playwriting and sat down one afternoon in 1908 to write the ideal performance of my first play . . . which, over two years later after being refused by a dozen publishers, was published in 1911 as *The Passionate Elopment*".

Dissatisfaction with the inevitability of actors and producers coming between the author's ideal conception of his characters and their stage realization thus committed Mackenzie to a literary career, which was to result in the appearance of over a hundred books.

His first success was *Carnival* (1912). Based on his second play, *Columbine*, (1920) it tells with tenderness and sympathy the story of a young Cockney dancer's life in the variety theatre, a background returned to in the sequel *Coral* (1925) and in *Figure of Eight* (1936).

His second success, and the book which established his reputation as a major British novelist, was *Sinister Street* (1913–14), a part-autobiographical tracing of the growth of a young man from childhood, through adolescence, Oxford and a first experience of London's underworld, to maturity. As a portrait of English society at the end of the Edwardian era, it is unsurpassed, the huge canvas of characters providing further material for *Sylvia Scarlet* (1918), *Sylvia and Michael* (1919) and *The Variety Girl* (1920). In between came that delightful idyll of love foredoomed *Guy and Pauline* (1915), the sharpness of character-observation and the mellifluous clarity of the prose nowhere more apparent.

It could be argued that Mackenzie's early and lasting achievement has nothing whatever to do with Scottish literature, if it is to be assumed that only some of the things Scots do while abroad are, in fact, the achievements of Scotsmen. But during the 1920s, Mackenzie began to involve himself deeply with his ancestral country, and continued to do so, whether as founder member of the Scottish National Party, by championing the claims of inshore Scottish fishermen, or in old-age, as Governor-General of the Royal Stuart Society. Catholic convert and flamboyant romantic, his Scottish interests were deeply felt. His last home was on a corner of Drummond Place in Edinburgh's New Town. There is something symbolic of Scottish values in the fact that his home for a decade on the island of Barra (where he is buried) has been turned into a factory.

The width of his interests is deployed in *The Four Winds of Love* (1937–45). This long but splendid study of "four philosophies of love", as the author himself described it, ranges widely from Scotland to Europe and America, ecompassing his concerns for music, religion, literature, politics and the perennial ills of society. The huge cast of characters is deftly handled, the economical clarity of the prose compelling. *The Four Winds of Love* is undoubtedly a major masterpiece of the earlier half of its century.

Mackenzie claimed that to what he called his comic books and pot-boilers he had given as much "concentration and search for style" as in his serious books. In his later series of comic Highland novels, he is able to make us laugh with, rather than at, the characteristics he satirizes with kindliness. The series begins with *The Monarch of the Glen* (1941), an assault upon the self-importance of visiting sportsmen and their English-orientated Highland hosts, and continues with *Keep the Home Guard Turning* (1943), *Whisky Galore* (1947), its gentle take-off of the double standards of Highland morality made famous by a film in which the author himself appeared; a hilariously funny depiction of the American craze for pursuing folk-lore in *Hunting the Fairies* (1949); and, probably the only rational comment on a famous Loch Ness myth, in *The Rival Monster* (1952).

From his comparative old age came one last novel of importance; the serious and sympathetic treatment of the public and private disaster which, until recently, could befall a homosexual, *Thin Ice* (1956), a reflective counterpart to his earlier amused acceptance of Lesbianism in *Vestal Fire* (1927).

Mackenzie's many honours included his election as Rector of Glasgow University in 1931, the bestowal on him of an LLD the following year, and knighthood in 1952.

Another prolific novelist of the period, indubitably Scottish though never specifically associated with the Scottish Renaissance, was the Orca-dian, Eric Linklater (1899–1974). Born in South Wales, he was educated at Aberdeen Grammar School and Aberdeen University. His military career included service as a private with the Black Watch between 1917 and 1919, an experience he was later to put to fruitful use; and, in the Second World War, a spell as commander of the Orkney Fortress Royal Engineers, followed by four years on the staff of the Directorate of Public Relations in the War Office. In between, he had been Assistant Editor of the *Times of India*, lectured in English at his *alma mater*, and fulfilled academic fellow-ships at two American universities. For many years he lived at Dounby, Orkney. Later he moved to Ross-shire and finally to Aberdeenshire; but he never deserted the North.

White Maa's Saga, in which, like its author, students "played chess with words for queens and bishops and ideas for common pawns", a humorous tale the central incident of which deals with a pre-marital custom to ensure male issue once common to many Scottish farming communities, was followed by *Poet's Pub* (1930), an uproariously stylish farce, and *Juan in America* (1931), undoubtedly one of the most accomplished pieces of fictional gaiety ever to be produced. Its sequel, *Juan in China* (1937), lacks something of the *brio* of the original. Both use the device of foreign travel to hold up a mirror to some of the more ludicrous aspects of the British way of life.

In between came *The Men of Ness: The Saga of Thorlief Coalbiter's Son* (1932), another new stylistic departure and a reminder of the importance which Linklater placed upon his Norse descent. *Magnus Merriman* (1934), its prose punctuated by amusingly bawdy verse in what was yet another new departure, matching manner with matter—in this case the comic aspects of Scotland's cultural revival—will surely remain, at least for Scottish readers, one of the funniest books in their literature. Adaptation of an Aristophanes comedy is the starting point for the humour of *The Impregnable Women* (1938), localized fantasy for *Laxdale Hall* (1951). *Private Angelo* (1946), in some ways the most comic of all his novels, its hero symbolically representative of soldiers everywhere, gives plain enough evidence of his hatred of war, a fact which may surprise some of those who deliberately undervalue Linklater because they misunderstand his recurring interest in soldiers of all ranks (who are, in any case, the servants and the ultimate safeguarders of society).

Linklater's sense of comedy has links with both Smollett and Rabelais, yet is different in that his situations are never simply picaresque. Comic characters are inevitably larger, or smaller, than life, whether their creator be poet or novelist, since it is in the implications of such distortion in relation to the common view of normality that the essence of comedy lies. Yet Linklater's comic characters rarely become caricatures, retaining enough of humanity to make them a mirror of countless anonymous prototypes and attitudes.

Linklater's virtue as a prose-writer is his ability to overlay humorous situations with serious implications and producing, often couched in sensuous imagery, new tangential circumstances, themselves original and arresting. Its most obvious fault is his fondness for the purple passage, the careful placing of the recondite word; faults that increased in the later novels. His ability to handle wit and pathos in condensed situations is evidenced in the collected *Short Stories of Eric Linklater* (1968). As a dramatist he was less successful, both wordy dialogue and over-contrived situation in *Love in Albania* (1949) and *Breakspear in Gascony* (1958) too often showing the seams of his stagecraft. An all-round professional, Linklater's volumes of autobiography, particularly *The Man on My Back* (1941), with its vivid portrait of his friend and fellow-novelist Mackenzie at work by night on Barra to the sound of the gramophone, are valuable records of his time, and much livelier than the formal histories of Scotland in times past written during his last years. His knowledge of, and affection for, the Norse islands of Scotland is reflected in *Orkney and Shetland: An Historical, Geographical, Social and Scenic Survey* (1965), unlikely to be surpassed for many years to come.

The kind of rich comicality in which Linklater excelled, but which nevertheless probes the question of what we are both as human beings and as Scots, has its parallel in one aspect of the work of Bruce Marshall (b. 1899), an Edinburgh-born writer who lost a leg in the 1914–18 war, qualified as a chartered accountant, and who has since lived mostly in France. His best Scottish novels are *The Uncertain Glory* (1935) and *Father Malachy's Miracle* (1935).

Father Malachy Murdoch, sent to Edinburgh from his Highland monastery to help tighten up plain-chant, is often so affronted by the sins of the heedless city world, especially as manifested in a *palais de danse* called *The Garden of Eden*, that he persuades God to transplant the establishment to the Bass Rock, in order to inspire the backsliders. The poor man soon discovers that practical miracles are not wanted in a country whose official religion depends upon them. Even Rome disapproves, so there is nothing for it but to restore the building to its original situation. Marshall's gallery of religious and secular characters is wittily drawn. Priests, Anglican clergymen, tycoons and newspapermen are all gently satirized; but the real target is human hypocrisy.

The novels of Robert Kemp (1908–1967) indulge in gentler comedy deployed, in the best of them, against Edinburgh's upper-middle-class culture vultures in *The Maestro* (1956), and against the former vagaries of Scottish marriage law in *Gretna Green* (1961).

In still slighter vein are the novels of Cliff Hanley (b. 1922), whose fictional study of adolescence in and around Glasgow, *A Taste of Too Much* (1960), shows sensitive knowledge of how young people think and feel. It has been followed by *The Hot Month* (1967), a distant kinsman to Mackenzie's Highland fantasies, though Ochie is far removed from the kilt-wearing haunts of Ben Nevis and his friends. Hanley's personal brand of humour is apt to make his characters jest with his voice rather than their own. *The Redhaired Bitch* (1969), based on the absurdity of producing a musical comedy with Mary, Queen of Scots as heroine, does deal in serious terms with problems of human relationships nurtured in that hot-house of egocentric feelings, the theatre.[22]

The national identity may be probed in other ways than through comedy. There is nothing humorous about *A Scots Quair* by "Lewis Grassic Gibbon", the pen name of J. Leslie Mitchell (1901–35), yet plenty about the effect of the soil and the climate of the North-east of Scotland upon those who are reared to it.

Grassic Gibbon was born at the farm of Hillhead of Segget, near Auchterless, Aberdeenshire, the third son of John Mitchell, a farmer, and his wife, Lilias. When the boy was in his eighth year, his parents' lease expired and the family moved to Aberdeen. They soon returned to farming, this time at Bloomfield, Kincardineshire, in the heart of the Mearns country. It was later to provide the background for his finest work.

From Arbuthnot school, where he had a sympathetic teacher and where he distinguished himself as a schoolboy essayist, he moved on to Mackie Academy, Stonehaven. Here, he was profoundly unhappy, and, apparently after some kind of classroom scene,[23] soon walked out. He got a job as a junior reporter on the *Aberdeen Journal*. In February 1919, he moved to Hill Street, Glasgow, where he wrote for the *Scottish Farmer*, from which he was dismissed for falsifying his expense account.[24] After an attempt at suicide and ensuing medical treatment, he returned home to face his unsympathetic parents.

Journalism now being closed to him, since he lacked a referee, he joined the Royal Army Service Corps in August 1919, with which he served until March 1923. In this way he saw much of Central Asia, Persia and Egypt, and although he was never anywhere near actual fighting, claimed, as a result, to have acquired "a keen distaste for that snarling cry of a machine gun which sends a man clawing earthwards".

After leaving the army, he spent five frustrating months as a civilian before rejoining the services, this time as a RAF Orderly Clerk. He had married by the time of his release in 1929. Between his return to civilian life and his death eight years later, he was to write sixteen books and several short stories. The books included non-fictional works, such as *Hanno: Or The Future of Exploration* (1928), *Nine Against the Unknown* (1934), and a lively if deliberately provocative volume shared with Hugh MacDiarmid, *Scottish Scene* (1934). He also produced a series of novels written under his own name, the finest of which is the historical story *Spartacus* (1933); too good, indeed, to be quite forgotten.

A Scots Quair, by far his finest achievement, unfolds on several levels. Outwardly, it tells the life story of Chris Guthrie, the daughter of a crofter, divided in her passionate personal attachments and loyalties, torn between the culture of England and that of her native country, but finally settling for the values of the Scottish land.

Gibbon also takes account of social history. In the first part, *Sunset Song* (1932), he uses as background the impact of the 1914–18 war, which broke up for ever the already declining economic crofting pattern. In the second part, *Claude Howe* (1933), we are made aware of the disintegration of small-town society, brought about, Gibbon suggests, by lack of understanding between the crofters and the "urban" workers. This is a difficult theory to sustain, and marks the beginning of the disintegration of the trilogy as a whole, since Mitchell increasingly imposes his own private dogma on his characters. This process is even more apparent in the final novel, *Grey Granite* (1934), where he portrays the surge and turmoil of city life, and those restless discontents out of which Communism grows.

In the end, Gibbon comes down on behalf of a fancied mythological cycle, nothing ultimately enduring but the land. This romantic theory might seem less unacceptable were it not itself vitiated by Gibbon's belief, symbolized by the Standing Stones, in a distant, primeval past before social organization had begun to poison human relationships. Romanticism run riot is the only way to describe his vision of the hunters who had "roamed those hills, naked and bright, in a Golden Age, without fear or hope or hate or love, living high in the race of the wind and the race of life, mating as simple as beasts or birds, dying with a little keen simpleness." Lyrical as is the "sing" of Mitchell's prose, the "keen simpleness" of dying in a damp cave, bones gnarled by rheumatoid arthritis and smelling like an animal, is not immediately apparent.

Sunset Song, with its strong characterization of the dour North-east farm-folk bred to the harshness of the land, and its passionate reaction to the destructive social and personal localized side-effects of a world for the first time at war, is undoubtedly a great novel. Munro is right when he says that it "possesses something of the quality of an impressionist painting or a tone-poem".[25] Yet, because of Mitchell's growing obsessions with Marxism, anthropology and plain old-fashioned Celtic twilight mysticism, the trilogy as a whole remains a flawed monument to a great but overworked talent. Consequently, the attempt by Kurt Wittig and others to make of Chris Guthrie "Chris Caledonia", a kind of Scottish Kathleen na Houlihan, is quite unsustainable. Scotland has no oneness of personality to give validity to the creation of what would be so emotionally useful a personification: the divisions of our history, languages and culture have seen to that.

Some of Gibbon's least forced qualities are also to be found in the best of the recently collected essays and stories, *A Scots Hairst* (1969).

Gibbon's most able follower is Edinburgh-born Fred Urquhart (b. 1912), whose short stories, collected as *The Dying Stallion* (1967) and *The Ploughing Match* (1968), reflect the earthy vigour of the farming-folk belonging to the generation of Chris Guthrie's grandchildren. Urquhart's understanding of the social forces that bind together a small agricultural community does not have to struggle with any of the inbred *isms* that blunted Gibbon's perception. Urquhart's range of characters is wide, his realization of them always most acute when the localities in which they are set takes on a more general significance. He is usually at his weakest in those urban stories in which he allows his portrayal of the pathetic and limited ambitions of the tawdry or the deprived to become doused with music-hall comicality, a fault from which his sensitive novel depicting an Edinburgh adolescence, *Time Will Knit* (1938), is happily free.

One of the strengths of Gibbon and Urquhart is the way in which they look at history in the past or in the making, as it is evolved by those ordinary people whose actions normally go unrecorded. Edinburgh-born Naomi Mitchison (b. 1897), sister of the scientist J. B. S. Haldane, uses the history of her Haldane forbears as material for her Jacobite novel *The Bull Calves* (1947), thus attempting an actuality view of the aftermath of the great events of the '45 as they must have seemed through the eyes of Gleneagles folk in 1747.

Her output has included children's books, notably *The Big House* (1950), a tale in which the magic of childhood, the attractions of the supernatural and the forces of history are combined to produce an impressive statement of a coherent life-view in a Scottish setting. Her modern Scottish folk-parable *Five Men and a Swan* (1958) is as notable for its clarity of style as for its condemnation of human stupidity and cupidity.

Her masterpiece, however, is *The Corn King and the Spring Queen* (1931). It traces the story of Erif and Berris Der, a brother and sister from Marob, which practises fertility rites, and where she is Spring Queen, having been first raped and then married by Tarrik, the Corn King. Marob has connections with Sparta just before the moment of its decline. The story moves there, and to the cruel, disillusioned Egypt of Ptolemy, where the last of the Spartan heroes die upon their own swords.

The success of Lady Mitchison's comprehension of the recurring nature of human ills and the flesh's brief glory is as vast as her sense of tolerance and compassion.

Although her home has been at Carradale, Kintyre, since 1937, and she has played an active part in local authority work, she has nevertheless remained a slightly aloof figure on the Scottish literary scene. This may partly be because of her international interests, which have resulted in her being awarded the Palmes de l'Academie Française and adopted as Tribal Adviser and Mmarona (mother) to the Bakgatha of Botswana.

An even more isolated position is that of David Lindsay (1878–1945). His father was Scottish, his mother English. He himself was educated at Blackheath and for a short period at Jedburgh. Although he won a university scholarship, he was not allowed to take it up by his grandmother, by then in charge of Lindsay and his elder sister and brother. Instead, he became a clerk with a firm of Lloyd's underwriters, doing work which he disliked yet accomplished so well that he was about to be made a director when he decided to make writing his fulltime occupation. In the meantime, however, he served during the First World War with the Grenadier Guards. He married in 1916, and on demobilization settled with his wife in north Cornwall.

His first book, the metaphysical fantasy *A Voyage to Arcuturus*, (1920) derives in style and conception from Macdonald's *Lilith*, likewise suffering such shared defects as stretches of flat prose-writing. Yet Macdonald's idea of shaking his reader out of the complacencies of his day-to-day physical experience is projected with much greater power and skill by Lindsay. At one level, *Arcturus* is a tale of science fiction in which Maskull, a human, finds himself propelled by rocket to another planet, Tormance. Yet this is no mere diversion of an escapist kind. It is a work of art which leads the sympathetic reader to question the very basis of what he understands as reality. Systematically, all conventional points of human reference are destroyed. The people of Tormance have physical characteristics additional to those with which we are equipped. The names of some of the Tormantic characters whom Maskull encounters are compounded in such a way that while some appear to have overtones of human significance—Joiwind and Sullenbode, apparently representing two aspects of female love: Nightspore and Oceaxe, human behavioural characteristics—others, like Tydomin and Digrung, apart from suggesting remote roots from the languages out of which English was compounded, mean nothing. The apparently authoritive scientific information is, in fact, non-information. The philosophical generalizations, delivered in the solemn manner similar to the offerings of distilled wisdom in *Lilith*, do not relate to the premises they stem from.

For example, one of the higher Tormantic characters remarks: "Thire cannot exist without Amfuse, and Amfuse cannot exist without Faceny". "That must be so", replies Maskull: "Without life there can be no love, and without love no religious feeling." The deduction appears more or less logical, but it is drawn from a meaningless symbolic comparison. Characters establish an identity, then later turn out also to be other characters in different contexts. In the end, the reader would find himself utterly on his own in the middle of a conceivable, terrifying, yet ultimately impossible nightmare of systematic subtraction, were it not for the clues that emerge in the final scenes. As Maskull and Krag—Pain, according to Lindsay the evolutionary force behind the known, who has an intimate guiding relationship to Maskull rather like the disguised Mephistopheles to Faust—approach Muspel, the ultimate destination in Crystalman's world, they meet Gangnet, "small, dark and pleasing"—the regular use of three nonrelated adjectival characteristics is another of Lindsay's techniques of detachment—with a face "not disfigured by any special organs", there is a greeting for Maskull but not for Krag. Krag protests. Replies Gagnet:

"I know you, Krag. There are few places where you are welcome."

"And I know you, Gangnet—you man-woman. . . . Well, we are here together, and you must make what you can of it. We are going down to the Ocean."

The smile faded from Gangnet's face. "I can't drive you away, Krag—but I can make you the unwelcome third."

Krag threw back his head, and gave a loud, grating laugh. "That bargain suits me all right. As long as I have the substance, you may have the shadow, and much good may it do you."

"Now that it's all arranged so satisfactorily," said Maskull, with a hard smile, "permit me to say that I don't desire any society at all at present. . . . You take too much for granted, Krag. You have played the false friend once already. . . . I presume I'm a free agent?"

"To be a free man, one must have a universe of one's own," said Krag, with a jeering look. "What do you say, Gangnet . . . is this a free world?"

"Freedom from pain and ugliness should be every man's privilege," returned Gangnet tranquilly. "Maskull is quite within his rights, and if you'll engage to leave him I'll do the same."

"Maskull can change face as often as he likes, but he won't get rid of me so easily. Be easy on that point, Maskull."

"It doesn't matter," muttered Maskull. "Let everyone join in the procession. In a few hours I shall be finally free, anyhow, if what they say is true."

"I'll lead the way," said Gangnet. "You don't know this country, of course, Maskull. When we get to the flat lands some miles further down, we shall be able to travel by water, but at present we must walk, I fear."

"Yes, you fear—you fear!" broke out Krag, in a high-pitched, scraping voice. "You eternal loller!"

Maskull kept looking from one to the other in amazement. There seemed to be a determined hostility between the two, which indicated an intimate previous acquaintance.

They set off through a wood, keeping close to its border, so that for a mile or more they were within sight of the long, narrow lake which flowed beside it. The trees were low and thin; their dolm-coloured leaves were all folded. There was no underbrush—they walked on clean, brown earth. A distant waterfall sounded. They were in shade, but the air was pleasantly warm. There were no insects, to irritate them. The bright lake outside looked cool and poetic.

Gangnet pressed Maskull's arm affectionately.

"If the bringing of you from your world had fallen to me, Maskull, it is here I would have brought you, and not to the scarlet desert. Then you would have escaped the dark spots, and Tormance would have appeared beautiful to you."

"And what then, Gangnet? The dark spots would have existed all the same."

"You could have seen them afterwards. It makes all the difference whether one sees darkness through the light, or brightness through the shadows."

"A clear eye is the best. Tormance is an ugly world, and I greatly prefer to know it as it really is."

"The devil made it ugly, not Crystalman. These are Crystalman's thoughts, which you see around you. He is nothing but Beauty and Pleasantness. . . . Even Krag won't have the effrontery to deny that."

"It's very nice here," said Krag, looking around him malignantly. "One only wants a cushion and half a dozen houris, to complete it."

Maskull disengaged himself from Gangnet.

"Last night, when I was struggling through the mud in the ghastly moonlight . . . then I thought the world beautiful. . . ."

"Poor Sullenbode!" said Gangnet, sighing.

"What! You knew her?"

"I know her through you. . . . By mourning for a noble woman, you show your own nobility. . . . I think all women are noble."

"There may be millions of noble women, but there's only one Sullenbode."

"If Sullenbode can exist," said Gangnet, "the world cannot be a bad place."

"Change the subject. . . . The world's hard and cruel, and I am thankful to be leaving it."

"On one point, though, you both agree," said Krag, smiling evilly. "Pleasure is good, and the cessation of pleasure is bad."

Gangnet glanced at him coldly. "We know your peculiar theories, Krag. You are very fond of them, but they are unworkable. The world could not go on being, without pleasure."

"So Gangnet thinks!" jeered Krag.

It depends upon individual temperament how much importance is placed upon the kind of metaphysical quasi-philosophizing which makes up *A Voyage to Arcturus*. Parallels have been drawn between it, The *Pilgrim's Progress* and also the character of Milton's Satan.[26] Condemnation of pleasure was certainly a Calvinistic as well as a Puritanical mistrust, and the dismissal of pleasure has, in human practice, almost invariably led to the glorification of the excesses of arrogance, or some other form of selfishness. However the interpretation of Lindsay's strange work may be viewed, indisputably it is a masterpiece of its allegorical kind.

Lindsay is concerned with the metaphysical connection between Pleasure and Evil, by the oneness of the shadow with the substance, and the belief that there exists a spiritual wholeness which transcends good or evil. It is perhaps significant that in his second book, *The Haunted Woman* (1922), one of his characters is imagined "climbing the great chords of Beethoven's staircase", Beethoven in his late string quartets being supposed by some to have been preoccupied with a similar spiritual search.

This story recounts the strange tale of Isbel Lamont and Henry Judge. Though she is engaged to another and Judge is fifty-eight, they fall in love, see each other frequently (mostly to converse), and eventually meet in Judge's large Elizabethan manor that Isbel's aunt proposes to buy. It was built on goblin-haunted ground, on the site of an older house occupied by an "ancient Saxon". The builder had been carried off by trolls, together with half his rooms. Judge, and others, believe that from time to time these rooms have been seen as if they were still there. The two lovers manage to enter the mysterious rooms by a secret stair, and afterwards decide that while there, they have been "enabled temporarily to drop the mask of convention, and talk to each other more humanly and truthfully".

The malicious Mrs Richborough, who suspects a conventional liaison, agrees to enter a room Isbel is afraid to enter, leaving the lovers, freed from inhibition, to indulge in amatory exchanges. A pallid Mrs Richborough reappears, having seen out of the window of the secret room a man with his back to her. When he turns round, she finds that his face is indescribable. The lovers go up to the room, discover that it looks out upon unknown country, and that in it is a strange man; Pleasure, or God to some, but another version of the mysterious Crystalman of *Arcturus*.

The Haunted Woman is a powerful book, which, in spite of its slacker tension than *Arcturus*, shakes the well-mapped senses, and again reveals Lindsay's abnormal reaction against sexual relations.

None of the succeeding books match up to *Arcturus*. *The Haunted Woman*, republished in 1964, was succeeded by what may be a self-portrait, *Sphinx* (1923); an impossible costume-piece, *The Adventures of M. de Mailly* (1926); and the turgid *Devil's Tor* (1932), which reflects some of the nastier aspects of the philosophies of Nietzsche and Schopenhauer. These are also two unpublished novels, *The Violet Apple* and *The Witch*.

None of Lindsay's books enjoyed any commercial success during his lifetime. Now, *Arcturus* has become the object of a paperback cult in America, and has received at least some recognition in Scotland, the country where the author liked to walk, whose Calvinistic fear of sexual pleasure he inherited, yet whose identity he rejected.

Foremost among twentieth-century Scottish novelists whose finest work arises out of concern for the personal relationships and social and cultural *mores* of the Highlands is Neil M. Gunn (1891–1974).

Gunn was born at Dunbeath, Caithness, the son of the skipper of a fishing vessel and the seventh of nine children who survived. After being educated formally at the village school—and, more importantly, informally, as he himself put it, alone, the "prehistoric boy in a modern strath . . . the nut-cracking young savage on his river stone"—he became in 1906 a civil servant, working on the income tax side, first in London and then in Edinburgh. Having achieved establishment, he underwent a course of training for the Customs and Excise department, and was posted, as he had wished, to Inverness.

From 1911 to 1921 there followed what he himself called "ten years of wandering" throughout the Highlands and Islands. Latterly, one of his colleagues was the Irish novelist Maurice Walsh. In 1937, to the dismay of some of his friends and colleagues who saw the action as forfeiting a pension for want of a few more years in official harness, Gunn left the Civil Service to devote himself entirely to writing. By then he had seven books to his credit, and had newly been awarded the James Tait Black Memorial Prize for *Highland River* (1937).

His first novel, *The Grey Coast* (1926), and *The Lost Glen* (1932), both deal with Highland life. They would have been remembered with interest had Gunn not done better things later; novels in which he explained less in expository terms, allowing his argument to expand through the action of his characters.

Morning Tide (1931), though in date of composition it lies between these two, is undoubtedly the first of the great novels. Ostensibly, it is about Hugh, a boy bred for the sea; his reaction to the skill and bravery of his brother and father, especially after the storm, which is magnificently described; and of the economic disintegration of the old way of life which leads Alan, Hugh's brother, to set sail for Australia, leaving behind him the regrets and the implications of social defeat that emigration implies: "Ther a great slackness came upon the people. They stood in groups, moved listlessly, drifted away, talking all the time in easy tones. 'Oh, they'll get on all right, the same lads!' They smiled. 'Trust them for that!' But their smiles were weary, as though there was a final element in them of defeat."

Hugh, however, survives to grow up, and go on living.

Sun Circle (1933) probes back into what must have been one of the crisis-points of Highland history: how Pictish tribal society had to face up to the invasions of the Vikings. The innocence of the Picts leads to their defeat. Because "they feel that by going forward they leave their true riches behind", they chose Haakon, the victorious young Viking chief, to be their new leader, having him marry Nessa, daughter of their slain chief, Drust.

It is a saga-like account of the fusing of Picts and Vikings, Druids and Christians, counterpointed with a contest for the affection of the Druid Master's favourite pupil, Aniel, between Breeta, who has embraced Christianity, and Nessa, who represents a purely physical response. But Breeta symbolizes for Aniel the master's teaching, the search for light:

> As the sun put a circle round the earth and all that it contained, so a man of vision put a circle round himself. At the centre of this circle, his spirit sat and the centre of his spirit was a serenity for ever watchful. Sometimes the watchfulness gave an edged joy in holding at bay the demons and even the vengeful lesser Gods and sometimes it merged with the Sun's light into pure timeless joy.

That passage may have little enough to do with the Viking invasion, but it typifies the search for wholeness which was Gunn's lifelong preoccupation. In *Sun Circle*, the Highland world was still new and optimistic. In *Butcher's Broom* (1934), what had now become the old archetypal world is powerfully etched with a striking sentence: "In the centre of this gloom was the fire, and sitting round it, their knees drawn together, were the old women, like fate, the young women like love, and the small boy with the swallow of life in his hand." The archetypal world is represented by Dark Mairi, one of the "innumerable women whose suffering and endurance were like little black knots holding the web of history together", just before it is about to be vanquished in a physical sense by the Clearances.

A glimpse of Dark Mairi, "the human mother carrying on her ancient solitary business with the earth", gives some idea of the lift and lilt of Gunn's prose style:

> The old woman stood on the Darras, the doorway between the bright sea and the dark hills; and when at last she turned from the sea and lifted her burden to her back, the door closed behind her. But the vacant glitter remained in her eyes and they held their stare until the valley began to pour slowly into them its dark comfort.

For a long time she was like one who had turned into her own house and found it empty, and walked in a silence that was a hearkening to presences withdrawn beyond the walls and fading away.

Every now and then there was a glint in this vagueness, for she had been born by the sea, and sea-water readily curls over and breaks on the shore of the mind. Looked at from a great distance childhood is little more than the breaking of small bright waves on a beach. And whatever of pain and cold-ness there may have been, the brightness keeps a certain wild strangeness, a restless fly-away, that the hills do not know and never quite conquer.

The sea had been in a good mood that morning, had had that pleasant scent that is the breath of fine weather. A person could always tell what the weather is to be by smelling the sea. There is the grey dark smell, cold inside the nostrils, ominous; the damp raw smell, husky to the throat, unsettled; the keen dry lifting tang of wind; but when good weather has newly come, how the sea brims and sways and breathes its sweet fragrance on the air! This morning, too, there had been the extra exhilaration of autumn, that indes-cribable quickening that the skin takes in a shiver.

All of that sea she now carried in her basket as she went back among the companionable hills. For in addition to fish she had many kinds of weed and shell. The clear pink dulse, gathered not off other sea-plants but off the rocks, was one of her most useful specifics. Eaten raw, it had a cleansing effect; boiled, with a pinch of butter added to the infusion, it acted as a tonic, brac-ing the flesh, making it supple, and drawing taut the muscles of the stomach. It could be preserved, too, by drying. A man working in a field could put a dry blade or two in his mouth and chew away at them. At first they were tasteless as gristle, but in a very short time they yielded back their juices, which began to run about the gums and fill the whole mouth with a richness that had to be frequently swallowed. When the dried dulse was ground into a powder and taken fasting, it sickened and expelled worms. Other ailments, like the stone and colic, yielded to it. . . .

She had a reputation for healing among the people of that land. . . . They knew, of course, that she had got her healing knowledge largely from her grandmother, who had been carried away from one of the Islands of the West by the famous smuggler called Black MacIver. Not that they could have called Mairi in her mainland home a foreign or strange woman. She was rather like a little woman from the hills, from any of the small inland glens, and her kind was not uncommon even in townships near the sea. Only Mairi seemed to have in her an older knowledge than was common to the rest of her ancient kind in these places.

As the light mellowed into late afternoon the hills grew darker and the winding valley began to fill itself with an imponderable calm. The frost in the morning had stilled the wind, and it might come again and lay a clear hand on the night. Already the outlines of the hills were sharp and held the eye for unknowing moments.

These outlines and these hills, the winding valley, the many valleys, the breasts of the hills, the little birch woods, the knolls, the humps and hillocks and boulders, the gravel faces, the black bogs, and always for movement the streams winding like snakes in the green or grey-green bottoms. To know one valley amongst these northern uplands was to know all. That was true! as Mairi might say with her thin polite smile. And she might even act as though she believed it. For there are times when all persons are beings moving about in a valley and looking from a little distance as different from one another as does not matter. And no irony is caught in the eye that stares unwinking and, throwing the valley itself out of focus in space, makes it change and curve in the backflow of time.

The backflow of time that is frozen at last in the Ice Age.

The poetry, the surge of sounding myth, and the sensitivity with which is portrayed the tearing up of human roots brought about by this social tragedy, are beautifully portrayed. By comparison, they make both *The Albannach* (1932) and *And the Cock Crew* (1945) by Tom Macdonald (Fionn MacColla) seem somewhat shrill, although the description of the burning of crofts in his second book presents a memorable picture, even if marred by improbably melodramatic detail.

Gunn's next novel, *Highland River* (1937), is once again a study of the boy with the "swallow of life" in his hand: an examination of the moment of delight, Kenn's hunting of the salmon (the fight with which is magnificently described) being also the "salmon of knowledge". Even the river, though a real river that Kenn is exploring upwards to its source, is also the river of life. The circle symbol, already used by Gunn, recurs, and the symbol of the serpent makes its appearance. One is also more strongly aware than ever of animism, the belief in the oneness of all things, repeatedly expressed also by Grassic Gibbon. Thus, Gunn has Kenn, curled up in bed, reflect:

> It was great fun to be so safe in this warm hole, while the dark cold river rolled on its way to the distant thunder of the sea . . . animals, furry and warm, were curled up in their dens . . . curled up, like himself, and heard, waking or sleeping, the rushing of the river. . . . The picture made him snuggle in his own den, and smell the thick warmth of his own pelt.

The Silver Darlings (1941) deals with the social situation resulting from the sweeping of the people from the strath to the coast, and the resultant development of the fishing industry, particularly in the Moray Firth. Here, Finn—also the name of Finn MacCoul, the hero of the Ossianic Fians—is the boy whose development from adolescence to manhood we follow. Like all the other major characters, he is archetypal, and seen to be so by the other characters again and again, as when Roddie, glancing through the window of Kirsty Mackay's house, sees Catrine's features "against the red glow, warm and soft, not only with her own beauty, but with all woman's beauty.'[27]

The Silver Darlings is a magnificent tribute to the indomitable spirit of the Gael, yet at the same time an adventure story with the terrible pace and authority of authenticity. It is a vast canvas of a book, packed with human insight and the smell and sound and touch of Highland life. Whether or not it is Gunn's best novel, it undoubtedly numbers amongst the finest novels of the Scottish Renaissance; indeed, by European standards, of the century.

The middle period Gunn novels leave behind them even the trappings of history, and explore entirely the landscape of the mind. *The Green Isle of the Great Deep* (1944) carries Young Art and Old Hector (themselves the title-characters of an earlier novel) in pursuit of the hazelnuts of knowledge and the salmon of wisdom, the boy's intuitive freedom being both the ultimate value and the quality against which society masses itself. It is a dream-tale which allows Gunn to present his visions of God. But the symbolism is carried to such a length that it becomes incredible, and so overlays the surface of the story. Old Hector calls on God, and He obligingly appears. As Alexander Scott has remarked,[28] not even Christ on the cross was as lucky as that!

In *The Serpent* (1943) and *The Drinking Well* (1946), the placing of the symbolism is inherent in the title. In both novels, young men leave the Highlands to go to cities, in the one case Tom to Glasgow, in the other Iain to Edinburgh, eventually returning to their native places fuller of wisdom. It would be impossible here to attempt to summarize the ceaseless search for wholeness, or to describe the poetry both books evoke. Yet by self-consciously elaborating where earlier Gunn had done the thing and theo-rized afterwards, these two novels lack the narrative coherence of the best of their predecessors, and are unconvincing in their oddly remote treat-ment of city life and its characters. In *The Drinking Well* for instance, credi-bility vanishes with the appearance of the American as a contemporary *deus ex machina*.

Gunn's final novels deal mostly with the problem of violence and its im-pact on individuals and society. No longer is it with "the swallow of life" in the hand of an adolescent that Gunn is concerned, but with the impli-cations and impact of the ending of a life: with murder, in fact. Yet his slow-moving, image-carrying prose style is unsuited to the fast pace of this particular contemporary preoccupation.

The Shadow (1948) deals with the robbery and murder of an old hermit, and its effect on a woman who has come north to her aunt to escape the "living figure of destruction" by "omen-shaped shapes flying across the sky". The result is a relapse from which, reanimated by the victory of inner light, she eventually returns to London cured.

The Key of the Chest (1945) centres on the strangulation of a Swedish seaman during a rescue operation as his ship is sinking off the Highland coast. Charlie, the rescuer, who has had a love affair with the minister's daughter, Flora, is suspected of the murder, while his crude shepherd brother Dugald is suspected of stealing money from the dead man's chest, the key of which cannot be found. Both have been in conflict with the minister, who, after pursuing Flora and Charlie as they flee together, finds that society is on their side and not on his.

Bloodhunt (1952) describes the search for a young man for the murder of a rival who got the girl pregnant. An old man, Sandy, tries to feed and hide the hunted fugitive but, weak and ill, the latter is caught and killed. But Sandy likes Liz, the girl, and takes comfort in her baby, born in his barn:

> The manger and the hay and life's new cry: beyond it, that hunt. Of all the stories man had made only two were immortal; the story of Cain and the story of Christ.

There is no doubt about Gunn's concern in these novels with the wider implications of violence upon society, or the rightness of his condemnation:

> More and more . . . nearer and nearer . . . violence upon violence, increasing violence . . . until the teeth champed and the juices ran about the gums. . . . Then satisfaction, the satisfaction after the orgy . . . until the hunt did not need a murder.
>
> Could substitute something else, an *ism* or *ology* that stood for the murderer, providing a wider hunt, a greater kill, more blood.

If one feels that the later novels are seriously flawed, it is partly because his increasing preoccupation with the theories of Ouspensky's *In Search of the Miraculous* and Zen Buddhism blurred his practical sense of purpose. Too often, as he grew older, he was content to retreat into a personal mysticism which was not fortified by the strength of the archetypal symbols he had earlier used so powerfully.

Nevertheless the notion, sometimes voiced, that Gunn is a limited, "regional" novelist is not tenable. His deep awareness of man's oldest instincts, his feeling for the strength of man's primitive roots, his poetry of language and his ceaseless search for human wholeness through the interaction on each other of closely-observed characters, are the preoccupations and achievements of a major artist. In *Morning Tide, Highland River, The Silver Darlings*, and in his interesting, if over-mystical, autobiography *The Atom of Delight* (1956), Gunn seems to be just that.

Where one comes up against his limitation is in his failure to accept urban civilization in any of its aspects. His norm is some idealized rural North. For Gunn, contemplating the brochs and the archetypal Picts and Celts, it is all very well to cry out: "It is a far cry to the golden age, to the blue smoke of the heather fire and the scent of the primrose! Our river took a wrong turning somewhere. But we haven't forgotten the source . . ." Perhaps not: but it is irretrievably lost.

To believe otherwise is to indulge in the same escapism as did Grassic Gibbon, with his belief in the Golden Age of happy instinct-hunting. Man's energies and efforts to build up a civilization capable of sustaining a Grassic Gibbon or a Gunn, and efficiently printing and distributing their books, has its nobility too, as well as its sordidness, and cannot be so easily dismissed.

The Scottish Renaissance writer most fascinated by the evils and the benefits of functionalism is George Blake (1893–1961), who was born in Greenock. He began his adult life by reading law at Glasgow University, but got caught up in the 1914–18 war, was wounded at Gallipoli and invalided out of the army. After a spell of journalism in Glasgow on Neil Munro's *Evening News*, he went to London in 1924 to edit the popular literary journal *John o' London's Weekly*, and in 1928 took over the *Strand* magazine. In 1930, he became a director of the publishing house of Faber, which incorporated the Porpoise Press, the publishers of Gunn's first novels. In 1932, Blake returned to Scotland and settled in Helensburgh, until the 1939–45 war took him back to London and the Ministry of Information. His last years were spent in Glasgow. Blake is best known for his novel *The Shipbuilders* (1935), a brilliant fictional realization of the disasters that all but overcame 'red' Clydeside before and after the Slump. He has an acute understanding of the social distinction, real or fancied, which in these islands separates men and women into "classes". For this, as for his open acceptance of our industrial civilization, he has been both criticized and undervalued.

By the end of the twentieth century it is highly probable that about sixty-five per cent of the world's population will be urban dwellers. The river will not unloop nor the hunter return to the sparsely populated hill. Short of atomic disaster, urban civilization is here to stay. A writer who chronicles as powerfully as does Blake the hopes and loves and fears and hurts of those generations and social classes who made Garvel (his Greenock) a microcosm of the wider industrial world from the end of the eighteenth century to the 1940 blitz, as he does in *The Constant Star* (1945) and its sequel *The Westering Sun* (1946), deserves our admiration. I know of no novel that so touchingly reflects the social tragedies of the "Kaiser's war" as does Blake's *The Valiant Heart* (1940), at once a chronicle of that war's impact on a small community and a condemnation of its futility in human terms:

Down the steep street of the Clydeside town the workers streamed in thousands from the factory that topped the rise like an outsize convict prison in red brick. Behind the factory the unspoiled hills of Lennox rose green and rock-browed and detached, but the urban area below was dominated by that long range of four-storey blocks, its windows as regularly sized and spaced, and as soulless, as a set of squares on a sheet of graph paper. The tide of humanity pouring down the slopes towards the shops and the houses confessed the dominance of the factory over the economic and social life of a sizeable community.

That evening crowd of released workers was made up of young, noisy girls, with a leaven of middle-aged and even elderly men. In times of peace the factory had produced a typewriting machine of world-wide repute, and the American brains behind the business had so equipped the place with machinery for the mass-production of typewriter parts that, when war came, it was not much more than an overnight job to switch the plant over to the production of time-fuses, torpedo parts and other fine contributions to the art of killing.

The machine was very nearly complete master in that enormous barracks. Hot-blooded girls and sentient men minded lathes and such that performed certain mechanical actions and shaped fragments of metal, of which the operatives hardly knew the ultimate use. How could a girl, dreaming of her boy and of silk next her skin, think with every action of her hand that the result was possibly to be the mangling of the bodies of six Germans, the grief of a woman, the starvation of children, and then not much else but a stink and a wooden cross commemorating the unimportant?

But it was Work, it was Money . . .

That, and not a harking back through brave hunting symbolism and archetypal folk-imagery, is the reality facing modern man. Blake copes with it by convincing character-drawing, the manipulation of the reflection of national and international events on the private lives of the people who make up his stories, a sure knowledge of local, historical and social detail, and a firm command of dialogue and narrative. He is, indeed, a regional novelist, but a very good one: much better, for instance, than Alexander McArthur (1901–1947), the pathetic, unsuccessful journalist who dragged himself out of the slums to achieve, with the aid of a ghostwriter, *No Mean City* (1935), and then, having lifted the lid off the fester of the notorious Gorbals, sank back into it again. Blake is also a more powerful writer than either James Barke (1905–1958),* at his most sincere in *The Land o' the Leal* (1939), or Guy F. McCrone (b. 1899), whose trilogy *Wax Fruit* (1947) and its successors, though somewhat cliché-ridden, re-capture at an agreeable surface level the ups and downs of Glasgow middle-class life from mid-Victorian times into the twentieth century.

Among the most successful novels of what our Victorian ancestors would have called "the lower orders" in Glasgow is *Dance of the Apprentices* (1948) by Edward Gaitens (1897–1966). It depicts the Macdonnel family in the inter-war years. Idealized politics are discussed against a background of seductive triviality, the "dispiriting background of the Gorbals".

When Jimmy, the sailor son, comes home from a voyage and gets engaged to a "good-living" girl, he promises to give up drink, a promise

---

* At his worst in his novels about Burns, where slovenly prose vies with sexual voyeurism.

which horrifies father Macdonnel, who had been anticipating the usual drunken party on Jimmy's return, until the sailor's pay was exhausted. Three hours later, brother Eddy, who had been inspired by Jimmy's unexpected conversion, looks out into the street to see Jimmy, wearing his Aunt Kate's hat, and their father staggering arm-in-arm:

Large bottles of whisky waggled from the pockets of the two men. Behind them, laughing like witches, came Mrs Macdonnel and Aunt Kate with the sailor's hat on, followed by six of Jimmy's pals who were carrying between them three dozen crates of bottled beer.

In the orgy that followed, Eddy decided that:

. . . human behaviour had passed his understanding. He was thinking of Jeannie Lindsay and wishing he might find her standing at her close mouth in South Wellinton Street. But it was very late. He hurried round the corner in a queer emotional tangle of sexual shame and desire, his romantic thoughts of Jeannie mingled with the shameful memory of his mother dressing up in men's clothes and Bridget Delaney pulling up her skirts to the hips to show her bare legs to the men.

Sex and drink are not the prerogatives of working-class city-dwellers. In Linklater-land (and Gunn-land) people both practised "bundling" and got drunk. Gaitens shows what happens when physical customs idealized by non-urban novelists are transported to an urban setting during an industrial depression.

Dealing with similar raw material is Greenock-born Alan Sharp (b. 1934), only two volumes of whose planned trilogy have so far appeared. A Green Tree in Gedde (1965) presents Gedde as an up-dated Garvel, focusing on the intimate sexual details of an ordinary family and their friends. Its sequel, The Wind Shifts (1967), depicts the landscape of that aimless London of underground journeys and wintry parks to which the young are attracted, and where some of the relationships implied in the earlier volume are worked out. But the alert observation, the affectionate unintellectual sensuousness of the ordinary, baffled folk of whom Sharp writes, are more muted in his second book.

Archie Hind (b. 1928) has produced only one book The Dear Green Place (1966). Its scenes of Glasgow boyhood are authentically vivid. Basically, it is a book about a man writing a book. The kind of people who inhabit the Gaitens/Sharp/Hind world cannot aspire to do this successfully without a larger infusion of out-of-the-ruck credibility than this author is able to supply.

More completely of a piece is From Scenes Like These (1968) by Gordon M. Williams (b. 1934), in which a boy of talent, Duncan Logan, has his abilities extinguished by the brutal West of Scotland life-style: mindless labour relieved only with mindless football, fornication and drunkenness. Williams shows that "old Scotia's grandeur" has indeed fallen on debased days. Wisely, he is content to present the lower levels of industrial society without either moralizing, or inferring the existence of some allegedly suppressed political nostrum.

Though prone to clever prosing in place of dialogue, William McIlvaney (b. 1936) has shown himself to be the most promising of the younger Scots novelist with *Docherty* (1975).[29]

The most sensitive prober of west of Scotland relationships is Robin Jenkins (b. 1912), who was born in Cambuslang—then a Lanarkshire suburb of Glasgow—and educated at Hamilton Academy and Glasgow University before himself teaching at Dunoon Grammar School. Latterly, he has spent much of his time teaching abroad in places as different as Kabul and Barcelona.

His first novel, *So Gaily Sings the Lark* (1951), came from the Scottish Renaissance publishing house of William Maclellan, and immediately established Jenkins's position as a writer who could stand his ground, and had some ground to look to. It is the daily terrain of ordinariness. For Jenkins in his earlier Scots novels, this if often the world of the deprived child and his teacher; routine punctuated by brief interuptions of tragedy, usually logically led up to, sometimes melodramatic (as tragedy must inevitably seem to its victims at the moment of strike), but which retrospectively also appears insignificant in its ordinariness.

Jenkins himself once wrote of his work: "We have been a long time in acquiring our peculiarities: in spite of ourselves they are profound, vigorous and important: and it is the duty of the Scottish novelist to portray them."[30]

Some would think that we have been a long time in not getting rid of our more unpleasant peculiarities, including Scottish Calvinism and its dismal physical and spiritual side-effects. Yet, as the old madman tells the hopeful youngster in *So Gaily Sings the Lark*: "A man kens in his heart that this is an unfinished sort of place, not perfect like heaven; and when he sees something that he thinks is complete he looks round, without meaning to, for the disappointment."

Happy for the Child (1953) is a sensitive evocation of a Scottish childhood. His first novel of real, if flawed, distinction is *The Cone-Gatherers* (1955). In it, the themes of vulnerability and the hollowness of privilege are probed from different angles. Two brothers, one of them deformed, are gathering seed-cones in a Highland forest, part of the Runcie-Campbell estate, during wartime. Runcie-Campbell is on war service, and the gamekeeper is the symbol of hired male authority to whom Lady Runcie-Campbell turns. The brothers form a bond of attachment with the young son of the house, a relationship which provokes the gamekeeper's animosity. He himself has a crippled wife. Against his ill-will, the brothers have no defence. The gamekeeper's resentment at his wife's affliction centres on the hunch-back brother. When the son gets dangerously stuck up a tree, the gamekeeper is powerless to do what is expected of him and effect a rescue. Only the hunch-back brother, in whom the son has confidence, is able to do what is needed. In the *dénouement*, stung beyond endurance by his inadequacy, the gamekeeper kills the hunchback, and, somewhat improbably, Lady Runcie-Campbell kneels in tears among the pine-cones.

Guests of War (1952) deals with the confrontation of respectable middle-class country folk faced with an influx of deprived city children evacuated because of the war. Adjustments are made on both sides, but the arrival of visiting parents proves the influence of heredity stronger than that of the new enviroment.

The Changeling (1958), in my view the best of Jenkins's Scottish novels, examines the situation in reverse. Charlie Forbes, a "do-gooding" progressive teacher, decides, against his wife's wishes, to take Tom Curdie, the intelligent product of a mixed Glasgow slum family, with his own children to the coast on holiday. Forbes believes that Tom's propensity for thieving is an outcome of his environment and the influence of his degraded family. Tom steals while on holiday to prevent himself becoming too closely identified with the Forbes ambience, which he increasingly enjoys but to which he bitterly realizes he can never belong. Only Forbes's daughter, Gillian, understands, and helps Tom escape to a hilly hut when the police arrive just before Tom's return in disgrace to the appalling slum-family in Donaldson's Court. Tom, however, hangs himself in the hut. While it is the case that in Jenkins's novels melodrama is often an aid to resolution, here again it is entirely justified. Charlie Forbes's intervention merely created the kind of expectation gap that society is discovering with increasing urgency it has no way of filling. The story is thus a microcosm of the central dilemma of modern industrial society. Suicide, of course, is not the usual response of those confronted with such a dilemma; but then most of them are not blessed—or cursed—with Tom Curdie's superior intelligence and sensitivity of response.

Scotland in the twentieth century does not provide a good background (in commercial terms) for a novelist to work against for too long. In 1960, Jenkins moved abroad with *Some Kind of Grace*. His finest mature achievement, however, is *Dust on the Paw* (1961), set in Afganistan, called in the novel Nurania, on the borders of Russia. Nurania is a backward country seeking to modernize itself, but in which American dollars and Soviet roubles vie for a controlling influence against the passionate desire of the Nuranians to indulge in their own form of nationalism.

The book has two heroes. One is the poet and teacher Harold Moffat, whose mind accepts racial equality, but whose emotions make him passionately resist it, to the point of denying his own beautiful Chinese wife, Lan, a child, since it would be half-caste. Moffat's disgust with himself in the end leads him to some kind of acceptance of his own imperfections. The other hero, Manchester-educated Abdul Wahab, comes home to Nurania engaged to an English woman teacher, who turns out to be older than himself and lame. Wahab, as Alexander Scott remarks, "lives on a see-saw of emotions, one eye on his ideals and the other on the main chance."[31] Accidentally, he quells a youthful revolution, and wins both self-acceptance and acceptance for his wife from the corrupt but well-meaning Nurianian authorities, as well as from the seedy British and American embassy set. But for how long, one is left wondering at the end of the book?

The characterization is penetrating, and although the novel invites comparison with studies of similar overseas situations created by Graham Greene, Jenkins's cynicism is that of accurate reportage, not, as with Greene, arising out of his own emotional reaction to the attitudes of his characters.

Some of Jenkins's later novels have allowed melodrama too much of a head, a let-out which also mars many of the stories in his collection *Far Cry from Bowmore* (1973). The best of the six is "Bonny Chung", a wry portrait of a Chinese immigrant on the make in a racially mixed society.

Poets do not always distinguish themselves as novelists, the technique of compression required for the one differing radically from that required for the other. Yet two Scottish Renaissance poets have achieved some distinction with creative prose, though more markedly through their short stories than in the more extended form of the novel.

George Mackay Brown's focus, in prose as in poetry, is firmly fixed upon his native Orkney. With a wide emotional range at his command, he examines a diversity of characters with sympathy and understanding, both in *A Calendar of Love* (1967) and *A Time to Keep* (1969), relating their lonelinesses not only to present-day communal activity, but, in an odd way, to the traditions of those from whom they have stemmed. *Greenvoe* (1972), his first so-called novel, is really a collection of accurate, yet never satirical or unkindly, portraits centred on a single community.

Brown became a convert to Roman Catholicism in 1961, and while this at first resulted in a further strengthening of his understanding of communal customs and myths, it has become something of a fall-back in some of his later verse. It is also present in his second novel *Magnus* (1974), which deals with the treacherous murder of Earl Magnus by Earl Hakon on the island of Egilsay in 1106, an event which made Magnus the patron saint of Orkney. The character of Magnus obviously fascinates Brown, for Magnus is also the subject of one of Brown's earlier Muir-influenced poems, "Saint Magnus on Egilsay". The sparse, original telling of the murder in the *Orkneyinga Saga* is not really bettered by Brown's extended re-telling, although, as always with this writer, the novel reveals still further surprises about the "feel" of the islands, a characteristic also of his less concentrated *An Orkney Tapestry*, (1969).

As far as the novels and stories of Iain Crichton Smith (and, indeed, the plays) are concerned, those in Gaelic do not come within the bounds of this survey. It is not so much with the physical or spiritual loneliness of people as it affects many of Brown's characters that Smith is primarily concerned; rather the sheer difficulty of communication between one person and another. This difficulty forms the general theme of Smith's first collection of stories, *Survival Without Error* (1970). "Je t'aime" and "Joseph", emotionally far apart, are particularly penetrating examples of his insight and manner of expression. His short novel *Consider the Lilies* (1968), with its evocative Highland-sounding prose, is a view of the Clearances through the eyes of his grandparents and their generation. Although it does contain several obvious—and, on the whole, unimportant—anachronisms, it portrays the upright but narrow character of the old woman who is the main protagonist in considerable depth. We are made sharply aware of the pathos of a way of life on the verge of disintegration.

Where Smith's tale fails is in its inability to see the other side of the story; to identify those social and economic currents that created the conditions which made the Duke of Sutherland's actions at least intelligible, and would have forced the depopulation of the Highlands by natural, slower means. (On the other hand, even Scott was at times a partial story-teller.)

Malcolm, the central character of *The Lost Summer* (1969), has depth and credibility. Yet the book, which is apparently autobiographical, again impresses more through Smith's ability to create atmosphere than to draw fully credible subsidiary characters.

My Last Duchess (1971) also has an autobiographical ring and some concentrated scenes; but it has serious faults of construction, its two parts giving the impression that they were conceived at different times. The relationships between the schoolmaster hero and women are also singularly unconvincing. Many of the lesser characters speak as if they were projections of the author rather than out of their own fully imagined separate identities.

It would seem that the intensity of Smith's observation, as with Brown's, operates most effectively in the short story; which, in an organizational sense at least, is really a kind of prose poem.

The final category of twentieth-century novelists is made up of those who write of Scotland from outside, looking in. Robert Bontine Cunninghame Graham (1852–1936)—grandson of that Robert Graham (1735?–1797?) who became Receiver General in Jamaica, Rector of Glasgow University and the author of "If doughty deeds my lady please"—though born in London, was the son of a Scottish laird. Leaving Harrow in his seventeenth year, he went to South America and married a Chilean poetess, Gabriela de la Balmondière. When he inherited Gartmore, the Perthshire family estate, it was so burdened with debt that he had to sell it, settling on the much smaller estate of Ardoch, on the Clyde. Although he travelled extensively in South America, he was for six years a Scottish Member of Parliament, co-founder with Keir Hardie of the Scottish Labour Party, and in 1928 the first President of the Scottish National Party.

His prose works are vivid, whether he is occupied in story-telling against a South American or a Scottish background. His travel books—notably *Mogreb-el-Acksa* (1898), about Morocco, and *El Río de la Plata* (1914)— breathe the enthusiasm and sharp insights of a man with so broad a range of interests that literature alone could not satisfy him. Most of the stories are to be found in *Success* (1902), *Faith* (1909), *Hope* (1911), *Charity* (1912) and *Scottish Stories* (1914). "Beattock for Moffat" deserves its wonted place in most anthologies of the Scottish short story. In it, as in many others, the narrative strand is strong, the characterization broad and colourful rather than psychologically subtle. Although his output amounts to some thirty books, he wrote no novels.

Frederick Niven (1878–1944), the son of a Glasgow manufacturer of "sewed muslins" and grandson of a Glasgow librarian, was born at Valparaíso, Chile, but came to Scotland in early childhood and was educated at Hutcheson's Grammar School, the prototype of Caruthers Academy in *The Three Marys* (1930). In his autobiography *Coloured Spectacles* (1938), he writes warmly of the city that became his second home. He studied at the Glasgow School of Art, but found himself insufficiently talented to become a painter, as he had planned. Not surprisingly, his novels abound in painterly detail. Since he did not enjoy working in his father's store, he emigrated to Canada at the age of twenty. There, he spent several years wandering about, and working in lumber and railway camps in the far West. He also traced old Indian trails up into the hills (all of which provided material for his final novel, *The Transplanted* (1944)).

Then followed a period of journalizing in Glasgow, Edinburgh, Dundee and London. He revisited Canada in 1912. Back again in London, he discovered that he had a heart condition, so worked during the 1914–18 war for the Ministries of Food and Information. Soon after, he left Britain for good, settling in British Columbia, where he died.

His own varied life-experience provided directly the themes for his novels. The early stories are novels of manners. George Blake described *Justice of the Peace* (1914) as "a more than worthy picture of conditions in a Glasgow warehouse in a bourgeois society in the still expanding city". *The Staff at Simson's* (1937) provides a readable account of the work and interests of those who operated John Simson's of Cochrane Street, manufacturers of shirtings, wincies, flanalettes and fancy goods, for customers who were still mostly clad in the Edwardian remnants of nineteenth-century snobbery. The love story of Robert Barclay for the girl from the marmalade factory in *The Three Marys* is handled with remarkable frankness for the times in which it was written. After reading *A Tale That is Told* (1920), Rebecca West hailed Niven as "a Scottish Chekov", adding: "No-one before Niven has ever dealt with Scotland's grey floridity, its pulpit theatricality, its extravagancies that break out in the very places one would have thought were committed to primness."

His memory of Glasgow detail never deserted him, whether remembering Kate Cranston—she of tea-room fame and patron of Charles Rennie Mackintosh—"rustling down Buchanan Street" in the '90s, or the appearance of the fascias of once-famous Glasgow shops like Edward's, the jewellers, or Porteous's bookshop.

Triumph (1934), set partly in South America and partly in Scotland, is dedicated to Cunninghame Graham. It deals with the career of a Scottish music-master whose native prickliness brings him into conflict with the conventions of overseas English behaviour.

Some of Niven's novels are set in Canada. *The Transplanted* deals with the fortunes of Robert Wallace and Jock Galbraith, and reflects the pioneering qualities which took so many Scots out of their own country. Wallace is the entrepreneur who opened up the lonely Elkhorn valley, Galbraith, a Gorbals man who becomes Wallace's foreman. Galbraith saves Wallace's life on the mountains, and in turn has his own life saved by his friend when Galbraith gets implicated in the murder of one of those violent cheats whom virgin lands always attract.

Niven's evocation of the differing Scots qualities of character against the background of physical hardships facing those who, emulating Galt, emigrated to tame Canada's lonely places, worthily celebrates in fiction that often ambiguously-motivated figure, the Scot abroad.

Edinburgh-born Muriel Spark (b. 1918) has achieved wide recognition as a result of the successful film version of *The Prime of Miss Jean Brodie* (1961), a witty account of the career of a spinster teacher with advanced ideas planted in the environs of a middle-class school in the '30s. Her ill-digested views on the latest intellectual fads of the day get passed on to her pupils, and in the end bring about her downfall. The book is very funny at surface level. At another level, the spectacle of a lonely woman seeking, and failing, to sublimate her physical unfulfilment through the cultivation of "progressive" notions, is handled with tact and sympathy. When a pupil and the teacher both fall in love with the school art-master, Miss Brodie finds the general pupil-trust she believes she enjoys to be false. As an outcome of bitchy jealousy, reactionary authority is provided with the necessary excuse for getting rid of this inconvenient liberal who tries to practise values to which others merely give lip-service.

Although *The Ballad of Peckham Rye* (1960) centres upon a Scottish eccentric, Mrs Spark's later novels ornament the literature of England rather than Scottish literature.

James Kennaway (1928–1968), whose regimental celebration *Tunes of Glory* (1956)—also filmed—scarcely rises above the level of well-turned popular fiction, showed remarkable talent for pace, narrative dialogue, and a deep understanding of the corrupting power of egotism in *Some Gorgeous Accident* (1967). His own untimely death in a car accident soon after ended what promised to be a novelist's career of considerable brilliance, his posthumous short novel *The Cost of Living Like This* (1969), the story of the love-tug a man dying of cancer finds himself helplessly caught in being full of touching human insight.

III

Drama is still the sickly child of the Scottish Renaissance family. Neil Gunn, in *Choosing a Play*, suggests that this is because whereas the writer of a novel has ample opportunity of correcting any misinterpretation the reader may initially have made, once an audience has laughed the play will be labelled a comedy. There has been no dearth of kitchen comedy, the oldest surviving example of which is *Bunty Pulls the Strings* (1911*) by Graham Moffat (1866–1951).

The forerunners of so-called "working-class" drama are the plays of Joe Corrie (1894–1968), who began life as a miner. Indeed *In Time of Strife* (1929) is about the miners' strike of 1926, and by far his best play. But *The Shillin'-a-week Man* (1927), *Kye Amang the Corn* (1933) and *The Gaberlunzie* (1947) all enjoyed considerable popularity, especially with amateur drama companies, by whom they are still occasionally revived. The limitations of Corrie's ability to draw the fullest implications from his socially aware themes also characterize his verse, the best of which is to be found in *Image o' God* (1928).

Scottish dramatists have shown a singular reluctance to tackle major issues on the stage, except on an obviously class or sectarian basis. This, no doubt, is yet another working-out of the national dichotomy. It is also partly a hang-up from the Reformation (assuming that it shaped the Scots temperament since 1560, and not that the Reformation was itself a product of the Scots temperament). The Scot does not like to show his feelings too openly in the public arts, whatever relaxing he may be prepared to make for the privately absorbed arts of reading, or looking at painting or sculpture.

After Barrie, the first dramatist to attract more than passing attention was "John Brandane" (Dr John MacIntyre) (1869–1947), an isleman with the sound of Gaelic-coloured English in his ears and the example of the Anglo-Irish revival in his mind. In his autobiography, Bridie remarked: "John Brandane was for the pure milk of the gospel. He considered that the [Scottish National Theatre] Society should produce a Scottish drama by Scottish authors, that the Society's sole function was to evoke one . . ."

The Glen is Mine (1925), which uses a pibroch to sound the theme, tried to do just that. It uncovers, but does not explore in any depth, the problem of the "romantic" Highland past set against the industrial present: the old weary labour in all sorts of weather amidst the healthy heather and the deer, against the drudgery and slumdom of "emigration" to a job in Glasgow. Angus, the central figure, is, however, an effective piece of character-drawing.

* But only published in 1932.

To claim, as some have done, Gordon Bottomley (1874–1968)—a York-shireman with a Scottish mother—as anything other than an English *fin de siècle* contemporary of Yeats who never developed, except towards refin-ing the dubious art of verse-speaking for polite drawing-rooms, is to stretch a point that will not bear the strain. His pageant-play *Kate Kennedy* (1945), however, has become an annual feature of student life in the Uni-versity of St Andrews.

The only figure after Barrie with an output of any quantity or sustained individuality in English is "James Bridie", Dr O. H. Mavor, (1888–1951). A Glasgow man, he qualified as a medical doctor at his native Univer-sity—where certain jovial rhymes, notably that chilly satire on timid middle-class wooing "The West End Perk", are still gratefully remem-bered—practised in Glasgow until 1938, and served in the R.A.M.C. in both wars. He first became known in Scotland as a dramatist with *The Sun-light Sonata* (1928) and *What it is to Be Young* (1929), both of which showed a talent for crisp wit and character-drawing rather than a flair for con-struction. But his eyes were set on the London Theatre, and in 1930, with *Tobias and the Angel*, he achieved his aim. It was to be the first of many of his plays to enjoy a long London run. Then followed, among others, *The Ana-tomist* (1930), *Jonah and the Whale* (1932), *The Sleeping Clergyman* (1933), *Susannah and the Elders* (1937), *Mr Bolfry* (1943), *The Forrigan Reel* (1944)—a fantasy that has always proved too Scottish for West End London audi-ences—*Dr Angelus* (1947), *The Baikie Charivari* (1949) and *Daphne Laureola* (1952).

Bridie, like Shaw, uses conversation to get his theme across. Like Shaw, too, his *point de départ* is often a Biblical or a classical legend re-interpreted in modern terms. There, the resemblance ends. While Bridie is at his best when dealing with the problems of individualists in a conformist society, he does not indulge in dogma. Shaw always offers us witty dogmatic an-swers, or pseudo-answers. Bridie, in the manner of Brecht, is usually con-tent to tease out the questions, examine the ambiguities of alienation, and leave the audience to provide its own answers. In *Daphne Laureola*, Lady Katherine Pitts is condemned to live her life in a world of her own ima-gining because of her inability to face up to reality. The examination of character which Bridie carries out to justify this disorientation is in marked contrast to the work of the "anyone for tennis" school popular in the between-the-wars period. He is concerned with the degradation of civilization, whether at the hands of men like Dr Angelus, who have gone on a moral holiday; or like Dr Knox, who carry a narrow zeal for their profession too far.

Indeed, in *John Knox* (1947), and in his best play, *The Queen's Comedy* (1950), where Bridie did attempt to provide answers—in the one case by means of a dialogue on the steps of heaven between Knox and his old antagonist, Mary Queen of Scots, and, in the other (an updated version of the Trojan War), through an explanation by Jupiter—the endings are ineffectual, if not actually embarrassing.

For all his sophistication, as a Lowland Scot Bridie was much exercized by the conundrums of good against evil, sin opposed to righteousness, dignity contrasted with ludicrousness.

As Edwin Morgan puts it, this: ". . . awareness of how thoroughly mixed good and evil are in the world implies that Bridie was no social reformer. . . . His peculiar quality is to suggest, though not to insist on, a certain trust in human adaptability and continuance."[32]

These are, of course, the virtues of that most stable element in society, the middle class. Bridie was thoroughly middle-class. His half-mock attitude to his own work, as revealed in his autobiography *One Way of Living* (1939), the fun-poking pretentiousness of *Tedious and Brief* (1944), and *Mr Bridie's Alphabet for Little Glasgow Highbrows* (1934) makes this plain enough:

> A play is a method of passing an interval of time. A stage play is a method of passing an interval of time by putting an actor or actors on a platform and causing them to say or do certain things. . . .

or again:

> The Play is not important to us today; not nearly so important as the films, for one thing. It would be fun if it was. . . .

Bridie, the shy unapproachable man—who once remarked, in response to a justified criticism of the construction of his third acts: "Only God could write the perfect Third Act, and he hasn't done it yet", and when responding at a press conference to a critic who had attacked Glasgow Citizens Theatre* suggesting that what Mr Bridie really wanted was not criticism but praise, burst out: "Yes, praise, damn you, praise"—may not have thought his method of communication all that important in itself. But he did value wit, the continuing attempt to keep alive an awareness of life's ambiguities, and the dour drollery of his Scots inheritance. He is therefore an essential corner-stone of whatever national theatre the defeat of the inhibitions of Calvinism may allow future generations of Scots to bring forth.

It may seem improbable that these products will bear much relationship to the linguistically pure Scots plays of Robert MacLellan (b. 1907). *Jamie the Saxt* (1937) provided a marvellous vehicle for that prince among Scots comedy actors Duncan Macrae (1912–1967). Macrae had only had to lift up his lugubrious chin to make an audience dissolve into laughter. As with Alexander Scott's *Right Royal* (1954), *Jamie the Saxt* is something of a concerto of a play, requiring the right comic virtuoso fully to realize it.

The trouble about writing plays in linguistically pure Scots is that the

* Of which Bridie was a founder.

playwright excludes the possibility of dealing with contemporary situations at every social level. MacLellan's *Jeddart Justice* (1934) and *Toom Byres* (1936) both stem from period tales, while *The Laird o' Torwattlie* (1946) and *The Flowers o' Edinburgh* (1947) remain pleasantly decorative period pieces with few relevant modern overtones.

Alexander Reid (b. 1914) perhaps achieves a higher level of contemporary significance, though a lower level of dramatic effectiveness and a less consistent Scots, in *The World's Wonder* (1953). Like MacLellan, Reid resorts to the skilful re-telling of an old tale in *The Lass Wi' the Muckle Mou'* (1950).

If there have been few makers of neatly made plays to please a Scots or a London audience as skilful as William Douglas Home (b. 1912), with his *The Chiltern Hundreds* and many others, plays which sacrifice credibility to left-wing dogma have proliferated, ranging from the work of Ewan Mac-Coll in the '50s to that of John McGrath in the '70s. The theatre, however, is neither the place to preach nor to proselytize if the dramatist seeks more than the equivalent of journalistic success. In gentler vein, *The Other Dear Charmer* (1957), Robert Kemp's play about Burns and Clarinda, seems likely to retain currency because of the skill with which he handles a love-story of continuing human interest.

Stewart Conn (b. 1936) has achieved some success in the theatre, but his plays, like his poems, are essentially derivative. *The Burning* (1973), perhaps the most effective on the stage, is, in stock-breeder's parlance, MacLellan's *Jamie the Saxt* out of Miller's *The Crucible*, while *Thistledown* (1975) is Brecht out of Joan Littlewood. Why listen regularly to the symphonies of Vanhal or Pleyel when you can experience those of Haydn?

Roddie MacMillan (b. 1923) in *All in Good Faith* (1954) and *The Bevellers* (1973) and Bill Bryden (b. 1942) with *Willie Rough* (1972) have managed more successfully than most to present Scottish life at a humbler level without rancour or the bias of class caricature.

The Scot, however, has yet to prove himself a master of the theatre. Sir David Lyndsay's *Ane Satire of the Thrie Estatis* remains our solitary major masterpiece; and it was written more than four hundred years ago.

IV

There are a few works of general literature which seem likely to retain their interest. MacDiarmid's prose—apart from the shorter pieces collected in *The Uncanny Scot* (1968)—is as erratic as his later verse, and considerably more vindictive. His ability to construct sentences that fill a page, and to avoid justifying his own opinions by quoting at length from the books of other writers, makes his autobiography *Lucky Poet* (1943) wearisome reading justified only by the forcefulness of character that comes through almost in spite of the author. Its successor, *The Company I've Kept* (1966), if less turgid, is not much above the level of day-to-day journalism.

Muir's *An Autobiography* (1954), an extended version of what first appeared as *The Story and the Fable* (1940), is a reflective record of a kindly life. His memories of his unpleasant youthful urban industrial experiences are much more telling than when fictionalized in his novel *Poor Tom* (1932).

Linklater's three autobiographical volumes, *The Man on my Back* (1941), *A Year of Space* (1953) and *Fanfare for a Tin Hat* (1970), flaunt his particular brand of gaiety. The final volume contains some interesting revelations about his own views on his work.

Cliff Hanley's *Dancing in the Streets* (1958), the autobiography of a clever boy who "made good" in Glasgow, is one of the funniest books ever written arising out of life in a city where objective gaiety is by no means a common commodity. It is in every way superior to his novels, which tend merely to reproduce himself thinly disguised.

Without doubt, the most astonishing autobiography in Scottish literature, if not in the English language, is Sir Compton Mackenzie's *My Life and Times* (1963–71) published, with glorious disregard for musical terminology, in ten "octaves". Unlike the seemingly endless and uneven journals and diaries of Boswell emerging from the editing of the Malahide papers, Mackenzie's work has shape and consistent interest. Edmund Gosse, Henry James, D. H. Lawrence, Churchill, de Valera, Ramsay Macdonald and Ethel Smythe are only some of the dozens of famous men and women who pass through Mackenzie's pages, leaving something of themselves behind etched in memorable detail. There are magnificent set-pieces, like his account of the Abdication row which broke out over his book *Windsor Tapestry*. There is a zest for living astonishing for an author in his eighties.

In the last quarter of the twentieth century, the writing of history has become so specialized that accuracy of detail almost inevitably takes the place of literary quality. In the same way, criticism has become so much an academic industry that its practitioners scarcely rank as purveyors of literature, however necessary their function.

One is left with a few non-fictional books which are basically concerned with facts, but where the quality is such that their atmosphere lingers long in the reader's memory. One such book is *Brother Scots* (1927) by Donald Carswell (1882–1940), who is also remembered for his play about the last years of Prince Charles Edward Stuart, *Count Albany*, a one-act minor masterpiece rescued from the wreck of a three-act play. *Brother Scots* manages to bring to life people as diverse as the evangelical theologian Henry Drummond, Keir Hardie, and Lord Overtoun, amongst others, using them to illuminate various unchanging aspects of the Scottish character.

William Roughead's (1870–1952) *Twelve Scots Trials* (1913) and *The Riddle of the Ruthvens* (1919) achieve a similar effect by the accurate yet colourful narration of the stories of the life and crimes of some of Scotland's inventive murderers.

More peaceably, *A Farmer's Boy* (1935) by John R. Allan (b. 1907), an account of a North-east childhood, is already rightly regarded as a minor Scottish classic. Moray Maclaren (1901–1971), though a versatile and prolific man of letters, seems likely to be best remembered for two books: *Return to Scotland* (1932), a luminous telling of the re-discovery of his native land and the qualities of its people after a period abroad; and *The Capital City* (1950), his account of his native place, which, though uneven, evokes as does nothing else the quality of New Town life just before its great Georgian homes were converted into more workable flats. Another successful re-creation of the "feel" of Scotland is *Summer in Scotland* (1952) by Ivor Brown (1891–1974), drama critic, author of several books on the meaning of words, and one-time editor of *The Observer*. *Summer in Scotland* invites comparison with Alexander Smith's *A Summer in Skye*, written a century earlier.

Doubtless other readers will remember their own choice of similar books with equal affection, since when one reaches the threshold of to-day, even the fairest-minded critic of Scottish literature is bound to be somewhat subjective in his judgments.

CHAPTER SEVEN

. . . And After

I

The Scottish Renaissance movement came into being almost imperceptibly during the early twenties at about the same time as the Scottish National Party. In a similar manner, it gradually rounded itself off during the latter half of the eighties. By 1991, Robert Crawford (b.1959) was able to declare (in the magazine *Chapman*) that Hugh MacDiarmid's ideas on Scotland were already "curiously antique . . . anglophobic . . . a strident rewriting of the story of Scotland as encyclopaedic and fierce, internationally orientated and chauvinistically macho". While, equally sweepingly, his friend W.N. Herbert (b.1961) could assert, in *Severe Burns* (1986) that: "Modernism has become an Alexandria of fastidious iconoclasm, politically suspect ideologies, linguistically imperialist techniques: all the —ists, —asms and —isms in a loggiam of hypnotic interest to its successors. Very well, let us be the neoteroi; the poets, who, by submitting themselves to a tradition of radicalism, free what is fecund from the sprawling mass that chokes up the latter part of this century—into Scots!" Even making due allowance for the customary arrogant air of most youthful manifestos, this one seems particularly unremarkable for its clarity of practical intention.

Many of the "second wind" Scottish Renaissance writers did undoubtedly produce good work in the eighties; in some cases, indeed, their finest work. One by one, however, their achievements were monumentalised into *Collected Poems*, their ranks gradually thinned by death.

Robert Garioch died in 1981. His *Collected Poems* appeared in 1977, consolidating his position as the wittiest of the Lallans Makars who remained linguistically firmly within a still-spoken Scots idiom. His fellow makar Alexander Scott, also an upholder of genuine spoken Scots, died in 1989, leaving an unpublished volume to be included in his *Collected Poems*, currently being edited by David Robb. If the late poems break little new ground, the vigour of Scott's refreshingly downright manner remains characteristically direct. His teaching influence, as the first holder of a specifically designated Scottish Literature appointment in a Scottish University, was very considerable, though it received inadequate academic recognition during his lifetime.

Of those who wrote only in English, Ruthven Todd died in 1978 without adding significantly to the poems collected in his *Garland For a Winter Solstice* (1962). Like so many poets who seek escape through exile, once he removed himself from the fricative clash of personal and national identity *vis-à-vis* the sights, sounds and traditions of the country of his upbringing, the quality of his verse declined. The quietly thoughtful, and undervalued, G.S. Fraser's *Collected Poems* came out in 1981, the year after his death. Sydney Tremayne, who in his work reflected musically so many of the colours and shades of the Scottish landscape, died in 1986. A *Collected Poems* is in his case still awaited.

Edwin Morgan's *Collected Poems* was published to mark his seventieth birthday in 1990. It further confirmed his breadth of interests, liveliness of mind and plasticity of rhythms, expressed in verse ranging from formal sonnets to so-called "concrete poetry". His excellence as a critic was simultaneously established in a companion volume, *Crossing the Border*, a collection of essays on Scottish literature. Morgan's ready appeal to, and identity with, the young has resulted in his becoming probably the most widely read of all twentieth century Scottish poets.

Norman MacCaig's *Collected Poems* (1990) marked his eightieth birthday, and consolidated his reputation as a poet of brilliant sleight-of-hand, colourful, metaphysical, "me-based" imagery. The reviewer who patronisingly declared that MacCaig "did one thing but did it well," failed to add that the "one thing",—throwing a new and perceptive light on familiar features and creatures—happens to be a "thing" enjoyed by many.

The present writer's *Collected Poems 1940–1990* added yet another to the tally of 1990 poetic round-ups, leading Iain Crichton Smith to remark on it as being the work of "a poet of the quotidian, of the random sparkle of everyday". George Mackay Brown's seventieth birthday was marked in 1991 by the re-publication of his *Selected Poems*, with additional poems from his subsequent volumes, *Voyages* (1983) and *The Wreck of the Archangel* (1989). In these later volumes, the grim saga-like *vers libre* manner becomes increasingly prosy, the counterpointing of pre-Reformation imagery with lyricism much less telling. Nevertheless, although it could be said, as of the Belgian composer César Franck, that in his later work Mackay Brown simply recomposes what he has already written, he has undoubtedly provided Orkney with a recognisable Islands voice, a wholly convincing "speak" which, at its best, has wider overtones, though more so, perhaps, in his later short story collections—*Andrina* (1983), *A Time to Keep* (1987), *The Masked Fisherman* (1989) and the novel *Magnus* (1973) —than in his later poetry.

Iain Crichton Smith's own *Collected Poems* came out in 1992, impressing with the cumulative evidence of the power of his quiet classicism tensioned by his handling of the modern conflicts that affect the Gaelic way-of-life and culture under late twentieth-century pressures.

Of the other writers more or less connected with the Scottish Renaissance, Stewart Conn's increasing mastery of subject-matter relating to the ambiguities of existence has become increasingly evident with successive volumes, notably *Under the Ice* (1978), *In the Kibble Palace* (1987) and *The Luncheon of the Boating Party* (1991). George Bruce's *Perspectives* (1987) records some of the impressions gained on lecture tours in the United States and Australia, but also includes a vigorous and highly amusing pseudo-lament on the much-heralded demise of the Scots tongue.

James Aitchison (b.1938), a fair-minded liberal critic as well as an impressively sure-footed poet, in *Sounds Before Sleeping* (1972), *Spheres* (1975) and *Second Nature* (1990) intensifies the perceptions of a compassionate voice and a seeing eye for nature. His latest collection, *Second Nature* (1990) further develops his fastidious music and quiet skill over a widening range of experience, as in "I Watched You Walk":

You stepped in and out of twenty years,
walking away from them, and yet bringing them with you,
the you of then so easily in step
with the you of now. You waved again.

It took me a few seconds to respond
before I grinned, waved back, and dropped the book,
startled at being recognised by both of you
and through so many walls.

The versatile and prolific Alan Bold (b.1943) began as a poet influenced by the worst features of MacDiarmid's latter-day style of political declamation, but had found his own voice and compassionate yet inquiring tone by the time he wrote his beautiful elegy on his father, *A Memory of Death*, which appeared in *A Perpetual Motion Machine* (1969). Among later volumes are *This Fine Day* (1979) and *In This Corner: Selected Poems 1963–83*. From *A Perpetual Motion Machine* also comes the charming poem to his daughter, Valencia:

The earth turns round and tells that our
    Precarious point in space
Is not forever—but these sour
Predictions vanish every hour
    We chatter face to face.

Bold's *MacDiarmid: A Critical Biography* (1990), though not perhaps the totally objective final word on its controversial genius of a subject, pulls few punches and is undoubtedly both a valuable study in itself, as well as a distinguished contribution to the biographer's craft. Bold's

Summoned by Knox (1985) illustrates his Scots writing, but the poet Bold is really more convincing in English.

Duncan Glen (b.1933) has written nearly forty collections of Scots verse, out of which now and again an occasional piece comes alive. Such a one is "My Faither"—a Scots figure, "My Faither," when alive, an Englished one, "My Father," when lying his coffin—illustrating the persistent association between the English tongue and religion forged when the reformer John Knox established English rather than Scots as the language for the vernacular Bible. Glen's longer philosophical pieces, however, rarely manage to transmute his domestic imagery into the stuff of poetry. His *Hugh MacDiarmid and the Scottish Renaissance* (1962), the earliest full-length study of its kind, remains a valuable source-book. He founded and edited the enterprising magazine *Akros* from 1965 to 1983.

The gradual move away from the idealistic nationalism of the Scottish Renaissance writers—whether expressly defined or simply reflected in choice of subject-matter or use of tone and imagery— towards radical social realism, is much more obvious in fiction and drama than in poetry. Nevertheless, the poetic sands also began sifting a decade or two before the older movement conspicuously ebbed away in the eighties.

Tom Leonard (b.1944), though a poet of varied styles, is best known for his poems in the Glasgow dialect, many of which reflect a kind of "alternative" folk humour. His anti-establishment outspokenness on religion, sex and politics, and his frequent use of "bad language," for a time laid him under suspicion in some establishment quarters. Though his dialect poems must be more or less incomprehensible to English readers, his characteristically detached irony is also deployed in his "straight" English poems, well represented in his collection *Intimate Voices: Writing 1965–83* (1984). The "alternative" way of looking at things was also wittily reflected in the early work of Alan Jackson (b.1938), though his *Collected Poems 1960–89* suggests a falling away into a more self-conscious introspection.

Among women poets Liz Lochhead (b.1947), though probably of more importance as a playwright, stands out from her sister-writers for the freshness of her style and the gradual extension of her verse-range, from *Memo for Spring* (1972) to the more ambitious *True Confessions and New Clichés* (1985). Of the same generation is the militant and somewhat over-praised Douglas Dunn (b.1942) whose proclaimed intention to refuse to pay his community charge (thereby leaving others to do so for him) in the *Glasgow Herald* was given an added literary dimension through his pamphlet *Poll Tax: the Fiscal Facts (1990)*. After the sub-Larkin Marxist-flavoured *Terry Street*, already referred to, his most successful achievement is his ruggedly honest *Elegies* (1985), inspired by the death of his first wife; a collection happily free from the somewhat whipped-up air of rather cold contrivance that has characterised much of his later work.

Of the younger writers, the most promising is probably Robert Crawford, quoted at the beginning of this chapter. His collection *The Scottish Assembly* (1990) wittily and satirically brought under scrutiny a number of well-established Scottish attitudes. Whether or not his powers will develop to carry him beyond his present sharp-edged youthful cleverness—he sometimes gives the impression of condescending to his readers—remains to be seen. The heavily mannered volume in a highly synthetic and iconoclastic phonetically spelt Scots, *Sharawaggi* (1990), the authorship of which Crawford shares with his fellow academic W.N. Herbert, and where sometimes the glossary occupies more space on the page than the verse it seeks to explicate, appears to carry both writers down a linguistic cul-de-sac. Their contrived artificiality contrasts unfavourably with the living Scots used with skill by (despite his Italian name), a young Arbroath writer, Raymond Vettese (b.1950), in *The Richt Noise and Ither Poems* (1988).

Three other poets should be chronicled: one, an older writer who has quietly built himself a reputation, almost unnoticed, another older writer sadly neglected over many years, and a vigorous newcomer.

William Neill (b.1922) uses English and Scots (and also Gaelic, I am told) with equal vigour and felicity. He hits thus at sartorial nationalism in *Scotland's Castle* (1969):

> North Britons wear their philabegs on Sunday
> (Like siller bridles on the heids o aires★)
> And press their suits for sordid gain on Mondays.

Wild Places (1980) and *Making Tracks* (1988), range over the increasingly Anglo-Scottish aspects of contemporary Scottish life with a mordant wit. Some of the academic writers already mentioned might take to heart his "Battle Hymn" from *Wild Places*:

> We are the learned young
> we, who know all,
> no questions to ask,
> no angels to fall.

Aberdeen-born Ken Morrice (b.1924), professionally a consultant psychiatrist, is a writer who has been almost totally overlooked, probably because he works securely in the traditional mainstream and exhibits no fashionable idiosyncrasies to attract attention. He has brought a poetically sensitive understanding to the clinical situations with which he has had to deal. Two of his later collections are among his

★ old horses.

best, *For All I Know* (1981) and *When Truth Is Known* (1986). There is an admirable antidote to what George Bruce has called "the emotional indulgence television has deployed on hospitals" in Morrice's "The Institute":

I was appointed to the Institute
and given a cure of minds,
"Start here," said the Superintendent,
"where all humanity winds
up sooner or later. Such is fate. Just
do what you can do. And remember, if you
please, the forms in triplicate."

Again, also from *Where Truth Is Known*, in "Coronation for a Black Prince" there is a similar sense of social disturbance:

In class one day he rose and said
"I am Jesus". Schoolmasters on the whole
are not well versed in this kind of metaphor.
Hurriedly he was consigned to the Head
who failed to notice the cross he carried.

Frank Kuppner (b.1951), using mostly unrhymed quatrains, displays a restless refusal to settle for certainties, even to the point of sometimes providing his poems with alternative part-lines. *A Bad Day for the Sung Dynasty* (1984), with its succession of Chinese-like cameos, is frequently very funny. He can also write in an oddly moving way, as in "An Old Guide Book to Prague" from *The Intelligent Observation of Naked Women* (1987).

Every twilight, the city has departed;
It has crept away into the tourists' memories,
And its quieter sister has slipped into its place;
The next day it returns, with a slight hangover.

Lights are on the statues, lights are on the porticoes,
Lights are on the monuments, lights are in the towers;
Lights show at most of the windows in the street;
But it is the lights in the street that go out first.

The content of his verse is perhaps best self-described in *Ridiculous, Absurd, Disgusting* (1989) as being "something worth speaking over the phone to somebody rung up more or less at random".

As we approach the end of the twentieth century the poetry scene in Scotland hosts no obvious figure among the younger writers of the imaginative stature of MacDiarmid or Muir, or, for that matter, even MacCaig or Morgan. It reflects the hesitancies and self-doubtings of a century that has encompassed a faster pace of scientific invention than any before it, yet also contained more far-reaching famines and "great" and "little" bloody wars than any of its predecessors; a century, too, in which Scotland has wakened up to the value of its national identity without (so far, at any rate) willing the political measures to ensure its survival.

Perhaps the spread of classless universal higher education, surely welcomed here in Scotland as elsewhere throughout Europe, may result in the production of many more future minor poetic talents, though few major ones. Some belief in the "everyone is famous for fifteen minutes" dictum of the American pop-artist and self-publicist Andy Warhol, together with an increasing teaching emphasis on self-expression rather than received information, is helping to downgrade the status of the great writers of the past; indeed, in the very concept of great art. At the least, largely thanks to the liberating impetus of the Scottish Renaissance, it seems reasonable to assert that Scotland is certainly not poetically voiceless as we approach the arrival of the twenty-first century, even if there may be some doubts as to the ultimate value of much that is being uttered.

II

It is difficult to chart the course of late twentieth-century Scottish fiction with any critical certainty of judgment, if for no other reason than because at various levels there is now so much of it. At what point, for example, does a novel become literature, and cease being merely entertainment? Once upon a time, the borderline was fairly obvious. Now, it is more than likely to be a matter of dispute, particularly with "post modernist" critics who challenge the existence of any kind of identifiable "reality".

Some of the writers mentioned in the previous chapter have continued producing—notably Robin Jenkins, from *Fergus Lamont* (1954), the story of a man who adhered consistently to false social values, to the charming if slightly improbable, *Poverty Castle* (1991). Iain Crichton Smith, too, has developed his skill in drawing reasonably convincing characters, as his kindly sympathies as a teller of autobiographically based tales has increased with the years, notably in *Murdo and Other Stories* (1981), *The Tenement* (1985), and *In the Middle of the Wood* (1987).

Radical social realism, the reflection of a far from divine discontent, becomes the keynote sounded by most of the post-Jenkins/Crichton Smith novelists and writers of short stories; a form, incidentally, in which many recent Scottish writers excel, as if in reaction to the ceaseless and so far unavailing urging of their critics to produce "the great Scottish novel". The distinguished critic Douglas Gifford has noted that, for whatever reason, these new creative writers do not "share the mood of political devolution," but instead, have become "increasingly exiles within their own society. The paradox presents itself that this new wave, this revival of Scottish writing," is "in essence about failed living".

George Friel (1910–1975), when already the author of three earlier novels, produced his minor masterpiece *Mr Alfred M.A.* (1975), the sad saga of a seedy alcoholic schoolmaster who transfers from a bad school to a worse one. William McIlvaney (b.1936), already mentioned, captures the images of a tough underworld that probably no longer exists in quite the way it is portrayed in *Docherty* (1975), *Laidlaw* (1977), *The Papers of Tony Veitch* (1983) and *Strange Loyalties* (1991), all of them basically stories of detection. Well-written and vigorously atmospheric though they be, they remain less than wholly credible as works of literature because the clever voice of the author keeps sounding so unmistakably through the dialogue of his much less clever characters. By far his most convincingly sympathetic achievement has been his collection of short stories, *Walking Wounded* (1989), all of the characters in which suffer from some or other form of "failed living".

Allan Spence (b.1942), in his short story sequence *The Colours They Are Fine* (1977), depicts the "development" of a Glasgow character from a more or less deprived childhood into becoming a "hard man". ("Hard" men have for too long been something of a Glasgow speciality). After a long interval, he followed his first book with *The Magic Flute* (1991), a study of religious bigotries.

Allan Massie (b.1938), Alasdair Gray (b.1934) and James Kelman (b.1946), however, have dominated the fictional scene throughout the eighties, joined, more recently, by the promising Janice Galloway (b.1956). Massie is the odd man out—neither apparently an unqualified supporter of devolution nor a writer preoccupied with the recording of failure. He is, indeed, a cosmopolitan man-of-the-world and a straight-speaking newspaper columnist, as at home with the problems of ancient Rome as with those of Scotland and modern Europe. His *Augustus: the Memoir of the Emperor* (1986), followed by its sequel, *Tiberius* (1990), are both period-costume imaginary "autobiographies" very little, if at all, inferior to *I, Claudius* and the other classical novels of Robert Graves. By far Massie's finest achievement is *A Question of Loyalties* (1989), which deals with the misguided idealism and conflicting demands of the moral choice facing Etienne de Balafre after the fall of France before the advancing German army in 1940.

He followed *A Question of Loyalties* with *The Sins of the Father* (1991), again a study of guilt and responsibility—centred on Rudi, a lukewarm Nazi, and Dr Czinner, a somewhat naive collaborator—with acutely observed characterisation, a skilfully handled plot and an overall concern for moral values which is the hallmark of a major writer.

Unlike Massie, two of whose novels have been set in Scotland, William Boyd (b.1953) has not used a Scottish setting for his mature novels so far. He has, however, produced several compellingly readable novels, from *An Ice-Cream War* (1982) to *Brazzaville Beach* (1990), thereby, like the later books of Muriel Spark, enriching "British" rather than specifically Scottish literature, if such a distinction has to be insisted upon.

Alasdair Gray, like Edwin Morgan at present rather a cult figure, is also something of a maverick. His original discipline was art rather than literature. For three years he was a theatrical scene-painter, a fact which perhaps accounts for the somewhat Baroque-like, stagey constructional methods by which he often contrives his literary effects. His large-scale minor masterpiece *Lanark: A Life in Four Books* (1981) contains a realistic and often very funny study of a young man growing up in Glasgow, contrasted with a piece of science fiction depicting either another young man, or perhaps the same fellow, progressing through a dreadful city which we are meant to identify as a possible future Glasgow. The two are then counterpointed in a manner some find masterly, others boring. There is no denying the vigour, cleverness and wit of the writing, even if, despite the enthusiastic critical advocacy of Dr Gifford, the sections of the book do not really seem to add up to a completely credible entity. One trouble is that the reductive view of Glasgow as seen by Gray (and, more understandably, in the deprived fictional world of James Kelman), is no longer really a true one.

"What is Glasgow to most of us?," asks Gray. "A house, the place we work, a football park, a golf course, some pubs and connecting streets. That's all. No, I'm wrong, there's also the cinema and the library. And when our imagination needs exercise we use these to visit London, Paris, Rome under the Caesars, the American West at the turn of the century, anywhere but here and now. Imaginatively Glasgow exists as a music-hall song and a few bad novels. That's all we've given to the world outside. It's all we've given ourselves."

Gray seems not to have noticed that time has moved on. The long overdue abandonment of Glasgow's traditional belief that it and nineteenth-century heavy industry were synonymous, the attracting of many new light industries, and the rediscovery of its cleaned and well-restored major (by European standards) architectural heritage have led not only to the development of a significant tourist industry in Glasgow (where previously there was virtually none), but to a renaissance of the city's self-confidence, now widely recognised and acknowledged at home and abroad.

Janine (1982), a further sequential often amusing piece of subjective counterpointing, is ultimately even less convincing than its predecessor. *The Fall of Kevin Walker* (1985) tells the story of an ordinary man, a

Scotsman on the make, who is accidentally elevated to television "fame" as a tough interviewer. When he has outlived his usefulness to his creators by showing signs of becoming independent, he is then publicly destroyed before the cameras by his promotor, a denouement with a totally improbable ring. The near soft-porn *Something Leather* (1990), with its apparent contempt for women, (whose cause, oddly enough, Gray elsewhere champions) is, quite simply, embarrassingly awful. Several volumes of short stories, notably *Unlikely Stories, Mostly* (1983), show Gray's quirky, imaginative talent operating at its readable best. Like many prose writers, he has also turned his hand occasionally to verse, his *Old Negatives* (1989) indulging in a kind of neo-Blakean line of prophecy, illustrated by his own line drawings.

James Kelman, more distinctively and single-mindedly than the others, gives voice to the socially deprived. Unfortunately, what they have to say, for all his descriptive abilities and gifts as a dialogue-reporter, is not always very interesting. He established his reputation with his collection of stories and short—sometimes very short—cameos, *Not, not while the giro* (1983), (as one critic★ observed, somewhat in the style of Damon Runyon), and consolidated it with his novels *The Busconductor Hines* (1984), *A Chancer* (1985) and *A Disaffection* (1989). Another collection of stories and sketches, *Greyhound for Breakfast* followed in 1987 and *The Burn* in 1990, by which time the influence of Samuel Beckett seems to have replaced that of the American writer. *The Busconductor Hines*, in some ways perhaps Kelman's most memorable portrait, depicts a decent man who balances precariously between the crushing pressures of his life. *A Chancer* is the study of a compulsive gambler whose addiction gradually takes precedence over his duty to his family, his friends and his work.

Kelman's third and best novel, *A Disaffection* (1989), deals with the disillusion of a reluctant schoolmaster, Patrick Doyle, and his unsuccessful attempts to have sex with a married fellow-teacher, Alison Houston. The novel's main strength lies in its unadulterated and unvarnished replication of Glasgow dialogue, as used among the educationally disadvantaged, distinguished by its frequent use of different declensions of the verb "to fuck". (Incidentally, it has always seemed odd to me that the Anglo-Saxon word for one of life's more pleasurable physical activities should have been appropriated as a general purpose term of contemptuous emphasis or an angry expletive! Perhaps Mrs Mary Whitehouse, with whom I rarely find myself in agreement, was right when she suggested that the next stage after swearing is inevitably the extension to physical violence.) However authentic, read or heard constantly, it is dialogue of a sort that appears completely to

★ James Aitchieson.

accept its own purility.

But to return to *A Disaffection*. Patrick, after spending an evening discussing his predicament with his brother and sister-in-law, Nicola,—she being a woman of common sense, aware that commitment necessarily means accepting a routine—Patrick is persuaded that he has had too much to drink to drive home. So he sets out on foot, hoping to find a bus or taxi.

> Along at the corner of the street he approached was this national bank from whose topmost windows beamed a nightlight and this was the window Patrick's brick would smash. And as he progressed towards Cowcaddens he could be smashing in the windows of each and every bank he chanced upon. And also those of building societies and insurance offices—anything at all connected with the financial institutions of the Greatbritish rulers . . . There was a pair of polis across the street who needless to report were observing him openly and frankly and not giving a fuck about who was noticing. But now they watched him watching them . . . Why were there no bloody damn taxis. No bloody damn fucking taxis just when you fucking needed one quite desperately, when you just needed one, and there wasn't one, just like they said about the polis as well, when you wanted one you couldni get one, just like with a bus, when you wanted one of them you couldn't bloody get one, there weren't any because they just bla bla bla and he was fucking running, steadily, and not too fast, his right hand gripping the edges of his jacket where it buttoned, shoulders hunched and head bowed. A large and wide expanse of water, huge puddle, ahead, and he splashed straight through the bloody centre rather than attempting to either jump it or skirt roundabout it in case of skidding on something and falling. The polis watching him now in a serious and suspicious manner. About to give chase. Catch the bastard, there he goes.

The Kelman short story or cameo usually has no significant narrative. A character comes into a pub, meets, talks with others and leaves. Nothing much happens. As in the novels (and in real life at a certain level,) "fuckings" and "bloodies" abound, expressing otherwise inarticulate pressures. It is almost as if in itself merely to endure was seen as some sort of achievement—which, at a certain hopeless level, it probably is. Nevertheless, however skilfully and sensitively done, such grinding nihilism in literary terms becomes in the long run self-defeating and numbingly oppressive.

The youngest writer of fiction to attract wide attention is Janice Galloway (b.1956), a Kelman disciple with a slightly social up-market range of human interests. While her short stories *Blood* (1991) do chronicle cameos of failure and despair, they also celebrate a more positive attitude. Her stream-of-consciousness novel *The Trick is to Keep Breathing* (1989) is an account from the inside of the mind of a drama teacher in the process of cracking up.

I recently found myself, somewhat surprisingly, described as that *rara avis*, a twentieth-century Scottish poet "resolutely resistant to the throes of modernism" who "walks the fragmented streets with an eighteenth century sense of balance."★ "Modernism" is a term used by every generation to justify a change of fashion; tricksiness, often for its own visual sake—scattering words about a page or splitting up lines in the middle for example, or shaping words into patterns of flowers or other objects. It is a term, which, retrospectively, nearly always comes to seem slightly absurd. Art is not exclusively about the pursuit of superficial newness for its own isolated sake. It is very much about content, choice and balance. Without a sense of balance, indeed, you fall, either off or in—something which the next century and its writers will doubtless sort out for themselves. Meanwhile, one may wonder if the future of Scotland is to be some kind of a "falling off"? The celebration of "failed living," however perhaps necessary as a corrective to the middle-class assumptions of Bridie, Gunn, Blake and Linklater, must surely, sooner or later, give place to more positive concerns if twenty-first-century literature is not to succumb to the celebration of its own frustrations and the contemplation of the body-politics lack of a political navel.

<h1 style="text-align:center">III</h1>

Some of the post-Bridean drama referred to in the previous chapter was already beginning to reflect the radical social realism which also prevailed in the Scottish Theatre of the sixties, seventies and early eighties: a kind of up-market more highly pressurised version of the homely "kitchen-sink" dramas purveyed by Joe Corrie and others in the twenties.

Robert MacLellan died in 1985, leaving a heritage of finely crafted historical plays. Alexander Reid, who worked a similar if shallower vein, died in 1982. Successful also in creating spoken stage Scots was Robert Kemp (1908–1967), not so much with his original plays like *The Penny Wedding* (1957) or *The Perfect Gent* (1962) as in his adaptation of Molière's *Let Wives Tak Tent* (1946). He also wrote three pageant plays, of which *The Saxon Saint*, staged at Dunfermline Abbey in 1949, was probably the most effective. He was also responsible for the acting version of the highly successful revival of Sir David Lyndsay of the Mount's 16th-century morality play, *Ane Satire of the Thrie Estatis*—Scotland's one undoubted stage masterpiece.

Characteristic of the post-war urban mood was the single play of the journalist Robert McLeish (b.1912), *The Gorbals Story* (1946). In *Gold in his Boots* (1967) George Munro (the dates of whose earthly passage appear to be unrecorded by our libraries) dealt with the heady urban Scottish intermix of football, so-called glory and religious bigotry. "I

★ Roderick Watson in *A History of Scottish Literature*, Vol. 4, 1988.

hate and detest this religious bigotry," one of its characters protests. "People are so busy fighting for mansions in the sky they've lost contact with middens on earth." Munro's *Gay Landscape* (1958) traced the fortunes of three generations of a family whose memories of a Highland home were relentlessly eroded by the grimness of Glasgow. Eva Lamont Stewart (b.1912) wrote effectively of the real conditions of the poorly paid post-war nursing profession in *Starched Aprons* (1965), and of the family tensions created by the stresses of poverty in *Men Should Weep* (1947).

The work of the actor/playwright Roddie MacMillan, who died in 1979, like that of Bill Bryden, has already been mentioned. Bryden scored a further success after *Willie Rough* (1972) with *Benny Lynch* (1974) and, more recently, with *The Ship* (1990), thought by many to be the dramatic high-point of Glasgow's year as Cultural Capital of Europe.

Ronald Mavor (b.1925) followed in the footsteps of his father, James Bridie, with *The Keys of Paradise* (1959) and a study of the moral dilemma facing the great Scots radical hero of the eighteenth century, *Muir of Huntershill* (1962).

The two playwrights who perhaps diverted us most regularly and rewardingly during the sixties and seventies were Newcastle-born Stanley Eveling (b.1925), who has long since settled permanently in Scotland, but sadly, no longer writes for the stage, and C.P. Taylor (1929–1981). Eveling's *Come and be Killed* (1967) dealt with the moral dilemma of abortion and where responsibilities should now lie in a world no longer regulated by religious belief. *Dear Janet Rosenberg, Dear Mr. Kooning* (1963), described by one reviewer as an "evaluation of meaning", reduces a more or less recognisable world to an abstract dimension through the awed adoration of a young girl for a writer.

Glasgow-born C.P. Taylor wrote in all more than sixty plays. While *The Ballachulish Beast* (1966), among his most powerful, satirises the world of pop music, it is also a parable demonstrating how violence and corruption almost inevitably arise out of any political programme, however initially idealistic. His later plays of ideas include *Bread and Butter* (1966), demonstrating how vainly ideas struggle to emerge through the inescapably mundane conditions of the life of the poor, and *Walter* (1977), wherein a Jewish entertainer confuses his own experiences of an impoverished Glasgow childhood with the socialist aspirations of the radical politician and "folk-hero", John Maclean.

Tom Gallacher (b.1934) reflects an almost Ibsen-like preoccupation with present experiences that have become clouded by past events in both *Our Kindness to Five Persons* (1981) and *The Only Street* (1973).

Hector Macmillan, in *The Rising* (1973), justified dramatically the cause of the Lowland weaver "rebels" of the 1820s. In *The Sash* (1974), he examines the working-class religious hatred that exists between

Glasgow Catholics and Protestants in the context of the Northern Irish situation, suggesting a hope of escape from this Scots-derived bigotry (not, alas, so far justified by events) through the younger generation.

Stewart Conn, earlier referred to (and underestimated)★ has produced, in *The Aquarium* (1973), a powerful study of the once-dominant middle-class Glaswegian in decay and, among other fine thought-provoking plays, *Hecuba* (1981/82), *Hugh Miller* (1988) and *By the Pool* (1988), several of which have been staged outside Scotland.★

Others creatively active are Tom McGrath (b.1940), with *The Hard Man* (1977), written in collaboration with Jimmy Boyle (with whose former career as one of Scotland's most wanted violent criminals it deals), and the almost wordless *Animals* (1979): Donald Campbell (b.1940) particularly for *The Jesuit* (1976): John Byrne (b.1940) for *The Slab Boys* (1978) and *Still Life* (1982), and John McGrath (b.1935) whose *The Cheviot, the Stag and the Black, Black Oil* (1974) is a highly diverting misrepresentational satire with caricature upper-class puppets as the greedy villains of the piece and idealised peasants as the heroes. This is political radicalism at its most wittily dishonest, though perhaps now viewable in a new more relaxed light following the disintegration of most of the Communist states formerly based on enforced Marxist dream-principles.

Among the many younger Scottish playwrights writing for the stage, mention should be made of the witty Liz Lochhead, whose *Mary Queen of Scots Got Her Head Chopped Off* (1987) and *Patter Merchant* (1988) both show a fine ear for dialogue and a good sense of stagecraft. Her Glasgow monologues, published in *Bagpipe Muzak* (1991), though funnier when declaimed by her then in print, are nevertheless remarkable studies in female characterisation. The three odes included in the book show, incidentally, a marked deepening of her lyric talent.

The Scottish dramatist writing for today's "live" theatre has to come to terms with more insidious competition than the post-war dramatists faced. While his (or her) predecessors had the competition of a cinema where virtually none of the films were of Scottish origin, native competition now comes constantly from the dramas and "soap operas", required to feed the insatiable maw of Scottish-produced mass-audience television, a medium which requires a flow of undemanding, mostly ephemeral, new material. After one initial screening, a play written for television is unlikely to be reshown more than once or twice (if that) and even more unlikely to be revised for production at some later date. Television by its very nature, thus cannot primarily be the medium for serious dramatic statement. In these circumstances, what is likely to be

---

★ In which connection, the answer to my rhetorical question on page 000 is that both Vanhal and Pleyel are worth listening to in their own right, as well as for the light they throw on the wider-ranging genius of Haydn.

the course followed by a future Barrie, Bridie or MacLellan? Write at two different levels, perhaps: the level of easy convention for television and a more creative level for the stage?

Twenty years ago, Sir Compton Mackenzie prophesied that by the year two thousand, television would virtually have done away with the practice of reading. This does not look like happening. Indeed, more books are now published than ever before; libraries have never been more widely used. Possibly, therefore, this active increase in the reading habits of the public in Scotland also offers reasonable encouragement for the survival of live stage drama. Let us hope so. The prospect of a television service increasingly dominated by the competition of "market forces" is hardly an encouraging portent for anyone concerned with the survival of fundamental human values, in Scotland or anywhere else.

SOURCE NOTES

CHAPTER I:

1   *An Historical Survey of Scottish Literature to 1714*, London, 1933.
2   *Scottish Vernacular Literature: A History*, London, 1898.
3   Ibid.
4   *Studies in Scottish Literature*, Vol. IV, No. 3.
5   Translated from the Latin by Agnes Mure Mackenzie for her *Scottish Pageant*, Vol. 1: Edinburgh and London, 1948.
6   In *Hary's Wallace*, Scottish Text Society, 1968.
7   *Studies in Scottish Literature*, Vol. II, No. 1.
8   Edwin Muir: *Essays on Literature and Society*, revised edition, London, 1965.
9   Edited by David Laing (Edinburgh).
10 *Studies in Scottish Literature*, Vol. II, No. 3.
11 *An Historical Survey of Scottish Literature*.
12 In *The Scottish Tradition in Literature*, Edinburgh and London, 1958, Kurt Wittig would have us believe that internal rhyme, apparently regarded as an aid to the memorizing of orally transmitted verse, like the revival of alliteration, was as much the result of Gaelic influence as of Latin, French or English. It may have been so. We simply do not have one single piece of evidence to prove or disprove such a claim.
13 *How to Read*.
14 The full text is to be found in the Early English Text Society's volume *Ratis Raving*, Edinburgh, 1870.

CHAPTER II:

1   Laing: "The Poetical Works of Sir David Lyndsay" (1879).
2   Reproduced in full in *Sir David Lyndsay* by W. Murison (1938).
3   Charteris's whole preface is quoted in David Laing's edition of *The Works of Sir David Lyndsay* (1879).
4   Volume XV in the series *Musica Britannica*, edited by K. Elliot and H. M. Shire, 2nd edition, London, 1964. Between 1562 and 1590 Wode made a musical anthology of part-song, secular and sacred—"musick fyne" as it was called.
5   Introduction to *Ballattis of Luve* edited by John MacQueen, Edinburgh, 1970.
6   Ibid.
7   *Song, Dance and Poetry of the Court of Scotland under King James VI*, Cambridge, 1969.

8 D. J. Durkan: "Cultural background in sixteenth-century Scotland", *The Innes Review*, No. 2, 1959.
9 *See* Elliot and Shire: *Music of Scotland, 1500–1700.*
10 "The Form and Matter of 'The Cherrie and the Slae' ", *University of Texas, Studies in English*, XXXVIII, 1958.
11 1974.
12 *Music of Scotland 1500–1700,* recorded on the disc "Musick Fyne", Volume 2 of the Saltire Society's *A History of Scottish Music* (1974).
13 *A Book of Scottish Verse*: World Classics Series. O.U.P. edited by R. L. Mackie; revised edition, 1968, edited M. Lindsay.
14 Like Stewart of Baldynneis's lines, to be found in the Oxford University Press World Classics series anthology *A Book of Scottish Verse.*
15 *Calvin and Art* (1938).
16 *The Scottish Tradition in Literature.*
17 Reviewing Peter Arnot's *The Byzantines and Their World: The Sunday Times,* 6th June 1973.
18 An extract from *Chamaeleon*, together with a sample of *The Pretended Conference*—which is, however, sometimes attributed to Thomas Maitland, the third member of the Lethington family—and which sets out the "overhearing" of an imaginary meeting at which the Regent Moray, Lord Lindsay, John Knox and two others plan the overthrow of the young James, are to be found in R. D. S. Jack's anthology *Scottish Prose: 1550–1700* (1971).
19 Pitscottie's *History*. S.T.S. (1899–1911).
20 The most recent edition of Melville's *Memorials* is that of the Folio Society (1973).

CHAPTER III:

1 *Music of Scotland 1500–1700,* No. 71.
2 A variant of this text is in *The Green Garden*, ed. Fergusson, Edinburgh and London, 1946.
3 *The Ballad and the Folk*, London, 1972.
4 London, 1973.
5 *Last Leaves of Traditional Ballads and Ballad Airs*, Aberdeen, 1925, and the Greig MSS.
6 *Selected Prose, 1500–1700,* edited by R. D. S. Jack, 1971, where several of Rutherford's letters are reproduced.

CHAPTER IV:

1 *The Works of Allan Ramsay*, Vol. IV, S.T.S., Edinburgh and London, 1970.
2 Original unpunctuated text to be found in S.T.S. edition, Vol. IV.
3 Appendix J, *Robert Fergusson 1750–74*, edited by S. G. Smith, Edinburgh, 1954.
4 "Fergusson and Ruddiman's Magazine" in Appendix J, *Robert Fergusson 1750–74*, edited by S. G. Smith, Edinburgh, 1954.
5 A fuller account of the books Burns studied is to be found in my *Burns: The*

Man: His Work: The Legend, 2nd revised edition, London, 1971, pages 33–36.

6   *Letters of Robert Burns,* edited by J. de Lancey Ferguson, Oxford, 1931.

7   *Burns: A Study of the Poems and Songs,* Edinburgh and London, 1960.

8   *My Life:* Oscar Kokoschka, London, 1974.

9   *Scott and Scotland,* London, 1936.

10 "Tam o' Shanter" in *Robert Burns: New Judgments,* edited by William Montgomerie, Glasgow, 1947.

11 *Scottish Poetry: A Critical Survey,* edited by James Kinsley, London, 1953.

12 *James Thomson: Poet of "The Seasons",* London, 1951.

13 Charles Burke: *Life, Writings and Genius of Akenside,* London, 1832.

14 *Transactions of the Gaelic Society of Inverness,* Vols xi and xii: Inverness and Edinburgh, 1886.

15 "Die Ossianische Heldenlieder", trans. J. L. Robertson, in *Transactions of the Gaelic Society of Inverness,* Vol. xxii, 1897–1898.

16 *Before Jane Austen,* London, 1965.

17 *Life of Smollett,* London, 1898.

18 *The Journals of Arnold Bennett,* Vol. 1, London, 1932.

19 Introduction to *Mordaunt,* edited by W. L. Renwick, London, 1965.

20 *Miscellaneous Prose Works,* Vol. iv.

CHAPTER V:

1   *Letters of Sir Walter Scott,* edited by Sir H. C. Grierson, London, 1937.

2   *Studies in Scottish Literature:* "Sir Walter Scott and Ballad Forgery", Vol. VIII, No. 1, 1970.

3   M. R. Dobie, *The Development of Scott's Minstrelsy,* London, 1940.

4   *Scott,* Edinburgh and London, 1965.

5   *Letters from and to C. K. Sharpe,* edited by Alexander Allardyce, Edinburgh and London, 1888.

6   *The Ballads,* London, 1950.

7   *Scott,* Edinburgh and London, 1965.

8   *Life of Scott,* Vol. II.

9   *James Hogg: A Critical Study,* Edinburgh and London, 1962.

10 "The History of the Reformation", *Transactions of the Gaelic Society of Inverness,* Vol. ii, Inverness and Edinburgh, 1885.

11 *Robert Burns and other Essays and Sketches,* London and Glasgow, 1926.

12 *The Poems of John Davidson,* Edinburgh and London, but which does not include the verse plays.

13 *John Davidson: A Selection of His Poems:* Preface by T. S. Eliot Edited by Maurice Lindsay with an Introduction by Hugh MacDiarmid, London, 1961.

14 *Selected Poems:* edited by Maurice Lindsay with a Personal Memoir by Helen B. Cruickshank, Edinburgh, 1950.

15 "Scott's Historical Fiction and Relative Truth", *Scottish Literary News,* Vol. 3, No. 2.

16 *Studies in Scottish Literature,* Vol. IV, Nos. 2, 3 and 4.

17 *Prose Works*, **XIX**, p. 55.
18 *Prose Works*, **XVIII**, review of John Galt's *The Omen*.
19 *Chronicles of the Canongate*, p. 143.
20 Lockhart's *Life of Scott*, Vol. III, p. 126.
21 *Sir Walter Scott*, London, 1932.
22 Stephen Gwynn, *Life of Sir Walter Scott*, London, 1930.
23 *A Critical History of English Literature*, London, 1960.
24 *Studies in Scottish Literature*, Vol. IV, Nos. 2, 3 and 4.
25 *Essays in Literary Criticism*, London,
26 *A Critical History of English Literature*, London, 1960.
27 Introduction to *Miss Marjoribanks*; London, 1969.
28 *Autobiography and Letters of Mrs Margaret Oliphant*, Leicester, 1974.
29 *Henry James and Robert Louis Stevenson*, edited by Janet Adam Smith, London, 1948.
30 *The Genesis of The Master of Ballantrae*, in the Edinburgh edition and in *The Art of Writing*, London, 1905.
31 *John Davidson: Poet of Armageddon*, New York, 1961.
32 Everyman's Library, London.
33 Brother of the more famous Charles, quoted in *Carlyle on Cromwell and others*, by D. A. Wilson, London, 1925.
34 *Miscellanies*.
35 *The Open Society and its Enemies*, London, 1962.
36 *The Rise and Fall of the Man of Letters*, John Gross, London, 1969.

CHAPTER VI:
1   Article "Poets at Loggerheads", in *Scotland's Magazine*, Vol. 50, No. 8, 1954.
2   *Hugh MacDiarmid and the Scottish Renaissance*; Duncan Glen, Edinburgh and London, 1964.
3   *MacDiarmid: A Festschrift*, Edinburgh, 1962.
4   *Hugh MacDiarmid (C. M. Grieve)*, Edinburgh and London, 1964.
5   Preface to 2nd edition, *A Drunk Man Looks at the Thistle*.
6   *Hugh MacDiarmid (C. M. Grieve)*, Edinburgh and London, 1964.
7   *MacDiarmid: A Festschrift*, Edinburgh, 1962.
8   *The Hugh MacDiarmid Anthology*, edited by Alexander Scott and Michael Grieve, London, 1972.
9   *Still Life*; Alexander Scott, Edinburgh and London, 1958.
10 Many of them to be found in the misleadingly titled *Collected Poems*, edited by MacDiarmid (1948), which omitted many of the poet's best pieces and retarded the spread of his reputation; a matter which W. R. Aitken's *Poems in Scots and English* (1961) helped to put right.
11 *Diaries of a Dying Man*, edited by Alexander Scott, Edinburgh and London, 1954.
12 *The Scottish Tradition in Literature*, Edinburgh, 1958.
13 In *Encounter*, June 1952.
14 Preface to *New Lines* (1956), in which, incidentally, the attack on Lallans

shows complete misunderstanding of a living Scots tradition. I pass no comment upon Mr Conquest's strange notions of the ingredients that make up music.

15 1 to 3: Glasgow, 4: Edinburgh.

16 1946, London, revised 2nd edition, 1966; revised 3rd edition, Manchester, 1976.

17 London, 1972.

18 The Cygnet Press, Burford, Oxford.

19 London.

20 "Two Modern Makars", *The Glasgow Review*, Vol. IV, No. 4, February 1974.

21 The best work of these and other new writers of the 1960s and the first half of the '70s may be found in *Scottish Poetry I–VI* (edited annually by George Bruce, Edwin Morgan and the present writer, who also with Alexander Scott and Roderick Watson, edited *Scottish Poetry VII and VIII*.).

22 Alexander Scott, "Clifford Hanley", *Contemporary Novelists of the English Language*, Chicago and London, 1970. He also writes on Mitchison, Jenkins, Mackay Brown and Gunn.

23 *Leslie Mitchell: Lewis Grassic Gibbon*, Ian S. Munro, Edinburgh and London, 1966.

24 Ibid.

25 Ibid.

26 By E. H. Visiak in the London 1946 re-issue of *Arcturus*.

27 See *Neil M. Gunn: The Man and the Writer*, edited by Alexander Scott and Douglas Gifford, Edinburgh, 1973.

28 Ibid.

29 His first two novels are *Remedy is None* (1967) and *A Gift from Nessus* (1969).

30 *Saltire Review*, 1955.

31 "Robin Jenkins", *Contemporary Novelists of the English Language*, Chicago and London, 1970.

32 *Essays*; Cheadle, 1974.

33 *Brother Scots*, London, 1927.

Selective Bibliography

The works included in this Bibliography represent some of the books referred to in the writing of this *History*. The works of the authors mentioned in the text are in general not listed here. The editions used for most of the material discussed in the earlier chapters are those of the Scottish Text Society or the Early English Text Society, although where neither sense nor sound were affected, the spelling of quotations has been modernized in the interests of easier intelligibility. *Rauf Coilyear, Cockelbie's Sow* and *The Pystil of Swete Susane*, discussed in Chapter One, are to be found in *Ancient Popular and Romance Poetry of Scotland*, edited by D. Laing (1875). The Maitland, Bannatyne, Asloan and Makulloch Manuscripts are all published by the Scottish Text Society. For Ramsay and Fergusson, I have also basically used the Scottish Text Society edition, and for Burns, Professor James Kinsley's three volume definitive edition (Oxford, 1968), though again, modifying occasionally misleading antique orthography.

I have not thought it necessary to draw attention to the relevant material to be found in the *Dictionary of National Biography* and the *Encyclopaedia Britannica*, or to stress the importance of the *Dictionary of the Older Scottish Tongue*, still in progress, or the completed *Scottish National Dictionary*. For the reader anxious to acquire his own Scots dictionary, *Chamber's Scots Dialect Dictionary* is easily available.

For the convenience of readers who may wish to sample rather than read works in their entirety, a number of anthologies are included. At the time of writing, a series of studies and anthologies which should usefully fill gaps has been announced for publication by Carcanet Press, Manchester. These are:

Aitken, A. J. and Murison, D.: *The Scottish Language*
Buthlay, K. (ed.): *Scottish Verse from the Reformation to 1707*
Campbell, I. (ed.): *Nineteenth-Century Scottish Fiction: A Critical Anthology*
Crawford, T. (ed.): *The Eighteenth-Century Scottish Lyric*
Morgan, E. (ed.): *Scottish Satirical Verse: An Anthology*
Scott, A.: *Modern Scottish Literature: A Critical History*

GENERAL

Chambers, R.: *A Biographical Dictionary of Eminent Scotsmen* Glasgow and London, 1835
Craig, D.: *Scottish Literature and the Scottish People* London, 1961
Daiches, David: *A Critical History of English Literature* London, 1960
———: *The Paradox of Scottish Culture: The Eighteenth-Century Experience* Oxford, 1964

Davie, G.: *The Democratic Intellect* Edinburgh and London, 1951

Dibdin, J. C.: *The Annals of the Edinburgh Stage* Edinburgh, 1888

Dickinson, W. C.: *Scotland from the Earliest Times to 1603* Edinburgh, 1961

Elliott, K. and Shire, H. M.: *Music of Scotland 1500–1700* (Vol. XV of *Musica Britannica*) London 1957

Fox, D.: "The Scottish Chaucerians" in *Chaucer and Chaucerians* Alabama, 1966

Geddie, W. (ed.): *A Bibliography of Middle Scots Poets* S.T.S. 1912

Glen, D. (ed.): *A Bibliography of Scottish Poetry from Stevenson to 1974* Preston, 1974

Greirson, H. J. C. (ed.): *Edinburgh Essays on Scots Literature* Edinburgh and London, 1933

Gross, J.: *The Rise and Fall of the Man of Letters* London, 1969

Henderson, T. F.: *Scottish Vernacular Literature: A History* Edinburgh, 1898

Irving, D.: *Lives of the Scottish Poets* Edinburgh, 1804

Jack, R. D. S.: *The Italian Influence on Scottish Literature* Edinburgh, 1970

Kinsley, J. (ed.): *Scottish Poetry: A Critical Survey* London, 1955

Lawson, Robb: *The Story of the Scots Stage* Paisley, 1917

MacKenzie, A. M.: *An Historical Survey of Scottish Literature to 1714* London, 1933

Maclaine, A.: "The *Christis Kirk* Tradition: Its Evolution in Scots Poetry to Burns" S.I.S.L. Vol. II, 1/2

Millar, J. H. (ed.): *A Literary History of Scotland* London, 1903

Muir, E.: *Scott and Scotland* London, 1936

Neilson, W. A.: "The Origins and Sources of the Court of Love" *Harvard Studies* VI, 1969

Ramsay, M. P.: *Calvin and Art* Edinburgh, 1938

Ramsay, J., of Ochtertyre: *Scotland and Scotsmen in the Eighteenth Century* Edinburgh and London, 1888

Ross, J. M.: *Scottish History and Literature to the Period of the Reformation* Glasgow, 1884

Saintsbury, G.: *Essays in English Literature* London, 1890

——: *History of Criticism and Literary Taste in Europe* Edinburgh and London, 1900–04

Shire, H. M.: *Song, Dance and Poetry at the Court of Scotland under King James VI* Cambridge, 1969

Sibbald, J.: *Chronicle of Scottish Poetry from the thirteenth century to the Union of the Crowns* Edinburgh, 1802

Smith, G. G.: *Scottish Literature: Character and Influence* London, 1919

Smith, J. M.: *The French Background of Middle Scots Literature* Edinburgh, 1934

Society of Ancient Scots: *The Lives of Eminent Scotsmen* London, 1821–2

Speirs, J.: *The Scots Literary Tradition* rev. ed. London, 1962

Veitch, J.: *The Feeling for Nature in Scottish Poetry* Edinburgh and London, 1887

Walker, H.: *Three Centuries of Scottish Literature* Glasgow, 1893

Watt, L. MacL.: *Scottish Life and Poetry* London, 1912

Wilson, Sir J.: *The Dialects of Central Scotland* London, 1926

Wittig, K.: *The Scottish Tradition in Literature* Edinburgh, 1958

Young, D.: *Plastic Scots and the Scots Literary Tradition* Glasgow, 1946

ANTHOLOGIES

GENERAL

Dixon, W. Macneile: *The Edinburgh Book of Scottish Verse* Edinburgh, 1910

Douglas, Sir George: *The Book of Scottish Poetry* London and Leipzig, 1911

Eyre-Todd, G.: *Abbotsford Series of Scottish Poets* Edinburgh, 1896

Fergusson, J.: *The Green Garden* Edinburgh and London, 1946

Fyfe, J. G.: (Introduction by R. S. Rait) *Scottish Diaries and Memoirs 1550–1746* Stirling, 1927

Fyfe, J. G.: (Introduction by J. D. Mackie) *Scottish Diaries and Memoirs 1746–1843* Stirling, 1942

Lindsay, M.: *Scotland: An Anthology* London, 1974; New York, 1975

MacDiarmid, H.: *Golden Treasury of Scottish Poetry* London, 1941

Mackenzie, A. M.: *A Garland of Scottish Prose* Glasgow, London and Toronto, 1956

Mackie, R. L., revised Lindsay, M.: *A Book of Scottish Verse* rev. ed. Oxford, 1967

MacQueen, J. and Scott, T.: *The Oxford Book of Scottish Verse* Oxford, 1956

Oliver, J. W. and Smith, J. C.: *A Scots Anthology* Edinburgh and London, 1949

FIFTEENTH TO EARLY SEVENTEENTH CENTURY

Gray, M. M.: *Scottish Poetry from Barbour to James VI* London, 1935

FIFTEENTH AND SIXTEENTH CENTURIES

Smith, G. G.: *Specimens of Middle Scots* Edinburgh and London, 1902

SIXTEENTH CENTURY

MacQueen, J. (ed.): *Ballattis of Luve* Edinburgh, 1970

Scott, T.: *Late Medieval Scots Poetry: A Selection from the Makars and their Heirs down to 1610* London, 1967

SEVENTEENTH CENTURY

Jack, R. D. S.: *Scottish Prose 1550–1700* London, 1971

Child, F. J.: *The English and Scottish Popular Ballads* Boston and New York, 1883–98

NINETEENTH AND TWENTIETH CENTURIES

Gifford, T. D.: *Scottish Short Stories 1800–1918* London, 1970

Young, D.: *Scottish Verse 1851–1951* London, Paris, Melbourne, Toronto, 1959

TWENTIETH CENTURY

Lindsay, M.: *Modern Scottish Poetry: An Anthology of the Scottish Renaissance* London, 1946, rev. 1966, Manchester, Rev. 1976

MacCaig, N. and Scott, A.: *Contemporary Scottish Verse 1959–69* London, 1970

CHAPTER I: *The Fifteenth Century and Before*

ANON
Beattie, W. (ed.): *The Taill of Rauf Coilyear printed by Robert Lekpreuik at St Andrews in 1572: A facsimile of the only known copy* Edinburgh, 1966
MacKenzie, A. M. (tr.): "Declaration of Arbroath" *Scottish Pageant*, Edinburgh, 1946
Scheps, W.: "The Thematic Unity of *Lancelot of the Laik*" *Studies in Scottish Literature*, Vol. V., 3
Templeton, J. M.: "Seventeenth-century Versions of *Christis Kirk on the Grene and The Wyf of Awchtermwchty*" S.I.S.L. Vol. IV, 3–4

BARBOUR, JOHN
Kinghorn, A. M.: "Scottish Historiography in the Sixteenth Century: A New Introduction to Barbour's *Bruce*" S.I.S.L. Vol. VI, 3

DOUGLAS, GAVIN
Coldwell, D. F. C.,: *Selections from Gavin Douglas* Oxford, 1964
Smith, S. G. (ed.): *Gavin Douglas: a Selection from his Poetry* Edinburgh, 1959
Watt, L. MacL.: *Douglas's Aeneid* Cambridge, 1920

DUNBAR, WILLIAM
Anon (Society of Ancient Scots): *Lives of the Scottish Poets* London, 1822
Baxter, J. W.: *William Dunbar: A Biographical Study* Edinburgh and London, 1952
Hyde, I.: "Primary Sources and Associations of Dunbar's Aureate Imagery" *Modern Language Review*, LI
——: "Poetic Imagery, a Point of Comparison Between Henryson and Dunbar" S.I.S.L. Vol. II, 1
Jack, R. D. S.: "Dunbar and Lydgate" S.I.S.L. Vol. VIII, 4
Kinsley, J. (ed.): Introduction to *William Dunbar: Selected Poems* Oxford, 1958
MacKenzie, W. M.: Introduction to *The Poems of William Dunbar* Edinburgh, 1932
Morgan, E.: "Dunbar and the Language of Poetry", *Essays* Cheadle Hulme, 1974
Schipper, J.: *William Dunbar: Sein Leben* Berlin, 1884
Scott, T.: *Dunbar: A Critical Exposition of the Poems* Edinburgh and London, 1966
Taylor, R. A.: *Dunbar the Poet and his Period* London, 1931

HARRY, BLIND
Harward, V.: "Hary's *Wallace* and Chaucer's *Troilus and Criseyde*" S.I.L.S. Vol. X, 1
Schepps, W.: "Middle English Poetic Usage and Blind Harry's *Wallace*" Chaucer Review, 4

HENRYSON, R.
Dolores, L. N.: "*The Testament of Cresseid*: Are Christian Interpretations Valid?" S.I.S.L. Vol. IX, 1
Elliott, C. (ed.): *Poems* Oxford, 1963
Fox, D. (ed.): *The Testament of Cresseid* London, 1968
Jamieson, I. W. A.: "The Minor Poems of Robert Henryson" S.I.S.L. Vol. IX, 2–3

Kinghorn, A. M.: "The Minor Poems of Robert Henryson" S.I.S.L. Vol. III, 1

Macdonald, D.: "Narrative Art in Henryson's *Fables*" S.I.S.L. Vol. III, 2

MacQueen, J.: *Robert Henryson: A Study of the Major Narrative Poems* Oxford, 1967

Muir, E.: *Essays on Literature and Society* London, rev. ed. 1965

Toliver, H. E.: "Robert Henryson: from Moralitas to Irony" Englische Studien, 46, 1965

Wood, H. H. (ed.): *The Poems and Fables of Robert Henryson* Edinburgh, 1933

HOLLAND, RICHARD

McDiarmid, M. P.: "Richard Holland's *Buke of the Howlat*: an Interpretation" Medium Aevum XXXVIII, 3

Stewart, M. M.: "Holland of the *Howlat*" Innes Review 23, 1

JAMES I, KING

Bain, C. E.: "A Valentine for Queen Joane" E.U.Q. 17, 1961

Brown, I.: "The Mental Traveller—A Study of the *King's Quair*" S.I.L.S. Vol. V, 4

McDiarmid, M. P. (ed.): *The Kingis Quair of James Stewart* London, 1973

Schepps, W.: "Chaucerian Synthesis: the Art of *The Kingis Quhair*" S.I.S.L. Vol. VIII, 3

Von Hendy, A.: "The Free Thrall: a Study of *The Kingis Quair*" S.I.S.L. II

CHAPTER II: *The Sixteenth Century*

FOWLER, WILLIAM

Jack, R. D. S.: "William Fowler and Italian Literature" M.L.R. 65, 3

HUME, ALEXANDER

Fergusson, R. M.: *Alexander Hume: An Early Poet-Pastor of Logie, and his Intimates* Paisley and London, 1899

Lindsay, D. W.: "'Of the Day Estivall': A Textual Note" S.I.S.L. Vol. IV, 2

Scott, T.: "A Note on Alexander Hume" S.I.S.L. Vol. II, 2–3

KNOX, JOHN

Dickinson, W. C. (ed.): *History of the Reformation* London, 1949

Lang, A.: *John Knox and the Reformation* London, 1905

Muir, E.: *John Knox* London, 1930

Ridley, J.: *John Knox* Oxford, 1968

LYNDSAY, SIR D.

Aschenberg, H.: *Sir David Lyndsay's Leben und Werke* München Gladbach, 1891

Kantrowitz, J. S.: "Encore: Lindsay's *Thrie Estatis*, Date and New Evidence" S.I.S.L. Vol. X, 1

MacQueen, J.: "Ane Satyre of the Thrie Estatis" S.I.S.L. Vol. III, 3

Murison, W.: *Sir David Lyndsay* Cambridge, 1938

MONTGOMERIE, ALEXANDER

Jack, R. D. S.: "The Lyrics of Alexander Montgomerie" R.E.S. Vol. XX, 78

Jack, R. D. S.: "Montgomerie and the Pirates" S.I.S.L. Vol. V, 2

Shire, H. M.: "The Oppositione of the Court to Conscience. 'Court and Conscience walis not weill'" S.I.S.L. Vol. III, 3

MURE, SIR WILLIAM

Jack, R. D. S.: "Scottish Sonneter and Welsh Metaphysical: A Study of the Religious Poetry of Sir William Mure and Henry Vaughan" S.I.S.L. Vol. III, 4

SCOTT, ALEXANDER

Durkan, D. J.: "Cultural Background in Sixteenth-century Scotland" *The Innes Review*, 2, 1959

MacQueen, J.: "Alexander Scott and Scottish Court Poetry of the Middle Sixteenth Century" P.B.A. Vol. 54

STEWART, JOHN, OF BALDYNNEIS

Nelson, T. G. A.: "John Stewart of Baldynneis and *Orlando Furioso*" S.I.S.L. Vol. VI, 2

CHAPTER III: *The Seventeenth Century*

ALEXANDER, SIR W.

Insh, G. P.: *Scottish Colonial Schemes, 1620–1686* Glasgow, 1922

McGrail, T. H.: *Sir William Alexander: A Biographical Study* Edinburgh and London, 1940

Rogers, C.: *Memorials of the Earl of Stirling and the House of Alexander* Edinburgh, 1877

Smith, G. G. (ed.): *Elizabethan Critical Essays* Oxford, 1904

BALLAD

Buchan, D.: *A Scottish Ballad Book* London, 1973

Buchan, D.: *The Ballad and the Folk* London, 1972

Entwhistle, W.: *European Balladry* rev. ed. Oxford, 1951

Hodgart, M. J. C.: *The Ballads* London, 1950

Mackenzie, M. L.: "The Great Ballad Collectors: Percy, Herd and Ritson" S.I.S.L. Vol. II, 4

Montgomerie, W.: "A Bibliography of the Scottish Ballad Manuscripts, 1730–1825" S.I.S.L. Vols. VI–VII

DRUMMOND, WILLIAM, OF HAWTHORNDEN

Jack, R. D. S.: "Drummond of Hawthornden: the Major Scottish Sources". S.I.S.L. Vol. VI, 1

MacDonald, R. H.: "Amendments to L. E. Kastner's Edition (S.T.S.) of Drummond's Poems". S.I.L.S. Vol. VII, 1–2

Masson, D.: *Drummond of Hawthornden*, London, 1873

URQUHART, SIR THOMAS

Kidde, Constance: "Sir Thomas Urquhart and 'The Admirable Crichton'". S.I.S.L. Vol. IX, 2–3

CHAPTER IV: *The Eighteenth Century*

BEATTIE, JAMES

Forbes, M.: *Beattie and His Friends* London, 1904

King, E. H.: "James Beattie's *The Minstrel*: Its Influence on Wordsworth" S.I.S.L. Vol. VIII, 1

BLAIR, HUGH

Schmitz, R. M.: *Hugh Blair* New York, 1948

BLAIR, ROBERT

Means, J. A.: "The Composition of *The Grave*" S.I.S.L. Vol. X, 1

BOSWELL, JAMES
    Dowling, W. C.: "The Boswellian Hero" S.I.S.L. Vol. X, 2
    Pottle, F. A.: *James Boswell: The Earlier Years* New York, 1966
BRUCE, MICHAEL
    Snoddy, T. G.: *Michael Bruce: Shepherd-Poet of the Lomond Braes* Edinburgh
    and London, undated
BURNS, ROBERT
    Angellier, A.: *Robert Burns: La Vie, Les Oeuvres* Paris, 1893
    Barke, J. and Smith, S. G.: *The Merry Muses of Caledonia* Edinburgh, 1959
    Daiches, D.: *Robert Burns* rev. ed. London, 1966
    Crawford, T.: *Burns, A Study* Edinburgh and London, 1960
    Egerer, J. W.: *A Bibliography of Robert Burns* Southern Illinois, 1965
    Farmer, H. G. (ed.): *The Songs of Robert Burns* and *Notes on Scottish Songs by
    Robert Burns* (by J. C. Dick), with *Annotations of Scottish Songs by Robert
    Burns* (by Davidson Cook) Folklo:e Associates, Hatoboro, Pennsylvania,
    1962
    Ferguson, De L.: *Letters* Oxford, 1931
    Fitzhugh, R. T.: *Robert Burns, His Associates And Contemporaries. . . . With The
    Journal of the Border Tour* Ed. by J. De Lancey Ferguson, North Carolina,
    1943
    Harder, H.: *Allan Ramsay, Robert Fergusson, Robert Burns in ihrer Stellung zu
    Gemeinschaft und Gesellschaft* Freiburg, 1922
    Hecht, H. (translated Jane Lymburn): *Robert Burns* London, 1936
    Johnson, J.: *The Scots Musical Museum* Folklore Associates, Hatoboro,
    Pennsylvania, 1962
    Kingsley, J.: *The Poems and Songs of Robert Burns* (definitive text and commen-
    tary) Oxford, 1968
    Legman, G.: *The Merry Muses of Caledonia and in part written by Robert Burns*
    New York, 1965
    Lindsay, M.: *The Burns Encyclopedia* rev. ed. London, 1970
    Lindsay, M.: *Burns: The Man, his Work, the Legend* rev. ed. London, 1971
    Lockart, J. G.: *The Life of Robert Burns* enlarged ed. London, 1892
    Low, D. A. (ed.): *Robert Burns: The Critical Heritage* London, 1974
    Meyerfeld, M.: *Robert Burns, Studien zu seiner dichterischen Entwickelung* Berlin,
    1899
    Montgomerie, W. (ed.): *New Judgements: Essays* Glasgow, 1947
    Thornton, R. D.: *James Currie: The Entire Stranger and Robert Burns* Edinburgh
    and London, 1963
    Snyder F. B.: *The Life of Robert Burns* New York, 1932
FERGUSSON, ROBERT
    Fairley, J. A.: *Bibliography of Robert Fergusson* Glasgow, 1915
    Gray, J.: *The Poems of Robert Fergusson. With A Life Of The Author and Remarks
    On His Genius And Writings* Edinburgh, 1821
    Grossart, A. B.: *Robert Fergusson: Famous Scots Series* Edinburgh, 1898
    Irving, D.: *The Poetical Works of Robert Fergusson, With the Life of the Author*
    Glasgow, 1800
    MacLaine, A. H.: "Robert Fergusson's *Auld Reekie* and the Poetry of City
    Life" S.I.S.L. Vol. I, 2
    MacLaine, A. H.: *Robert Fergusson* New York, 1965

McDiarmid, M. P.: *The Poems of Robert Fergusson* S.T.S. Edinburgh and London, 1950–56

Peterkin, A.: *The Works of Robert Fergusson: To Which Is Prefixed, A Sketch of The Author's Life* London, 1807

Smith, S. G. (ed.): *Robert Fergusson 1750–1774* Edinburgh, 1952

Sommers, T.: *The Life of Robert Fergusson, the Scottish Poet* Edinburgh, 1803

HUME, DAVID

Cavendish, A. P.: *David Hume* New York, 1958

Mossner, E. C.: *Life of David Hume* Oxford, 1954

Pears, D. F. (ed.): *David Hume: A Symposium* London, 1963

MACPHERSON, JAMES

Dunn, J. J.: "Coleridge's Debt to Macpherson's Ossian" S.I.S.L. Vol. VII, 1–2

Thomson, D.: *The Gaelic Sources of Macpherson's Ossian* Aberdeen, 1952

MACKENZIE, HENRY

Jenkins, R. E.: "The Art of the Theorist: Rhetorical Structure in *The Man of Feeling*" S.I.S.L. Vol. IX, 1

MOORE, J.

Renwick, W. L.: Introduction to *Mordaunt* London, 1965

RAMSAY, ALLAN

Martin, B.: *Allan Ramsay: A Study of his Life and Works* Cambridge, Mass., 1931

Oliver, J. W., Martin, B., Kinghorn, A. M., and Law, A. (eds.): *The Works of Allan Ramsay* S.T.S. Edinburgh and London, 1974

ROSS, ALEXANDER

Wattie, M. (ed.): *The Scottish Works of Alexander Ross* S.T.S. Edinburgh and London, 1935

SMOLLETT, TOBIAS

Boucé, R. G.: *Les Romans de Smollett, Etude critique* Paris, 1971

Giddings, R.: *The Tradition of Smollett* London, 1967

Goldberg, M. A.: *Smollett and the Scottish School* Albuquerque, New Mexico, 1959

Hannay, D.: *Life of Smollett* London, 1898

Kahrl, G. M.: *Tobias Smollett: Traveler-Novelist* Chicago, 1945

Klukoff, P. J.: "Smollett and the *Critical Review*: Criticism of the Novel, 1756–1763" S.I.S.L. Vol. IV, 2

Knapp, L. M. (ed.): *The Letters* Oxford, 1970

Rice, S.: "The Satiric Persons of Smollett's *Travels*" S.I.S.L. Vol. X, 1

Steers, R. H.: *Before Jane Austen* London, 1965

THOMSON, JAMES

Cohen, K.: *The Unfolding of "The Seasons"* Baltimore, 1969

Grant, D.: *James Thomson. The Poet of the Seasons* London, 1951

CHAPTER V: *The Nineteenth Century*

BAILLIE, JOANNA

Carhart, M. S.: *The Life and Work of Joanna Baillie* Newhaven, 1923

BLACKWOOD, WILLIAM

Oliphant, M.: *William Blackwood and His Sons* Edinburgh, 1897

CAMPBELL, THOMAS

Macauley, P. S.: "Thomas Campbell: A Revaluation" E.S. Vol. L, 1

CARLYLE, THOMAS

Campbell, I. (ed.): *Reminiscences* London, 1972

Campbell, I.: *Thomas Carlyle* London, 1974

Collis, J. S.: *The Carlyles* London, 1971

De Laury, D. J. (ed.): *Victorian Prose, A Guide to Research* London, 1973

Harrold, C. F.: "The Nature of Carlyle's Calvinism" *Studies in Philology* 33, 3, 1936

Holme, T.: *The Carlyles at Home* London, 1965

Lindberg, J.: "The Decadence of Style: Symbolic Structure in Carlyle's Later Prose." S.I.S.L. Vol. I, 3

Masson, D.: *Edinburgh Sketches and Memories* Edinburgh, 1892

Popper, Sir K.: *The Open Society and its Enemies* London, 1962

Sandes, C. K. (ed.): *The Collected Letters of Thomas and Jane Welsh Carlyle* Duke-Edinburgh Edition, 1970

Siegel, J. P. (ed.): *Carlyle: The Critical Heritage* London, 1971

Tennyson, G. B.: *Sartor called Resartus* London, 1965

Wilson, D. A.: *Life of Carlyle* London, 1923–29

FERRIER, SUSAN

Bushnell, N. S.: "Susan Ferrier's *Marriage* as Novel of Manners" S.I.S.L. Vol. V, 4

Doyle, J. A.: *Memoir and Correspondence of Susan Ferrier* London, 1898

Parker, W. M.: *Susan Ferrier and John Galt* London, 1965

Saintsbury, G.: *Collected Essays and Papers* London, 1923

GALT, JOHN

Aberdein, J.: *John Galt* London, 1936

Costain, K. M.: "The Prince and the Provost" S.I.S.L. Vol. VI, 1

Gordon, I. A.: *John Galt: The Life of a Writer* London, 1972

Gordon, R. K.: *John Galt* Toronto, 1920

Hall, L. B.: "Peripety in John Galt's *The Entail*" S.I.S.L. Vol. V, 3

Klinck, C. F.: "John Galt's Canadian Novels" Ontario History, 1957

Lumsden, H.: "The Bibliography of John Galt" Records of Glasgow Bibliographical Society, 1931

Lyell, F. H.: *A Study of the Novels of John Galt* Princeton, 1942

HOGG, JAMES

Batho, E. C.: *The Ettrick Shepherd* Cambridge, 1927

Campbell, I.: "Author and Audience in Hogg's *Confessions of a Justified Sinner*" S.I.S.L. Vol. II, 4

Eggenschwiller, D.: "James Hogg's *Confessions* and the Fall Into Divisions" S.I.S.L. Vol. IX, 1

Gifford, T. D. (ed.): *The Three Perils of Man* Edinburgh and London, 1972

Lee, L. L.: "The Devil's Figure: James Hogg's *Justified Sinner*" S.I.S.L. Vol. III, 6

Mack, D. S.: "The Development of Hogg's Poetry" S.I.S.L. Vol. III, 1

Mack, D. S. (ed.): *James Hogg, Memoir of the Author's Life and Familiar Anecdotes of Sir Walter Scott* London, 1972

Mack, D. S. (ed.): *James Hogg: Selected Poems* Oxford, 1970
Simpson, L.: *James Hogg: A critical study* Edinburgh and London, 1962

JEFFREY, FRANCIS

Cockburn, H.: *Life of Francis Jeffrey* Edinburgh, 1852
Greig, J. A.: *Francis Jeffrey of the Edinburgh Review* Edinburgh and London, 1948
Morgan, P. F.: "Principles and Perspective in Jeffrey's Criticism" S.I.S.L. Vol. IV, 3–4

LANG, ANDREW

Green, R. L.: "'Dear Andrew', and 'Dear Louis'" *Scots Magazine*, 1945
Green, R. L.: *Andrew Lang* Leicester, 1946
The Andrew Lang Lectures (Delivered at the University of St Andrews) Oxford, 1927 onwards

LOCKHART, JOHN GIBSON

Craig, D. (ed.): *Adam Blair* Edinburgh, 1963
Hart, F.: *Lockhart as Romantic Biographer* Edinburgh, 1971
Hilyard, M. C.: *Lockhart's Literary Criticism* Oxford, 1931
Lang, A.: *The Life and Letters of John Gibson Lockhart* London, 1897
Lockhead, M.: *John Gibson Lockhart* London, 1954

MACDONALD, GEORGE

Lewis, C. S. (ed.): *Lilith and Phantastes* London, 1971
Lewis, C. S. (ed.): *George Macdonald: An Anthology* London, 1946
Manlove, C. N.: "George MacDonald's Fairy Tales: Their Roots in MacDonald's Thought" S.I.S.L. Vol. VIII, 2

NORTH, CHRISTOPHER

Swann, E.: *Christopher North (John Wilson)* Edinburgh and London, 1934

OLIPHANT, MRS. M.

Autobiography and Letters of Mrs Margaret Oliphant Leicester, 1974
Leavis, Q. D. (ed.): *Introduction to Miss Marjoribanks* London, 1969

SCOTCH REVIEWERS

Clive J.: *Scotch Reviewers: The Edinburgh Review 1802–1815* London, 1957

SCOTT, SIR WALTER

Anderson, J.: "Sir Walter Scott as Historical Novelist" S.I.S.L. Vol. IV/V
Anderson, W. E. K. (ed.): *The Journal of Sir Walter Scott* Oxford, 1972
Buchan, J. (Lord Tweedsmuir): *The Life of Sir Walter Scott* London, 1932
Bushnell, N. S.: "Sir Walter Scott's Advent as Novelist of Manners" S.I.S.L. Vol. I, 1
Bushnell, N. S.: "Scott's Mature Achievement as Novelist of Manners" S.I.S.L. Vol. III, 1
Clark, A. M.: *Sir Walter Scott: The Formative Years* Edinburgh and London, 1969
Cockshut, A. J.: *The Achievement of Sir Walter Scott*, London, 1965
Crawford, T.: *Scott* Edinburgh and London, 1965
Daiches, D.: "Sir Walter Scott and History" *Etudes Anglaises*, 24, 4
Dobie, M. R.: *The Development of Scott's Minstrelsy* London, 1940
Grierson, Sir H. with Coole, D., and Parker, W. M.: *The Letters of Sir Walter Scott* Oxford, 1932
Gwynn, S.: *Life of Sir Walter Scott* London, 1930
Hart, F. R.: *Scott's Novels: The Plotting of Historic Survival* Virginia, 1966

Hayden, J. (ed.): *Scott: The Critical Heritage* London, 1970
Jeffares, W. (ed.): *Scott's Mind and Art* Edinburgh, 1969
Johnson, E.: *Sir Walter Scott: The Great Unknown* London, 1970
Jordan, F. Jr.: "Walter Scott as a Dramatic Novelist" S.I.S.L. Vol. V, 4
Lockhart, J. G.: *Memoirs of the Life of Sir Walter Scott* Edinburgh 1837/8
Pearson, Hesketh: *Walter Scott: His Life and Personality* London, 1954
Reizou, B.: "Scott's Historical Fiction and Relative Truth" S.I.S.L. Vol. 3, 2
Trevor-Roper, H.: "Sir Walter Scott and History" *The Listener*, 19th August 1971
Zug III, C. G.: "Sir Walter Scott and the Ballad Forgery" S.I.S.L. Vol. VIII, 1

SHARPE, C. K.

Allardyce, A. (ed.): *Letters from and to C. K. Sharpe* Edinburgh and London, 1888

STEVENSON, R. L.

Adcock, St. J. (ed.): *Robert Louis Stevenson: His Work and Personality* London 1924
Balfour, G.: *The Life of Robert Louis Stevenson* London, 1901
Butts, D.: *R. L. Stevenson* London, 1960
Colvin, Sir S. (ed.): *Letters to his Family and Friends* London, 1901
Daiches, D.: *Robert Louis Stevenson* Glasgow, 1947
Eignor, E. M.: *Robert Louis Stevenson and the Romantic Tradition* Princeton, 1960
Furnas, J. C.: *Voyage to Windward* London, 1952
Kiely, R.: *Robert Louis Stevenson and the fiction of adventure* Cambridge, Mass., 1964
Kilroy, J. F.: "Narrative Techniques in *The Master of Ballantrae*" S.I.S.L. Vol. V, 2
Lang, A.: *Adventures Among Books* London, 1905
Masson, R. (ed.): *I Can Remember Robert Louis Stevenson* London and Edinburgh, 1925
Smith, J. A. (ed.): *Henry James and Robert Louis Stevenson* London, 1948
Steuart, J. A.: *Robert Louis Stevenson: Man and Writer* London, 1924

THOMSON, JAMES ("B.V.")

Power, W.: *Robert Burns and Other Essays and Sketches* Glasgow and London, 1926

CHAPTER VI: *The Scottish Renaissance . . .*

ANGUS, MARION

Lindsay, M. (ed.): and Cruickshank, H.: *Selected Poems . . . with a Personal Memoir by Helen B. Cruickshank* Edinburgh, 1950

BARRIE, SIR J. M.

Blake, G.: *Barrie and the Kailyard School* London, 1951
Dunbar, J.: *J. M. Barrie: The Man Behind the Image* London, 1970
McGraw, W. R.: "Barrie and the Critics" S.I.S.L. Vol. 1, 2

BRIDIE, JAMES

Bannister, W.: *James Bridie and his Theatre* London, 1955
Morgan, E.: "James Bridie" *Essays* Cheadle Hulme, 1974
Greene, Anne: "Bridie's Concept of The Master Experimenter" S.I.S.L. Vol. II, 2

Luyben, H. L.: *James Bridie: Clown and Philosopher* Philadelphia, 1965

BROWN, GEORGE DOUGLAS

McClure, J. D.: "Dialect in 'The House with the Green Shutters'" S.I.S.L. Vol. IX, 2–3

Smith, I. C.: "The House with the Green Shutters" S.I.S.L. Vol. 7, 1–2

Veitch, J.: *George Douglas Brown* London, 1952

BROWN, GEORGE MACKAY

Scott, A.: "George Mackay Brown" *Contemporary Poets* London and New York, 1975

BRUCE, G.

Lindsay, M.: "George Bruce" *Contemporary Poets* London and New York, 1975

Scott, A.: "Myth-Maker: The Poetry of George Bruce" *Akros* 29, 1975

BUCHAN, JOHN (Lord Tweedsmuir)

Smith, J. A.: *John Buchan: A Biography* London, 1965

BUCHAN, T.

Bruce, G.: "Tom Buchan" *Contemporary Poets*, London and New York, 1975

DAVIDSON, JOHN

Gallienne, R. Le: *The Romantic '90s* London, 1926

Lindsay, M. (ed.): *John Davidson: A Selection of his Poems* (Preface by T. S. Eliot, Essay by Hugh McDiarmid) London, 1961

Mix, K. L.: *A Study in Yellow* Kansas and London, 1960

Townsend, J. B.: *John Davidson: Poet of Armageddon* Yale, 1961

FRASER, G. S.

Deutsch, B.: *Poetry in Our Time*, New York, 1963

Lindsay, M.: "G. S. Fraser" *Contemporary Poets* London and New York, 1975

Garioch, R.: "Robert Garioch", *Contemporary Poets* London and New York, 1975

GIBBON, LEWIS GRASSIC

Macaree, D.: "Myth and Allegory in Lewis Grassic Gibbon's *A Scots Quair*" S.I.S.L. Vol. II, 1

Munro, I. S.: *Leslie Mitchell: Lewis Grassic Gibbon* Edinburgh 1968

Young, D.: *Beyond the Sunset* Aberdeen 1974

GRAHAM, W. S.

Dickey, J.: *Babel to Byzantium*, New York, 1968

Morgan, E.: "W. S. Graham's Threshold" *Nine* 3, London 1950

GRAY, SIR ALEXANDER

Scott, A.: "Sir Alexander Gray, 1882–1968" S.I.S.L. Vol. VIII, 2

GUNN, NEIL

Hart, F.: "The Hunter and the Circle: Neil Gunn's Fiction of Violence" S.I.S.L. Vol. I, 1

Scott, A. and Gifford T. D. (eds.): *Neil M. Gunn: The Man and the Writer* Edinburgh, 1973

HANLEY, C.

Scott, A.: "Clifford Hanley" *Contemporary Novelists of the English Language* London and Chicago, 1971

JENKINS, ROBIN

Morgan, E.: "The Novels of Robin Jenkins" *Essays* Cheadle Hulme, 1974

Scott A.: "Robin Jenkins" *Contemporary Novelists of the English Language* London and Chicago, 1971

HAY, J. MACDOUGAL
    Hart, F. R.: "Reviewing Hay's *Gillespie*" S.I.S.L. Vol. II, 1
LINDSAY, DAVID
    Extracts from his unpublished work, Lines Review 40
    McClure, D.: "Language and Logic in *A Voyage to Arcturus*" S.L.J. 1
    Pick, J. B.: "The Work of David Lindsay" S.I.S.L. Vol. I, 3
    Pick, J. B., Wilson, C. and Visiok, E. H. *The Strange Genius of David Lindsay: An Appreciation* London, 1970
LINDSAY, M.
    Bruce, G.: Review of *Comings and Goings, Akros* 17, 1971
    Campbell, D.: "A Different Way of Being Right" *Akros* 1974
    Nye, R.: "Maurice Lindsay" *Contemporary Poets* London and New York,
    Scott, A.: "Two Modern Makars", *The Glasgow Review*, Glasgow, 1974
MACCAIG, N.
    MacCaig Issue *Akros* 7, 1968
MACDIARMID, HUGH
    Buthlay, K.: *Hugh MacDiarmid (C. M. Grieve)* Edinburgh and London, 1964
    Glen, D.: *Hugh MacDiarmid and the Scottish Renaissance* Edinburgh and London, 1964
    Glen, D. (ed.): *MacDiarmid Double Issue of Akros, Akros* 13/14, 1970
    Glen, D. (ed.): *Hugh MacDiarmid: A Critical Survey* Edinburgh and London, 1972
    Duval, K. and Smith, S. G. (eds.): *Hugh MacDiarmid: A Festschrift* Edinburgh, 1962
    Lindsay, M.: "Hugh MacDiarmid" *Contemporary Poets* London and New York, 1975
    Smith, I. C.: "*Sangschaw* and *A Drunk Man Looks at the Thistle*" S.I.S.L. Vol. 7, 3
    Morgan, E.: "Poetry and Knowledge in MacDiarmid's Later Work" *Essays* Cheadle Hulme, 1974
MACKIE, A.
    Mason, L.: *Two North-East Makars* Preston, 1975
    Mitchison, N.: "Naomi Mitchison", *Contemporary Novelist of the English Language*, London and Chicago, 1971
MORGAN, E.
    Buchan, T.: "Edwin Morgan" *Scottish International* Edinburgh, 1968
    Lindsay, M.: "Edwin Morgan" *Contemporary Poets* London and New York, 1975
MUIR, E.
    Butter, P.: *Edwin Muir: Man and Poet* Edinburgh and London, 1966
    Butter P. H.: *Selected Letters of Edwin Muir* London, 1974
    Huberman, E.: *The Poetry of Edwin Muir: The Field of Good and Ill* London, 1971
    Mellown, E. W.: "Bibliography of the Writings of Edwin Muir" Alabama, 1964; London, 1966
    Butter, P. H.: *Edwin Muir* Edinburgh and London, 1962
    Bruce, G.: "Edwin Muir: Poet" *The Saltire Review*, Edinburgh, 1959
    Grice, F.: "The Poetry of Edwin Muir" *Essays in Criticism* London, 1955
    Hollander, R.: *A Textual and Bibliographical Study of the Poems of Edwin Muir*

Unpublished, National Library of Scotland

Hamburg, M.: "Edwin Muir" *Encounter*, London, 1960

Raine, K.: "Edwin Muir: An Appreciation" *Texas Quarterly*, IV, 1961

Bruce, G.: "The Poetry of Alexander Scott", *Akros* 19, 1972

Buchan, D.: "New Dimensions," *The Library Review*, Vol. 25, 2, 1975

SCOTT, A.

MacCaig, N.: "Alexander Scott" *Contemporary Poets* London and New York, 1975

MacIntyre, L.: "Alexander Scott: Makar Extraordinary" *Akros* 25, 1974

Mason, L.: *Two North-East Makars* Preston, 1975

SMITH, IAIN CRICHTON

Morgan, E.: "The Raging and the Grace" *Essays* Cheadle Hulme, 1974

——. Bibliography. Lines Review 29, 1969

Thomson, D. S.: "Iain Crichton Smith" *Contemporary Poets* London and New York, 1975

SMITH, S. G.

Sydney Goodsir Smith, special number, including articles by Hugh Mac-Diarmid and A. Scott *Akros* 10, 1969

Crawford, T.: "The Poetry of Sydney Goodsir Smith" S.I.S.L. Vol. VII, 1–2

——. "Goodsir Smith: The Auk" of the Mandrake Hert, *The Scottish Review*, Vol. I, 2, Glasgow, 1976

Scott, A.: "A Rejoinder" S.I.S.L. Vol. VIII, 1

Lindsay, M.: "Sydney Goodsir Smith" *Contemporary Poets* London and New York, 1975

MacCaig, N.: "The Poetry of Sydney Goodsir Smith" *The Saltire Review*, 1, Edinburgh, 1954

MacDiarmid H.: "Sydney Goodsir Smith" *The Uncanny Scot* London, 1968

Scott, A.: "Daylight and the Dark.: Edinburgh in the Poetry of Robert Fergusson and Sydney Goodsir Smith" *Lines* 3, Edinburgh, 1953

Anon (ed.): Various writers: *For Sydney Goodsir Smith* Loanhead, 1975

SOUTAR, WILLIAM

Goodwin, K. L.: "William Soutar, Adelaide Crapsey, and Imagism" S.I.S.L. Vol. III, 2

Scott, A.: *Still Life: William Soutar* Edinburgh and London, 1958

Scott, A.: *The Macdiarmid Makars 1923–1972*, Preston, 1972

CHAPTER VII: . . . *And After*

GENERAL

Burgess, Moira: *The Glasgow Novel*, 2nd Edition, Glasgow, 1986

Craig, Cairns (ed.): *A History of Scottish Literature* (4 vols) 1987–8, Aberdeen

Gifford, Douglas: *The Dear Green Place: The Novel in the West of Scotland*, 1985, Glasgow

GUNN, NEIL M.

Russell, Francis and Pick, J.B.: *A Highland Life*, 1981, London

LINKLATER, ERIC

Parnell, Michael: *Eric Linklater*, 1984, London

MACCAIG, NORMAN
Hendry, J. and Ross R. (eds): *Norman MacCaig: Critical Essays*, 1990, Edinburgh
MACDIARMID, HUGH
Bold, A. (ed): *The Letters of Hugh MacDiarmid*, 1984, London
Bold, A.: *MacDiarmid: Christopher Murray Grieve: A Critical Biography*, 1988, London
MACKENZIE, SIR COMPTON
Linklater, A.: *Compton Mackenzie: A Life*, 1987, London
MUIR, EDWIN
Crawford, R., and Whyte, H. (eds): *About Edwin Morgan*, 1990, Edinburgh

Most Scottish contemporary poets are the subject of useful explicatory essays in *Contemporary Poets*, 5th Edition, 1991, Chicago and London.

Index

Principal references are in bold type

Supplementary Index
(including additional bibliography)